THE
GOOD HOUSEKEEPING
ILLUSTRATED
COOKBOOK
Revised & Expanded
EDITION

THE
GOOD HOUSEKEEPING
ILLUSTRATED
COOKBOOK
Revised & Expanded
EDITION

HEARST BOOKS, a divison of
Sterling Publishing Co., Inc.
New York

Good Housekeeping

Editor-In-Chief	John Mack Carter
Executive Editor	Mina W. Mulvey
Institute Director	Mary E. Powers

Food Department

Director	Mildred Ying
Associate Director	Susan Deborah Goldsmith
Associates	Ellen H. Connelly
	Marianne Zanzarella
	Carol Ann Barbetta
	Anna Brandenburger

Revised Edition

Editors	Elizabeth Wolf-Cohen
	Jillian Somerscales
Editorial Assistants	Maria Adams
	Christiane Gunzi
	Irene Lyford
Art Editors	Helen Claire Young
	Sue Storey
Designer	Sally Hibbard
Editorial Director	Amy Carroll
Art Director	Denise Brown

Acknowledgments (Revised Edition)

Color illustration	Gilly Newman
Photography	Clive Streeter
Home Economist	Lyn Rutherford
Stylist	Sue Russell
Research Dietician	Wendy Doyle

10 9 8 7 6 5 4 3 2 1

Published by Hearst Books, a division of
Sterling Publishing Company, Inc.
387 Park Avenue South, New York, N.Y. 10016
© 1989 and 1980 by Hearst Communications, Inc.
Distributed in Canada by Sterling Publishing
c/o Canadian Manda Group, One Atlantic Avenue, Suite 105
Toronto, Ontario, Canada M6K 3E7
Distributed in Great Britain and Europe by Cassell PLC
Wellington House, 125 Strand, London WC2R 0BB, England
Distributed in Australia by Capricorn Link (Australia) Pty. Ltd.
P.O. Box 704, Windsor, NSW 2756 Australia
Printed in China
All rights reserved

ISBN 1-58816-187-0

FOREWORD

Cooking is easier when an expert shows, step-by-step, how to prepare a recipe. We planned this cookbook so that even a beginning cook could successfully use our recipes simply by following the diagrams of the steps along with the recipe itself. In this collection of recipes, we demonstrate all the fundamental cooking techniques, from folding in egg whites, to kneading bread, rolling piecrusts, decorating cakes and cookies, even boning certain cuts of meat and poultry and filleting fish. We've included recipes that are often considered difficult as well as everyday ones.

Since recipe selection and meal planning are easier when a picture shows exactly how the food will look, all of our recipes (except the microwave recipes) are shown in the large color picture index at the beginning of the book. You can browse through these pages and select the recipe best suited for your specific occasion. The color pictures also suggest how to garnish and serve the dish. Captions provide information on the recipe seasonings, cooking methods used, time needed to prepare the food, number of servings and so on. For the first time in a cookbook, menu planning is made easier as the pictures are arranged according to the course of the meal, starting with appetizers and going through to main dishes, salads, breads and desserts.

Many of these recipes are classics, direct from the pages of *Good Housekeeping* Magazine. Others are newly developed for this book. All have met the strict standards of *Good Housekeeping*'s food department. The staff checked and rechecked these recipes, trying several brands of ingredients, eliminating extra steps, using fewer utensils, confirming the cooking times, making sure they are nutritionally sound and, most importantly, that they tasted as good as they looked.

The popularity of microwave ovens and an increasing concern with nutritional values have been the major factors to affect cooking since the book was first published. In this revised edition, we have included a chapter of microwave recipes as well as color photographs of microwave techniques and equipment.

Each recipe in the book is now accompanied by a calorie count, and many include additional nutritional information, such as whether a recipe is high in fiber or low in cholesterol or fat. More general information on healthy eating is given in the back of the book.

To help make entertaining and menu-planning easier and more exciting we include menus for seasonal celebrations; large color photographs illustrate seasonal ingredients, a special seasonal menu and a step-by-step guide to preparation.

All of us hope that this unique cookbook provides the inspiration for many good-tasting, easily prepared meals to serve your friends and family.
Mildred Ying, Director, Food Department,
Good Housekeeping Institute

HOW TO USE THIS BOOK

The Color Index pages in this book are organized in menu order, so all you have to do is choose a dish from each course and then turn to the appropriate page and find the recipe.

First, look at the Color Index and find a dish you'd like to prepare. The captions to the photographs will tell you what each recipe contains, how many it will serve, and the page on which it appears in the book.

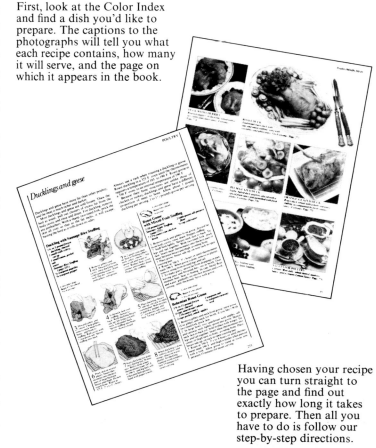

Having chosen your recipe you can turn straight to the page and find out exactly how long it takes to prepare. Then all you have to do is follow our step-by-step directions.

Contents

BEFORE YOU COOK

Before you begin to prepare a recipe for the first time, read it through carefully to make sure that you have allowed enough preparation time. Before actually beginning cooking, assemble and measure all the ingredients and utensils needed for the recipe to be sure you have everything you need. Avoid substituting key ingredients, product forms (such as regular or instant) or package sizes, unless the recipe suggests an alternative. Be cautious, too, about doubling or halving any recipe: although some can be increased successfully, many more cannot. For best results, therefore, make up the recipe as given and, if necessary, repeat it until the required amount is obtained. Seasonings and spices can be varied according to taste, but it's a good idea to follow the recipe directions exactly the first time.

Do as much advance preparation as possible before you start mixing and cooking. Measure and mix ingredients using the correct equipment (pages 8 and 10). Advance preparation of utensils is just as important as assembling ingredients: grease and flour a pan if directed and when a preheated oven is called for, turn it on when called for in the recipe, which will be at least 10 minutes before putting in the food to allow it to preheat to the required temperature. For best results, cook at the temperature specified in the recipe; start checking for doneness towards the end of cooking time; and lastly, get into the habit of cleaning up as you work.

Below: A selection of useful cookware
Top row: 3-quart saucepan, steamer, ramekin, soufflé dishes
Middle row: Dutch oven, omelet pan, tartlet pan, loose bottom tart pans, springform pan
Bottom row: non-stick loaf pan, wire rack, non-stick pie plate, pastry cutter, pastry brush, pastry wheel, muffin pan, cake pan

Cutting and grating

A basic collection of cutting and grating tools is vital in any well-equipped kitchen. A good cook's ability to work skillfully depends upon using the right tool for the job. Keep knives sharp, use them only for the purpose for which they are intended, and store in a safe place.

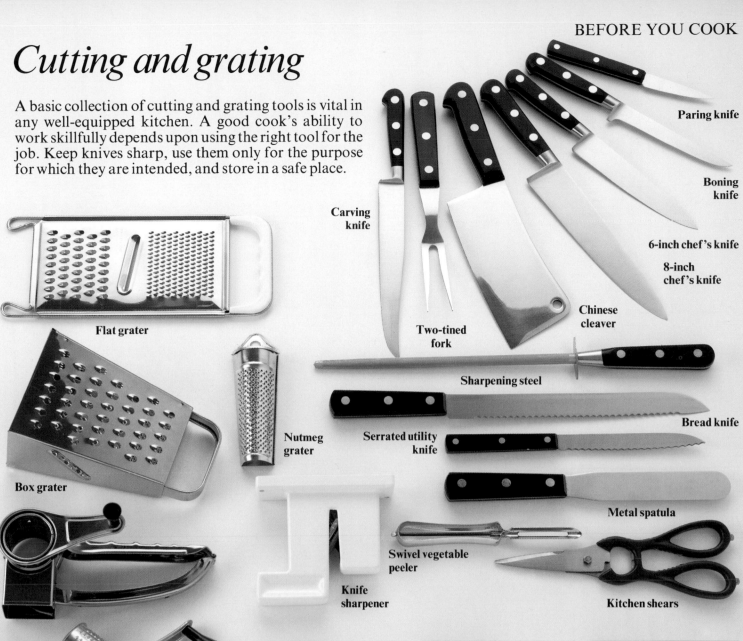

Paring knife

Boning knife

6-inch chef's knife

8-inch chef's knife

Carving knife

Two-tined fork

Chinese cleaver

Sharpening steel

Bread knife

Nutmeg grater

Serrated utility knife

Flat grater

Box grater

Rotary grater

Metal spatula

Swivel vegetable peeler

Knife sharpener

Kitchen shears

CUTTING TERMS

Cutting can be done with a sharp knife on a chopping board, or in a blender or food processor.

Chop: To cut food into small, irregularly-shaped pieces.
Cube: To cut food into square chunks.
Dice: To cut food into very small pieces.
Mince: To cut food into very small, irregular pieces.
Peel: To remove outer covering of foods by trimming away with a knife or vegetable peeler.
Score: To cut shallow slits in the surface of foods to tenderize or decorate.
Shred: To cut food into slivers or slender pieces.

Slicing an onion: Peel the onion and place on flat surface. With a chef's knife, cut crosswise in ¹/4-inch slices.

Dicing an onion: Cut onion in half lengthwise. With cut side down, cut onion crosswise in ¹/4-inch thick slices.

Hold onion firmly in place and give quarter turn; cut in ¹/4-inch pieces. Repeat with other onion half.

Grating: Rotary graters are useful for using up small pieces of food without a risk to fingers. Fill with cheese, nuts or chocolate and turn handle.

Coring: Using a small knife with a 2- to 4-inch-long blade, carefully remove any stem and all of the seeds from the center of cut pieces of fruit.

Cutting strips: Place vegetables on a board. Using a chef's knife, cut the vegetables lengthwise into matchstick-thin (julienne) strips.

Mixing and measuring

Using the correct measuring and mixing equipment ensures good results each time you cook. When measuring dry ingredients (see below), level excess into small bowl; then add measured amount to mixing bowl.

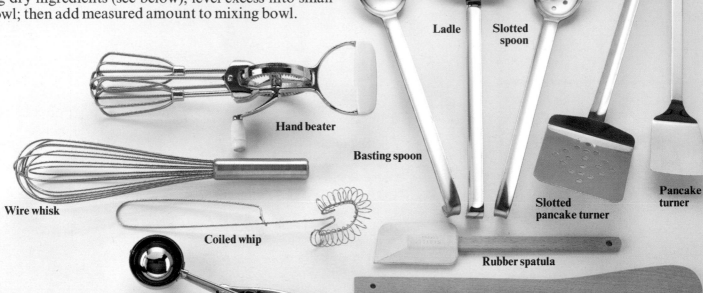

Ladle

Slotted spoon

Basting spoon

Slotted pancake turner

Pancake turner

Rubber spatula

Wooden spatula

Wooden spoon

Hand beater

Wire whisk

Coiled whip

Ice cream scoop

Shown below (*clockwise from left*): food processor; blender; stand-mounted mixer; hand-held electric mixer; graduated measuring cups for dry ingredients ($\frac{1}{4}$-, $\frac{1}{3}$-, $\frac{1}{2}$- and 1-cup); liquid measuring cup

Folding in: To avoid losing air, add lighter ingredients to heavier ones. With a rubber spatula or wire whisk, cut down through the center, across the bottom and up the side of the bowl. Turn the bowl as you work.

Beating: Using a wooden spoon, tip the bowl toward you and beat the mixture rapidly until smooth. Beating incorporates as much air as possible into the mixture and also helps to eliminate any lumps from the mixture.

Measuring flour: Over small bowl, lightly spoon flour from the canister into a measuring cup or spoon. Level off surplus flour with the straight edge of a metal spatula or small kitchen knife; never pack or shake flour down.

Measuring shortening, soft butter or margarine: Pack in firmly to the top of a measuring cup or graduated spoon; level off with metal spatula or knife. **For hard butter or margarine:** Follow the cutting marks on the wrapper.

Measuring liquids: When using a liquid measuring cup, place the cup on a level surface and slowly pour in the liquid until it reaches the desired line. If using measuring spoons, pour liquid just to the top of the spoon without letting it spill over.

Spices

Spices should be stored in containers with well-fitting lids in a dark cool place, away from the heat of the stove. Red spices hold their color and keep their flavor longer if refrigerated. Whole spices retain their aroma and flavor almost indefinitely.

Shown directly below are five spices that have become available in more recent years due to the popularity of Indian and Oriental cooking.

Cinnamon
Reddish-brown sticks of rolled bark also used ground. Cinnamon has a sweet, pungent aroma and is used with sweet vegetables (baked beans, sweet potatoes) and in fruit dishes, pickles, breads, cakes, cookies, and desserts.

Ginger
Whole root used crystallized (candied), fresh, preserved in syrup, or dried and ground. Used in Oriental-style meat, poultry, seafood, and vegetable dishes, and with fruit.

Curry powder　　**Cumin seed**　**Star anise**　**Chinese five-spice**　**Turmeric**

Allspice
Whole or ground berries with a flavor resembling a blend of cloves, cinnamon and nutmeg. Used in baking, some meat dishes, pickles, and relishes.

Chili powder
Dried chili peppers blended with ground cumin seeds, garlic powder, oregano and, usually, salt. Used in Mexican- and Spanish-style meat dishes.

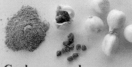

Cardamom seed
Whole pods containing small brown seeds. Pods and seeds or seeds only are ground. Used in Indian and Scandinavian cooking, coffee, coffee-cakes, and cookies.

Sesame and poppy seed
Sesame seeds are flat with a nut-like flavor; they are used in Chinese-style dishes, breads, snacks, and candy. Poppy seeds are crunchy with a sweet, mild, nutty flavor. Used whole in breads, pastries, and cakes.

Cloves
Closed flower buds used ground or whole in sweet and savory dishes, breads, desserts, and spiced wine.

Saffron
Dried stamens of a crocus used ground or as strands in poultry and fish dishes, and in rice.

Vanilla bean
The unripe seed pod of an orchid used to flavor sweet sauces, cakes, and puddings. Vanilla beans are tasteless when picked but develop a strong, sweet flavor after curing. The beans may be used grated if they dry out. Vanilla essence is a concentrated extract used sparingly in confectionery, cakes, and ice cream.

Caraway seed
Whole seeds with a warm, slightly sharp taste. Related to anise, they are used in breads, sweet pickles, cheese spreads, and dips.

Pickling spice and juniper berries
A mixture of mustard seed, black peppercorns, allspice, cloves, chili pepper and other spices, usually tied in cheesecloth; used in pickles and vinegars. Dried juniper berries are used to flavor game and pork dishes.

Pepper
Black pepper is made from dried pepper berries; used whole, cracked or ground.
White pepper, made from mature pepper berries, is milder.
Ground red pepper (cayenne) and *crushed red pepper* are made from dried, hot chilies.
Green peppercorns are fresh berries freeze-dried or packed in water or brine.
Szechwan peppercorns ("anise pepper") have a mild taste and are used in Oriental cooking.

Paprika
Ground pods of sweet chilies or peppers, mildly hot to mild and sweet in flavor. Used in meat, poultry, and cheese dishes.

Mace and nutmeg
Mace is the dried, net-like casing around nutmeg. Both spices are used ground in breads, cookies, cakes, and custards.

BEFORE YOU COOK
Herbs

Fresh herbs keep in the refrigerator for a few days or in the freezer for up to 1 year. Store dried herbs in tightly-closed containers in a cool place. The flavor of dried herbs does not hold up well during lengthy cooking, so add them toward the end of cooking time.

Basil
Fresh or dried leaves with a faintly anise-like flavor and sweet aroma. Used in tomato dishes and pesto sauce.

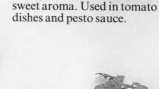

Bay leaves
Fresh or dried leaves used in meat and poultry dishes; their strong flavor mellows during long cooking. Remove whole leaves before serving.

Chervil
Lacy leaves with a delicate flavor reminiscent of tarragon. Used dried or fresh in fish and egg dishes.

Chives
Fresh, freeze-dried or frozen leaves with a delicate onion flavor. Used in egg, cheese, fish, and poultry dishes.

Coriander
Fresh, lacy leaves also known as cilantro and Chinese parsley. Used in Chinese- and Mexican-style dishes. Coriander seeds are available whole or ground.

Dill
Fresh, feathery leaves used in fish dishes. Also available dried (dill weed). Dill seeds are used whole or ground.

Marjoram
Bittersweet fresh or dried leaves used in meat, poultry, and Italian-style dishes.

Oregano
Aromatic leaves similar in flavor to marjoram. Used fresh or dried in Italian- and Mexican-style dishes.

Mint
Leaves with a sweet aroma and cool aftertaste. Used fresh or dried with vegetables, fruits, and desserts, and in jelly and sauces.

Using a chef's knife: Place the herbs on a board; rock the blade rapidly up and down over the herbs until finely chopped.

Using a rotary mincer: Place the herbs on a board; roll the mincer over the herbs, turning occasionally, until chopped.

Using a cup and scissors: Place the herbs in the cup. Pointing the scissors into the cup, snip herbs until well chopped.

Using a food processor: Place the herbs in the bowl. With steel blade attached, process the herbs until chopped.

Parsley
Flat-leaved (Italian) or curly-leaved parsley are used fresh or as dried flakes to flavor and garnish many non-sweet dishes.

Rosemary
Needle-shaped, bittersweet leaves used fresh or dried with lamb, poultry, and fish dishes.

Sage
Fresh or dried aromatic leaves. Used rubbed or ground in stuffings and with liver, pork, poultry and cheese dishes.

Savory
Winter savory (above) and summer savory are the most common varieties. Used fresh or dried in meat, egg, and rice dishes.

Tarragon
Long, pointed leaves with an anise-like flavor. Used fresh or dried in chicken, cheese, and egg dishes, and with vegetables.

Thyme
There are many varieties of this herb. The small, fragrant, gray-green leaves are used fresh or dried in sauces, soups, stews, casseroles, and stuffings.

Microwave equipment and utensils

Microwave ovens have made it possible to perform many techniques — such as steaming, simmering, roasting, defrosting and reheating — in much less time than it would take using a conventional oven. Using the right microwave equipment and utensils and the correct cooking techniques (pages 15 and 16) will ensure successful results each time you use the microwave.

Many containers already in your kitchen — such as heat-safe glassware, glass-ceramic dishes, china and pottery — are suitable for microwave use, providing they do not contain metal (unless special directions are given in your owner's manual). Other useful items include cooking bags, waxed paper, plain white napkins and paper plates, cups, cartons and towels. Wood and wicker containers can be used to heat food briefly and dishwasher-safe plastic containers can be used for short-term reheating. For general microwave cooking, use plastic containers marked specifically for microwave use; many have been designed especially for cooking food in the microwave.

Below: A selection of microwave equipment and utensils

Testing containers or utensils for microwave safety: Measure 1 cup cold water into a glass measuring cup and place alongside dish or utensil. Cook at HIGH (100% power) 1 minute. After this time, the dish should be cool and the water warm; do not use dish if warm.

Microwave-cooking techniques

Microwave energy cooks food quickly but not always evenly. Microwaves cook from the outer edges toward the center. Without applying special techniques, you can overcook or burn the outside edges of food while the center remains underdone. Microwaves penetrate food to a depth of up to 1¹/₂ inches; cooking the food all the way through in a microwave oven depends on manip-

ulation of the food by stirring or rearranging it or by heat conduction — covering the food and letting it stand after cooking to complete the cooking process.

Arranging: Place thicker, meatier parts of food toward edge of dish, where they will receive more microwave energy.

Arrange even-sized pieces of food such as potatoes or tomatoes in a circle, leaving a space between them for more even cooking.

Size of food: Small, even-sized pieces of food cook more evenly than large pieces. Cut vegetables into smaller pieces that are roughly similar in size.

Piercing: Pierce the skin of vegetables such as acorn squash, potatoes, sweet potatoes and whole tomatoes to prevent them from bursting during cooking.

Elevating: Raise the cooking dish slightly off the oven floor using a microwave-safe meat rack, trivet, inverted pie plate or saucer. This allows microwave energy to

cook the center-bottom of food. Use a meat rack in a roasting pan to keep a roast from stewing in its own juices.

Covering with lid: Casserole lids hold in moisture during cooking and are useful when steaming vegetables that do not need added moisture. Microwave-safe plates may be used instead of lids.

Plastic wrap: This can be used in place of a lid or plate. A build up of steam can cause plastic wrap to split; to avoid this, leave the wrap unsealed at one edge of the dish so steam can escape.

Waxed paper: This forms a loose cover and is suitable for foods that do not need steam to tenderize. Waxed paper is also useful for covering foods like bacon that tend to splatter.

Paper towels: These allow steam to escape, absorb excess moisture and prevent foods such as bacon from splattering. Always use plain white paper towels as dye can be transferred onto the food.

Microwave-cooking techniques

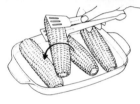

Rearranging: Foods that cannot be stirred should be rearranged, turned over or rotated during cooking. To rearrange, move pieces of food from the center to the outside of the dish and vice versa. Whole foods such as ears of corn or potatoes should be turned over.

Rotating: Whole foods such as baked apples can be rotated in the dish. To rotate the entire dish a half turn, turn it until the side facing the back of the oven is to the front. For a quarter turn, turn the dish so that the side that faced the back faces the side of the oven. Always rotate the dish in one direction only.

Stirring: Stir foods such as stews and soups from the outer edge – where the food cooks first – toward the center of the dish, pushing the cooler food at the center toward the edge.

Whisking: Whisking scrambled eggs and sauces during cooking helps break up the thickened edge and mix it with the unthickened liquid. For best results, whisk often and briskly.

Standing time: Foods cooked in the microwave continue to cook by internal heat after they are removed from the oven. Many dishes such as scrambled eggs call for a "standing time" at the

end of cooking to prevent overcooking. Always allow food to stand as directed in the recipe before testing for doneness. Standing roasts also makes for easier carving.

COLOR INDEX

APPETIZERS

COLD CANAPES (left to right): CAVIAR-EGG ROUNDS; SMOKED SALMON SQUARES; CURRIED-TUNA CANAPES; WATERCRESS CREAM-CHEESE TRIANGLES; TUNA-DILL ROUNDS; BLUE-CHEESE-AND-ASPIC CANAPES; ANCHOVY-CHEESE CIRCLES; ASPARAGUS CANAPES. Pages 115 to 116

PATE DE CAMPAGNE
Ground pork and chicken, cooked with mushrooms, sherry, herbs and bacon. 16 servings; day ahead. Page 122

TIDBITS
CHINESE FRIED WALNUTS (left). *Early in day.* CURRIED ALMONDS *Early in day.* CRISP CHEESE TWISTS Page 114

PORK RILLETTES
Pork roast, cooked with marjoram and thyme, then shredded and served with French bread. 12 servings; early in day. Page 124

GUACAMOLE
Mashed avocado with tomato, onion, garlic, chilies and lemon juice, served with potato chips. 1 hour. Page 124

SPINACH PATE
Chilled loaf of spinach mixture, flavored with basil and cayenne, garnished with Carrot Flowers. 10 servings; day ahead. Page 122

CHICKEN-LIVER PATE
Cooked chicken livers, blended with onion, butter and brandy, then chilled. 16 servings; 3 1/2 hours. Page 122

RADISH SPREAD (left). *15 minutes.* Page 293. CHEESE SPREADS (front, rear and right). Page 124

HOMEMADE PEPPER-HERB CHEESE
Homemade cheese seasoned with herbs and coated with cracked pepper. 5 days ahead. Page 123

GREEN-ONION DIP (left). *15 minutes.* Page 124. **BLUE-CHEESE DIP** (center). *15 minutes.* Page 124. **YOGURT-CHEESE DIP** *15 minutes.* Page 125

BAGNA CAUDA
Hot, creamy, garlic and anchovy dip, served with crisp vegetables. 12 servings; 1½ hours. Page 125

CHILI DIP WITH FRESH VEGETABLES
Chilled fresh vegetables served with a spicy, blended dip; early in day. Page 125

DUCK PATE IN SHERRY ASPIC
Duckling meat, pork, chicken livers, mushrooms and peas baked and topped with gelatin. 10 servings; day ahead. Page 123

PEPPERY DIP WITH VEGETABLES
Mayonnaise-based dip with chili sauce, curry and vinegar, served with cauliflowerets and carrot. Several hours ahead. Page 124

TUNA DIP
Tuna, blended with mayonnaise, anchovies, lemon juice and paprika and served with chips or crackers. Early in day. Page 125

STEAK BITES
Broiled top round steak pieces, served in a mustard-Worcestershire mixture. 24 servings; 2 hours. Page 119

SWEDISH MEATBALLS
Meatballs cooked in consommé and cream. 40 appetizers; 1 hour. Page 119

19

TINY HAM-STUFFED TOMATOES
Cherry tomatoes, filled with deviled ham, sour cream and horseradish. 20 appetizers; early in day. Page 126

SAUSAGE-STUFFED MUSHROOMS
Baked mushrooms stuffed with sausage, mozzarella cheese and bread crumbs. 30 appetizers; 1 hour. Page 117

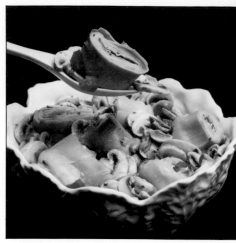

MARINATED ARTICHOKE HEARTS AND MUSHROOMS *Artichoke hearts, mushrooms and pimentos marinated in spicy dressing. 8 servings; early in day.* Page 319

CHICKEN WING APPETIZERS
Chicken wings and green onions cooked in spicy soy sauce; served warm or chilled. 36 appetizers; 1 hour. Page 121

CAPONATA
Italian-style chilled vegetables in tangy dressing. 12 servings; 4 hours. Page 299

CELERY HEARTS VINAIGRETTE
Cooked celery in pimento marinade, served over romaine lettuce. 8 servings; 6 hours. Page 321

NIPPY CARROTS *12 servings; day ahead.* **PICKLED ONIONS** *16 servings; day ahead.* **HERBED MUSHROOMS** *12 servings; day ahead. All* page 126

SPANAKOPITAS
Phyllo triangles with chopped spinach, cheese and egg filling, baked until golden. 20 servings; 2¼ hours. Page 121

TOSTADA APPETIZERS
Corn tortilla pieces, topped with beef in spicy tomato sauce, with cheese, lettuce and olives. 36 appetizers; 1 hour. Page 118

ANTIPASTO
Platter: Selection of cold meat, fish and cheese on platter. Includes mortadella, ham, salami, sardines and provolone.
In bowls (clockwise): MARINATED EGGPLANT; MARINATED ITALIAN GREEN BEANS; MARINATED TUNA
AND RED CABBAGE; MARINATED CAULIFLOWERETS. *18 appetizer servings; early in day.* Page 126

APPETIZER AVOCADOS
Avocado slices with a warm, spicy sauce, garnished with crumbled bacon. 6 servings; 35 minutes. Page 302

HAWAIIAN FRUIT SALAD
Papayas and bananas in lime-flavored syrup, topped with coconut and ginger. 8 servings; 20 minutes. Page 322

STEAMED ASPARAGUS
Tender, cooked asparagus, topped with Hollandaise Sauce. 8 servings; 15 minutes. Page 277

PISSALADIERE
Sliced onions, anchovies, olives, oregano and Swiss cheese, baked on yeast-dough base until golden. 18 servings; 2¼ hours. Page 117

HOT APPETIZERS: *Individual Broccoli Quiches. Hot Mushroom Turnovers. Cheesy Shrimp Canapés. Pumpernickel-Muenster Triangles. Pages 116 to 118*

SAUSAGE EN CROUTE
Country-style pork sausages, baked in pastry. 32 appetizers; 2½ hours. Page 121

GRAVAD LAX
Scandinavian-style fresh salmon, coated with pepper and dill and served chilled, with Mustard Sauce. 14 servings; 2 to 3 days ahead. Page 119

RUMAKI
Marinated chunks of chicken liver and water chestnuts, wrapped in bacon and broiled. 18 appetizers; 1½ hours. Page 121

BRIE-IN-BRIOCHE
Whole brie cheese set into a brioche "basket" Served cold with grapes. 24 servings; day ahead. Page 120

BROILED GRAPEFRUIT
Halved grapefruits, dotted with brown sugar and butter and broiled until golden.
2 servings; 15 minutes. Page 305

GINGERED MELON WEDGES
Honeydew wedges, sprinkled with confectioners' sugar and ground ginger.
8 servings; 2 hours. Page 309

TORTELLINI IN CREAM SAUCE
Homemade pasta filled with chicken mixture. Served with cream sauce and cheese.
12 servings; 3 hours. Page 335

BRUNCH EGGS FLORENTINE
Scrambled eggs served over sliced tomatoes and spinach-soufflé mixture, garnished with dill. 12 servings; 1^1/2 hours. Page 144

STUFFED EGGS and VARIATIONS
Hard-cooked egg yolks, softened with mayonnaise and flavored. 12 halves; 45 minutes. Page 141

EGGS EN GELEE
Hard-cooked eggs garnished with olive and pimento pieces, served chilled in a gelatin mixture. 12 servings ; day ahead. Page 141

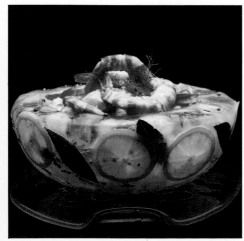

PICKLED SHRIMP AND CRYSTALLINE ICE BOWL *Marinated shrimp, served in homemade ice bowl. 20 servings; day ahead. Page 120*

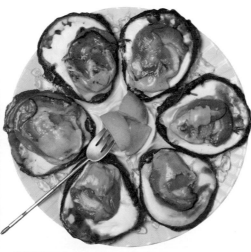

OYSTERS ON THE HALF-SHELL
Freshly-opened oysters served with lemon wedges on bed of crushed ice. 5–6 oysters each serving. Page 161

SHRIMP COCKTAIL WITH TANGY DIP
Chilled fresh-cooked shrimp served on lettuce leaves and topped with cocktail sauce.
6 servings ; early in day. Page 164

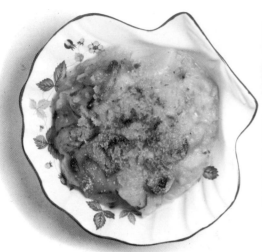

COQUILLES ST. JACQUES
Scallops in a mushroom-and-onion mixture baked in a shell with buttered crumbs and cheese. 8 servings; 50 minutes. Page 163

BACON BROILED SCALLOPS
Bacon slices wrapped around scallops, broiled then seasoned. 8 servings; 20 minutes. Page 163

OYSTERS ROCKEFELLER
Oysters on the half-shell, baked with herbed spinach topping, bacon and grated cheese. 6 servings; 30 minutes. Page 161

QUENELLES IN WINE SAUCE
Poached, ground-fish fillets, served with vermouth sauce and topped with melted cheese. 9 servings; 3 hours. Page 182

FISH MOUSSE
Mixture of poached fish, cream and salad dressing, decorated with olives and pimentos. 8 servings; 6 hours. Page 183

PAN-FRIED OYSTERS
Shucked oysters sprinkled with crushed saltines and fried until golden. 6 servings; 20 minutes. Page 161

MUSSELS MARINIERE
Mussels simmered in wine sauce, served garnished with parsley. 4 servings; 1¼ hours. Page 160

BLINI WITH CAVIAR
Tiny buckwheat pancakes, topped with sour cream and caviar. 24 servings; 55 minutes. Page 118

INDIVIDUAL ASPARAGUS SOUFFLES
Fresh cooked asparagus in a soufflé mixture, baked in ramekins until puffy. 6 servings; 1 hour. Page 149

FRENCH ONION SOUP GRATINEE
Sliced onions cooked in wine and broth; serve garnished with cheese slices on French bread. 4 servings; 45 minutes. Page 130

AVGOLEMONO
Cooked chicken broth and long-grain rice with eggs and lemon juice added, topped with lemon slices. 6 servings; 30 minutes. Page 130

SHRIMP BISQUE
Shrimp, vegetables, white wine, rice, chicken bouillon and spices cooked together with cream added. 10 servings; 1 hour. Page 130

CREAM OF MUSHROOM SOUP
Fresh mushrooms blended with oniony-bouillon mixture and heavy cream added. 8 servings; 45 minutes. Page 131

GAZPACHO
Tomatoes, tomato juice, cucumber, onion, green pepper, and spice blended until finely chopped, chilled. 4 servings; 2½ hours. Page 129

CHILLED CUCUMBER SOUP
Cooked cucumbers, onions, and spices in chicken-broth base, chilled, blended and strained. 6 servings; 4 hours. Page 129

PEA SOUP
Lettuce, onions and seasonings blended with peas and garnished with mint leaves. 10 servings; 45 minutes. Page 130

CREME VICHYSSOISE
Chopped leeks and potatoes simmered in chicken-flavor bouillon, blended until smooth, enriched with milk and cream, chilled, then garnished with fresh dill. Crème vichyssoise is also delicious hot. 12 servings; early in day. Page 129

SEAFOOD GUMBO
Spicy, Creole mixture of onion, shrimp and crab, served with a scoop of rice. 8 servings; 2 hours. **Page 136**

NEW ENGLAND CLAM CHOWDER
Traditional soup of chopped clams and potatoes with a milk base. 4 servings; 30 minutes. **Page 135**

MANHATTAN CLAM CHOWDER
Clams, bacon, potatoes and carrots in a classic herbed tomato base. 8 servings; 1½ hours. **Page 135**

BOUILLABAISSE, AMERICAN STYLE
Bass fillets, littleneck clams and shrimp in a highly seasoned tomato soup. 10 servings; 1 hour. **Page 136**

SHRIMP CHOWDER
Shrimp, cheese and cubed potatoes combined with milk and garnished with chopped parsley. 8 servings; 1 hour. **Page 136**

FISH CHOWDER
Chunks of flounder fillets, potatoes and onions simmered with herbs in creamy wine sauce. 8 servings; 50 minutes. **Page 135**

CHICKEN SOUP WITH RIVELS
Tiny dumplings added to a rich chicken and vegetable soup. 8 servings; 1½ hours. **Page 134**

HUNGARIAN GOULASH
Beef stew meat and veal heart cooked with potatoes and onions and seasoned with paprika. 12 servings; 2½ hours. **Page 133**

GERMAN LENTIL SOUP
Lentils, carrots, onions and celery simmered with leftover ham bone and bay leaves. 6 servings; 1½ hours. **Page 132**

NAVY BEAN AND BACON SOUP
Dry navy beans cooked with bacon, celery and tomatoes. 8 servings; 3½ hours. Page 135

SPLIT-PEA SOUP
Leftover ham bone simmered in water with spice bag, split peas, sliced carrots and onion. 6 servings; 1 hour. Page 133

HEARTY BORSCHT
Beets, chunks of beef and shredded cabbage served with a sour-cream topping. 4 servings; early in day. Page 132

CREAMY CHEDDAR-CHEESE SOUP
Shredded cheese stirred into milk and broth mixture, garnished with pumpernickel-bread cubes. 6 servings; 45 minutes. Page 134

MULLIGATAWNY SOUP
Hearty Indian-style, curry-flavored soup, topped with rice. 6 servings; 1½ hours. Page 134

OLD-FASHIONED BEEF-VEGETABLE SOUP *Chunks of beef and zucchini added to a rich mixture of onion, celery, carrots, cabbage and beans. 10 servings; 1 hour.* Page 132

MINESTRONE
Classic Italian vegetable soup, including kidney beans, zucchini and tomatoes; serve with grated cheese. 8 servings; 2 hours. Page 133

HARD- AND SOFT-COOKED EGGS
Eggs cooked to taste. Solid yolk and firm white or barely-set yolk and creamy white. 1 or 2 eggs per person. Page 140

CREOLE EGGS
Hard-cooked eggs simmered in a spicy tomato-and-green-pepper sauce, spooned over rice. 4 servings; 45 minutes. Page 142

EGGS DIVAN
Stuffed eggs arranged with broccoli spears and topped with a cheese spread, baked. 3 servings; 1 hour. Page 142

SCRAMBLED EGGS
Two eggs, stirred with dash of water or milk, cooked in buttered skillet until set; served here on toast. 2 eggs per person; 5 minutes. Page 144

SHRIMP SCRAMBLE
Shrimp cooked with beaten eggs and served on toasted English muffin halves. 2 servings; 15 minutes. Page 144

FRENCH OMELET
Classic dish of beaten eggs, cooked and folded in half for serving. Serve plain or with a filling. 3 eggs per person; 30 minutes. Page 145

FRIED EGGS
Whole eggs cooked in a little butter and basted until of desired doneness. Two eggs per person; 5 minutes. Page 143

BAKED EGGS
Two eggs in a buttered ramekin, seasoned with salt, pepper and paprika before baking. 2 eggs per person. 30 minutes. Page 143

EGGS MORNAY
Eggs baked for 15 minutes in a mustardy cheese sauce. 4 servings; 40 minutes. Page 143

CLASSIC CHEESE SOUFFLE
Shredded Cheddar cheese and a light white sauce, baked until puffy and golden. 6 servings; 1¼ hours. Page 148

SPINACH SOUFFLE
Puree of chopped spinach and onion in a light white sauce; baked here in individual ramekins. 6 servings; 1½ hours. Page 149

SALMON PUFF
Canned salmon, stirred into a mustard and Worcestershire-flavored egg mixture before baking. 4 servings; 1¼ hours. Page 149

CHEESE-AND-BACON SOUFFLE
Crumbled fried bacon with cheese and egg-white mixture, baked until golden. 2 servings; 1¼ hours. Page 149

CHICKEN SOUFFLE
Chicken-and-mushroom mixture, baked until puffy and golden brown. 6 servings; 1½ hours. Page 149

PUFFY OMELET
Beaten egg whites folded with beaten yolks, then baked in the oven. Can contain a filling. 2 servings; 30 minutes. Page 146

POACHED EGG
Egg simmered a few minutes in water, drained and served immediately, shown on toast. 2 eggs per person; 5 minutes. Page 142

EGGS BENEDICT
Poached eggs with slices of ham or bacon on English muffin halves, topped with Hollandaise Sauce. 4 servings; 30 minutes. Page 142

SHRIMP CURRY CREPES (top). *1 hour.*
SPINACH CREPES *30 minutes.*
6 servings each. Page 147

CLASSIC SWISS FONDUE
Traditional Swiss cheese-wine mixture served hot at the table with bread chunks. 4 servings; 25 minutes. Page 155

CHEDDAR-CHEESE FONDUE
Thick Cheddar cheese variation for serving with French bread chunks. 6 servings; 30 minutes. Page 155

BAKED CHEESE FONDUE
Slices of white bread, topped with American cheese and egg mixture and baked until puffy. 4 servings; 2 hours. Page 155

RACLETTE
Baked cheese from Switzerland, served hot with potatoes, pickles and onions. 4 servings; 20 minutes. Page 154

ITALIAN CHEESE TOAST
Broiled, sliced, Italian bread, topped with mozzarella cheese and an anchovy-caper sauce. 4 servings; 25 minutes. Page 154

WELSH RABBIT
Thick, Cheddar-cheese-sauce topping for warm toast. 6 servings; 20 minutes. Page 154

WELSH RABBIT WITH BEER
American cheese, dry mustard and beer cooked until smooth and served over toast. 4 servings; 20 minutes. Page 154

SWISS-CHEESE-AND-TOMATO BAKE
Baked croutons topped with sliced tomatoes, shredded Swiss Cheese and a mustardy egg mixture. 4 servings; 1¼ hours. Page 154

QUICHE LORRAINE
Classic flan of cheese, bacon, eggs and cream baked in a pie shell. 6 servings; 1½ hours. Page 156

ITALIAN CHEESE-AND-HAM PIE
Cottage, ricotta and Parmesan cheeses mixed with diced ham and eggs and baked in a two-crust pie. Serve cold and cut into wedges. 10 servings; early in day. Page 157

SWITZERLAND CHEESE-AND-ONION PIE *Chopped onion with Swiss cheese and egg mixture, baked in a piecrust. 6 servings; 1¼ hours.* Page 157

CHEESE-SPINACH-SAUSAGE PIE
Chopped sausage links with spinach, mozzarella and ricotta cheese, baked in a 2-crust pie. Serve hot or cold. 10 servings; 2 hours. Page 156

FRIED CHEESE PATTIES
Crumb-coated, Swiss-cheese mixture served with Spaghetti Sauce. 6 servings; early in day. Page 157

FONDUE BREAD
Yeast dough filled with Muenster cheese, topped with sliced almonds and baked until golden. 8 servings; 2 hours. Page 446

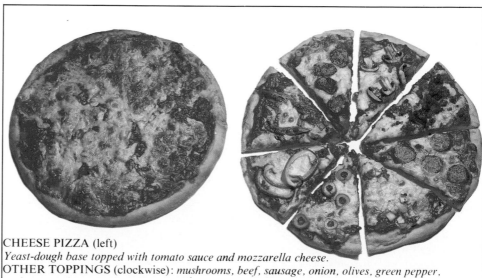

CHEESE PIZZA (left)
Yeast-dough base topped with tomato sauce and mozzarella cheese.
OTHER TOPPINGS (clockwise): *mushrooms, beef, sausage, onion, olives, green pepper, anchovies and pepperoni. 8 servings; 2½ hours.* Page 454

SPAGHETTI WITH FOUR CHEESES
Cooked spaghetti, topped with creamy sauce of mozzarella, fontina, provolone and Parmesan cheeses. 4 servings; 45 minutes. Page 331

BAKED MACARONI AND CHEESE
Elbow macaroni, covered with a thick cheese sauce, topped with buttered bread crumbs and baked. 4 servings; 45 minutes. Page 332

SKILLET MACARONI AND CHEESE
Elbow macaroni, cooked with onion and green pepper, then stirred with cheese and olives. 4 servings; 45 minutes. Page 332

BACON AND EGGS SPAGHETTI
Spaghetti, tossed with crisp bacon and onion, then stirred with beaten eggs and cheese. 4 servings; 30 minutes. Page 331

SPAGHETTI WITH HAM AND PEAS
Quick spaghetti dish, with ham, peas and cheese in a cream sauce. 4 servings; 45 minutes. Page 331

RAVIOLI and JUMBO RAVIOLI
Regular- and large-sized stuffed pasta in Marinara Sauce. 4 servings; 3 hours. Page 333

SPAGHETTI AND MEATBALLS
Small meatballs made of ground beef and bread crumbs in herbed tomato sauce accompany spaghetti. Serve with grated Parmesan cheese; garnished here with parsley. 6 servings; 2$^{1}/_{4}$ hours. Page 331

CAVATELLI WITH MEAT SAUCE
Small, homemade pasta, served topped with meat sauce and grated cheese. 4 servings; 4 hours. Page 332

HEARTY MANICOTTI
Manicotti shells, stuffed with cheese mixture, topped with sausage-beef sauce and baked. 8 servings; 2½ hours. Page 334

MANICOTTI
Cheese-stuffed pasta pancakes, baked in a ground veal and tomato sauce. 8 servings; 3 hours. Page 334

CANNELLONI
Squares of pasta, filled with meat, rolled and baked in cheese sauce. 8 servings; 2 hours. Page 335

LASAGNA
Wide noodles, layered with ricotta-cheese mixture, mozzarella and meat sauce, baked. 8 servings; 2½ hours. Page 336

VEAL LASAGNA
Creamy version of classic dish, with cubes of boneless veal baked in a sauce with lasagna noodles. 10 servings; 2½ hours. Page 336

EGGPLANT LASAGNA
Baked layers of noodles, bread-crumbed eggplant slices, tomato sauce and mozzarella cheese. 8 servings; 2¼ hours. Page 336

STUFFED SHELLS
Jumbo macaroni shells, stuffed with a cheese mixture, baked in herbed tomato sauce. 10 servings; 2½ hours. Page 334

PUERTO RICAN BEANS AND RICE
Pink beans cooked with salt pork and green pepper and flavored tomato sauce, served on rice. 6 servings; 3 hours. Page 278

EGGPLANT PARMIGIANA
Layers of sliced eggplant, tomato mixture, Parmesan and mozzarella, baked. 6 servings; 1½ hours. Page 298

33

PAELLA
Classic, Spanish, one-pan meal of seafood, sausage, chicken and saffron rice, served at the table. 8 servings; 2½ hours. **Page 165**

STEAMED CLAMS
In-shell clams steamed open and served with their own broth and melted butter. 6 servings; 1 hour. **Page 162**

CLAM FRITTERS
Chopped clams dipped in batter, fried until golden; served with Tartar Sauce. 4 servings; 45 minutes. **Page 162**

PAN-FRIED CLAMS
Cherrystone clams, dipped in egg and then bread crumbs and fried until golden. 6 servings; 30 minutes. **Page 162**

SCALLOPS BONNE FEMME
Scallops in a creamy wine sauce, topped with parsley and cheese and served with toast points. 4 servings; 40 minutes. **Page 163**

INDIAN SHRIMP CURRY
Fried shrimp in a spicy yogurt mixture, served over rice. 8 servings; 30 minutes. **Page 165**

SHRIMP SCAMPI
Broiled shrimp covered with garlic-flavored butter sauce, garnished with parsley and lemon. 6 servings; 20 minutes. **Page 164**

STIR-FRIED SHRIMP
Tender-fried large shrimp, served over Chinese cabbage, pea pods and straw mushrooms, in a soy- and ginger-flavored sauce. 8 servings; 1½ hours. **Page 165**

BROILED LOBSTER
Whole lobster, split open, brushed with melted butter and broiled. 1 small lobster per serving; 25 minutes. Page 169

LOBSTER THERMIDOR
Cooked lobster meat mixed with creamy sherry sauce. Mixture is returned to shells and broiled with cheese topping until hot. 4 servings; early in day. Page 169

BROILED ROCK LOBSTER TAILS
Broiled lobster tails, served with melted butter or favorite sauce. 1 large tail per serving; 15 minutes. Page 169

PAN-FRIED SOFT-SHELL CRABS
Cooked, whole crabs, served with butter sauce and lemon wedges. 4 servings; 15 minutes. Page 167

CRAB CAKES
Fried patties of cooked crab meat, bread crumbs and spices served with Tartar Sauce. 4 servings; 30 minutes. Page 167

CRAB IMPERIAL
Alaska King crab meat in sherry-egg sauce, baked in a casserole. 8 servings; 1 hour. Page 167

BLUEFISH WITH BUTTERY LEMON SAUCE *Broiled or grilled, pan-dressed fish, basted with lemon sauce during cooking. 8 servings; 20 minutes. Page 174*

BAKED RED SNAPPER WITH OYSTER STUFFING *Whole fish, with chopped oyster, celery and bread-cube stuffing. 8 servings; 1½ hours. Page 176*

POACHED SALMON WITH ASPIC
Whole salmon poached in wine and water. Serve with homemade aspic made from cooking liquid and herb mayonnaise. 12 servings; early in day. Page 176

BROILED SESAME TROUT
Marinated pan-dressed fish, basted with sesame-seed mixture and served with lemon slices and parsley. 6 servings; 4 hours. Page 174

PAN-FRIED SMELTS
Breaded pan-dressed smelts, fried until golden and served with lime wedges. 6 servings; 1½ hours. Page 175

STRIPED BASS WITH PUNGENT SAUCE
Chinese-style fried fish, served with spicy sauce and stir-fried vegetables. 6 servings; 1½ hours. Page 175

BROILER-BARBECUED FISH DINNER
Seafood-Barbecue Sauce-topped haddock or cod fillets, broiled with mushrooms, cheese and zucchini. 4 servings; 55 minutes. Page 177

FILLETS OF SOLE THERMIDOR
Sole or other white fish fillets poached in milk then broiled in a cheese and sherry sauce until golden. 8 servings; 45 minutes. Page 178

MEDITERRANEAN COD WITH VEGETABLES *Fried fillets, served with mixture of eggplant, onions, peppers and tomatoes. 8 servings; 1½ hours.* Page 178

SHRIMP-STUFFED ROLL-UPS
Sole or other fillets, stuffed with shrimp-and-mushroom mixture, simmered and topped with creamy sauce. 6 servings; 40 minutes. Page 180

BROILED TARRAGON FISH
Flounder or other fillets, broiled with tarragon dressing and served with lemon wedges and parsley. 4 servings; 20 minutes. Page 177

CLAM-STUFFED FILLETS
Flounder, ocean perch or other fillets, stuffed with minced-clam mixture and baked in custard cups. 4 servings; 50 minutes. Page 179

CODFISH STEW
Cod fillets, cooked in seasoned tomato-mixture with potatoes, bacon and onion. 4 servings; 55 minutes. Page 180

POACHED SOLE WITH HOLLANDAISE SAUCE *Sole fillets, simmered in court bouillon, topped with sauce and parsley. 4 servings; 50 minutes.* Page 179

BAKED SOLE WITH LEMON SAUCE
Cooked fillets, covered with thick lemon sauce and garnished with fresh dill. 8 servings; 30 minutes. Page 179

CREAMED FINNAN HADDIE
Chunks of Finnan haddie simmered in cream sauce, served on toast, garnished with sieved egg yolk. 8 servings; 30 minutes. Page 180

FRIED FISH A LA MARGHERITA
Sole, flounder or other fillets, in herbed tomato sauce. 8 servings; 50 minutes. Page 178

FISH FRY
Batter-coated flounder, turbot or other fillets, fried until golden; serve with Sweet-Sour Sauce. 4 servings; 55 minutes. Page 177

MARINATED SWORDFISH STEAKS
Fish steaks, covered in a tarragon-flavored vinegar marinade and broiled. 6 servings; early in day. Page 182

CHILLED SALMON STEAKS WITH MARINATED CUCUMBER *Cooked steaks served with thin cucumber slices and Green Mayonnaise. 6 servings; 4 hours.* Page 181

HALIBUT STEAK WITH EGGPLANT SAUCE *Broiled, butter-basted fish, served with simmered eggplant sauce. 6 servings; 30 minutes.* Page 181

CODFISH STEAK
Fried steaks accompanied by cooked spinach and mushroom mixture. 4 servings; 40 minutes. Page 182

COLD SALMON MOUSSE
Molded canned salmon, mayonnaise, gelatin, flavorings and cream, decorated with radish slices. 6 servings; 4 hours. Page 184

SALMON BURGERS
Seasoned and fried canned-salmon patties, served with Hollandaise Sauce on English muffins. 6 servings; 45 minutes. Page 183

TUNA PIE
Tuna, broccoli, water chestnuts, mushrooms and cheese mixture, topped with pastry and baked. 6 servings; 1½ hours. Page 184

TUNA TETRAZZINI
Cooked spaghetti in cheese sauce, mixed with canned tuna before baking. 8 servings; 1 hour. Page 184

TUNA LOAF WITH CUCUMBER SAUCE
Canned-tuna and saltine mixture, baked in loaf pan and topped with sauce. 8 servings; 1½ hours. Page 183

ROAST TURKEY WITH MOIST
BREAD STUFFING AND
GIBLET GRAVY *Turkey with
homemade stuffing, roasted until
golden and served with Giblet Gravy.
16 servings; 6$^1/_2$ hours.* Page 249

TURKEY MOLE
*Mexican dish of cooked turkey, topped
with chocolate-sesame-seed sauce, garnished
with avocado. 12 servings; 3 hours.* Page 266

TURKEY ROLL WITH SPINACH
STUFFING *Boned turkey breast, cut in half
and rolled jelly-roll fashion around stuffing
before roasting. 16 servings; 3 hours.* Page 250

SAUCY TURKEY WINGS
*Turkey wings braised in celery sauce until
tender and garnished with fresh parsley.
6 servings; 2$^1/_2$ hours.* Page 259

TURKEY SAUSAGE KABOBS
*Chunks of marinated turkey breast, brown-and-serve sausages, canned
pineapple chunks and green onions. 6 servings; 1 hour.* Page 262

39

TURKEY-ROQUEFORT SALAD
*Cooked turkey mixed with Roquefort cheese
and sour cream, served on a canned peach-half.
6 servings; early in day. Page 268*

CHICKEN SALAD
*A simple salad of chicken, celery, green pepper
and onion, coated with a mayonnaise dressing.
8 servings; early in day. Page 268*

TURKEY IN CHAMPAGNE SAUCE
*Braised turkey meat, in a mushroom, half-and-
half and champagne sauce, served with toast
flowers. 6 servings; 2 hours. Page 259*

TURKEY-TAMALE CASSEROLE
*Mexican-style dish of braised turkey with
kidney beans, chili and herbed cornmeal-
batter topping. 6 servings; 4 hours. Page 259*

APRICOT-GLAZED TURKEY DRUMSTICKS
*Turkey drumsticks glazed with an apricot preserve and served with canned apricot halves,
shown here with rice, green beans and watercress sprigs. 4 servings; $2^1/2$ hours. Page 259*

CHICKEN CORDON BLEU
Boned chicken breasts, filled with sliced Swiss cheese and cooked ham; served here with green salad. 6 servings; 1¹/4 hours. Page 256

HERB-ROASTED CAPON
Unstuffed bird, lightly covered with a herbed seasoning and left overnight before roasting. 8 servings; day ahead. Page 250

CHICKEN DINNER WITH SOUR-CREAM GRAVY *Braised chicken with carrots and celery served with gravy and hot rice. 4 servings; 45 minutes. Page 254*

CHICKEN OPORTO
Portuguese dish of boneless chicken breasts, braised in white port with mushrooms and cream. 4 servings; 35 minutes. Page 256

CHICKEN PAPRIKA WITH SPAETZLE
Small, homemade dumplings served with paprika-flavored chicken pieces in a creamy sauce. 6 servings; 45 minutes. Page 253

CHICKEN CURRY, SOUTHERN STYLE
Chicken pieces in a curried sauce with almonds and currants, shown with rice. 5 servings; 1 hour. Page 254

CHICKEN SEVILLE
Richly-herbed chicken pieces cooked in a vegetable mixture and finished with olives. 6 servings; 1¹/2 hours. Page 255

NUT-STUFFED CHICKEN BREASTS WITH CREAMY GRAVY *Baked chicken breasts stuffed with chopped peanuts. 6 servings; 2 hours. Page 251*

BEER-BATTER CHICKEN
Chicken fried in batter; served here with French fries. 4 servings; 55 minutes. Page 263

41

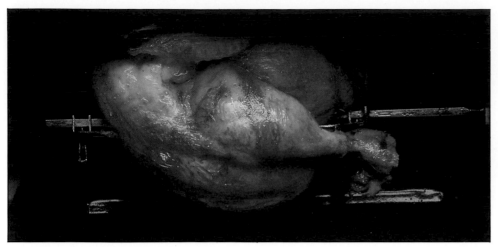

ROTISSERIED CHICKEN
Whole chicken, grilled on a spit and basted during cooking with melted butter. Allow 3/4 to 1 pound per person. Page 260

FESTIVE CHICKEN WITH ASPARAGUS
Chicken breasts braised with asparagus in cream-of-chicken soup, white wine and blue cheese. 6 servings; 1 1/2 hours. Page 258

CHICKEN CHORIZO
Spicy dish of braised chicken pieces with ham, Spanish sausage and garlic. 6 servings; 1 hour. Page 255

CHICKEN WITH CUCUMBERS
Simmered chicken quarters with cucumber, mushroom and sour cream sauce, topped with cucumber. 4 servings; 1 1/4 hours. Page 254

SOUR CREAM CHICKEN ENCHILADAS
Fried tortillas, filled with chicken meat, chilies and mushrooms, baked in sour cream and topped with cheese. 6 servings; 1 hour. Page 269

SAVORY CHICKEN
Chicken quarters marinated with garlic, dry mustard and Worcestershire; garnished with watercress. 8 servings; 3 1/2 hours. Page 260

CHICKEN CACCIATORE
Classic Italian dish of chicken with onions, tomatoes, green pepper and herbs, in red wine. 4 servings; 1 hour. Page 254

PARTY SHRIMP AND CHICKEN
Chicken breasts braised in a rich sauce of shrimp, tomatoes, port wine and herbs. 6 servings; 45 minutes. Page 257

CHICKEN PERIGORD-STYLE
Boned chicken breasts simmered in a rich fresh mushroom sauce. 8 servings; 1 hour.
Page 256

CHICKEN BREASTS WITH SAUSAGE-WALNUT STUFFING
Stuffed chicken breasts simmered in broth, served with sautéed zucchini. 8 servings; 1¹/₂ hours. Page 257

CHICKEN DELHI
Roast spiced chickens, basted during cooking with a yogurt sauce; served over rice. 8 servings; 2¹/₂ hours. Page 250

CHICKEN OROBIANCO
Tender chicken breasts teamed with robust pork sausages and cooked with mushrooms and white wine. 8 servings; 1¹/₄ hours. Page 258

CHICKEN WITH ENDIVES
Braised, boned chicken breasts and endives, topped with cheese sauce and buttered crumbs. 4 servings; 45 minutes. Page 256

ROAST CHICKEN WITH SAUSAGE-APPLE STUFFING
Tender roast chicken, stuffed with sausage-apple mixture. 6 servings; 4 hours. Page 250

CHICKEN AVGOLEMONO
Boneless chicken breasts and sliced zucchini served with egg-yolk and lemon sauce and Orzo-Rice Pilaf. 8 servings; 1 hour. Page 258

CHICKEN SALADS:
WALDORF (left).
10 servings. WALNUT (right).
8 servings. HAM *8 servings; all early in day.* Page 268

43

PAN-FRIED CHICKEN WITH CREAM GRAVY *Chicken pieces shallow-fried in oil until the skin is crisp, served with a milk-based gravy. 4 servings; 1 hour.* Page 262

BAKED CHICKEN
Chicken, dipped first in a flour coating, then melted butter or margarine, and baked. 8 servings; 1 hour. Page 251

SIMMERED CHICKEN
Stewing chicken in a vegetable seasoned broth, served here with dumplings. 6 servings; 3 hours. Page 266

COQ AU VIN
Classic French dish of chicken pieces, mushrooms and onions braised in herbs and red wine. 4 servings; 1^1/$_2$ hours. Page 266

CHICKEN IMPERIAL
Chicken breasts, braised in heavy cream and dry sherry, with mushrooms and minced onion. 8 servings; 1^1/$_4$ hours. Page 257

CHEESE AND ANCHOVY BROILED CHICKEN BREASTS *Anchovy-stuffed chicken breasts topped with cheese; served here with salad. 6 servings; 1 hour.* Page 262

CHICKEN BREASTS WITH ARTICHOKE HEARTS *Baked chicken in a creamy, brandy and lemon sauce, finished with artichoke hearts. 6 servings; 1^1/$_2$ hours.* Page 258

ARROZ CON POLLO
Rice and chicken in a Spanish-style dish with tomatoes, pimentos, olives, sausages and peas. 8 servings; 1^3/$_4$ hours. Page 253

CHICKEN KIEV
Boned chicken breast stuffed with chive and parsley butter then deep-fried in a crisp bread-crumb-coating. 6 servings; 3 hours. Page 264

MOO GOO GAI PAN
Sliced chicken, walnuts, straw mushrooms, bamboo shoots and snow peas, stir-fried, Chinese style. 4 servings; 35 minutes. Page 265

STIR-FRIED CHICKEN
Strips of chicken lightly fried with Oriental-style vegetables and topped with toasted almonds. 4 servings; 45 minutes. Page 265

CHICKEN WITH ORANGE PEEL SZECHUAN STYLE *Marinated chicken, stir-fried in a little oil and garnished with fried orange peels. 4 servings; 1 hour. Page 265*

BROILED LEMON-CHICKEN
Chicken quarters, basted with a lemony butter mixture, accompanied by broiled tomatoes. 4 servings; 50 minutes. Page 261

SAUCY CHICKEN WITH AVOCADO
Topping of avocado slices in a creamy sauce for chicken braised in sherry. 4 servings; 45 minutes. Page 255

CHICKEN TETRAZZINI
Cooked chicken in a creamy sauce, spooned over spaghetti. 8 servings; 2 hours. Page 267

CHICKEN FRICASSEE
Chicken in white wine sauce, garnished here with curls of fried bacon and parsley. 8 servings; 3$^1/2$ hours. Page 255

OVEN-FRIED CHICKEN
Cracker-meal-coated chicken pieces, fried in the oven until crisp. 4 servings; 1$^1/4$ hours. Page 263

CHICKEN A LA KING
Cooked chicken and mushrooms in a rich cream sauce, served in patty shells. 8 servings; 40 minutes. Page 268

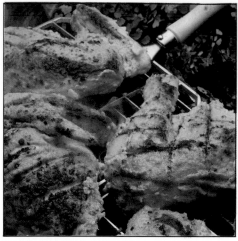

TANDOORI CHICKEN
Chicken marinated in yogurt, spices and lemon juice, barbecued outdoors or broiled in the oven. 4 servings; day ahead. Page 260

CHICKEN POT PIE
Simmered chicken, combined with vegetables in a creamy sauce and baked with a pastry topping. 8 servings; 2 hours. Page 267

CRUNCHY DRUMSTICKS
Chicken drumsticks marinated in orange juice, then rolled in oats and butter and baked until crisp. 8 servings; early in dav. Page 263

CHICKEN CROQUETTES
4 servings; early in day. Page 269

CHICKEN MARINATED IN CHILI SAUCE *Chicken pieces marinated in a spicy sauce and then broiled or barbecued. 4 servings; early in day.* Page 261

LEMON CHICKEN ON SPINACH LEAVES *Lightly fried, boned chicken breasts, served on shredded raw spinach with lemon sauce. 6 servings; 45 minutes.* Page 263

CREAMY CHICKEN HASH
Cubed cooked chicken and potatoes, served in a thick sauce. 4 servings; 25 minutes. Page 268

CRISPY CHICKEN ROLLS
Halved, boned chicken breasts stuffed with cooked shrimp, dipped in batter and fried until golden. 6 servings; 2$^1/_2$ hours. Page 264

CHICKEN SAUTERNE
Chicken halves marinated in white wine and salad oil with green onions and parsley and baked. 4 servings; early in day. Page 251

CHICKEN LIVERS SAUTE
Chicken livers, sautéed with onion and stirred into a sherry-flavored sauce to serve on toast triangles. 6 servings; 30 minutes. Page 269

LEMON-GLAZED ROCK CORNISH HENS *Rotisseried Rock Cornish hens, finished with glaze of lemon peel, apple juice and light corn syrup. 4 servings; 1¹/₂ hours. Page 271*

CHICKEN LIVERS ALOHA
Chicken livers cooked with vegetables and served Hawaiian-style, with pineapple chunks and rice. 4 servings; 30 minutes. Page 269

ROCK CORNISH HENS WITH MINCEMEAT DRESSING *Roast hens finished with a sweet glaze of corn syrup and sherry. 4 servings; 2 hours. Page 271*

BROILED ROCK CORNISH HEN
A halved hen, broiled with pineapple slices and served with herbed rice. 2 servings; 50 minutes. Page 271

ROCK CORNISH HENS WITH RED RAISIN SAUCE
Roasted Rock Cornish hens with a wheat germ and celery stuffing; served with a hot, fruity sauce. 4 servings; 1³/₄ hours. Page 270

ROCK CORNISH HENS WITH DRESSING *Roast hens stuffed with mushroom- and shallot-flavored rice. 4 servings; 2³/₄ hours. Page 270*

47

STANDING RIB ROAST WITH YORKSHIRE PUDDING
Beef rib roast small end, served with individual Yorkshire Puddings and Horseradish Sauce. 18 servings; 2 to 4 hours. Page 191

SESAME CHUCK STEAK
Chuck blade steak, marinated in sesame-seed mixture, broiled and served with cooked sliced onions. 10 servings; early in day. Page 198

NEW ENGLAND "BOILED" DINNER
Simmered boneless fresh beef brisket with cooked vegetables. 16 servings; 3 1/2 hours. Page 205

CREAMY TOP BLADE STEAKS
Braised steaks served with noodles and topped with dilled sour-cream sauce. 6 servings; 1 3/4 hours. Page 200

BARBECUED POT ROAST
Beef chuck 7-bone pot roast braised in a spicy tomato and onion sauce. 12 servings; 4 hours. Page 195

CALIFORNIA BEEF STEW
Stewed beef chunks, with onions, mushrooms, peas and olives. 8 servings; 3 hours. Page 203

BRAISED STEAK CAESAR-STYLE
*Beef eye round steaks, braised in
Worcestershire-anchovy sauce and served on
toast. 4 servings; 1¾ hours. Page 201*

LONDON BROIL
*Seasoned flank steak, broiled with halved
tomatoes and mushrooms. 4 servings;
30 minutes. Page 196*

MEAT LOAF (top) *and variation,*
PINEAPPLE MEAT LOAF. *Each 8 servings;
2 hours. Page 206*

**FILETS MIGNONS WITH MUSTARD-
CAPER SAUCE** *Fried beef tenderloin steaks,
served with creamy, vermouth-flavored mustard
and caper sauce. 6 servings; 30 minutes.
Page 195*

**POT ROAST WITH SWEET AND SOUR
CABBAGE** *Braised beef chuck eye roast,
served with cooked red cabbage. 10 servings;
3½ hours. Page 194*

ZITI BAKE
*Baked macaroni, ground beef, ricotta and
Spaghetti Sauce, topped with mozzarella
cheese. 8 servings; 1½ hours. Page 209*

VEGETABLE-TOPPED ROAST BEEF
*Beef round tip roast, topped with shredded
carrots and celery and served with wine gravy.
18 servings; 3½ hours. Page 191*

CELERY-STUFFED FLANK STEAK
*Flank steak, rolled jelly-roll fashion around
fresh celery stuffing and braised. 8 servings;
2½ hours. Page 201*

CARBONNADES A LA FLAMANDE
*Beef chunks simmered in beer with bacon and
onions and garnished with fresh thyme.
10 servings; 2¾ hours. Page 199*

51

BARBECUED SHORT RIBS
Precooked beef ribs, grilled with spicy catchup sauce. 8 servings, day ahead. Page 204

SAUERBRATEN
Marinated bottom round roast, cooked with vegetables and served with gravy. 16 servings; 2 days ahead. Page 193

SPICY BEEF CHUCK STEAK
Chuck underblade steak, braised in steak sauce, brown sugar, mustard and lemon juice. 10 servings; 2 hours. Page 199

DEVILED ROUND STEAK
Breaded beef top round steak, grilled until golden. 12 servings; 1^1/2 hours. Page 197

WHOLE STUFFED CABBAGE
Cooked cabbage shell, filled with spicy ground-beef and rice mixture and baked with tomato sauce. 6 servings; 3 hours. Page 209

BEEF WITH LEEKS AND CARROTS
Chuck 7-bone steak, braised with leeks and carrots. 8 servings; 2 hours. Page 199

BEEF STEW
Chunks of meat, carrots, potatoes and peas simmered in bouillon. 10 servings; 3^1/2 hours. Page 202

BEEF STEAK STROGANOFF
Chuck top blade boneless steaks with onion and mushrooms, served with noodles and sour cream sauce. 1^3/4 hours. Page 201

COUNTRY POT ROAST
Beef chuck cross rib pot roast braised in tomato juice with vegetables, served with gravy. 20 servings; 5 hours. Page 192

FRUITED POT ROAST
Boneless beef chuck eye roast, braised with apple cider, cloves, dried apricots and prunes. 14 servings; 4 hours. Page 193

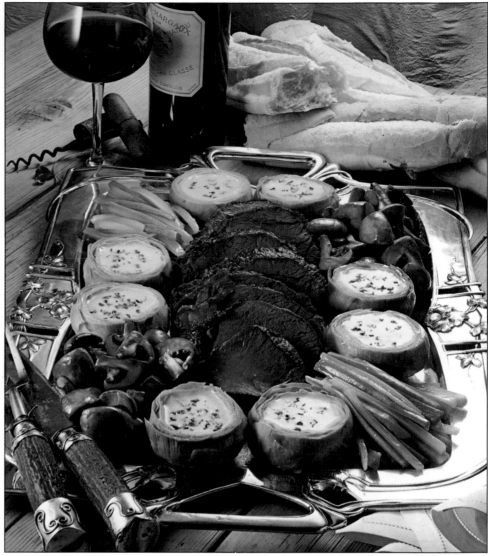

BEEF SHANKS WITH VEGETABLES
Beef shanks, stewed in tomato soup with carrots, onions and lima beans. 8 servings; 4 hours. Page 204

CHATEAUBRIAND
Broiled beef tenderloins, served with ARTICHOKES BEARNAISE (page 276) *and sautéed mushrooms, carrots and celery. 8 servings; 1¹/2 hours.* Page 195

BAKED POT ROAST WITH VEGETABLES *Beef round rump roast, braised in oven with parsnips and lima beans. 10 servings; 4 hours.* Page 193

SWISS STEAK WITH TOMATO
Chuck arm steak, braised with onions and green pepper in tomato sauce. 10 servings; 2¹/2 hours. Page 200

CONTINENTAL BEEF STEAK
Broiled beef top round steak, flavored with herbs; served with peppers, olives, tomatoes and capers. 12 servings; 1 hour. Page 197

WHOLE SMITHFIELD HAM
Simmered whole Smithfield ham, brushed with corn syrup and baked in the oven until glazed; serve whole ham with biscuits and bread for a party, letting each guest help him- or herself. 60 party servings; day ahead. Page 221

GLAZED HAM PLATTER
Baked ham, glazed with horseradish and mustard sauce, served with apples and acorn squash. 18 servings; 3 hours. Page 220

BARBECUED CANNED HAM AND PEACHES *Canned ham, baked with fresh peaches and homemade barbecue sauce. 12 servings; 1³/₄ hours.* Page 220

SMOKED PORK WITH SWEET POTATOES *Pork shoulder roll coated with brown sugar mixture, baked with canned sweet potatoes. 10 servings; 2 hours.* Page 222

**PINEAPPLE-GLAZED BAKED HALF
HAM** *Baked, smoked half ham, with
pineapple and brown sugar glaze.
20 servings; 2³/4 hours.* **Page 220**

FRUIT-SAUCED HAM SLICES
*Slices of ham, simmered with orange juice,
dried apricots and prunes. 6 servings;
30 minutes.* **Page 222**

CHOUCROUTE GARNI
*Simmered smoked and fresh pork, onions,
potatoes, bratwurst and sauerkraut served
together. 20 servings; 3 hours.* **Page 222**

HAM STEAK HAWAIIAN
*Smoked ham center slice and bananas, cooked
in brown sugar and vinegar sauce. 6 servings;
30 minutes.* **Page 221**

LEMONY HAM STEAKS
*Ham slices, broiled with a fresh-lemon and
mustard glaze. 8 servings; 20 minutes.*
Page 222

GLAZED HAM LOAF
*Ground ham, carrot and onion loaf, baked with
pineapple glaze and decorated with pineapple
slices. 5 servings; 1³/4 hours.* **Page 223**

BAKED PICNIC
*Baked smoked pork shoulder picnic, glazed and
decorated with oranges and cloves.
16 servings; 3¹/2 hours.* **Page 220**

COUNTRY HAM STEAK
*Shredded, stir-fried cabbage, baked with
smoked ham and pancake syrup. 6 servings;
1 hour.* **Page 222**

LEFTOVER HAM IDEAS (from top)
**HAM CASSEROLE; HAM CHEF'S
SALAD; HAM FRUIT SALAD;
GLAZED KABOBS. Page 223**

LEMON-TARRAGON VEAL ROAST
*Boneless veal shoulder, roasted with tarragon and lemon and served with pan gravy.
14 servings; 3¼ hours. Page 234*

SPICY VEAL RUMP ROAST
Veal rump roast, braised with apple juice, onion and pickling spice and garnished with apples. 14 servings; 3 hours. Page 235

SALTIMBOCCA
Fried cutlets, baked with strips of prosciutto ham and raclette cheese. 4 servings; 40 minutes. Page 236

VEAL STEW MILANESE
Veal chunks, stewed with red wine with tomatoes, carrot, celery and basil, garnished with lemon peel. 6 servings; 2 hours. Page 239

VEAL PICCATA
Thin cutlets, simmered in white wine and lemon juice and topped with lemon slices. 8 servings; 1¼ hours. Page 236

VEAL PAPRIKA
Veal, stewed with onions, paprika and sour cream and served over noodles. 8 servings; 2½ hours. Page 239

VEAL RIB ROAST MARSALA
Seasoned roast veal, served with Marsala and mushroom gravy. 10 servings; 3¼ hours. Page 234

VEAL PARMIGIANA
Fried veal cutlets, topped with Marinara Sauce and mozzarella and Parmesan cheeses. 6 servings; 1 hour. Page 236

WIENER SCHNITZEL
Bread-crumbed veal cutlets, fried in butter and garnished with lemon and parsley. 6 servings; 45 minutes. Page 236

SCHNITZEL A LA HOLSTEIN
Wiener Schnitzel topped with a fried egg, anchovy fillets and capers. 6 servings; 45 minutes. Page 236

TOMATO-PAPRIKA VEAL
Braised veal, sliced and served with noodles and creamy tomato-paprika sauce. 14 servings; 3 hours. Page 235

COUNTRY-STYLE VEAL RUMP ROAST
Boneless roast, braised in mushroom soup with carrots, onion and herbs. 16 servings; 3¹/4 hours. Page 234

BLANQUETTE DE VEAU
Veal stew meat in a creamy sauce, served over noodles and garnished with dill. 10 servings. 3 hours. Page 239

VEAL AND PEPPERS
Veal cutlets cooked in butter with red and green peppers and flavorings including basil and oregano. 8 servings; 1 hour. Page 235

SALADE NICOISE
Classic tuna, egg, anchovy and vegetable salad.
4 servings; early in day. Page 324

CHEF'S SALAD
Chicken, cheese, ham, hard-cooked eggs and
tomatoes on lettuce base. 6 servings;
30 minutes. Page 324

CRAB LOUIS (top). *4 servings; 1 hour.*
PINEAPPLE-CHEESE SALAD *4 servings;*
30 minutes. Page 325

CHUNKY EGG SALAD
Hard-cooked eggs, celery and green pepper,
tossed with mayonnaise mixture and served on
lettuce leaves. 4 servings; 1 hour. Page 325

SMOKED CHICKEN SALAD
Sliced chicken, tomatoes and cheese served
on spinach and topped with mustard dressing.
8 servings; 30 minutes. Page 325

BROWN RICE, WESTERN STYLE
Flavored cooked rice mixed with cooked ham,
green pepper and corn. 6 servings; 1 hour.
Page 325

HERRING SALAD
Rich salad of chopped pickled herring, diced
potatoes and pickled beets in heavy cream.
6 servings; early in day. Page 324

SHRIMP SALAD (left) *and variations. Cooked, shelled shrimp tossed in a*
French-dressing and mayonnaise mixture with celery, walnuts, olives and
onion, served on lettuce. **TUNA SALAD** (center) *and* **SALMON**
SALAD. *4 servings; 1 hour.* Page 325

CAULIFLOWER POLONAISE
Whole, cooked cauliflower, topped with mixture of bread crumbs, chopped egg and lemon juice. 6 servings; 20 minutes. **Page 282**

BAKED CREAMED SPINACH
Cooked spinach, mixed with a light, creamy sauce and baked. 8 servings; 1 hour. **Page 293**

RATATOUILLE
Eggplant, peppers, zucchini, onion and tomato, flavored with garlic; serve hot or cold. 8 servings; 45 minutes. **Page 297**

GREEN BEANS WITH ZUCCHINI (top).
6 servings; 30 minutes. **Page 298**
STIR-FRIED ZUCCHINI *4 servings; 15 minutes.* **Page 294**

SUMMER SQUASH MEDLEY
Tender-crisp strips of zucchini and straightneck squash, tossed with butter and lemon. 6 servings; 15 minutes. **Page 294**

CANDIED SWEET POTATOES (left).
6 servings; 30 minutes. **SHERRIED SWEET POTATOES** *6 servings; 50 minutes.* **Page 295**

CREAMED ONIONS (left). *10 servings; 30 minutes.* **Page 289. GLAZED ONIONS** *4 servings; 30 minutes.* **Page 288**

FRENCH-FRIED ONIONS (left).
8 servings; 30 minutes. **PAN-FRIED ONIONS** *4 servings; 15 minutes.* **Page 289**

BAKED ONIONS
Sliced onions baked in honey and butter until tender and golden brown. 8 servings; 1 hour. **Page 288**

BOSTON BAKED BEANS
Navy beans, baked with molasses, brown sugar, onions and salt pork. 12 servings; early in day. Page 277

BLACKEYE BEANS (left). *Cooked with salt pork. 6 servings; day ahead.* BEAN RELISH *Tangy kidney beans and corn. 9 cups; 4 1/2 hours.* Page 278

WHOLE GREEN AND WAX BEANS WITH PARSLEY SAUCE *Tender fresh green and wax beans served together in a thick parsley sauce. 8 servings; 30 minutes.* Page 278

BRAISED FENNEL
Halved fennel bulbs simmered in bouillon and served with buttery sauce and fennel leaf garnish. 4 servings; 30 minutes. Page 285

SPICED CARROTS (top). *12 servings; 45 minutes.* GLAZED CARROTS *4 servings; 25 minutes.* Page 282

MASHED TURNIPS
Cooked turnips, mashed with butter, seasoned with salt, sugar and pepper. 8 servings; 40 minutes. Page 296

PARSLEY CREAMED PARSNIPS
Cooked, sliced parsnips with a creamy orange-flavored sauce, garnished with chopped parsley. 6 servings; 30 minutes. Page 289

HARVARD BEETS
Cooked beets served hot in an onion-vinegar sauce or, if preferred, a piquant orange sauce. 6 servings; 20 minutes. Page 279

LIMA BEANS SMITANE (left). *4 servings; 25 minutes.*
ZESTY LIMA BEANS *4 servings; 2 hours.* Both page 279

EGGPLANT WITH CARAWAY SEED
(top). *25 minutes.* SAUTEED EGGPLANT
SLICES *15 minutes; 4 servings each.* Page 284

SUMMER VEGETABLE BOWL
*Corn, onions, green pepper, green beans,
zucchini and celery, garnished with bacon and
tomato. 8 servings; 1 hour.* Page 297

SAUTEED MUSHROOMS (left).
4 servings; 20 minutes. MUSHROOMS IN
SOUR CREAM. *12 first-course servings;
30 minutes.* Both page 287

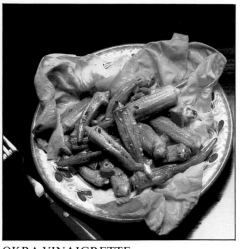

OKRA VINAIGRETTE
*Chilled tender-crisp okra and chopped pimento
in a vinaigrette sauce. Served on Boston
lettuce. 6 servings; 4 1/2 hours.* Page 288

STIR-FRIED CABBAGE AND ZUCCHINI
*Finely-sliced cabbage and zucchini, stir-fried
in garlic-flavored oil until tender-crisp.
8 servings; 15 minutes.* Page 298

VEGETABLE TRIO
*Carrots, green beans and mushrooms, braised
with thyme butter until tender-crisp.
5 servings; 25 minutes.* Page 297

ENDIVES WITH SWISS CHEESE
*Belgian endives, simmered until tender, then
baked with topping of Swiss cheese and half-
and-half. 6 servings; 1 hour.* Page 285

SAUTEED CARAWAY-CABBAGE
*Coarsely-shredded green cabbage, sautéed in
oil with caraway seed until tender-crisp.
6 servings; 15 minutes.* Page 281

CABBAGE RELISH (left). *3 hours.* RED
CABBAGE AND APPLES (enter). *1 hour.*
SKILLET CABBAGE *30 minutes. All
8 servings.* Page 281

FLAVORED BUTTERS FOR CORN
Serve corn-on-the-cob with butters flavored with chili powder, chives, or dill weed.
Page 283

STIR-FRIED ASPARAGUS
Fresh asparagus cut diagonally and stir-fried, Chinese-style, in salad oil and salt until tender-crisp. 6 servings; 10 minutes. Page 277

LEEKS AU GRATIN
Leeks simmered in water, topped with cheese mixture and broiled until golden. 4 servings; 45 minutes. Page 286

MARINATED PEPPERS (top). *6 servings; early in day.* **HERB SAUTEED GREEN PEPPERS** *4 servings; 15 minutes.* Page 290

VEGETABLE-STUFFED GREEN PEPPERS (left). *4 servings; 15 minutes.* Page 299. **PEPPER-AND-TOMATO SAUTE** *10 servings; 30 minutes.* Page 298

STIR-FRIED VEGETABLE MIX
Carrots, onion and broccoli stir-fried in hot oil, then simmered with mushrooms until tender-crisp. 6 servings; 25 minutes. Page 298

SAUTEED CUCUMBER RINGS
Peeled cucumber slices with seeds removed, sautéed in butter until tender-crisp. 4 servings; 30 minutes. Page 284

PEAS AMANDINE
Shelled peas, mixed with chopped bacon, minced onion, slivered almonds and heavy cream. 4 servings; 40 minutes. Page 290

CARROTS AND CELERY
Diagonally sliced fresh carrots and celery simmered with light seasonings until tender-crisp. 8 servings; 30 minutes. Page 297

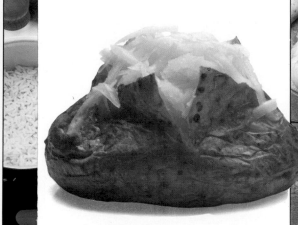

HOT F BAKED POTATOES
20 min Fork-tender potatoes, served with choice of
4 servir sour cream, butter or shredded cheese.
6 servings; 1 hour. Page 291

COOKED POTATOES:
PAN-ROASTED (left). *6 servings; 1¹/₄ hours.*
MASHED (center). *6 servings; 50 minutes.*
FRENCH-FRIED *8 servings; 30 minutes.* All page 291

BAKEI HASH BROWN POTATOES (top).
Uncook 6 servings; 45 minutes. Page 292;
green p HOME-FRIED POTATOES *4 servings;*
cheese 25 minutes. Page 291

POTATOES AU GRATIN (top). *6 servings;*
55 minutes. POTATOES ANNA *4 servings;*
1¹/₂ hours. Page 292

CONFETTI VEGETABLES
Shredded zucchini, carrots and parsnips,
cooked until tender-crisp. 12 servings;
30 minutes. Page 297

RICE F SAUTEED CELERY
Cooked Sliced celery, cooked quickly in salad oil with
packed bay leaves and thyme. 6 servings;
serving. 20 minutes. Page 283

CHEESY KOHLRABI
Cooked, sliced kohlrabi with cheese sauce,
sprinkled with allspice and parsley. 6 servings;
45 minutes. Page 286

SWEET-AND-SOUR BRUSSELS
SPROUTS (left). *10 servings; 30 minutes.*
BAKED BRUSSELS SPROUTS *6 servings;*
1 hour. Page 280

71

HERBED ORANGE RICE
Long-grain or parboiled rice cooked with orange juice, onion, celery and thyme. 6 servings; 45 minutes. Page 338

CURRIED RICE AND ONIONS
Hot cooked rice stirred with half-and-half and seasoned with onions, curry powder and nutmeg. 4 servings; 35 minutes. Page 339

CHINESE FRIED RICE
Cooked rice fried with oil, scrambled eggs, crumbled bacon and soy sauce and topped with green onions. 6 servings; 2½ hours. Page 341

RISOTTO ALLA MILANESE
Long-grain rice cooked with saffron, minced onion and chicken broth, baked with Parmesan cheese. 6 servings; 45 minutes. Page 339

FETTUCINI ALFREDO
Medium egg noodles in a creamy mixture of butter, Parmesan and half-and-half. 8 servings; 30 minutes. Page 330

HOMEMADE NOODLES *Homemade pasta dough, cut into strips and cooked until tender.* Page 330. **EGG** (left), *served here with Pesto (page 337); garnished with fresh basil. 6 servings; 3½ hours.* **SPINACH** (right), *here served with Shrimp Marinara Sauce* (page 337). *8 servings; 3 hours.*

74

CAESAR SALAD
Anchovy fillets, raw egg and Parmesan cheese tossed with romaine lettuce, topped with Garlic Croutons. 6 servings; 30 minutes. Page 318

TOSSED SALAD WITH LEMONY-MUSTARD DRESSING *Spinach, Boston lettuce and Belgian endives, coated with fresh dressing. 10 servings; 45 minutes.* Page 318

CUCUMBERS IN SOUR CREAM
Thinly sliced cucumbers, with chives or onions in sour cream, served chilled. 6 servings; early in day. Page 319

CALIFORNIA SALAD
Avocados and lettuce in zesty, seasoned sauce, garnished with California walnuts. 8 servings; 30 minutes. Page 318

TOMATOES VINAIGRETTE
Overlapping tomato slices, sprinkled with oregano-flavored dressing. 6 servings; 2 hours. Page 319

POTATO-VEGETABLE SALAD
Overlapping cucumber slices cover a potato-carrot-and-pea-mixture, arranged on Boston lettuce. 8 servings; 1 hour. Page 320

COLONEL'S LADY'S SALAD BOWL
Green salad of lettuce, cucumber, celery, onions and peas, tossed with spicy dressing. 12 servings; 20 minutes. Page 318

DANISH CUCUMBER SALAD
Thin slices of cucumber in dilled vinegar. 8 servings; 5 hours. Page 319

GERMAN HOT-POTATO SALAD
Cooked potatoes and bacon, tossed in a sweet-sour mixture and topped with parsley. 6 servings; 45 minutes. Page 320

DELUXE COLESLAW
Cabbage, celery, green pepper, carrot and onion, tossed with a creamy dressing. Can be served in Coleslaw Bowl made of cut-out cabbage (above left) or dish. 8 servings; 1½ hours. Page 319

PERFECTION SALAD
Shredded cabbage with celery and pimentos in lemony-vinegar gelatin mixture. 8 servings; 4 hours. Page 323

CRANBERRY-NUT MOLD
Cranberries, celery and walnuts in a wine and lemon-flavored gelatin; served with sour cream dressing. 10 servings; 6 hours. Page 323

BRAISED LEEKS VINAIGRETTE
Cooked leeks marinated in a spiced pimento-oil-vinegar mixture. 8 servings; 6 hours. Page 321

GERMAN SAUERKRAUT SALAD
Grated apple and sauerkraut, marinated an hour ahead. 8 servings; 1½ hours. Page 321

THREE-BEAN SALAD
Green, wax and kidney beans, chilled in an oil and vinegar dressing. 8 servings; early in day. Page 321

TURKISH BEAN SALAD
Cooked dry beans in a herby tomato and ripe olive dressing. 10 servings; 5 hours. Page 321

TOMATO ASPIC
Molded tomato salad, chilled and served with a yogurt-dill dressing. 8 servings; 4 hours. Page 323

WALDORF SALAD
Diced apple, celery, walnut and raisin mixture, tossed with lemony mayonnaise and served on lettuce leaves. 8 servings; 20 minutes. Page 322

ZESTY TANGELO SALAD
Tangelo segments, celery and pimentos, tossed in Italian salad dressing and served on romaine leaves. 6 servings; 40 minutes. Page 314

SALAD DRESSINGS
Salad dressings, flavored with herbs, spices, garlic, cheese and anchovies. 10 to 15 minutes. Page 326

GREEK SALAD
Ripe olives, cucumbers, anchovy fillets, capers, tomatoes, onions and feta cheese with chicory and iceberg lettuce, dressed with olive oil and red wine vinegar. 10 servings; 30 minutes. Page 320

WHITE BREAD
Simple, everyday yeast loaf made using basic breadmaking techniques. 2 loaves; 4 hours. Page 434

WHOLE-WHEAT BREAD
Loaves made from whole-wheat- and all-purpose-flour, sweetened with molasses. 2 loaves; 4½ hours. Page 434

ROUND RYE BREAD
Caraway seed and buttermilk flavor this rye and all-purpose flour loaf which is baked on a cookie sheet. 2 loaves; 4½ hours. Page 435

WHOLE-GRAIN BREAD
Bran, wheat germ, whole-wheat and rye flour dough topped with caraway. 1 loaf; 5 hours. Page 436

MARBLED LOAF
Two different doughs, rolled up jelly-roll fashion and then baked. 2 loaves; 4½ hours. Page 435

PUMPERNICKEL AND WHOLE-WHEAT BRAID
Braid of dark pumpernickel and honey-sweetened whole-wheat doughs. 1 loaf; 4½ hours. Page 437

BRAIDED HERB BREAD
Rosemary flavors a plain dough, which is rolled into pieces and braided. 2 loaves; 4 hours. Page 437

ITALIAN BREAD
Traditional long Italian loaves, topped with an egg-white glaze. 2 loaves; 4 hours. Page 436

SOURDOUGH BREAD
Favorite American bread, using a fermented yeast "starter" to give bread its traditional sour taste. 2 loaves; 4 days. Page 441

OATMEAL BATTER BREAD (above and right). *Quick-cooking oats, stirred with a yeast batter and baked in a shallow casserole. 2 loaves; 4½ hours. Page 438*

CHEESE CASSEROLE BREAD (left).
All-purpose flour yeast batter, flavored with shredded, sharp Cheddar cheese, baked in a casserole. 1 loaf; 4½ hours. Page 438

SESAME PAN BREAD
Kneaded, white-bread dough, glazed with milk, sprinkled with sesame seeds and baked in cake pans. 2 loaves; 3 hours. Page 438

POTATO BREAD
Mashed potato flavored yeast dough, baked in a shallow casserole until well browned. 2 loaves; 4½ hours. Page 438

79

DINNER ROLLS *24 rolls; 3¹/₂ hours.*
Pages 439 to 440

VIENNA ROLLS

DOUBLE TWISTS

DINNER BUNS

FAN-TANS

CRESCENTS

PINWHEELS

POSIES

KNOTS

PAN ROLLS

REFRIGERATOR PAN ROLLS
*Dough, made ahead and refrigerated, then
shaped into balls and let rise before baking.
30 rolls; 6 hours.* Page 441

PARKER HOUSE ROLLS
*Dough from Refrigerator Pan Rolls, cut into
circles, dipped in butter, folded and baked.
40 rolls; 6 hours.* Page 441

RAISIN BREAD
Sweet loaf, flavored with raisins. 1 loaf;
4½ hours. Page 442

TURTLE BREAD
Novelty bread, easily made from pieces of
sweet dough. 1 turtle, 4½ hours. Page 442

HOT CROSS BUNS
Easter bread flavored with raisins and orange peel and
criss-crossed with sugar icing.
12 buns; 4½ hours. Page 442

KOLACKY
Blueberry, Cherry, Cream-cheese, Lemon,
Orange and Pineapple fillings top a circle of
sweet dough. 1 coffeecake; 4½ hours. Page 443

APRICOT COFFEECAKE
Strips of sweet dough laced across a dried
apricot filling before baking and glazing.
1 coffeecake; 4½ hours. Page 443

CINNAMON ROLLS
Pecan- and raisin-filled dough, rolled jelly-roll
fashion, cut into slices and then baked and
glazed. 15 rolls; 4½ hours. Page 444

FRUTTED BRAID
Raisins, candied orange peel and candied citron
flavor a braided dough which is glazed and then
baked. 1 braid; 4½ hours. Page 444

LEMON BUBBLE RING
Rounds of yeast dough, sprinkled with grated
lemon peel, sugar and mace and baked into a
ring in a tube pan. 1 loaf; 4 hours. Page 444

81

**APRICOT BUTTERFLY
ROLLS** *20 rolls;
4½ hours. Page 445*

BRIOCHES
*36 brioches; day
ahead. Page 447*

CROISSANTS
*12 croissants;
8 hours. Page 448*

PARTY DOUGHNUTS
36 doughnuts; 4 hours. Page 449. JELLY
DOUGHNUTS *(right). 36 doughnuts;
4 hours. Page 449*

BABAS AU RHUM
*Individual breads, topped
with Rum Sauce.
24 babas; 4 hours.
Page 450*

DANISH PASTRY
Selection of pastries with choice of Jam, Almond or Cream-Cheese Filling. (From left): PINWHEEL,
FOLDOVER, ENVELOPE, COCKSCOMB. *24 pastries; 5 hours. Page 451*

PITA (POCKET BREAD)
*Middle-Eastern style, baked "pocket" bread.
6 breads; 3 hours. Page 447*

WHOLE-WHEAT "SUGAR" BEARS
*Shaped sweet dough. 3 bears; 4 hours.
Page 445*

CHALLAH
*Traditional, Jewish, braided egg bread.
2 loaves; 5½ hours. Page 453*

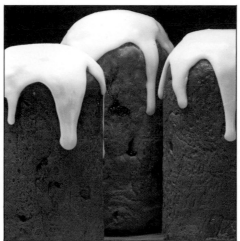

CARDAMOM CHRISTMAS WREATH
Special occasion bread made from decorated yeast dough with hint of lemon. 1 wreath; 4½ hours. Page 453

STOLLEN
Traditional fruit-and-nut-filled yeast dough. 3 stollens; 5 hours. Page 452

ENGLISH MUFFINS
Traditional, cornmeal-coated yeast-dough muffins, browned in a skillet, toasted and served hot. 18 muffins; 3½ hours. Page 446

KULICH
Traditional, Russian Easter bread, made from fruited dough and baked in a coffee can. 3 loaves; 5 hours. Page 452

POPPY-SEED POTICAS
Special yeast dough, filled with poppy seed and walnut mixture and baked. 2 loaves; 6 hours. Page 448

OLD-FASHIONED ROLLS
Yeast dough, shaped into rolls, brushed with melted butter or Egg Glaze and baked until golden. 24 rolls; 3½ hours. Page 439

IRISH SODA BREAD
Traditional, buttermilk-flavored, coarse-textured casserole bread. 1 loaf; 5 hours. Page 429

ZUCCHINI BREAD
Grated zucchini- and chopped-walnut-flavored baked loaf. Serve warm or cold. 2 loaves; 2 hours. Page 429

LEMON LOAF
Sweet loaf brushed with lemon juice after baking. 1 loaf; 2 hours. **Page 428**

CHOCOLATE DATE-NUT LOAF
Pitted dates, walnuts and chocolate pieces in baked loaf. 1 loaf; day ahead. **Page 429**

NUT BREAD
Chopped California walnuts flavor a traditionally-shaped loaf. 1 loaf; day ahead. **Page 428**

CORN BREAD
Cornmeal batter, baked and cut into squares for serving. 9 servings; 35 minutes. **Page 428**

CORN STICKS
Corn Bread batter is used for making these corn sticks. 14 sticks; 35 minutes. **Page 428**

BUTTERMILK WAFFLES
Buttermilk-flavored batter, baked in waffle baker. 5 waffles; 30 minutes. **Page 427**

SILVER DOLLAR PANCAKES
Small amounts of pancake batter, cooked on a hot griddle to make tiny pancakes; serve with syrup. 24 pancakes; 30 minutes. **Page 427**

PANCAKES
Thin batter, cooked in hot skillet until bubbly and golden. 12 pancakes; 30 minutes. **Page 426**

POTATO PANCAKES
Shredded potato and onion, mixed with egg and flour and fried until golden. 16 pancakes; 1¼ hours. **Page 426**

**PEACH-FILLED
COFFEECAKE**
12 servings; 1½ hours.
Page 430

CHERRY COFFEECAKE
9 servings; 2 hours.
Page 430

**SOUR-CREAM
COFFEECAKE**
10 servings; 2 hours.
Page 430

GIANT POPOVERS
*Egg batter, baked in pottery custard cups.
8 popovers; 1½ hours.* Page 427

BISCUITS *and* **MUFFINS**
Quickly made, individual muffins (top left) *and
biscuits. 12 muffins, 18 biscuits; each
35 minutes.* **Pages 423 and 424**

MUFFIN VARIATIONS (clockwise from
left): **WHOLEWHEAT, BLUEBERRY,
ORANGE, BRAN, CORN.**
12-16 muffins; 35-45 minutes. Page 424

**OLD-FASHIONED DOUGHNUTS AND
DOUGHNUT "HOLES"** *Deep-fried dough
circles and centers, sprinkled with sugar.
24 doughnuts; 2½ hours.* Page 425

BEIGNETS
*French-style fried dough served with a sweet
syrup. 8 servings; 45 minutes.* Page 425

BOSTON BROWN BREAD
*Coffee cans are used to shape this bread
flavored with molasses and raisins. 2 loaves;
2½ hours.* Page 429

POORI (left). *Indian-style fried bread.
20 poori; 1¾ hours.* **ONION THINS**
32 baked crackers; 1½ hours. Page 431

DEEP-DISH PEACH PIE
Sliced peaches, cinnamon and butter-dotted filling in a piecrust, topped with pastry strips. 10 servings; early in day. Page 348

CHOCOLATE CREAM PIE
Rich chocolate mixture, chilled and served here in a baked piecrust, topped with whipped cream. 8 servings; 5½ hours. Page 350

BLACKBERRY PIE
Fresh blackberries in old-fashioned piecrust. 6 servings; 2 hours. Page 346

CHERRY PIE
Pitted tart fresh cherries in scalloped-edged piecrust. 6 servings; 2 hours. Page 346

APPLE PIE
Sliced cooking apples, baked in spicy mixture in piecrust. 6 servings; 2 hours. Page 346

PUMPKIN PIE
Unbaked piecrust, filled with spicy pumpkin mixture, baked and served with Brandy Hard Sauce. 6 servings; early in day. Page 349

PECAN PIE
Traditional baked pie, with pecan halves arranged in single layer on unbaked piecrust; serve cool. 10 servings; early in day. Page 356

PRUNE AND APRICOT PIE
Baked piecrust, filled with prunes, dried apricots and grated peel, garnished with walnuts. 8 servings; early in day. Page 347

LEMON CHIFFON PIE
Light, lemon filling in baked piecrust, garnished with whipped cream and shredded lemon peel. 8 servings; early in day. Page 352

DEEP-DISH PLUM PIE
Fresh plums sprinkled with almond extract, sugar and flour, baked in deep-dish pastry crust, topped with pastry strips. 10 servings; 2 hours. Page 348

FRUIT CREAM TARTS
Homemade cream filling in baked tart shells, topped with a variety of fresh fruits. 12 tarts; early in day. Page 357

RICH BAVARIAN PIE
Baked piecrust, filled with egg-cream mixture flavored with vanilla, served topped with chocolate. 8 servings; early in day. Page 353

RICH BAVARIAN PIE VARIATIONS
Fresh strawberry (left) and coffee variations of Rich Bavarian Pie. 8 servings each; early in day. Page 353

BLUEBERRY COBBLER
Spiced blueberry filling in a deep pie plate topped with crust and baked until golden brown. 8 servings; 2 hours. Page 346

CHOCOLATE CHIFFON PIE
Chocolate-Wafer Crumb-Crust base, filled with light chocolate-chiffon mixture, served with cream. 8 servings; 4 hours. Page 353

WALNUT TARTS
Egg- and corn-syrup mixture over chopped walnuts in tart shells, baked and topped with cream. 12 tarts; early in day. Page 357

DELUXE APPLE TART
Sliced apples and applesauce baked in sweetened pastry and glazed with apricot mixture. 8 servings; early in day. Page 348

STREUSEL-TOPPED PEAR PIE
Fluted-edged crust, filled with fresh pears and topped with brown sugar, shredded cheese and spices. 8 servings; 2 hours. Page 347

PEACH PIE
Fresh peaches in piecrust, topped with pastry strips. 6 servings; 2 hours. Page 347

ORANGE CHIFFON PIE
Light, creamy orange filling in prepared piecrust, served with whipped cream and orange sections. 8 servings; early in day. Page 352

CUSTARD PIE
Milk custard, baked in piecrust and sprinkled with nutmeg. 6 servings; early in day. Page 349

DOUBLE PEANUT PIE
Creamy peanut butter, peanuts and corn syrup baked in piecrust and garnished with whipped cream. 12 servings; early in day. Page 356

CHERRY CREAM TART
Light, cherry-flavored whipped-cream mixture, served chilled in baked crust, topped with whole cherries. 8 servings; early in day. Page 355

PUMPKIN CHIFFON PIE
Spicy pumpkin filling in graham-cracker and coconut crust, served with whipped cream and coconut. 10 servings; early in day. Page 354

FUDGE-NUT PIE
Chocolate-egg mixture with California walnuts, baked in a piecrust and served with ice cream. 8 servings; early in day. Page 356

RASPBERRY RIBBON PIE
Raspberry mixture layered with cream-cheese mixture and served in baked piecrust. 8 servings; day ahead. Page 354

BLACK BOTTOM PIE
Baked, crumb crust, filled with chocolate- and rum-flavored custards. 8 servings; early in day. Page 355

COFFEE CORDIAL PIE
Coffee-flavored chiffon mixture in a baked crumb crust. 8 servings; 4½ hours. Page 354

LEMON MERINGUE PIE
Baked piecrust filled with lemon peel and juice mixture, topped with meringue then baked. Serve chilled. 6 servings; 6 hours. Page 351

PEACH MERINGUE TARTS
Sliced peaches, tapioca and lemon juice filling, baked in tart shells, topped with egg whites and baked again. 12 tarts; 3 hours. Page 357

NESSELRODE PIE
Rum-flavored candied fruit filling, served in Graham-cracker crumb crust and garnished with cream. 8 servings; early in day. Page 355

MINCE TARTS
Mincemeat, apples, walnuts and brown sugar in individual tart shells, served warm with Brandy Hard Sauce. 12 tarts; day ahead. Page 357

VANILLA CREAM PIE
Baked crumb crust, filled with vanilla-flavored egg-custard mixture and topped with whipped cream. 8 servings; 5½ hours. Page 350

BANANA CREAM PIE
Baked piecrust filled with vanilla-flavored egg-custard and bananas, topped with grated lemon. 8 servings; 5½ hours. Page 350

DEVIL'S FOOD CAKE
Dark-chocolate two-layer cake, topped with Quick Fudge Frosting. 10 servings; early in day. Page 384

SILVER-WHITE CAKE
White cake, filled and frosted with Mocha Butter-Cream Frosting. 8 servings; early in day. Page 385

SPICY GINGERBREAD
Gingerbread batter, baked and then cooled, topped with whipped cream. 9 servings; early in day. Page 387

GERMAN GOLD POUNDCAKE
Traditional cake baked in loaf or Bundt pan. 16 servings; early in day. Page 386

ORANGE CHIFFON CAKE
Beaten egg whites folded with batter, baked and topped with fluffy orange frosting. 16 servings; early in day. Page 389

DELUXE MARBLE CAKE
Vanilla and chocolate mixtures, cut through to create a design and baked. 12 servings; early in day. Page 386

SACHERTORTE
Chocolate-cake layers, filled with apricot preserves and glazed with chocolate. 12 servings; 6 hours. Page 394

LANE CAKE
Four-layer white cake with fruit and nut filling and cooked frosting. 16 servings; early in day. Page 387

SUGAR BUSH WALNUT CAKE
Maple-flavored chiffon cake made with finely chopped California walnuts. 12 servings; early in day. Page 389

DARK CHRISTMAS FRUITCAKE
Traditional fruit and nut cake with apple jelly glaze. One 5-pound fruitcake; several weeks ahead. Page 393

JELLY ROLL
Jam-filled sponge, rolled and sprinkled with confectioners' sugar. 10 servings; early in day. Page 391

MOCHA-CREAM ROLL
Baked cake roll, spread with Mocha-Cream Filling with Chocolate Icing and Sugar Glaze. 10 servings; 2 hours. Page 391

HOLIDAY PETITS FOURS
Small sponge cakes with Almond Paste filling iced and decorated. 30 petits fours; early in day. Page 392

ANGEL-FOOD CAKE
Favorite cake made fluffy with beaten egg whites; served with berries and ice cream. 12 servings; early in day. Page 390

SPICE CAKE
Spicy layers, filled and frosted with Whipped-Cream Frosting. 8 servings; early in day. Page 387

FILBERT TORTE
Delicate cake layers, filled and frosted with vanilla flavored, whipped cream and garnished with ground nuts. 12 servings; 3 hours. Page 395

MERRYFIELD APPLE CAKE
Cooking apples, walnuts and raisins baked in a cake and sprinkled with sugar. 18 servings; early in day. Page 387

YELLOW CAKE
Two-layer cake, filled and frosted with Butter-Cream Frosting. 10 servings; early in day. **Page 384**

PINEAPPLE-UPSIDE-DOWN CAKE
Pineapple chunks and cherries, baked with yellow cake batter and inverted to serve. 12 servings; early in day. **Page 384**

COFFEE CLOUD CAKE
Coffee-flavored sponge batter, baked with chopped California walnuts. 12 servings; early in day. **Page 392**

BRAZIL-NUT SENSATION FRUITCAKE
Brazil nuts, dates and maraschino cherries baked in batter and chilled. One 3-pound cake; several weeks ahead. **Page 393**

CHOCOLATE CHIFFON CAKE
Cocoa-flavored batter, baked in tube pan and sprinkled with sugar. 12 servings; early in day. **Page 389**

BLACK FOREST CHERRY TORTE
Chocolate cake, layered with whipped cream and tart cherries and richly garnished. 12 servings; 4 hours. **Page 395**

BANANA CAKE *Banana-flavored cake layers, filled and frosted with whipped cream frosting. 10 servings; early in day.* **Page 388**

FRESH COCONUT CAKE *Filled with Custard Filling flavored with shredded fresh coconut. 16 servings; 3 hours.* **Page 386**

WALNUT-FUDGE CAKE *Light layer cake, flavored with walnuts and semisweet chocolate, filled and glazed. 16 servings; early in day.* **Page 388**

GOLDEN FRUITCAKE
Candied fruit, raisins and nuts in light batter, baked, then glazed. One 7-pound cake; day ahead. Page 393

DAFFODIL CAKE
Yellow and white cake, baked in tube pan and topped with Orange-Lemon Icing. 12 servings, early in day. Page 390

PARTY CAKE
Three-tiered cake, with Lemon-Butter-Cream Filling and Vanilla-Butter-Cream Frosting, decorated. 62 servings; day ahead. Page 396

CHOCOLATE CAKE *and* **CHOCOLATE CUPCAKES**
The same cocoa batter can be used for 24 individual cupcakes or for a chocolate layer cake (10 servings). Both are coated with Coffee Cream-Cheese Frosting; early in day. Page 385

SIX-LAYER EGGNOG CAKE
Cake layers, filled with rum-flavored whipped cream and topped with chocolate. 12 servings; 4 hours. Page 394

DESSERTS

DELUXE STRAWBERRY SHORTCAKE
Shortcake, sliced in half horizontally, filled and topped with layers of whipped cream and berries. 12 servings; 4 hours. Page 369

STRAWBERRY SOUFFLE
Chilled mixture of strawberries, gelatin, egg whites and cream, prepared in collared soufflé dish. 12 servings; 6 hours. Page 361

POTS DE CREME AU CHOCOLAT
Rich mousse of semisweet chocolate, egg yolks, and half-and-half, chilled and served with whipped cream. 6 servings; 5 hours. Page 362

APPLE STRUDEL
Phyllo pastry filled with apples, raisins, walnuts and spices and baked in the oven. 10 servings; 3 hours. Page 370

FLOATING ISLAND
Vanilla custard topped with soft meringue and decorated with sugar syrup. 4 servings; 1½ hours. Page 365

CREAM PUFF RING
Choux pastry, filled with almond pastry cream and topped with chocolate glaze and strawberries. 10 servings; early in day. Page 367

CREPES SUZETTE
Classic French crêpes, heated at the table in orange sauce and flamed in orange liqueur. 6 servings; early in day. Page 368

DESSERT CREPES WITH ORANGE SAUCE *Sour cream-filled crêpes, topped with orange sauce. 6 servings; 1 hour.* Page 368

SYLLABUB
Half-and-half beaten until frothy and mixed with lemon juice, Chablis and brandy. 16 servings; 10 minutes. Page 369

CHOCOLATE SOUFFLE
Mixture of chocolate, egg yolks, milk and egg whites, baked. 8 servings; 2 hours. Page 363

INDIVIDUAL CHOCOLATE SOUFFLES
Chocolate and egg mixture, baked until puffy and brown, served with whipped cream and chocolate syrup. 6 servings; 1 hour. Page 363

CREAM PUFFS
Baked pastry shells filled with chilled Vanilla Pastry Cream and topped with confectioners' sugar. 12 servings; early in day. Page 366

SWANS
Choux pastry shapes with vanilla custard filling. 36 pastries; early in day. Page 367

APRICOT-CREAM FLAN
Egg custard in walnut-crumb crust, topped with apricots and melted apple jelly. 8 servings; 5 hours. Page 360

CHOCOLATE CUPS WITH STRAWBERRY CREAM *Handmade chocolate shells, filled with fresh strawberries and cream. 8 servings; 2 hours.* Page 370

BAVARIAN CREAM
A molded mixture of custard and whipped cream, garnished with sliced strawberries and nectarines. 8 servings; early in day. Page 360

SURPRISE ANGEL PECAN PIE
Crustless, pecan-soda-cracker and egg-white pie with whipped cream topping. 8 servings; 4 hours. Page 365

BANANA SOUFFLE
Purée of bananas in nutmeg-and-egg-white-sauce, baked until puffy and brown. Serve with whipped cream. 8 servings; 1 hour. Page 364

CHOCOLATE-CHERRY SOUFFLE
Chocolate, cherry and whipped-cream mixture, chilled in soufflé dish, with cream and cherry topping. 12 servings; early in day. Page 361

ALMOND-CREAM BOMBE
Almond liqueur-soaked cake triangles filled with chocolate-cream mixture. 8 servings; day ahead. Page 375

CHOCOLATE FANCY
Whipped-cream-topped cake, covered with strawberry-cream and chocolate sheet. 16 servings; early in day. Page 374

GALATOBOUREKO (front). *Phyllo with cream filling and syrup topping. 2¹/₂ hours.* **BAKLAVA** *Phyllo with walnuts and honey. 3 hours; each 24 servings.* Page 371

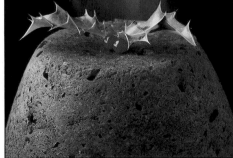

STEAMED PUDDING
Traditional Christmas fruit-filled dessert, flamed before serving. 12 servings; 4 hours. Page 375

CREME CARAMEL
Individual, baked vanilla custards served chilled in own syrup. 8 servings; early in day. Page 359

CHOCOLATE-CINNAMON TORTE
Baked cookie circles layered with chocolate cream filling and topped with grated chocolate. 16 servings; day ahead. Page 373

CREME BRULEE
Chilled egg custard, topped with brown sugar and broiled; served cold with sliced fruit. 10 servings; early in day. Page 359

STRAWBERRY MERINGUES
Individual meringues, filled with ice cream and topped with strawberries. 6 servings; early in day. Page 365

FROSTY LIME SOUFFLE
Chilled soufflé flavored with fresh lime juice. 8 servings; early in day. Page 362

ZABAGLIONE
Light, frothy egg-yolk, sugar and Marsala dessert, cooked in double-boiler and served warm. 6 servings; 20 minutes. Page 360

CHOCOLATE ANGEL PIE
Meringue pie shell, filled with rich chocolate and whipped cream filling. 10 servings; early in day. Page 365

ORANGE LIQUEUR SOUFFLE
Soufflé of custard sauce, orange liqueur and egg whites, baked and served hot with bowl of whipped cream. 6 servings; 1¼ hours. Page 364

STRAWBERRY SHORTCAKE
Plain shortcake, split in half and buttered, then filled and garnished with whipped cream and strawberries. 8 servings; 45 minutes. Page 369

SHERRY TRIFLE
Macaroons and sherry-soaked cake, layered with jam, custard, cream, cherry and almond topping. 8 servings; early in day. Page 372

ECLAIRS
Baked choux pastries filled with Vanilla Pastry Cream and topped with a semisweet-chocolate glaze. 10 éclairs; early in day. Page 366

CRANBERRY SOUFFLE
Chilled fresh cranberry soufflé served topped with whole sugared berries. 10 servings; early in day. Page 362

APPLE TURNOVERS (top). *8 filled pastry turnovers; 5 hours.* Page 372. **CREAMY RICE PUDDING** *Sweetened rice mixture with cream. 10 servings; 4½ hours.* Page 341

CHEESE BLINTZES
Cottage- and cream cheese-filled crêpes, baked until heated and topped with strawberries. 6 servings; early in day. Page 368

STRAWBERRY DESSERT OMELET
Baked sweet omelet filled with fresh strawberries and sprinkled with sugar. 4 servings; 30 minutes. Page 146

NO-BAKE CHEESECAKE
Creamed cottage cheese-gelatin mixture in unbaked crumb crust, garnished with canned fruit. 12 servings; early in day. Page 159

DELUXE BAKED CHEESECAKE
Filling of cream cheese, sugar and eggs, baked in rich crust, chilled and topped with sour cream. 16 servings; day ahead. Page 158

CHOCOLATE CHEESECAKE (top).
18 servings; early in day. **CHERRY CHEESECAKE** *12 servings; day ahead.*
Page 158

DELUXE PEACH-CHEESE PIE
Softened cream cheese in crumb crust, refrigerated and garnished with sliced peaches in apricot glaze. 8 servings; 6 hours. Page 159

CREAM-CHEESE RHUBARB PIE
Rhubarb sauce topped with cream cheese and eggs, baked in piecrust with sour cream and almond garnish. 8 servings; 6 hours. Page 159

ICED CHERRY SOUP
Made with canned, tart cherries. 6 servings ; early in day. **Page 137**

COLD RASPBERRY SOUP
Made with frozen raspberries. 6 servings ; early in day. **Page 137**

STRAWBERRY SOUP
Made with fresh strawberries. 3 servings ; early in day. **Page 137**

STRAWBERRY-RHUBARB SOUP
Chilled blend of rhubarb, strawberries and orange sections in sweetened orange juice, garnished with strawberry slices. 4 servings ; 3 hours.
Page 137

BLENDER BLUEBERRY SOUP
Blueberries blended with sour cream and served chilled. 2 servings ; 20 minutes. **Page 137**

CINNAMON APRICOTS IN CREAM
*Halved, unpeeled apricots, baked until tender
in sugar and cinnamon syrup and finished in
heavy cream. 4 servings; 35 minutes.* Page 301

STRAWBERRIES ROMANOFF
*Fresh strawberries in orange-flavor liqueur,
orange juice and brandy, topped with whipped
cream. 4 servings; 1½ hours.* Page 303

FREEZER STRAWBERRY TOPPING
*Sauce of fresh strawberries and orange juice,
shown here over pound cake, cheesecake, ice
cream and yogurt. 2 days ahead.* Page 303

BRANDIED CHERRY SAUCE (left).
30 minutes. Page 304. **BLUEBERRY
SAUCE** *20 minutes.* Page 303

STEWED PLUMS (top left). *20 minutes.*
PLUMS IN PORT SAUCE (right).
6 servings; day ahead. **CREAMY PLUM
DRESSING** *on fruit; 1¼ hours.* Page 313

PAPAYAS WITH LEMON CREAM
*Halved papayas with lemon-flavored, whipped-
cream filling, chilled and garnished with lemon
slices. 6 servings; 1 hour.* Page 311

VERY-BERRY COMPOTE
*Strawberries, raspberries and blueberries,
topped with ice cream and grated orange peel.
10 servings; 2½ hours.* Page 303

GRAPEFRUIT AMBROSIA
*Grapefruit sections, drained and tossed with
honey and flaked coconut. 4 servings;
5 minutes.* Page 305

STEWED PEACHES (top). *6 servings;
20 minutes.* **BUTTERY BAKED PEACHES**
6 servings; 1 hour. Page 311

POACHED PEARS IN SAUTERNE (top).
6 servings; 4 hours.
PEARS IN CHOCOLATE SAUCE
2 servings; 30 minutes. Page 312

MINTED GRAPES
*Seedless green grapes, marinated in honey,
lime juice and chopped mint. 4 servings; early
in day.* Page 306

BAKED APPLES (top). *Topped with cream.
6 servings; 1 hour.* **APPLESAUCE** *Chunky or
smooth. 30 minutes.* Page 300

GINGERED KIWI FRUIT
*Sliced kiwi fruit and orange sections in ginger
syrup, served cold. 4 servings; 2¹/2 hours.*
Page 306

BANANA POPS
*Banana pieces on wooden ice-cream-bar sticks,
rolled in melted chocolate and coconut.
12 pops; 2 hours.* Page 302

MARINATED WATER MELON (top).
16 servings; 4 hours. **CANTALOUPE ICE**
5 cups; day ahead. Page 309

RHUBARB SAUCE (top). *20 minutes.*
RHUBARB CRUMBLE *6 servings;
50 minutes.* Page 314

**FRESH FRUIT BOWL WITH
CARDAMOM DRESSING** *Bowl of melons
and summer fruit with smooth dressing.
12 servings; 30 minutes.* Page 322

SACRAMENTO FRUIT BOWL
*Pineapple, melon, oranges, nectarines, plums,
grapes and limes, chilled in anise seed syrup.
10 to 12 servings; early in day.* Page 322

HOMEMADE VANILLA ICE CREAM
Egg custard, flavored with vanilla and frozen in ice-cream freezer. Early in day. Page 376

HOMEMADE ICE-CREAM VARIATIONS *Just add flavorings to the basic ice-cream mixture* (left to right): *Spiced Banana; Strawberry; Chocolate; Pistachio; Peach; early in day.* Page 377

PEPPERMINT-CANDY ICE CREAM
Ice-cream mixture flavored with crushed peppermint candies; 6 hours. Page 377

NESSELRODE ICE-CREAM MOLD
Molded of candied fruit, raisins and walnuts mixed with vanilla ice cream, layered with ladyfingers. 10 servings; day ahead. Page 379

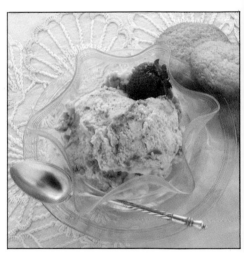

STRAWBERRY ICE MILK
Frozen crushed-strawberry mixture. Early in day. Page 378. *Served here with* REFRIGERATOR COOKIES. Page 411

PINEAPPLE SHERBET
Blended fresh pineapple, sugar, lemon juice and egg whites, frozen until firm. Early in day. Page 380

BAKED ALASKA PIE
Vanilla ice cream and frozen raspberries in a ladyfinger crust, topped with meringue, baked. 12 servings; 5 hours. Page 378

ORANGE MILK SHERBET (left). *Early in day.* Page 380. **CANTALOUPE SHERBET** *Early in day.* Page 380

STRAWBERRY-ORANGE ICE
Frozen strawberries, fruit juices and liqueur. Early in day. Page 381. *Served here with* CANDIED ORANGE PEEL. Page 310

RAINBOW ICE-CREAM TORTE
Layered ice creams and sweet cherries in gingersnap crust. 12 servings; early in day. Page 379

MINTED SHERBET RING WITH BERRIES *Lemon sherbet, flavored with crème de menthe and decorated for serving. 10 servings; early in day.* Page 380

LEMON ICE IN LEMON CUPS
Hollowed lemons filled with sweetened fresh lemon juice mixture, garnished with mint sprigs. Early in day. Page 381

WATERMELON ICE
Blended watermelon chunks, lemon juice and confectioners' sugar, frozen in freezing compartment. Early in day. Page 381

ICE-CREAM BOMBE LES DAMES D'ESCOFFIER
Molded strawberry and vanilla ice cream with almond brickle-chip center, decorated with whipped cream and strawberries and served with chocolate sauce. 12 servings; early in day. Page 379

103

SPRITZ AND VARIATIONS: RINGLET COOKIES (top). *32 cookies;* SPRITZ (center). *108 cookies;* RASPBERRY THUMB-PRINTS *72 cookies; 3½ hours.* Page 410

CHOCOLATE-DIPPED BUTTER COOKIES *Sour-cream dough, pressed through a tree shaped plate, baked and then glazed. 120 cookies; 4 hours.* Page 410

SANDWICH COOKIES *Rolled vanilla cookies with colored frosting. 42 cookies; 3 hours.* Page 412

CANDY APPLES *Red Delicious apples, dipped in corn-syrup mixture and left to harden. 8 apples; 2 hours.* Page 301

LOLLIPOPS *Hard candies and corn-syrup mixture, hardened in paper cup molds. 12 lollipops; 3 hours.* Page 417

POPCORN BALLS *Popped corn and candied cherries, coated with syrup mixture. 12 balls; 2 hours.* Page 418

CHOCOLATE FUDGE *36 pieces; 2½ hours.* Page 415

PEANUT BRITTLE *1 pound; 2 hours.* Page 418

NUTTY BUTTERSCOTCH FUDGE *49 pieces; 1½ hours.* Page 415

MAPLE KISSES *24 pieces; 1½ hours.* Page 415

MOLASSES TAFFY ¾ *pound;*
2 hours. Page 416.

MARZIPAN FRUITS 4¼ *pounds;*
day ahead. Page 419.

DIVINITY
1½ pounds; 1½ hours.
Page 417.

PECAN PENUCHE
2 pounds; 2½ hours.
Page 415.

BONBONS
1 pound; 7 hours.
Page 418.

FONDANT
1 pound; 5 hours.
Page 417

WALNUT CRUNCH
1½ pounds; 3½ hours. Page 418.

PEPPERMINT PATTIES
64 patties; 3 hours
Page 419.

ORANGE-ALMOND CARAMELS
50 pieces; 1½ hours.
Page 416.

NOUGATS
2¼ pounds; day ahead.
Page 416

**CHOCOLATE-DIPPED
FRUIT** *and* **NUTS** *Orange segments,
peanuts and strawberries covered in melted
chocolate. 1½ hours.* Page 420

**MELT-AWAY
CHOCOLATE MINTS**
*Semisweet chocolate squares
flavored with peppermint. 2½ hours.* Page 420

TRUFFLES
*Sweetened condensed milk and chocolate
rounds, rolled in cocoa. 36 truffles; 2 hours.*
Page 420

107

OPEN-FACE STEAK SANDWICHES
Cubed steaks on toasted bread, served with gravy and garnished with watercress. 4 servings; 20 minutes. Page 457

WESTERN SANDWICHES (left). *Ham, green pepper and onion cooked in an omelet and served on toast. 4 sandwiches; 35 minutes. Page 456*

CANADIAN-BACON BUNS *Lightly fried Canadian bacon in toasted hamburger buns. 6 sandwiches; 15 minutes. Page 456*

CURRIED BEEF IN PITA
Curried ground beef, onion, chopped apple, and raisins in pita bread, served with yogurt. 12 sandwiches; 3 hours. Page 457

CROQUE MONSIEUR
Ham, Swiss cheese and mustard on white bread, toasted in the oven until golden. 16 sandwiches; 45 minutes. Page 455

SLOPPY JOES
Ground beef, cooked with onion, green pepper and canned pork and beans, served in long rolls. 6 sandwiches; 30 minutes. Page 456

BARBECUED PORK SANDWICHES
Chunks of pork, cooked with onion and peppers in spicy sauce, served in rolls with lettuce and tomato. 10 sandwiches; 3½ hours. Page 455

MOZZARELLA LOAF
Mozzarella cheese and olives in a long Italian loaf, baked until cheese is melted. 6 servings; 40 minutes. Page 455

REUBEN
Swiss cheese, corned beef and sauerkraut in rye-bread, browned in a skillet. 4 sandwiches; 45 minutes. Page 456

ITALIAN HERO SANDWICHES
Sweet Italian sausages, cooked with onions and peppers and served in hard rolls. 4 sandwiches; 45 minutes. **Page 457**

TACOS (with CORN TORTILLAS)
Taco shells with chicken or beef filling, served with lettuce, tomato, shredded cheese and hot pepper sauce. 12 sandwiches; 1 hour. **Page 456**

POOR BOY
Ham, Swiss cheese, cucumber, tomato and dressing in French bread. 6 servings; 20 minutes. **Page 457**

CLUB SANDWICHES
Layers of toast with crisp bacon, turkey, lettuce, tomato and mayonnaise filling. 2 servings; 20 minutes. **Page 457**

WATERCRESS-WALNUT SANDWICHES
(bottom). *30 minutes.* **KEEP TRIM SANDWICHES: CURRIED SHRIMP** (left) and **CRUNCHY TUNA.** All page 458

RIBBON SANDWICHES (top).
50 sandwiches; 3½ hours.
DEVILED HAM PINWHEELS
30 sandwiches; 30 minutes. **Page 459**

OPEN SANDWICHES
(Top row, left to right) *Egg, caviar and red pepper; shrimp on mayonnaise; Danish Blue, black grapes and walnuts; marinated herring and onion on lettuce.*

(Bottom row, left to right) *Rare roast beef with crumbled fried onion; smoked salmon on lettuce; salami and cucumber twists; cold roast pork with orange twists and crumbled bacon.* Page 458

CAFFE ESPRESSO (left). *4 servings;*
15 minutes. CAFE AU LAIT *1 serving;*
15 minutes. Page 467

IRISH COFFEE (left). *1 serving;*
15 minutes. CAFE BRULOT *8 servings;*
15 minutes. Page 467

ICE-CREAM SODAS (back): *Flavored syrups added to milk, ice cream*
and club soda. 1 serving; 5 minutes. STRAWBERRY SODA. *1 serving;*
5 minutes. All page 469

CHOCOLATE-ORANGE SODAS (left).
8 servings. EGG CREAM. *1 serving; both*
5 minutes. Page 469

EGGNOG (top). *38 servings; 2 hours.*
Page 470. PARTY ORANGE SODA
16 servings; 15 minutes. Page 469

ICED COFFEE
Double-strength coffee, poured over ice; serve
with cream and sugar, if desired. 15 minutes.
Page 467

HEARTY HOT COCOA
Hot cocoa, milk, vanilla and sugar, topped with marshmallow. 6 servings; 15 minutes. Page 468

CHOCOLATE *and* BANANA MILK SHAKES *Chocolate: ice cream, blended with syrup and milk; banana: blended with vanilla ice cream. 2 servings; 10 minutes.* Page 469

MOCHA FLOAT
Chocolate-milk mix, coffee powder and club soda, with ice-cream scoops. 1 serving; 5 minutes. Page 469

FRENCH HOT CHOCOLATE
Rich drink of hot milk and chocolate, beaten with heavy cream. 8 servings; 50 minutes. Page 468

BLACK COW
Chilled root beer topped with scoop of vanilla ice cream. 1 serving; 5 minutes. Page 469

ICED TEA, FAMILY STYLE
Steeped tea, poured over ice cubes and served with sugar and lemon slices. 8 servings; 15 minutes. Page 468

STRAWBERRY SHAKES
Low-calorie, strawberry-and-nonfat-dry-milk-powder shake. 4 servings; 5 minutes. Page 469

SPARKLING STRAWBERRY PUNCH
Strawberries in rosé wine, lemonade and club soda, garnished with orange slices. 36 servings; 10 minutes. Page 471

SANGRIA
Chilled, fruit-filled, Spanish wine-and-soda-water punch. 8 servings; 5 minutes. Page 471

LEMONADE (left). *16 servings; 2 hours.*
EASY-WAY LEMONADE *5 servings; early in day.* Page 470

HOT MULLED WINE
Red wine heated with cinnamon, cloves, orange and lemon slices. 36 servings; 30 minutes. Page 471

WASSAIL BOWL WITH BAKED APPLES
Baked apples in hot, spicy apple cider and juice. 36 servings; 45 minutes. Page 472

FROZEN DAIQUIRIS (left). FROZEN
WHISKEY SOURS *Both 13 servings; day ahead.* Page 472

WHISKEY-SOUR PUNCH (left). *32 servings; 25 minutes.* GOLDEN PUNCH *Non-alcoholic. 20 servings; 10 minutes.* Page 471

GLOGG
Warm alcoholic punch, flamed and topped with almonds. 20 servings; day ahead. Page 471

COCKTAILS (from left): ALEXANDER; MINT JULEP; MARGARITA; OLD-FASHIONED; TOM COLLINS; MANHATTAN;
STINGER; MARTINI; BLOODY MARY *and* COMPANY BLOODY MARY. *5 minutes.* Pages 472–3

RECIPES

APPETIZERS

Little nibblers to go with cocktails, dainty canapés to be passed on a tray, colorful appetizers to serve as the first course at dinner, all reflect the skill of the cook and help create an elegant setting for the occasion. The appetizers in this chapter include some to be made ahead, some that are light, crunchy and low in calories and other heartier appetizers for those occasions when the party you are planning is almost a meal.

Tidbits

Crisp Cheese Twists

1¹/4 cups all-purpose flour
1/2 cup yellow cornmeal
1/2 teaspoon salt
1¹/4 cups shredded Cheddar cheese (5 ounces)
1/4 cup shortening
water
grated Parmesan cheese

Color index page 18

Begin 45 mins ahead or early in day

96 appetizers or 24 servings

18 cals per appetizer

1. In large bowl, mix flour, cornmeal and salt. With pastry blender or 2 knives used scissor-fashion, cut in Cheddar cheese and shortening until mixture resembles coarse crumbs. With fork, stir in ⅓ cup water. With hands, shape dough into ball. (If mixture is too dry, add more water, a teaspoon at a time, until moist enough to hold together.) Preheat oven to 425°F.
2. Between two 15-inch-long sheets of waxed paper, with rolling pin, roll half of pastry into 12″ by 10″ rectangle. With knife, cut dough into 5″ by ½″ strips. Remove each strip; holding ends, make twist by turning ends in opposite directions. Lay on cookie sheet; press ends to sheet to prevent curling.
3. Bake twists 6 to 8 minutes until golden. When done, sprinkle lightly with Parmesan cheese; cool twists on racks. Repeat with remaining dough.

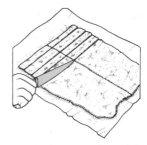

Cutting the strips: Roll half dough into 12″ by 10″ rectangle, then cut into 5″ by ½″ strips. Repeat.

Making a twist: Hold strip and turn ends in opposite directions to make twist; lay on cookie sheet.

Chinese Fried Walnuts

6 cups water
4 cups California walnuts
1/2 cup sugar
salad oil
1/8 teaspoon salt

Color index page 18

Begin early in day

4 cups

204 cals per 1/4 cup

1. In 3-quart saucepan over high heat, heat water to boiling; add walnuts; reheat to boiling; cook 1 minute. Rinse under running hot water; drain.
2. In large bowl, toss walnuts in sugar.
3. Meanwhile, in electric skillet, heat about 1 inch salad oil to 350°F. With slotted spoon, add about half of walnuts to oil; fry 5 minutes or until golden, stirring often.
4. With slotted spoon, place walnuts in coarse sieve over bowl to drain; sprinkle with salt; toss lightly to keep walnuts from sticking together. Transfer to waxed paper to cool. Fry remaining walnuts. Store in tightly covered container.

Curried Almonds

2 cups blanched whole almonds
1¹/2 tablespoons butter or margarine, melted
1 tablespoon curry powder
1 teaspoon salt

Color index page 18

Begin early in day

2 cups

230 cals per 1/4 cup

Good source of calcium, iron

Preheat oven to 300°F. In 8- or 9-inch cake pan, combine almonds and melted butter. Toast in oven 30 minutes, stirring occasionally. Add curry powder and salt; toss until thoroughly coated. Transfer to waxed paper to cool. Store almonds in tightly covered container.

289 cals per 1/4 cup

HOT-PEPPER PECANS: Prepare as above but use *2 cups pecan halves, 1¹/2 tablespoons butter* or margarine, melted, *1 teaspoon salt, 2 teaspoons soy sauce* and *dash hot pepper sauce.* (Makes 2 cups.)

243 cals per 1/4 cup

CASHEWS WITH CHILI: Prepare as above but use *2 cups salted cashews, 1¹/2 tablespoons butter* or margarine, melted, *1 tablespoon chili powder* and omit salt. (Makes 2 cups.)

Cold canapés

Color index
page 22

Begin 2¼ hrs
ahead

36 appetizers
or 18 servings

124 cals per
serving

Low in
cholesterol

Color index
page 18

Begin 2 hrs
ahead

40 appetizers

56 cals each

Color index
page 20

Begin 1 hr
ahead

30 appetizers

36 cals each

Curried-Tuna Canapés

Choux paste:
¼ cup butter or
   margarine
½ cup water
⅛ teaspoon salt
½ cup all-purpose flour
2 eggs
Filling:
1 6½- to 7-ounce can
   tuna
2 hard-cooked eggs
½ cup mayonnaise
¼ cup minced celery
1 tablespoon curry
   powder
¼ teaspoon salt
⅔ cup chopped parsley

1 Grease large cookie sheet. Preheat oven to 375°F. Prepare *choux* paste: In 1-quart saucepan over medium heat, heat butter, water and salt until mixture boils. Remove from heat. Add flour all at once. With wooden spoon, vigorously stir until mixture forms a ball and leaves side of pan. Add eggs, one at a time, beating well after each addition, until smooth. Allow mixture to cool slightly; carefully spoon into pastry bag fitted with round tube.

2 Squeeze *choux* paste through pastry bag onto greased cookie sheet to make 20 mounds, each about 2 teaspoonfuls and about 1 inch apart.

3 Bake puffs 20 to 25 minutes, until browned; cool puffs on wire rack.

4 Meanwhile, prepare Filling: In small bowl with fork, stir tuna and its oil until finely flaked; chop hard-cooked eggs.

5 Into flaked tuna, stir mayonnaise, minced celery, chopped hard-cooked eggs, curry powder and salt; cover and chill.

6 When puffs are cool, with sharp knife, cut each puff horizontally in half to make 2 shells.

7 Spoon about 1 rounded teaspoon of mixture into each shell; garnish with chopped parsley.

Caviar-Egg Rounds

Color index
page 18

Begin 30 mins
ahead

12 appetizers

51 cals each

6 pumpernickel-bread
  slices
2 hard-cooked
  eggs

3 pitted ripe olives
  mayonnaise
1 tablespoon red
  caviar

1. Using a 2-inch round cookie cutter, cut 2 circles from each of the bread slices.
2. With sharp knife, cut each hard-cooked egg into 6 thin slices. Cut each olive into 4 slices.
3. Spread a dab of mayonnaise on center of each circle and top with a slice of hard-cooked egg. Garnish with some caviar and a slice of olive.

Tuna-Dill Rounds

Color index
page 18

Begin 45 mins
ahead

28 appetizers

76 cals each

1 1-pound loaf
  pumpernickel-bread,
  sliced
mayonnaise
1 medium cucumber,
  thinly sliced
1 6½- to 7-ounce can
  tuna, drained

¼ cup sour cream
1 teaspoon dill weed
1 teaspoon lemon
  juice
⅛ teaspoon pepper
1½ teaspoons minced
  pimento

1. With 2-inch round cutter, cut 2 rounds from each bread slice; spread with some mayonnaise; top with cucumber slice. Chop any leftover cucumber.
2. In small bowl, mix chopped cucumber, 3 tablespoons mayonnaise, tuna and next 4 ingredients. Spoon some mixture on each round; top with some minced pimento.

Watercress Cream-Cheese Triangles

Color index
page 18

Begin 15 mins
ahead

20 appetizers

34 cals each

1 3-ounce package cream
  cheese, softened
5 thin white-bread slices,
  crusts removed

1 bunch watercress,
  washed and trimmed

Spread cheese on bread slices. Cut each slice into 4 triangles. Top each with 2 sprigs watercress.

Smoked Salmon Squares

Color index
page 18

Begin 30 mins
ahead

20 appetizers

39 cals each

5 thin white-bread slices
1 3-ounce package
  cream cheese,
  softened

3 ounces sliced smoked
  salmon
strips of peel cut from 2
  large lemons

1. Toast bread; trim crusts. Spread bread with cream cheese; cut each slice into quarters.
2. Cut salmon slices to fit on toast; top toast with slices. Garnish with strips of lemon peel.

Anchovy-Cheese Circles

Color index
page 18

Begin 15 mins
ahead

20 appetizers

44 cals each

10 pumpernickel-bread
  slices
1 5-ounce jar Old English
  cheese spread
2 teaspoons horseradish

5 anchovy fillets, cut into
  strips
5 pimento-stuffed olives,
  sliced

1. Using 2-inch round cookie cutter, cut 2 circles from each pumpernickel-bread slice.
2. In small bowl, mix cheese spread and horseradish; spread some mixture on each circle. Top with strip of anchovy fillet and olive slice.

First-course soups

Avgolemono

Color index
page 25

Begin 30 mins
ahead

6 servings or
5½ cups

110 cals per
serving

**3 13¾-ounce cans
chicken broth**
**¼ cup regular long-
grain rice**

4 eggs
**3 tablespoons lemon
juice**
lemon slices (optional)

1. In 3-quart saucepan over high heat, heat broth and rice to boiling. Reduce heat to low; cover and simmer 15 minutes or until rice is tender.
2. In small bowl with wire whisk or hand beater, beat eggs and lemon juice together until frothy.
3. Into egg mixture, stir small amount of hot broth; pour egg mixture into broth, stirring. Cook over low heat, stirring, until soup is hot (do not boil).
4. Serve topped with lemon slices, if you wish.

Pea Soup

Color index
page 25

Begin 45 mins
ahead

10 servings
or 5 cups

111 cals per
serving

Low in
cholesterol

¼ cup butter
4 cups shredded lettuce
½ large onion, chopped
**1 tablespoon all-purpose
flour**
1 teaspoon sugar
**¼ teaspoon ground
coriander**

**3 13¾-ounce cans
chicken broth**
**2 10-ounce packages
frozen peas**
1 cup milk
**mint leaves for garnish
(optional)**

1. In 3-quart saucepan over medium heat, in hot butter, cook lettuce and onion until tender, stirring often. Add flour, sugar and coriander. Slowly stir in broth; add peas, reserving a few for garnish; cook, covered, 15 minutes.
2. In covered blender container, blend mixture, a cup at a time; return it to the pan. Add milk; reheat. Garnish with reserved peas and mint, if you wish.

Shrimp Bisque

Color index
page 25

Begin 1 hr
ahead

10 servings
or 8½ cups

395 cals per
serving

Good source
of calcium,
iron,
vitamin A

3 tablespoons olive oil
**1½ pounds medium
shrimp, shelled and
deveined (reserve
shells)**
¼ cup butter
1 large onion, diced
1 carrot, chopped
1 celery stalk, chopped
2½ cups water

1 cup dry white wine
**¼ cup regular long-
grain rice**
1 bay leaf
½ teaspoon salt
¼ teaspoon cayenne
**3 chicken-flavor
bouillon cubes**
1 16-ounce can tomatoes
2 cups heavy cream

1. In 4-quart Dutch oven over medium-high heat, in hot olive oil, cook shrimp shells until pink, stirring constantly with slotted spoon. Discard shells, leaving flavored oil in Dutch oven.
2. Add shrimp to oil and cook, over medium-high heat, stirring frequently, until shrimp turn pink, about 3 minutes; spoon into bowl.
3. Reduce heat to medium; add butter, onion, carrot and celery; cook, stirring occasionally, until tender.
4. Stir in next 7 ingredients and heat to boiling. Reduce heat to low; cover and simmer 15 minutes or until rice is tender. Remove Dutch oven from heat.
5. Discard bay leaf. Drain juice of tomatoes into rice mixture. Remove seed from tomatoes; stir tomatoes into rice mixture and add cooked shrimp.
6. In covered blender container at high speed, blend one half of mixture at a time until smooth.
7. Return shrimp mixture to Dutch oven; stir in cream. Over medium heat, heat just to boiling.

French Onion Soup Gratinée

Color index
page 25

Begin 45 mins
ahead

4 servings or
6 cups

644 cals per
serving

Good source
of calcium,
iron,
vitamin A

**¼ cup butter or
margarine**
**3 large onions, sliced
(about 4 cups)**
1 teaspoon sugar
**1 tablespoon all-
purpose flour**
2½ cups water
½ cup red cooking wine
**2 10½-ounce cans
condensed beef broth**
**1 long loaf French
bread**
**1 8-ounce package
Swiss cheese slices**

1 In 4-quart saucepan over medium heat, in hot butter, cook onions and sugar for 10 minutes.

2 Stir in flour until well blended with the onions and the pan juices.

3 Add water, wine and undiluted beef broth; heat to boiling. Reduce heat to low; cover and simmer 10 minutes.

4 Cut four 1-inch-thick slices of bread from loaf; save remaining bread to eat with soup. Toast the bread slices in 325°F. oven just until lightly browned, about 10 minutes.

5 Ladle soup into four 12-ounce oven-safe bowls and place 1 slice toasted bread on surface of soup in each bowl.

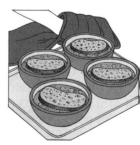

6 Fold Swiss cheese slices and fit onto toasted bread slices in soup.

7 Place soup bowls in jelly-roll pan for easier handling. Bake in 425°F. oven 10 minutes or just until cheese is melted.

Cream of Mushroom Soup

Color index
page 25

Begin 45 mins
ahead

8 servings or
7 cups

225 cals per
serving

Good source
of vitamin A

1 pound mushrooms
½ cup butter or
margarine
1 teaspoon lemon juice
1 small onion, sliced
⅓ cup all-purpose flour
3½ cups water
3 chicken-flavor bouillon
cubes or envelopes
1 teaspoon salt
¼ teaspoon pepper
1 cup heavy or whipping
cream

1 Trim tough stem ends of mushrooms; remove stems; set aside. With knife, slice mushroom caps thinly.

2 In 4-quart saucepan over medium-high heat, in hot butter or margarine, cook sliced mushrooms and lemon juice until mushrooms are just tender, stirring.

3 Reduce heat to medium-low; with slotted spoon, remove mushrooms to bowl. In saucepan in remaining butter, cook onion and stems; cook until onion is tender.

4 Stir in flour until blended; cook 1 minute, stirring the mixture constantly.

5 Gradually stir in water and bouillon; cook, stirring constantly, until mixture is thickened.

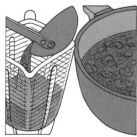

6 Into blender container, ladle half of mixture; cover and at high speed, blend until smooth. Repeat with other half.

7 Return mixture to saucepan; stir in salt, pepper, cream and mushroom slices; reheat just until soup is boiling.

GARNISHES FOR SOUPS

A well-chosen garnish such as a sprinkling of finely chopped parsley or chives, a slice of lemon or a few paper-thin slices of cucumber can turn an otherwise ordinary soup into something quite special. For a more decorative effect, swirl a tablespoon of cream lightly into each bowl to marbleize the surface. Grated cheese should be served separately so that each person can help himself.

CHOPPED
HARD-COOKED EGG

LEMON SLICES

MEATBALLS

CROUTONS

SLICED
CAULIFLOWERETS

CARROT AND
CELERY STICKS

WHIPPED OR
SOUR CREAM

GRATED CHEESE

BACON BITS

SLICED ALMONDS

Croutons can be passed around in a separate bowl to be added to each portion of soup at the very last moment. You can use any light or dark bread slices for making croutons.

Trim off the crusts and cut the bread into small even-sized cubes.

Fry cubes in salad oil, a mixture of butter and oil or bacon drippings until crisp and golden, stirring constantly while frying.

Main-dish soups

A main-dish soup makes a first-class informal lunch or family supper. It is substantial and filling with crusty hot bread and butter as an accompaniment. Serve a tossed salad or fresh vegetable relishes to complete the menu.

The flavors of fish, meat and chicken soups can be enhanced by adding a small amount of red table wine or cooking wine or a lemon slice and gently reheating for a minute or two to bring out the flavor. Make sure not to cook the soup for too long after adding the red wine or lemon slice, or the flavor will be lost.

Small portions of these substantial soups can also be served as a first course before a light main dish.

Hearty Borscht

Color index page 27

Begin early in day or day ahead

4 servings or 8 cups

260 cals per serving

Good source of calcium, iron, vitamin C

3 cups hot water
1 pound beef brisket, cut into 1-inch chunks
2 medium carrots, sliced
1 medium onion, sliced
1 stalk celery, cut into chunks
1 bay leaf
3 medium beets

salt
½ 6-ounce can tomato paste
1½ teaspoons sugar
½ small head cabbage, shredded
1 tablespoon cider vinegar
½ cup sour cream

1 To 5-quart saucepot or Dutch oven over medium-low heat add water, beef, carrots, onion, celery, bay leaf, 2 sliced beets and 1½ teaspoons salt.

2 Cover and simmer 2 hours. Shred remaining beet and, with tomato paste, sugar and 1 teaspoon salt, stir into soup.

3 Cover again and simmer 20 minutes. Remove pan from heat and discard bay leaf. Chill.

4 *About 20 minutes before serving:* Remove hardened fat from surface of chilled soup.

5 Over medium heat, heat soup to boiling. Add cabbage; cook 15 minutes. Stir in vinegar.

6 Serve in large soup plates or wide bowls, each portion garnished with some sour cream.

German Lentil Soup

Color index page 26

Begin 1½ hrs ahead

6 servings or 11 cups

312 cals per serving

Low in cholesterol

Good source of iron

4 bacon slices, diced
2 medium onions, sliced
2 medium carrots, sliced
1 cup sliced celery
1 ham bone
1 16-ounce package lentils

½ teaspoon pepper
½ teaspoon thyme leaves
2 bay leaves
8 cups hot water
salt
2 tablespoons lemon juice

1. In 5-quart Dutch oven or large saucepot over medium-high heat, fry bacon until lightly browned; push to side of pan.
2. Add onions, carrots and celery and over medium heat, cook until onions are tender, about 5 minutes.
3. Add ham bone, lentils, pepper, thyme, bay leaves, hot water and 2 teaspoons salt.
4. Cover; simmer over low heat 1 hour or until lentils are tender. Discard bay leaves.
5. Remove ham bone to cutting board and cut off any meat; cut into small pieces.
6. Stir meat, lemon juice and salt to taste into soup.

Old-fashioned Beef-Vegetable Soup

Color index page 27

Begin 1 hr ahead

10 servings or 16 cups

189 cals per serving

Good source of iron

¼ cup salad oil
1 small onion, diced
3 celery stalks, sliced
2 medium carrots, sliced
½ small head cabbage, shredded
1 medium zucchini, cut into ½-inch chunks
1½ pounds beef for stew, cut into ½-inch chunks

6 medium potatoes
1 28-ounce can tomatoes
6 cups water
1 16-ounce can cut green beans, drained
1 8-ounce can baby lima beans, drained
3 teaspoons salt
½ teaspoon pepper
½ teaspoon basil

1. In 8-quart Dutch oven or saucepot over high heat, in very hot salad oil, cook onion, celery, carrots, cabbage and zucchini until vegetables are lightly browned, stirring frequently. With slotted spoon, remove vegetables to medium bowl; set aside.
2. In same Dutch oven over high heat, in remaining oil, cook beef chunks, stirring frequently, until meat is well browned on all sides.
3. Meanwhile, peel potatoes; shred 1 potato and cut remaining 5 potatoes into 1-inch cubes. To meat chunks add reserved vegetable mixture, potatoes, tomatoes with their liquid and remaining ingredients; heat to boiling. Reduce heat to low; cover and simmer 25 to 30 minutes or just until beef chunks and medium potatoes are fork-tender.

Split-Pea Soup

1 ham bone (left over from whole or half ham, preferably with enough meat left to make 1½ cups)
1 16-ounce package split peas
2 carrots, thinly sliced
1 medium onion, chopped
7 cups water
¼ teaspoon whole allspice
¼ teaspoon peppercorns
1 bay leaf
salt

Color index page 27

Begin 1 hr ahead

6 servings or 7 cups

290 cals per serving

Low in cholesterol

Good source of iron, thiamine

1 In 5-quart Dutch oven over medium heat, heat bone, split peas, carrots, onion and water to boiling.

2 Tie allspice, peppercorns and bay leaf in piece of cheesecloth. Add to bone mixture.

3 Reduce heat to low; cover; simmer 1 hour. Discard spice bag; add salt if necessary.

4 Remove bone to cutting board. Cut off meat and discard bone.

5 Cut meat into bite-size chunks and return to soup for serving.

SOUP ACCOMPANIMENTS
Crisp accompaniments contrast pleasantly with any soup. Choose from a selection of the following: hot crusty bread or toast with garlic, herb or onion butter; plain or seasoned bread sticks or melba toast; cheese, rye, wheat or oyster crackers; potato or corn chips and saltines or soda crackers.

Making melba toast: Cut unsliced loaf of bread into ⅛-inch-thick slices. If you like, remove crusts, then cut slices diagonally into triangles. Place on cookie sheet; bake 15 minutes or until golden, crisp and curled, turning once.

Minestrone

⅓ cup olive or salad oil
¼ cup butter or margarine
1 large onion, diced
2 large carrots, diced
2 stalks celery, diced
2 medium potatoes, diced
½ pound green beans, cut into 1-inch pieces
6 cups water
½ small head cabbage, shredded
1 16-ounce can tomatoes
½ 10-ounce bag fresh spinach, coarsely shredded
2 medium zucchini, diced
6 beef-flavor bouillon cubes or envelopes, or 2 tablespoons beef-flavor stock base
1 teaspoon salt
1 16- to 20-ounce can white kidney (cannellini) beans, drained
1 16- to 20-ounce can red kidney beans, drained
½ cup grated Parmesan or Romano cheese

Color index page 27

Begin 2 hrs ahead

8 servings or 16 cups

289 cals per serving

Low in cholesterol

Good source of calcium, iron

1. In 8-quart Dutch oven or large saucepot over medium heat, in hot oil and butter or margarine, cook onion, carrots, celery, potatoes and green beans until vegetables are lightly browned, about 20 minutes, stirring occasionally .
2. Add water, cabbage, tomatoes with their liquid, spinach, zucchini, bouillon cubes and salt. Over high heat, heat to boiling, stirring to break up tomatoes.
3. Reduce heat to low; cover; simmer 40 minutes or until all the vegetables are very tender, stirring occasionally; do not overcook.
3. Stir in beans; cook 15 minutes longer or just until the soup is slightly thickened.
5.To serve: Ladle soup into bowls and pass cheese separately to sprinkle over each individual serving.

Hungarian Goulash

3 tablespoons lard or shortening
1½ cups fresh or frozen chopped onions
1 small green pepper, cut into ½-inch chunks
1 large garlic clove, crushed
6 cups water
1½ pounds beef stew meat, cut into ¾-inch cubes
1 veal heart (about 12 ounces) cut into ¾-inch cubes
2 tablespoons paprika
3 teaspoons salt
¼ teaspoon crushed red pepper
¼ teaspoon caraway seed
1½ pounds potatoes, peeled and cut into ¾-inch cubes
1 16-ounce can tomatoes

Color index page 26

Begin 2½ hrs ahead

12 servings or 15 cups

202 cals per serving

Good source of iron

1. In 5-quart Dutch oven over medium-low heat, in hot lard or shortening, cook onions, green pepper and garlic just until onion is tender, about 10 minutes, stirring occasionally.
2. Add water, beef, heart, paprika, salt, red pepper and caraway seed; heat to boiling. Reduce heat to low; cover and simmer 1½ hours or just until meat is fork-tender.
3. Add potatoes; cover and cook 10 minutes longer or until potatoes are tender.
4. Drain liquid from tomatoes and add to mixture in Dutch oven. With small knife, coarsely chop tomatoes; stir into mixture.
5. Cook soup just until heated through.
6. Ladle into warm soup plates and serve at once.

Scrambled eggs

Scrambled eggs must be cooked slowly if they are to stay creamy and, for the best results, the eggs should be at room temperature. By mixing 2 tablespoons milk, cream or water with every 2 eggs you can slow the cooking and make them fluffier and more tender. Eggs should not be stirred too often: frequent stirring breaks them into small pieces and they become dry and crumbly.

The size of the skillet you choose is important, too – the egg mixture should not be more than 1 inch deep, otherwise the portion that cooks at the beginning will have toughened before the remaining mixture has had a chance to thicken. The skillet should be made from a material that conducts heat evenly.

Scrambled Eggs

Color index
page 28

2 eggs
per person

291 cals per
serving

Good source
of iron,
vitamin A

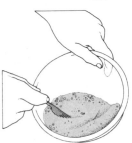 

1 Break *2 eggs* into bowl, add *2 tablespoons liquid* and sprinkle with *salt* and *pepper.* With a fork beat slightly just until mixed.

2 In 9-inch skillet over medium heat, melt *1 tablespoon butter* or margarine, tilting the skillet to coat both the base and side thoroughly

3 Pour in the egg mixture and as it begins to set, with spatula, stir slightly so thin, uncooked egg flows to bottom.

4 Cook the egg mixture gently until set but still very moist; remove from heat. Eggs will continue to cook from pan heat.

5 Pile eggs onto warmed plate, or hot buttered toast and serve the dish immediately.

Color index
page 28

Begin 15
mins ahead

2 servings

459 cals per
serving

Good source
of calcium,
iron,
vitamin A

Shrimp Scramble

4 eggs
2 tablespoons milk
1 4½-ounce can shrimp
½ teaspoon salt
⅛ teaspoon pepper

¼ teaspoon prepared
mustard
2 English muffins,
split
butter or margarine

1. In medium bowl with fork, beat eggs and milk. Drain shrimp and stir into eggs with salt, pepper and mustard. Toast muffins; butter and keep warm.
2. In 10-inch skillet, over medium heat, melt 1 tablespoon butter. Add egg mixture; cook, stirring lightly with fork.
3. When eggs are set and creamy, spoon over toasted muffin halves. Serve immediately.

Color index
page 23

Begin 1½ hrs
ahead

12 servings

273 cals per
serving

Good source
of calcium,
iron,
vitamin A,
riboflavin

Brunch Eggs Florentine

butter or margarine
1 small onion,
minced
¼ cup all-purpose
flour
salt
2 cups milk
18 eggs

4 10-ounce packages
frozen chopped
spinach, thawed
and drained
3 medium tomatoes,
sliced
⅛ teaspoon pepper
dill for garnish

1. In 3-quart saucepan over medium heat, melt 4 tablespoons butter; add onion and cook until tender, about 5 minutes, stirring occasionally. Stir in flour and 2 teaspoons salt; gradually stir in milk and cook until sauce thickens and boils, stirring constantly. Remove saucepan from heat.
2. Separate 4 eggs, placing whites in large bowl and yolks in small bowl; set whites aside. With fork, beat yolks slightly. Into yolks, stir small amount of hot sauce; slowly pour yolk mixture back into sauce, stirring rapidly to prevent lumping. Cook over low heat until mixture is very thick, stirring constantly (do not boil or mixture will curdle). Remove from heat; stir in spinach. Cover and refrigerate to cool slightly, about 15 minutes.
3. Preheat oven to 350°F. Grease 13″ by 9″ baking dish. With mixer at high speed, beat reserved egg whites until stiff peaks form. With rubber spatula or wire whisk, gently fold spinach mixture into beaten whites until blended. Pour mixture into prepared baking dish. Bake 30 minutes; remove baking dish from oven and arrange tomato slices, overlapping slightly, over spinach mixture. Return dish to oven and continue baking until knife inserted in center of spinach mixture comes out clean and tomatoes are heated through, about 10 minutes.
4. Meanwhile, prepare scrambled eggs: In large bowl, with wire whisk or fork, beat remaining 14 eggs, pepper, and 1 teaspoon salt until just blended. In 12-inch skillet over medium-high heat, melt 6 tablespoons butter. Add egg mixture and, as egg mixture begins to set, with rubber spatula, stir slightly so uncooked egg flows to bottom. Continue cooking until set but moist, stirring occasionally.
5. To serve, remove dish from oven; arrange scrambled eggs in row, down center, on top of spinach and tomatoes and garnish with dill.

Spring Picnic

We know Spring is here when strawberries, asparagus and new potatoes appear on supermarket shelves. Other fruits and vegetables synonymous with the season include rhubarb, young beets, peas and Chinese pea pods. Some more exotic fruits that are used now to add special interest to meals are mangoes, passion fruit and lychees.

Take advantage of the warm days of Spring to enjoy the picnic overleaf. Potato chips and peanuts are there for the family to nibble on while the Oven-fried Chicken and Corn Bread are being unpacked. The Potato-Vegetable Salad and Deluxe Coleslaw Bowl are variations of old favorites that contrast well with Okra Vinaigrette and cherry tomatoes. Individual Strawberry Shortcakes and Fudgy Brownies are delicious to eat out of hand and the pitcher of Lemonade is a real thirst quencher.

Clockwise from left: artichokes; asparagus; jumbo asparagus; strawberries; mangoes

Spring Picnic

Menu

Spring Picnic
8 people
* * *
Potato Chips and Peanuts
* * *
Oven-fried Chicken
(double recipe) page 263
Potato-Vegetable Salad
page 320
Deluxe Coleslaw Bowl
page 319
Okra Vinaigrette
page 288
Cherry Tomatoes
Corn Bread
page 428
* * *
Individual Strawberry Shortcakes
page 369
Fudgy Brownies
page 404
* * *
Lemonade
page 470

Making Strawberry Shortcakes

Strawberry shortcake is an all-time favorite dessert that can be enjoyed at outdoor get-togethers as well as at more formal gatherings.

For a change, prepare individual shortcakes and let the guests complete these by adding the strawberry mixture themselves.

1 Prepare shortcake batter as in step 1, page 369, but onto greased cookie sheet, drop dough in 8 equal mounds about 2 inches apart. Bake 10 minutes or until golden. Cool shortcakes completely.

2 Hull strawberries, reserving a few for garnish. Sprinkle remainder with 1/3 cup sugar; with a fork, mash slightly and refrigerate. Whip cream and refrigerate.

3 To assemble cakes, using a serrated knife, split shortcakes horizontally. Spread both cut surfaces with softened butter or margarine.

4 Onto the bottom half of the cake, spoon some of the mashed strawberry mixture; cover with top half to form a sandwich. Spoon whipped cream over the cake top.

5 Slice remaining whole strawberries and arrange on whipped cream. Or, garnish with whole berries and serve extra strawberries and cream.

Individual Strawberry Shortcakes
Prepare the shortcakes and put in a container when cool. Pack the strawberries and whipped cream separately in insulated containers to keep them cold, especially when serving outdoors.

Omelets

A French omelet should be shiny and delicately browned on the outside, moist and creamy in the center. You can serve it plain or with any one of the fillings on page 146. The puffy omelet, a cross between an omelet and a soufflé, is finished by baking in the oven. It, too, can be eaten plain or with fillings for a main dish, or it can be served with a sweet filling and eaten as a dessert. The eggs for a puffy omelet are separated, and the yolks mixed into the beaten whites.

Remember that the eggs should always be cooked over moderate to low heat. With practice, you can turn out a perfect omelet every time. Timing is important; have any fillings warm and get the plate ready before you start cooking the eggs. An individual omelet should not take more than a few minutes.

Always coat the pan lightly with butter or margarine to prevent sticking, and make sure the egg mixture is not more than ¼ inch deep in the pan. It is not necessary to turn the omelet over, but the edge should be raised with a spatula and the pan shaken gently to keep the uncooked mixture moving freely. When the omelet is almost set but still moist on the surface, increase the heat slightly to brown the bottom. Have a warmed plate handy to receive the folded omelet: an omelet should never wait. Add your choice of filling, if desired, and serve the omelet without delay.

THE OMELET PAN

An omelet can be made in any good skillet with a flared side and an easy-to-grip, heat-resistant handle. Easiest to use are those made from aluminum, copper or stainless steel (combined with aluminum, copper or carbon steel) because they conduct and distribute heat well. A nonstick coating in the pan is especially helpful for omelet making and enables you to reduce the amount of butter necessary for cooking the eggs.

OMELET PAN

Pan size is important. Too thin an omelet will cook too quickly and be tough; too thick an omelet will not completely "set" and will split and ooze when you attempt to fold it. A 7- or 8-inch top diameter (5- or 6-inch base diameter) pan is the size for a 3-egg omelet.

French Omelet

3 eggs
1 tablespoon cold
* water*
¼ teaspoon salt
⅛ teaspoon pepper
1 tablespoon butter
* or margarine*

Color index page 28
Begin 30 mins ahead
1 main-dish serving
352 cals

Good source of iron,
vitamin A, riboflavin

1 Break the eggs into a small bowl. Add the water, salt and pepper.

2 Beat the eggs vigorously with a wire whisk or fork – just enough to mix the egg yolks and whites.

3 In a 7-inch omelet pan or skillet over medium heat, melt butter or margarine; tilt the skillet so that the butter coats the entire surface of the pan.

4 Pour in eggs all at once. Let them set around edge. Shake pan occasionally to keep omelet moving freely over the bottom of the pan.

5 With a metal spatula lift edge as it sets, tilting skillet to allow uncooked egg mixture to run under omelet.

6 Continue to shake pan for a few seconds longer until you can feel the omelet sliding freely over the pan surface.

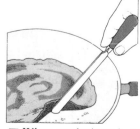

7 When omelet is set but still moist on the surface, increase heat slightly to brown bottom. Remove pan from heat.

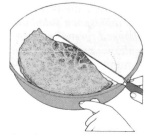

8 Tilt pan away from you and using the spatula, lift the edge of the omelet and quickly fold in half.

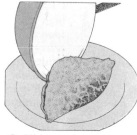

9 Slide omelet on to a warm plate, garnish if you wish. Serve the hot omelet immediately.

SHELLFISH

Shellfish fall into two main categories, mollusks such as oysters, clams, mussels and scallops, and crustaceans – lobsters, crabs and shrimp. Shellfish are particularly rich in minerals; they contain high-quality protein, are a good source of vitamins and are low in calories.

Fresh, uncooked shellfish should be bought live. Mollusks should be tightly closed. If the shells are slightly parted, a sharp tap should be enough to make them snap shut again. Shucked mollusks should be plump and shiny, free of odor and with little or no liquor (surrounding liquid). Crustaceans survive longer out of water but their movements become slow and languid. Crabs and lobsters should be lively; when picked up, the lobster tails should curl under, not hang down. The amount of shellfish to buy depends on whether or not it has been shelled or shucked. Where we give recommended amounts for individual servings of each shellfish, these should be used only as a guide. If in doubt, especially with crabs, discuss the number to buy with your marketman.

Store fresh shellfish loosely wrapped in the refrigerator and cook them within 1 day.

Mussels

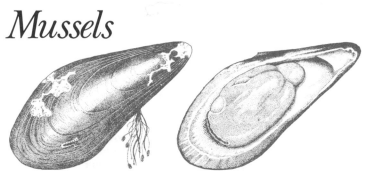

Mussels are sold fresh in the shells. Buy them from a reliable fish market or gather them fresh only when in season in your particular area. (They could be toxic if eaten out of season.)

Mussels must be alive when cooked, the shells unbroken and tightly closed, or they should close if touched. Rinse thoroughly under running cold water to remove all sand. Discard any that remain open. Scrub clean with a stiff metal brush, scraping off any loose barnacles with a knife. With shears, clip off beards.

To steam mussels, place them in a large pot in a small amount of boiling water. Tightly cover pot and simmer over medium heat 5 to 10 minutes until all the shells open up. Discard any unopened shells.

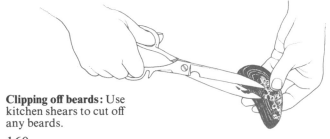

Clipping off beards: Use kitchen shears to cut off any beards.

Color index page 24

Begin 1¼ hrs ahead

4 servings

174 cals per serving

Good source of calcium, iron

Mussels Marinière

3 pounds mussels (about 5 to 6 dozen)
butter or margarine
3 shallots, minced
1 garlic clove, minced
½ cup dry white wine
¼ teaspoon salt
⅛ teaspoon pepper
1 tablespoon chopped parsley

1. Discard any mussels that remain open when tapped with fingers. Clean and remove beards.
2. In 5-quart saucepot or Dutch oven over medium-high heat, in 2 tablespoons hot butter or margarine, cook shallots and garlic 1 minute, stirring. Add wine and mussels; sprinkle mussels with salt and pepper. Cover and simmer 6 to 8 minutes until shells open, stirring occasionally.
3. With slotted spoon, remove mussels to bowl. (Discard any that remain unopened.) Without disturbing sediment in bottom of saucepot, pour stock into 1½-quart saucepan; heat.
4. Meanwhile, discard halves of mussel shells to which meat is not attached. Arrange mussels in shells, open side up, in soup plates. Into hot stock, stir 1 tablespoon butter or margarine; pour over mussels; sprinkle servings with parsley.

Cooking mussels: Simmer 6 to 8 minutes until shells open; remove to bowl.

Arranging shells in plates: Place mussels in half-shells, open side up.

Oysters

Oysters are sold live in the shell, fresh-shucked or shucked then frozen or canned. Eastern oysters are graded by size: "counts" are extra-large, "extra-selects" are large and "selects", the ones preferred for frying, are medium. "Standards", or very small oysters, are used for soups and stews. West Coast oysters include the tiny Olympia and the very large Pacific oyster.

Fresh oysters in the shell are sold by the dozen, shucked oysters by the pint or quart. For serving raw on the half-shell, allow 5 or 6 oysters per person. Oysters can also be cooked in stews or chowders, breaded and pan-fried or deep-fried.

A sturdy oyster knife or clamshucker tool is the ideal implement for shucking oysters; if you don't have one use a small blunt knife.

OPENING OYSTERS

First scrub oyster shells under running cold water with a vegetable brush to remove sand, then shuck them as shown below.

Hold oyster in one hand and with the other hand, insert oyster knife between shells near the hinge.

Run knife between shells until you reach the opposite end.

With twisting motions of the knife, pry shells apart. Remove top shell.

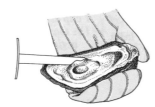

Insert knife under the oyster to cut meat loose from shell; retain as much liquor as possible. Remove any broken shell.

Oysters Rockefeller

Color index page 24

Begin 30 mins ahead

6 first-course servings

121 cals per serving

Low in cholesterol

Good source of calcium, iron

3 tablespoons butter or margarine
½ 10-ounce package frozen chopped spinach, slightly thawed
1 tablespoon instant minced onion
1 tablespoon chopped parsley
1 bay leaf, finely crumbled
¼ teaspoon salt
⅛ teaspoon cayenne pepper, hot pepper sauce or anisette
¼ cup dried bread crumbs
rock salt (optional)
18 large or 24 small oysters on the half-shell
2 bacon slices, diced
grated Parmesan cheese (optional)
lemon wedges for garnish

1. Preheat oven to 425°F. In 1-quart covered saucepan over medium heat, in melted butter, cook spinach, onion, parsley, bay leaf, salt and cayenne, stirring occasionally, until spinach is heated through. Toss in bread crumbs; set aside.

2. If you like, place enough rock salt in bottom of large shallow baking pan to keep oysters in shell from tipping over. Place oysters in baking pan and spoon on spinach mixture. Sprinkle with bacon and cheese. Bake 10 minutes or until bacon is crisp. Garnish with lemon. Serve with oyster forks.

Pan-fried Oysters

Color index page 24

Begin 20 mins ahead

6 first-course servings

197 cals per serving

Good source of calcium, iron

1 pint shucked "select" oysters
⅔ cup finely crushed saltines
3 tablespoons butter or margarine
3 tablespoons salad oil
lemon slices for garnish

1 Drain shucked oysters; then pat them dry with paper towels.

2 On waxed paper, sprinkle half of crushed saltines, then place oysters on crumbs.

3 Sprinkle the oysters with the remaining crushed saltines. Make certain that the oysters are thoroughly coated with crumbs before frying them.

4 In 10-inch skillet over medium-high heat, in hot butter and oil, fry half of oysters, turning once, 5 minutes or until golden brown. Repeat. Serve with lemon slices.

SHELLFISH
Crabs

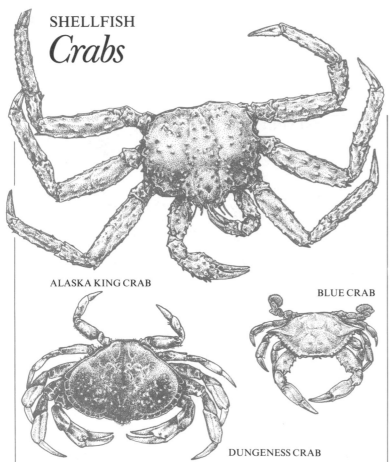

ALASKA KING CRAB

BLUE CRAB

DUNGENESS CRAB

The Atlantic and Pacific coasts of America offer a variety of crabs; the most popular is the small ⅓- to ½-pound blue crab from the Atlantic and Gulf coasts. The other principal types marketed are the 1¾- to 3½-pound Dungeness crab from the Pacific and the massive 6- to 20-pound King crab (only the legs are sold) caught off Alaska. There are also local specialities such as the stone crabs of Florida, snow and tanner crabs of Alaska, and the rock crab of the New England and Californian coasts. Soft-shell crabs are simply blue crabs that have shed their old shells (molted) and are in the process of growing new ones.

Crabs are available live, cooked in the shell, cooked and frozen in the shell, or as fresh cooked, frozen or canned crab meat. Live soft-shell crabs are in season during the summer months.

Live crabs should still be very active when you buy them; soft-shell crabs should be a rich bluish-gray color and cooked crabs will have bright red shells. When buying cooked crab meat, fresh or frozen, it should be clear white, tinged with pink, and have little or no odor.

Hard-shell crabs should be cooked before the meat is removed from the shell. Under running cold water, with rubber glove on hand, hold crab and scrub with stiff or metal brush to remove sand between shell and legs. Drop crab into a large pot of boiling salted water to cover. Reheat to boiling; reduce heat to medium; cover and cook 5 to 10 minutes, or until shells turn red. (Claws and legs may fall off during cooking.)

Soft-shell crabs are prepared differently (see opposite). They are usually pan-fried or broiled 5 minutes and basted occasionally with melted butter.

REMOVING THE MEAT FROM HARD-SHELL CRABS

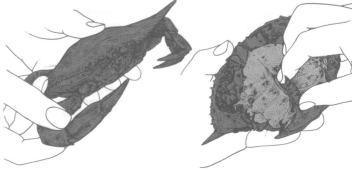

Break off all claws and legs. Crack; remove meat.

With fingers, pull off "apron" on underside.

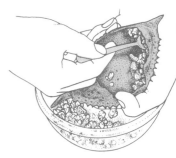

Holding crab in both hands, insert thumb under shell by the apron hinge. Remove the top shell from the body.

With spoon, scrape soft substance from shell into small bowl if you like. Discard shell.

From body, with fingers, remove and discard "deadman's fingers" and soft substance in the middle of the body.

With kitchen shears or both hands, break body in half down center. Cut off thin shell around edges.

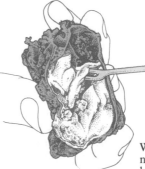

With fingers and lobster or nut pick, remove meat between sections.

Crab Imperial

Color index
page 35

Begin 1 hr
ahead

8 servings

171 cals per
serving

Good source
of vitamin A

3 tablespoons butter or
    margarine
2 tablespoons minced
    green pepper
1/4 cup all-purpose flour
3/4 teaspoon dry mustard
1/4 teaspoon salt
3/4 teaspoon
    Worcestershire

1/8 teaspoon paprika
1/8 teaspoon pepper
1 1/2 cups milk
2 tablespoons dry sherry
2 egg yolks
2 6-ounce packages
    frozen Alaska King
    crab meat, thawed and
    well drained

1. In 2-quart saucepan over medium heat, melt butter or margarine; add green pepper; cook until tender, about 5 minutes. Stir in flour, mustard, salt, Worcestershire, paprika and pepper until well blended. Continue cooking and slowly add milk and sherry, stirring constantly, until sauce thickens and comes to a boil. Remove saucepan from heat. Meanwhile, preheat oven to 350°F.
2. In cup, beat egg yolks slightly; stir in 1/4 cup hot sauce until blended. Slowly pour egg mixture back into saucepan, stirring rapidly to prevent lumping. Fold in crab meat.
3. Pour mixture into greased 1 1/2-quart casserole. Bake 25 to 30 minutes until mixture is hot.

Crab Cakes

Color index
page 35

Begin 30 mins
ahead

4 servings

726 cals per
serving

Good source
of calcium,
iron,
vitamin A

Tartar Sauce (page 185)
3 cups cooked crab meat
    (about 1 pound)
1/3 cup fresh bread
    crumbs
2 tablespoons
    mayonnaise
2 teaspoons minced
    parsley

1 teaspoon
    Worcestershire
1/4 teaspoon salt
1/2 teaspoon dry mustard
1/4 teaspoon pepper
1 egg
about 3 tablespoons
    butter or margarine
lemon wedges

1. Prepare Tartar Sauce. In large bowl with fork, break crab meat into fine shreds; mix in remaining ingredients except butter or margarine and lemon wedges. Divide mixture into 8 portions.
2. In 10-inch skillet over medium heat, into hot butter or margarine, spoon 4 portions; with pancake turner, lightly flatten portions into patties. Fry patties until golden on undersides; turn and brown other sides. Keep patties warm and repeat with other 4 portions. Serve crab cakes with Tartar Sauce and lemon wedges.

Adding mixture to skillet: Spoon portions of crab mixture into hot butter or margarine.

Forming the patties: With pancake turner, lightly flatten portions into patties.

CLEANING SOFT-SHELL CRABS

Before cooking, soft-shell crabs must be cleaned. With kitchen shears, cut across crab 1/4 inch behind eyes; discard. With fingers, remove the flat pointed appendage (apron) on the underside. Fold back but do not remove top shell from one of the points. Pull off spongy gills (dead-man's fingers); discard. Fold top shell back. Repeat on other side. Rinse crab in cold water.

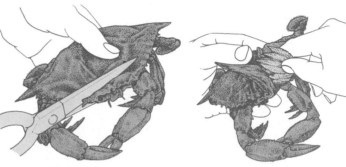

Cutting off head: Cut across crab 1/4 inch behind eyes.

Pulling off gills: Fold back top shell; pull off spongy gills.

Pan-fried Soft-shell Crabs

Color index
page 35

Begin 15 mins
ahead

4 servings

230 cals per
serving

Good source
of vitamin A

8 soft-shell crabs (about
    1 pound), cleaned
salt and pepper
1/4 cup butter or
    margarine
1 tablespoon chopped
    parsley

1 teaspoon lemon juice
1/8 teaspoon
    Worcestershire
toast points (optional)
lemon wedges (optional)

1 Sprinkle the cleaned crabs with salt and pepper. In 12-inch skillet, melt butter or margarine.

2 Over medium heat, fry crabs 3 minutes on each side or until golden. Remove crabs; keep warm.

3 Into butter left in skillet, stir chopped parsley, lemon juice and Worcestershire.

4 Pour sauce over crabs. If you like, serve on toast points with lemon. Entire crab is eaten.

167

SHELLFISH
Lobsters

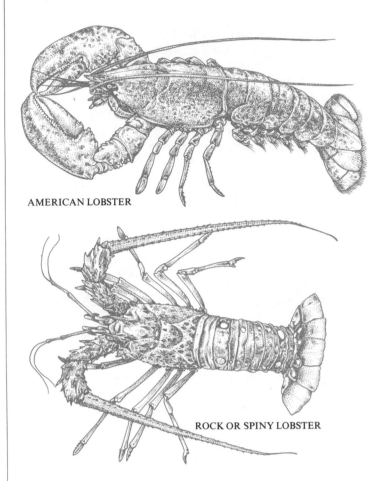

AMERICAN LOBSTER

ROCK OR SPINY LOBSTER

There are two types of lobster, the American lobster and the rock or spiny lobster. The American lobster from the north Atlantic coast, is the most popular. It's marketed live or cooked in the shell. When selecting a live lobster, pick it up near its head–it should curl its tail under and feel heavy for its size. Allow a 1- to 2-pound lobster for each serving.

Since most of the meat of a rock or spiny lobster (which is caught in warm, southern waters) comes from its tail, usually only the tail is sold. It's frozen in the shell or shelled and canned as lobster meat. Allow one 6- to 8-ounce tail, or 2 or 3 smaller ones per serving.

BOILING A LIVE LOBSTER

In large saucepot, heat 3 inches water (or enough to cover lobster) to boiling. Plunge lobster into pot head first. Reheat to boiling; reduce heat to medium; cover and simmer 12 to 15 minutes until shell is red, lifting lid occasionally to let steam escape.

REMOVING THE MEAT

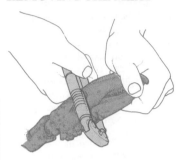

Cool cooked lobster slightly. Break off claws and legs. With lobster or nut cracker, crack the large claws; remove meat.

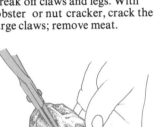

Cut along rounded backside of meat, about ¼ inch deep, to expose dark vein; remove vein and discard. Reserve any red roe (coral) or greenish-gray liver (tomalley) in a bowl. Cut meat into chunks; place in same bowl.

If you like, reassemble shells of head and tail to use as a server for lobster meat.

Twist off head from tail and, with kitchen shears, cut away thin underside shell from tail and discard; gently pull meat from shell.

With hand, lift out the bony portion from head shell; add any further roe or liver to lobster meat. Discard sac and spongy grayish gills from top of head.

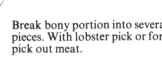

Break bony portion into several pieces. With lobster pick or fork pick out meat.

Lobster Thermidor

Color index
page 35

Begin early
in day

4 servings

672 cals per
serving

Good source
of calcium,
iron,
vitamin A

**4 1½-pound lobsters,
  cooked
6 tablespoons butter
3 tablespoons all-purpose
  flour
½ teaspoon salt
⅛ teaspoon ground
  nutmeg**

**⅛ teaspoon paprika
1½ cups half-and-half
3 tablespoons medium
  sherry
½ cup shredded Cheddar
  cheese
parsley for garnish**

1. Follow directions for removing lobster meat
(opposite), but leave shells whole; do not twist head
from tail and leave antennae on head. Wash and
drain lobster shells.
2. Place meat, roe and liver in large bowl. Cover
bowl and wrap shells; refrigerate both.
3. *About 25 minutes before serving:* In 3-quart
saucepan over medium heat, in butter, blend flour,
salt, nutmeg and paprika. Stir in half-and-half and
sherry; cook, stirring, until thickened. Add meat;
cook just until heated, stirring occasionally.
4. Preheat broiler if manufacturer directs. Place
shells on rack in broiling pan; fill with mixture;
sprinkle with cheese. Broil until mixture is hot. Place
lobsters on platter; garnish with parsley.

Making lobster filling:
Cook sauce until thick,
then add lobster meat.

Filling shells: Spoon
lobster mixture into shells
and sprinkle with cheese.

Broiled Rock- Lobster Tails

Color index
page 35

Begin at least
15 mins ahead
1 large or 2 or
3 small tails
per serving

437 cals per
serving

Good source
of calcium,
iron,
vitamin A

**frozen rock-lobster tails,
  thawed**

**melted butter or
  favorite sauce**

1. Preheat broiler if manufacturer directs. With
kitchen shears, cut away thin underside shell of each
tail. Insert skewer lengthwise through meat to prevent
curling. Place, shell side up, on rack in broiling pan.
2. Broil 7 to 9 inches from source of heat according
to timetable (below), turning once as indicated.
Baste occasionally with melted butter. Tails are
done when meat is opaque; remove skewer. Serve in
shell, with small dishes of melted butter or sauce.

TIMETABLE FOR BROILING ROCK-LOBSTER TAILS		
Weight of tail *(in ounces)*	**Broiling time** *(in minutes)*	
	Shell side	**Meat side**
2 to 3	3 to 4	2 to 3
4 to 5	5	3 to 4
6 to 8	5	6 to 8

Broiled Lobster

Color index
page 35

Begin at least
25 mins ahead

1 small or
½ large lobster
per serving

346 cals per
serving

Good source
of calcium,
iron,
vitamin A,
vitamin C

**1 small (1 pound) or ½
large (1¾ to 2¼
pounds) live lobster
per serving
melted butter or
  margarine
lemon wedges for
  garnish
parsley sprigs for
  garnish (optional)**

1 Place lobster on back.
Holding head, insert
point of sharp knife just
under mouth; quickly
bring knife down body.

2 With both hands, crack
the body of the lobster
open, splitting it in half.

3 Remove dark vein from
tail. Leave light-greenish
liver and dark roe.

4 With hammer or lob-
ster cracker, crack
large part of each large
claw. Preheat broiler if
manufacturer directs.

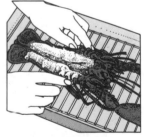

5 Place lobster, cut side
up, on rack in broiling
pan. Brush meat with
melted butter. Broil 7 to 9
inches from heat source.
Do not turn.

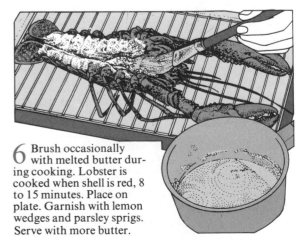

6 Brush occasionally
with melted butter dur-
ing cooking. Lobster is
cooked when shell is red, 8
to 15 minutes. Place on
plate. Garnish with lemon
wedges and parsley sprigs.
Serve with more butter.

FISH

Fish are usually divided into two categories, according to whether the flesh is "fat" or "lean". But even the so-called fat fish, e.g. salmon, mackerel, shad, herring and lake trout, contain no more than 15 percent fat, far less than most meats, while lean fish such as cod, flounder, halibut, haddock, hake and whiting, contain between 2 and 5 percent. Most of this fat is of the polyunsaturated type. As well as being an excellent low-calorie food, fish are also a good source of vitamins and minerals. In addition to fresh fish, canned fish is useful for dishes of all kinds, from soups and salads to main dishes.

One kind of fish may be substituted for another in most recipes as long as you remain within the fat or lean category. Similarly, fresh and frozen fish are usually interchangeable.

CHOOSING FRESH FISH
A fresh fish has clear, bulging eyes and bright red gills. Avoid any with sunken, cloudy eyes and faded pink gills. If the fish is very stale, the gills may even have turned gray or greenish-brown. The body of the fish should be firm and springy to the touch, the skin shiny and the scales bright and close-fitting. Fresh fish has a mild, fresh odor or none at all.

Pieces of fish, fillets and steaks should look freshly cut, the flesh moist and firm-textured, showing no signs of dryness or discoloration. Any visible bones should be firmly embedded in the flesh. With time, they become loose and tend to come away from the flesh. Again, any odor should be fresh and mild.

When you buy frozen fish, make sure that it is tightly wrapped and that the wrapping is moisture- and vapor-proof. The fish itself should be solidly frozen, clear in color and free of ice crystals, with a mild, fresh odor. Discoloration, a brownish tinge or a covering of ice crystals all indicate that the fish may have been thawed and refrozen. It is important that the surface of breaded fish should be dry and crisp.

HOW MUCH FISH TO BUY FOR EACH SERVING			
Whole or drawn	1 pound	Fillets	¼ to ⅓ pound
Dressed	½ to ¾ pound	Portions	¼ to ⅓ pound
Steaks	½ pound	Sticks	¼ to ⅓ pound

STORING FISH
Store fresh fish loosely wrapped in the refrigerator and cook it within a day. Bought frozen fish which is not to be used immediately should be stored in the freezer in its original wrapping. Do not thaw and refreeze it. Freezer storage times are as follows: fillets and steaks from lean fish (cod, haddock, flounder, sole), up to 6 months; fillets and steaks from fat fish (bluefish, mackerel, perch, salmon), up to 3 months; purchased breaded fish products (do not freeze home breaded), up to 3 months.

THAWING FROZEN FISH
In many cases, fish can be cooked from its frozen state. Unwrap and cut frozen fillets into equal-size portions with a serrated knife. (Frozen fish will usually require a little longer cooking time than fresh fish.)

The best way to thaw frozen fish is to leave it in the refrigerator, still in its original wrapping, just until portions can be separated easily. Or you can thaw it in running cold water. Thawing fish at room temperature can cause sogginess and spoil the texture; breaded fish should be cooked while it is still frozen.

Thawed fish should be drained well, blotted dry with paper towels and used immediately.

PREPARING FRESHLY CAUGHT FISH
Fish are usually sold cleaned and cut into pieces, steaks or fillets, ready for cooking. However, you may have to deal with a freshly caught fish, and it is useful to know how to clean it. To dress a whole fish, remove the scales. Then remove the entrails of the fish and cut off the head, tail and fins. Thoroughly wash the fish under running cold water then drain and blot it dry with paper towels. Filleting or cutting into steaks should be left to the end.

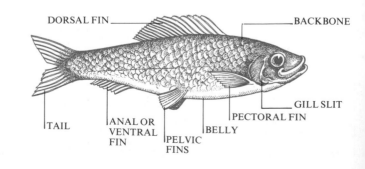

DORSAL FIN — BACKBONE — GILL SLIT — PECTORAL FIN — BELLY — PELVIC FINS — ANAL OR VENTRAL FIN — TAIL

SCALING FISH

Place fish on a board or in sink, grip the fish firmly by the tail and scrape scales off with the dull edge of a knife, a vegetable peeler or fish scaler, holding the knife almost at right angles to the body of the fish and working from the tail toward the head. Pay particular attention to the area around the fins and near the base of the head. Turn the fish over and remove scales from the other side working from tail to head in the same way. Rinse the fish thoroughly with cold water after scaling.

Scaling a fish: Lay the fish on a board and with one hand, hold it firmly by the tail. With a knife in the other hand, beginning at the tail and working toward the head, scrape off the scales. Turn the fish and repeat on the other side.

CLEANING FISH

With a sharp knife, slit the belly of the fish open from the vent (anal opening) to the head. Remove entrails and rinse the cavity clean. Often small fish are cooked with only the entrails removed or with entrails and head removed. Give the fish a final rinse with cold water making sure it is thoroughly clean inside and out and blot it dry with paper towels. It is now ready for cooking whole, cutting into steaks or filleting.

REMOVING HEAD AND FINS

With sharp knife, cut around pelvic fins; remove and discard. Next, cut off head above collarbone, together with pectoral fins. Cut off the tail.

Or, if fish is large with strong backbone, cut down each side of head to bone, lay fish on its back at edge of counter and bend head back until bone snaps. Cut through any remaining flesh to free head.

To remove dorsal fin, make deep incision on each side of fin. Rip fin out, with root bones, by pulling sharply in direction of head. Remove remaining fins in same way. Never trim them off as this leaves root bones.

FILLETING FISH

Fillets are removed in one piece from each side of the backbone of a fish. A knife with a sharp blade is essential for filleting fish. When filleting, there is no need to remove the head and tail. If the fillets are to be skinned, there is no need to remove the scales.

With sharp knife, cut through fish along the backbone from tail to just behind head, cutting right down to the bone.

Holding the blade almost flat and parallel with the body of the fish, cut the flesh away from the backbone to the tail, allowing the knife to run over the rib bones. Cut with clean, even strokes, being careful not to cut into the flesh.

Lift the fillet off in one piece. Turn the fish over and remove the other fillet.

SKINNING A FILLET

If you wish, you may skin the fillet; place it, skin side down, on a cutting board. Use the tip of your knife to loosen enough skin at the tail end to give you a good grip; be careful not to cut through the skin. Holding down the tail end of the skin securely with one hand, and with the knife held almost flat in the other hand, cut the flesh of the fish free from the skin.

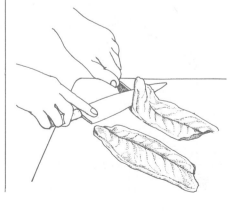

Grasping the tail end of the skin with one hand, with the knife held almost flat, cut the flesh free with the other.

FISH GLOSSARY

Court bouillon: Seasoned liquid in which fish may be poached. Usually a mixture of lightly salted water and white wine (or white wine vinegar), with seasonings such as onion, celery, carrot and herbs and spices – parsley, bay leaves, whole peppercorns and cloves. If available, some fish bones and trimmings may also be included. Before poaching fish, these ingredients are often simmered together in a covered pan for 20 to 30 minutes to extract their flavor.

Drawn fish: A whole fish with entrails removed but which is not boned.

Dressed fish: A fish that has been scaled and had entrails removed; it usually also has the head, tail and fins removed. Smaller fish prepared in this manner are described as pan-dressed.

Fillets: Sides of fish cut lengthwise from the backbone, so that they are boneless and ready for cooking. They are usually skinned. Butterfly fillets are whole fish split lengthwise down the front so that the backbone can be removed, and opened out flat, the two sides held together by the skin and a little uncut flesh.

Butterflying a fillet: Cut fish lengthwise down front; remove backbone and open out flat.

Steaks: Crosscut sections of a large dressed fish, usually cut at least ¾ inch thick from the thickest part of the fish.

Cutting steaks: After scaling and cleaning a large fish, cut off the head and fins; then, with sharp knife, starting at the head end, cut crosswise sections into steaks about ¾ to 1 inch thick.

Portions and sticks: Fish cut into uniform pieces. Usually sold breaded, partially cooked and frozen. Cook as package label directs.

CHOOSING CANNED FISH

Look for a dependable brand name and the variety that suits your needs. Most varieties of canned fish come in several forms, ranging from the kinds which are best for dishes such as party salads where color and texture play an important part, to varieties, often cheaper, which are more suitable for sandwich fillings and cooked dishes, where appearance is less important.

Salmon: Salmon is usually packed in 3¾-ounce, 7¾-ounce and 15½- and 16-ounce cans. There are several varieties available, differing slightly in color, texture and flavor. *Sockeye, Red* and *Blueback* are all the same species, deep salmon-pink in color, firm in texture and rich in oil. They break into medium flakes and are ideal for dishes such as salads and party casseroles in which firmness and good color are important. *King* and *Chinook* are rich in oil and break into large flakes but are rather softer in texture than Sockeye. Use them for salads. *Medium Red, Coho* and *Silver* are large-flaked and can be used in most recipes. Nearly half of all the canned salmon sold is *Pink*. It is small-flaked and goes well in entrees, soups and sandwiches. *Chum* and *Keta* are large-flaked and coarse-textured. Use them for casseroles and other cooked dishes where their lighter color is not important.

Tuna: Canned tuna comes packed in oil or water, solid- or fancy-pack, chunk-style and flaked or grated, in cans weighing 3¼ or 3½ ounces, 6½ or 7 ounces and 12½ or 13 ounces. Use the solid-pack for cold plates and party salads, chunks for salads and casseroles, and the flaked for appetizers and sandwich fillings. *Albacore* is the only white-meat canned tuna. It usually comes solid-pack or chunk-style and is more expensive than other tunas. *Yellowfin*, a light-meat variety, accounts for most of the available canned tuna and comes in chunk-, solid- or flake-style. *Skipjack* and *Bluefin* are also light-meat tunas available in chunk-, solid- and flake-style.

Mackerel: Like sardines, mackerel are not usually boned before canning since the bones soften during the canning process. Salted mackerel are available in 8-ounce cans, plain mackerel in 15-ounce cans.

Sardines: Sardines belong to the herring family and are usually sold canned in a variety of oils and sauces. The canning process softens the bones so that they can be eaten whole. Serve them as appetizers or as fillings in sandwiches. Sardines are usually sold in cans weighing 3¾, 4⅜, 5½, 8 and 15 ounces.

Anchovies: These tiny members of the herring family are sold cured, canned or bottled in oil or brine. They usually come in the form of flat fillets but the fillets may also be rolled up and the rolls stuffed with capers. Anchovies are usually sold in 2-ounce cans.

COOKING FISH

Fish needs very little cooking – just long enough to coagulate the protein and bring out its flavor; it is ready as soon as the flesh has lost its translucent appearance and turned opaque and milky right through. Test for doneness by inserting a fork deep into the thickest part and gently parting the flesh which should come up in thick flakes or layers. With a whole fish or steak the flesh should come away cleanly from the backbone.

Most kinds of fish, either fresh or frozen, can be prepared in any one of the following ways, and, provided you allow extra cooking time, many can be cooked from the frozen state.

BROILED OR GRILLED FISH

Steaks, fillets and pan-dressed whole fish, about 1 inch thick, are best for broiling. Thinner pieces tend to dry out too quickly, while thicker ones may brown on the surface before they are cooked through. Brush generously with melted butter or margarine, oil or sauce before and during broiling. Thicker pieces (pan-dressed fish or steaks) should be turned once halfway through broiling. Broiled fish will take 10 to 15 minutes.

PAN-FRIED FISH

Fillets, thin steaks and pan-dressed whole fish can all be pan-fried successfully. Fish is usually breaded before frying (see Breading Fish, below right). Fry over medium-high heat in about ⅛ inch of heated fat – vegetable shortening or oil is best because of its high smoking point. Turn the fish once halfway through frying. Fish cooked in this manner will be cooked in 8 to 10 minutes, depending on thickness.

OVEN-FRIED FISH

Individual portions of fish are first breaded (see Breading Fish), then oven-fried or baked in preheated 450°F. oven. Place the breaded fish in a well-greased baking pan (to simulate deep-fat frying), drizzle a little salad oil, melted butter or margarine over the fish if liked, and bake for 10 to 15 minutes, or until fish flakes easily with a fork. No turning or basting is necessary in this method of cooking; the breading of the fish prevents any of the flavorful juices escaping.

DEEP-FRIED FISH

Bread-crumb- or batter-coated fillets, steaks and pan-dressed fish may all be fried successfully in deep fat. Bread the fish and put on a rack to dry for a few minutes. Meanwhile, heat 2 inches of vegetable shortening or oil in a deep, heavy saucepan or deep-fryer to 350°F. Gently lower fish into saucepan with pancake turner, or arrange fish in fry basket in a single layer and carefully lower basket into hot fat. Fry fish until golden and cooked through, usually 3 to 5 minutes. Drain the fish thoroughly on paper towels.

BAKED FISH

Whole dressed fish, fillets or steaks, may all be baked in a preheated 350°F. oven. There is no need to turn them while baking. To prevent fish drying out while it is in the oven, brush with melted butter, margarine or oil, or cover with a sauce. A 3-pound dressed fish takes 30 to 35 minutes; steaks, fillets, 12 to 15 minutes. Stuffed fish will need an additional 20 to 30 minutes' baking. Fish cooked from the frozen state will take slightly longer.

POACHED FISH

Fish fillets, steaks and whole dressed fish cook quickly in simmering liquid in a covered skillet or pan. Lightly salted water, milk, a mixture of water and white wine, or a well-seasoned *court bouillon* are all suitable. After poaching the fish, some of this liquid may be strained and used to make a sauce for the fish. Fillets and steaks will be ready in 5 to 10 minutes. Thicker, dressed fish will take longer. Do not allow the poaching liquid to boil at any point as this will cause fish to be tough textured or might even cause the flesh to break up.

STEAMED FISH

Fish fillets, steaks and pan-dressed fish may all be steamed. Use a steam cooker or a deep pan with a rack and a tightly fitting cover. Pour water into pan to below level of steam cooker liner or rack; heat to boiling. Put fish in greased, shallow baking dish; place on rack; cover pan and simmer until fish flakes when tested with a fork. Fillets and steaks will take 5 to 10 minutes, thicker whole fish will need several minutes longer.

BREADING FISH

If fish is frozen, thaw it before breading. First pat the fish dry with paper towels. Then dip in milk or egg beaten with a little milk, allowing excess to drain off, and coat with fine dried bread crumbs, cornflake crumbs, cornmeal or flour. For a slightly more substantial coating, dust the fish with seasoned flour before dipping it in egg and coating it with crumbs. Let the coated fish dry on a rack a few minutes before following recipes for pan-frying, oven-frying or deep-frying.

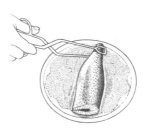

Dip fish in milk or egg beaten with a little milk. (For a thicker coating, first dust fish with seasoned flour.)

Coat fish with fine dried bread crumbs, cornflake crumbs, cornmeal or flour. Allow fish to dry on rack before frying.

Whole fish

Broiled Sesame Trout

Color index
page 36

Begin 4 hrs
ahead

6 servings

397 cals per
serving

Good source
of iron,
vitamin A

**6 serving-size rainbow
trout or other locally
available fish,
pan-dressed
½ cup lemon juice
3 teaspoons salt
¼ teaspoon pepper
¼ cup sesame seed
¾ cup butter or
margarine
lemon slices and
parsley sprigs
for garnish**

1 With sharp knife, make
3 light slashes on each
side of fish, without cutting
flesh too deep.

2 In 13" by 9" baking
pan, mix lemon juice,
salt and pepper. Add fish
and turn over to coat with
marinade. Cover; re-
frigerate at least 3 hours,
turning occasionally.

3 In 1-quart saucepan
over medium heat,
toast sesame seed until
golden, stirring and shaking pan occasionally. Add
butter or margarine and
heat until melted.

4 Place fish on rack in
broiling pan. Drain
marinade from baking pan
into sesame seed mixture.
Preheat broiler if manu-
facturer directs.

5 Broil fish about 5 minutes on each side,
basting frequently with
sesame seed mixture.

6 Test fish for doneness
with a fork. Trout are
cooked when their flesh
flakes easily.

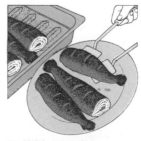

7 With pancake turners,
lift fish carefully onto
warm platter. Spoon hot
juices over and garnish.

Bluefish with Buttery Lemon Sauce

Color index
page 35

Begin 20 mins
ahead

8 servings

369 cals per
serving

Good source
of vitamin A

**1 cup butter or margarine
⅓ cup lemon juice
¼ cup chopped parsley
1 tablespoon grated
lemon peel
¾ tablespoon salt
1 teaspoon sugar
¼ teaspoon pepper
8 1-pound bluefish,
pan-dressed**

1. Preheat broiler if manufacturer directs. In 1-quart
saucepan over high heat, melt butter or margarine;
stir in lemon juice, parsley, lemon peel, salt, sugar
and pepper.
2. Place fish on rack in broiling pan and brush with
butter mixture. Cook about 5 minutes, then turn
and cook 5 minutes more or until fish flakes easily
when tested with a fork. During cooking, brush
bluefish frequently with butter mixture.

GRILLED BLUEFISH: Prepare outdoor grill for
barbecuing as manufacturer directs. Place *bluefish* in
folding wire grill and cook over hot coals, brushing
frequently with the *butter mixture* during cooking.

CARVING A WHOLE FISH

The directions below are for a whole, unstuffed fish. If the
fish is stuffed, remove and serve stuffing after cutting top of
fish and before removing bones to serve lower portion.

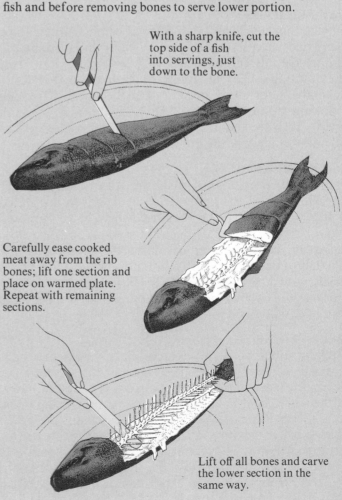

With a sharp knife, cut the
top side of a fish
into servings, just
down to the bone.

Carefully ease cooked
meat away from the rib
bones; lift one section and
place on warmed plate.
Repeat with remaining
sections.

Lift off all bones and carve
the lower section in the
same way.

Pan-fried Smelts

Color index page 36

Begin 1½ hrs ahead

6 servings

305 cals per serving

½ cup all-purpose flour
½ teaspoon salt
¼ teaspoon pepper
2 eggs
2 tablespoons water
½ cup dried bread crumbs
2 pounds smelts, pan-dressed
½ cup salad oil
2 tablespoons butter or margarine
lime or lemon wedges for garnish

1 On waxed paper, combine flour, salt and pepper. In pie plate with fork, beat eggs with water. Onto second sheet of waxed paper, pour bread crumbs.

2 Using tongs, coat fish one by one. Dip each first in flour mixture.

3 Then dip each fish in egg mixture, then coat well in bread crumbs.

4 Place coated fish on a rack over another sheet of waxed paper. Let dry 30 minutes.

5 In 12-inch skillet over medium heat, heat oil and butter or margarine. Fry the fish a few at a time, turning them after they have fried for 2 minutes.

6 Still over medium heat, fry smelts 2 minutes longer on other side or just until the flesh flakes easily when tested with a fork.

7 With pancake turner, lift cooked smelts onto warm platter and keep hot until all fish are cooked. Garnish with lime or lemon wedges.

Striped Bass with Pungent Sauce

Color index page 36

Begin 1½ hrs ahead

6 servings

500 cals per serving

Good source of calcium, iron

1 3½-pound whole striped bass or sea bass, dressed, with head and tail on
1 tablespoon dry sherry
salt
salad oil
cornstarch
1 small carrot, cut into 3-inch-long matchstick-thin strips
1 stalk celery, cut into 3-inch-long matchstick-thin strips
¾ cup sugar
½ cup white wine vinegar
½ cup catchup
2 tablespoons sweet pickle relish
2 teaspoons soy sauce
1¼ cups water
2 medium lemons, sliced, for garnish

1. Rinse fish under running cold water; pat dry. With sharp knife, cut fish crosswise into two pieces; score 3 crosswise slashes about ½ inch deep on both sides of each piece to help fish cook more evenly and reduce cooking time.

2. In small bowl, mix sherry and ½ teaspoon salt. With hand, rub mixture inside and outside of fish. Place fish on platter; cover; refrigerate 30 minutes.

3. In 6-quart Dutch oven or saucepot, over medium-high heat, heat about 1 inch salad oil to 350°F. on deep-fat thermometer.

4. Meanwhile, again pat fish dry; on waxed paper, coat fish inside and out with ⅓ cup cornstarch. Carefully slip 1 piece of fish into hot oil; cook 8 minutes or until underside is golden and fish flakes easily when tested with fork.

5. Turn fish over to brown other side, about 8 minutes. Drain on paper towels 1 minute; place on warm platter; keep warm. Repeat with second piece. Reassemble pieces to make a whole fish.

6. Meanwhile, in 2-quart saucepan over high heat, in 1 tablespoon hot oil, stir-fry (stirring quickly and constantly) carrot, celery and ½ teaspoon salt, 2 minutes or until vegetables are tender-crisp. Spoon into small bowl; set aside.

7. In same saucepan over medium-low heat, heat sugar, vinegar, catchup, pickle relish, soy sauce, water and 3 tablespoons cornstarch to boiling, stirring frequently with wire whisk. Continue cooking for 2 minutes, stirring frequently. Pour sauce over and around fish; sprinkle with carrot mixture; garnish with lemon.

Scoring fish pieces: With a sharp knife, make 3 crosswise slashes ½ inch deep on both sides of fish.

Reassembling fried fish: After frying, on warm platter, reassemble pieces to make whole fish.

Whole fish

Color index page 35
Begin 1½ hrs ahead
8 servings

276 cals per serving
Good source of
calcium, iron

Baked Red Snapper with Oyster Stuffing

1 4- to 4½-pound red
  snapper, dressed
salt
salad oil
1 cup water
¾ cup minced celery
¼ cup chopped
  onion
1 8-ounce container
  shucked oysters

3 cups day-old bread
  cubes
¼ cup butter or
  margarine, melted
1 teaspoon poultry
  seasoning
¼ teaspoon pepper

1 Sprinkle inside and outside of fish with salt; brush one side with oil. Brush large shallow roasting pan with oil; place fish, oiled side down, in pan.

2 Make stuffing: In 2-quart saucepan over high heat, in boiling water, cook celery and onion until tender; drain, reserving liquid. Put onion and celery in large bowl. Into 1-cup measuring cup, drain liquid from oysters; add celery liquid to make ½ cup. Cut up oysters; add to celery and onion. Stir in bread cubes, butter, poultry seasoning, pepper and celery-oyster liquid.

3 With spoon, lightly fill cavity with oyster stuffing mixture.

4 Skewer cavity closed with toothpicks. Brush other side of fish with salad oil.

5 Bake in 350°F. oven 1 hour 10 minutes brushing fish occasionally with salad oil; with 2 pancake turners, lift fish to warm platter. Remove toothpicks.

6 To serve: Cut top side of fish into squares just down to bone. Serve squares with some of stuffing. Lift off all bones and repeat with other side of fish.

Poached Salmon with Aspic

8 cups water
2 cups white table wine
4 carrots, sliced
2 medium onions, cut into
  thin wedges
2 stalks celery, sliced
2 teaspoons salt
1 teaspoon thyme leaves
½ teaspoon peppercorns
1 bay leaf
1 5- to 6-pound whole
  salmon, dressed, with
  head and tail on
3 envelopes unflavored
  gelatin

2 medium lemons, thinly
  sliced, for garnish
parsley or watercress
  sprigs for garnish
Herb Mayonnaise
  (page 185)

Color index page 36
Begin early in day or
  day ahead
12 servings
444 cals per serving

1 In 26-inch fish poacher over high heat, heat first 9 ingredients to boiling. (The poacher will require 2 heating units.)

2 Meanwhile, rinse salmon under running cold water. Cut head off salmon if you wish and add to poaching liquid.

3 Place salmon on poaching rack; lower into liquid. Cover; simmer 30 minutes or until fish flakes when tested with fork.

4 Remove rack from poacher and with 2 pancake turners, place salmon on large platter. Cover; chill well.

5 Meanwhile, ladle poaching liquid into cheesecloth-lined sieve over a large bowl; discard all vegetables.

6 Into 2-quart saucepan, measure 4 cups strained poaching liquid; refrigerate until cool.

7 Sprinkle gelatin over liquid; over medium heat, cook, stirring, until dissolved. Pour into 13" by 9" baking pan; cover; refrigerate until aspic is set.

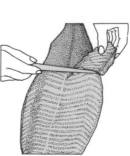

8 To serve: With small knife or kitchen shears, carefully cut skin around top half of salmon; remove and discard skin.

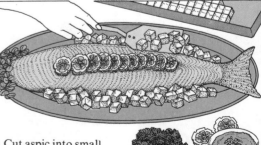

9 Cut aspic into small cubes; sprinkle around salmon. Garnish with lemon slices and parsley. Serve salmon with Herb Mayonnaise.

Fish fillets

Broiled Tarragon Fish

¼ cup salad oil
1 tablespoon lemon juice
½ teaspoon tarragon
½ teaspoon salt
⅛ teaspoon pepper
*1 16-ounce package
    frozen flounder,
    Greenland turbot, sole,
    whiting or other fish
    fillets, partially thawed*

*1 lemon, cut into
    4 wedges, for garnish
parsley sprigs for garnish*

Color index
page 37

Begin 20 mins
ahead

4 servings

180 cals per
serving

1 Preheat broiler if manu-facturer directs. In small bowl with fork, mix salad oil, lemon juice, tarragon, salt and pepper.

2 Place flounder fillets in broiling pan and broil, basting generously with oil mixture occasionally.

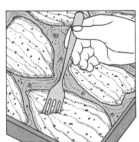

3 Broil 5 to 8 minutes until fish flakes easily when tested with a fork.

4 Lift fillets onto warm plate and garnish with lemon wedges and parsley

Broiler-barbecued Fish Dinner

Color index
page 36

Begin 55 mins
ahead

4 servings

369 cals per
serving

Good source
of calcium,
vitamin A

*Seafood Barbecue Sauce
    (below right)*
*¼ pound large
    mushrooms*
*4 small zucchini
melted butter
salt and pepper*

*grated Parmesan
    cheese*
*1 16-ounce package
    frozen haddock or cod
    fillets, partially
    thawed*

1. Prepare sauce. Grease broiling-pan rack. Remove mushroom stems (save for use another day). Place mushroom caps on rack. Halve zucchini lengthwise; place, cut side up, beside mushrooms.
2. Preheat broiler if manufacturer directs. Brush mushrooms and zucchini generously with melted butter or margarine; sprinkle lightly with salt and pepper. Sprinkle zucchini lightly with cheese. Cut fillets crosswise into 4 chunks and place on rack. Spoon barbecue sauce over fish.
3. Broil 10 to 12 minutes until fish flakes easily when tested with a fork and zucchini is tender; baste mushrooms occasionally with melted butter.

Fish Fry

*1 16-ounce package
    frozen flounder, sole or
    Greenland turbot or
    other fillets, partially
    thawed*
*Sweet-Sour Sauce
    (below)*
salad oil
¾ cup all-purpose flour
⅔ cup water
*1 teaspoon double-acting
    baking powder*
1 teaspoon salt

Color index
page 37

Begin 55 mins
ahead

4 servings

337 cals per
serving

1 Place unopened package of frozen fish in large pan; add enough cold water just to cover package. Let stand until flounder fillets are partially thawed, about 30 minutes. While fish is thawing in water, prepare Sweet-Sour Sauce. Keep sauce warm until needed.

2 Separate flounder fillets; pat dry with paper towels. In 12-inch skillet over medium heat, heat about 1 inch oil to 370°F. on deep-fat thermometer.

3 In medium bowl, mix flour, water, baking powder and salt, then using tongs, coat fillets with flour mixture.

4 Fry fish fillets in hot salad oil until golden, about 4 to 8 minutes, carefully turning fillets once.

5 When cooked, remove fillets to drain well on paper towels. Serve fillets with hot Sweet-Sour Sauce spooned over.

SWEET-SOUR SAUCE: In 1-quart saucepan with spoon, stir *2 tablespoons sugar, 1 tablespoon corn-starch* and *½ teaspoon chili powder* until well mixed; stir in *⅔ cup water, 3 tablespoons catchup* and *1 tablespoon cider vinegar* until smooth. Over medium-high heat, cook until mixture is thickened and boils, stirring constantly; cook 1 minute longer, stirring constantly. Remove from heat; stir in *¼ cup chopped sweet pickle* or pickle relish.

194 cals per
serving

SEAFOOD BARBECUE SAUCE: In 2-quart saucepan over medium heat, simmer *2 small onions*, sliced, *½ cup catchup, ⅓ cup salad oil, 2 tablespoons diced celery, 2 teaspoons dry mustard, ½ teaspoon salt, 2 teaspoons Worcestershire, 2 teaspoons lemon juice* and *¼ teaspoon pepper* for 10 minutes, stirring frequently, until vegetables are tender.

Fish fillets

Fried Fish à la Margherita

Color index
page 37

Begin 50 mins
ahead

8 servings

207 cals per
serving

2 16-ounce packages
  frozen sole, flounder or
  ocean perch fillets
1 15-ounce can tomato
  sauce
2 tablespoons finely
  chopped parsley

1 teaspoon oregano
  leaves
¼ cup olive or salad oil
¼ cup butter or
  margarine
parsley sprigs for
  garnish (optional)

1. Place unopened packages of frozen fish in large pan; add cold water to cover packages. Let stand until fillets are partially thawed, about 30 minutes. Carefully separate fillets; pat dry with paper towels.
2. In medium bowl, stir tomato sauce, parsley and oregano leaves until well mixed; set aside.
3. In 12-inch skillet over medium-high heat, in hot oil and butter or margarine, cook fillets 2 or 3 minutes on each side until fish flakes easily when tested with a fork.
4. Pour sauce over fish; cook 2 minutes, occasionally basting fish with sauce. Serve fish with sauce from skillet. Garnish with parsley, if you like.

Mediterranean Cod with Vegetables

Color index
page 36

Begin 1½ hrs
ahead

8 servings

329 cals per
serving

Good source
of vitamin C

2 16-ounce packages
  frozen cod or other
  fillets
⅔ cup salad oil
3 garlic cloves, slivered
1 medium eggplant, cut
  up
3 medium onions, cut into
  wedges
2 green peppers, cut up
¼ teaspoon pepper

¾ cup water
salt
1 egg
2½ cups fresh bread
  crumbs (5 white
  bread slices)
2 tablespoons chopped
  fresh dill or
  1 tablespoon dill weed
3 medium tomatoes, cut
  into wedges

1. Place unopened packages of frozen fish in large pan; add cold water to cover packages. Let stand until fillets are partially thawed, about 30 minutes.
2. In 12-inch skillet over medium-high heat, in ⅓ cup hot salad oil, cook garlic until golden; with slotted spoon, discard garlic. Add eggplant and onions; cook until vegetables are browned, stirring frequently, about 5 minutes. Stir in green peppers, pepper, water and 1 teaspoon salt; cover and cook 5 minutes longer, stirring occasionally. Remove cover; continue cooking until all the water has evaporated. Spoon vegetables into medium bowl; keep warm.
3. Meanwhile, bread fish: Cut each package of cod fillets crosswise into 4 pieces; sprinkle with ½ teaspoon salt. In pie plate with fork, beat egg. On waxed paper, combine bread crumbs and dill. Dip fish in egg; coat with bread-crumb mixture.
4. In same skillet over medium-high heat, heat remaining ⅓ cup salad oil; cook fish 10 minutes or until it flakes easily when tested with fork, turning fish once. Remove fish to warm large platter; keep warm while vegetables are heated.
5. Return vegetables to skillet; add tomatoes and cook, stirring frequently, until tomatoes are heated through. Remove vegetables to warm platter and arrange mixture next to fish.

Fillets of Sole Thermidor

Color index
page 36

Begin 45 mins
ahead

8 servings

254 cals per
serving

Good source
of calcium,
vitamin A

5 tablespoons butter
8 sole or other fillets
  (about 2 pounds)
2 teaspoons salt
½ teaspoon seasoned salt
⅛ teaspoon pepper
1¼ cups milk
3 tablespoons all-purpose
  flour
1 cup grated Cheddar
  cheese
3 tablespoons sherry
  (optional)
paprika

1 Preheat oven to 350°F. In 1-quart saucepan, melt 2 tablespoons butter; brush over sole fillets. Sprinkle with salt, seasoned salt and pepper.

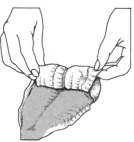

2 Roll up each fillet and place, seam side down, in 9″ by 9″ baking dish.

3 Pour ½ cup milk over fillets; bake in oven 25 minutes or until fish flakes easily when tested with fork.

4 Meanwhile, in 2-quart saucepan over medium heat, melt remaining butter. Stir in flour; gradually add remaining milk; cook, stirring, until thickened.

5 Reduce heat; stir in cheese and sherry. Preheat broiler if manufacturer directs.

6 Spoon liquid from cooked fish. Stir ¼ cup liquid into cheese sauce. (If not using sherry use extra 3 tablespoons liquid.)

7 Pour cheese sauce over fish; sprinkle with paprika. Broil about 1 minute, just until cheese sauce is slightly golden.

Baked Sole with Lemon Sauce

Color index
page 37

Begin 30 mins
ahead

8 servings

169 cals per
serving

2 16-ounce packages
frozen sole, ocean
perch, flounder or
other fillets, thawed
3/4 teaspoon salt
1/4 teaspoon pepper
*3 tablespoons butter or
margarine*

2 egg yolks
1 tablespoon water
*1 tablespoon all-purpose
flour*
3/4 cup chicken broth
2 tablespoons lemon juice
dill sprigs for garnish

1. Preheat oven to 350°F. Grease a large, shallow baking dish; arrange fillets in dish. Sprinkle fillets with salt and pepper; dot with 2 tablespoons butter or margarine. Bake 10 minutes or until fish flakes easily when tested with a fork.
2. Meanwhile, prepare sauce: In cup, mix egg yolks with water; set aside. In heavy 1-quart saucepan over medium heat, into 1 tablespoon hot butter or margarine, stir flour until well blended. Gradually stir in chicken broth and lemon juice and cook, stirring, until mixture is thickened; remove saucepan from heat.
3. Into egg yolks, stir small amount of hot sauce; slowly pour egg mixture back into the sauce, stirring rapidly to prevent lumping. Cook, stirring, until thickened (do not boil). Spoon off any liquid from fish. Pour sauce over fish and garnish with dill.

Clam-stuffed Fillets

Color index
page 37

Begin 50 mins
ahead

4 servings

339 cals per
serving

Good source
of calcium,
iron,
vitamin A

*1 8-ounce can minced
clams*
*1/4 cup butter or
margarine*
1/3 cup chopped celery
*1/4 cup chopped onion
salt*

3 cups white bread cubes
1 egg
1/8 teaspoon thyme leaves
*1 pound flounder, ocean
perch or Greenland
turbot fillets*
parsley sprigs for garnish

1. Grease four 6-ounce custard cups. Drain clams, reserving 2 tablespoons clam liquid; set aside. In 2-quart saucepan over medium heat, in hot butter, cook celery, onion and 1/4 teaspoon salt until celery is tender, about 5 minutes. Stir in clams, reserved liquid, bread, egg, thyme. Preheat oven to 350°F.
2. Pat fish fillets dry with paper towels and sprinkle with 1/4 teaspoon salt. Line custard cups with fillets, cutting fillets to fit if necessary. Spoon 1/2 cup clam mixture into center of each fillet-lined custard cup.
3. Place cups in 9-inch cake pan for easier handling. Bake 20 to 25 minutes until fish flakes easily when tested with a fork and stuffing is heated. To serve: Remove from cups; garnish.

Lining custard cups:
Add fillets to cups, cutting to fit if necessary.

Removing fillets: Use 2 spoons to gently lift fillets onto warm platter.

Poached Sole
with Hollandaise Sauce

Color index
page 37

Begin 50 mins
ahead

4 servings

373 cals per
serving

Good source
of iron,
vitamin A

Court bouillon:
1 carrot, sliced
1 stalk celery, sliced
1 small onion, sliced
*1 lemon, thinly
sliced*
4 peppercorns
2 bay leaves
2 parsley sprigs
1/2 teaspoon salt
2 cups water

*1 16-ounce package
frozen sole fillets,
partially thawed
Hollandaise Sauce
(page 463)
chopped parsley for
garnish
lemon wedges
for garnish*

1 To make *court bouillon:* In 12-inch skillet over high heat, heat carrot, celery, onion, lemon, peppercorns, bay leaves, parsley sprigs, salt and water to boiling.

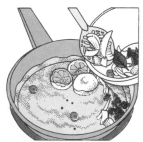

2 Cover, reduce heat and simmer 10 minutes. With a slotted spoon, remove the vegetables and spices; discard.

3 With serrated knife, cut fish into serving-size portions. Place fish portions in *court bouillon.*

4 Cover skillet and simmer fish over low heat 10 to 12 minutes, or until fish flakes easily when tested with a fork. Meanwhile, prepare Hollandaise Sauce.

5 With slotted pancake turner, carefully remove fish pieces and arrange on warm platter. Discard *court bouillon.*

6 To serve: Spoon Hollandaise Sauce over fish. Garnish platter with chopped parsley and lemon wedges.

FISH
Fish fillets

Shrimp-stuffed Roll-ups

*¼ cup butter or margarine
1 cup shelled, deveined and chopped shrimp
1 cup chopped mushrooms
¼ cup dried bread crumbs
½ teaspoon dill weed salt
6 sole or other fillets (about 2 pounds)
1 cup dry white wine
½ cup water
2 tablespoons cornstarch
½ cup half-and-half
1 egg*

Color index page 37

Begin 40 mins ahead

6 servings

314 cals per serving

1 In 10-inch skillet over medium heat, in butter, cook shrimp and mushrooms until shrimp turn pink. Stir in crumbs, dill and ¼ teaspoon salt.

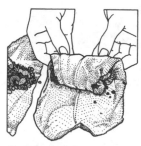

2 Spoon shrimp mixture onto center of each fillet; roll up. Secure with toothpicks.

3 In cleaned skillet over high heat, heat to boiling fillets, wine, water and 1 teaspoon salt.

4 Reduce heat to low; cover; simmer 12 to 15 minutes. With slotted spoon, remove fillets to warm platter. Remove toothpicks; keep fish warm until needed.

5 In small bowl, blend cornstarch and half-and-half; stir into fish liquid. Cook over medium heat, stirring, just until boiling and thickened.

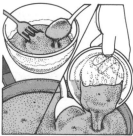

6 In small bowl, beat egg slightly; stir a little hot sauce into beaten egg; pour mixture back into sauce, stirring rapidly.

7 Cook, stirring, until thick, but do not boil. Spoon some sauce over fillets and pass remainder separately in sauce boat.

Codfish Stew

*1 16-ounce package frozen cod fillets
3 bacon slices
1 medium onion
1 16-ounce can whole white potatoes
1 16-ounce can tomatoes
¼ cup catchup
1 teaspoon Worcestershire
¼ teaspoon seasoned pepper
⅛ teaspoon thyme leaves*

Color index page 37

Begin 55 mins ahead

4 servings

243 cals per serving

Good source of iron

1. Place unopened package of frozen fish into large pan; add cold water to cover package. Let stand until fish fillets are partially thawed, about 20 minutes. Cut fillets into bite-size chunks; set aside.
2. Cut bacon into 1-inch pieces; thinly slice onion. Drain potatoes; cut each potato in half.
3. In 2-quart saucepan over medium heat, cook bacon until just limp; add onion and cook until onion is browned. Stir in potatoes, tomatoes with their liquid, catchup, Worcestershire, pepper and thyme; cook 5 minutes, stirring occasionally.
4. Add fish; cook about 10 minutes longer or until fish flakes easily when tested with a fork, stirring fish mixture often.

Creamed Finnan Haddie

*2 pounds Finnan haddie or smoked cod fillets, cut in large pieces
3 tablespoons butter or margarine
4 teaspoons all-purpose flour
2 cups milk
1 cup heavy or whipping cream
4 hard-cooked eggs
parsley for garnish
Holland rusks or toast points (optional)*

Color index page 37

Begin 30 mins ahead (Finnan haddie)
1½ hrs ahead (smoked cod)

8 servings

344 cals per serving

Good source of calcium, vitamin A

1. If using smoked cod: In large, shallow pan, place fillets and cover with cold water. Soak 1 hour, then drain thoroughly.
2. In 12-inch skillet over medium heat, into hot butter or margarine, stir flour until blended. Gradually stir in milk and cream and cook, stirring, until the flour mixture is slightly thickened and comes to a boil.
3. Add fish pieces; cover. Simmer 15 minutes or until fish flakes easily when tested with a fork.
4. Reserve 2 hard-cooked egg yolks for garnish; chop whites and other 2 egg yolks.
5. In the sauce, with fork, coarsely flake fish. Stir in chopped eggs and pour into warm dish.
6. Through coarse sieve, press reserved egg yolks over top. Garnish with parsley. Serve creamed fish on Holland rusks or toast points.

Flaking the fish: After poaching in sauce, flake fish coarsely with fork.

Garnishing: Press yolks through coarse sieve over Creamed Finnan Haddie.

180

Fish steaks

Halibut Steak with Eggplant Sauce

1 large green pepper
1 large onion
1 1-pound eggplant
⅓ cup salad oil
2 8-ounce cans tomato sauce
½ cup dry white wine
1 garlic clove, minced
1 bay leaf
¼ cup butter
2 tablespoons lemon juice
½ teaspoon salt
¼ teaspoon pepper
1 2-pound halibut steak

Color index
page 38

Begin 30 mins
ahead

4 servings

351 cals per
serving

Good source
of iron,
niacin,
vitamin C

1 With sharp knife, cut green pepper into ½-inch strips and thinly slice onion. With vegetable peeler, peel eggplant; cut eggplant into ½-inch cubes.

2 In 12-inch skillet over medium heat, in hot oil, cook green pepper and onion until tender; then add cubed eggplant.

3 Add tomato sauce, wine, garlic and bay leaf; simmer 15 minutes.

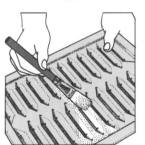

4 Meanwhile, grease broiling pan rack. Preheat broiler if manufacturer directs.

5 In 1-quart saucepan over low heat, melt butter with lemon juice, salt and pepper.

6 Place halibut steak on rack and brush generously with butter mixture. Broil 5 minutes; turn; lightly brush again with butter mixture.

7 Broil 5 minutes longer or just until fish flakes easily when tested with a fork. Serve halibut steak with hot eggplant sauce.

Chilled Salmon Steaks with Marinated Cucumber

4 cups water
salt
6 salmon steaks, about ½ inch thick (2 pounds)
2 large cucumbers, thinly sliced
½ cup white vinegar
2 tablespoons sugar
¼ teaspoon pepper
1 small onion, thinly sliced
romaine leaves and lemon wedges for garnish
Green Mayonnaise Dressing (page 185)

Color index
page 38

Begin 4 hrs
ahead

6 servings

886 cals per
serving

Good source
of calcium,
iron, niacin

1 In 12-inch skillet over high heat, heat to boiling water and 1 tablespoon salt. Add 3 salmon steaks. Reheat to boiling.

2 Reduce heat to low; cover; simmer 5 to 8 minutes or until fish flakes. Grease 15½" by 10½" jelly-roll pan.

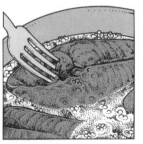

3 Remove each steak and drain over paper towels. Repeat with remaining steaks; place steaks in pan; cover; refrigerate.

4 Meanwhile, in medium bowl, toss cucumbers and 1 tablespoon salt. Let stand 30 minutes; drain in colander; press out liquid.

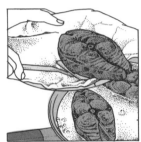

5 Discard liquid and return cucumbers to bowl; add vinegar, sugar, pepper and onion and mix well. Cover and refrigerate.

6 On each plate arrange salmon on romaine leaf with cucumbers and lemon. Pass Green Mayonnaise Dressing separately.

Fish steaks

Color index page 38
Begin early in day
6 servings

310 cals per serving
Good source of niacin

Marinated Swordfish Steaks

2 1½-pound swordfish or	*2 teaspoons salt*
halibut steaks	*1 teaspoon*
⅓ cup salad oil	*Worcestershire*
⅓ cup tarragon or cider	*¼ teaspoon tarragon or*
vinegar	*¾ teaspoon chopped*
2 bay leaves	*fresh tarragon*
2 tablespoons chopped	*¼ teaspoon pepper*
parsley	*1 lime*

1. Place the swordfish or halibut steaks in a large shallow dish.
2. In a measuring cup, combine oil, vinegar, bay leaves, parsley, salt, Worcestershire, tarragon and pepper for marinade; pour over fish. Cover the dish and refrigerate, turning the fish occasionally to coat in marinade.
3. *About 25 minutes before serving:* Preheat broiler if manufacturer directs.
4. Place fish steaks in broiling pan reserving marinade, and broil 15 minutes or until the fish flakes easily when tested with a fork. Baste swordfish or halibut steaks occasionally with marinade.
5. Meanwhile, cut lime into 6 wedges. With a pancake turner, carefully lift swordfish or halibut steaks to warm platter. Serve with lime.

Color index page 38
Begin 40 mins ahead
4 servings

312 cals per serving
Good source of iron, vitamin A

Codfish Steak

1 10-ounce bag spinach	*½ pound mushrooms,*
½ cup butter or	*sliced*
margarine	*2 tablespoons lemon*
1 1-pound cod, halibut or	*juice*
hake steak	*lemon wedges for*
½ teaspoon salt	*garnish*

1. Wash spinach well; drain in colander; pat dry with paper towels.
2. In 12-inch skillet over medium-high heat, in hot butter or margarine, place fish steak; sprinkle the steak with salt and cook until fish flakes easily when tested with a fork, about 10 minutes, turning once with a pancake turner. Remove fish to warm large platter and keep warm.
3. To drippings in skillet, add sliced mushrooms and lemon juice; cook until mushrooms are tender, about 5 minutes. With slotted spoon, spoon mushrooms into small bowl.
4. To remaining drippings in skillet, add spinach; cook 2 to 3 minutes until just tender, stirring occasionally. Stir in cooked mushrooms; heat mixture thoroughly
5. With slotted spoon, arrange spinach and mushroom mixture around fish; then pour liquid on fish and vegetable mixture. Garnish the platter with lemon wedges.

Ground fillets

Quenelles in Wine Sauce

Quenelles:
2 pounds flounder fillets, or 2 16-ounce packages frozen flounder or other fillets, thawed, cut into chunks
¼ cup butter or margarine
water
1 cup all-purpose flour
3 eggs, beaten
¼ teaspoon pepper
⅛ teaspoon ground nutmeg
salt
1 cup heavy cream

Wine Sauce:
3 tablespoons all-purpose flour
2 tablespoons butter or margarine, softened
½ cup dry vermouth
1 teaspoon lemon juice
¼ teaspoon salt
⅛ teaspoon pepper
1 cup shredded Swiss cheese

Color index page 24
Begin 3 hrs ahead
9 appetizer or
6 main-dish servings
396 cals per appetizer serving
Good source of calcium, vitamin A

1 Prepare quenelles: Pat fish dry with paper towels pressing out liquid. With food grinder, using fine cutting disk, grind fish into paste.

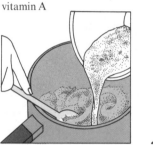

2 In 3-quart saucepan over medium heat, heat butter and 1 cup water to boiling. Remove from heat; add flour and beat until mixture forms ball.

3 Beat in eggs until thoroughly blended. Stir in fish, pepper, nutmeg and 1 teaspoons salt. Refrigerate mixture about 1½ hours.

4 Stir in 2 tablespoons cream. In deep 12-inch skillet over medium heat, boil 8 cups water and 1 tablespoon salt. Reduce heat to very low.

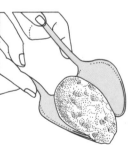

5 Divide half quenelle mixture into 9 equal portions. Using 2 spoons, shape portions into ovals.

6 Gently drop shaped quenelles into simmering water in skillet.

7 Cook, uncovered, 15 minutes until quenelles roll easily; drain on paper towels. Repeat. (Reserve 2 cups water.)

8 Arrange cooked and drained quenelles in 13" by 9" baking dish; keep quenelles warm.

9 Prepare sauce: In 2-quart saucepan over high heat, heat reserved poaching water to boiling. Boil 15 minutes to reduce by half. In small bowl, blend flour and butter; stir into liquid. Over medium heat, cook, stirring, until slightly thickened. Add vermouth, lemon juice, salt and remaining cream. Cook, stirring, about 5 minutes until thickened. Preheat oven to 475°F.

10 Spoon sauce over quenelles; sprinkle with cheese. Bake 5 to 8 minutes until cheese melts.

Fish Mousse

2¹/₂ cups water
2 envelopes unflavored
*   gelatin*
1 small onion, sliced
1 teaspoon salt
¹/₂ teaspoon peppercorns
¹/₂ teaspoon basil
1 16-ounce package
*   frozen flounder,*
*   pollock, sole or cod*
*   fillets*
¹/₂ cup salad dressing or
*   mayonnaise*
1 tablespoon lemon juice

¹/₄ teaspoon hot pepper
*   sauce*
¹/₂ cup heavy or whipping
*   cream*
pitted olives and
*   pimentos for garnish*

lettuce leaves
lemon wedges

Color index page 24

Begin 6 hrs or day ahead

8 appetizer or

4 main-dish servings

207 cals per appetizer serving

1 In 12-inch skillet, into water, sprinkle gelatin. Cook over low heat, stirring, until gelatin is dissolved.

2 Add onion, salt, peppercorns and basil; heat to boiling. Reduce heat to low; cover and simmer 5 minutes.

3 Add frozen fish fillets to skillet; heat to boiling. Reduce heat; simmer 15 minutes until fish flakes easily. With slotted spoon, remove fish from liquid.

4 Strain liquid into 4-cup measure, discarding onion and peppercorns. If needed add water to make 2¹/₄ cups liquid. Add fish; cover; refrigerate until thickened.

5 In covered blender container, at medium speed, blend until smooth fish mixture, salad dressing, lemon juice and hot pepper sauce.

6 Pour mixture into large bowl. Whip cream; fold into mixture. Pour into 5-cup fish-shaped mold; refrigerate until set, about 4 hours.

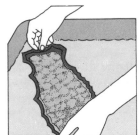

7 To serve: Unmold mousse by dipping mold into hot water for a few seconds.

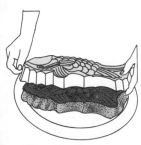

8 Place flat platter over mold; invert both together and lift off mold. With sharp knife, finely slice olives and pimentos.

9 Arrange lettuce leaves and lemon wedges around fish mousse and garnish with sliced pitted olives and pimentos.

Canned fish

Color index page 38
Begin 1¹/₂ hrs ahead
8 servings

361 cals per serving
Good source of calcium, iron, niacin

Tuna Loaf with Cucumber Sauce

Tuna Loaf:
18 saltine crackers, finely
*   crushed*
1 cup finely chopped
*   celery*
3 6¹/₂ - or 7-ounce cans
*   tuna, drained*
2 tablespoons grated
*   onion*
¹/₄ teaspoon pepper
¹/₂ teaspoon salt
1 cup milk
3 eggs, slightly beaten

Cucumber Sauce:
2 medium cucumbers,
*   peeled, seeded and*
*   chopped*
water
2¹/₂ tablespoons butter or
*   margarine*
2¹/₂ tablespoons all-
*   purpose flour*
¹/₂ teaspoon salt
1¹/₂ teaspoons grated
*   lemon peel*
1 teaspoon lemon juice
2 egg yolks

chopped parsley and
*   cucumber slices for*
*   garnish*

1. Preheat oven to 350°F. In large bowl, combine milk, eggs and crackers; let stand 5 minutes, stirring often. Stir in celery, tuna, onion, pepper and salt.

2. Pour tuna mixture into well-greased 10″ by 5″ by 3″ loaf pan. Bake tuna loaf for 1 hour or until knife inserted in center comes out clean. Cool slightly.

3. *About 15 minutes before serving:* Prepare Cucumber Sauce: In 2-quart saucepan, simmer cucumbers in 1 cup water until tender-crisp. Drain; add water to liquid to make 1³/₄ cups; set aside. In same saucepan, over medium heat, melt butter or margarine; add flour; stir until smooth. Slowly add reserved liquid; cook, stirring, until thickened. Add salt, lemon peel, juice and cooked cucumber; cook just until boiling. In small bowl, beat egg yolks slightly; stir in some hot liquid; slowly add mixture to pan; cook, stirring, until thickened (do not boil).

4. Loosen loaf from pan; invert onto platter; pour on some sauce; garnish. Pass remaining sauce.

Color index page 38
Begin 45 mins ahead
6 servings

531 cals per serving
Good source of calcium, iron, vitamin A

Salmon Burgers

3 eggs
1 16-ounce can salmon,
*   drained*
2¹/₂ cups fresh bread
*   crumbs (about 5*
*   slices)*
²/₃ cup chopped celery
¹/₃ cup chopped green
*   onions*

3 tablespoons salad
*   oil*
3 English muffins, split
*   and toasted*
1¹/₃ cups Hollandaise
*   Sauce (page 463)*

1. In large bowl with fork, beat eggs slightly. Add salmon, crumbs, celery and green onions and mix well. Shape mixture firmly into 6 patties.

2. In 12-inch skillet over medium heat, in hot oil, fry patties, turning once, 10 minutes until browned.

3. Top each muffin with a patty; spoon on sauce.

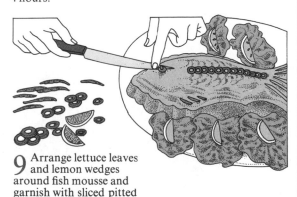

Canned fish

Tuna Pie

Color index
page 38

Begin 1½ hrs
ahead

6 servings

553 cals per
serving

Good source
of calcium,
iron,
vitamin A,
niacin,
vitamin C

1 10-ounce package
frozen broccoli spears,
thawed
1 8- to 8½-ounce can
water chestnuts,
drained
¼ cup butter or
margarine
¼ cup all-purpose
flour
½ teaspoon salt
½ teaspoon paprika

2¼ cups milk
½ cup shredded Swiss
cheese
½ pound mushrooms,
sliced
1 12½- to 13-ounce can
tuna, drained
pastry for 1-crust 9-inch
pie (page 344)
1 egg yolk
1 teaspoon water

1. Cut broccoli into 2-inch pieces; cut water chestnuts into ¼-inch slices; set aside.
2. In 3-quart saucepan over low heat, melt butter or margarine; stir in flour, salt and paprika until blended. Gradually stir in milk and cook, stirring constantly, until mixture is thickened and smooth.
3. With rubber spatula, gently stir in broccoli, water chestnuts, cheese, mushrooms and tuna; spoon mixture into 2-quart casserole.
4. Prepare pastry. On lightly floured surface with lightly floured rolling pin, roll pastry to a circle ⅛ inch thick and about 1 inch larger all around than casserole. Place pastry loosely over tuna mixture.
5. Preheat oven to 375°F. With kitchen shears, trim pastry edge, leaving 1-inch overhang; fold overhang under and press gently all around casserole rim to make a high stand-up edge. With sharp knife, cut slits in pastry top to allow steam to escape.
6. Reroll pastry trimmings. With leaf-shaped cookie cutter, cut several leaves. With tip of small knife, score several lines on leaves to resemble veins. Arrange the scored leaves in attractive pattern in the center top of pie.
7. In small bowl, mix well egg yolk with water. Brush pastry with egg-yolk mixture. Bake 30 to 35 minutes or until crust is golden and mixture is heated.

Tuna Tetrazzini

Color index
page 38

Begin 1 hr
ahead

8 servings

425 cals per
serving

Good source
of calcium,
vitamin A

1 8-ounce package
spaghetti, broken in
pieces
2 2½-ounce cans sliced
mushrooms
¼ cup all-purpose flour
¼ cup butter or
margarine
1¼ cups milk

¼ cup medium sherry
½ pound pasteurized
process cheese, cubed
(2 cups)
½ teaspoon seasoned salt
¼ teaspoon ground
nutmeg
2 6½- or 7-ounce cans
tuna, drained

1. Cook spaghetti as label directs; drain and set aside. Drain mushrooms, reserving ⅓ cup liquid. Preheat oven to 350°F.
2. For sauce, in 2-quart saucepan over low heat, stir flour into hot butter or margarine, until blended. Gradually stir in milk, sherry and mushroom liquid and cook, stirring, until thickened. Stir in cheese, seasoned salt and nutmeg until cheese melts.
3. Stir spaghetti, tuna and mushrooms into sauce. Pour mixture into 2½-quart, shallow baking dish. Bake in oven 20 minutes or until light golden.

Cold Salmon Mousse

Color index
page 38

Begin 4 hrs
or day ahead

6 main-dish
servings

424 cals per
serving

Good source
of calcium,
vitamin A

1 envelope unflavored
gelatin
water
salad oil
1 cup heavy or
whipping cream
1 15½-ounce can
salmon, drained and
flaked
½ cup mayonnaise
½ teaspoon salt

¾ teaspoon dill weed or 2
teaspoons chopped
fresh dill
½ teaspoon paprika
½ teaspoon hot pepper
sauce
1 bunch radishes
2 peppercorns
2 medium lemons, thinly
sliced, for garnish

1. In small bowl, mix gelatin with ¼ cup cold water. Let gelatin stand 5 minutes to soften. Add ½ cup *very hot* tap water to gelatin mixture and stir until gelatin is completely dissolved, about 3 minutes. Cover and refrigerate until slightly chilled.
2. With pastry brush, lightly brush 5½-cup fish or other favorite mold with salad oil.
3. In small bowl with mixer at medium speed, beat cream until stiff peaks form. In large bowl with mixer at medium-high speed, beat salmon, mayonnaise, salt, dill weed, paprika, hot pepper sauce and gelatin mixture until smooth, scraping bowl often with rubber spatula. Fold in cream. Spoon salmon mixture into mold; cover and refrigerate until set, about 3 hours.
4. *To serve:* Thinly slice radishes; cut slices in half. Unmold mousse onto large platter. Decorate head of fish with peppercorns for eyes. Carefully press radish slices overlapping slightly, about ⅛ inch deep, into mousse in rows to resemble scales, making sure that rounded end of each radish extends at a slight angle. Garnish platter with lemon slices.

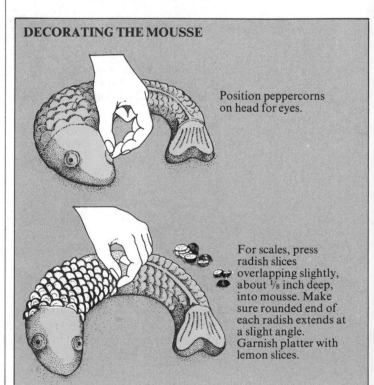

DECORATING THE MOUSSE

Position peppercorns on head for eyes.

For scales, press radish slices overlapping slightly, about ⅛ inch deep, into mousse. Make sure rounded end of each radish extends at a slight angle. Garnish platter with lemon slices.

Sauces for fish

Mustard Sauce

Begin 5 mins ahead

²/₃ cup

389 cals per ¹/₃ cup

½ cup mayonnaise
3 tablespoons milk
¼ teaspoon salt

1 tablespoon prepared mustard

1. In small bowl with spoon, mix well mayonnaise, milk, salt and prepared mustard.
2. Cover and refrigerate until serving time.

Tartar Sauce

Begin 15 mins ahead

1¼ cups

327 cals per ¼ cup

1 cup mayonnaise
2 tablespoons minced parsley
1 to 2 tablespoons minced dill pickle
1 to 2 tablespoons minced onion

1 tablespoon bottled capers
1 tablespoon minced pimento-stuffed olives (optional)

In small bowl with fork, stir together all ingredients until well mixed.

Green Mayonnaise Dressing

Begin early in day

2 cups

428 cals per ¼ cup

2 cups mayonnaise
¹/₃ cup chopped parsley
4 teaspoons tarragon vinegar

½ teaspoon tarragon
2 green onions, cut up

In covered blender container at medium speed, blend all ingredients until smooth, occasionally stopping blender and scraping sides. Refrigerate.

Horseradish Sauce

Begin 10 mins ahead

¾ cup

165 cals per ¼ cup

¹/₃ cup mayonnaise
¼ cup minced dill pickles
2 tablespoons horseradish

1 tablespoon milk
¹/₈ teaspoon pepper

1. In small bowl with spoon, combine mayonnaise, dill pickles and horseradish.
2. Stir in milk and pepper and blend well.

Shrimp Sauce

Begin 15 mins ahead

2¾ cups

141 cals per ¼ cup

6 tablespoons butter
½ 16-ounce package frozen shelled and deveined shrimp
6 tablespoons all-purpose flour

¹/₈ teaspoon paprika
¹/₈ teaspoon pepper
¼ teaspoon salt
1 cup half-and-half
½ cup sauterne

1. In 1-quart saucepan over medium-high heat, in hot butter, cook shrimp until tender, about 5 minutes. Blend in flour, paprika, pepper and salt.
2. Gradually stir in half-and-half and sauterne and cook, stirring constantly, until thickened.

Dill-Butter Sauce

Begin 10 mins ahead

1 cup

411 cals per ¼ cup

1 cup butter or margarine
1 teaspoon dill weed

¼ teaspoon salt

1. In 1-quart saucepan over low heat, melt butter or margarine.
2. Stir dill weed and salt into melted butter or margarine. Serve Dill-Butter Sauce hot.

Watercress Sauce

Begin 15 mins ahead

¾ cup

210 cals per ¼ cup

1 medium onion
¹/₃ cup butter or margarine
1 small garlic clove

1 bunch watercress, chopped
¼ cup white table wine

1. With sharp knife, slice onion thinly.
2. In 1-quart saucepan over medium-high heat, in hot butter or margarine, cook onion and garlic until onion is tender, about 5 minutes.
3. Discard garlic. Stir in chopped watercress and white table wine.
4. Cook until watercress is tender, about 3 minutes.

Herb Mayonnaise

Begin early in day

1½ cups

408 cals per ¼ cup

1½ cups mayonnaise
½ cup chopped parsley
¼ cup chopped watercress
¼ cup chopped chives
2 teaspoons chervil

1 teaspoon tarragon
½ teaspoon salt
¼ teaspoon pepper
parsley sprig for garnish

1. In covered blender container at high speed, blend all ingredients except parsley sprig until well mixed and mayonnaise is green.
2. Spoon into small bowl; cover and refrigerate until serving time.
3. To serve, garnish with parsley sprig.

Shrimp-Olive Sauce

Begin 15 mins ahead

2 cups

45 cals per ¼ cup

1 8-ounce can tomato sauce
½ pound shelled and deveined small shrimp, cooked

½ cup sliced pimento-stuffed olives
¹/₃ cup dry white wine

In 1-quart saucepan over medium heat, heat all ingredients, stirring.

Orange Sauce

Begin 10 mins ahead

¾ cup

131 cals per ¼ cup

¾ cup orange juice
1 tablespoon lemon juice
¹/₈ teaspoon salt
¹/₈ teaspoon ground nutmeg

2 tablespoons butter or margarine
2 tablespoons all-purpose flour

1. In measuring cup, combine orange juice, lemon juice, salt and nutmeg; set aside.
2. In 1-quart saucepan over medium heat, melt butter or margarine.
3. Add flour and cook, stirring constantly, until mixture is well blended.
4. Add juice mixture; cook, stirring constantly, until sauce is thickened.

Cucumber-Dill Sauce

Begin 10 mins ahead

2 cups

66 cals per ¼ cup

1 8-ounce container sour cream
1 medium cucumber, peeled and chopped
1 teaspoon dill weed

1 teaspoon sugar
¾ teaspoon salt
¹/₈ teaspoon pepper

In small bowl with spoon, mix well sour cream with cucumber, dill weed, sugar, salt and pepper.

MEAT

In one form or another, meat appears on the table in most homes at least once a day, providing good nutrition for every member of the family.

BUYING MEAT

Recognizing the cuts that come from each animal and knowing the best way to cook them is very important. But as the same cuts from animals of different quality will vary in tenderness, it is equally important to be able to judge the quality of the meat itself.

USDA marks: All fresh meat sold across state lines bears a circular mark with the legend "U.S. inspected and passed", indicating that the meat is wholesome, was processed under sanitary conditions and is accurately labeled. This stamp is applied only to large wholesale cuts, so it may not appear on smaller cuts packaged for retail sale. Meat that does not cross state borders may sometimes carry the inspection stamp of a state government agency.

USDA grade stamps, in the form of a small shield, indicate the quality of beef, veal and lamb, e.g. Prime, the top grade, usually sold to restaurants, and Choice, the quality most widely available. Prime and Choice are considered to be high quality grades, but certain Choice cuts may be less tender than others because of the wide range of cuts in this grade. USDA Good, a lower grade sometimes found in supermarkets, is leaner and often less juicy than higher-grade meat. Grades are usually not marked for pork since much pork, such as ham or sausage, carries a packer's brand.

HOW MUCH MEAT TO BUY

If the meat is boneless, plan on ¼ to ⅓ pound per serving. If it has a little bone, allow ⅓ to ½ pound per serving. If very bony, allow ½ to 1 pound per serving. Plan to have extra servings ready for hearty appetites.

STORING MEAT

Refrigerate fresh meat as soon as possible after purchase in the meat compartment or in the coldest part of the refrigerator. Store prepackaged meat in its original wrapping and use it within 2 days; or freeze it and use within 1 or 2 weeks. For longer freezer storage, overwrap package with freezer wrap. If meat has not been prepackaged, remove market wrapping paper, rewrap meat loosely in waxed paper or foil (tightly in the case of variety and ground meats), and refrigerate. Use ground beef, stew meat and variety meats within 1 or 2 days, other meats within 2 days. Frozen meat should be placed in the freezer or freezer compartment of your refrigerator as soon after purchase as possible.

FREEZING MEAT

Only freeze meat that is fresh and in top condition. Cut large pieces into meal-size portions. Trim excess fat from cuts and, wherever practical, remove bones to conserve freezer space. Enough chops, steaks or patties and small cuts such as short ribs for a single meal may be packaged together, with foil, plastic wrap or a double thickness of waxed paper between slices, so that they will be easy to separate while still frozen. Ground meat should not be seasoned before freezing (freezing intensifies flavors and hastens rancidity); simply shape it into patties or divide into amounts required for meat loaves or other recipes. Freeze gravy and stuffings separately from cooked meat.

Wrap meat tightly in freezer wrap; label with name of cut, weight or number of servings and date, and freeze as quickly as possible, at –10°F. or lower. Keep frozen meat at 0°F. or lower and use within recommended storage period.

COOKING MEAT

There are six basic ways of cooking meat. Most tender cuts are best cooked by dry heat: roasted or cooked on a rotisserie, broiled or grilled, pan-broiled or pan-fried. Less tender cuts should be cooked slowly in moist heat: braised or pot-roasted, or cooked in liquid. We give appropriate cooking methods for each cut throughout the chapter.

Roasting: Preheat oven to 325°F. for most meats. Season meat if desired and place fat side up on rack in open roasting pan. In some roasts (e.g. pork loin, standing rib roast), bones form a natural rack. Insert meat thermometer (page 188) and roast meat to desired degree of doneness. Roasts continue to cook after they are removed from the oven, so you may wish to stop cooking when thermometer reads about 5 degrees below reading for degree of doneness desired.

Cooking on a rotisserie: This is also a form of roasting. As with other dry-heat methods, low to moderate temperatures should be used. Meat cuts should be as uniform in shape and thickness as possible. Insert the spit through center of the roast lengthwise, fastening the meat securely so that it does not slip. Test for balance by rotating the spit in the palms of your hands. Insert the meat thermometer (see page 188). If it does not stay securely in position, after the approximate roasting time, stop the rotisserie, insert the thermometer and read the temperature. Following manufacturer's directions, cook the meat to the desired degree of doneness. Meat cooked on a rotisserie is self-basting, but it may be basted occasionally for added flavor and color. Sweet basting sauces should not be applied until the last half-hour of cooking.

Broiling or grilling: Steaks and chops should be at least 3/4 inch thick, ham slices at least 1/2 inch thick. Trim excess fat from meat and slash the edge of fat at 2-inch intervals so it won't curl during broiling. Preheat broiler if manufacturer directs, or prepare coals. Rub the broiling pan rack with a piece of fat trimmed from the meat. Place the meat on the rack, then place the pan in the broiler. Steaks, chops and patties 3/4 to 1 inch thick should be 2 to 3 inches from the heat; cuts 1 to 2 inches thick should be 3 to 5 inches from the heat. Broil meat until top is browned (lightly browned for cured and smoked pork). Season top if desired (ham and bacon will not need seasoning) and with tongs, turn meat. Broil until of desired degree of doneness; cut slit near bone and check color to test doneness.

Pan-broiling: The meat cut should be no more than 1 inch thick and it will take about half as long as if broiled in broiler. Place meat in an unheated heavy skillet or on a griddle. Most meats have enough fat to prevent sticking. However, if meat is very lean, pan may first be brushed lightly with fat or rubbed with a piece of fat trimmed from the meat. Over medium-low to medium heat, cook meat slowly, turning occasionally. Pour off fat as it accumulates so that meat does not fry. Brown meat on both sides.

Pan-frying: In a skillet, over medium to medium-high heat, using a little hot salad oil or other fat if necessary, brown the meat on both sides. (Add a little salad oil only if cut is low in fat, such as liver, or if meat is coated with flour or bread crumbs.) Season, if desired, and continue cooking over medium-low to medium heat, turning occasionally, until done. Do not cover, or crispness will be lost. Serve meat at once.

Braising: In a large, heavy skillet or Dutch oven over medium-high heat in a little hot salad oil or fat melted from meat, brown the meat on all sides; spoon off drippings. Season meat and add a little liquid if needed. Less tender cuts require liquid; tender ones, such as pork chops, may not. Cover the pan tightly to keep in the steam and simmer the meat over low heat or in a preheated 325°F. to 350°F. oven until fork-tender.

Cooking in liquid: Large cuts: In a large, heavy saucepot, over medium-high heat, brown meat on all sides to develop flavor and color. (Corned beef and other cured meats are not browned.) Add hot or cold liquid to cover the meat; season, if desired. Over high heat, heat liquid to boiling; reduce heat to low, cover pan and simmer (don't boil) until the meat is fork-tender. Add any vegetables just long enough before meat is done to cook them. If meat is to be served cold, chill it in the cooking liquid in the refrigerator to improve juiciness and flavor and reduce shrinkage.

Stewing: For a browned stew, in a heavy saucepan over medium-high heat, in a little hot salad oil, brown the pieces of meat on all sides, a few at a time, removing them as they brown. Meat may be coated with flour before browning. When all pieces are browned, return meat to the pan. For a light stew, omit flouring and browning. Add hot or cold liquid just to cover the meat. Season, if desired; cover and simmer (don't boil) until the meat is fork-tender. Add any vegetables just long enough before meat is done to cook them. When done, remove both meat and vegetables to a warm dish and keep hot: if desired, thicken the remaining liquid to make a gravy or sauce. Serve the gravy over the meat and vegetables or pass it in a gravy boat.

TENDERIZING MEAT

Meat tenderizers: These are derivatives of natural food-tenderizing agents found in some tropical fruits which soften meat tissue only while meat is cooking. Be sure to follow directions on the label: don't use more and don't leave it on longer than the label recommends, or meat surface might become mushy. Also, don't use it on naturally tender cuts, such as sirloin steak, or on beef tendered with papain.

Mechanical methods: Grinding makes meat tender, as does "cubing," which breaks down the connective tissue by machine. Pounding meat, as directed in some recipes, achieves the same results.

Beef "tendered with papain": This is a scientific commercial process that utilizes protein derivatives from such fruits as papaya (papain). The tendering develops only as the beef cooks, making it possible to cook more beef cuts by dry heat, and shortening cooking time for those cuts that must be cooked by moist heat.

Aging: This improves the tenderness of some beef cuts. At the storage plant, beef is hung for a specified time, in rooms with controlled temperature and humidity.

Marinating: Soaking meat, particularly in acid mixtures such as lemon juice or vinegar, tenderizes meat and adds flavor. Often herbs and spices are included in marinades.

Beef

USING A MEAT THERMOMETER

For meats that are roasted in an open pan, insert the thermometer so that its point is centered in the thickest part of the meat. Make sure that it is not resting on bone or in fat, or it will not register the correct temperature. If necessary, pierce the meat with a skewer first to make insertion of the thermometer easier.

When roasting frozen meat, insert thermometer about halfway through the roasting period, when meat is partially thawed (check first with a skewer).

For rotisserie cooking, the dial type of thermometer is recommended. Insert it at a slight angle or through the end of the roast halfway between the spit and the surface of the meat, making sure that its point is not resting on bone or fat, or touching the spit.

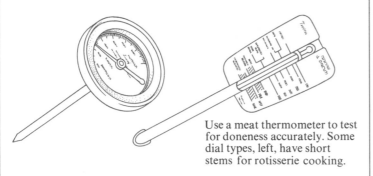

Use a meat thermometer to test for doneness accurately. Some dial types, left, have short stems for rotisserie cooking.

MAKING GRAVY

Remove the cooked meat and any vegetables to a warmed platter; keep warm while making gravy.

For roasts: Into 2-quart saucepan, measure ¼ cup fat from roasting pan (or use butter or margarine). Pour 1 cup water or bouillon into the roasting pan; stir to loosen the brown bits in the bottom of the pan. Into fat in saucepan over medium heat, stir ¼ cup all-purpose flour; cook, stirring constantly until brown. Slowly stir in liquid from the roasting pan; add 1 cup water and heat to boiling, stirring until thickened. If you like, add bottled sauce for gravy to make a rich color; add salt and pepper to taste. (Makes 2 cups.)

For pan-fried meat: In skillet over medium heat, in ¼ cup hot drippings (or butter or margarine), cook ¼ cup all-purpose flour until brown. Gradually stir in 2 cups water, milk or bouillon; heat to boiling, stirring until thickened. If you like, add bottled sauce for gravy to make a rich brown color; add salt and pepper to taste. (Makes 2 cups.)

For pot roasts and braised meat: Spoon fat from pan liquid; measure liquid and heat. For each cup liquid, in cup, blend 2 tablespoons all-purpose flour with ¼ cup water; stir into simmering liquid and cook, stirring, until thickened. Season if needed.

For stews: Thicken gravy as for pot roasts but use only 1 tablespoon flour for each cup liquid.

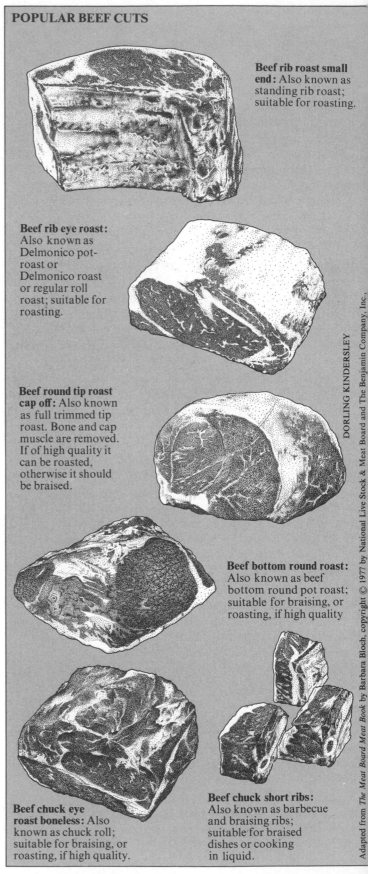

POPULAR BEEF CUTS

Beef rib roast small end: Also known as standing rib roast; suitable for roasting.

Beef rib eye roast: Also known as Delmonico pot-roast or Delmonico roast or regular roll roast; suitable for roasting.

Beef round tip roast cap off: Also known as full trimmed tip roast. Bone and cap muscle are removed. If of high quality it can be roasted, otherwise it should be braised.

Beef bottom round roast: Also known as beef bottom round pot roast; suitable for braising, or roasting, if high quality

Beef chuck eye roast boneless: Also known as chuck roll; suitable for braising, or roasting, if high quality.

Beef chuck short ribs: Also known as barbecue and braising ribs; suitable for braised dishes or cooking in liquid.

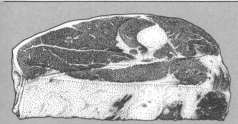

Beef chuck arm pot roast: Also known as round bone pot roast; suitable for pot roasts and other braised dishes.

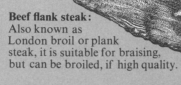

Beef flank steak: Also known as London broil or plank steak, it is suitable for braising, but can be broiled, if high quality.

Beef top loin steak: Popular names include Shell, club, strip and Delmonico steak; suitable for broiling, pan-broiling and pan-frying.

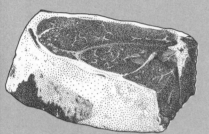

Beef chuck shoulder pot roast boneless: Also known as shoulder or English roast; suitable for pot roasts and other braised dishes.

Beef chuck under blade steak: Also known as bottom chuck steak; suitable for braising, or broiling, pan-broiling and pan-frying, if high quality.

Beef porterhouse steak: Contains tenderloin of at least 1¼ inches diameter; suitable for broiling, pan-broiling and pan-frying.

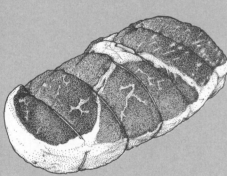

Beef round rump roast boneless: Usually found tied; suitable for braised dishes but may be roasted, if high quality.

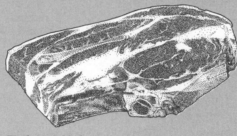

Beef chuck blade steak: Also known as blade steak or blade cut; suitable for braising or broiling or pan-broiling, if high quality.

Beef pin bone sirloin steak: Otherwise known as sirloin steak; suitable for broiling, pan-broiling and pan-frying.

Beef chuck 7-bone steak: Also known as center chuck steak; suitable for braising.

Beef rib eye steak: Also known as Delmonico and fillet steak; suitable for broiling, pan-broiling and pan-frying.

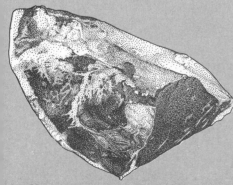

Beef bottom rump round roast: Also known as round tip roast, it is an irregular, thick cut suitable for braising, roasting, if high quality.

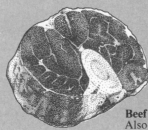

Beef shank cross cuts: Also known as center beef shank; suitable for braising.

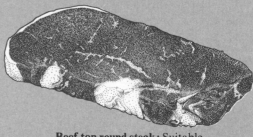

Beef top round steak: Suitable for braising or broiling, pan-broiling and pan-frying, if high quality.

Beef

From succulent steaks and tender, juicy roasts to hearty hamburgers and spicy meat loaves, beef provides us with a greater variety of cuts and more ways of cooking than any other meat.

BUYING BEEF

Beef should be a uniform bright color, varying from light to deep red. The texture of the meat should be fine rather than coarse, firm and slightly moist, and the bones should be red and porous. The color of the fat varies with age, feed and breed of the animal, and cannot be taken as a guide to quality.

Some beef, usually cuts such as roasts and some steaks, is aged to increase its tenderness. Always check if the meat you are buying has been aged so you will know whether or not to tenderize it. Beef may also be pretendered with papain. If this has been done, the label on the package will carry special cooking directions and it is important that you follow these.

TESTING FOR DONENESS

Roast and broiled beef may be cooked rare, medium or well done according to taste. Rare beef cooked to an internal temperature of 140°F. is reddish-pink inside with an abundance of clear red juice of a lighter color. Medium beef is cooked to 160°F. Beef is well done when the meat thermometer reads 170°F. and is a uniform brown color throughout, with clear, golden juices. Cooked braised or simmered beef should be fork-tender.

The table below is intended as a guide for roasting beef; times are for roasting meat straight from the refrigerator.

TIMETABLE FOR ROASTING BEEF			
Weight *(in pounds)*	Approximate cooking time* *(in hours)*		Oven Temperature
	Rare 140°F.**	Medium 160°F.**	Well done 170°F.**	
Rib roast 4 to 6 6 to 8	1¾ to 2½ 2¼ to 3	2¼ to 3½ 2¾ to 3½	2¾ to 4 3¼ to 4¼	325°F. 325°F.
Rib eye roast 4 to 6	1¼ to 1¾	1¼ to 2	1½ to 2¼	350°F.
Tenderloin (whole) 4 to 6	45 to 60 mins			425°F.
Tenderloin (half) 2 to 3	45 to 50 mins			425°F.
Rump roast boneless 4 to 6		1¾ to 2½		325°F.
Tip roast 3½ to 4 6 to 8		2 to 2¼ 3 to 4		325°F. 325°F.

*Remove meat from oven when internal temperature is 5 to 10 degrees below desired doneness as meat continues cooking
**Temperature on meat thermometer*

CARVING BEEF

Rib roast of beef: Place the beef on a cutting board or warm platter with the large end down and the ribs to your left. Insert carving fork, tines down, between the top and second rib of the roast. With the carving knife, carefully cut across the meat toward the rib bone, making a slice about ¼ inch thick.

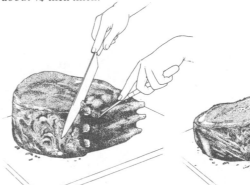

Remove knife and, with tip, cut down along side of rib bone to release meat; place the slice on a warm dinner plate.

Continue cutting slices, removing each rib bone as it is exposed.

Boneless roast: Place the roast on a board or warm platter. Cut away any strings (or, if the roast starts to fall apart, leave one or two in place to help the roast hold its shape). Using a fork to anchor the meat, start cutting crosswise across the fibers (grain) of the meat into slices ¼ to ½ inch thick.

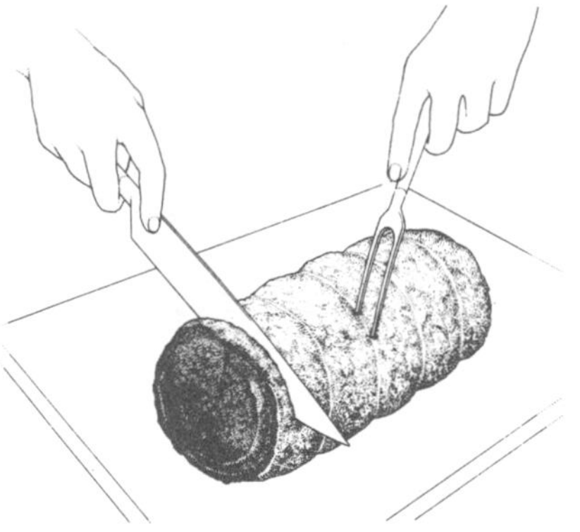

Steak or arm or blade pot roast: With the roast on a cutting board and using a fork to anchor the meat, cut between muscles and around bones. Carve one section at a time, turning to cut across the grain of the meat. Cut the pieces into slices of desired thickness. Repeat with remaining sections of meat.

Tender roasts

Standing Rib Roast with Yorkshire Pudding

Color index page 50

Begin 2 to 4 hrs ahead

18 servings

200 cals per serving

1 2- to 3-rib beef rib roast small end (4 to 6 pounds)
salt and pepper
2 eggs
1 cup milk
½ teaspoon salt
1 cup all-purpose flour
Horseradish Sauce (page 463)
parsley sprigs for garnish

1 Place roast on rib bones in open roasting pan. Sprinkle with salt , pepper.

2 Insert meat thermometer into thickest part, making sure it is in center of roast and not resting on bone or fat.

3 Roast in 325°F. oven until internal temperature reaches 140°F. for rare (1¾ to 2½ hours); 160°F. for medium (2¼ to 3½ hours); 170°F. for well done (2¾ to 4 hours). When roast is done, allow it to stand at room temperature 15 minutes for easier carving. Place on warm platter and garnish with parsley. About 5 minutes before end of roasting time, prepare Yorkshire Pudding.

4 In medium bowl with wire whisk, beat eggs until foamy; beat in milk and ½ teaspoon salt; gradually beat in flour until batter is smooth.

5 When roast is done, spoon off 2 tablespoons drippings and divide into twelve 3-inch muffin cups; tilt to coat evenly; turn oven to 400°F.

6 Heat muffin pan in oven 5 minutes; pour 2½ tablespoons batter in each greased muffin cup. Bake 30 minutes.

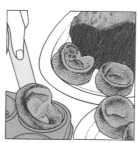

7 Loosen Yorkshire Pudding; transfer to platter with roast and serve immediately with Horseradish Sauce.

STANDING RIB ROAST AU JUS: Prepare Standing Rib Roast. After removing roast from pan, spoon off fat from meat juices in pan; use 2 tablespoons fat for Yorkshire Pudding; discard remaining fat. Into meat juices in pan, pour a little *water* (about ⅓ to ½ cup). Over medium-high heat, heat mixture to simmering, stirring and scraping until browned bits are dissolved; strain mixture. Serve over slices of meat.

Vegetable-topped Roast Beef

Color index page 51

Begin 3½ hrs ahead

18 servings

134 cals per serving

1 4½-pound beef round tip roast cap off
2 tablespoons prepared mustard
¼ teaspoon pepper
salt
1 cup shredded carrots
½ cup minced celery leaves
1 teaspoon thyme leaves
1 cup water
⅓ cup dry red wine

1. Place round tip roast on a small wire rack in a medium open roasting pan. Spread the top of roast with the mustard; sprinkle with pepper and ½ teaspoon salt. On waxed paper, combine the shredded carrots, celery leaves and thyme. Reserve ¼ cup of the vegetable mixture. With hands, evenly press the remaining vegetable mixture on top of the mustard and seasoning on roast.
2. Insert meat thermometer into the center of the beef roast. Roast in 325°F. oven for 1 hour. Cover the roast beef loosely with a tent of folded foil, leaving the thermometer uncovered and continue roasting until the thermometer reaches 160°F. for medium (about 2 hours) or until of desired doneness.
3. When roast is done, place on warm large platter or carving board; sprinkle top with reserved vegetable mixture; keep warm.
4. Remove the wire rack from the roasting pan. Spoon off any fat from the pan; discard the fat. Into the pan, pour the water and the dry red wine; add ¼ teaspoon salt; stir until the brown bits on the bottom of the pan are loosened.
5. Over medium-high heat, heat the mixture to boiling, stirring constantly and scraping until the brown bits are dissolved.
6. To serve: Slice the roast beef. Spoon the gravy over individual portions.

Coating meat: Spread on mustard and sprinkle with salt and pepper; then evenly press vegetable mixture on top of roast.

Making foil tent: To prevent topping burning, cover roast loosely with tent of folded foil; leave thermometer uncovered.

191

Tender roasts

Individual Beef Wellingtons

1 pound medium mushrooms	*2 eggs, separated water*
¼ cup butter or margarine	*curly endive for garnish*
1 medium onion, minced	*preserved or fresh kumquats for garnish (optional)*
3 cups fresh bread crumbs	
½ teaspoon pepper	Color index page 52
¼ teaspoon thyme leaves	Begin early in day
salt	10 servings
pastry for 4 2-crust pies (page 344)	1220 cals per serving
1 4-pound beef rib eye roast	Good source of calcium, iron, niacin

1 Remove stems from 10 mushrooms; set mushrooms aside. Mince remaining mushrooms and the extra stems.

2 In 12-inch skillet over medium heat, in hot butter, cook minced mushrooms and onion 5 minutes, until all liquid is evaporated.

3 Stir in bread crumbs, pepper, thyme and 1 teaspoon salt; cool. Prepare pastry; divide into 5 equal pieces.

4 Trim fat off roast; cut meat in half lengthwise; slice each half crosswise into 5 equal pieces. Dry with paper towels.

5 On floured surface with floured stockinette-covered rolling pin, roll 1 piece pastry to 14″ by 11″; cut 2 rectangles 6½″ by 10″; reserve scraps.

6 Place ⅓ cup of mushroom mixture in center of pastry rectangle. Top with piece of meat.

7 Sprinkle meat lightly with salt; top with 1 whole mushroom. In bowl with fork, beat egg whites with 2 teaspoons water; brush pastry edges.

8 Fold pastry over meat and mushroom; overlap edges; press to seal; place on cookie sheet. Refrigerate while preparing remainder.

9 Roll out pastry scraps; with sharp knife, cut into designs. Brush backs with egg white; arrange on pastry. Refrigerate.

10 *About 35 minutes before serving:* Preheat oven to 400°F. In cup, beat egg yolks with 2 teaspoons water; brush over pastry. Bake 25 minutes for rare, 27 minutes for medium-doneness. With pancake turner, place Wellingtons on warm platter. Garnish the platter with curly endive and, if you wish, preserved or fresh kumquats. These may be either sliced or left whole, if you prefer. Serve immediately.

Less tender roasts and pot roasts

Color index page 54
Begin 5 hrs ahead
20 servings

162 cals per serving
Good source of iron

Country Pot Roast

2 garlic cloves	*2 medium onions, cut up*
1 5-pound beef chuck cross rib pot roast boneless or bottom rump round roast	*1 cup thinly sliced celery*
	1 tablespoon salt
	1 teaspoon oregano leaves
¼ cup all-purpose flour	*¼ teaspoon pepper*
¼ cup salad oil	*celery leaves or parsley sprigs for garnish*
1 cup tomato juice	
2 medium carrots, sliced	

1 Crush garlic; rub onto roast. On waxed paper, coat meat with flour.

2 In 8-quart Dutch oven over high heat, in hot salad oil, cook pot roast until it is evenly browned on all sides.

3 Add tomato juice and remaining ingredients except celery leaves; heat to boiling. Reduce the heat to low.

4 Cover Dutch oven and simmer for 4 hours or until the meat is fork-tender, turning it occasionally. Transfer the meat to a warm platter.

5 Fill blender three-fourths full with liquid and vegetables; cover; blend at high speed; pour into large bowl; repeat until all is blended.

6 Return the blended mixture to the Dutch oven; heat to boiling. Garnish the roast with celery leaves and serve with the hot gravy.

Sauerbraten

3 medium onions,
  sliced
3 medium carrots,
  sliced
2½ cups dry red wine
2 cups water
¼ cup red wine vinegar
2 large celery stalks,
  sliced
2 bay leaves
6 peppercorns
¼ teaspoon mustard
  seed
1 5-pound beef bottom
  round roast
2 tablespoons all-purpose
  flour

¼ teaspoon cracked
  black pepper
salt
¼ cup salad oil
  or shortening
⅓ cup fine gingersnap
  crumbs
½ cup sour cream

Color index page 54

Begin 2 to 3 days ahead

16 servings

249 cals per serving

Low in sodium

Good source of iron

1 In 3-quart saucepan over medium heat, heat 2 onions, 1 carrot and next 7 ingredients to boiling. Reduce heat to low; cover saucepan; simmer 10 minutes.

2 Pour into large bowl, cover and cool. Add roast, turning to coat. Cover and refrigerate 2 to 3 days, turning the meat each day.

3 About 4 hours before serving: Remove meat; dry with paper towels; coat with flour, pepper and 1 teaspoon salt. Strain marinade, reserving liquid.

4 In 8-quart Dutch oven over medium-high heat, in hot oil, cook meat until browned, 15 to 20 minutes. Remove meat; pour off all but 1 tablespoon of the drippings.

5 In drippings over medium heat, cook rest of vegetables 3 minutes, stirring. Add the meat.

6 Add marinade; heat to boiling. Reduce heat to low; cover; simmer 3½ hours, turn occasionally.

7 Remove meat to warm platter; keep warm. Spoon off and discard the fat from gravy.

8 Add cookie crumbs and ½ teaspoon salt. Over medium-high heat, stir until mixture thickens.

9 With a wire whisk, blend in sour cream. Cook, stirring, until heated through (do not boil).

10 Spoon some of the sour-cream gravy over the meat and pass remaining gravy separately.

Color index page 55
Begin 4 hrs ahead
10 servings
284 cals per serving
Good source of iron

Baked Pot Roast with Vegetables

1 3-pound beef round
  rump roast
  boneless
1 large onion, sliced
1 garlic clove,
  crushed
2 tablespoons
  Worcestershire
3 teaspoons salt
1 teaspoon sugar

¼ teaspoon cracked
  black pepper
2 cups water
4 medium parsnips,
  cut into chunks
1 24-ounce bag frozen
  lima beans
parsley sprigs for garnish
  (optional)

1. In 5-quart Dutch oven, place beef round rump roast. Add onion, garlic, Worcestershire, salt, sugar, pepper and water. Cover and bake in 350°F. oven for 2 hours.

2. Add the parsnip chunks and the lima beans to the Dutch oven and continue baking 1 to 1½ hours more until the vegetables and the meat are fork-tender, turning the meat occasionally.

3. Transfer the meat to a warm platter. Remove the strings and discard them.

4. With slotted spoon, arrange vegetables around meat. With large spoon, skim fat from the liquid in Dutch oven. Serve liquid over meat and vegetables. Garnish with parsley if you like.

Color index page 55
Begin 4 hrs ahead
14 servings
262 cals per serving
Good source of iron

Fruited Pot Roast

2 tablespoons shortening
  or salad oil
1 4-pound beef chuck eye
  roast boneless
2 medium onions, sliced
1 cup apple cider or juice
2 tablespoons brown
  sugar
2 teaspoons salt

1 teaspoon seasoned
  pepper
¼ teaspoon ground
  cloves
1½ cups dried apricots
1½ cups pitted prunes
2 tablespoons all-purpose
  flour (optional)
¼ cup water (optional)

1. In 5-quart Dutch oven over medium-high heat, in hot shortening, cook chuck roast until well browned on all sides.

2. Add onions, apple cider, brown sugar, salt, seasoned pepper and cloves; heat to boiling. Reduce heat to low; cover and simmer 3½ hours or until meat is almost fork-tender, turning meat occasionally and adding more cider during cooking if necessary.

3. Add the apricots and the pitted prunes to the mixture in the Dutch oven. Continue cooking 20 minutes or until the meat is fork-tender. Place the meat on a warm platter.

4. Spoon the fat from liquid in the Dutch oven. If you like, blend flour and water until smooth; gradually stir into the pan liquid and cook over medium heat, stirring constantly, until the mixture is thickened. Serve sauce with the meat.

Less tender roasts and pot roasts

Pot Roast with Sweet and Sour Cabbage

Color index page 51

Begin 3½ hrs ahead

10 servings

229 cals per serving

Good source of iron

2 tablespoons salad oil
1 3-pound beef chuck eye roast boneless, cut 2 inches thick
2 medium onions, sliced
½ cup red wine vinegar
3 teaspoons salt
4 teaspoons light brown sugar
1 teaspoon caraway seed
½ teaspoon cracked black pepper
water
1 medium head red cabbage
2 tablespoons all-purpose flour

1. In 8-quart Dutch oven over medium-high heat, in hot oil, cook roast until well browned on all sides. Stir in onions, vinegar, salt, sugar, caraway seed, pepper and ¼ cup water; heat to boiling. Reduce heat to low; cover and simmer 2½ hours or until meat is fork-tender, turning meat occasionally. Meanwhile, coarsely shred cabbage; discard any tough ribs; set aside.
2. When meat is done, remove meat to large platter; keep warm. Skim off fat from liquid in Dutch oven. Add cabbage; over medium-high heat, heat to boiling. Reduce heat to low; cover and simmer 30 minutes or until cabbage is tender, stirring often.
3. In cup, stir flour and ¼ cup water until blended. Gradually stir flour mixture into cabbage in Dutch oven. Cook over medium heat, stirring gently, until mixture is thickened. Spoon cabbage around meat.

Pepper Beef Pot Roast

Color index page 53

Begin 3 hrs ahead

10 servings

221 cals per serving

Good source of iron, vitamin C

2 tablespoons salad oil
3 large sweet red and/or green peppers, cut in ½-inch strips
1 3-pound beef chuck underblade pot roast, cut 1½ inches thick
1 medium onion, thinly sliced
¼ cup dry sherry
2 tablespoons soy sauce
water
1 tablespoon cornstarch
1 teaspoon sugar

1. In 8-quart Dutch oven over medium-high heat, in hot oil, cook pepper strips, stirring constantly with slotted spoon until tender-crisp, about 3 minutes. Remove peppers to medium bowl; cover; chill.
2. In oil remaining in Dutch oven, over medium-high heat, cook roast until browned on both sides. Add onion, sherry, soy sauce and 2 tablespoons water; heat to boiling. Reduce heat to low; cover and simmer 2 to 2½ hours until meat is fork-tender, adding more water, if necessary, and turning meat occasionally.
3. Place roast on warm large platter; keep warm. Pour pan liquid into 2-cup measure (set pan aside); let stand a few seconds until fat separates from meat juices. Skim 1 tablespoon fat from juices; return to Dutch oven. Spoon off and discard excess fat; add water to juices if necessary, to make 1½ cups.
4. Into fat in Dutch oven, stir cornstarch and sugar until blended; gradually stir in pan juices. Cook over medium heat, stirring, until thickened. Return peppers to Dutch oven; heat through.
5. To serve, spoon peppers around roast and pour remaining sauce on top of roast.

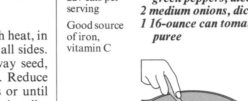

Mexican-style Pot Roast

Color index page 52

Begin 2¾ hrs ahead

12 servings

227 cals per serving

Good source of iron, vitamin C

1 tablespoon salad oil
3 medium garlic cloves, each cut in half
1 3-pound beef chuck arm pot roast, cut 1½ inches thick
4 medium, hot red or hot green peppers, diced
2 medium onions, diced
1 16-ounce can tomato puree
¼ cup red wine vinegar
1 tablespoon sugar
2 teaspoons salt
1 teaspoon oregano leaves
4 medium green peppers, each cut into quarters
2 10-ounce packages frozen whole-kernel corn

1 In 8-quart Dutch oven over medium-high heat, in hot salad oil, cook the halved garlic cloves until lightly browned; discard garlic cloves.

2 Add beef chuck arm pot roast and cook until well browned on all sides. Remove the meat to a plate and set aside.

3 In same Dutch oven in drippings over medium heat, cook hot peppers and onions 10 minutes or until tender, stirring frequently.

4 Return meat to Dutch oven; add tomato puree, vinegar, sugar, salt and oregano; over high heat, heat to boiling. Reduce heat to low; cover and simmer 1 hour.

5 Add the quartered green peppers; cover and simmer 1 hour longer or until the meat is fork-tender. Carefully skim off the fat from juices remaining in Dutch oven.

6 Add the corn to the meat mixture; over high heat, heat to boiling. Reduce heat to low; cover and simmer 5 minutes or until the kernels of corn are tender.

Tenderloin

Barbecued Pot Roast

Color index
page 50

Begin 4 hrs
ahead

12 servings

257 cals per
serving

Good source
of iron

2 tablespoons salad oil
*1 5-pound beef chuck 7-
    bone (center cut) pot
    roast, cut 2½ inches
    thick*
2 medium onions, sliced
1 garlic clove, minced
*1 8-ounce can tomato
    sauce*
*1 6-ounce can tomato
    paste*

*²/₃ cup packed light
    brown sugar*
½ cup cider vinegar
2 teaspoons salt
*2 tablespoons
    Worcestershire*
1 teaspoon dry mustard
¼ teaspoon pepper
2 bay leaves
parsley sprigs for garnish

1. In 8-quart Dutch oven over medium-high heat, in hot salad oil, cook pot roast until well browned on both sides. Remove meat to platter.
2. In same Dutch oven over medium heat, in drippings, cook onions and garlic until lightly browned, about 5 minutes, stirring occasionally. Spoon off drippings from Dutch oven. Stir in tomato sauce and remaining ingredients except parsley. Return meat to Dutch oven. Over high heat, heat to boiling. Reduce heat to low; cover and simmer 3¼ hours or until meat is fork-tender, turning meat once.
3. To serve: Place meat on platter. Skim fat from liquid; discard bay leaves; spoon liquid into gravy boat. Garnish roast with parsley.

Mushroom Sherry Pot Roast

Color index
page 52

Begin 3 hrs
ahead

10 servings

195 cals per
serving

Good source
of iron

1 tablespoon salad oil
*1 2¾-pound beef
    chuck shoulder
    pot roast boneless,
    cut 1½ inches thick*
¾ pound mushrooms
*⅓ cup dry sherry
    water*

1 teaspoon salt
1 bay leaf
*1 tablespoon butter or
    margarine*
*1 tablespoon all-purpose
    flour*
parsley sprigs for garnish

1. In 12-inch skillet over medium-high heat, in hot oil, cook roast until well browned on both sides. Reserve 6 large mushrooms for garnish; remove stems. Dice stems and remaining mushrooms.
2. Add diced mushrooms, sherry, ⅓ cup water, salt and bay leaf to skillet; heat to boiling. Reduce heat to low; cover and simmer 2 hours until meat is fork-tender, turning once.
3. *About 15 minutes before meat is done:* Flute reserved mushroom caps: Hold mushroom, top up. Beginning at center-top of mushroom and rotating cap, cut curved slit from center of cap to outside edge. Space several curved slits around cap. Cut second set of slits parallel to the first to make thin wedges. Lift out wedges; add to skillet.
4. In small skillet over medium-low heat, in hot butter, cook mushroom caps, turning once, until golden brown, about 5 minutes; keep warm.
5. When roast is done, place on warm platter; keep warm. In cup, blend flour and 2 tablespoons water. Gradually stir into liquid in skillet; cook, stirring, until slightly thickened; discard bay leaf.
6. To serve, pour some gravy over roast. Garnish with fluted mushrooms and parsley. Pass remaining gravy in gravy boat.

Filets Mignons with Mustard-Caper Sauce

Color index
page 51

Begin 30 mins
ahead

6 servings

420 cals per
serving

Good source
of iron,
niacin

3 tablespoons butter
*6 loin tenderloin steaks,
    each cut 1½ inches
    thick*
½ cup dry vermouth
*2 tablespoons chopped
    green onions*
½ cup water
*½ cup heavy or whipping
    cream*

2 tablespoons capers
*2½ teaspoons prepared
    mustard*
¾ teaspoon salt
*½ teaspoon coarsely
    ground black pepper*
*1 beef-flavor bouillon
    cube or envelope*
watercress for garnish

1. In 12-inch skillet over medium-high heat, in hot butter, cook steaks until underside is browned, about 4 minutes; turn and cook about 5 minutes longer for rare. Remove steaks to warm platter and keep warm.
2. Reduce heat to medium. To drippings in skillet add vermouth and green onions; cook about 2 minutes, stirring to loosen brown bits on bottom of skillet. Stir in water, heavy cream, capers, prepared mustard, salt, coarsely ground black pepper and bouillon cube; heat sauce to boiling.
3. To serve: Garnish platter with watercress. Pass sauce in gravy boat.

Châteaubriand

Color index
page 55

Begin 1½ hrs
ahead

8 servings

501 cals per
serving

Good source
of iron,
vitamin A,
niacin

8 large artichokes
*2 2-pound beef
    loin tenderloin
    roasts*

2 teaspoons salt
*Béarnaise Sauce
    (page 463)*

1. Prepare artichokes (page 276), but cut off two-thirds of tops, leaving 1-inch bottoms. Cook bottoms; cool slightly; with spoon, scoop out and discard fuzzy "chokes." Return the artichokes to cooking liquid and keep them warm.
2. Preheat the broiler if manufacturer directs. Sprinkle roasts with salt. Place both pieces of meat on rack in the broiling pan; broil 30 minutes for rare or until of the desired doneness, turning once.
3. Prepare Béarnaise Sauce.
4. To serve: With slotted spoon, remove artichoke bottoms from cooking liquid; drain on paper towels; spoon some Béarnaise Sauce into center of each. Slice meat thickly. Arrange meat slices on center of warm large platter and surround them with the stuffed artichokes.

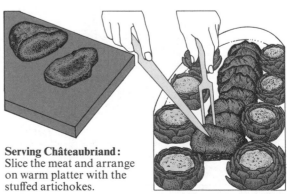

Serving Châteaubriand:
Slice the meat and arrange
on warm platter with the
stuffed artichokes.

Tender steaks

London Broil

*1 1½-pound high-
    quality beef flank
    steak*
seasoned salt
seasoned pepper
2 medium tomatoes
*bottled Italian
    dressing*
6 large mushrooms

Color index
page 51

Begin 30 mins
ahead

4 servings

308 cals per
serving

Good source
of iron,
niacin

1 Preheat broiler if
manufacturer directs.
With sharp knife, score
both sides of the
steak; place on rack in
broiling pan.

2 Sprinkle steak with ½
teaspoon seasoned salt,
⅛ teaspoon seasoned pep-
per. Cut tomatoes in half.

3 Brush tomatoes with
Italian dressing and
arrange, cut side up,
around steak; broil 5
minutes. Meanwhile, wash
and slice mushrooms.

4 With tongs, turn steak;
sprinkle with ½ tea-
spoon seasoned salt, ⅛
teaspoon seasoned pepper.

5 Arrange mushroom
slices in overlapping
rows on broiler rack; brush
with Italian dressing.

6 Broil the steak 5
minutes more for rare
or 6 minutes for medium.
To check the doneness,
with a knife, make a small
cut in the center of meat.

7 With knife in slanting
position, carve thin
slices across width of
steak. Serve slices with
broiled vegetables. Spoon
drippings over, if you like.

Marinated Porterhouse Steak

*1 4-pound beef loin
    porterhouse or pin bone
    sirloin steak, cut about
    1½ inches thick*
½ cup red Burgundy

*2 teaspoons seasoned
    salt*
*¼ teaspoon seasoned
    pepper*

Color index
page 52

Begin early in
day or
day ahead

12 servings

192 cals per
serving

Good source
of iron

1. In large, shallow baking dish, place steak. For
marinade, pour wine over steak. Cover and refrigerate at least 4 hours or overnight, turning meat
occasionally.
2. *About 40 minutes before serving:* Preheat broiler if
manufacturer directs. With tongs, place steak on
greased rack in broiling pan; reserve marinade.
Sprinkle steak with seasoned salt and pepper.
3. Broil steak 30 minutes for rare or until of desired
doneness, basting occasionally with marinade and
turning once.

ZESTY MARINADE: Prepare as above, but in step
1, omit wine; substitute mixture of *⅓ cup bottled
steak sauce, 3 tablespoons lemon juice, 2 tablespoons
salad oil* and *1½ teaspoons sugar.* In step 2, omit
seasoned salt and seasoned pepper; sprinkle steak
with *½ teaspoon salt* and *¼ teaspoon pepper.*

Steak Diane

*4 beef rib eye steaks,
    each cut about ½ inch
    thick*
salt
pepper
*4 tablespoons butter or
    margarine*

¼ cup brandy
2 small shallots, minced
*3 tablespoons chopped
    chives*
½ cup dry sherry

Color index
page 52

Begin 20 mins
ahead

4 servings

365 cals per
serving

Good source
of iron,
vitamin A,
niacin

1. On cutting board, with meat mallet, edge of plate
or the dull edge of French knife, pound the steaks
until about ¼ inch thick, turning occasionally.
Sprinkle each of the steaks with salt and pepper.
2. In chafing dish over high heat, in 1 tablespoon hot
butter or margarine, cook one steak just until both
sides are browned.
3. Pour 1 tablespoon brandy over steak and with
match set aflame. When the flaming stops, stir in ¼
each of shallots and chives; cook, stirring constantly, until the shallots are tender, about 1 minute.
Add 2 tablespoons sherry; heat through.
4. Place the steak on a warm dinner plate and pour
sherry mixture over it. Keep warm. Repeat with
remaining steaks.

Pounding steaks: Use a
meat mallet to pound
steaks to ¼ inch thick.

Flaming steaks: Pour over
brandy then use long
match to set steaks aflame.

Deviled Round Steak

Color index
page 54

Begin 1½ hrs
ahead

12 servings

274 cals per
serving

Good source
of iron

1 4-pound beef top round
  steak, cut 1½ inches
  thick
6 tablespoons butter or
  margarine, softened
1 tablespoon
  Worcestershire
1 teaspoon dry
  mustard
½ teaspoon curry
  powder
¼ teaspoon salt
¼ teaspoon pepper
1 cup dried bread crumbs

1. Prepare outdoor grill for barbecuing. Meanwhile, trim any excess fat from the round steak. In small bowl, mix the butter or margarine with the Worcestershire, dry mustard, curry powder, salt and pepper; set mixture aside.
2. Place steak on grill over medium coals; grill 35 minutes for rare or until of the desired doneness, turning occasionally.
3. Remove the steak from the grill. With narrow metal spatula, spread one side of steak with ½ of butter mixture and pat on ½ of bread crumbs. Repeat with remaining butter mixture and bread crumbs on other side of steak.
4. Return steak to grill; continue grilling 5 minutes longer or until crumbs are golden, turning once.

TO BROIL IN OVEN: About 1 hour before serving, preheat broiler if manufacturer directs. Place steak on rack in broiling pan. About 3 to 5 inches from source of heat, broil steak 35 minutes for rare or until of desired doneness, turning once. Remove steak from broiler and season on both sides as above with butter mixture and bread crumbs. Return steak to broiler; broil 3 to 5 minutes on each side or until crumbs are golden.

Continental Beef Steak

Color index
page 55

Begin 1 hr
ahead

12 servings

254 cals per
serving

Good source
of iron,
vitamin C

1 4-pound beef top round
  steak, cut about 1½
  inches thick
unseasoned instant meat
  tenderizer
½ teaspoon oregano
¼ teaspoon seasoned
  pepper
1 garlic clove, minced
3 large green or red
  peppers
3 tablespoons salad oil
1½ cups thinly sliced
  celery
2 14½-ounce cans sliced
  baby tomatoes,
  drained
1 10-ounce jar colossal
  stuffed olives, drained
  and halved
2 tablespoons capers,
  drained

1. Preheat broiler if manufacturer directs. With sharp knife, lightly score both sides of steak. Use meat tenderizer as label directs; sprinkle both sides of steak with oregano, seasoned pepper and minced garlic. Place steak on greased rack in broiling pan; broil 35 minutes for rare or until of desired doneness, turning once.
2. Meanwhile, slice the green peppers crosswise into rings; discard the seeds.
3. In 12-inch skillet over medium-high heat, in hot salad oil, cook peppers and celery 10 minutes or until tender-crisp. Add tomatoes, olives and capers; heat through.
4. Place steak on warm large platter; with slotted spoon, spoon vegetables around it.

Steak Medici

Color index
page 53

Begin 25 mins
ahead

4 servings

416 cals per
serving

Good source
of iron,
vitamin A,
riboflavin,
niacin

4 tablespoons butter or
  margarine
4 beef top loin steaks
  boneless, each cut
  ¾ inch thick
½ pound mushrooms, cut
  into ¼-inch slices
½ teaspoon salt or
  seasoned salt
¼ cup red port wine
chopped parsley for
  garnish

1 In 12-inch skillet over medium-high heat, in 2 tablespoons hot butter, brown steaks on both sides. Use tongs to turn them.

2 Cook until of the desired doneness, about 3 minutes per side for rare. Remove the steaks to a large warm platter and keep warm.

3 In same skillet over medium heat, melt the remaining butter.

4 Add the sliced mushrooms together with the salt and cook, stirring, until the mushrooms are just tender.

5 Stir in wine, scraping to loosen brown bits from bottom of skillet.

6 Pour mushroom and wine mixture over steaks; garnish steaks with chopped parsley and serve immediately.

Tender steaks

Sesame Chuck Steak

Color index page 50

Begin early in day or day ahead

10 servings

293 cals per serving

Good source of calcium, iron

½ cup salad oil
⅓ cup sesame seed
4 medium onions
½ cup soy sauce
¼ cup lemon juice
1 tablespoon sugar
¼ teaspoon cracked black pepper
2 garlic cloves, crushed
1 2½-pound beef chuck blade steak, cut 1 inch thick
watercress sprigs for garnish

1 In 10-inch skillet over medium-high heat, in hot salad oil, cook sesame seed until golden, stirring. Slice onions thickly.

2 In 13" by 9" baking dish, mix sesame-seed-oil mixture and onions. Add next 5 ingredients.

3 Trim excess fat from steak; add meat to marinade; turn to coat; cover; chill at least 8 hours, turning occasionally.

4 *45 minutes before serving:* Preheat broiler if manufacturer directs. Place steak on rack in broiling pan. Drain onions; set aside; reserve marinade.

5 Broil steak 25 minutes for rare or as desired, brushing frequently with the marinade. Turn steak once.

6 In 10-inch skillet over medium heat, cook onions and remaining marinade until tender, stirring occasionally.

7 To serve, arrange the steak and sliced onions on a heated large platter. Garnish with sprigs of watercress.

Cubed Steaks with Fresh Tomato Sauce

Color index page 53

Begin 45 mins ahead

8 servings

241 cals per serving

Good source of iron

¼ cup salad oil
2 pounds beef or veal cubed steaks
6 medium tomatoes
cold water
¼ cup chopped green onions

2 tablespoons sugar
1 teaspoon salt
2 teaspoons basil
2 tablespoons cornstarch

1. In 10- or 12-inch skillet over medium-high heat, in hot salad oil, cook steaks, a few at a time, 2 or 3 minutes on each side or until of desired doneness; place on warm platter and keep warm. Chop 3 tomatoes and slice the rest.

2. Reduce heat to medium; to same skillet, add ¼ cup water, chopped tomatoes, green onions, sugar, salt and basil. Blend cornstarch and ¼ cup water until smooth; gradually stir into tomato mixture and cook, stirring, until thickened. Add sliced tomatoes; cook until heated through. Spoon tomato mixture over steaks.

Teriyaki Beef Kabobs

Color index page 53

Begin 4 hrs ahead or early in day

8 servings

207 cals per serving

Good source of iron

1 2-pound beef top round steak, cut about 1 inch thick
¼ cup packed light brown sugar
¼ cup soy sauce
2 tablespoons lemon juice
1 tablespoon salad oil

¼ teaspoon ground ginger
1 garlic clove, minced
1 small pineapple, cut into 1-inch chunks

1. Trim any excess fat from steak and cut meat into 1-inch chunks.

2. Prepare marinade: Combine brown sugar, soy sauce, lemon juice, oil, ginger and garlic; stir in beef chunks. Cover and refrigerate at least 3 hours, stirring meat often.

3. *About 30 minutes before serving:* Preheat broiler if manufacturer directs. Thread meat and pineapple chunks alternately on 12-inch metal skewers. (Pineapple quickly tenderizes meat, so thread skewers just before broiling; if done earlier, meat becomes mushy.)

4. Broil 15 minutes until rare or of desired doneness, basting occasionally with marinade and turning once. To check doneness make slit in center of meat.

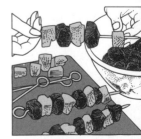

Marinating beef: Stir meat into marinade; cover; refrigerate 3 hours, stirring mixture often.

Threading skewers: Just before broiling, thread meat and pineapple alternately on skewers.

Less tender steaks

Carbonnades à la Flamande

Color index
page 51

Begin 2³/₄ hrs
ahead

10 servings

260 cals per
serving

Good source
of iron

*4 slices bacon, cut into
1-inch pieces
3 large onions (about
1¹/₂ pounds), sliced
3 pounds beef for stew,
cut into 2-inch chunks
salad oil
2 tablespoons all-purpose
flour
1 12-ounce can beer
¹/₂ cup water
1 beef-flavor bouillon
cube or envelope or 1
teaspoon beef-flavor
instant bouillon*

*1 small bay leaf
2 teaspoons sugar
³/₄ teaspoon salt
¹/₄ teaspoon thyme
leaves
¹/₈ teaspoon coarsely
ground black pepper
2 tablespoons red-wine
vinegar
fresh thyme sprigs
for garnish*

1. In 12-inch skillet over medium heat, cook bacon pieces until browned, stirring occasionally; with slotted spoon, remove bacon to 3-quart casserole. In drippings remaining in skillet, cook onions until tender and lightly browned (about 5 minutes), stirring occasionally. With slotted spoon, remove onions to casserole.
2. In drippings remaining in skillet, over medium-high heat, cook beef chunks, a few pieces at a time, until well browned on all sides (adding salad oil if necessary); remove beef chunks to the casserole as they brown.
3. In same skillet over medium heat, into 2 tablespoons hot salad oil, stir flour until well blended; cook, stirring constantly, until flour and salad oil mixture is dark brown. Gradually stir in beer and water; cook until sauce thickens slightly and boils, stirring constantly. Stir in bouillon, bay leaf, sugar, salt, thyme leaves, and coarsely ground black pepper.
4. Pour sauce over meat in casserole; mix well. Bake, covered in 350°F. oven, stirring occasionally, for 1³/₄ hours or until meat is fork-tender. Using a basting spoon or ladle, carefully skim fat from sauce in casserole. Discard bay leaf. Stir in wine vinegar.
5. If you like, transfer meat and sauce to large heated serving dish; garnish with fresh thyme sprigs and serve.

Browning the bacon: In 12-inch skillet over medium heat, cook 1-inch bacon pieces, stirring occasionally, until browned.

Adding the beer: When the salad oil and flour mixture is dark brown, gradually add beer and water; cook, stirring constantly, until sauce thickens and boils.

Spicy Beef Chuck Steak

Color index
page 54

Begin 2 hrs
ahead

10 servings

216 cals per
serving

Good source
of iron

*1 tablespoon salad oil
1 beef chuck underblade
steak (about 3 pounds),
cut 1 inch thick
¹/₂ cup bottled steak
sauce
¹/₄ cup water*

*3 tablespoons brown
sugar
2 tablespoons prepared
mustard
1 teaspoon lemon juice
parsley sprigs for garnish*

1. In 12-inch skillet over medium-high heat, in hot salad oil, cook chuck steak until well browned on both sides.
2. Meanwhile, in cup, combine steak sauce, water, brown sugar, mustard and lemon juice until blended. Pour mixture over steak; heat to boiling. Reduce heat to low; cover and simmer steak 1¹/₂ hours or until fork-tender, turning steak once.
3. To serve, with 2 pancake turners, remove steak to warm large platter; garnish with parsley. With a spoon, skim fat from liquid in skillet and discard. Pour liquid over steak or serve separately.

197 cals per
serving

BEEF STEAK CREOLE: Prepare as in step 1, above, but use 8-quart Dutch oven and in step 2, omit steak sauce, water, brown sugar, prepared mustard and lemon juice. Remove meat from Dutch oven and into hot fat, stir *¹/₄ cup all-purpose flour*, stirring constantly until flour is dark brown (mixture will be thick). Add *2 large celery stalks*, diced, *1 medium green pepper*, diced and *1 medium onion*, diced; cook over medium heat until vegetables are tender, about 10 minutes. Add *one 16-ounce can stewed tomatoes, 1 tablespoon sugar, 1 teaspoon salt* and *¹/₂ teaspoon hot pepper sauce.* Add meat and cook.

Beef with Leeks and Carrots

Color index
page 54

Begin 2 hrs
ahead

8 servings

214 cals per
serving

Good source
of iron

*1 tablespoon salad
oil
1 beef chuck
7-bone steak
cut 1 inch thick
(about 2¹/₂ pounds)
1 beef-flavor bouillon
cube or envelope
1 bay leaf
¹/₂ teaspoon salt*

*¹/₄ teaspoon thyme
leaves
¹/₈ teaspoon pepper
water
3 large leeks
6 large carrots
1 tablespoon all-purpose
flour*

1. In 8-quart Dutch oven over medium-high heat, in hot salad oil, cook chuck steak until well browned on both sides. Add bouillon, bay leaf, salt, thyme, pepper and 1 cup water; heat to boiling. Reduce heat to low; cover and simmer steak 1¹/₄ hours or until almost fork-tender.
2. Meanwhile, cut off roots and discard tough outer green leaves from leeks. Cut leeks lengthwise in half; rinse under running cold water to remove sand. Cut leeks crosswise into 2-inch pieces. Thinly slice carrots.
3. Place leeks and carrots in liquid around steak. Cover and cook 20 minutes longer or until steak and vegetables are fork-tender; discard bay leaf. In cup, combine flour and ¹/₄ cup water until blended. Stir flour mixutre into hot liquid in pan. Cook over medium heat, stirring until slightly thickened.

Less tender steaks

Swiss Steak with Tomato

Color index page 55

Begin 2½ hrs ahead

10 servings

211 cals per serving

Good source of iron

1 2½- to 3-pound beef chuck arm steak boneless, cut about 1 inch thick
2 tablespoons all-purpose flour
3 tablespoons salad oil
2 large onions, thinly sliced
1 small green pepper, diced
1 8-ounce can tomato sauce
1 small garlic clove, minced
¾ teaspoon salt
¼ teaspoon pepper
1 bay leaf
hot mashed potatoes, buttered cooked noodles or cooked rice (optional)
celery leaves for garnish (optional)

1 Cut off any excess fat from arm steak. On cutting board, coat meat on one side with half of flour.

2 With a meat mallet, pound the meat well. Turn meat over and repeat the flouring and pounding with the mallet on the other side.

3 In 12-inch skillet over medium-high heat, in hot salad oil, cook meat until well browned on both sides. Remove meat.

4 To drippings in skillet, add onions and green pepper and cook, stirring frequently, until onions are lightly browned, about 5 minutes.

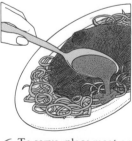

5 Add tomato sauce, next 4 ingredients and meat; heat to boiling. Reduce heat to low; cover and simmer about 2 hours or until meat is fork-tender, turning meat once.

6 To serve, place meat on warm platter. Discard bay leaf; spoon fat from liquid in skillet. Serve meat and liquid with mashed potatoes. If you like, garnish with celery leaves.

Oriental Anise Beef

Color index page 53

Begin 2¼ hrs ahead

8 servings

358 cals per serving

Good source of iron

1 bunch green onions
½ cup dry sherry
¼ cup soy sauce
1 tablespoon sugar
2 teaspoons anise seed
½ teaspoon ground ginger
water
1 beef chuck shoulder steak boneless, cut 1½ inches thick (about 2 pounds)
2 teaspoons cornstarch
hot cooked rice

1. Cut off roots from onions; cut onions into 1-inch pieces. In 10-inch skillet, place half of the onion pieces; stir in sherry, soy sauce, sugar, anise seed, ground ginger and ¼ cup water. Add the steak. Over high heat, heat to boiling. Reduce heat to low; cover and simmer steak 1¾ hours or until fork-tender, turning steak once.
2. When steak is done, remove to platter; keep warm. In cup, combine ¼ cup water and cornstarch until blended. Gradually stir cornstarch mixture into liquid in skillet. Cook over medium heat, stirring constantly, until thickened. Stir in remaining half of onion pieces. Spoon sauce over steak. Cut steak into thin slices to serve. Serve with rice.

Creamy Top Blade Steaks

Color index page 50

Begin 1¾ hrs ahead

6 servings

325 cals per serving

Good source of iron

1 tablespoon salad oil
4 beef chuck top blade steaks boneless, each cut 1 inch thick (about 1½ pounds)
⅓ cup water
1 beef-flavor bouillon cube or envelope
¼ teaspoon salt
⅛ teaspoon pepper
¾ 8-ounce package medium egg noodles
1 8-ounce container sour cream
½ teaspoon dill weed
watercress for garnish

1. In 12-inch skillet over medium-high heat, in hot oil, cook steaks until well browned on both sides. Stir in water, bouillon, salt and pepper; heat to boiling. Reduce heat to low; cover and simmer steaks 1¼ hours or until fork-tender, turning steaks with tongs once during cooking.
2. Prepare noodles as label directs.
3. When steaks are done, remove to warm large platter. Drain noodles; place on platter; keep warm. Stir sour cream and dill into hot liquid in skillet. Cook, stirring, until slightly thickened (do not boil). Spoon some sauce over steaks; pass remainder in sauceboat. Garnish platter with watercress.

Serving steaks: Spoon some sauce over meat and noodles. Pass remainder separately. Garnish platter with watercress.

Braised Steak Caesar-style

Color index
page 51

Begin 1¾ hrs
ahead

4 servings

472 cals per
serving

Good source
of iron,
niacin

⅓ cup olive or salad oil
2 garlic cloves, sliced
4 diagonal slices French
  bread, each cut ½ inch
  thick
4 beef eye round steaks,
  each cut 1 inch thick
  (about 1½ pounds)
1 2-ounce can anchovy
  fillets, drained

1 tablespoon
  Worcestershire
1 teaspoon lemon juice
¼ teaspoon dry mustard
  water
1 tablespoon all-purpose
  flour
chopped parsley for
  garnish

1. In 10-inch skillet over medium heat, in hot oil, brown garlic; discard garlic. Spoon all but 1 tablespoon oil into a small bowl.
2. In remaining oil, cook bread until golden on both sides, adding a little more garlic-flavored oil if needed. Remove bread to platter.
3. In same skillet over medium-high heat, heat remaining garlic-flavored oil. Add steaks; cook until well browned on both sides. Meanwhile, mince enough anchovies to make 1 tablespoon.
4. When steaks are browned, stir in minced anchovies, Worcestershire, lemon juice, mustard and ⅓ cup water; heat to boiling. Reduce heat to low; cover and simmer steaks 1¼ hours or until fork-tender, turning once.
5. Place 1 steak on each piece of toast; keep warm. In cup, blend flour and ¼ cup water. Stir into hot liquid in skillet. Cook over medium heat, stirring until thickened. Spoon some sauce over steaks; pass remainder in sauceboat. Garnish with parsley and remaining anchovies.

Beef Steak Stroganoff

Color index
page 54

Begin 1¾ hrs
ahead

6 servings

315 cals per
serving

Good source
of iron,
niacin

1 tablespoon butter
4 beef chuck top blade
  steaks boneless, each
  cut 1 inch thick (about
  1½ pounds)
1 medium onion, sliced
¾ teaspoon salt
⅛ teaspoon pepper
water
2 4- or 4½-ounce cans
  whole mushrooms

1 8-ounce package wide
  egg noodles
1 tablespoon all-purpose
  flour
½ cup sour cream
1 tablespoon chopped
  parsley for garnish
  (optional)

1. In 12-inch skillet over medium-high heat, in hot butter, cook steaks and onion until meat is well browned on both sides, about 10 minutes. Add salt, pepper, ¼ cup water and liquid from mushrooms; heat to boiling. Reduce heat to low; cover and simmer 1¼ hours or until steaks are fork-tender. Add mushrooms; heat through.
2. About 20 minutes before steaks are done, prepare noodles as label directs; drain. Spoon noodles onto warm platter.
3. Remove steaks and mushrooms to platter with noodles; keep warm. In cup stir flour and ¼ cup water until blended. Gradually stir into liquid in skillet. Cook over medium heat until sauce is thickened, stirring. Stir in sour cream; heat through (do not boil). Spoon sauce over steaks and noodles. Sprinkle with parsley if you like.

Celery-stuffed Flank Steak

Color index
page 51

Begin 2½ hrs
ahead

8 servings

207 cals per
serving

Good source
of iron

1 2-pound beef flank
  steak
pepper
1 cup fresh bread crumbs
¾ cup diced celery
1 small onion, minced
butter or margarine
½ teaspoon salt

⅛ teaspoon thyme leaves,
  crushed
water
all-purpose flour
1 tablespoon cornstarch
¼ teaspoon ground
  ginger

1. With a large sharp knife, score the steak to make a diamond pattern on both sides; sprinkle the steak with pepper.
2. In medium bowl, combine bread crumbs, celery, onion, 1 tablespoon melted butter or margarine, salt, thyme, ⅛ teaspoon pepper and 2 tablespoons water; spread evenly on one side of steak, leaving a 1-inch border. Roll steak from a long side, jelly-roll fashion; secure with toothpicks or string. On waxed paper, coat meat lightly with flour.
3. In 5-quart Dutch oven over medium-high heat, in 2 tablespoons hot butter or margarine, cook the meat until well browned on all sides. Add 1 cup water; heat to boiling. Reduce heat to low; cover and simmer 2 hours or until meat is fork-tender, stirring liquid and adding water, if necessary. Place meat on warm platter: remove toothpicks or string and keep meat warm.
4. In cup, blend cornstarch and ginger with 2 tablespoons cold water until smooth; stir into hot liquid in Dutch oven and cook over medium heat, stirring constantly, until mixture is thickened. Stir in more water, if necessary. Serve gravy separately in sauceboat, to eat with steak.

Scoring steak: Use a sharp knife to score both sides of the flank steak in a diamond pattern.

Stuffing steak: Spread stuffing then roll up from long side jelly-roll fashion. Secure with toothpicks.

Serving steak: Cut the steak into slices and serve with gravy passed separately in sauceboat.

Stew meat

Beef Stew

2¹/₂ pounds beef for stew
¹/₃ cup all-purpose flour
¹/₃ cup salad oil
1 large onion, chopped
1 garlic clove, minced
3 cups water
4 beef-bouillon cubes
³/₄ teaspoon salt
¹/₂ teaspoon
   Worcestershire
¹/₄ teaspoon pepper
5 medium potatoes,
   cut in chunks
1 16-ounce bag carrots,
   cut in chunks
1 10-ounce package
   frozen peas

Color index
page 54

Begin 3¹/₂ hrs
ahead

10 servings

307 cals per
serving

Good source
of iron

1 Cut meat into 1¹/₂-inch chunks. On waxed paper, coat stew meat with flour; reserve leftover flour. In 6-quart Dutch oven over medium-high heat, heat oil.

2 Brown meat all over in oil, a few pieces at a time; remove pieces as they brown. Reduce heat to medium.

3 To drippings in pan, add onion and garlic; cook 3 minutes, stirring, until onion is almost tender. Stir in reserved flour.

4 Gradually add water, bouillon, salt, Worcestershire, pepper; cook, stirring, until mixture is slightly thickened.

5 Add meat; heat to boiling, stirring. Reduce heat to low; cover; simmer 2¹/₂ hours until almost tender, stirring occasionally.

6 Add potato and carrot chunks; over medium heat, heat to boiling. Reduce heat to low; cover and simmer 20 minutes.

7 Stir in frozen peas; cover and simmer 5 to 10 minutes or until all the vegetables are tender. Serve immediately.

Beef Bourguignon

1 8-ounce package sliced
   bacon, cut into 1-inch
   pieces
20 small white onions
3 pounds beef for stew,
   cut into 2-inch chunks
all-purpose flour
1 large carrot,
   chopped
1 large onion,
   chopped
¹/₄ cup brandy

2 garlic cloves,
   crushed
1¹/₂ teaspoons salt
¹/₂ teaspoon thyme
   leaves, crushed
¹/₄ teaspoon pepper
1 bay leaf
3 cups red Burgundy
butter or margarine
1 pound mushrooms,
   sliced

Color index
page 53

Begin 4¹/₂ hrs
ahead

10 servings

387 cals per
serving

Good source
of iron,
niacin

1. In 6-quart Dutch oven over medium-high heat, cook the bacon pieces until browned. With a slotted spoon, remove the bacon to paper towels to drain; set aside.

2. Discard all but 3 tablespoons drippings. In drippings in Dutch oven, cook small white onions until lightly browned, stirring occasionally. With slotted spoon, remove the onions and place in a small bowl; set aside.

3. Meanwhile, on waxed paper, coat meat chunks with 3 tablespoons flour. In drippings in Dutch oven over medium-high heat, cook meat, several pieces at a time, until well browned on all sides, removing pieces as they brown.

4. To drippings in the Dutch oven, add the chopped carrot and onion and cook over medium heat, stirring frequently, until tender, about 5 minutes. Return the beef to Dutch oven; pour brandy over all and set aflame with match. When flaming stops, add reserved bacon, garlic, salt, thyme leaves, pepper, bay leaf and Burgundy. Cover and bake in 325°F. oven 3¹/₂ hours or until fork-tender.

5. About 1 hour before meat is done, in 10-inch skillet over medium heat, in 2 tablespoons hot butter or margarine, cook mushrooms until golden brown, about 7 minutes.

6. Meanwhile, in small bowl with spoon, mix 2 tablespoons softened butter or margarine and 2 tablespoons flour until smooth.

7. Remove Dutch oven from oven. Into hot liquid in Dutch oven, add flour mixture, ¹/₂ teaspoon at a time, stirring after each addition, until blended. Add reserved onions and mushrooms to Dutch oven. Cover and bake until onions are fork-tender. Serve immediately.

Flaming beef: Pour brandy over beef, carrot and onion and immediately set aflame with a long match.

Thickening sauce: Stir in flour mixture, ¹/₂ teaspoon at a time, until blended; return to oven.

Color index page 50
Begin 3 hrs ahead
8 servings
248 cals per serving
Good source of iron, niacin

California Beef Stew

3 bacon slices, diced
2 pounds beef for stew,
*   cut in 1½-inch chunks*
water
1 cup dry red wine
1 beef-flavor bouillon
*   cube*
2 garlic cloves, minced
½ small onion, minced
1 teaspoon salt

¼ teaspoon thyme leaves
1 strip orange peel
18 small white onions
¾ pound small
*   mushrooms*
2 tablespoons cornstarch
1 10-ounce package
*   frozen peas*
½ cup pitted ripe olives,
*   drained*

1. In 6-quart Dutch oven over medium-high heat, fry bacon until crisp; push bacon to side of pan.
2. To drippings in pan, add stew meat and cook until well browned. Stir in 1 cup water, wine and next 6 ingredients; heat to boiling. Reduce heat to low; cover and simmer 2½ hours or until meat is fork-tender, stirring occasionally.
3. Meanwhile, in covered, 2-quart saucepan over high heat, in about 1 inch boiling salted water, cook onions 10 minutes; add mushrooms; cook 5 more minutes; drain.
4. Blend cornstarch and 3 tablespoons water; stir into stew; cook over medium heat, stirring, until thickened. Add onions, mushrooms, frozen peas and olives; cover; cook 10 minutes or until peas are fork-tender. Serve immediately.

Color index page 52
Begin early in day
8 servings
192 cals per serving
Good source of iron

Pressure-cooked Beef Stew

½ cup red table wine
2 tablespoons salad oil
2 pounds beef for stew,
*   cut into 1½-inch chunks*
¼ pound lean salt pork,
*   cut into ½-inch cubes*
1 16-ounce can tomatoes
1 large onion, minced
1 large carrot, minced
1 celery stalk, minced

½ garlic clove, minced
1 bay leaf
1½ teaspoons salt
1 teaspoon thyme leaves
3 parsley sprigs
12 stuffed olives, halved
1 3-ounce can whole
*   mushrooms, drained*
hot cooked noodles
*   (optional)*

1. Prepare marinade: In large bowl, combine wine and salad oil. Add beef chunks and turn over to coat with marinade. Cover and refrigerate at least 4 hours, turning often.
2. *About 30 minutes before serving:* Drain meat, discard marinade. In 4-quart pressure cooker over medium-high heat, fry salt pork until golden; add beef and cook until well browned. Add tomatoes and their liquid and remaining ingredients except mushrooms. Cover and bring cooker to 15 pounds pressure as manufacturer directs; cook 20 minutes. Remove cooker from heat and reduce pressure quickly as manufacturer directs before uncovering. Add mushrooms and heat. Discard parsley and bay leaf. Serve over noodles if you like.

Steak and Kidney Pie

1 beef kidney (about 1
*   pound)*
2½ pounds beef for stew,
*   cut into 1-inch chunks*
¼ cup all-purpose
*   flour*
salad oil
1 large onion, chopped
½ cup dry red wine or
*   beer*
water
2 beef-flavor bouillon
*   cubes or envelopes*
2 teaspoons
*   Worcestershire*

¼ teaspoon pepper
pastry for 9-inch
*   Unbaked Piecrust*
*   (page 344)*
1 egg yolk

Color index page 53
Begin 3¾ hrs ahead
10 servings
440 cals per serving
Good source of iron, riboflavin, niacin

1 Wash kidney; remove membrane and hard white parts and with sharp knife, cut into 1-inch chunks.

2 On waxed paper, coat kidney and beef chunks with flour. In 5-quart Dutch oven over medium-high heat, heat 3 tablespoons oil.

3 Cook kidney and beef chunks, several pieces at a time, until well browned. Remove pieces as they brown and add more oil, as needed.

4 Reduce heat to medium; add onion to drippings. Cook until onion is almost tender, about 3 minutes, stirring occasionally.

5 Stir in wine, ½ cup water, bouillon, Worcestershire and pepper, stirring to dissolve bouillon cubes.

6 Add meat and heat to boiling; reduce heat to low. Cover and simmer 2 hours or until meat is fork-tender.

7 Spoon mixture into 2-quart round shallow casserole. Preheat oven to 400°F. Prepare pastry; roll into circle 1 inch larger than casserole.

8 Fit crust loosely over meat mixture; trim back pastry overhang to about 1 inch and make a fluted edge.

9 Beat egg yolk with 1 teaspoon water. Brush pastry with egg-yolk mixture. With point of knife, make slits in crust.

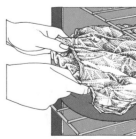

10 Bake pie 40 minutes until browned and bubbly. Cover loosely with foil if crust browns too quickly.

Short ribs and shanks

Herbed Short Ribs

Color index page 53

Begin 3 hrs ahead

4 servings

510 cals per serving

Good source of iron, niacin

all-purpose flour
3 pounds beef chuck short ribs
2 tablespoons salad oil or shortening
water
1 small onion, chopped
2 tablespoons catchup
1½ teaspoons salt
¼ teaspoon pepper
¼ teaspoon thyme leaves, crushed

1 In ¼ cup flour on waxed paper, with tongs, coat the chuck short ribs well on all sides.

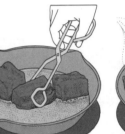

2 In 12-inch skillet with ovensafe handle over medium-high heat, in hot oil or shortening, cook meat until well browned on all sides.

3 Add ½ cup water, onion, catchup, salt, pepper and thyme to meat in the skillet.

4 Cover skillet. Bake in 350°F. oven 2½ hours or until meat is fork-tender, stirring once or twice during cooking.

5 With slotted spoon, remove meat to warm platter; keep warm while making gravy.

6 Spoon off all but 3 tablespoons drippings from skillet, leaving browned bits in pan; over medium heat, stir in 2 tablespoons flour.

7 Gradually stir in 1¼ cups water and cook, stirring constantly, until mixture is smooth and thickened. Spoon gravy over the meat.

Barbecued Short Ribs

Color index page 54

Begin early in day or day ahead

8 servings

401 cals per serving

Good source of iron, vitamin A

5 pounds beef chuck short ribs
water
1½ cups catchup
½ cup white vinegar
⅓ cup packed brown sugar
1 tablespoon Worcestershire

2 teaspoons grated lime peel
1½ teaspoons dry mustard
¾ teaspoon garlic salt
¼ teaspoon pepper

1. In 8-quart Dutch oven, cover beef short ribs with water; over high heat, heat to boiling. Reduce heat to low; cover and simmer 2 hours or until ribs are fork-tender. Remove ribs to platter; cover and refrigerate.

2. *About 1 hour before serving:* Prepare outdoor grill for barbecuing. Meanwhile, in small bowl combine catchup and remaining ingredients. Place cooked ribs on grill over medium coals; cook 20 to 25 minutes until heated through, brushing occasionally with catchup mixture and turning often.

Precooking ribs: Simmer ribs 2 hours until fork-tender. Remove to platter; cover and refrigerate.

Grilling ribs: Heat through ribs, brushing with catchup mixture and turning often.

TO BROIL IN OVEN: Precook ribs as above. About 40 minutes before serving, preheat broiler if manufacturer directs. Prepare catchup mixture as above. Place ribs on rack in broiling pan; broil ribs 20 to 25 minutes until heated through, brushing with catchup mixture occasionally and turning ribs once.

Beef Shanks with Vegetables

Color index page 55

Begin 4 hrs ahead

8 servings

457 cals per serving

Good source of calcium, iron, niacin

3 tablespoons salad oil
8 beef shank cross cuts, each cut about 1 inch thick
2 10¾-ounce cans condensed tomato soup
water
¼ cup sugar

1 tablespoon salt
¼ teaspoon pepper
10 large carrots, cut crosswise in half
6 small onions, cut in half
1 10-ounce package frozen lima beans

1. In 8-quart Dutch oven over medium-high heat, in hot oil, cook shanks until well browned.

2. Add undiluted soup, 2 cups water, sugar, salt and pepper; heat to boiling. Reduce heat to low; cover and simmer 2¼ hours, stirring occasionally.

3. Add carrots and continue cooking 40 minutes. Add onions and cook 30 minutes. Stir in beans and simmer 10 minutes more until meat and vegetables are tender. Serve immediately.

Brisket

Ground beef

New England "Boiled" Dinner

*1 4- to 5-pound beef
   brisket flat half
   boneless
1 garlic clove
1 bay leaf
1/2 teaspoon peppercorns
water
1 medium rutabaga
1 medium head cabbage
16 medium carrots
16 small red potatoes*

Color index
page 50

Begin 3½ hrs
ahead

16 servings

209 cals per
serving

Good source
of iron

1 In 8-quart Dutch oven, place beef, garlic, bay leaf, peppercorns and enough water to cover meat. Over high heat, heat to boiling.

2 Reduce heat to low; cover; simmer 3 to 3½ hours until meat is fork-tender. Remove meat with slotted spoon and keep it warm.

3 Cut rutabaga and cabbage into wedges and add with remaining vegetables to liquid in Dutch oven.

4 Over high heat, heat to boiling. Reduce heat to low; cover and simmer about 30 minutes or until the vegetables are fork-tender.

5 To serve, slice beef and arrange on warm large platter with rutabaga, cabbage, carrots and small red potatoes.

CORNED BEEF AND CABBAGE: Prepare as above but, for meat, use *one 4- to 5-pound corned beef brisket flat half boneless* and, for the vegetables, use only *1 large head cabbage*, cut into thin wedges; cook 3 to 3½ hours or until the meat is fork-tender. Add the cabbage wedges 15 minutes before the end of cooking time.

140 cals per
serving

OTHER VEGETABLES: Substitute the vegetables in the recipe above with a selection of the following: 1 10-ounce container Brussels sprouts, 1 pound whole green beans, 8 small white onions, 4 medium parsnips, cut in 2-inch chunks, and 4 medium turnips, cut in halves.

When beef is ground from a specific cut, it may carry the name of the cut, as "ground beef round." Beef ground from less tender cuts, is labeled "ground beef." Labels may also indicate proportion of fat to lean.

Ground beef—approximately 75% lean, the least expensive kind, is suitable for hamburgers, meat sauces and any dish during the preparation of which you will have an opportunity to spoon off excess fat.

Lean ground beef—approximately 80% lean, makes good, lean hamburgers, meat loaves, meatballs and any dishes which contain other ingredients such as bread crumbs or noodles to absorb fat as it cooks out.

Extra-lean ground beef—approximately 85% lean, is recommended in dishes for fat-controlled diets, where it is important to eliminate as much fat as possible.

Hamburgers

*1 pound lean ground beef
2 tablespoons minced
   onion
1 teaspoon salt
1/4 teaspoon pepper
catchup, mustard or relish*

*plain or toasted
   hamburger buns,
   toasted split
   English muffins,
   toasted white bread
   slices (optional)*

Color index
page 52

Begin 20 mins
ahead

4 servings

296 cals per
serving

Good source
of iron

1 With spoon, mix well ground beef, onion, salt and pepper.

2 Shape mixture gently into 4 patties, each about 1 inch thick.

3 Over medium heat, heat skillet until very hot. Cook patties 3 to 4 minutes each side, turning them once.

4 Serve Hamburgers plain or with one of the suggested toppings, in buns, if you like.

357 cals per
serving

BROILED HAMBURGERS: Preheat broiler if manufacturer directs. Prepare ground-beef mixture as above; shape into thick patties; arrange on rack in broiling pan. Broil about 2 inches from heat source, about 8 minutes, turning once. If you like, during last few minutes, top with one of the following: *Cheddar cheese slice* or catchup, chili or soy sauce.

Ground beef

HAMBURGER SERVING IDEAS

English burger: In small bowl, mix ½ *cup catchup*, ¼ *cup diced dill pickle* and *2 teaspoons prepared horseradish*. In *split broiled, buttered English muffin*, serve *cooked beef patty* topped with some of pickle mixture.

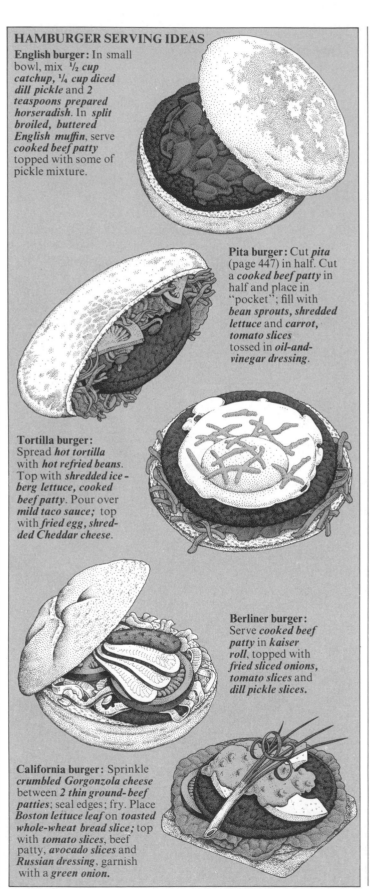

Pita burger: Cut *pita* (page 447) in half. Cut a *cooked beef patty* in half and place in "pocket"; fill with *bean sprouts, shredded lettuce* and *carrot, tomato slices* tossed in *oil-and-vinegar dressing*.

Tortilla burger: Spread *hot tortilla* with *hot refried beans*. Top with *shredded iceberg lettuce, cooked beef patty*. Pour over *mild taco sauce;* top with *fried egg, shredded Cheddar cheese*.

Berliner burger: Serve *cooked beef patty* in *kaiser roll*, topped with *fried sliced onions, tomato slices* and *dill pickle slices*.

California burger: Sprinkle *crumbled Gorgonzola cheese* between *2 thin ground-beef patties;* seal edges; fry. Place *Boston lettuce leaf* on *toasted whole-wheat bread slice;* top with *tomato slices*, beef patty, *avocado slices* and *Russian dressing*, garnish with a *green onion*.

Color index page 51

Begin 2 hrs ahead

8 servings

204 cals per serving

Good source of iron

197 cals per serving

312 cals per serving

210 cals per serving

208 cals per serving

Meat Loaf

2 pounds lean ground beef
2 cups fresh white or whole-wheat bread crumbs (about 4 bread slices)
½ cup milk
½ cup minced onion
2 eggs
2 teaspoons salt
¼ teaspoon pepper

1 In large bowl, mix well lean ground beef, fresh bread crumbs and remaining ingredients.

2 Spoon mixture into 9" by 5" loaf pan; with spoon, level top. Bake in 350°F. oven 1½ hours.

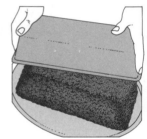

3 Let meat loaf stand 5 minutes at room temperature; pour off and discard drippings.

4 With spatula, loosen meat loaf from pan; invert onto warm platter and remove loaf pan.

FLAVORED MEAT LOAVES

GERMAN-STYLE MEAT LOAF: Drain *one 8-ounce can sauerkraut*, reserving liquid. Prepare Meat Loaf as above but omit milk and substitute *2 cups caraway-rye bread crumbs* for bread crumbs; add sauerkraut. To liquid, add *water* to make ½ cup; add to mixture.

MONTEREY MEAT LOAF: Prepare Meat Loaf as above but add ½ *teaspoon oregano* to mixture. In loaf pan, spread half of mixture; from *one 8-ounce package pasteurized process Monterey (Jack) cheese slices*, arrange 2½ cheese slices on meat. Top with remaining mixture. Bake loaf as directed but during last 10 minutes, remove from oven; repeat cheese layer; top cheese with *1 medium tomato*, peeled and sliced. Finish baking the loaf. With 2 pancake turners, lift meat loaf, top side up, to warm platter.

PINEAPPLE MEAT LOAF: Prepare Meat Loaf as above but omit milk and add juice drained from *one 8¼-ounce can sliced pineapple*. In shallow baking pan, shape mixture into 11" by 5" oval loaf; top with pineapple slices. Bake 1 hour.

CURRIED MEAT LOAF: Prepare Meat Loaf as above but add *1 cup shredded peeled apples*, ½ *cup minced celery* and *1 tablespoon curry powder* to mixture.

FILLED MEAT LOAF: Prepare meat-loaf mixture as left but spread half of mixture in loaf pan; top with *one of the following fillings:* 4 or 5 whole medium mushrooms; ¼ pound mushrooms, minced; 1 10-ounce package frozen chopped spinach, thawed and drained; 1 cup shredded mozzarella or scamorze cheese; 4 hard-cooked eggs; 2 frankfurters or ¼ pound knackwurst, cut lengthwise into fourths; 4 or 5 pasteurized process cheese slices (overlap slightly). Add remaining meat mixture. Bake as directed.

244 cals per serving

SPINACH-CHEESE MEAT LOAF: Prepare Meat Loaf as left but omit milk; add *one 8-ounce container creamed cottage cheese;* set aside. In medium bowl, combine *one 10-ounce package frozen chopped spinach*, thawed and drained, ¼ *cup minced onion*, ½ *teaspoon salt*, ⅛ *teaspoon ground nutmeg* and *1 egg*. In 10″ by 6″ baking dish, spread half of meat mixture; top with spinach mixture, then with remaining meat mixture; level top. Bake 1½ hours. (Makes 10 servings.)

MEAT LOAF ADDITIONS: Prepare Meat Loaf, opposite, but add *one or more of the following:* 1 garlic clove, minced, ½ teaspoon caraway seed, ½ teaspoon oregano, 1 tablespoon chili powder.

Lemon Barbecued Meat Loaves

Color index page 52

Begin 1 hr ahead

6 servings

263 cals per serving

Good source of iron

1½ pounds lean ground beef
2 cups fresh bread crumbs (about 4 bread slices)
¼ cup lemon juice
¼ cup minced onion
1 egg
2 teaspoons seasoned salt
½ cup catchup
⅓ cup packed brown sugar
1 teaspoon dry mustard
¼ teaspoon ground allspice
¼ teaspoon ground cloves
6 thin lemon slices

1. Preheat oven to 350°F. Grease 13″ by 9″ baking pan. In large bowl, mix well the ground beef, fresh bread crumbs, lemon juice, minced onion, egg and seasoned salt. Shape the mixture into 6 individual loaves; place in baking pan. Bake 15 minutes.

2. Meanwhile, prepare the sauce: In small bowl, combine the catchup, brown sugar, mustard, allspice and ground cloves. Mix well. Spoon the sauce over the loaves in the baking pan and top each one with a lemon slice; bake 30 minutes longer, basting occasionally with sauce from the baking pan. Serve sauce over the meat loaves.

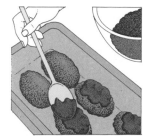

Shaping loaves: With hands, shape the meat mixture into 6 loaves.

Adding sauce: Spoon over sauce then top each loaf with a lemon slice.

Country Meat Loaf

Color index page 52

Begin 2 hrs or day ahead

8 servings

226 cals per serving

Good source of iron

2 tablespoons salad oil
1 medium onion, chopped
1 celery stalk, finely chopped
3 white- or whole-wheat bread slices
2 pounds lean ground beef
1 medium carrot, finely shredded
1½ teaspoons salt
¼ teaspoon cracked black pepper
1 egg
1 8-ounce can tomato sauce
1 tablespoon light brown sugar
1 tablespoon cider vinegar
1 tablespoon prepared mustard

1 In 2-quart saucepan over medium heat, to the hot salad oil, add the chopped onion and celery. Cook about 10 minutes, stirring occasionally with a slotted spoon.

2 Into large bowl, tear bread slices into small pieces; add onion and celery mixture.

3 To the bread and onion mixture add the lean ground beef, shredded carrot, salt, pepper, egg and one half of the can of tomato sauce. Stir thoroughly to mix.

4 In 12″ by 8″ baking dish, with hands, shape ground beef mixture into 8″ by 4″ loaf; set aside.

5 In cup with spoon, combine the light brown sugar, cider vinegar, prepared mustard and remaining tomato sauce. Mix thoroughly.

6 Spoon sauce over meat loaf in baking dish. Bake in 350°F. oven 1½ hours. Serve meat loaf warm; or cover and refrigerate to serve cold.

Ground beef

Dilled Meatballs

Color index
page 53

Begin 1 hr
ahead
6 main-dish
servings

317 cals per
serving

Good source
of iron

1½ pounds lean ground
beef
¾ cup quick-cooking
oats, uncooked
1 egg
1 teaspoon salt
¼ teaspoon pepper
dill weed
2 tablespoons salad oil
1 cup water
1 beef-flavor bouillon
cube or envelope
1 cup sour cream

1 In large bowl with
spoon, mix beef, oats,
egg, salt, pepper and
½ teaspoon dill weed.

2 With hands, form
the ground-beef
mixture into evenly
shaped 1-inch meatballs.

3 In 12-inch skillet over
medium-high heat, in
hot oil, cook meatballs, a
few at a time. Turn with a
spoon until well browned
on all sides.

4 With a slotted spoon,
remove the meatballs
to a large bowl as they
brown. When all are
browned, pour off any
remaining oil in the skillet.

5 Return meatballs to
skillet. Stir in water and
bouillon. Over medium
heat, heat to boiling.

6 Reduce heat to low;
cover the skillet and
simmer 15 minutes,
stirring the meatballs
and liquid frequently.

7 Stir in sour cream and 2
teaspoons dill weed to
the meatballs and liquid;
heat through (but be
careful not to boil).

Mushroom-Cheese Meatballs

Color index
page 53

Begin 1 hr
ahead
8 main-dish
servings

268 cals per
serving

Good source
of calcium,
iron

salad oil
¼ cup finely chopped
onion
¼ cup finely chopped
green pepper
1½ pounds lean ground
beef
1 egg
¾ teaspoon salt
¼ teaspoon cracked
black pepper

½ pound mushrooms,
sliced
2 tablespoons all-purpose
flour
2 cups water
1 8-ounce package
pasteurized process
cheese spread,
sliced
2 tablespoons cooking or
dry sherry

1. In 12-inch skillet over medium-high heat, in 2
tablespoons hot salad oil, cook onion and green
pepper until tender, about 5 minutes.
2. In large bowl, mix well onion mixture, ground
beef, egg, salt and pepper. Shape mixture into 1-inch
round meatballs.
3. In same skillet over medium-high heat, in 3 more
tablespoons hot salad oil, cook meatballs, a few at a
time, until well browned on all sides, removing
meatballs to large bowl as they brown. Pour off all
but 2 tablespoons drippings from skillet.
4. In drippings remaining in skillet over medium
heat, cook sliced mushrooms until tender, about
5 minutes.
5. In small bowl, blend flour with water. Return
meatballs to skillet; stir in flour mixture and cheese;
heat to boiling. Reduce heat to low; cover and
simmer 15 minutes, stirring occasionally. Add
sherry; heat through.

Burgundied Meatballs

Color index
page 53

Begin 45 mins
ahead
6 main-dish
servings

283 cals per
serving

Good source
of iron

1 pound lean ground beef
¾ cup dried bread
crumbs
¾ cup milk
1 egg
1 small onion, minced
½ teaspoon salt
¼ cup salad oil

2 tablespoons all-purpose
flour
1 cup water
1 cup red Burgundy
1 beef-flavor bouillon
cube
¾ teaspoon sugar

1. In large bowl, mix well first 6 ingredients; shape
mixture into 1-inch meatballs.
2. In 12-inch skillet over medium-high heat, in hot
salad oil, cook meatballs, a few at a time, until well
browned on all sides. With slotted spoon, remove
them to plate as they brown.
3. Into drippings remaining in skillet over medium
heat, stir flour until blended. Gradually stir in water,
Burgundy, bouillon and sugar and cook, stirring
constantly, until mixture is thickened. Add meatballs; heat to boiling. Reduce heat to low; cover and
simmer 15 minutes.

TO DO AHEAD: Up to 1 month ahead, prepare
meatballs as in steps 1 and 2 above; place in freezer-
safe container or freezer-weight plastic bag with
metal tie or zip top. Freeze. *Day before serving*, thaw
meatballs overnight in refrigerator. About 20 minutes before serving, prepare sauce as above but use
2 tablespoons salad oil instead of drippings. Return
meatballs to sauce in skillet and heat through.

Summer Barbecue

Summer, the most bountiful season, offers a cornucopia of fruits – peaches, nectarines, apricots, mangoes and melons. All kinds of berries, too, are at their best as well as the array of fresh vegetables. For salads, choose from green and lima beans, corn, jícama, tomatoes and garden lettuces.

The summer celebration of choice is a barbecue. A welcoming drink of refreshing Sangria gets things off to a good start, and while the grill is heating up there's Guacamole served with plenty of fresh vegetables and corn chips. For something special we've chosen Marinated Butterflied Lamb, which we cook on the grill as for Barbecued Short Ribs. Garlic bread; Brown Rice, Western Style; Corn-on-the-cob; and Tomatoes Vinaigrette are colorful and tangy accompaniments. A cooling Cantaloupe Sherbet is a welcome refresher, especially when served with berries and sliced fruit and the more substantial Marbled Fudge Bars cater for heartier appetites.

Clockwise from left: curly-leaved parsley; corn-on-the-cob; raspberries; blackberries; wild strawberries; apricots; peaches; nectarines; chives; dill; garden lettuce

Summer Barbecue

Menu

Summer Barbecue 10 people

* * *

Sangria
(double recipe)
page 471

* * *

Guacamole
(with fresh vegetables and corn chips)
page 124

* * *

Marinated Butterflied Lamb
(barbecued)
page 226
Barbecued Short Ribs
page 204

Brown Rice, Western Style
page 325
Tomatoes Vinaigrette
(double recipe) page 319
Corn-on-the-cob
page 283
Garlic Bread

* * *

Cantaloupe Sherbet
(with tropical fruits and berries)
page 380
Marbled Fudge Bars
page 405

Preparing Tropical Fruits

Markets across America are overflowing with exciting new fruits from faraway places. Combine these exotic and colorful new additions with traditional favorites in fruit salads, desserts, ice creams, and sherbets. These tropical fruits may also be used in fish and poultry dishes and in sauces.

Kiwi fruit: With sharp knife or swivel vegetable peeler, peel off skin and cut in wedges or slices. Alternatively, cut unpeeled fruit lengthwise in half to eat with spoon.

Persimmons: When ripe, remove stem cap; cut crosswise in slices to eat pulp. Or, place on plate with stem end downward; cut gashes through top skin and eat pulp with spoon.

Carambola and Passion fruit: Slice carambola (star fruit) crosswise for its star shape. Cut passion fruit crosswise and scoop out pulp to eat or to strain and use juice.

Papayas: Using a sharp knife, cut in half lengthwise; scrape out seeds. With spoon, scoop out flesh to eat. Or, peel and cut up or slice.

Mangoes: With sharp knife, cut a lengthwise slice from each side of the long flat seed as close to the seed as possible; set aside seed section. Peel skin from cut off pieces; slice lengthwise. Cut skin from seed section and slice off remaining fruit.

Tropical Fruits
This combination of fruits makes a delicious, refreshing dessert. *From left to right:* carambola (star fruit), strawberries, persimmons, guava, passion fruit, green seedless grapes, mango, kiwi fruit, black grapes, papaya, tamarillo, cape gooseberries (center).

Ziti Bake

Color index page 51
Begin 1½ hrs ahead
8 servings

553 cals per serving
Good source of calcium, iron, vitamin A, vitamin C

Spaghetti Sauce
(page 337)
1 16-ounce package
ziti macaroni
1 pound lean ground
beef
1 15-ounce container
ricotta cheese
½ cup grated Parmesan
cheese

¼ cup finely chopped
parsley
1 egg, slightly beaten
¾ teaspoon salt
¼ teaspoon pepper
1 8-ounce package
mozzarella or
scamorze cheese,
shredded

1. Prepare Spaghetti Sauce.
2. Meanwhile, in 8-quart Dutch oven, prepare ziti macaroni as label directs; drain. Set aside.
3. In same Dutch oven over medium-high heat, cook ground beef until well browned, about 10 minutes, stirring occasionally. Preheat oven to 350°F.
4. Remove Dutch oven from heat; stir in ricotta, next 5 ingredients and half of Spaghetti Sauce until well mixed. Add ziti and toss gently to coat well.
5. Spoon mixture into 13" by 9" baking pan; pour remaining Spaghetti Sauce evenly over ziti mixture; sprinkle with mozzarella cheese. Bake 20 minutes or until hot and bubbly.

Chili con Carne

Color index page 52
Begin 1½ hrs ahead
10 servings

224 cals per serving
Good source of iron

1 tablespoon salad oil
2 pounds lean ground
beef
1 cup coarsely chopped
onions
¼ cup diced green
pepper
2 large garlic cloves,
minced

2 16-ounce cans tomatoes
or 4 cups chopped,
peeled fresh tomatoes
¼ to ⅓ cup chili powder
1 teaspoon salt
2 16- or 17-ounce cans
red kidney or pinto
beans
Accompaniments (below)

1. In 5-quart Dutch oven over medium-high heat, in hot salad oil, cook ground beef, onions, green pepper and garlic until onion is tender, about 10 minutes, stirring frequently.
2. Add tomatoes and their liquid, chili powder and salt; heat to boiling. Reduce heat to low; cover and simmer 1 hour, stirring occasionally.
3. Stir in beans and their liquid; heat. Serve in soup bowls with a choice of accompaniments.

ACCOMPANIMENTS: Shredded mild Cheddar or Monterey (Jack) cheese, shredded iceberg lettuce, diced avocados, minced onions, chopped green pepper, chunks of French bread, saltine crackers, hot Corn Tortillas (page 431), tortilla or corn chips.

TEXAS-STYLE CHILI: For ground beef, substitute *1 2-pound beef chuck underblade steak boneless*, cut into ½-inch cubes. Cook as in steps 1 and 2 above, but simmer 1½ hours or until fork-tender. Omit beans, serve as above. (Makes 6 to 8 servings.)

Whole Stuffed Cabbage

1 28-ounce can tomatoes
1 6-ounce can tomato
paste
1 tablespoon brown
sugar
½ teaspoon
Worcestershire
⅛ teaspoon ground
allspice
salt
1 medium head green
cabbage

1 pound ground beef
1 medium onion, diced
1 garlic clove, minced
½ teaspoon pepper
1 cup cooked rice
2½ cups water

Color index page 54
Begin 3 hrs ahead
6 servings
182 cals per serving
Good source of iron, vitamin C

1 In 3-quart saucepan, combine tomatoes and their liquid, the tomato paste, brown sugar, Worcestershire, allspice and ½ teaspoon salt. Mix together thoroughly. Over high heat, heat to boiling, stirring constantly; reduce heat to low, cover the saucepan and simmer 20 minutes, stirring the mixture occasionally.

2 Discard tough outer leaves from cabbage. Carefully remove 2 large leaves and reserve. With sharp knife, cut out stem and center of cabbage, leaving a 1-inch-thick shell.

3 Discard the stem from the cabbage; with sharp knife, evenly dice cut-out cabbage center.

4 In 5-quart Dutch oven over medium-high heat, cook beef, onion, garlic, pepper, ½ teaspoon salt and 1 cup diced cabbage about 15 minutes.

5 Stir in rice and 1 cup tomato mixture. Remove from heat. Carefully spoon off any excess fat from surface of the mixture.

6 Fill cabbage shell with beef mixture; cover opening with the large reserved leaves.

7 With string, tie cabbage securely to hold leaves firmly in position.

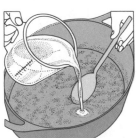

8 Into same Dutch oven, stir water, scraping pan to loosen brown bits at the bottom. Add the remaining diced cabbage and the tomato mixture; mix well.

9 Place cabbage, stem end down, in sauce. Over high heat, heat to boiling. Reduce heat to low; cover; simmer 2 hours, basting occasionally with sauce.

10 To serve, place cabbage, stem end down, on deep, warm platter; discard string. Spoon over sauce and cut the cabbage in wedges. Serve immediately.

209

Pork

POPULAR FRESH PORK CUTS

Pork shoulder arm picnic: Also known as picnic, this is suitable for baking and roasting.

Pork leg whole: Also known as fresh ham, this cut contains the hind leg bone and is suitable for roasting.

Pork shoulder arm roast: Also known as pork arm roast, this has the shank removed and is suitable for roasting.

Pork loin rib chops: Also known as center cut pork chops, they are suitable for roasting, baking and broiling.

Pork loin center rib roast: Also known as center cut pork roast, it contains the loin eye muscle and rib bones.

Pork loin chops: Also known as loin end chops, they are suitable for braising, and pan-frying.

Pork loin tenderloin and slices: Very tender roast and slices are suitable for braising and baking.

Pork loin sirloin chops: Also known as sirloin pork chops, they are suitable for braising and broiling.

Pork loin sirloin cutlets: Boneless tender slices cut from sirloin end of loin are suitable for braising and broiling.

Pork loin blade roast: Also known as 5- or 7-rib roast and rib end roast, this is suitable for roasting.

Pork shoulder blade roast: Also known as Boston butt roast or pork butt, this is the top portion of the shoulder and is suitable for roasting.

Pork shoulder blade steak: This is suitable for braising and broiling.

Pork shoulder blade roast boneless: It is usually tied with string or placed inside elastic netting. Suitable for roasting.

Pork loin country style ribs (Country ribs): These contain either rib bones or backbones and can be baked, braised or cooked in liquid.

Pork spareribs: These long rib bones with a thin covering of meat are suitable for baking and broiling.

POPULAR SMOKED PORK CUTS

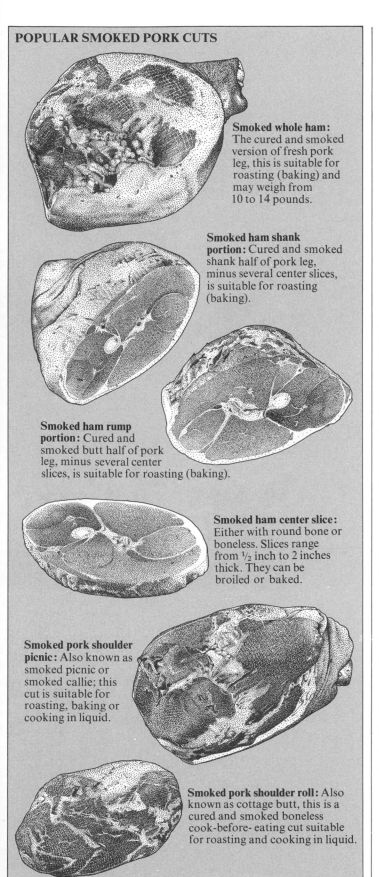

Smoked whole ham: The cured and smoked version of fresh pork leg, this is suitable for roasting (baking) and may weigh from 10 to 14 pounds.

Smoked ham shank portion: Cured and smoked shank half of pork leg, minus several center slices, is suitable for roasting (baking).

Smoked ham rump portion: Cured and smoked butt half of pork leg, minus several center slices, is suitable for roasting (baking).

Smoked ham center slice: Either with round bone or boneless. Slices range from ½ inch to 2 inches thick. They can be broiled or baked.

Smoked pork shoulder picnic: Also known as smoked picnic or smoked callie; this cut is suitable for roasting, baking or cooking in liquid.

Smoked pork shoulder roll: Also known as cottage butt, this is a cured and smoked boneless cook-before-eating cut suitable for roasting and cooking in liquid.

Unlike beef, cuts of fresh pork vary little in tenderness and most can be successfully cooked by one of the dry heat methods, roasting, broiling, pan-broiling and frying (see pages 186–87). See pages 218–19 for information on smoked pork.

BUYING FRESH PORK

Choose meat that has a high proportion of lean to fat and bone. The fat should be solid and white, the lean firm and fine-textured, grayish pink to light red.

TESTING FOR DONENESS

Pork is always cooked well-done and should be a uniform light gray color throughout. When the meat is broiled, pan-broiled or pan-fried, make a small slit in the center of the meat or near the bone to check the color. For roast pork, use a meat thermometer. It should register 170°F. Braised pork and pork cooked in liquid should be fork-tender.

TIMETABLE FOR ROASTING FRESH PORK *				
Type of cut	Weight (in pounds)	Meat thermometer reading	Approximate cooking time** (in hours)	Oven temperature
Loin roasts center rib or loin	3 to 5	170°F.	1½ to 2½	325°F.
loin half	5 to 7	170°F.	2¾ to 4	325°F.
loin blade or sirloin	3 to 4	170°F.	2 to 2¾	325°F.
top loin, boneless (double)	3 to 5	170°F.	1¾ to 2¾	325°F.
Crown roast	4 to 6	170°F.	2¼ to 3½	325°F.
Shoulder arm picnic bone-in	5 to 8	170°F.	2½ to 4	325°F.
boneless	3 to 5	170°F.	1¾ to 2¾	325°F.
Shoulder blade (Boston) roast	4 to 6	170°F.	2¾ to 4	325°F.
Shoulder arm roast	4 to 6	170°F.	2¾ to 4	325°F.
Leg (fresh ham) half bone-in	5 to 8	170°F.	2¾ to 4¾	325°F.
whole boneless	10 to 14	170°F.	4 to 5½	325°F.
whole bone-in	12 to 16	170°F.	4½ to 5¾	325°F.
Tenderloin	½ to 1		¾ to 1	325°F.

Meat at refrigerator temperature
** *Remove meat from oven when internal temperature is 5 to 10 degrees below desired doneness as meat continues cooking*

CARVING LOIN ROAST

After roasting, cut backbone from ribs and discard. Place roast on cutting board with rib side facing you. Anchor meat with a fork, cut closely along each side of every rib; one slice will contain the rib, next one will be boneless.

Roast pork

Roast Pork

*1 3-pound pork loin
   center rib roast*
salt
pepper
*butter or margarine
   (optional)*
*water or chicken
   broth*
*¼ cup all-purpose
   flour or 2 tablespoons
   cornstarch*

Color index
page 56

Begin 2 hrs
ahead

8 servings

192 cals per
serving

Good source
of thiamine

1 Place roast, fat side up, on rib bones in open roasting pan. Sprinkle meat lightly with salt and pepper.

2 Insert meat thermometer into center of roast. Roast in 325°F. oven 1½ to 1¾ hours, until thermometer reaches 170°F. Remove roast to platter.

3 Into 2-cup measure, pour pan drippings (set pan aside). Let stand a few seconds until fat separates from meat juice.

4 Skim ¼ cup fat from the drippings into 1-quart saucepan. (Add butter or margarine, if necessary, to make ¼ cup.)

5 Add ½ cup water to roasting pan; stir until brown bits are loosened; add to meat juice in cup and add enough water or chicken broth to make 2 cups liquid. Into fat in saucepan over medium heat, blend flour or cornstarch, 1 teaspoon salt and ¼ teaspoon pepper. Gradually stir in meat-juice mixture and cook, stirring constantly, until gravy is thickened. Pour into gravy boat to serve hot with roast.

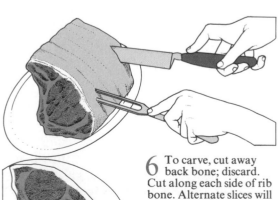

6 To carve, cut away back bone; discard. Cut along each side of rib bone. Alternate slices will contain rib bone.

Prune-stuffed Roast Pork

*½ 12-ounce package
   pitted prunes*
1 cup boiling water
*1 4½- to 5-pound pork
   loin center rib roast*
¼ teaspoon pepper
salt
ground ginger
*3 tablespoons all-purpose
   flour*
½ cup half-and-half
*1 teaspoon red currant
   jelly*

Color index
page 56

Begin 3 hrs
ahead

14 servings

221 cals per
serving

Good source
of iron,
thiamine

1 In medium bowl, soak the prunes in boiling water for 30 minutes.

2 Drain the prunes thoroughly and pat them dry on paper towels.

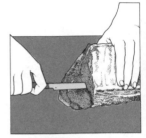

3 With a long, narrow, sharp knife, pierce through center of roast from one end to the other, twisting the knife slightly as you cut to form a long slit in the meat.

4 Pack prunes into slit with the handle of a wooden spoon or fingers.

5 Sprinkle roast with pepper, 1 teaspoon salt and 1 teaspoon ginger. Place the roast, fat side up, in a shallow open roasting pan.

6 Insert meat thermometer, being careful not to touch bone or stuffing. Roast in 325°F. oven 2 to 2½ hours until thermometer reaches 170°F.

7 When done, place meat on heated platter and make gravy: Pour drippings into 2-cup measure; let stand a few seconds until fat separates. Return 3 tablespoons of fat to pan; spoon off any remaining fat. Over low heat, stir in flour. Add enough water to drippings to make 1 cup; stir into flour mixture, scraping to loosen brown bits. Stir in half-and-half, jelly, ¼ teaspoon ginger and salt to taste; cook until gravy is thickened. Pass gravy separately.

Tenderloin

Pork Roast with Piquante Sauce

Color index
page 57

Begin 3 hrs
ahead

12 servings

156 cals per
serving

Good source
of thiamine

1 4-pound pork loin blade roast
1 8-ounce can tomato sauce
¼ cup packed light brown sugar
¼ cup cider vinegar
¼ cup dark corn syrup
1 tablespoon cornstarch
½ teaspoon salt
⅛ teaspoon pepper
¼ cup water

1. Place pork roast, fat side up, on rack in open roasting pan. Insert meat thermometer into center of roast, being careful not to touch bone. Roast in 325°F. oven about 2¾ hours or until thermometer reaches 170°F.
2. Meanwhile, prepare the sauce: In 1-quart saucepan over medium-high heat, cook remaining ingredients, stirring constantly, until mixture is smooth and thickened; set aside. During the last 30 minutes of roasting time, brush the meat generously two or three times with tomato-sauce mixture.
3. To serve, place the roast on a warm platter. Let stand 15 minutes for easier carving. Pour sauce into a sauceboat and pass separately.

Pork-and-Onion Kabobs

Color index
page 57

Begin 4½ hrs
ahead or
early in day

4 servings

428 cals per
serving

Good source
of iron,
thiamine,
niacin

2 pounds pork shoulder blade (Boston) roast, boneless
¼ cup soy sauce
2 tablespoons chili sauce
2 tablespoons honey
1 tablespoon salad oil
1 tablespoon minced green onion
1 teaspoon curry powder
3 medium onions, each cut into chunks

1. Trim excess fat from pork roast, cut meat into 1-inch cubes.
2. For marinade, in medium bowl, combine soy sauce and the next 5 ingredients. Stir in the meat cubes. Cover and refrigerate at least 3 hours, stirring meat occasionally.
3. *About 1 hour before serving:* Prepare outdoor grill for barbecuing. Meanwhile, on 4 long skewers (about 18 inches), thread pork cubes alternately with onion (reserving marinade).
4. Place skewers on grill over medium coals; cook 20 minutes or until pork is tender, basting meat and onion frequently with reserved marinade and turning skewers occasionally.

Threading the skewers:
Alternately thread pork cubes and onion chunks onto each skewer. Reserve the marinade for basting.

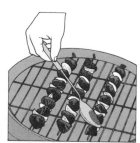

Basting the kabobs:
During cooking, frequently baste both the meat and onion with reserved marinade.

Breaded Pork Tenderloin

Color index
page 56

Begin 25 mins
ahead

3 servings

422 cals per
serving

Good source
of iron,
thiamine

1 pork tenderloin (about ¾ pound)
1 egg
2 tablespoons water
½ teaspoon salt
¼ teaspoon rosemary, crushed
⅛ teaspoon pepper
¾ cup dried bread crumbs
3 tablespoons salad oil

1. With sharp knife, cut tenderloin lengthwise almost in half, being careful not to cut all the way through. Open and flatten to "butterfly." On cutting board, with meat mallet or dull edge of French knife, pound meat to about ¼ inch thickness; cut into 3 serving pieces.
2. In pie plate with fork, beat together egg with water, salt, crushed rosemary and pepper. On waxed paper place the bread crumbs. With tongs, dip meat into egg mixture, turning to coat both sides dip in crumbs. Repeat until each piece is coated twice.
3. In 12-inch skillet over medium-high heat, in hot oil, cook meat until well browned and fork-tender, about 10 minutes, turning once.

Cutting tenderloin: With sharp knife, cut meat lengthwise almost in half, but not all the way through.

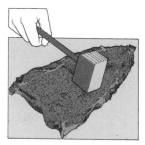

Pounding meat: Open like a butterfly and with meat mallet or dull edge of French knife, pound ¼ inch thick.

Stir-fried Pork and Vegetables

Color index
page 57

Begin 30 mins
ahead

6 servings

356 cals per
serving

Good source
of iron,
thiamine,
niacin

¼ cup soy sauce
1 tablespoon dry sherry
2½ teaspoons cornstarch
1¼ teaspoons sugar
½ teaspoon minced fresh ginger
2 pork tenderloins, thinly sliced (each about ¾ pound)
salad oil
1 pound asparagus or ½ bunch broccoli, cut into bite-size pieces
½ pound mushrooms, sliced
¼ teaspoon salt
2 tablespoons water

1. In medium bowl, mix well first 5 ingredients; add pork and toss lightly to coat.
2. In 5-quart Dutch oven or 12-inch skillet over high heat, in ¼ cup hot oil, cook asparagus, mushrooms and salt, stirring quickly and frequently (stir-frying) until vegetables are coated; add water and stir-fry until asparagus is tender-crisp. Place vegetables and liquid on heated platter; keep warm.
3. In same Dutch oven over high heat, heat 6 more tablespoons oil until very hot; add meat mixture and stir-fry until meat loses pink color, about 2 minutes. Return vegetables to Dutch oven; stir-fry until heated through. Serve immediately.

Chops and steaks

Skillet-braised Pork Chops

4 to 6 pork chops, any cut, or shoulder steaks, any cut; all cut ³⁄₄ to 1 inch thick
¹⁄₂ teaspoon salt
¹⁄₄ teaspoon pepper
¹⁄₂ cup water, chicken broth, or dry or semisweet white wine

Color index page 57

Begin 1 hr ahead

6 servings

308 cals per serving

Good source of thiamine, niacin

1 Trim a piece of fat from edge of one pork chop. In 10- or 12-inch skillet over medium-high heat, rub fat over bottom of skillet to grease; discard fat.

2 Add the pork chops to the skillet; cook until browned on both sides. Sprinkle chops with salt and pepper.

3 Add water; reduce heat to low. Cover; simmer 45 minutes. Skim fat from pan liquid and spoon pan liquid over chops.

24 cals per serving

PAN GRAVY FOR SKILLET-BRAISED PORK CHOPS: Blend *¹⁄₄ cup water* and *1 tablespoon all-purpose flour* until smooth. Remove chops from skillet; skim off fat, leaving pan liquid; stir in flour mixture and cook over medium heat, stirring, till mixture is thickened. Serve with chops.

BRAISED PORK-CHOP VARIATIONS: Prepare Skillet-braised Pork Chops as above but, after browning chops, use one of these variations.

APPLE: Substitute *¹⁄₂ cup apple juice* for water and use *³⁄₄ teaspoon salt*. During last 5 minutes, top chops with *4 to 6 thick cooking-apple slices*.

GARDEN: Substitute *¹⁄₂ cup cocktail vegetable juice* for water. During last 5 minutes, top chops with *4 to 6 thin green-pepper rings* and *4 to 6 thin onion slices*.

PEACH-CHILI SAUCE: Substitute ¹⁄₄ cup syrup drained from *one 16-ounce can cling-peach halves*, *¹⁄₄ cup chili sauce* and *2 tablespoons lemon juice* for water. During last 5 minutes, add peach halves.

PLUM: Substitute *¹⁄₃ cup syrup from one 17-ounce can purple plums* and *3 tablespoons cider vinegar* for water. During last 5 minutes, add plums.

TOMATO-THYME: Add *¹⁄₈ teaspoon thyme leaves*, crushed, with water. During last 5 minutes, top chops with *6 thick tomato slices*; sprinkle with *salt*.

Thin Pork Chops Orientale

¹⁄₂ cup soy sauce
¹⁄₄ cup sake or dry sherry
¹⁄₄ cup salad oil
1 garlic clove, finely chopped
1 teaspoon ground ginger or 2 teaspoons finely chopped fresh ginger
1¹⁄₂ pounds thinly sliced pork loin chops, each cut about ¹⁄₂ inch thick
hot cooked rice (optional)

Color index page 57

Begin 4¹⁄₂ hrs ahead or early in day

6 servings

227 cals per serving

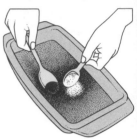

1 In shallow baking dish, for marinade, combine soy sauce, sake, oil, garlic and ginger.

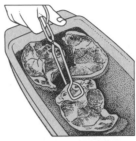

2 Add pork chops to marinade and turn to coat. Cover; refrigerate at least 4 hours, turning meat in marinade occasionally.

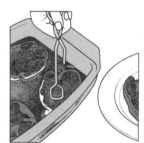

3 *About 15 minutes before serving:* With tongs, remove chops from marinade and drain slightly. Trim piece of fat from one chop.

4 In 12-inch skillet over medium-high heat, rub fat over skillet to grease well; discard fat.

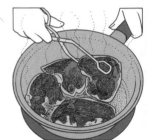

5 Cook chops a few at a time until well browned and fork-tender, about 10 minutes, turning once. Serve with rice, if desired.

Barbecued Pork in Buns

Color index page 56

Begin 20 mins ahead

6 servings

400 cals per serving

Good source of calcium, iron, thiamine

2 tablespoons salad oil
6 pork loin sirloin cutlets, each cut about ¹⁄₄ inch thick
1 teaspoon salt
¹⁄₄ teaspoon pepper

6 hamburger buns, split and toasted
¹⁄₂ cup catchup
3 tablespoons molasses
1 tablespoon lemon juice

1. In 12-inch skillet over medium-high heat, in hot salad oil, cook pork cutlets until well browned, turning once and sprinkling with salt and pepper. Place cutlets in toasted buns and keep warm.
2. Reduce heat to medium; into drippings in skillet, stir catchup, molasses and lemon juice and heat to boiling, stirring. Spoon some sauce over each cutlet.

Color index page 57
Begin 55 mins ahead
6 servings
323 cals per serving
Good source of thiamine

Orange Pork Chops

6 pork loin rib chops, each cut ½ *inch thick*	*1 cup orange juice*
	½ *cup sugar*
	1 tablespoon
¾ *cup water*	*cornstarch*
½ *teaspoon paprika*	½ *teaspoon ground*
¼ *teaspoon pepper*	*cinnamon*
salt	*12 whole cloves*
1 medium orange	

1. Trim several pieces of fat from edge of pork chops. In 12-inch skillet over medium-high heat, heat fat until lightly browned; rub fat over bottom of skillet to grease it; discard fat.

2. In the greased skillet, over high heat, cook pork chops until well browned on both sides. Add next 3 ingredients and 1 teaspoon salt; heat to boiling. Reduce heat to low; cover; simmer about 35 minutes, turning once.

3. Meanwhile, prepare orange sauce: Grate 1 tablespoon peel from stem end of orange; then from other end, cut 6 thin slices; set aside. In 1-quart saucepan over medium-high heat, cook orange peel, orange juice, next 4 ingredients and ¼ teaspoon salt until thickened, stirring. Add orange slices; cover; remove from heat and keep warm.

4. To serve, top pork chops with orange sauce.

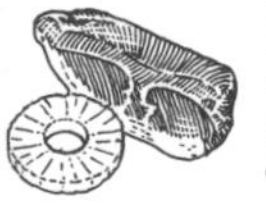

Color index page 57
Begin 4 hrs ahead or early in day
6 servings
395 cals per serving
Good source of iron, thiamine

Grilled Pork Steaks with Pineapple

1 20-ounce can sliced pineapple	*1 tablespoon brown sugar*
½ *cup soy sauce*	*6 pork shoulder blade*
⅓ *cup salad oil*	*steaks, each cut*
¼ *cup minced onion*	½ *inch thick*
½ *garlic clove, crushed*	

1. Drain 6 pineapple slices and reserve with ¼ cup liquid from pineapple.

2. In 13″ by 9″ metal baking pan, combine reserved pineapple liquid with next 5 ingredients. Place steaks in marinade; cover and refrigerate at least 3 hours, turning once.

3. *About 40 minutes before serving:* Prepare grill or preheat broiler if manufacturer directs. Arrange steaks on grill (or in large broiling pan); grill 15 minutes, brushing with marinade once.

4. Meanwhile, place pineapple slices in pan of marinade, turning to coat both sides; place pan on grill while steaks are cooking to heat pineapple slices. If in broiler, heat pineapple on top of steaks during last 3 or 4 minutes.

5. Turn steaks and grill 15 minutes more, spooning remaining marinade over steaks once, until meat is thoroughly cooked and fork-tender. Serve a hot pineapple slice with each pork steak.

Stuffed Pork Chops with Apple Dressing

2 tablespoons butter or margarine	*salt and pepper*
	⅔ *cup hot water*
½ *cup diced onion*	*1 beef-flavor bouillon*
½ *cup diced celery*	*cube or envelope*
*6 pork loin rib chops, each cut about 1*½ *inches thick*	¼ *cup diced carrots*
	6 peppercorns
	1 bay leaf
1 cup diced dried white bread	*chopped parsley for garnish*
1 medium apple, peeled, cored and diced	
1 egg, beaten	
¼ *teaspoon sage*	
⅛ *teaspoon basil*	
⅛ *teaspoon ground thyme*	

Color index page 56
Begin 2½ hrs ahead
6 servings
352 cals per serving
Good source of iron, thiamine

1 In 10-inch skillet over medium heat, in hot butter, cook ¼ cup onion and ¼ cup celery until vegetables are tender, about 5 minutes.

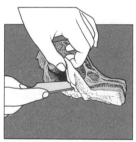

2 Meanwhile, with sharp knife, form pocket in meat by cutting horizontally through each chop almost to the bone.

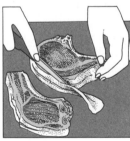

3 Remove skillet from heat; stir in next 6 ingredients, ½ teaspoon salt and ⅛ teaspoon pepper.

4 Use skillet mixture to stuff chops; sprinkle meat on both sides with salt and pepper. Wash the skillet.

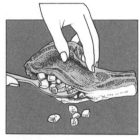

5 Trim piece of fat from edge of one of the pork chops. In skillet over medium-high heat, rub fat over bottom of skillet to grease well; discard fat.

6 Add chops, a few at a time, to skillet. Cook until browned on both sides, turning once with tongs. Set aside.

7 In 13″ by 9″ metal baking pan, stir water and bouillon until bouillon is dissolved. Add carrots, peppercorns, bay leaf, rest of onion and celery.

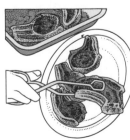

8 Arrange browned, stuffed chops in baking pan on top of the vegetable-herb mixture.

9 Cover with foil; bake in 325°F. oven 1½ hours, or until fork-tender. Turn once during cooking.

10 Place chops on platter; garnish with parsley; strain liquid; serve separately as gravy.

Spareribs and country style ribs

Barbecued Spareribs

4 pounds pork spareribs
water
1 medium onion, sliced
1½ cups catchup
3 tablespoons cider vinegar
2 tablespoons dark corn syrup
1 teaspoon salt
1 teaspoon paprika
¾ teaspoon chili powder
parsley sprigs for garnish

Color index page 56

Begin early in day or day ahead

4 servings

876 cals per serving

Good source of iron, vitamin A, thiamine, niacin

1 Use a sharp knife to cut spareribs into 2- or 3-rib portions.

2 Place ribs in 8-quart Dutch oven, then add cold water to cover and sliced onion.

3 Over high heat, heat to boiling. Reduce heat to low; cover; simmer 1 hour or until almost tender. Drain; cover and chill until ready to grill.

4 *About 50 minutes before serving:* Prepare out-door grill for barbecuing. In medium bowl, combine catchup and remaining ingredients for sauce.

5 Place ribs on grill over medium coals. Grill 20 minutes or until fork-tender, brushing often with sauce and turning occasionally. Serve with remaining sauce; garnish.

990 cals per serving

GLAZED BARBECUED SPARERIBS: Prepare as above but in step 4, omit sauce ingredients and prepare glaze: In 1-quart saucepan over medium heat, heat *one 10-ounce jar red currant jelly, ½ cup lemon juice, 3 tablespoons cornstarch, 2 teaspoons salt, 1 tablespoon grated lemon peel* and *1 minced garlic clove,* until mixture is thickened and jelly melted, stirring constantly. Use melted glaze to brush spareribs.

TO BROIL: Precook spareribs as in steps 1 to 3; mix catchup and remaining ingredients in step 4. Preheat broiler if manufacturer directs. Broil ribs 20 to 30 minutes until fork-tender, basting often with mixture and turning occasionally.

Pork-Rib Dinner

4 pounds pork loin country style ribs, cut into serving pieces
⅓ cup all-purpose flour
2 tablespoons salad oil
1½ cups apple juice
2 teaspoons salt
½ teaspoon pepper
2 pounds small red potatoes
1 16-ounce bag carrots, cut into 2-inch pieces
1 pound small whole onions
1 small head cabbage, shredded

Color index page 56

Begin 2½ hrs ahead

8 servings

545 cals per serving

Good source of iron, thiamine, niacin

1. On waxed paper, thoroughly coat pork ribs with flour; reserve any leftover flour.
2. In 8-quart Dutch oven with ovensafe handles over medium-high heat, in hot salad oil, cook meat, a few pieces at a time, until well browned on all sides, removing pieces to plate as they brown. Reduce heat to medium.
3. Into drippings in Dutch oven, stir reserved flour until blended. Gradually stir in apple juice. Return browned meat pieces to Dutch oven; add salt and pepper; heat to boiling.
4. Cover Dutch oven and bake in 350°F. oven 30 minutes. Add potatoes, carrots and onions; cover; bake 30 minutes. With spoon, skim off fat from liquid in Dutch oven.
5. Add the shredded cabbage; cover and bake 1 hour longer or until the vegetables and meat are fork-tender, stirring occasionally.

Pork Back Ribs with Sauerkraut

2½ pounds pork loin back ribs
1 tablespoon salad oil
1 12-ounce can beer
salt
4 cups well-drained sauerkraut
2 tablespoons dark brown sugar
chopped parsley for garnish

Color index page 56

Begin 2¼ hrs ahead

6 servings

388 cals per serving

Good source of iron, thiamine

1. Cut back ribs into 2- or 3-rib portions.
2. In 12-inch skillet over medium-high heat, in hot salad oil, cook ribs, a few pieces at a time, until well browned, removing pieces as they brown. Pour off drippings from skillet.
3. Return all ribs to skillet; add beer and ½ teaspoon salt; heat to boiling. Reduce heat to low; cover and simmer 30 minutes. Stir in sauerkraut, brown sugar and ½ teaspoon salt. Cover and simmer 1 hour longer or until ribs are tender, stirring occasionally. Garnish with parsley.

Browning back ribs: Cook ribs, a few pieces at a time, removing pieces with tongs as they brown.

Adding sauerkraut: Stir in sauerkraut, brown sugar and ½ teaspoon salt, then simmer 1 hour longer.

Hocks and stew meat

Hocks and Navy-Bean Stew

4 fresh pork hocks
1½ tablespoons salt
¼ teaspoon pepper
2 garlic cloves, crushed
1 bay leaf
water
3 cups dry navy beans
(1½ 16-ounce
packages)
4 whole cloves
1 pound small white
onions (about 12)
1 pound carrots, cut in
chunks
2 tablespoons lemon
juice

Color index
page 57

Begin 3½ hrs
ahead

12 cups or
6 servings

541 cals per
serving

High in fiber

Good source
of calcium,
iron,
thiamine,
niacin

1 In 8-quart saucepot over high heat, heat to boiling first 5 ingredients and 5 cups water. Reduce heat to low; cover; simmer 1½ hours, skimming off fat.

2 Meanwhile, rinse navy beans in running cold water, discarding any small stones or discolored or shriveled pieces.

3 In 4-quart saucepan over high heat, in 9 cups boiling water, heat beans to boiling; boil 2 minutes. Remove from heat; cover; soak 1 hour; drain thoroughly.

4 Add beans to hocks; simmer 30 minutes more. Stick cloves into 1 onion. Add all onions and carrots to saucepot; over high heat, heat to boiling.

5 Reduce heat to low; cover; simmer 1 hour until meat and vegetables are fork-tender. Add lemon juice in last ¼ hour. Discard bay leaf, cloves.

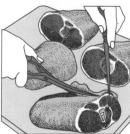 

6 Remove hocks to cutting board and discard skin and bones.

7 Cut meat in bite-size pieces; return to pot. Reheat before serving.

Easy Pork Stew

¼ cup all-purpose flour
salt
¼ teaspoon pepper
¼ teaspoon ground
ginger
3 pounds pork cubes
¼ cup salad oil
¾ cup water
½ cup cooking sherry
½ teaspoon sugar
1¼ pounds tiny white
onions
2 10-ounce packages
frozen lima beans,
thawed
1½ pounds yellow
straight-neck squash,
cut in 1½-inch chunks

Color index
page 57

Begin 2½ hrs
ahead

12 servings

300 cals per
serving

Good source
of iron,
thiamine

1. On waxed paper, mix flour, 1 tablespoon salt, pepper and ginger; toss pork with mixture to coat.
2. In 6-quart Dutch oven with ovensafe handles over medium-high heat, in hot oil, brown pork well, pushing cubes aside as they brown. Spoon off any excess fat. Add water, sherry, sugar and onions. Heat to boiling, stirring to loosen brown bits. Cover; bake in 350°F. oven 1 hour, stirring occasionally.
3. Add lima beans, squash and 2 teaspoons salt. Continue baking 45 minutes or until squash is tender-crisp, stirring occasionally. Skim off fat.

Burritos

salad oil
1 pound beef for stew, cut
into ½-inch chunks
½ pound pork pieces, cut
into ½-inch chunks
1 cup chopped onions
1 garlic clove, minced
salt
water
4½ cups all-purpose flour
½ cup lard or shortening
1 15½-ounce can refried
beans
¼ cup shredded longhorn
or Cheddar cheese
1 4-ounce can diced green
chilies

Color index
page 57

Begin 2½ hrs
ahead

10 servings

439 cals per
serving

Good source
of calcium,
iron

1. In 10-inch skillet over medium-high heat; in 2 tablespoons hot salad oil, cook beef and pork chunks until browned; add onion, garlic, ½ teaspoon salt and 1½ cups water; heat to boiling. Reduce heat to low; cover and simmer 2 hours or until meat is fork-tender and begins to fall apart. Meanwhile, prepare Flour Tortillas.
2. In bowl, mix 4 cups flour with 2 teaspoons salt; cut in lard until blended. Add 1 cup warm water; mix well. Turn dough onto floured surface; knead until smooth, about 3 minutes, adding more flour if needed.
3. Divide dough into 10 pieces; cover. On floured surface with rolling pin, roll one dough piece into 10-inch circle. In ungreased 12-inch skillet over medium-high heat, cook tortilla 1 minute until brown specks appear; turn, cook 30 seconds. Place between sheets of foil; keep warm. Repeat with rest of pieces.
4. About 5 minutes before meat mixture is done, in 2-quart saucepan over medium heat, in 1 tablespoon hot oil, heat refried beans and cheese until hot and cheese is melted, stirring occasionally.
5. When meat is done, add chilies and, with spoon, gently flake meat. Continue cooking until mixture is thickened and all liquid has evaporated.
6. In center of each tortilla, spread about 2 tablespoons bean mixture in a thin layer. Spoon on about 2 tablespoons meat mixture. Fold tortilla over filling to make a "package." Eat sandwich-style.

Smoked pork

A wide and varied choice of smoked pork products is available, ranging from large holiday hams to economical, everyday cuts—smoked hocks, spareribs and bacon. Half and whole hams should be stored in the refrigerator for no more than a week before use; ham steaks for 3 to 4 days; sliced boiled ham and prosciutto for up to 3 days; and bacon for 5 to 7 days.

SMOKED HAMS AND PICNICS

Both hams and picnics are usually sold fully cooked and ready-to-serve. Flavor and texture are improved by heating them to an internal temperature of 140°F. or as label directs. Some cook-before-eating hams are sold; cook hams to an internal temperature of 160°F., picnics to 170°F.

Fully cooked hams include the following:
Bone-in ham or its two halves—butt half and shank half. If sold as portions, several center slices probably would have been removed.
Partially boned hams are either shankless or semi-boneless. In the latter case, both shank bone and aitchbone will have been removed, leaving only the leg.
Boneless hams, known as "rolled", "shaped" or "formed" hams, are sold whole, weighing 7 to 14 pounds, in halves, quarters, pieces and slices or steaks.
Canned hams are always boneless and fully cooked, and may be smoked or unsmoked. Some are also flavored.
Boiled ham is sold sliced by the pound or prepackaged.
Prosciutto is an Italian-style pressed ham, deep red in color, with a strong flavor. It is sold in paper-thin slices.
Cook-before-eating hams are usually sold bone-in. They include the "country" hams—"Smithfield", "Tennessee", "Kentucky" and "Virginia". Country hams are usually heavily cured and smoked, and require soaking and precooking unless label directs otherwise.
Smoked picnics are sold whole and usually fully cooked. When sold boneless they are called pork shoulder roll.

COOKING HAMS AND PICNICS

Roasting: Roast a fully cooked ham or picnic according to timetable. A cook-before-eating ham should be cooked to an internal temperature of 160°F., a picnic to 170°F. Plan to have the meat ready about 15 minutes before it is to be served so it can "set" for easier carving. To decorate a ham, score surface lightly in a diamond pattern and stud each diamond with a clove before it goes into the oven. If meat is to be glazed, plan to start glazing it about 30 minutes before the end of cooking.
Cooking in liquid: Place picnic in a large saucepot and cover with water. Over high heat, heat to boiling. Reduce heat to low; cover and simmer until meat is tender, 3½ to 4 hours. Drain.
Glazing after simmering: Place picnic on rack in roasting pan and bake in preheated 400°F. oven for 15 to 30 minutes, brushing 2 or 3 times with glaze.

TIMETABLE FOR ROASTING SMOKED PORK*				
Type of cut	Weight (in pounds)	Meat thermometer reading	Approximate cooking time** (in hours)	Oven temperature
Fully cooked				
Smoked ham whole	10 to 14	140°F.	2½ to 3½	325°F.
half or portion	5 to 7	140°F.	1½ to 2	325°F.
Boneless smoked ham whole	7 to 10	140°F.	2½ to 3	325°F.
	10 to 12	140°F.	3 to 3½	325°F.
	12 to 14	140°F.	3½ to 4	325°F.
half	5 to 7	140°F.	2 to 2¼	325°F.
portion	3 to 4	140°F.	1½ to 1¾	325°F.
Semi-boneless smoked ham whole	10 to 12	140°F.	3 to 3½	325°F.
half	4 to 6	140°F.	1¾ to 2½	325°F.
Canned ham	1½ to 3	140°F.	1 to 1½	325°F.
	3 to 7	140°F.	1½ to 2	325°F.
	7 to 10	140°F.	2 to 2½	325°F.
	10 to 13	140°F.	2½ to 3	325°F.
Smoked shoulder arm picnic	5 to 8	140°F.	2 to 3¼	325°F.
Smoked shoulder roll (butt)	2 to 4	170°F.	1¼ to 2¼	325°F.
Canadian-style bacon	2 to 4	160°F.	1¼ to 2¼	325°F.
Cook before eating				
Smoked ham whole	10 to 14	160°F.	3 to 4¼	325°F.
	5 to 7	160°F.	1¾ to 2½	325°F.
half or portion	3 to 4	160°F.	1¾ to 2¼	325°F.
Smoked shoulder arm picnic	5 to 8	170°F.	2½ to 4	325°F.

*Meat at refrigerator temperature
**Remove meat from oven when internal temperature is 5 to 10 degrees below desired doneness as meat continues cooking

SMOKED SHOULDER ROLLS

Roasting: Before roasting remove any casing then follow directions for hams; internal temperature should be 170°F. A 2- to 4-pound shoulder roll will take 1¼ to 2¼ hours. If desired, glaze as for hams.
Cooking in liquid: Cook and glaze as for picnics. A 2- to 4-pound shoulder roll takes 1½ to 2 hours to simmer. Then, place roll in baking dish; glaze.

HAM SLICES

Center-cut slices usually are cut from fully cooked ham. Ham slices 1 to 2 inches thick may be baked, broiled or braised. Slices 1 inch thick may also be pan-broiled. Broil or pan-broil slices ½ to ¾ inch thick.

Broiling: Slash fat around edge of ham slice in several places to prevent curling. Place slice on rack in broiling pan and broil 2 to 3 inches from heat until browned on both sides, turning once. Ham slices 1 inch thick will take 16 to 20 minutes; slices ½ inch thick are done in 10 to 12 minutes.

Pan-broiling: Rub surface of skillet with a piece of fat trimmed from edge of ham slice. Slash fat around edge of ham slice in several places to prevent curling. In skillet over medium heat, cook ham slice until well browned on both sides, turning occasionally and pouring off fat as it accumulates in pan.

Braising: Over medium heat, rub bottom of heavy skillet or Dutch oven with a piece of fat trimmed from edge of ham slice. Add ham and cook until well browned on both sides. Add a little liquid; reduce heat to low; cover tightly and cook until ham is tender.

BACON

Bacon is sold in slices, varying in thickness according to whether it is thin-sliced, regular-sliced or thick-sliced, or in pieces, with the rind left on (slab bacon), for slicing as needed. The flavor depends on the curing and smoking process used, and the bacon may be lean or fat, depending on the cut from which it comes. Sliced bacon may be baked, broiled, pan-broiled, or pan-fried.

Baking: Arrange bacon slices on rack in open roasting pan, overlapping lean edge of each slice with fat edge of the next. Bake in a preheated 400°F. oven until browned and crisp, 10 to 12 minutes.

Broiling: Separate bacon slices carefully so they do not tear and place on rack in broiling pan. Broil 3 inches from heat for 3 to 4 minutes until browned; turn and brown other side, taking care not to burn bacon. Drain on paper towels.

Pan-frying: In a cold, heavy skillet lay the number of slices required in one piece without separating them. (A 10-inch skillet will hold one 8-ounce package of bacon slices at one time.) Over medium heat, cook bacon 5 to 8 minutes, separating slices with tongs so they lie flat in the pan and turning them occasionally to brown them evenly on both sides. When browned, remove from pan and drain on paper towels.

CANADIAN-STYLE BACON

Canadian-style bacon is the large rib-eye muscle of the pork loin, cured and smoked. It is boneless and usually lean, and is sold in 2- to 4-pound pieces or sliced. Roast large pieces. Broil, pan-broil or pan-fry slices until lightly browned on both sides, turning occasionally.

SMOKED PORK LOIN AND CHOPS

A smoked pork loin should be roasted. Chops up to ½ inch thick may be pan-broiled or pan-fried; if cut thicker, they should be broiled or baked.

CARVING HAM

Whole ham: Place on cutting board or warm platter, fat side up, with shank to your right. Using a fork to anchor meat, cut a few slices from thin side; steady ham on this surface.

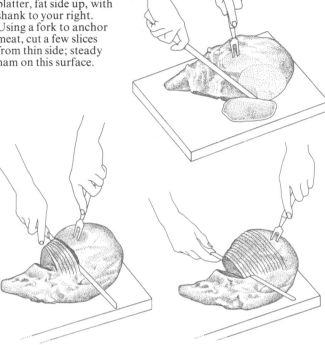

Starting at shank end, slicing down to bone, cut out small wedge of meat. Continue cutting down to bone in slices ¼ inch thick until you reach aitchbone at other end.

Starting at shank end, release meat slices by cutting along leg bone. For more servings, turn ham to its original position and cut slices to bone.

Rump half ham: Place ham on its cut surface. Using a fork to anchor meat, cut down along aitchbone to remove chunky boneless piece of meat.

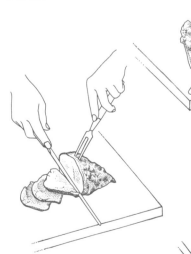

Place piece on its freshly cut surface and cut uniform slices about ¼ inch thick down to board.

Hold remaining piece, slice across, then cut along bone to free each slice.

219

Smoked ham and picnics

Pineapple-glazed Baked Half Ham

1 5-to 7-pound fully cooked smoked rump or shank half ham
1 8-ounce can crushed pineapple, well drained
½ cup packed brown sugar

Color index page 59

Begin 2¾ hrs ahead

20 servings

294 cals per serving

Good source of iron, thiamine

1. Place ham on rack in open roasting pan. Insert meat thermometer into center of meat, being careful not to allow it to touch bone or fat. Bake in 325°F. oven 1 to 1½ hours.
2. Meanwhile, in bowl, combine crushed pineapple with the brown sugar.
3. Remove ham from oven; carefully cut off any tough outer skin from it and discard. With spoon, evenly pat the prepared pineapple mixture on ham. Bake 30 minutes longer or until meat thermometer reaches 140°F.

Removing skin: Before adding glaze cut off any tough outer skin from the ham; discard skin.

Adding the glaze: Use a spoon to pat the prepared pineapple mixture onto the ham.

Baked Picnic

1 5- to 8-pound fully cooked smoked pork shoulder arm picnic
½ cup orange marmalade
1½ teaspoons prepared mustard
1 small orange whole cloves

Color index page 59

Begin 3½ hrs ahead

16 servings

398 cals per serving

Good source of iron, thiamine, niacin

1. Place picnic on rack in open roasting pan. Insert meat thermometer from top center of the thickest part, making sure pointed end is in center of picnic and not resting on bone or fat.
2. Bake at 325°F. 1½ to 2¾ hours; remove picnic from oven and, with sharp knife, cut skin and excess fat from picnic, leaving thin fat covering.
3. Meanwhile, prepare orange glaze: In 1-quart saucepan over low heat, heat orange marmalade and mustard until marmalade is melted.
4. With a pastry brush, brush half of the prepared orange glaze evenly over the picnic. Return the picnic to the oven and bake 20 minutes longer until the internal temperature reaches 140°F.
5. Remove picnic from oven; remove meat thermometer. Cut oranges into very thin slices and halve them; arrange in rows over picnic overlapping them slightly and fastening with cloves. Brush remaining warm glaze over orange slices.
6. Return the picnic to the oven and bake 10 minutes more until the orange slices are heated through. Allow the Baked Picnic to cool slightly to serve warm or serve cold later.

Barbecued Canned Ham and Peaches

1 3-pound canned ham
½ cup sugar
½ cup chili sauce
1 tablespoon lemon juice
2 teaspoons Worcestershire
½ teaspoon chili powder
½ cup water
5 medium peaches, peeled and halved

Color index page 58

Begin 1¾ hrs ahead

12 servings

199 cals per serving

1. Remove any gelatin from ham. Place ham in 12" by 8" baking dish; insert meat thermometer into center of ham. Bake in 325°F. oven 1¼ hours.
2. Meanwhile, in 2-quart saucepan over medium heat, heat to boiling sugar, chili sauce, lemon juice, Worcestershire, chili powder and water, stirring occasionally. Remove sauce from heat; add peaches and gently stir to coat well.
3. Spoon peaches into baking dish and pour remaining sauce over ham. Bake ham and peaches about 20 minutes more, basting occasionally with sauce, until thermometer reaches 140°F. Place ham on warm platter; arrange peaches around it.

Glazed Ham Platter

1 5- to 6-pound fully cooked smoked semi-boneless half ham
½ cup pineapple preserves
½ cup apple jelly
2 tablespoons prepared horseradish
2 tablespoons prepared mustard
1 cup packed light brown sugar
½ cup maple-flavor syrup
¼ teaspoon ground cinnamon
⅛ teaspoon ground allspice
water
3 medium acorn squash, cut into ¾-inch wedges
butter or margarine
3 large red cooking apples, cut into ½-inch wedges

Color index page 58

Begin 3 hrs ahead

18 servings

409 cals per serving

Good source of iron, thiamine

1. Place ham on rack in open roasting pan. Insert meat thermometer, avoiding bone or fat. Bake ham in 325°F. oven 1 to 1½ hours.
2. Meanwhile, make glaze: In 1-quart saucepan over low heat, combine pineapple preserves, apple jelly, horseradish and mustard until jelly melts. Brush over ham and bake ham 30 minutes longer until thermometer reads 140°F, brushing often with glaze.
3. Meanwhile, in 1-quart saucepan combine sugar, syrup, cinnamon and allspice; set aside. In 12-inch skillet over medium heat, heat ½ inch water and squash to boiling. Reduce heat to low; cover; simmer about 10 minutes until squash is fork-tender; drain. To squash in skillet add ¼ cup butter and half sugar mixture. Over medium heat, cook until butter and sugar melt and squash is glazed, stirring gently; keep warm.
4. In another 12-inch skillet over medium-high heat, in ¼ cup hot butter, cook apples until tender, about 5 minutes, stirring. Add remaining sugar mixture and continue cooking until sugar is melted and apples are glazed, stirring gently with rubber spatula. Place ham on warm large platter; arrange squash and apples around ham. Pour any remaining glaze over squash and apples.

Ham slices

Whole Smithfield Ham

1 10- to 12-pound cook-before-eating Smithfield ham or country ham
water
dark corn syrup
little hot biscuits or assorted sliced breads

Color index page 58

Begin day ahead

60 appetizer servings

132 cals per serving

1 Place the ham, skin side down, in saucepot large enough to hold the whole ham; add enough water to cover the ham completely. Allow to stand at room temperature for at least 12 hours or overnight.

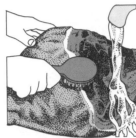

2 *About 5 hours before serving:* Discard water; scrub ham; rinse. Again cover ham with water. Over high heat, heat to boiling.

3 Reduce heat to low; cover; simmer 20 minutes per pound until bone on small end feels loose. Preheat oven to 325°F.

4 Remove ham to rack in open roasting pan; discard water. Cool ham 20 minutes. Remove skin; trim fat leaving about ¼ inch fat.

5 Brush ham with dark corn syrup. Bake 15 minutes or until ham is evenly glazed.

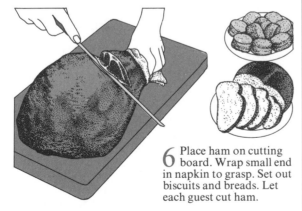

6 Place ham on cutting board. Wrap small end in napkin to grasp. Set out biscuits and breads. Let each guest cut ham.

LEFTOVER SMITHFIELD HAM

CHICKEN SOUP: Add minced ham to chicken soup.

SEASONING: Add small chunks of ham to vegetables as they are cooking.

APPETIZER: Put slices of ham on melon wedges.

Ham Steak Hawaiian

½ cup packed light or dark brown sugar
¼ cup butter or margarine
¼ cup red or white wine vinegar
1 smoked ham center slice, cut ½ to ¾ inch thick (about 1½ pounds)
4 firm medium bananas

Color index page 59

Begin 30 mins ahead

6 servings

348 cals per serving

Good source of iron, thiamine

1 In 12-inch skillet over medium heat, heat brown sugar, butter or margarine and vinegar until sugar is melted, stirring frequently.

2 Add ham slice to sugar mixture; cook 5 minutes on each side or until heated through.

3 With pancake turner, arrange ham on heated platter; keep warm.

4 Remove skillet from heat. Cut bananas into 1½-inch chunks. Add bananas to the sugar mixture in the skillet.

5 Cook over medium heat, basting bananas with sauce until bananas are heated through, about 5 minutes.

6 With spoon, carefully spoon banana chunks onto platter to surround ham slice. Spoon sauce remaining in skillet over ham and banana mixture. Serve Ham Steak Hawaiian immediately.

Ham slices

Smoked shoulder rolls

Lemony Ham Steaks

Color index
page 59

Begin 20 mins
ahead

8 servings

255 cals per
serving

Good source
of iron,
thiamine

*³/₄ cup packed light
  brown sugar*
*3 tablespoons prepared
  mustard*
*1¹/₂ tablespoons lemon
  juice*
*³/₄ teaspoon grated
  lemon peel*

1 lemon, thinly sliced
*2 smoked ham boneless
  center slices, each
  cut about ³/₄ inch thick
  (about 1 pound each)*

1. Preheat broiler if manufacturer directs. Make glaze: In small bowl, combine first 4 ingredients. Cut lemon slices in half; set aside.
2. Place ham slices in large broiling pan. Broil 2 minutes, brush with some of glaze and broil 5 minutes more. Turn and broil 2 or 3 minutes.
3. Arrange lemon slices on steaks; brush with rest of glaze; broil 5 minutes more or until glaze is bubbling and steaks are heated through.

Fruit-sauced Ham Slices

Color index
page 59

Begin 30 mins
ahead

6 servings

484 cals per
serving

Good source
of iron,
thiamine,
niacin

*6 smoked ham boneless
  center slices, each
  about ¹/₂ inch thick*
1 cup pitted dried prunes
1 cup dried apricots

1³/₄ cups orange juice
¹/₄ cup sugar
1 tablespoon cornstarch
2 tablespoons water

1. Trim piece of fat from ham slice; slash edges of ham slices. In 12-inch skillet over medium-high heat, heat piece of fat until lightly browned, rubbing fat on bottom of skillet to grease it; discard piece of fat. Cook ham slices, a few at a time, until lightly browned on both sides, removing the slices as they brown.
2. Into skillet, stir prunes, apricots, orange juice and sugar. Return ham to skillet, overlapping slices to fit; spoon some juice over slices; heat to boiling. Reduce heat to low; cover; simmer 20 minutes or until apricots are tender. Place ham slices on warm platter; keep warm.
3. In cup, blend cornstarch and water until smooth; stir into hot mixture in skillet and cook over medium heat, stirring constantly, until mixture is thickened and boils. Serve fruit sauce with ham.

Country Ham Steak

Color index
page 59

Begin 1 hr
ahead

6 servings

296 cals per
serving

Good source
of iron,
thiamine,
vitamin C

¹/₄ cup butter
*1 small head cabbage
  (about 1¹/₂ pounds),
  coarsely shredded*
¹/₂ teaspoon salt

*1 smoked ham center
  slice, cut about
  1 inch thick*
*2 tablespoons pancake
  syrup*

1. Preheat oven to 350°F. In 12-inch skillet over medium-high heat, in hot butter, cook the coarsely shredded cabbage and salt, stirring quickly and frequently, until cabbage is tender-crisp, about 5 minutes. Spoon cabbage evenly into 13" by 9" baking dish.
2. Place ham slice on top of cabbage; drizzle syrup over ham and cabbage.
3. Bake in oven 30 minutes or until ham is heated through, stirring cabbage occasionally so that it does not stick. Serve immediately.

Choucroute Garni

Color index
page 59

Begin 3 hrs
ahead

20 servings

219 cals per
serving

Good source
of iron

*1 2- to 2¹/₂-pound smoked
  pork shoulder roll*
*1 2- to 2¹/₂-pound pork
  shoulder blade
  (Boston) roast
  boneless*
2 cups dry white wine
*1 13³/₄-ounce can chicken
  broth*

*8 juniper berries or 2
  tablespoons gin*
6 medium onions, halved
*8 medium potatoes,
  halved*
*6 fresh bratwurst or
  frankfurters*
*4 cups well-drained
  sauerkraut*

1. In 10- to 12-quart saucepot, heat to boiling smoked pork shoulder roll (remove any casing), pork shoulder blade roast, wine, canned chicken broth and juniper berries or gin. Reduce heat to low; cover and simmer 1¹/₂ hours.
2. Add remaining ingredients in layers: first the onions, then potatoes, bratwurst and sauerkraut; cover tightly and simmer for 35 to 40 minutes until the meat and vegetables are fork-tender.
3. With slotted spoon, place the sauerkraut, bratwurst, potatoes and onions on warm large platter. Slice the shoulder blade roast and smoked pork roll and arrange on the same platter. Drain fat from the pan liquid; discard the juniper berries. Serve liquid over meat and vegetables and pass the remainder separately in a gravy boat.

Serving Choucroute Garni:
Spoon some pan liquid
over meat and vegetables.
Pass rest in gravy boat.

Smoked Pork with Sweet Potatoes

Color index
page 58

Begin 2 hrs
ahead

10 servings

333 cals per
serving

Good source
of iron,
thiamine

*1 2¹/₂- to 3-pound smoked
  pork shoulder roll*
*1 cup packed light brown
  sugar*
*¹/₂ teaspoon ground
  nutmeg*

3 tablespoons water
*2 17-ounce cans
  vacuum-packed
  sweet potatoes*

1. Remove any casing from smoked shoulder roll. Place meat in open roasting pan. Insert meat thermometer into center of meat. Roast in 325°F. oven 30 minutes.
2. Meanwhile, in small bowl, blend the light brown sugar, ground nutmeg and water.
3. Remove roasting pan from oven; place the sweet potatoes in one layer around meat; brush meat and potatoes with brown-sugar mixture. Roast about 1 hour longer or until meat thermometer reaches 170°F., brushing occasionally with the pan liquid. Place the meat and potatoes on warm platter; spoon pan liquid over all. Serve immediately.

Glazes and leftover ham

GLAZES

ORANGE-MINCEMEAT: In covered blender container at low speed, blend ½ *cup drained mincemeat* and ¼ *cup orange marmalade* until glaze is smooth. (Makes about ¾ cup.) 405 cals total

CURRY-ORANGE: In small bowl with fork, stir ⅔ *cup light corn syrup, 1 tablespoon curry powder* and *1 tablespoon grated orange peel* until blended. (Makes about ⅔ cup.) 482 cals total

TOMATO-ONION: In 1-quart saucepan over medium heat, in *1 tablespoon butter* or margarine, cook *2 tablespoons minced onion* until tender, about 3 minutes, stirring occasionally. Stir in *one 8-ounce can tomato sauce, 2 tablespoons dark brown sugar* and *1 teaspoon Worcestershire*; heat to boiling. Reduce heat to low; simmer 5 minutes or until glaze is slightly thickened. (Makes about 1 cup.)

267 cals total

LEFTOVER HAM

GLAZED KABOBS: Alternately skewer *chunks of ham* with *thick wedges of apple*, brush with *orange marmalade* diluted with *lemon juice*; broil, until kabobs are glazed.

HAM DIP: Combine *finely chopped ham* with *sour cream, mayonnaise, Worcestershire* and *salt*; mix until of spoonable consistency; use as dip.

HAM AND SWISS SPREAD: Combine *ground ham* with *shredded Swiss cheese* and *softened cream cheese*, thinned with *milk* and seasoned with ⅛ *teaspoon hot pepper sauce*; use as sandwich filling.

CREAMED VEGETABLES WITH HAM: Stir *bits of ham* or matchstick-size strips of ham into *creamed potatoes*, cauliflower or leeks; eat as a main dish.

HAM CHEF'S SALAD: Arrange *chunks or slivers of ham, tomato slices, olives, cucumber sticks* and *sliced radishes* over *macaroni* or *potato salad*.

HAM PATTIES: Combine *ground ham* with an *egg* and add *bread crumbs*, ⅛ *teaspoon ground sage* and ⅛ *teaspoon pepper*; shape into small patties and fry in *butter*; serve in buns as a main dish if you like.

HAM FRUIT SALAD: Combine *diced ham* with *chopped walnuts* or almonds and *sliced celery*, moistened with *mayonnaise*; fill a halved *avocado*, cantaloupe or papaya.

HAM AND WATERCRESS SOUP: Heat homemade or canned *chicken broth* to boiling; add *sliced mushrooms, slivered pieces of ham* and *watercress*; reheat to boiling; serve as first course.

HAM CASSEROLE: Combine *kidney beans* or canned pork and beans, *catchup, brown sugar, mustard* and *diced green pepper* with *chunks of ham*; bake until mixture is bubbly.

MINCED HAM TOPPINGS: Serve *minced ham* over scrambled eggs, cooked vegetables, tossed salads, potato salads, bean or vegetable soup.

Color index page 59

Begin 1¾ hrs ahead

5 servings

292 cals per serving

Good source of iron, thiamine

Glazed Ham Loaf

1 pound ground smoked ham
1 large carrot, grated
1 small onion, minced
1 cup fresh bread crumbs
2 eggs
2 tablespoons chopped parsley
2 teaspoons prepared mustard

1 8-ounce can pineapple slices in juice
2 tablespoons light brown sugar
2 teaspoons cornstarch
1 tablespoon butter or margarine
1 tablespoon lemon juice

1 In medium bowl with fork, mix well first 7 ingredients. Grease 11″ by 7″ baking pan.

2 In pan, shape ham mixture into 7″ by 3″ loaf. Bake in 350°F. oven 30 minutes. Into 1-quart saucepan, drain the pineapple juice and reserve the pineapple slices.

3 Into pineapple juice, stir brown sugar and cornstarch until completely smooth. Over medium heat, stir the mixture until thickened and boiling.

4 Remove from heat; stir in butter or margarine and lemon juice until well blended.

5 Remove ham loaf from oven; with a pastry brush, carefully brush the meat loaf all over with the pineapple and lemon juice glaze.

6 Overlap pineapple slices on top. Bake 30 minutes longer, brushing occasionally with glaze. Let loaf stand 5 minutes for easier slicing.

Lamb

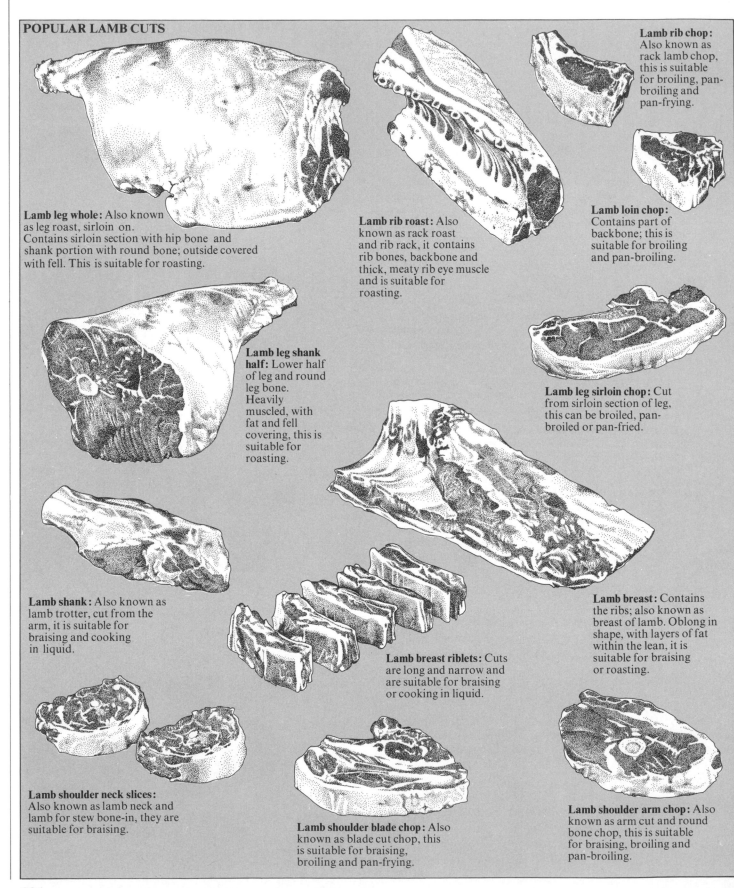

POPULAR LAMB CUTS

Lamb leg whole: Also known as leg roast, sirloin on. Contains sirloin section with hip bone and shank portion with round bone; outside covered with fell. This is suitable for roasting.

Lamb rib roast: Also known as rack roast and rib rack, it contains rib bones, backbone and thick, meaty rib eye muscle and is suitable for roasting.

Lamb rib chop: Also known as rack lamb chop, this is suitable for broiling, pan-broiling and pan-frying.

Lamb loin chop: Contains part of backbone; this is suitable for broiling and pan-broiling.

Lamb leg shank half: Lower half of leg and round leg bone. Heavily muscled, with fat and fell covering, this is suitable for roasting.

Lamb leg sirloin chop: Cut from sirloin section of leg, this can be broiled, pan-broiled or pan-fried.

Lamb shank: Also known as lamb trotter, cut from the arm, it is suitable for braising and cooking in liquid.

Lamb breast riblets: Cuts are long and narrow and are suitable for braising or cooking in liquid.

Lamb breast: Contains the ribs; also known as breast of lamb. Oblong in shape, with layers of fat within the lean, it is suitable for braising or roasting.

Lamb shoulder neck slices: Also known as lamb neck and lamb for stew bone-in, they are suitable for braising.

Lamb shoulder blade chop: Also known as blade cut chop, this is suitable for braising, broiling and pan-frying.

Lamb shoulder arm chop: Also known as arm cut and round bone chop, this is suitable for braising, broiling and pan-broiling.

LAMB

Lamb is a tender, lean meat with a delicate yet distinctive flavor which is enhanced by seasonings and flavorings of all kinds, ranging from garlic and herbs and spices to fruit and nuts.

BUYING LAMB

The meat of high-quality lamb is pink to light red in color, firm and fine-textured, with red, porous bones. The color of the fat cannot be taken as a guide to quality because it varies according to the animal's age, breed and feed; the fat should not be too thick in relation to lean meat.

The thin, papery skin that surrounds chops, steaks and roasts should feel fresh, moist and pliable, not dry or wrinkled, This skin, known as the "fell," should be left on roasts to help them hold their shape during cooking. However, if it has not been removed from steaks and chops when you buy them, pull it off yourself before you cook them. When buying rib roasts, ask the meatman to loosen the backbone from the ribs to make carving easier.

Some lamb cuts, such as rib crown roast, are expensive and are suitable only for special occasions, but there are a number of lamb cuts which are excellent value for everyday budget meals. These include riblets and shanks, which are very economical. If planning to serve kabobs, the cubes can be cut from any thick, solid piece of boneless lamb. You can cut the cubes at home from an unrolled boneless shoulder roast.

COOKING LAMB

Most lamb cuts are tender enough to be cooked by one of the dry heat methods, roasting, broiling, pan-broiling or pan-frying (see pages 186–87), but lamb is also delicious braised or cooked in liquid.

Whichever method you choose, it is always important to remember to keep temperatures low to moderate so that the meat will not cook too quickly and will be as tender, juicy and flavorful as possible.

TESTING FOR DONENESS

Roast lamb can be served rare, medium or well done. For rare lamb, the thermometer should read 140°F. and the meat will be reddish inside. For medium lamb, the thermometer should read 160°F. and the meat will be brownish-pink with a tinge of red. For well-done lamb, the thermometer should register 170°F. and there will be no sign of pink in the meat. Remember to let lamb stand 15 minutes when you take it out of the oven. This will make for much easier carving.

To test broiled, pan-broiled and pan-fried lamb for doneness, make a small slit in the center of the meat or near the bone and check the color. Braised lamb or lamb cooked in liquid should be fork-tender.

TIMETABLE FOR ROASTING LAMB *				
Weight (in pounds)	Approximate cooking time** (in hours)			Oven temperature
	Rare 140°F.	Medium 160°F.	Well done 170°F.	
Leg whole				
5	1¾	2	2½	325°F.
7	2¼	3	3½	325°F.
9	3	3¾	4½	325°F.
Leg shank half				
3 to 4	1¼ to 1¾	1½ to 2	1¾ to 2¼	325°F.
Leg sirloin half				
3 to 4	1 to 1¼	1¼ to 1¾	1½ to 2	325°F.
Leg roast boneless				
3	1¼	1½	1¾	325°F.
5	2	2½	3	325°F.
7	3	3½	4	325°F.
Rib roast (rack)				
1½ to 2	¾	1	1¼	375°F.
2 to 3	1	1¼	1½	375°F.
Shoulder roast square cut whole				
4 to 6		1¾ to 2½	2 to 3	325°F.
Shoulder roast boneless				
3½ to 5	1¾ to 2½	2 to 3	2⅓ to 3¼	325°F.

*Meat at refrigerator temperature.
**Remove meat from oven when internal temperature is 5 to 10 degrees below desired doneness as meat continues cooking.

CARVING A LEG OF LAMB

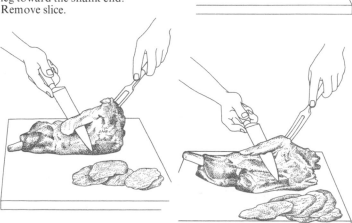

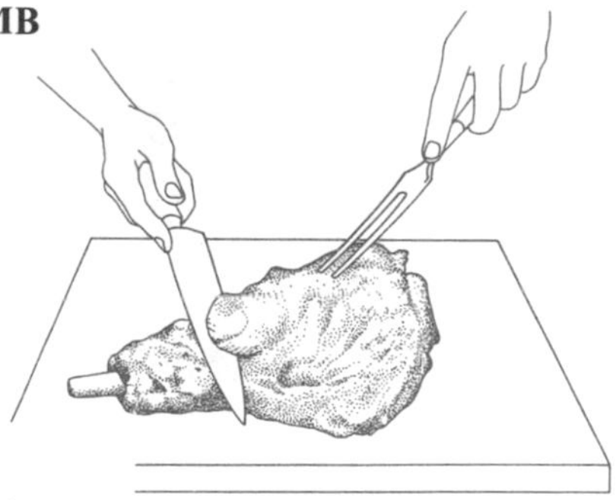

Place leg of lamb on cutting board or warm platter with leg or shank bone to your right. Using a fork to anchor meat, and holding knife in a slanting position almost parallel to the surface of lamb, make a ¼-inch-thick slice about a third of the way along the leg toward the shank end. Remove slice.

Cut next slice ¼ inch farther toward the large end and cut parallel to the bone. Continue cutting slices until you reach the bone.

After removing the top slices, turn leg slightly and carve the sides in long slender slices.

Lamb roasts

Roast Leg of Lamb

3 juniper berries
2 teaspoons dry mustard
1/4 teaspoon pepper
salt
water
1 5-pound lamb leg whole
12 small potatoes,
*   peeled*
1/4 cup gin (optional)
1/2 cup red currant
*   jelly*
2 tablespoons cornstarch

Color index
page 60

Begin 3 hrs
ahead

15 servings

192 cals per
serving

Good source
of iron

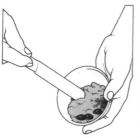

1 Crush juniper with mustard, pepper, 1 teaspoon salt and 2 teaspoons water. Spread on lamb.

2 Place lamb, fat side up, on rack in open roasting pan. Insert meat thermometer into center of thickest part of meat, taking care not to touch bone. Roast 1⅔ to 2½ hours in 325°F. oven, until meat thermometer reaches 140°F. for rare or 160°F. for medium or 170°F. for well done. Meanwhile, cut potatoes into 1-inch-thick slices. About 45 minutes before meat is done, sprinkle the potato slices with 1 teaspoon salt.

3 Put potatoes on rack around meat; cook until fork-tender, brushing with drippings. Place potatoes, meat on platter.

4 Pour pan liquid into 2-cup measure; let stand until fat separates; spoon fat from liquid; discard.

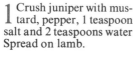

5 Add 1¼ cups water to pan; cook over medium heat, stirring to loosen bits; add to liquid in cup with gin. Add water to make 1¾ cups.

6 In 2-quart saucepan over medium heat, heat measured liquid and jelly to boiling, stirring constantly until the jelly is melted.

7 Blend cornstarch, ¼ teaspoon salt and ¼ cup water; stir into liquid in pan until thickened. Carve lamb. Serve sauce separately.

Marinated Butterflied Lamb

1 4-pound lamb leg
*   shank half*
1 tablespoon peppercorns
1/3 cup Burgundy
3 tablespoons olive oil
1 teaspoon salt

1 1/2 teaspoons oregano,
*   crushed*
1 large garlic clove,
*   slivered*
parsley sprigs
*   for garnish*

Color index
page 61

Begin day
ahead

12 servings

227 cals per
serving

Good source
of iron

1. Butterfly leg of lamb (see below).
2. On cutting board, between double thickness of waxed paper, with meat mallet or clean hammer, pound peppercorns until coarsely cracked.
3. For marinade, in 12" by 8" baking dish, combine peppercorns and next 5 ingredients. Add butterflied lamb; turn over to coat evenly. Cover with plastic wrap; refrigerate at least 12 hours, turning meat occasionally.
4. *About 45 minutes before serving:* Preheat broiler if manufacturer directs. Drain lamb, reserving marinade. Place lamb on rack in broiling pan. Broil about 5 inches from source of heat (or at 450°F.) for 10 minutes, occasionally basting with marinade. Turn and broil 15 minutes longer for rare or until meat is of desired doneness. Place on carving board; garnish lamb with sprigs of parsley.

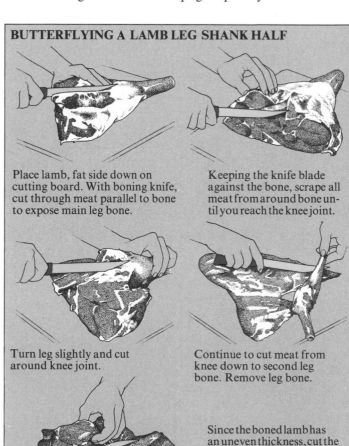

BUTTERFLYING A LAMB LEG SHANK HALF

Place lamb, fat side down on cutting board. With boning knife, cut through meat parallel to bone to expose main leg bone.

Keeping the knife blade against the bone, scrape all meat from around bone until you reach the knee joint.

Turn leg slightly and cut around knee joint.

Continue to cut meat from knee down to second leg bone. Remove leg bone.

Since the boned lamb has an uneven thickness, cut the thicker muscles almost in half and open like a butterfly to make it flatter for a more even thickness. It will have an irregular shape. Trim excess fat from meat.

Marinated Leg of Lamb Olé

Color index page 60

Begin day ahead

10 to 12 servings

12 servings

254 cals per serving

Good source of iron

salt
$^1/_2$ cup orange juice
$^1/_2$ cup dry red wine
$^1/_2$ cup chili sauce
2 tablespoons salad oil
1 small onion, minced
1 garlic clove, minced
2 tablespoons sugar
2 teaspoons chili powder
1 teaspoon basil
1 4-pound lamb leg shank half
water
3 tablespoons all-purpose flour

1. In large shallow pan, for marinade, mix 1 teaspoon salt and remaining ingredients except leg of lamb, water and flour. Add lamb and turn over to coat with marinade. Cover with plastic wrap and refrigerate at least 12 hours, turning lamb occasionally.

2. *About 3$^1/_2$ hours before serving:* Place lamb, fat side up, on rack in open roasting pan; reserve marinade. Insert meat thermometer into center of meat, being careful thermometer does not touch bone. Roast in 325°F. oven about 1$^2/_3$ hours or until meat thermometer reaches 140°F. for rare, 160°F. for medium or 170°F. for well done, basting occasionally with marinade. Place meat on warm platter; let rest 15 minutes.

3. Meanwhile, make gravy: Pour pan liquid into a 4-cup measure or medium bowl (set pan aside); let stand a few minutes until fat separates from meat liquid. Skim 3 tablespoons fat from liquid into 2-quart saucepan; skim remaining fat and discard. Add 1$^1/_2$ cups water to roasting pan; cook over medium heat, stirring until brown bits are loosened; add mixture and reserved marinade to liquid in cup. (Add more water if needed to make 2$^1/_2$ cups.) Over medium heat, into hot fat in saucepan, stir flour and $^1/_4$ teaspoon salt until blended; gradually stir in liquid mixture and cook, stirring, until thickened. Serve gravy with lamb.

Rotisseried Leg of Lamb

Color index page 61

Begin day ahead

16 to 18 servings

18 servings

217 cals per serving

$^1/_2$ cup salad oil
$^1/_2$ cup white wine
$^1/_2$ cup red wine vinegar
1 garlic clove, crushed
1 teaspoon salt
$^1/_2$ teaspoon rubbed sage
$^1/_2$ teaspoon ground ginger
$^1/_4$ teaspoon pepper
1 5-pound lamb leg roast boneless
Mint Sauce (page 243)

1. In large, shallow dish, for marinade mix well all ingredients except lamb and Mint Sauce. Add lamb; coat well with marinade. Cover and refrigerate, turning lamb occasionally.

2. *About 3 hours before serving:* Place lamb on rotisserie skewer as manufacturer directs; reserve marinade. Insert meat thermometer into center of lamb, being careful thermometer does not touch skewer or heating element or oven as it turns. Roast on rotisserie about 2 to 3 hours until meat thermometer reaches 140°F. for rare, 160°F. for medium or 170°F. for well done, brushing frequently with marinade. Meanwhile prepare Mint Sauce.

3. Remove skewer and strings. Let meat stand 15 minutes for easier carving. Serve with Mint Sauce.

Roast Rack of Lamb

Color index page 61

Begin 2 hrs ahead

4 servings

510 cals per serving

Good source of iron, niacin

$^1/_2$ teaspoon garlic salt
$^1/_4$ teaspoon salt
$^1/_8$ teaspoon pepper
1 8-rib lamb rib roast (about 2$^1/_2$ pounds)
$^1/_4$ cup apricot preserves
2 teaspoons lemon juice

1 Preheat oven to 375°F. Combine garlic salt, salt and pepper; rub into meat. Place lamb on rib bones in roasting pan.

2 Insert meat thermometer. Roast 1 hour or until thermometer reaches 140°F. for rare, 160°F. for medium or 170°F. for well-done meat.

3 Meanwhile, in 1-quart saucepan over medium heat, heat apricot preserves and lemon juice until preserves are melted.

4 During last 30 minutes of roasting, brush lamb with apricot mixture occasionally.

5 Remove roast to cutting board; let stand 10 minutes for easier carving; with sharp knife, cut backbone from ribs; discard.

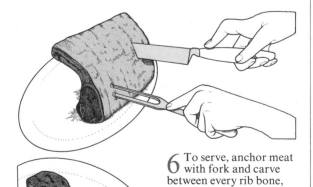

6 To serve, anchor meat with fork and carve between every rib bone, allowing 2 ribs for each individual serving.

Lamb cubes

Lamb Kabobs

Color index page 61

Begin early in day or day ahead

8 servings

261 cals per serving

Good source of iron, niacin, vitamin C

2 tablespoons butter
1/2 cup chopped onion
1 small green pepper, diced
1 celery stalk, diced
1 garlic clove, minced
1 8-ounce can tomatoes
1 6-ounce can tomato paste
1/4 cup water
2 tablespoons light brown sugar
1 1/2 teaspoons vinegar
1/2 teaspoon salt
1/2 teaspoon hot pepper sauce
1/4 teaspoon cracked pepper
1 medium eggplant
2 medium red peppers
2 pounds lamb cubes for kabobs

1 In 2-quart saucepan over medium heat, in hot butter, cook onion, green pepper, celery and garlic 10 minutes or until vegetables are tender.

2 Add tomatoes and their liquid and next 7 ingredients; heat to boiling. Reduce heat to low; simmer 5 minutes. Spoon mixture into large bowl; chill.

3 Cut eggplant lengthwise in half, then crosswise into 1-inch-thick slices. Cut red peppers into 2-inch pieces.

4 When tomato mixture is cool, add lamb, eggplant and red peppers; mix well; cover; chill 4 hours or overnight, stirring.

5 About 1 hour before serving: Prepare outdoor grill for barbecuing. On four 18-inch skewers, thread lamb alternately with vegetables. Spoon marinade into pan; cover.

6 Place skewers on grill over medium coals; cook 30 minutes or until lamb is of desired doneness, turning often. Heat marinade on same grill to serve with lamb.

Chops

Lamb Chops à l'Orange

Color index page 61

Begin 30 mins ahead

8 servings

375 cals per serving

Good source of iron

1 10-ounce jar orange marmalade
2 tablespoons butter or margarine
1 tablespoon dry sherry
1 garlic clove, minced
1 teaspoon salt
8 lamb shoulder arm chops, each cut about 1 inch thick

1. Preheat broiler if manufacturer directs. In 1-quart saucepan over low heat, heat all ingredients except chops until marmalade melts, stirring.
2. Place chops on rack in broiling pan; broil 10 to 15 minutes until of desired doneness, turning once and brushing occasionally with marmalade mixture.

Roquefort Lamb Chops

Color index page 61

Begin 1 1/4 hrs ahead

8 servings

347 cals per serving

Good source of iron, niacin

1/4 pound Roquefort cheese
1/2 teaspoon salt
1 teaspoon Worcestershire
1/8 teaspoon pepper
8 lamb 2-rib rib chops, each cut about 2 1/2 inches thick
1 10 1/2-ounce can condensed consommé, undiluted

1 Preheat oven to 325°F. Stir and mash Roquefort, salt, Worcestershire and pepper until mixed.

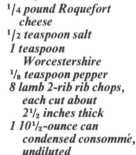

2 Trim chops, leaving thin layer of fat; over fat sides, to within about 1 inch of both ends, spread some Roquefort mixture.

3 Set chops on bones in 12″ by 8″ baking dish; add consommé. Bake 50 minutes or until of desired doneness, basting.

Broiled Gingery Lamb Chops

Color index page 61

Begin 30 mins ahead

6 servings

345 cals per serving

Good source of iron, niacin

2 tablespoons salad oil
1 1/2 teaspoons ground ginger
1/2 teaspoon salt
1/2 teaspoon garlic powder
6 lamb loin chops, each cut about 1 inch thick or 6 lamb leg sirloin chops, each cut about 1/2 inch thick
1 pound mushrooms, stems removed

1. Preheat broiler if manufacturer directs. Combine oil, ginger, salt and garlic powder.
2. Place chops on greased rack in broiling pan; brush one side with some oil mixture. Broil 5 minutes; turn chops and arrange mushroom caps around chops; brush both with remaining oil mixture; broil until of desired doneness. Serve chops immediately.

Breasts and riblets

Lamb Chops with Vegetable Gravy

Color index page 60

Begin 1¾ hrs ahead

6 servings

392 cals per serving

Good source of iron

6 lamb shoulder blade chops, each cut ¾ inch thick
¼ teaspoon pepper
salt
3 tablespoons all-purpose flour
¼ cup salad oil
3 medium carrots, sliced
1 large onion, diced
1 large celery stalk, sliced
1 garlic clove, minced
½ cup dry red wine

2 tomatoes, peeled, seeded and diced
1 beef-flavor bouillon cube or envelope
1 bay leaf
½ teaspoon thyme leaves
¼ teaspoon ground allspice
celery leaves for garnish

1 On waxed paper, sprinkle lamb chops with pepper and ½ teaspoon salt; using tongs, coat well with flour.

2 In 12-inch skillet over medium-high heat, in hot oil, cook chops, half at a time, until browned on both sides, removing chops to a platter as they brown.

3 In skillet over medium heat, in drippings, cook carrots, onion, celery and garlic 5 minutes, stirring occasionally. Add wine, next 5 ingredients and ¾ teaspoon salt. Add chops.

4 Heat to boiling. Reduce heat to low; cover; simmer 50 minutes or until chops are tender, turning once; remove to platter. Discard bay leaf and any bones.

5 Spoon mixture into blender container; skim fat from top. Cover; blend at medium speed until mixture is smooth.

6 Pour gravy into same skillet; over medium heat, heat to boiling; spoon over chops. Garnish with celery leaves.

Oven-barbecued Lamb Breast

Color index page 60

Begin 3½ hrs ahead

4 servings

470 cals per serving

Good source of iron, niacin, vitamin C

1 3-pound lamb breast
3 medium oranges
½ cup chili sauce
2 tablespoons honey
¾ teaspoon salt
1 teaspoon Worcestershire
¼ teaspoon cracked black pepper

1 Cut lamb breast into serving-size portions. Grate 1 tablespoon peel and squeeze ¼ cup juice from 1 orange.

2 In small bowl, mix well orange peel, juice, chili sauce and remaining ingredients; set aside.

3 Place lamb in open roasting pan; pour chili-sauce mixture over lamb portions.

4 Bake in 325°F. oven 2½ to 3 hours until fork-tender, basting with sauce occasionally. Meanwhile, slice rest of oranges crosswise.

5 During last 15 minutes of cooking time, add orange slices to lamb to heat through.

Lamb Riblets with Pineapple

Color index page 61

Begin 2½ hrs ahead

8 servings

448 cals per serving

Good source of iron, niacin

1 16-ounce can pineapple chunks
¼ cup honey
3 tablespoons white wine vinegar
1½ teaspoons salt
1 teaspoon Worcestershire

¼ teaspoon ground ginger
6 pounds lamb riblets

1. In 17¼" by 11½" roasting pan, mix liquid drained from pineapple with honey, vinegar, salt, Worcestershire and ginger. (Reserve pineapple.)
2. Add riblets; cover pan tightly with foil and bake in 325°F. oven 2 hours or until riblets are fork-tender. During last 10 minutes, add pineapple chunks.
3. Place riblets and pineapple on warm platter.

Shanks and neck slices

Lamb Shank Stew

Color index
page 60

Begin 2½ hrs
ahead

6 servings

700 cals per
serving

Good source
of calcium,
iron,
riboflavin,
niacin,
vitamin C

*12 medium tomatoes
(about 4 pounds)*
*6 lamb shanks (about 6
pounds)*
all-purpose flour
¼ cup salad oil
1 cup chopped onions
2 carrots, sliced
1 garlic clove, minced
¼ cup dry vermouth
*2 chicken-flavor bouillon
cubes or envelopes*

4 teaspoons sugar
1½ teaspoons salt
2 teaspoons rosemary
½ teaspoon pepper
*3 medium zucchini, cut
into 1½-inch chunks*
⅓ cup water
*1 tablespoon grated
lemon peel*
*3 cups hot cooked barley
or rice*

1. Peel 6 tomatoes; cut into quarters; set aside. Cut remaining tomatoes into wedges; cover and refrigerate. On waxed paper, coat lamb shanks with 2 tablespoons flour.

2. In 8-quart Dutch oven over medium-high heat, in hot salad oil, cook shanks, a few at a time, until well browned on all sides, removing the lamb shanks as they brown.

3. To oil remaining in Dutch oven, add onions, carrots and garlic; cook until lightly browned, about 10 minutes, stirring occasionally. Return meat to Dutch oven; add quartered tomatoes, vermouth, bouillon, sugar, salt, rosemary and pepper; heat to boiling. Reduce heat to low; cover and simmer 1¼ hours or until meat is almost tender, stirring mixture occasionally.

4. Add zucchini; cover and simmer 15 minutes or until zucchini is tender. In cup with fork, mix water and 3 tablespoons flour until smooth; gradually stir into hot liquid in Dutch oven and cook, stirring constantly, until slightly thickened. Add tomato wedges; heat through. Sprinkle stew with lemon peel; serve with hot cooked barley or rice.

Braised Lamb Neck Slices

Color index
page 60

Begin 1¼ hrs
ahead

4 servings

382 cals per
serving

Good source
of iron

*2 pounds lamb neck
slices, each cut
¾ inch thick*
*3 tablespoons all-purpose
flour*
1 tablespoon salad oil
1 cup water
1 cup pitted prunes

2 tablespoons sugar
*2 tablespoons cider
vinegar*
¾ teaspoon salt
*¼ teaspoon ground
cinnamon*
*¼ teaspoon ground
allspice*

1. On waxed paper, coat lamb neck slices with flour. In 12-inch skillet over medium-high heat, in hot salad oil, cook slices until well browned, turning once. Skim off fat from skillet.

2. Add water; heat to boiling. Reduce heat to low; cover and simmer 45 minutes. Turn neck slices and stir in prunes; cover and simmer 10 minutes. Add sugar and remaining ingredients. Cover and simmer 5 minutes longer or until meat is fork-tender. Serve slices and pan liquid in warm deep platter.

CARAWAY LAMB NECK SLICES: Prepare as above but omit prunes and remaining ingredients. Increase water to 1½ cups; add *1 teaspoon caraway seed* and *1 beef-flavor bouillon cube or envelope* with water. Cook 1 hour or until meat is fork-tender.

297 cals per
serving

Stew meat

Near-East Lamb Stew

Color index
page 61

Begin 3 hrs
ahead

12 servings

397 cals per
serving

Good source
of iron

*3 pounds lamb for stew,
cut into 1½-inch
chunks*
*¼ cup all-purpose
flour*
*¼ cup salad or
olive oil*
1 cup water
2 medium onions, diced
2 garlic cloves, minced
*1 tablespoon seasoned
salt*

*½ teaspoon seasoned
pepper*
*½ teaspoon thyme
leaves*
4 medium tomatoes
2 green peppers
1 medium eggplant
*hot cooked rice for
10 servings*

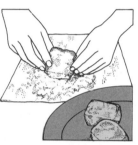

1 On waxed paper, coat chunks of lamb stew meat thoroughly with the flour.

2 In 6-quart Dutch oven over medium-high heat, in hot salad oil, cook lamb, several pieces at a time, until browned on all sides, removing pieces as they brown.

3 Return meat to Dutch oven; stir in water, onions, minced garlic, seasoned salt, seasoned pepper and thyme. Heat to boiling; reduce to low; cover; simmer 2 hours.

4 Peel tomatoes and cut into wedges; cut green peppers and eggplant into even-sized chunks.

5 Add tomato wedges, green pepper and eggplant chunks to Dutch oven and cook 30 minutes longer, stirring the stew occasionally.

6 When the meat and all the vegetables are fork-tender, remove Dutch oven from heat and serve the meat and vegetables over hot cooked rice.

Ground lamb

Lamb Curry

Begin 2½ hrs
ahead

8 servings

445 cals per
serving

Good source
of iron

**2 pounds lamb for stew,
cut into 1-inch chunks**
**¼ cup all-purpose
flour**
salad oil
**2 medium onions,
sliced**
1 garlic clove, minced
**1 to 3 tablespoons curry
powder**
1½ teaspoons salt
**¼ teaspoon ground
cinnamon**

**¼ teaspoon ground
cloves**
**⅛ teaspoon coarsely
ground pepper**
**1 beef-flavor bouillon
cube or envelope**
1 cup water
½ cup tomato juice
**hot cooked rice for
6 servings**
**Curry Accompaniments
(below)**

1. On waxed paper, coat lamb pieces with flour. In 12-inch skillet over medium-high heat, in 2 tablespoons hot salad oil, cook lamb until well browned, removing pieces as they brown and adding more oil if necessary.
2. Into drippings in skillet, stir the sliced onions, minced garlic and curry powder; cook over medium heat until onions are tender, about 5 minutes, stirring frequently.
3. Return meat to skillet; add salt, cinnamon, cloves, pepper, bouillon and water; heat to boiling. Reduce heat to low; cover and simmer 2 hours or until meat is fork-tender, stirring occasionally. Stir in tomato juice; heat through.
4. Serve on a bed of hot cooked rice; pass a selection of Curry Accompaniments.

CURRY ACCOMPANIMENTS: In separate small bowls, place two or more of these accompaniments, to be sprinkled over individual servings of Lamb Curry: chutney, raisins, tomato wedges, salted almonds or peanuts, chopped parsley, pineapple chunks, banana slices, fried onion rings, crisp bacon bits, currant jelly, chopped hard-cooked eggs, sweet or sour pickles, flaked coconut, sliced avocado, finely shredded orange peel.

Lamb Stew Rosé

Begin 3 hrs
ahead

6 servings

514 cals per
serving

Good source
of iron,
niacin

**1 tablespoon salad
oil**
**2 pounds lamb for stew,
cut into 1½-inch
chunks**
1 cup rosé
2 garlic cloves, minced
1 teaspoon salt
¼ teaspoon pepper

**¼ teaspoon rosemary,
crushed**
1 pint cherry tomatoes
**1 3-ounce jar almond- or
pimento-stuffed olives,
drained**
**hot cooked buttered
rice for 6 servings**

1. In 12-inch skillet over medium-high heat, in hot salad oil, cook lamb stew meat, half at a time, until meat is well browned on all sides, removing pieces as they brown.
2. Return all browned meat to skillet. Stir in rosé, minced garlic, salt, pepper and crushed rosemary; heat to boiling. Reduce heat to low; cover and simmer about 2½ hours until the meat is fork-tender, stirring occasionally.
3. Add tomatoes and olives; heat 5 minutes. Serve with hot cooked rice.

Persian-style Lamb with Almonds

Begin 25 mins
ahead

4 servings

380 cals per
serving

Good source
of calcium,
iron

1 tablespoon salad oil
½ cup slivered almonds
1 pound ground lamb
1½ cups chopped onions
**1 beef-flavor bouillon
cube**
½ teaspoon salt
½ teaspoon garlic salt
¼ teaspoon pepper
**1 tablespoon lime or
lemon juice**
1 teaspoon dried mint
spinach leaves
**1 medium tomato, cut
into wedges**

1 In 10-inch skillet over medium heat, in hot salad oil, cook slivered almonds, stirring, until golden brown. Remove almonds to plate.

2 Over medium-high heat, in oil remaining in skillet, cook ground lamb and next 5 ingredients, stirring, until meat is browned, about 10 minutes.

3 To lamb, add almonds, lime juice and mint. Stir mixture to blend well.

4 Line platter with spinach leaves; spoon meat mixture onto spinach leaves and garnish with tomato wedges.

Lamburgers

Begin 25 mins
ahead

6 servings

266 cals per
serving

Good source
of iron

6 ground lamb patties
½ teaspoon salt

¼ teaspoon pepper
6 bacon slices

1. Preheat broiler if manufacturer directs. Sprinkle lamb patties with salt and pepper. Wrap edge of each patty with bacon slice, securing with toothpick. Place patties on greased rack in broiling pan; broil 5 minutes.
2. With pancake turner, turn patties. Broil 5 minutes longer or until patties are of desired doneness. To serve, remove and discard toothpicks. Arrange lamb patties on large warm platter.

Veal

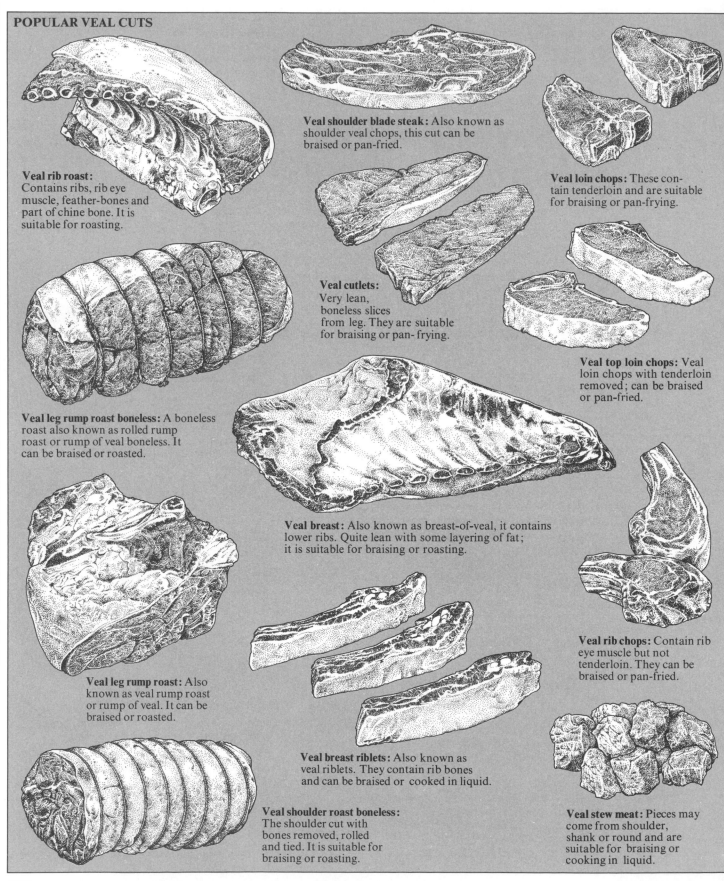

POPULAR VEAL CUTS

Veal rib roast: Contains ribs, rib eye muscle, feather-bones and part of chine bone. It is suitable for roasting.

Veal shoulder blade steak: Also known as shoulder veal chops, this cut can be braised or pan-fried.

Veal loin chops: These contain tenderloin and are suitable for braising or pan-frying.

Veal cutlets: Very lean, boneless slices from leg. They are suitable for braising or pan-frying.

Veal top loin chops: Veal loin chops with tenderloin removed; can be braised or pan-fried.

Veal leg rump roast boneless: A boneless roast also known as rolled rump roast or rump of veal boneless. It can be braised or roasted.

Veal breast: Also known as breast-of-veal, it contains lower ribs. Quite lean with some layering of fat; it is suitable for braising or roasting.

Veal rib chops: Contain rib eye muscle but not tenderloin. They can be braised or pan-fried.

Veal leg rump roast: Also known as veal rump roast or rump of veal. It can be braised or roasted.

Veal breast riblets: Also known as veal riblets. They contain rib bones and can be braised or cooked in liquid.

Veal shoulder roast boneless: The shoulder cut with bones removed, rolled and tied. It is suitable for braising or roasting.

Veal stew meat: Pieces may come from shoulder, shank or round and are suitable for braising or cooking in liquid.

Veal is the most delicate of all meats, with a subtle flavor and texture. This almost bland flavor makes it perfect for seasoning with herbs and other, more distinctively flavored, ingredients. Because veal comes from young animals only, it is always very lean, with no marbling and only a thin external layer of fat. It also has a comparatively large amount of connective tissue. Like beef, better grades of veal carry federal grade stamps.

BUYING VEAL

The lean of good-quality veal is firm and fine-textured, ranging in color from creamy white to the palest pink. Avoid veal which is flabby or brightly colored. Any visible fat should also be pale, almost white, and bones should be soft and very red.

COOKING VEAL

Because of its lack of fat and the large proportion of connective tissue in the meat, veal calls for careful, thorough cooking at low to moderate temperatures. Otherwise, it can easily toughen and become dry. For the same reason, veal should never be broiled.

TESTING FOR DONENESS

Roast veal to an internal temperature of 170°F. (Use a meat thermometer to avoid guesswork.) The exterior will be reddish-brown, the interior a uniform creamy white. To test pan-fried veal for doneness, make a small slit in the center of the meat or near the bone to check that the color is creamy white throughout. Braised veal and veal cooked in liquid should be tender when pierced with a fork.

CUTTING VEAL FOR SCALOPPINE

Scaloppine, sometimes called "escalopes" or "scallops" are thin, boneless slices of veal cut from leg round roast or loin. With boning knife, separate roast into muscles, removing bone, membrane and any fat. With knife in a slanting position, cut thin-as-possible slices across width of each muscle. Place the veal between sheets of waxed paper and with a meat mallet or the dull edge of a French knife, pound them to 1/8 to 1/16 inch thickness. The scaloppine can then be pan-fried, stuffed, rolled and braised, or they can be used in recipes for cutlets on pages 235 to 236.

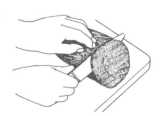

Cutting scaloppine: With knife in slanting position, slice meat across grain into 1/4 inch slices.

Pounding veal: On cutting board with meat mallet, pound veal slices between sheets of waxed paper to 1/8 inch thickness.

TIMETABLE FOR ROASTING VEAL*				
Type of cut	Weight (in pounds)	Meat thermometer reading	Approximate cooking time** (in hours)	Oven temperature
Leg rump or round roast	5 to 8	170°F.	2 to 3 1/4	325°F.
Loin roast	4 to 6	170°F.	2 to 3	325°F.
Rib roast	3 to 5	170°F.	1 3/4 to 3	325°F.
Shoulder roast boneless	4 to 6	170°F.	2 3/4 to 4	325°F.

* Meat at refrigerator temperature
** Remove meat from oven when internal temperature is 5 to 10 degrees below desired doneness, as meat continues cooking

CARVING VEAL

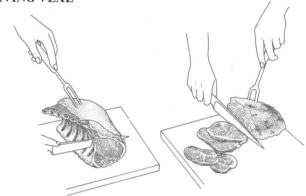

Rib roast: Remove backbone, leaving as little meat on it as possible, before bringing roast to table. Place roast on platter with rib side facing you. Insert a fork in top of roast to anchor meat, then cut closely alongside of each rib. One slice will contain a rib, the next will be boneless.

Boneless roast: Place meat on board or warm platter as it was roasted. Remove all strings (or leave one or two in place if roast starts to fall apart). Using a fork to anchor meat, start cutting right side of roast into slices 1/4 to 1/2 inch thick.

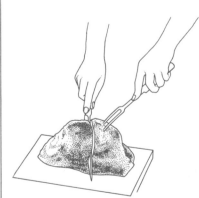

Leg round roast: Place roast on cut surface. Anchor with fork and cut along aitchbone to remove boneless piece of meat; place piece on its cut surface and cut into 1/4-inch-thick slices.

Anchoring remaining half, slice across meat until knife strikes aitchbone; cut down along bone to release each slice.

233

Veal roasts

Lemon-tarragon Veal Roast

2 teaspoons salt
2 teaspoons grated lemon peel
1 teaspoon tarragon leaves
1 4-pound veal shoulder roast boneless
water
¼ cup all-purpose flour
1 beef-flavor bouillon cube or envelope

Color index page 62

Begin 3¼ hrs ahead

14 servings

148 cals per serving

Good source of niacin

1 In small bowl with a spoon, stir together salt, grated lemon peel and tarragon leaves.

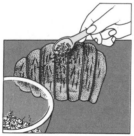

2 With tip of sharp knife, make about 2 dozen slits, about 2½ inches deep, over top and sides of veal shoulder roast, taking care not to cut string.

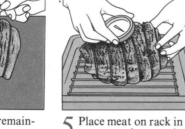

3 Into each slit in the meat, with spoon, insert some of salt mixture.

4 Sprinkle any remaining salt mixture over the veal roast.

5 Place meat on rack in open roasting pan; insert meat thermometer into center of thickest part of meat. Roast in 325°F. oven 2¾ hours or until temperature is 170°F.

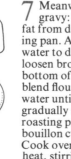

6 Place veal on warm platter; let stand 15 minutes for easier carving. With knife, carefully remove strings.

7 Meanwhile, prepare the gravy: Spoon off any fat from drippings in roasting pan. Add 1½ cups water to drippings; stir to loosen brown bits at the bottom of the pan. In cup, blend flour with ½ cup water until smooth; gradually stir into liquid in roasting pan. Stir in the bouillon cube or envelope. Cook over medium heat, stirring constantly until the gravy is smooth and thickened; serve over the meat.

Veal Rib Roast Marsala

1 4-pound veal rib roast
1 teaspoon salt
¼ teaspoon pepper
¼ teaspoon thyme leaves, crushed
1 bay leaf, finely crumbled
1¼ cups water
¼ pound mushrooms, thinly sliced
1 shallot, minced
2 tablespoons all-purpose flour
¼ cup dry Marsala

Color index page 62

Begin 3¼ hrs ahead

10 servings

191 cals per serving

Good source of iron, niacin

1. In shallow roasting pan, place roast on rib bones. In small bowl or cup, combine salt, pepper, thyme and bay leaf; rub over meat.
2. Insert meat thermometer into center of thickest part of roast. Roast in 325°F. oven 2½ hours or until meat thermometer reaches 170°F. Cut off backbone and discard. Place meat on warm platter.
3. For gravy, into 2-quart saucepan, spoon 2 tablespoons fat from drippings in roasting pan; spoon off any remaining fat from drippings and discard. Into roasting pan over medium heat, stir water and cook, stirring to loosen brown bits at the bottom of the roasting pan.
4. In hot fat, in saucepan over medium heat, cook mushrooms and shallot until mushrooms are tender. Stir in flour until blended. Gradually stir in water mixture and Marsala and cook, stirring, until thickened; boil 1 minute; serve with meat.

Seasoning the meat: Combine salt, pepper, thyme and bay leaf and rub over meat.

Removing backbone: When meat is done, cut off backbone and discard.

Country-style Veal Rump Roast

1 4-pound veal leg rump roast boneless
3 medium carrots, diced
1 medium onion, chopped
⅔ cup water
1 10¾-ounce can condensed cream of mushroom soup
1 teaspoon salt
¼ teaspoon coarsely ground black pepper
¼ teaspoon marjoram leaves
1 bay leaf

Color index page 63

Begin 3¼ hrs ahead

16 servings

148 cals per serving

1. In 8-quart Dutch oven over medium-high heat, cook veal leg rump roast until well browned on all sides. Push roast to one side of Dutch oven; add carrots and onion; cook, stirring occasionally, about 5 minutes. Skim off any excess fat.
2. Add water, undiluted soup, salt, pepper, marjoram leaves and bay leaf; heat to boiling, stirring constantly. Reduce heat to low; cover and simmer 2½ to 3 hours until meat is fork-tender, stirring.
3. To serve, place meat on warm platter; discard bay leaf. Pour pan liquid into gravy boat.

Cutlets

Spicy Veal Rump Roast

Color index
page 62

Begin 3 hrs
ahead

14 servings

240 cals per
serving

Good source
of iron,
niacin

2 tablespoons salad oil
1 5-pound veal leg rump
    roast
1 tablespoon mixed
    pickling spice
1 medium onion, diced
1 teaspoon curry powder
1³/₄ cups apple juice
2 teaspoons salt

¼ teaspoon pepper
5 small red cooking
    apples
¹/₃ cup water
3 tablespoons all-purpose
    flour
celery leaves for garnish

1. In 8-quart Dutch oven over medium-high heat, in hot salad oil, cook veal roast until well browned on all sides.

2. Meanwhile, cut a double-thickness of cheesecloth, 5 inches square. On it, place pickling spice. Pull corners up to form small bag; tie securely with color-fast or undyed cotton string.

3. When veal is browned, remove to platter. In drippings in Dutch oven, cook onion and curry, stirring occasionally, until onion is tender, about 5 minutes. Stir in apple juice, salt, pepper and spice bag; return veal to Dutch oven; heat to boiling. Reduce heat to low; cover and simmer 2½ hours or until veal is fork-tender, turning veal occasionally.

4. About 10 minutes before veal is done, core and cut apples into thick wedges. When veal is done, place on platter; keep warm. Discard spice bag from liquid in Dutch oven; add apples.

5. In cup, stir water and flour until blended. Gradually stir into liquid in Dutch oven; cook over medium heat, stirring constantly, until mixture is thickened and apples are tender.

6. To serve, with slotted spoon, spoon apples around meat; garnish with celery leaves. Pour gravy into gravy boat and pass with meat.

Tomato-paprika Veal

Color index
page 63

Begin 3 hrs
ahead

14 servings

400 cals per
serving

Good source
of iron,
niacin

2 tablespoons salad oil or
    shortening
1 5-pound veal leg rump
    roast
1 cup chopped onions
1 cup tomato juice
2 tablespoons paprika
1 teaspoon salt

¼ teaspoon crushed red
    pepper
2 tablespoons cornstarch
¼ cup water
½ cup sour cream
hot cooked noodles or
    mashed potatoes

1. In 5-quart Dutch oven over medium-high heat, in hot salad oil, cook rump roast until well browned on all sides; remove meat.

2. In drippings, over medium heat, cook onion until tender, about 5 minutes. Stir in tomato juice, paprika, salt and red pepper; return meat to Dutch oven and heat to boiling. Reduce heat to low; cover and simmer 2½ hours or until meat is fork-tender, turning meat occasionally. Place meat on warm platter; keep warm.

3. For sauce, in cup, blend cornstarch with water until smooth; gradually stir into hot mixture in Dutch oven and cook, stirring constantly, until sauce is thickened. Stir in sour cream until blended; heat (do not boil). Serve sauce over sliced veal and hot cooked noodles or mashed potatoes.

Veal and Peppers

Color index
page 63

Begin 1 hr
ahead

8 servings

345 cals per
serving

Good source
of iron,
niacin,
vitamin C

¹/₃ cup olive or salad oil
2 garlic cloves, sliced
2 medium onions, sliced
3 green peppers, sliced
3 red peppers, sliced
2 tablespoons red wine
    vinegar
1 teaspoon basil
½ teaspoon oregano
    leaves
salt and pepper
8 veal cutlets, each cut
    about ¼ inch thick
¹/₃ cup all-purpose flour
butter or margarine

1 In 12-inch skillet over medium-high heat, in hot oil, cook garlic until browned; discard. Add the sliced onions and peppers; cook 2 minutes, stirring.

2 Stir in vinegar, basil, oregano, 1 teaspoon salt and ¼ teaspoon pepper. Reduce heat to medium; cover; cook about 10 minutes.

3 With slotted spoon, remove vegetables to medium bowl; keep warm.

4 With meat mallet, pound cutlets until ¹/₈ inch thick; sprinkle with ½ teaspoon salt and ¼ teaspoon pepper.

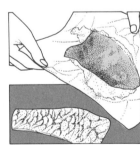

5 On waxed paper, coat cutlets with flour. In same skillet over medium-high heat, melt 3 tablespoons butter.

6 Cook meat, a few pieces at a time, until lightly browned on both sides, adding more butter if necessary.

7 When all of veal is cooked, arrange the meat with the peppers and onions on warm platter or serve in skillet.

Cutlets

Wiener Schnitzel

Color index page 63

Begin 45 mins ahead

6 servings

476 cals per serving

Good source of calcium, iron, vitamin A, niacin

6 large veal cutlets, each cut about 1/4 inch thick
2 eggs
1 teaspoon salt
1/2 teaspoon coarsely ground pepper
1/3 cup all-purpose flour
1 1/2 cups dried bread crumbs
1/2 cup butter or margarine

2 lemons, each cut into 8 wedges
3 tablespoons chopped parsley
6 anchovy fillets, drained (optional)
capers, well drained (optional)

1 On cutting board with meat mallet, pound veal cutlets to about 1/8 inch thickness, turning once.

2 In pie plate, beat eggs, salt and pepper. On waxed paper, place flour; on another sheet, place the bread crumbs.

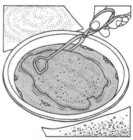

3 Coat veal in flour, then dip in eggs, then coat well with bread crumbs.

4 In 12-inch skillet over medium heat, in 1/4 cup hot butter, cook meat, a few pieces at a time, 3 or 4 minutes on each side till brown adding butter as needed. Remove to platter.

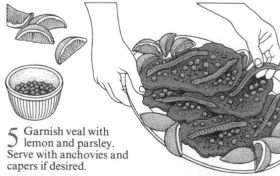

5 Garnish veal with lemon and parsley. Serve with anchovies and capers if desired.

604 cals per serving

A LA HOLSTEIN: Prepare veal cutlets as in the Wiener Schnitzel recipe, above, but serve each one topped with a *fried egg*.

Saltimbocca

Color index page 62

Begin 40 mins ahead

4 servings

562 cals per serving

Good source of calcium, iron, vitamin A, niacin

4 veal cutlets, each cut about 1/4 inch thick
1/4 cup butter
1/4 cup medium sherry

1/4 pound thinly sliced prosciutto, cut in thin strips
1/2 pound raclette

1. Preheat oven to 350°F. With meat mallet, pound cutlets until about 1/8 inch thick, turning once. In 12-inch skillet over medium-high heat, in hot butter, cook cutlets until lightly browned on both sides. Place in 12" by 8" baking dish.
2. To drippings in skillet, add sherry and stir to loosen brown bits; pour over meat. Arrange prosciutto strips over veal. Bake 5 minutes. Remove from oven; coarsely shred cheese and sprinkle over. Bake 4 to 5 minutes more until cheese is melted.

Veal Piccata

Color index page 62

Begin 1 1/4 hrs ahead

8 servings

292 cals per serving

Good source of iron

2 pounds veal cutlets, each cut 1/4 inch thick
salt and pepper
1/3 cup all-purpose flour
1/3 cup olive oil
2 tablespoons butter

1 cup water
1/2 cup dry white wine
1 chicken-flavor bouillon cube or envelope
2 medium lemons
parsley sprigs

1. With meat mallet, pound cutlets to 1/8 inch thickness. On waxed paper, sprinkle with 1/2 teaspoon salt and 1/4 teaspoon pepper; coat with flour.
2. In 12-inch skillet over medium-high heat, in hot olive oil and butter, cook veal, a few pieces at a time, until lightly browned on both sides, removing pieces as they brown and adding more oil if necessary.
3. Reduce heat to low. Into drippings in skillet, stir water, wine, bouillon and 1/2 teaspoon salt, scraping to loosen brown bits. Return veal to skillet; cover and simmer 15 minutes until cutlets are fork-tender. Cut 1 lemon in half; squeeze to remove juice; thinly slice the other. Overlap cooked cutlets on large platter; keep warm. Stir lemon juice into liquid in skillet. Over high heat, heat to boiling. Spoon liquid over cutlets; garnish with lemon slices and parsley.

Veal Parmigiana

Color index page 62

Begin 1 hr ahead

6 servings

513 cals per serving

Good source of calcium, iron, vitamin A, niacin

2 cups Marinara Sauce (page 337)
1 cup dried bread crumbs
3/4 teaspoon salt
1/8 teaspoon pepper
2 eggs
6 veal cutlets, each cut about 1/4 inch thick

3 tablespoons butter or margarine
1 8-ounce package mozzarella cheese, cut into 6 slices
1/4 cup grated Parmesan cheese

1. Prepare Marinara Sauce.
2. On waxed paper, mix bread crumbs, salt and pepper. In pie plate, beat eggs lightly. Dip cutlets in egg, then bread crumbs; repeat to coat each twice.
3. In 12-inch skillet over medium-high heat, in hot butter, fry cutlets, a few at a time, until browned on both sides, about 10 minutes. Arrange cutlets in skillet; spoon some sauce over each cutlet; top each with slice of mozzarella; sprinkle with Parmesan. Reduce heat to low; cover and cook until cheese is melted, about 5 minutes.

Chops and steaks

Veal Forestier

**6 veal rib chops, each cut
½ inch thick
¼ cup all-purpose flour
butter or margarine
1 garlic clove, halved**

**½ pound mushrooms,
thinly sliced
½ cup dry vermouth
1 teaspoon salt
⅛ teaspoon pepper**

Color index
page 64

Begin 45 mins
ahead

6 servings

351 cals per
serving

Good source
if iron,
vitamin A,
niacin

1. On waxed paper, coat chops lightly with flour. In 12-inch skillet over medium-high heat, in 2 tablespoons hot butter, cook garlic until brown; discard garlic. In butter remaining in skillet, cook chops, half at a time until well browned on both sides, removing chops as they brown to platter and adding a little more butter if needed.
2. Reduce heat to low. In same skillet, melt 2 tablespoons more butter; cook mushrooms until just tender. Stir in vermouth, salt and pepper, scraping to loosen brown bits. Return chops to skillet; cover; simmer 15 minutes until chops are fork-tender.
3. To serve, arrange chops on warm platter; pour mushroom mixture in skillet over chops.

Veal Chops with Avocado

**4 veal loin chops, each cut
about ¾ inch thick
2 tablespoons butter
¼ pound mushrooms,
sliced
¼ cup minced onion
2 tablespoons medium
sherry
¾ teaspoon salt**

**dash hot pepper
sauce
1 small ripe avocado
2 teaspoons cornstarch
½ cup heavy or whipping
cream
1 teaspoon chopped fresh
dill**

Color index
page 64

Begin 1½ hrs
ahead

4 servings

507 cals per
serving

Good source
of iron,
vitamin A,
riboflavin,
niacin

1. Preheat oven to 350°F. Slash fat on edge of chops. In 10-inch skillet with ovensafe handle, over medium heat, in hot butter, cook mushrooms and onion until tender, about 5 minutes.
2. Arrange chops in skillet. Add sherry, salt and hot pepper sauce; heat to boiling. Cover and bake 1 hour or until meat is fork-tender.
3. Cut avocado in half; remove seed and skin. Slice avocado and arrange over chops. Bake, uncovered, 10 minutes or until avocado is heated through. Place chops on warm platter.
4. Blend cornstarch and 1 tablespoon cream until smooth; stir in remaining cream. Gradually stir into hot liquid in skillet and cook over medium heat, stirring until thickened. Stir in dill. Serve chops immediately with sauce.

Slashing fat: Cut through fat on edge of chops in several places.

Adding avocado: Arrange avocado slices over veal chops in skillet.

Veal Chops in Tomato Sauce

**6 veal top loin chops,
each cut ½ inch thick
¼ cup all-purpose flour
butter or margarine
3 medium tomatoes
(about 1 pound),
peeled, seeded and
cubed**

**¼ cup water
1 chicken-flavor bouillon
cube or envelope
1 teaspoon basil
½ teaspoon sugar
1 tablespoon chopped
parsley**

Color index
page 64

Begin 45 mins
ahead

6 servings

367 cals per
serving

Good source
of iron,
vitamin A,
niacin

1. On waxed paper, coat loin chops lightly with flour. In 12-inch skillet over medium-high heat, in 3 tablespoons hot butter, cook chops until well browned on both sides, removing chops as they brown and adding a little more butter if needed.
2. Reduce heat to low. In same skillet, melt 2 tablespoons more butter. Stir in tomatoes, water, bouillon cube, basil and sugar, scraping to loosen brown bits. Return chops to skillet; over high heat, heat to boiling. Reduce heat to low; cover and simmer 15 minutes or until meat is fork-tender.
3. To serve, arrange chops on warm platter; pour tomato sauce over chops; sprinkle with parsley.

Veal Steaks with Spaghetti

**2 veal shoulder arm
steaks, each cut about
1 inch thick
2 tablespoons all-purpose
flour
2 tablespoons olive oil
1 8-ounce can stewed
tomatoes
1 6-ounce can tomato
paste**

**1 teaspoon seasoned
salt
1 teaspoon sugar
¼ teaspoon seasoned
pepper
¼ teaspoon oregano,
crumbled
1 8-ounce package
spaghetti, cooked**

Color index
page 64

Begin 1¼ hrs
ahead

4 servings

538 cals per
serving

Good source
of iron,
niacin,
vitamin C

1. On waxed paper, coat veal steaks with flour. In 12-inch skillet over medium-high heat, in hot oil, cook meat until well browned on both sides.
2. Add remaining ingredients except spaghetti; heat to boiling. Reduce heat to low; cover and simmer 1 hour or until steaks are fork-tender, turning once. Serve with spaghetti.

Veal Steak Marsala

**4 veal shoulder blade
steaks, each cut
¾ inch thick
½ teaspoon salt
¼ teaspoon pepper
2 tablespoons all-purpose
flour**

**butter or margarine
½ cup dry Marsala
½ cup water
chopped parsley for
garnish**

Color index
page 64

Begin 1¼ hrs
ahead

4 servings

334 cals per
serving

Good source
of iron,
niacin

1. On waxed paper, sprinkle veal steaks lightly with salt and pepper; coat well with flour.
2. In 12-inch skillet over medium-high heat, in 3 tablespoons hot butter, cook steaks until well browned on both sides, adding more butter if needed. Remove steaks to platter; keep warm.
3. Reduce heat to low. Stir wine and water into drippings, scraping to loosen brown bits. Return veal to skillet; cover; simmer 45 minutes or until veal is fork-tender. Arrange on warm platter; pour liquid in skillet over steaks. Garnish with parsley.

Breast and riblets

Deviled Veal Riblets with Saucy Noodles

Color index page 64

Begin 2 hrs ahead

6 servings

777 cals per serving

Good source of iron, niacin

1 13¾-ounce can chicken broth
1 carrot, cut up
1 celery stalk, cut up
1 small onion, cut up
¼ teaspoon pepper
salt
5 pounds veal breast riblets
⅓ cup mayonnaise
¼ cup dry mustard
4 garlic cloves, minced

2 tablespoons milk
¾ cup dried bread crumbs
¼ cup butter or margarine, melted
Saucy Noodles (right)
1 small tomato, cut into wedges for garnish

1 At high speed, blend broth, carrot, celery, onion, pepper and 1½ teaspoons salt until vegetables are finely chopped.

2 In 6-quart Dutch oven over high heat, heat to boiling veal breast riblets and blended vegetable-broth mixture.

3 Reduce heat to low; cover; simmer 1 hour, occasionally turning riblets. Remove riblets; let cool about 15 minutes. Reserve meat juice in Dutch oven.

4 Preheat broiler if manufacturer directs. In 10" by 6" baking dish, combine mayonnaise, mustard, garlic, milk, and ½ teaspoon salt.

5 Dip riblets into mayonnaise mixture; on waxed paper, coat with bread crumbs. Place on rack in broiling pan; drizzle with half of butter. Broil 15 minutes.

6 Turn riblets; drizzle with remaining butter. Broil 15 minutes more. Prepare Saucy Noodles; arrange with riblets on platter; garnish with tomato wedges.

SAUCY NOODLES: Prepare *one 8-ounce package broad egg noodles* as label directs; drain. Meanwhile, pour reserved meat juice into small bowl; let stand a few seconds until fat separates from meat juice. Skim 3 tablespoons fat from meat juice into same Dutch oven; skim off and discard any remaining fat. Into fat in Dutch oven over medium heat, stir *3 tablespoons all-purpose flour* until blended; gradually stir in 1½ cups meat juice; cook, stirring constantly, until mixture is thickened. Add hot noodles and *2 tablespoons chopped parsley*; gently stir noodles to coat well.

Braised Breast of Veal and Peaches

Color index page 64

Begin 3¼ hrs ahead

672 cals per serving

Good source of iron, niacin

1 4-pound veal breast
1 garlic clove, cut in thin slivers
½ cup dry sherry
2 tablespoons soy sauce
½ cup packed dark brown sugar

4 teaspoons prepared mustard
1 29-ounce can cling-peach halves, well drained
thin slices French or Italian bread

1. With tip of sharp knife, make 1-inch-long slits on fatty side of veal breast and insert garlic.
2. Place meat, fat side up, in 13" by 9" baking pan; pour on sherry and soy sauce. Cover pan tightly with foil and bake in 325°F. oven 2½ to 3 hours until meat is fork-tender.
3. Preheat broiler if manufacturer directs. Remove meat from oven. Spoon pan drippings into gravy boat; let stand until fat separates. Spoon off fat and discard. Keep pan drippings warm.
4. In small bowl, blend brown sugar and mustard until smooth. Arrange peach halves, cut sides up, around meat. Spread brown-sugar mixture on top of meat and peaches. Broil 3 to 5 minutes until brown-sugar mixture melts and peaches are hot. Serve meat with French bread and pan drippings.

Inserting garlic: With a sharp knife, make slits on fatty side of breast and insert garlic.

Adding brown-sugar mixture: Spread mixture over top of meat and cut sides of peaches.

611 cals per serving

VEAL BREAST WITH PLUM GLAZE: Prepare as steps 1 and 2 above; remove from oven and omit steps 3 and 4. In covered blender container, blend *one 17-ounce bottle chutney, 4 large plums*, peeled and cut up, and *¼ teaspoon salt* until smooth; place in same bowl. Turn oven control to broil. Place veal breast, bone side up, on rack in broiling pan; brush with some mixture. Broil 10 to 15 minutes until glaze is lightly browned. Turn veal over and baste; broil 10 to 15 minutes longer.

Stew meat

Blanquette de Veau

Color index
page 63

Begin 3 hrs
ahead

10 servings

421 cals per
serving

Good source
of iron,
niacin

1 stalk celery, diced
1 carrot, diced
2 whole cloves
1 bay leaf
2½ pounds veal for stew,
cut into 1½-inch
chunks
½ cup dry vermouth or
other dry white wine
2 teaspoons salt
1 pound small white
onions

1 pound small
mushrooms
4 egg yolks
½ cup heavy or whipping
cream
hot cooked egg noodles
or rice, or mashed or
boiled potatoes
chopped dill or parsley
for garnish

1 Prepare bouquet garni:
Cut double-thickness of
cheesecloth into 8-inch
square. On it, place first 4
ingredients; pull up
corners and tie securely
with undyed cotton string.

2 In 5-quart Dutch oven
over medium-high heat,
heat to boiling bouquet
garni, veal, vermouth
and salt. Reduce heat to
low; cover and simmer
1½ hours.

3 Add onions and mushrooms. Over high heat,
heat to boiling. Reduce
heat to low; cover and simmer 30 minutes or until
fork-tender. Discard the
bouquet garni.

4 In small bowl with wire
whisk, mix egg yolks
and cream; stir in about
½ cup hot broth from
Dutch oven.

5 Slowly pour egg-yolk
mixture into stew, stir-
ring rapidly to prevent
lumping. Cook, stirring,
until mixture is thickened
(do not boil).

6 Serve stew over hot
cooked egg noodles,
rice, or mashed or boiled
potatoes. Garnish with a
sprinkling of chopped
dill or parsley.

Veal Paprika

Color index
page 62

Begin 2½ hrs
ahead

8 servings

295 cals per
serving

Good source
of iron,
niacin

3 tablespoons butter or
margarine
2 pounds veal for stew,
cut into 1-inch chunks
2 large onions, diced
1 tablespoon paprika
1¾ teaspoons salt
water

1 8-ounce package
medium egg noodles
1 tablespoon all-purpose
flour
½ cup sour cream
chopped parsley for
garnish

1. In 5-quart Dutch oven over medium-high heat, in
hot butter or margarine, cook veal stew meat,
several pieces at a time, until well browned on all
sides, removing pieces as they brown.
2. Reduce heat to medium; add onions and paprika
to drippings in Dutch oven and cook until onions
are tender, about 10 minutes, stirring occasionally.
3. Return meat to Dutch oven; add salt and ½ cup
water; heat to boiling. Reduce heat to low; cover
Dutch oven and simmer 1¼ hours or until meat is
fork-tender.
4. Meanwhile, cook noodles as label directs; drain.
5. In cup, blend flour and 2 tablespoons water until
smooth; gradually stir into hot liquid in Dutch oven
and cook over medium heat, stirring constantly,
until mixture is thickened. Stir in sour cream; heat
(do not boil). Serve over noodles. Garnish with
chopped parsley.

Veal Stew Milanese

Color index
page 62

Begin 2 hrs
ahead

6 servings

543 cals per
serving

Good source
of calcium,
iron, niacin

¼ cup olive or salad
oil
2 pounds veal for stew,
cut into 1¼-inch
chunks
1 large onion, diced
1 large carrot, diced
1 large stalk celery,
diced
1 garlic clove,
minced
⅓ cup white chianti or
other dry white wine
1 16-ounce can tomatoes

1 teaspoon salt
½ teaspoon basil
¼ teaspoon coarsely
ground black pepper
1 bay leaf
1 chicken-flavor bouillon
cube or envelope
Risotto alla Milanese
(page 339)
(optional)
1 tablespoon chopped
parsley
1½ teaspoons grated
lemon peel

1. In 5-quart Dutch oven over medium-high heat, in
2 tablespoons hot oil, cook veal, ⅓ at a time, until
well browned on all sides, removing pieces with
slotted spoon as they brown and adding more oil if
necessary.
2. In same Dutch oven over medium heat, in
drippings, cook onion, carrot, celery and garlic until
lightly browned, about 5 minutes, stirring occasionally. With spoon, stir in wine, tomatoes with
their liquid, and next 5 ingredients, breaking up
tomatoes into small pieces.
3. Return veal to Dutch oven; heat to boiling.
Reduce heat to low; cover and simmer 1¼ hours or
until veal is fork-tender, stirring occasionally.
4. Meanwhile, prepare the Risotto alla Milanese, if
desired; keep warm.
5. To serve, spoon veal into serving dish; discard bay
leaf. Sprinkle with parsley and lemon peel. Serve
with risotto.

Variety meat

Variety meats are highly nutritious, are generally economical, and contain little or no fat or gristle, so there is little waste. However, they are highly perishable and should be cooked, or at least precooked, as soon as possible after purchase. Sweetbreads, brains and tripe are especially perishable.

Liver: Veal, calves' and lamb liver are the most delicate; beef and pork liver have the strongest flavor; beef liver is the least tender. Before cooking, remove any membrane from the liver. Veal and lamb liver may be broiled, pan-broiled or pan-fried. Pork and beef liver are best braised. Allow 1 pound for 4 servings.

Sweetbreads, a great delicacy, are tender and subtly flavored. They are the thymus gland of veal, calf or young beef. If not to be used immediately, they should be precooked. Sweetbreads should be soaked and peeled before cooking; then broiled, braised or cooked in liquid. If cooked in water, the membrane may be removed after cooking.

Tongue may be purchased fresh, smoked, corned or pickled, also canned. A less tender meat, it needs long, slow cooking in liquid. Smoked or pickled tongue may also need soaking for several hours before cooking. To prepare cooked tongue for serving, see recipes. One beef tongue makes 12 to 16 servings; 1 veal tongue, 3 to 6 servings; 1 pork tongue, 2 to 4 servings; 1 lamb tongue, 2 to 3 servings.

Brains: Beef, veal, lamb and pork brains are tender and delicately flavored. They should be soaked and peeled before cooking, then broiled, braised or cooked in liquid. If cooked in water, membrane may be removed after cooking. If they are not to be served immediately, they should be precooked; reheat in a sauce or pan-fry. Allow 1 pound for 4 servings.

Kidneys: Veal, lamb and pork kidneys are tender enough to be broiled. Beef kidneys are less tender, more strongly flavored, and should be braised or cooked in liquid. To prepare kidneys for cooking, remove membranes and hard white part. One beef kidney makes 4 to 6 servings; 1 veal kidney, 3 to 4 servings; 1 pork kidney, 1 to 2 servings; 1 lamb kidney, ½ to 1 serving.

Heart is a firm-textured meat, with little waste. A less tender meat, it should be braised, cooked in liquid or ground and used in recipes. To trim heart, see Beef Heart Stew, page 241. One beef heart makes 10 to 12 servings; 1 pork or veal heart, 2 to 3 servings; 1 lamb heart, 1 serving.

Tripe: Plain, honeycomb and pocket tripe, all from beef, are sold fresh, pickled or canned. Honeycomb is considered the best. Fresh tripe is sold partially cooked and requires about 1½ hours further cooking in salted water, tightly covered, to make it tender. Pickled tripe is sold thoroughly cooked and need only be soaked before use. Allow 1 pound for 4 servings.

Color index page 65

Begin 20 mins ahead

4 servings

433 cals per serving

Good source of iron, vitamin A, riboflavin, niacin

Pan-fried Liver and Bacon

1 8-ounce package bacon slices
1 pound calves' liver, sliced about ¼ inch thick
2 tablespoons all-purpose flour

¼ teaspoon salt
4 lemon wedges (optional)
chopped parsley for garnish

1 In 10-inch skillet over medium heat, fry bacon until crisp; drain on paper towels; keep warm. Pour off all but 2 tablespoons fat from skillet.

2 Trim any membrane from edges of liver slices. On waxed paper, coat liver with flour.

3 Over medium heat, in hot fat, cook liver 4 minutes, turning once, until crisp and brown on outside, delicate pink inside.

4 Sprinkle with salt; squeeze over a little lemon juice. Place liver and bacon on warm platter; garnish with parsley.

Color index page 65

Begin 1¼ hrs ahead

8 servings

350 cals per serving

Low in cholesterol

Good source of iron, vitamin A, riboflavin, niacin, vitamin C

Liver Jardinière

2 pounds beef liver, sliced about ¼ inch thick
3 tablespoons all-purpose flour
1 8-ounce package bacon slices

3 medium onions, thinly sliced
3 large green peppers, thinly sliced
1½ teaspoons salt
¼ teaspoon pepper
1 16-ounce can tomatoes

1. On waxed paper, lightly coat liver slices with flour. In 12-inch skillet over medium heat, fry bacon until crisp; drain on paper towels; crumble; set aside. Pour off drippings and reserve.

2. Over medium heat, in ¼ cup bacon drippings, fry liver, a few pieces at a time, until lightly browned on both sides. Remove from pan.

3. Meanwhile, to skillet, add 2 or 3 tablespoons more bacon drippings, onions, next 3 ingredients and brown lightly. Add juice from tomatoes (reserve tomatoes); place liver on top; cover; cook over low heat 25 minutes or until liver is tender. During last minutes, add tomatoes to heat through. To serve, sprinkle bacon on top.

Sweetbreads Meunière

Color index page 65

Begin 45 mins ahead

4 servings

384 cals per serving

Good source of iron, vitamin A

1 pound veal sweetbreads
hot water
salt
lemon juice
vinegar (optional)
¼ teaspoon ground ginger (optional)
½ cup butter or margarine
⅓ cup dried bread crumbs
chopped parsley for garnish

1. Wash sweetbreads. Precook: In 3-quart saucepan, place sweetbreads with hot water to cover. For each 4 cups water, add 1 teaspoon salt and 1 tablespoon lemon juice or vinegar. If you like, add ginger. Over high heat, heat to boiling. Reduce heat to low; cover tightly; simmer 20 minutes; drain. Place in cold water; remove membrane. Cut out veins and connective tissue. Halve sweetbreads lengthwise.

2. Meanwhile, preheat broiler if manufacturer directs. In 1-quart saucepan over low heat, melt butter. Place bread crumbs on waxed paper. Dip sweetbreads in butter, then in bread crumbs; reserve leftover butter. Place sweetbreads on greased rack in broiling pan and broil 8 to 10 minutes until lightly browned, turning once. Place on warm platter.

3. Reheat butter; stir in 2 tablespoons lemon juice; pour over sweetbreads. Garnish with parsley.

"Boiled" Fresh Tongue

Color index page 65

Begin 3½ hrs ahead

14 servings

189 cals per serving

Good source of iron

1 3½-pound fresh beef tongue
1 medium onion, sliced
1½ tablespoons salt
½ teaspoon mustard seed
½ teaspoon peppercorns
5 whole cloves
1 bay leaf
hot water
Creamy Cucumber Sauce or Spicy Cranberry Sauce (page 243)

1. In 8-quart Dutch oven over high heat, heat to boiling first 7 ingredients and enough hot water to cover. Reduce heat to low; cover and simmer 3 hours or until meat is fork-tender.

2. Plunge tongue into cold water and remove skin, bones and gristle as shown below. Serve hot or cold with sauce. To serve cold, cover and refrigerate in cooking liquid to cool (it will be juicier).

REMOVING SKIN, BONES AND GRISTLE FROM "BOILED" TONGUE

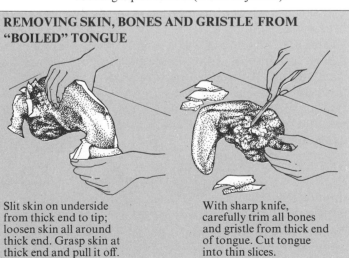

Slit skin on underside from thick end to tip; loosen skin all around thick end. Grasp skin at thick end and pull it off.

With sharp knife, carefully trim all bones and gristle from thick end of tongue. Cut tongue into thin slices.

Brains au Beurre Noir

Color index page 65

Begin 1 hr ahead

4 servings

437 cals per serving

Good source of iron, vitamin A

2 beef brains, halved (about 1½ pounds)
water
salt
lemon juice or white vinegar
2 tablespoons all-purpose flour
6 tablespoons butter or margarine
4 French bread slices, toasted
2 tablespoons chopped parsley
1 teaspoon capers, drained

1. Wash brains. Precook: In 3-quart saucepan or Dutch oven, place brains with water to cover. For each 4 cups water, add 1 teaspoon salt and 1 tablespoon lemon juice or vinegar; over high heat, heat to boiling. Reduce heat to low; cover and simmer 20 minutes; drain. Cover with cold water to cool quickly; drain. Carefully remove membrane, being careful to keep brains in one piece. Pat dry with paper towels.

2. On waxed paper, coat brains with flour.

3. In 10-inch skillet over medium heat, in hot butter, cook brains until lightly browned on all sides, turning with pancake turner. Carefully place each brain on a French bread slice on warm platter. Sprinkle with parsley; keep warm.

4. Into drippings in skillet, stir 1 tablespoon white vinegar and capers; pour over brains.

LAMB BRAINS: Use *4 lamb brains* (about 1 pound), instead of beef; do not halve.

Beef Heart Stew

Color index page 65

Begin 3½ hrs ahead

10 servings

142 cals per serving

Good source of iron, riboflavin

1 beef heart
1 29-ounce can tomatoes
2 medium onions, chopped
1 tablespoon salt
1 teaspoon basil
½ teaspoon thyme leaves
¼ teaspoon pepper
2 bay leaves
1 garlic clove, minced
3 medium carrots, cut into ½-inch pieces
3 celery stalks, cut into ½-inch pieces

1. With kitchen shears, split heart open; remove fat and white tubes; wash heart. With sharp knife, cut meat into 1-inch chunks.

2. In 5-quart Dutch oven over high heat, heat meat, tomatoes, onions, salt, basil, thyme, pepper, bay leaves and garlic to boiling. Cover and bake in 350°F. oven 1½ hours.

3. Add carrots and celery pieces and bake 1 hour.

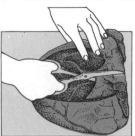

Cutting open heart: Use kitchen shears to split heart open.

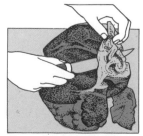

Removing fat and tubes: Cut away all fat and white tubes, leaving only meat.

Variety meat

Sautéed Veal Kidneys

2 veal kidneys
3 tablespoons butter
¼ pound mushrooms, sliced
2 green onions, sliced
½ cup chicken broth
2 tablespoons Madeira
¼ teaspoon salt
toast points
chopped parsley

Color index page 65

Begin 50 mins ahead

6 servings

211 cals per serving

Good source of iron, vitamin A, riboflavin, niacin

1. Cut kidneys into 1-inch chunks, removing membrane and hard white parts.
2. In 10-inch skillet over medium-high heat, in hot butter, cook mushrooms and onions until tender, about 5 minutes. With slotted spoon, remove from skillet; set aside. In drippings in skillet, cook kidneys until lightly browned, about 3 minutes, stirring kidneys occasionally.
3. Add mushroom mixture, chicken broth, Madeira and salt; heat to boiling. Reduce heat to low; cover and simmer 30 minutes or until kidneys are fork-tender. Serve with toast points. Garnish mixture with chopped parsley.

Lamb Kidneys Madeira

8 lamb kidneys
2 tablespoons Madeira
1 teaspoon drained green peppercorns
⅓ cup butter or margarine, softened
¼ cup minced onion
3 tablespoons chopped parsley
1 teaspoon Worcestershire
½ teaspoon dry mustard
¼ teaspoon garlic salt
toast points

Color index page 65

Begin 1 hr ahead

4 servings

258 cals per serving

Good source of iron, vitamin A, riboflavin, niacin

1. Remove membranes from kidneys. Firmly grasp kidney. With knife, begin splitting kidney lengthwise, cutting about two-thirds of way down into kidney, exposing thin white veins; repeat on other side of white piece. Insert knife under each vein; cut vein loose. (Be careful not to cut kidney into pieces.) Discard white piece and veins. Wash kidney.
2. Spread kidney open and place, cut side up, on greased rack of broiling pan. Repeat with remaining kidneys. Sprinkle over Madeira.
3. Preheat broiler if manufacturer directs. In small bowl with pestle, crush peppercorns. Add butter and remaining ingredients except toast points; mix well. Spoon mixture over kidneys.
4. Broil kidneys about 6 minutes for rare, 8 minutes for medium and 10 minutes for well done. Serve with toast; spoon pan drippings over kidneys.

Splitting kidney: With knife next to white piece, split kidney lengthwise.

Adding Madeira: Arrange kidneys on greased rack and sprinkle over Madeira.

Sausage

The many different types of sausages available, both fresh and cooked, make a useful and popular standby for quick meals, snacks and sandwiches. Sausage is meat that is ground and seasoned. It is grouped according to the way it is made. Varieties include:

Fresh sausage: Usually made of pork, sometimes beef. Refrigerate and use within 2 or 3 days.
Uncooked smoked sausage: Refrigerate and use as above. Includes kielbasa and mettwurst.
Cooked sausage: Made from fresh, not cured, meat; is ready-to-serve. Unsliced pieces may be refrigerated for 4 to 6 days before use. Sliced pieces should be eaten within 2 to 3 days. Blood sausage and liverwurst are examples.
Cooked, smoked sausage: Made of fresh meat, smoked, and fully cooked. Refrigerate and eat within 4 to 5 days. If sliced, use within 2 or 3 days. See below on how to serve hot. Frankfurters and some salami are types.
Dry and semi-dry sausages: Smoked or unsmoked, these are ready-to-eat. Refrigerate and use within 2 to 3 weeks. They include salami, pepperoni and cervelat.
Cooked meat specialities: Include a variety of ready-to-serve meat products. Most are presliced and packaged; some are spreadable. Use within 2 or 3 days.

COOKING FRESH AND UNCOOKED SMOKED SAUSAGE
Make sure that sausage links or patties are cooked thoroughly; turn links with tongs during cooking so that you avoid piercing the casings.
Pan-frying: Place links in cold skillet with 2 to 4 tablespoons water; cover tightly and, over low heat, cook 5 to 8 minutes, depending on size. Remove cover of skillet and cook the links until they are browned, turning them occasionally. Cook sausage patties in a skillet over medium heat until they are browned, turning them frequently with pancake turner.
Broiling: Place sausage links on rack in a broiling pan and broil until well done, turning and brushing them occasionally either with sauce or with butter or margarine. Uncooked bratwurst and bockwurst should be placed in a pan of water, heated to boiling and left to stand about 10 minutes before broiling. Drain them thoroughly before broiling as above.
Baking: Place links or patties on rack in open roasting pan and bake in preheated 400°F. oven 20 to 30 minutes, depending on size.

HEATING COOKED SMOKED-SAUSAGE LINKS
Cooked smoked-sausage links may be heated through in simmering water; pan-fried over medium heat in 1 or 2 tablespoons hot salad oil, butter or margarine until browned on all sides; or brushed with melted fat, placed on rack in broiling pan and broiled 3 inches from heat until links are evenly browned on all sides.

Homemade Sausages

2 pounds pork shoulder blade roast boneless, cut into 1-inch cubes
¹/₄ cup chopped parsley
2 teaspoons salt
1 teaspoon rubbed sage
¹/₂ teaspoon pepper
2 yards natural sausage casing
water

Color index page 65

Begin 5 hrs ahead

8 main-dish servings

167 cals per serving

Good source of thiamine

1 With food grinder, using coarse cutting disk, grind cubed pork into large bowl.

2 Add chopped parsley, salt, rubbed sage and pepper; mix well. Refrigerate mixture until well chilled, about 3¹/₂ hours.

3 Rinse casing in several changes of warm water; slip one end of casing over faucet and run warm water through it.

4 Cover casing with warm water and let soak 30 minutes until it is supple.

5 Remove cutting disk from meat grinder and attach sausage horn as manufacturer directs,

6 Place some of meat mixture in grinder and grind just until meat reaches the end of the sausage horn.

7 Slip entire length of sausage casing onto horn, allowing 2 inches to extend over end; tie end of casing in knot.

8 To fill casing, gradually grind meat mixture into casing, pulling casing gently to fill evenly. Do not overfill casing.

9 Twist casing at 5-inch intervals or at desired lengths to form links, pressing meat away from twists. With kitchen shears, cut into links. Cover; refrigerate.

10 To cook: In covered 12-inch skillet over low heat, in ¹/₄ cup simmering water, cook links 5 minutes; uncover; brown over medium heat 20 minutes.

Sausage Patties: *About 1 hour before serving:* Prepare the meat mixture as for Homemade Sausages, above, but in step 2 do not refrigerate; shape the meat mixture into patties. In 12-inch skillet over medium-low heat, cook the patties about 25 minutes or until they are browned and well done. Carefully turn the patties occasionally with pancake turner to ensure they cook and brown evenly. (Makes 8 main-dish servings.)

Sauces for meat

Begin 1¹/₂ hrs ahead   16 cals per serving
1 cup or 6 servings

Mint Sauce

2 bunches mint
¹/₄ cup cider vinegar
4 teaspoons sugar

2 tablespoons boiling water

1. Rinse mint well in cold water; drain thoroughly. Trim any tough stems. On cutting board, finely chop mint to make 1 cup.
2. In small bowl, combine mint with remaining ingredients. Let stand 1 hour to blend flavors. Serve with roast or broiled lamb.

Begin 15 mins ahead   296 cals per ¹/₃ cup
1²/₃ cups

Spicy Cranberry Sauce

1 16-ounce can whole-cranberry sauce
2 tablespoons butter
1 tablespoon light brown sugar
1 tablespoon horseradish

¹/₂ teaspoon dry mustard
¹/₄ teaspoon ground allspice

In 2-quart saucepan over medium heat, heat to boiling all ingredients, stirring occasionally. Reduce heat and simmer about 5 minutes. Serve with sliced tongue, roast pork or baked ham.

Begin 10 mins ahead   77 cals per ¹/₄ cup
1¹/₂ cups

Raisin Sauce

¹/₂ cup water
¹/₂ cup dark seedless raisins
¹/₃ cup currant jelly
¹/₂ teaspoon grated orange peel
¹/₈ teaspoon salt

¹/₈ teaspoon ground allspice
1 tablespoon cornstarch
¹/₃ cup orange juice

In 1-quart saucepan over medium-high heat, heat to boiling water, raisins, jelly, orange peel, salt and allspice. In cup, blend cornstarch with orange juice; stir into raisin mixture and cook, stirring, until thickened and clear. Serve with baked ham, sliced tongue or roast pork.

Begin 15 mins ahead or early in day   86 cals per ¹/₄ cup
1¹/₂ cups

Creamy Cucumber Sauce

1 medium cucumber, peeled and seeded
1 cup sour cream

1 teaspoon grated onion
¹/₂ teaspoon salt

Onto waxed paper shred cucumber; pat dry. In medium bowl, stir cucumber and remaining ingredients until blended. Cover and refrigerate. Serve with sliced tongue, roast beef or baked ham.

POULTRY

Poultry, which includes turkey, chicken, duckling, goose and Rock Cornish hens, is plentiful fresh or frozen the year around – and in a form to meet the needs of every cook. Birds range from 1-pound Rock Cornish game hens to massive turkeys weighing 24 pounds and more. There is also a wide choice of "parts" – halves, quarters, breasts, legs, thighs and drumsticks – and boneless roasts. In the case of long-roasting turkeys, some need little watching since they are sold prebasted, injected with fat or broth to keep them moist.

Holidays and festivals are traditionally celebrated with a roast bird, but poultry is equally at home fried or baked at family meals, or combined with other flavors to make excitingly different dishes for more formal occasions. When it comes to cooking, then, there are few meats to match poultry for versatility. Poultry is also one of the most economical sources of high-quality protein and, serving for serving, chicken and turkey are actually lower in calories than most other meats.

CHOOSING POULTRY

When choosing poultry, you will find many items carry helpful information on the label or wrapper. Poultry processors as well as supermarkets label products to indicate the quality; sometimes cooking directions are also included. A United States Department of Agriculture circular mark proves that the bird has been inspected for wholesomeness and has met rigid federal standards. Birds of the highest quality of meatiness and appearance also have a shield-shaped label stating that they are USDA "Grade A". The age of the bird may also be indicated; age determines its tenderness. Young poultry has tender meat and can successfully be broiled, barbecued, fried or roasted. Older or "mature" birds are more richly flavored, but the meat is less tender and should be tenderized by braising or simmering in liquid. Choose a whole bird with a plump, well-rounded breast and clear skin free of blemishes and bruising. (Skin color may vary from white to yellow according to what the bird was fed and is not an indication of quality.)

STORING UNCOOKED POULTRY

Store uncooked fresh poultry in its plastic wrap in the refrigerator and use within 2 or 3 days. If wrapped in meat market paper, unwrap it, place it on a platter and cover loosely with waxed paper before refrigerating. Wrap and refrigerate giblets separately. Frozen unstuffed poultry should be kept in the freezer just until time to thaw and roast. Remember that commercially stuffed frozen poultry should always be kept strictly according to label directions.

THAWING FROZEN POULTRY

Frozen poultry is best thawed gradually in the refrigerator, but to speed up the process if you are in a hurry, use the cold water method.

Refrigerator method: Place the bird, in its plastic wrap, on a tray in the refrigerator. The exact thawing time will depend on the size of the bird and the temperature of the refrigerator, but it can be estimated as follows:

REFRIGERATOR METHOD FOR THAWING POULTRY			
Weight *(in pounds)*	Thawing time *(in hours)*	Weight *(in pounds)*	Thawing time *(in days)*
1 to 2	12	6 to 12	1½ to 2
2 to 4	12 to 24	12 to 20	2 to 3
4 to 6	24 to 36	20 to 24	3 to 3½

Cold water method: Place bird in its original plastic wrap in a large pan or in the sink and cover with cold water. Change the water regularly as its temperature drops until bird thaws. Small chickens and Rock Cornish hens will thaw within about 1 hour, 4- to 12-pound birds in 3 to 6 hours. A 12- to 20-pound turkey will take 6 to 8 hours to thaw and a 24-pounder should be ready for cooking within approximately 10 hours.

STORING AND FREEZING COOKED POULTRY

Cooked poultry should stand at room temperature no more than about 1½ hours after cooking. Store loosely wrapped in the refrigerator and use within 2 or 3 days. Store stuffing and gravy separately in covered containers. Gravy should be reheated to boiling and poured into a warmed gravy boat just before serving.

Before freezing cooked poultry, cool and separate the meat, stuffing and gravy. Freezer-wrapped cooked poultry will retain its quality for about 2 months. Stuffing and gravy should always be used within 1 month of freezing.

TYPES OF POULTRY

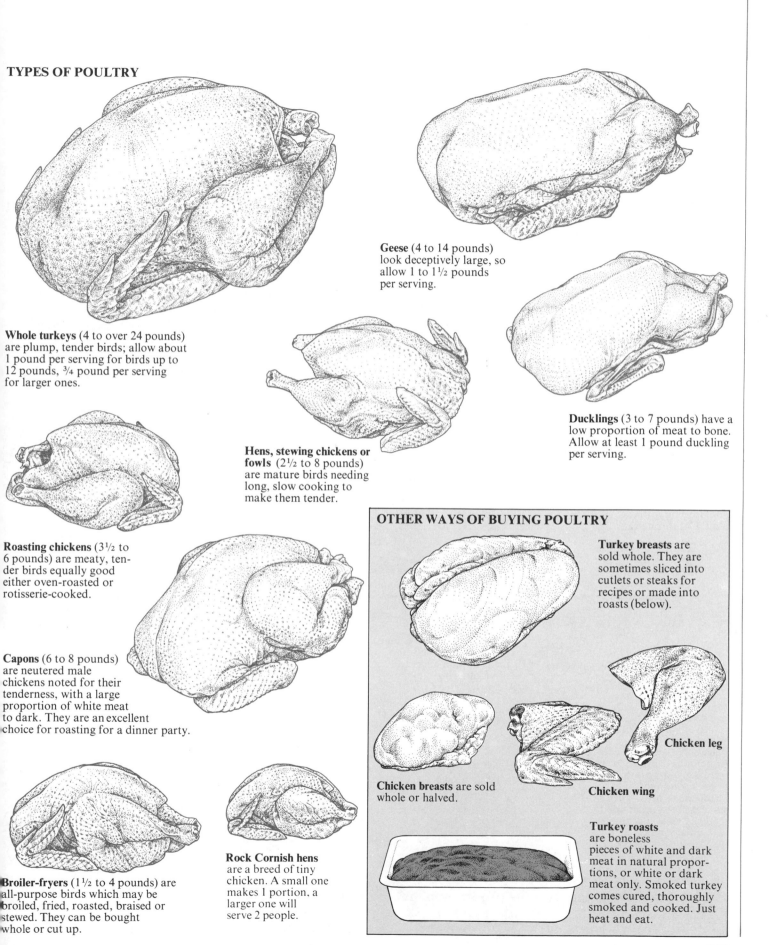

Whole turkeys (4 to over 24 pounds) are plump, tender birds; allow about 1 pound per serving for birds up to 12 pounds, ¾ pound per serving for larger ones.

Geese (4 to 14 pounds) look deceptively large, so allow 1 to 1½ pounds per serving.

Hens, stewing chickens or fowls (2½ to 8 pounds) are mature birds needing long, slow cooking to make them tender.

Ducklings (3 to 7 pounds) have a low proportion of meat to bone. Allow at least 1 pound duckling per serving.

Roasting chickens (3½ to 6 pounds) are meaty, tender birds equally good either oven-roasted or rotisserie-cooked.

Capons (6 to 8 pounds) are neutered male chickens noted for their tenderness, with a large proportion of white meat to dark. They are an excellent choice for roasting for a dinner party.

Broiler-fryers (1½ to 4 pounds) are all-purpose birds which may be broiled, fried, roasted, braised or stewed. They can be bought whole or cut up.

Rock Cornish hens are a breed of tiny chicken. A small one makes 1 portion, a larger one will serve 2 people.

OTHER WAYS OF BUYING POULTRY

Turkey breasts are sold whole. They are sometimes sliced into cutlets or steaks for recipes or made into roasts (below).

Chicken breasts are sold whole or halved.

Chicken wing

Chicken leg

Turkey roasts are boneless pieces of white and dark meat in natural proportions, or white or dark meat only. Smoked turkey comes cured, thoroughly smoked and cooked. Just heat and eat.

245

POULTRY

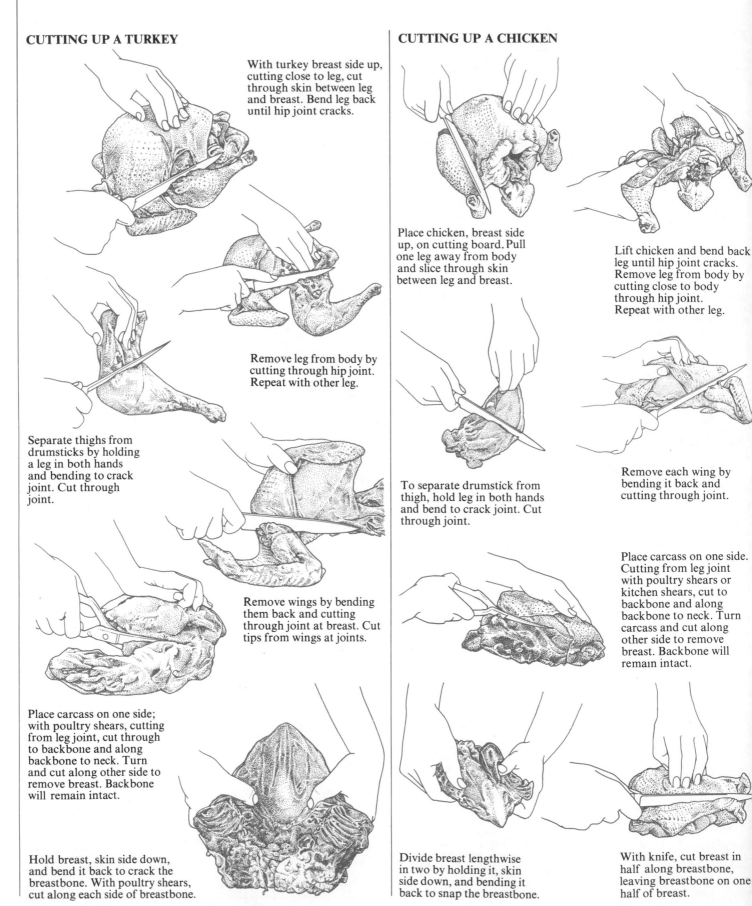

CUTTING UP A TURKEY

With turkey breast side up, cutting close to leg, cut through skin between leg and breast. Bend leg back until hip joint cracks.

Remove leg from body by cutting through hip joint. Repeat with other leg.

Separate thighs from drumsticks by holding a leg in both hands and bending to crack joint. Cut through joint.

Remove wings by bending them back and cutting through joint at breast. Cut tips from wings at joints.

Place carcass on one side; with poultry shears, cutting from leg joint, cut through to backbone and along backbone to neck. Turn and cut along other side to remove breast. Backbone will remain intact.

Hold breast, skin side down, and bend it back to crack the breastbone. With poultry shears, cut along each side of breastbone.

CUTTING UP A CHICKEN

Place chicken, breast side up, on cutting board. Pull one leg away from body and slice through skin between leg and breast.

Lift chicken and bend back leg until hip joint cracks. Remove leg from body by cutting close to body through hip joint. Repeat with other leg.

To separate drumstick from thigh, hold leg in both hands and bend to crack joint. Cut through joint.

Remove each wing by bending it back and cutting through joint.

Place carcass on one side. Cutting from leg joint with poultry shears or kitchen shears, cut to backbone and along backbone to neck. Turn carcass and cut along other side to remove breast. Backbone will remain intact.

Divide breast lengthwise in two by holding it, skin side down, and bending it back to snap the breastbone.

With knife, cut breast in half along breastbone, leaving breastbone on one half of breast.

HALVING A CHICKEN

Place chicken breast up; with poultry shears or kitchen shears, starting at body cavity and holding meat with other hand, cut straight along one side of breastbone to neck cavity.

Spreading chicken open, cut along one side of backbone to make two halves. If you like, cut along other side of bone to remove bone. Because shears may not be sharp enough, if you like, first cut through skin and flesh with knife before cutting through bone.

QUARTERING A CHICKEN

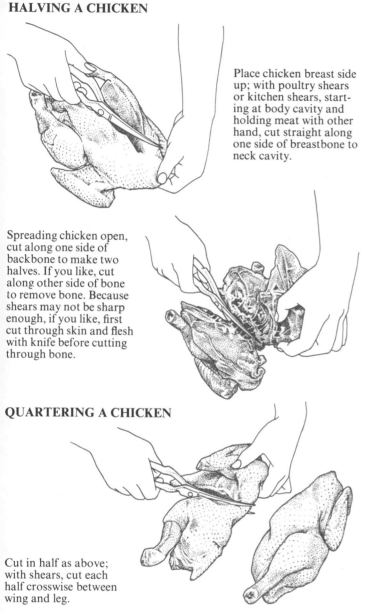

Cut in half as above; with shears, cut each half crosswise between wing and leg.

BONING A CHICKEN OR TURKEY BREAST

With sharp knife, working with one side of breast, starting parallel and close to large end of rib bone, cut and scrape meat away from bone and rib cage, gently pulling back meat in one piece as you cut. Repeat with remaining side of breast; discard bones.

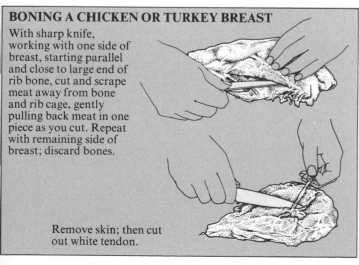

Remove skin; then cut out white tendon.

QUARTERING A DUCKLING

Place duckling breast side up; with poultry shears or kitchen shears, cut off excess skin beyond neck cavity and discard. Pull off clusters of excess fat in body cavity; discard.

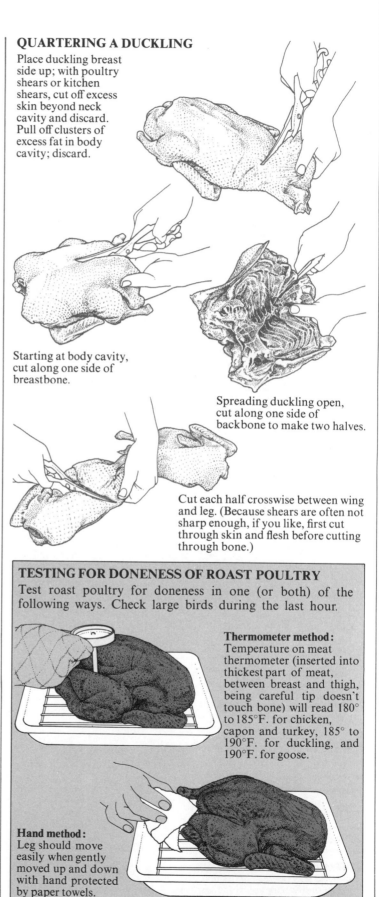

Starting at body cavity, cut along one side of breastbone.

Spreading duckling open, cut along one side of backbone to make two halves.

Cut each half crosswise between wing and leg. (Because shears are often not sharp enough, if you like, first cut through skin and flesh before cutting through bone.)

TESTING FOR DONENESS OF ROAST POULTRY

Test roast poultry for doneness in one (or both) of the following ways. Check large birds during the last hour.

Thermometer method: Temperature on meat thermometer (inserted into thickest part of meat, between breast and thigh, being careful tip doesn't touch bone) will read 180° to 185°F. for chicken, capon and turkey, 185° to 190°F. for duckling, and 190°F. for goose.

Hand method: Leg should move easily when gently moved up and down with hand protected by paper towels.

Roast poultry

Stuffing for roast poultry should be spooned in loosely just before cooking. Do not bother to stuff the neck of a bird under 4 pounds. For unstuffed birds, skewer the neck skin to the back; tie the legs together across the tail or use a stuffing clamp.

To keep the breast meat moist, cover the bird with a foil "tent" during the last hour of roasting. Never partially roast any poultry one day and complete it the next: bacteria are likely to grow under such conditions. Unless you are roasting a prebasted turkey, spoon pan drippings, melted butter, margarine or salad oil over bird at intervals while roasting. A bird will be easier to carve if it is taken out of the oven and allowed to rest – about 30 minutes for a turkey, less for smaller birds.

When the meal is over, cover and refrigerate the stuffing, gravy and meat separately and use within a day or so. Or, wrap separately and freeze poultry meat up to 3 months, the stuffing and gravy up to 1 month.

TIMETABLE FOR ROASTING POULTRY

Ready-to-cook weight (in pounds)	Oven temperature	Cooking time (in hours)	Internal temperature
Turkey, stuffed			
8 to 12	325°F.	3½ to 4	180 to 185°F.
12 to 16	325°F.	4 to 4½	
16 to 20	325°F.	4½ to 5	
20 to 24	325°F.	5 to 6	
Turkey, unstuffed: allow about ½ hour less			180 to 185°F.
Capon, stuffed			
5 to 6	325°F.	2½ to 3	180 to 185°F.
6 to 8	325°F.	3 to 4	
Capon, unstuffed: allow about ½ hour less			180 to 185°F.
Chicken, stuffed or unstuffed			
2 to 2½	325°F.	1½	180 to 185°F.
2½ to 3	325°F.	2	
3 to 4	325°F.	2½	
4 to 6	325°F.	2½ to 3½	
Rock Cornish hen, stuffed or unstuffed*			
1 to 2	350°F.	1 to 1½	
Whole duckling, stuffed or unstuffed			
3½ to 5½	325°F.	2 to 2½	185 to 190°F.
Goose, stuffed			
9 to 11	350°F.	3¼ to 4	190°F.
11 to 13	350°F.	4 to 4½	
Goose, unstuffed: allow about ½ hour less			190°F.

Bird is too small to use meat thermometer. Test for doneness by moving legs up and down and pinching with fingers protected with paper towels. Leg will move easily and feel soft.

TRUSSING POULTRY

Truss as follows, but for some brands of turkey push drumsticks under band of skin or use stuffing clamp.

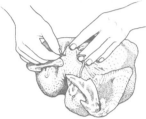

With bird breast side up, fold neck skin under turkey. Lift wings up toward neck, then fold under back of bird so they balance bird and keep neck skin in place.

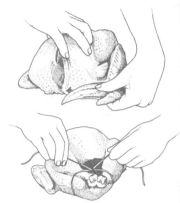

Fasten skin to back with 1 or 2 skewers, if necessary.

Tie drumsticks and tail together with string.

CARVING

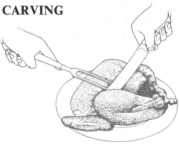

Place roasted bird on warm platter or cutting board 15 to 30 minutes to allow it to "set" for easier carving. Place bird directly in front of you with breast of bird at your left. With sharp carving knife and long-tined fork, cut drumstick and thigh from body.

Disjoint it by bending it down with hand.

Remove drumstick to a separate plate and slice dark meat from bone.

Insert fork securely into upper part of wing; make a long deep cut above wing joint through breast to bird's frame.

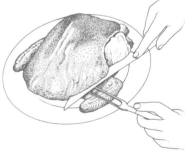

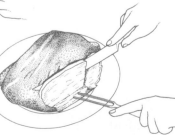

From halfway up breast, carve downward with a straight motion; when knife reaches slice made across from wing, poultry slices will fall free. Carve enough thin slices for serving. Carve more as needed.

Roast Turkey with Moist Bread Stuffing

1 12- to 16-pound frozen
ready-to-stuff
prebasted turkey,
thawed
Moist Bread Stuffing
(page 252)
salad oil
Giblet Gravy (below)

Color index page 39
Begin 6½ hrs ahead
16 servings

633 cals per serving

Good source of iron,
vitamin A, niacin

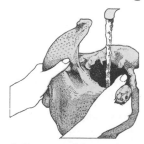 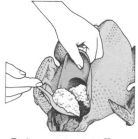 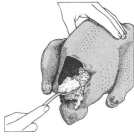
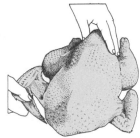

1 Remove giblets and neck from inside turkey and reserve for gravy. Rinse bird with running cold water; drain well.

2 Spoon some stuffing lightly into neck cavity (do not pack). Fold neck skin over and fasten to back with 1 or 2 skewers.

3 With bird breast side up, lift wings up toward neck, then fold under back of bird so they stay flat and keep neck skin in place.

4 Spoon remaining stuffing lightly into body cavity. Close by folding skin lightly over opening; skewer closed.

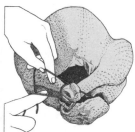 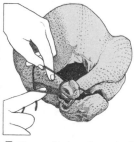  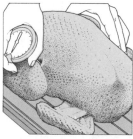  

5 Depending on brand of bird, with string, tie legs to tail; or push drumsticks under band of skin or use stuffing clamp.

6 On rack in open roasting pan, place bird breast side up. Brush skin lightly with salad oil.

7 Insert meat thermometer into meat between breast and thigh, being careful that pointed end does not touch bone.

8 Roast at 325°F. 4 to 4½ hours, covering with a "tent" of foil when bird turns golden. Check doneness during last 30 minutes.

9 Toward end of roasting, remove foil; coat bird with drippings. Bird is done when thermometer reads 180° to 185°F.

Giblet Gravy

reserved giblets
and neck
1 celery stalk, cut up
½ cup chopped
onion
salt
water
turkey pan drippings
6 tablespoons all-purpose
flour

Begin 2 hrs ahead
5 cups

116 cals per ½ cup

Good source of vitamin A

1 While turkey is roasting, in 3-quart saucepan over high heat, heat to boiling giblets, neck, celery, onion, ½ teaspoon salt and water to cover.

2 Reduce heat to low; cover; simmer 1 hour until giblets are tender. Drain, reserving broth; discard celery and onion. Chop neck meat and giblets.

3 When turkey is done, remove rack from pan; pour pan drippings into a 4-cup measure; let drippings stand until fat separates from meat juice.

4 Skim ⅓ cup fat from drippings into 2-quart saucepan; skim off and discard any fat remaining on surface of drippings.

5 Add reserved broth to roasting pan; stir until brown bits are loosened.

6 Add liquid to meat juice in cup to make 4 cups (add water if necessary).

7 Into fat in saucepan over medium heat, stir flour and 1½ teaspoons salt.

8 Gradually stir in meat-juice mixture; cook, stirring until thickened.

9 Add reserved chopped giblets and neck meat; cook until heated through.

Roast turkey

Turkey Roll with Spinach Stuffing

*Spinach stuffing
(page 252)
1 6-pound turkey breast,
boned, halved and
skinned (reserve
skin)
1 teaspoon salt
¼ cup butter or
margarine, melted*

**Gravy: 2 cups water,
2 tablespoons all-purpose
flour, ½ teaspoon salt,
⅛ teaspoon pepper**

**Color index
page 39**

**Begin 3 hrs
ahead**

16 servings

**286 cals per
serving**

**Good source
of iron,
niacin**

1 Prepare stuffing. Place each half-breast, cut side up, on board. Starting at long side, cut horizontally in half, but not all the way through; open out meat like a butterfly.

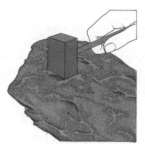

2 Spread meat open. With meat mallet or dull edge of French knife, pound until about 10" by 9" and ¼ inch thick.

3 Sprinkle with half of salt then cover with half of stuffing. Starting at narrow end, roll up jellyroll fashion. Place one piece of skin on top of roll.

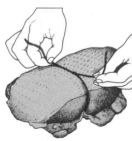

4 Tie roll with string. Repeat steps 2–4 with remaining half-breast.

5 Place rolls, skin side up, on rack in roasting pan. Brush with butter. Insert meat thermometer in center of one roll.

6 Roast at 325°F. until thermometer reads 185°F., about 1¾ hours; remove the strings.

7 Make gravy: Pour drippings into 4-cup measure; let stand until fat separates. Pour 2 tablespoons fat into 1-quart saucepan; skim off and discard remaining fat. Add water to roasting pan; stir to loosen brown bits; add to meat juice in cup. Into fat in saucepan, over medium heat, stir flour, salt, pepper and meatjuice; cook, stirring until the gravy is thick.

Roast Chicken with Sausage-Apple Stuffing

**Color index
page 43**

**Begin 4 hrs
ahead**

6 servings

**652 cals per
serving**

**Good source
of iron,
niacin**

*Sausage-Apple Stuffing
(page 252)
1 5- to 5½-pound
roasting chicken*

*salad oil, butter or
margarine*

1. Prepare the stuffing. Remove giblets and neck from inside bird. Rinse bird with running cold water and drain well. Spoon some stuffing lightly into neck cavity. Fold neck skin over stuffing. With bird breast side up, lift wings up toward neck, then fold under back of bird to balance it.

2. Spoon remaining stuffing into body cavity; fold skin over opening; rub bird with salad oil. Bake any leftover stuffing in covered, greased small casserole during last 30 minutes of roasting chicken.

3. Insert meat thermometer into thickest part of meat between breast and thigh (do not touch bone). Place chicken, breast side up, on rack in open roasting pan. Roast, uncovered, in 325°F. oven 2½ to 3 hours.

4. When chicken turns golden cover loosely with a "tent" of folded foil. Remove foil during last hour of roasting time. Brush bird generously with pan drippings, oil or melted butter. Chicken is done when thermometer reads 180° to 185°F. Start checking for doneness during the last 30 minutes.

Herb-roasted Capon

**Color index
page 41**

**Begin day
ahead**

8 servings

**188 cals per
serving**

**Good source
of niacin**

*1 6- to 8-pound capon
¼ cup salt
1 teaspoon parsley flakes
¾ teaspoon thyme leaves*

*½ teaspoon rubbed sage
⅛ teaspoon cracked
pepper
salad oil*

1. Prepare capon as for Roast Chicken (above) but do not stuff. Mix salt and next 4 ingredients and rub over outside and in body cavity. Cover and refrigerate at least 12 hours or overnight.

2. Brush skin with oil, roast, uncovered, in 325°F. oven 3 to 4 hours, basting frequently.

Chicken Delhi

**Color index
page 43**

**Begin 2½ hrs
ahead**

8 servings

**469 cals per
serving**

**Good source
of calcium,
niacin**

*2 3-pound broilerfryers
1½ teaspoons ground
ginger
⅛ teaspoon ground
coriander
⅛ teaspoon pepper
3 tablespoons butter*

*1 cup minced onions
1 cup plain yogurt
1 cup half-and-half
1 tablespoon turmeric
1½ teaspoons salt
about 6 cups hot cooked
rice*

1. Remove giblets and neck from chickens. (Use giblets and neck for broth, if you like.) Rinse and drain chicken well. With string, tie legs and tail of each chicken together. Combine ginger, coriander and pepper; rub into birds and place in open roasting pan.

2. In 2-quart saucepan over medium heat, melt butter; stir in next 5 ingredients; pour over birds. Roast in 325°F. oven about 2 hours or until forktender, basting frequently.

3. Lift chickens to warm platter; remove strings. Spoon pan sauce over rice; serve with chicken.

Baked chicken

Baking chicken is the same cooking technique as roasting chicken – the whole bird or parts are baked, uncovered, with uniform heat. However, the oven temperature is usually higher for baking than for roasting. Sometimes chicken pieces are marinated in a sauce before baking, then, during cooking, the remaining marinade is spooned over the pieces. Among the many good tasting sauces to use for marinating are barbecue sauce, French, Italian or other favorite salad dressing, red or white wine, or one of the marinade recipes from page 261. Stuffed chicken breasts can also be baked and are equally good cooked in a marinade.

Baked Chicken

Color index page 44

Begin 1 hr ahead

8 servings

309 cals per serving

Good source of vitamin A, niacin

½ cup butter or margarine
½ cup all-purpose flour
1½ teaspoons salt

2 teaspoons paprika
¼ teaspoon pepper
2 3-pound broiler-fryers, each cut into quarters

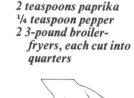

1 In a large roasting pan in 425°F. oven, melt the butter or margarine.

2 Meanwhile, in pie plate, combine flour, salt, paprika and pepper. Coat the chicken quarters evenly with the mixture.

3 In roasting pan, place the chicken pieces, skin side down, in melted butter. Bake 30 minutes.

4 Turn the chicken pieces and bake 15 minutes more until pieces are fork-tender.

Chicken Sauterne

Color index page 46

Begin early in day or day ahead

4 servings

353 cals per serving

Good source of iron, niacin

¾ cup sauterne
2 tablespoons salad oil
2 tablespoons chopped parsley
2 tablespoons chopped green onions

1 teaspoon salt
¼ teaspoon paprika
2 2-pound broiler-fryers, each cut in half

1. In 13″ by 9″ baking dish, for marinade, mix all ingredients except chicken. Add chicken; coat with marinade. Cover and refrigerate at least 4 hours.
2. *About 1 hour before serving:* Preheat oven to 375°F. Place chicken, skin side down, in marinade. Bake 25 minutes, basting occasionally; turn; bake 25 minutes more or until fork-tender, basting occasionally. Pour drippings into cup; spoon off fat; discard. Serve remaining liquid over chicken.

Nut-stuffed Chicken Breasts with Creamy Gravy

Color index page 41

Begin 2 hrs ahead

6 servings

454 cals per serving

Good source of calcium, iron, vitamin A, niacin

⅓ cup finely chopped salted peanuts
¼ cup minced parsley
salt
6 medium whole chicken breasts, each skinned, boned and cut in half
butter or margarine
½ teaspoon paprika

2 tablespoons all-purpose flour
1 chicken-flavor bouillon cube or envelope or 1 teaspoon chicken- flavor stock base
1¼ cups milk
parsley for garnish

1. In small bowl, combine peanuts, minced parsley and ½ teaspoon salt; set aside.
2. With meat mallet or dull edge of French knife, pound each chicken piece until ¼ inch thick.
3. To stuff chicken breasts: Overlap two pieces about 1 inch; sprinkle with a generous tablespoonful of peanut mixture to within ½ inch of edges; fold the two long sides slightly toward the middle; roll chicken breast in the opposite direction, jelly-roll fashion; fasten seam with two toothpicks.
4. Repeat this process with each of the remaining pieces of chicken breast.
5. In 13″ by 9″ baking dish, melt ½ cup butter or margarine in 400°F. oven; stir in paprika and ½ teaspoon salt until well mixed. Arrange stuffed chicken breasts, seam side down, in baking dish; brush with butter mixture in pan. Bake 40 minutes or until chicken is fork-tender, basting occasionally with pan drippings.
6. Spoon 3 tablespoons pan drippings into 1-quart saucepan. Over medium heat, into drippings, stir flour, bouillon and ½ teaspoon salt until blended. Gradually stir in milk; cook, stirring constantly, until mixture is thickened.
7. Discard toothpicks from stuffed chicken breasts; arrange on warm platter.
8. To serve: Garnish with finely chopped parsley Pour gravy into gravy boat; pass separately.

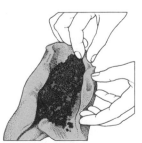

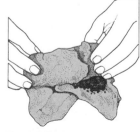

Folding the edges: Fold long sides of chicken toward middle.

Rolling the chicken breast: Roll each stuffed breast up, jelly-roll fashion.

Stuffings

When stuffing whole birds, prepare stuffing just before roasting. You will need ¾ to 1 cup stuffing per pound of bird. Stuffing expands during cooking, so pack it lightly into the bird. If you wish, bake extra stuffing in a covered, greased casserole along with the bird during the last 30 to 45 minutes of roasting time.

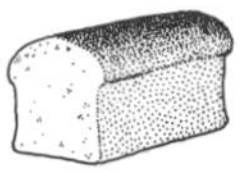

Moist Bread Stuffing

Begin 30 mins ahead

10 cups

215 cals per ½ cup

1 cup butter or margarine
2 cups diced celery
1½ cups chopped onions
¼ cup minced parsley
2 teaspoons salt
2 teaspoons poultry seasoning
½ teaspoon pepper
18 cups white bread cubes
3 eggs, slightly beaten

1. In 8-quart Dutch oven over medium heat, in hot butter or margarine, cook celery and onions until tender, about 10 minutes.
2. Add parsley, salt, poultry seasoning and pepper; stir well until thoroughly mixed.
3. Stir in bread cubes and eggs; mix together well.

Mixed-Fruit Stuffing

Begin 45 mins ahead

8 cups

150 cals per ½ cup

Low in fat, cholesterol

1 12-ounce package mixed dried fruit, cut in pieces
water
1 medium onion, minced
1 16-ounce package cranberries
1 cup sugar
5 cups lightly packed, day-old bread cubes
1 teaspoon salt
½ teaspoon ground allspice

1. If prunes have pits, remove and discard. In 2-quart saucepan over high heat, heat 2 cups water, fruit and onion to boiling. Reduce heat to low; simmer 15 minutes or until fruit is tender; pour mixture into large bowl.
2. In same pan over medium heat, heat ¼ cup water, cranberries and sugar to boiling. Reduce heat to low; simmer 7 minutes or until berries pop, stirring occasionally. Drain liquid from berries. Pour berries into fruit mixture.
3. Add remaining ingredients; toss lightly.

Chestnut Stuffing

Color index page 49

Begin 1¼ hrs ahead

11 cups

178 cals per ½ cup

Low in cholesterol

1½ pounds chestnuts
water
1 cup butter
1½ cups diced celery
1 cup chopped onions
2 teaspoons salt
1 teaspoon thyme leaves
1 teaspoon marjoram
½ teaspoon seasoned pepper
8 cups fresh bread crumbs

1. With tip of sharp knife, mark an "X" in flat side of each chestnut. In 3-quart saucepan, cover chestnuts with water.
2. Over high heat, heat to boiling; cook 1 minute. Remove pan from heat. With slotted spoon remove 3 or 4 chestnuts at a time; remove shells and skins. Coarsely chop chestnuts; set aside.
3. In 6-quart Dutch oven over medium heat, in hot butter, cook celery and next 5 ingredients about 10 minutes or until vegetables are tender.
4. Remove pan from heat. Stir in chestnuts and bread crumbs; mix all ingredients together well.

Rice-Raisin Stuffing

Color index page 49

Begin 45 mins ahead

14 cups

150 cals per ½ cup

Low in cholesterol

2½ cups long-grain rice
1 8-ounce package sliced bacon
¾ cup dark seedless raisins
⅓ cup boiling water
¾ cup butter
4 cups diced celery
2 cups diced onions
2 teaspoons salt
½ teaspoon pepper

1. Prepare rice as label directs. Meanwhile, in 12-inch skillet over medium-low heat, cook bacon; drain on paper towels; crumble into pieces. In bowl, combine raisins with water.
2. In 8-quart Dutch oven over medium heat, in hot butter, cook celery, onions, salt and pepper 10 minutes, stirring often.
3. Remove celery mixture from heat; stir in rice, bacon pieces and seedless raisins.

Sausage-Rice Stuffing

Begin 25 mins ahead

3 cups

217 cals per ½ cup

Low in cholesterol

¾ cup regular long-grain rice
½ pound sweet Italian sausage links, casings removed
1 green onion, thinly sliced
⅛ teaspoon pepper

1. Prepare rice as label directs; meanwhile, in 10-inch skillet over medium heat, cook sausage until well browned, breaking apart with fork. Drain.
2. Toss rice with sausage, onion and pepper.

Sausage-Apple Stuffing

Color index page 49

Begin 45 mins ahead

6¼ cups

105 cals per ¼ cup

Low in cholesterol

1 pound pork-sausage meat
3 large apples, peeled, cored and chopped
1 large onion, chopped
1 cup chopped celery
4 cups fresh bread crumbs
2 eggs
1½ teaspoons salt
1 teaspoon poultry seasoning

1. In 4-quart saucepan over medium heat, cook sausage meat until browned, breaking apart with fork. Remove meat to medium bowl.
2. Pour off drippings but return ¼ cup to pan. In drippings over medium heat, cook apples, onion and celery until celery is tender, about 10 minutes.
3. Remove from heat. Add sausage meat and remaining ingredients. Stir until well mixed.

Spinach Stuffing

Begin 30 mins ahead

3½ cups

246 cals per ½ cup

Good source of calcium, iron, vitamin A

1 10-ounce package frozen chopped spinach, thawed
½ cup butter or margarine
¼ pound mushrooms, thinly sliced
1 cup diced celery
½ cup chopped onion
3 cups fresh bread crumbs
½ 15-ounce container ricotta cheese (1 cup)
1 egg
1 tablespoon minced parsley
1 teaspoon salt
½ teaspoon poultry seasoning
⅛ teaspoon pepper

1. Squeeze spinach dry with paper towels.
2. In 4-quart saucepan over medium heat, in hot butter or margarine, cook mushrooms, celery and onion until tender, about 5 minutes, stirring occasionally; remove from heat.
3. Add remaining ingredients and spinach; mix well.

Braised chicken

Braising usually involves two cooking techniques. First, most recipes call for cooking the food in hot fat until well browned on all sides. Next, flavorings and a small quantity of liquid, such as water, chicken broth, tomato juice or wine, are added. The skillet is then tightly covered and the poultry simmered over low heat until it is fork-tender. Sometimes, the covered skillet is transferred to the oven to complete cooking (be sure the handle of the skillet is ovensafe). Whatever the method. braising is a *slow-cooking method* and should never be hurried.

Select the pan for braising according to the recipe and the shape and size of the poultry. For poultry pieces a deep, heavy skillet with a close-fitting lid will often do well. For larger quantities a Dutch oven is more suitable. Select a pan large enough to hold the bird, its liquid and other ingredients comfortably.

Only a small quantity of liquid is used for braising, usually ½ to 1 cup. During long braising times, therefore, it is best to check the liquid occasionally during cooking, adding a few tablespoons more liquid if it has evaporated too much.

Arroz con Pollo

Color index
page 44

Begin 1¾ hrs
ahead

8 servings

476 cals per
serving

Good source
of iron,
niacin

¼ cup salad oil
1 4- to 5-pound roasting
   chicken, cut up
1 cup chopped onion
1¼ cups water
1 16-ounce can tomatoes
1 4-ounce jar diced
   pimentos
1 2-ounce jar pimento-
   stuffed olives
2 cups regular long-grain
   rice
2 teaspoons salt
¼ teaspoon pepper

2 chicken-flavor
   bouillon cubes or
   envelopes or
   2 teaspoons chicken-
   flavor stock base
½ pound fresh pork-
   sausage links, cut
   into ½-inch
   pieces
1 10-ounce package
   frozen peas,
   thawed

1 In 8-quart Dutch oven over medium-high heat, in hot oil, brown chicken, a few pieces at a time; set aside. In drippings, over medium heat, cook onion until it is tender.

2 Add chicken, water, tomatoes, pimentos and olives and all their liquids and remaining ingredients except peas; heat to boiling.

3 Reduce heat to low. Cover Dutch oven and simmer chicken mixture 30 minutes or until chicken is almost fork-tender, occasionally lifting rice with fork.

4 Add thawed peas to Dutch oven and cook 10 minutes more. (If mixture seems dry when peas are added, cook covered; if it seems moist, cook uncovered.)

Chicken Paprika with Spaetzle

Color index
page 41

Begin 45 mins
ahead

6 servings

376 cals per
serving

Good source
of calcium,
iron

1 2½- to 3-pound
   broiler-fryer, cut up
⅓ cup all-purpose flour
2 tablespoons salad oil
2 medium onions, thinly
   sliced
1½ teaspoons salt

1 tablespoon paprika
⅛ teaspoon pepper
1½ cups water
1 chicken-flavor bouillon
   cube or envelope
Spaetzle (below)
½ cup sour cream

1. Coat chicken with flour; reserve remaining flour. In 12-inch skillet over medium-high heat, in hot salad oil, cook chicken until browned on all sides, about 7 to 10 minutes. Remove chicken.

2. To oil in skillet, add remaining flour and onions; cook, stirring constantly, for 2 minutes. Stir in salt, paprika, pepper, water and bouillon. Return chicken to skillet; cover and reduce heat to medium; simmer 25 minutes or until chicken is fork-tender, turning once.

3. Meanwhile, prepare the Spaetzle. With tongs, remove chicken to large platter. Spoon fat from gravy in pan; stir in sour cream until blended.

4. To serve: Add Spaetzle and heat through: spoon around chicken.

SPAETZLE: In 6-quart Dutch oven over high heat, heat **4 quarts water** and **1 teaspoon salt** to boiling. Meanwhile, in medium bowl with wire whisk or spoon, beat **2 cups all-purpose flour,** ½ **cup water, 3 eggs** and ½ **teaspoon salt** until smooth. Reduce heat to medium. Over boiling water with rubber spatula, press batter through colander or spaetzle maker. Stir water gently so spaetzle will not stick together. Boil 5 minutes or until tender but firm *(al dente);* drain.

Making spaetzle with a colander: Press batter through colander if you have no spaetzle maker.

Cooking the spaetzle: While cooking, stir water gently to keep spaetzle from sticking.

Braised chicken

Chicken Cacciatore

1 tablespoon salad oil
1 3- to 3¹/₂-pound
* broiler-fryer, cut up*
* into serving-size pieces*
1 16-ounce can tomatoes
¹/₂ cup Chianti or other
* dry red wine*
1¹/₂ teaspoons garlic salt

³/₄ teaspoon basil
¹/₄ teaspoon pepper
12 small white onions,
* peeled*
2 large green peppers,
* cut into ¹/₂-inch strips*
1 tablespoon cornstarch
1 tablespoon water

Color index
page 42

Begin 1 hr
ahead

4 servings

303 cals per
serving

Good source
of iron,
niacin,
vitamin C

1. In 12-inch skillet over medium-high heat, in hot salad oil, cook the chicken pieces until well browned on all sides.
2. Stir in tomatoes with their liquid, wine, garlic salt, basil and pepper; heat to boiling. Reduce heat to low; cover and simmer 15 minutes.
3. Add onions and green peppers; cover and simmer 15 minutes longer or just until vegetables are fork-tender.
4. In cup, stir cornstarch and water until smooth; gradually stir into chicken mixture and cook, stirring frequently, until mixture is boiling and thickened and chicken is fork-tender.

Chicken Curry, Southern Style

1 3- to 3¹/₂-pound broiler-
* fryer, cut up*
¹/₄ cup all-purpose
* flour*
¹/₄ cup salad oil
2 garlic cloves,
* halved*
2 medium onions, thinly
* sliced*
¹/₂ cup chopped celery
1 medium green pepper,
* chopped*
1 tablespoon curry
* powder*

1 teaspoon salt
1 29-ounce can
* tomatoes*
1 cup regular long-
* grain rice*
¹/₂ cup currants or
* dark seedless*
* raisins*
1 tablespoon butter or
* margarine*
¹/₃ cup blanched whole
* almonds*
chopped parsley for
* garnish*

Color index
page 41
Begin 1 hr
ahead
5 servings

480 cals per
serving

Good source
of calcium,
iron,
niacin,
vitamin C

1. On waxed paper, coat chicken with flour. In 12-inch skillet over medium-high heat, in hot salad oil, cook chicken until browned on all sides; remove chicken from skillet.
2. In drippings in skillet, over medium heat, cook garlic, onions, celery, green pepper, curry powder and salt until vegetables are tender, about 10 minutes, stirring occasionally. Stir in tomatoes and their liquid; add chicken pieces and heat to boiling. Reduce heat to low; cover and simmer 40 minutes or until chicken is fork-tender.
3. Meanwhile, prepare rice as label directs; add currants to rice.
4. In 10-inch skillet over medium heat, in hot butter or margarine, cook almonds until golden, shaking skillet occasionally to brown them evenly.
5. To serve Southern-style curry, arrange chicken pieces and cooked rice on warm serving platter. Remove garlic pieces from sauce then spoon some sauce over chicken pieces.
6. Sprinkle chicken and rice with almonds and chopped parsley. Pass remaining sauce separately in gravy boat.

Chicken Dinner with Sour-Cream Gravy

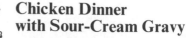

3 tablespoons salad oil
1 2¹/₂- to 3-pound
* broiler-fryer, cut up*
2 teaspoons salt
¹/₄ teaspoon pepper
¹/₂ cup water
2 cups diagonally sliced
* celery*

2 cups diagonally sliced
* carrots*
1 cup regular long-grain
* rice*
1 8-ounce container sour
* cream*

Color index
page 41

Begin 45 mins
ahead

4 servings

542 cals per
serving

Good source
of calcium,
iron,
niacin

1. In 12-inch skillet over medium-high heat, in hot salad oil, cook chicken pieces until browned on all sides. Sprinkle chicken with salt and pepper. Add water and heat to boiling. Reduce heat to low. Cover and simmer 20 minutes.
2. Add celery and carrot slices. Cover and simmer 15 minutes more or until chicken and vegetables are fork-tender, stirring occasionally.
3. Meanwhile, prepare rice as label directs. Spoon onto warm platter and keep warm.
4. With slotted spoon, arrange chicken and vegetables on cooked rice.
5. To prepare sour-cream gravy: Spoon fat from drippings remaining in skillet. Into drippings, stir sour cream. Over medium heat, heat through, scraping any bits from bottom of pan. Do not allow mixture to boil or sour cream will curdle.
6. Pour sour-cream gravy over chicken and vegetables and serve immediately.

Chicken with Cucumbers

2 tablespoons salad
* oil*
1 2¹/₂- to 3-pound
* broiler-fryer,*
* quartered*
¹/₄ pound mushrooms,
* sliced*
1 garlic clove, minced
3 tablespoons all-purpose
* flour*

¹/₄ cup dry sherry
2 chicken-flavor bouillon
* cubes or envelopes or 2*
* teaspoons chicken-*
* flavor stock base*
1 teaspoon salt
1¹/₂ cups water
2 large cucumbers
1 8-ounce container sour
* cream*

Color index
page 42

Begin 1¹/₄ hrs
ahead

4 servings

425 cals per
serving

Good source
of calcium,
iron,
niacin

1. In 12-inch skillet over medium-high heat, in hot salad oil, cook chicken until browned on all sides; remove from skillet.
2. To drippings in skillet, add mushrooms and garlic; cook about 2 minutes. Stir in flour until blended. Gradually stir in sherry, bouillon, salt and water; cook, stirring constantly, until mixture is slightly thickened.
3. Add chicken; heat to boiling. Reduce heat to low; cover and simmer 30 minutes, stirring.
4. Meanwhile, cut half of a cucumber into very thin slices; set aside for garnish. Peel remaining cucumbers and cut into large chunks.
5. Add cucumber chunks to chicken and continue cooking 15 to 20 minutes until chicken is fork-tender and cucumber is tender-crisp. Stir in sour cream; cook until heated through but do not boil.
6. Arrange chicken pieces on warm platter, surround with chunks of cucumber and pour on sauce. Garnish with cucumber slices.

Chicken Fricassee

Color index page 45

Begin 3½ hrs ahead

8 servings

207 cals per serving

Good source of niacin

1 5- to 6-pound stewing chicken, cut up
1 cup liquid (dry vermouth or other dry white wine or chicken broth or diluted canned condensed cream of celery, mushroom or chicken soup)

1 small onion, sliced
1 stalk celery, thinly sliced
1 tablespoon salt
½ teaspoon pepper
½ teaspoon paprika
⅓ cup cold water
3 tablespoons all-purpose flour

1. In 12-inch skillet over medium-high heat, heat chicken and remaining ingredients except water and flour to boiling.
2. Reduce heat to low; cover skillet and simmer 2½ hours or until chicken is fork-tender. With slotted spoon, remove chicken pieces to warm platter; keep chicken pieces warm.
3. In cup, stir water into flour until smooth; gradually stir into pan juices and cook over medium heat, stirring constantly, until mixture is thickened.
4. To serve: Pour mixture over chicken.

272 cals per serving

Good source of niacin

BROWN CHICKEN FRICASSEE: Prepare as above but before cooking, on waxed paper, coat chicken with about *½ cup all-purpose flour* and in 12-inch skillet over medium-high heat, in *¼ cup hot salad oil,* cook chicken, a few pieces at a time, until browned on all sides, removing pieces as they brown. Return pieces to skillet. Add liquid (dry vermouth or other dry white wine or chicken broth or diluted canned condensed cream of celery, mushroom or chicken soup), onion, celery, salt, pepper and paprika; heat to boiling. Reduce heat to low; cover and simmer as in step 2., above. Remove chicken pieces to warm platter and in cup, stir *¼ cup cold water* into *1 tablespoon all-purpose flour* and add to skillet to thicken pan juices.

OTHER FLAVORINGS: Thyme leaves; rosemary; sliced green onions; a few whole cloves or celery tops; 1 tablespoon lemon juice; ⅛ teaspoon nutmeg; curry powder.

Saucy Chicken with Avocado

Color index page 45

Begin 45 mins ahead

4 servings

565 cals per serving

Good source of calcium, iron, vitamin A, niacin

2 tablespoons butter or margarine
1 2½- to 3-pound broiler-fryer, cut up
⅔ cup dry sherry
2 tablespoons all-purpose flour

¾ teaspoon salt
⅛ teaspoon paprika
1¼ cups half-and-half
1 large avocado
watercress for garnish

1. In 12-inch skillet over medium heat, in hot butter or margarine, cook chicken until pieces are browned on all sides.
2. Stir in sherry. Heat to boiling. Reduce heat to low; cover and simmer 25 minutes or until chicken is fork-tender. Remove chicken to warm platter.
3. Into liquid in skillet, stir flour, salt and paprika until well blended. Gradually stir in half-and-half; cook, stirring constantly, until thickened.
4. Peel and seed avocado; cut into slices and add gently to sauce; heat through.
5. To serve: Spoon sauce over chicken pieces. Garnish with watercress.

Chicken Seville

Color index page 41

Begin 1½ hrs ahead

6 servings

302 cals per serving

Good source of iron, niacin, vitamin C

¼ cup olive or salad oil
1 3½- to 4-pound broiler-fryer, cut up
2 medium green peppers, cut in strips
1 large onion, sliced
½ cup minced cooked ham
2 garlic cloves, minced
1 28-ounce can tomatoes, drained
¾ teaspoon salt
¼ teaspoon pepper

⅛ teaspoon fennel seed
⅛ teaspoon marjoram leaves
⅛ teaspoon thyme leaves
1 3¼- to 3½-ounce can pitted, large ripe olives, drained and halved
1 10-ounce jar colossal pimento-stuffed olives, drained and halved

1. In 12-inch skillet over medium-high heat, in hot oil, brown chicken; remove to plate.
2. In same skillet over medium heat, in remaining oil, cook green peppers, onion, ham and garlic, stirring occasionally, until vegetables are tender, about 5 minutes. Spoon oil from skillet and discard.
3. To vegetables in skillet, add chicken, tomatoes and next 5 ingredients. Over high heat, heat to boiling. Reduce heat to low; cover; simmer 20 minutes or until chicken is fork-tender. Add olives; cook 5 minutes longer.
4. When chicken is done, with fork, remove to warm platter; keep warm.
5. Increase heat to high and cook vegetable mixture until thick and reduced by half, about 5 minutes, stirring often; spoon over chicken.

Chicken Chorizo

Color index page 42

Begin 1 hr ahead

6 servings

336 cals per serving

Good source of niacin

2 tablespoons olive or salad oil
3 small garlic cloves, minced
1 3½- to 4-pound broiler-fryer, cut up
2 chorizos (Spanish sausage) or ¼ pound pork-sausage links
1 cup cubed cooked ham

½ cup chicken broth
⅓ cup packed dark brown sugar
⅓ cup red wine vinegar
¾ teaspoon salt
½ teaspoon pepper
1½ teaspoons cornstarch
2 tablespoons water

1. In 12-inch skillet over medium heat, in hot oil, cook garlic and chicken until chicken is browned on all sides. Remove chicken to plate; set aside.
2. Cut chorizos into ¼-inch-thick slices. In same skillet over medium heat, in remaining oil, cook chorizos and ham, stirring frequently, until lightly browned. With slotted spoon, remove chorizo mixture; set aside.
3. Spoon off fat from skillet; add chicken broth, brown sugar and wine vinegar to skillet; stir until brown bits are loosened. Add chicken and chorizo mixture; sprinkle with salt and pepper.
4. Over high heat, heat to boiling. Reduce heat to low; cover and simmer 15 to 20 minutes until chicken is fork-tender. With slotted spoon, remove mixture to warm platter; keep warm.
5. In cup, mix cornstarch and water; gradually stir into liquid remaining in skillet and cook until thickened, stirring. Pour over chicken.

Braised chicken

Chicken Oporto

Color index
page 41

Begin 35 mins
ahead

4 servings

864 cals per
serving

Good source
of iron,
vitamin A,
niacin

½ cup butter
½ pound mushrooms,
thinly sliced
¼ cup all-purpose flour
1 teaspoon salt
¼ teaspoon pepper
¼ teaspoon ground
nutmeg

4 medium whole chicken
breasts, skinned and
boned
1½ cups heavy or
whipping cream
⅓ cup white port wine

1. In 12-inch skillet over medium-high heat, in hot butter, cook mushrooms 5 minutes. With slotted spoon, remove to small bowl; set aside.
2. On waxed paper, combine flour, salt, pepper and nutmeg; use to coat chicken breasts. In same skillet in remaining butter, over medium-high heat, cook the chicken breasts until browned on all sides.
3. Stir in cream, port and mushrooms; heat to boiling. Reduce heat to low; cover and simmer 15 minutes or until chicken is fork-tender.

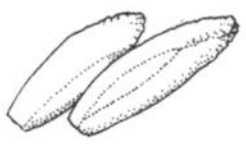

Chicken with Endives

Color index
page 43

Begin 45 mins
ahead

4 servings

452 cals per
serving

Good source
of calcium,
iron,
vitamin A,
niacin

4 medium whole chicken
breasts, skinned
and boned
water
butter or margarine
1 teaspoon salt
4 small Belgian endives,
trimmed
2 tablespoons lemon juice

2 tablespoons drained
bottled capers
½ cup fresh bread
crumbs
1 tablespoon all-purpose
flour
¼ pound natural Swiss
cheese, shredded
(about 1 cup)

1. Tuck under edges of chicken breasts for a more attractive shape. In 10-inch skillet over medium-low heat, heat ½ cup water and 2 tablespoons butter until melted. Arrange chicken in skillet; sprinkle with salt and place 1 endive on each breast; sprinkle endives with lemon juice.
2. Cover skillet; simmer 25 minutes or until chicken and endives are fork-tender. Remove endive-topped chicken to platter. Sprinkle with capers.
3. Meanwhile, in small skillet over medium heat, heat 2 tablespoons butter and bread crumbs until crumbs are browned, stirring frequently; set aside.
4. In cup, blend flour and 2 tablespoons water until smooth; gradually stir into hot liquid in skillet (there should be about ⅔ cup liquid left in skillet) and cook over medium heat, stirring constantly, until mixture is thickened. Remove from heat; stir in cheese until melted; pour over chicken; top with bread crumbs.

Adding the endives:
Sprinkle with salt and put
an endive on each breast.

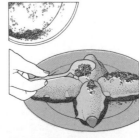

Serving the chicken: Pour
melted cheese sauce over
and top with bread crumbs.

Chicken Cordon Bleu

Color index
page 41

Begin 1¼ hrs
ahead

6 servings

526 cals per
serving

Good source
of calcium,
vitamin A,
niacin

6 medium whole chicken
breasts, skinned and
boned
1 8-ounce package Swiss
cheese slices
1 8-ounce package sliced
cooked ham
3 tablespoons all-purpose
flour
1 teaspoon paprika

6 tablespoons butter or
margarine
½ cup dry white wine
1 chicken-flavor bouillon
cube or envelope or
1 teaspoon chicken-
flavor stock base
1 tablespoon cornstarch
1 cup heavy or whipping
cream

1. Spread chicken breasts flat; fold cheese and ham slices to fit on top; fold breasts over filling and fasten edges with toothpicks.
2. On waxed paper, mix flour and paprika; use mixture to coat chicken pieces.
3. In 12-inch skillet over medium heat, in hot butter or margarine, cook chicken until browned on all sides. Add wine and bouillon. Reduce heat to low; cover and simmer 30 minutes or until fork-tender; remove the toothpicks.
4. In cup, blend cornstarch and cream until smooth; gradually stir into skillet. Cook, stirring constantly, until thickened; serve over chicken.

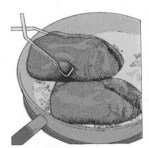

**Assembling the chicken and
filling:** Fold chicken
breasts over the cheese and
ham slices and fasten
securely with toothpicks.

Frying the chicken: In
12-inch skillet over
medium heat, in hot butter
or margarine, brown
chicken on all sides.

Chicken Périgord-Style

Color index
page 43

Begin 1 hr
ahead

8 servings

351 cals per
serving

Good source
of vitamin A,
niacin

½ cup butter or
margarine
8 whole chicken breasts,
skinned and boned
½ pound mushrooms,
sliced

⅓ cup all-purpose flour
¼ teaspoon salt
1 13¾-ounce can
chicken broth
2 tablespoons
half-and-half

1. In 12-inch skillet or 6-quart Dutch oven over medium-high heat, in 6 tablespoons hot butter or margarine, cook chicken, a few pieces at a time, until browned on all sides. Set chicken aside.
2. In drippings over medium heat, in remaining 2 tablespoons butter, cook mushrooms until golden, about 5 minutes. With slotted spoon, remove mushrooms to small bowl.
3. Into drippings, over medium heat, stir flour and salt until blended. Gradually stir in chicken broth and half-and-half and cook, stirring constantly, until mixture is thickened.
4. Place chicken and mushrooms in sauce. Reduce heat to low; cover and simmer 25 minutes.

Chicken Breasts with Sausage-Walnut Stuffing

*1 pound sweet Italian
  sausage links, casings
  removed*
*½ cup chopped
  California walnuts*
⅓ cup chopped celery
¼ cup chopped onion
*½ cup fresh bread
  crumbs*
1 egg
*8 small whole chicken
  breasts, boned*
¼ cup all-purpose flour
½ teaspoon paprika
2 tablespoons salad oil

*2 chicken-flavor bouillon
  cubes or envelopes*
1½ cups water
*2 tablespoons butter or
  margarine*
*4 medium zucchini, sliced
  salt and pepper*
1 tablespoon cornstarch
*2 tablespoons white table
  wine*

Color index page 43

Begin 1½ hrs ahead

8 servings

592 cals per serving

Good source of iron, niacin

1 In 8-quart Dutch oven over medium-high heat, cook sausage, nuts, celery and onion until meat is browned, stirring often.

2 Add fresh bread crumbs and egg; stir until well mixed. Set mixture aside until needed.

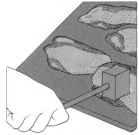

3 Place each breast, skin side up, on cutting board. With meat mallet or dull edge of French knife, pound breast to ¼-inch thickness.

4 Top half of each breast with a scant ½ cup of sausage mixture. Fold other half over filling and fasten edges of breast with toothpicks.

5 On waxed paper, mix flour and paprika. Coat breasts with mixture. In same Dutch oven over medium heat, in hot oil, brown breasts.

6 Add bouillon and water. Reduce heat to low; cover and simmer 30 minutes or until chicken is fork-tender.

7 Meanwhile, in 12-inch skillet, in melted butter, cook zucchini, stirring frequently, until tender. Sprinkle with salt and pepper to taste.

8 Transfer zucchini to warm serving dish; arrange chicken on top. Remove the toothpicks.

9 In cup, blend the cornstarch with wine. Stir into liquid in Dutch oven and cook until thickened.

10 Pour into gravy boat and serve with chicken and zucchini.

Color index page 44 406 cals per serving

Begin 1¼ hrs ahead Good source of
8 servings vitamin A, niacin

Chicken Imperial

*4 large whole chicken
  breasts, halved and
  skinned*
all-purpose flour
*½ cup butter or
  margarine*
*1 pound small
  mushrooms,
  quartered*

*1 tablespoon minced
  onion*
*1 cup heavy or whipping
  cream*
¼ cup dry sherry
1½ teaspoons salt
⅛ teaspoon pepper
2 tablespoons water

1. On waxed paper, coat chicken breasts with ¼ cup flour. In 12-inch skillet over medium heat, in hot butter or margarine, cook chicken, a few pieces at a time, until lightly browned on all sides. Set chicken breasts aside.
2. In drippings in skillet over medium heat, cook mushrooms and onion 5 minutes, stirring frequently. Stir in cream, sherry, salt and pepper and stir to blend well. Return chicken to skillet.
3. Reduce heat to low; cover skillet and simmer 20 minutes or until chicken is fork-tender. Remove chicken to warm platter.
4. In cup, blend 1 tablespoon flour with water. Gradually add to pan liquid, stirring constantly, and cook until mixture is thickened.
5. To serve: Spoon sauce over chicken.

Color index page 42 280 cals per serving

Begin 45 mins ahead Good source of
6 servings calcium, iron, niacin

Party Shrimp and Chicken

*¼ cup butter or
  margarine*
1 cup chopped onion
*1 small garlic clove,
  minced*
*3 medium whole chicken
  breasts, halved*
1 teaspoon salt
½ teaspoon pepper
*1 8-ounce can tomato
  sauce*

¼ cup port wine
1 teaspoon basil
*¼ cup chopped
  parsley*
*1 16-ounce package
  frozen, shelled
  and deveined
  shrimp*

1. In 12-inch skillet over medium heat, in hot butter or margarine, cook onion and garlic until tender, about 5 minutes. With slotted spoon, remove mixture to small bowl.
2. Rub chicken breasts with salt and pepper. In butter remaining in skillet, cook chicken breasts until golden on all sides.
3. Stir in tomato sauce, wine, basil, 3 tablespoons parsley and reserved onion mixture; heat to boiling. Reduce heat to low; cover and simmer 10 minutes or until chicken is tender.
4. Add frozen shrimp; over high heat, heat to boiling. Reduce heat to low; simmer 2 or 3 minutes until shrimp is just pink and tender, stirring often. Skim off fat, if you like.
5. To serve: Spoon mixture into deep dish; sprinkle lightly with the remaining chopped parsley.

Braised chicken

Chicken Orobianco

¼ cup olive oil
2 garlic cloves, quartered
4 medium whole chicken breasts, halved
2 pounds hot Italian sausage links or pork-sausage links
2 cups Orobianco or light muscat
½ pound mushrooms, sliced
1 teaspoon salt
toast points
2 tablespoons cornstarch
¼ cup water

Color index page 43

Begin 1¼ hrs ahead

8 servings

670 cals per serving

Good source of iron, niacin

1. In 12-inch skillet over medium heat, in hot oil, cook garlic until golden; with slotted spoon, remove garlic; discard. In drippings in skillet over medium-high heat, cook chicken and sausages, a few pieces at a time, until browned. Spoon off all but 2 tablespoons drippings. Return chicken and sausage to skillet. Stir in Orobianco, sliced mushrooms and salt; heat mixture to boiling.
2. Reduce heat to low; cover skillet and simmer 30 minutes or until chicken is fork-tender, basting occasionally with liquid in skillet. On warm platter, arrange toast points; with tongs, place chicken and sausage on toast; keep warm.
3. In cup, blend cornstarch and water; gradually stir into hot liquid and cook over medium heat, stirring constantly, until mixture is thickened.
4. To serve: Spoon some of sauce over chicken. Pass remaining sauce in gravy boat.

Chicken Avgolemono

Orzo-Rice Pilaf (below)
2 tablespoons butter
2 garlic cloves, sliced
4 large whole chicken breasts, boned and halved
water
2 medium zucchini, sliced
5 egg yolks
1 tablespoon cornstarch
1½ teaspoons salt
⅛ teaspoon cayenne pepper
1 chicken-flavor bouillon cube or envelope
5 tablespoons lemon juice

Color index page 43

Begin 1 hr ahead

8 servings

616 cals per serving

Good source of iron, vitamin A, niacin

1. Prepare Orzo-Rice Pilaf. In 12-inch skillet over medium-high heat, in hot butter, cook garlic until brown; discard garlic. In same skillet, in remaining butter, cook chicken breasts until browned on all sides. Add ½ cup water; heat to boiling. Reduce heat to low; cover; simmer 10 minutes. Add zucchini; cook 10 minutes longer or until chicken and zucchini are tender.
2. Meanwhile, in 1-quart heavy saucepan with wire whisk, beat egg yolks, cornstarch, salt and cayenne pepper until blended; stir in 1½ cups water and chicken bouillon. Over medium-low heat, heat mixture, stirring until thickened (do not boil), about 10 minutes. Stir in lemon juice.
3. Arrange chicken mixture on warm platter; spoon on sauce. Serve with Orzo-Rice Pilaf.

ORZO-RICE PILAF: In 2-quart saucepan over medium-high heat, melt ½ cup butter or margarine. Add 1 cup orzo (rice-shaped pasta); cook until golden, stirring often, about 10 minutes. Stir in 4 cups water, 1 cup regular long-grain rice and 3 chicken-flavor bouillon cubes; heat to boiling. Reduce heat to low; cover and simmer 30 minutes or until liquid is absorbed and orzo and rice are tender.

Festive Chicken with Asparagus

3 medium whole chicken breasts, halved
2 tablespoons all-purpose flour
3 tablespoons salad oil
¼ cup dry white wine
¼ cup blue cheese, crumbled (1 ounce)
1 10¾-ounce can condensed cream of chicken soup
½ teaspoon salt
¼ teaspoon pepper
1 pound asparagus

Color index page 42

Begin 1½ hrs ahead

6 servings

266 cals per serving

Good source of niacin

1. On waxed paper, coat chicken breasts with flour. Preheat oven to 375°F. In 12-inch skillet over medium-high heat, in hot salad oil, cook chicken pieces until lightly browned on all sides.
2. Meanwhile, in shallow, 3-quart casserole, mix well wine, blue cheese, undiluted cream of chicken soup, salt and pepper. Arrange chicken in soup mixture and spoon some mixture over chicken to coat it. Bake in oven 30 minutes.
3. Meanwhile, prepare asparagus: Hold base of asparagus stalk firmly and bend stalk; end will break off at spot where it becomes too tough to eat. Discard ends; trim scales if stalks are gritty. Cut each asparagus spear crosswise in half; rinse under running cold water; drain.
4. Remove casserole from oven and arrange asparagus between chicken pieces. Cover casserole tightly with foil or lid and bake 30 minutes longer or until chicken is fork-tender and asparagus is tender-crisp. Serve in casserole.

Chicken Breasts with Artichoke Hearts

3 medium whole chicken breasts, halved
all-purpose flour
2 tablespoons salad oil
2 tablespoons butter or margarine
¾ teaspoon salt
⅛ teaspoon white pepper
3 tablespoons brandy
2 teaspoons lemon juice
1½ cups water
2 chicken-flavor bouillon cubes or envelopes or 1 teaspoon chicken-flavor stock base
1 cup sour cream
2 9-ounce packages frozen artichoke hearts, thawed and well drained

Color index page 44

Begin 1½ hrs ahead

6 servings

343 cals per serving

Good source of calcium, iron, niacin

1. On waxed paper, coat chicken breasts with ¼ cup flour. In 12-inch skillet over medium-high heat, in hot salad oil, cook chicken until lightly browned on all sides. Place chicken in 12″ by 9″ baking dish; set aside. Preheat oven to 350°F.
2. In 2-quart saucepan over low heat, in melted butter or margarine, stir 2 tablespoons flour with salt and pepper until smooth. Gradually stir in brandy, lemon juice, water and chicken bouillon; cook, stirring constantly, until thickened and smooth. With wire whisk, gradually blend in sour cream; pour mixture over chicken.
3. Cover baking dish tightly with foil and bake chicken 45 minutes.
4. Remove foil from baking dish and add artichoke hearts. Cover and return to oven; continue baking 15 minutes longer or until chicken and artichoke hearts are fork-tender.

Braised turkey

Turkey in Champagne Sauce with Toast Flowers

Color index page 40

Begin 2 hrs ahead

6 servings

629 cals per serving

Good source of calcium, iron, vitamin A, riboflavin, niacin

1 tablespoon salad oil	*1½ cups half-and-half*
2 2- to 2½-pound turkey legs (thigh and drumstick)	*3 tablespoons butter or margarine*
4 cups water	*½ pound mushrooms, sliced*
1 large onion, thinly sliced	*1 split dry champagne (about 6 ounces)*
1¼ teaspoons salt	*⅓ cup minced parsley*
½ teaspoon pepper	*Toast Flowers (below)*
⅓ cup all-purpose flour	

1. In 12-inch skillet over medium-high heat, in hot salad oil, cook turkey legs until well browned on all sides. Add water, onion, salt and pepper; heat to boiling. Reduce heat to low; cover and simmer 1½ hours or until turkey is fork-tender.
2. Remove turkey from skillet; cool slightly until easy to handle. Cut turkey meat into 1-inch pieces; discard skin and bones. Meanwhile, over high heat, cook turkey broth in skillet until it reduces to about 1½ cups.
3. In small bowl with spoon, blend flour with ½ cup half-and-half; gradually stir into broth until smooth; stir in remaining half-and-half. Cook, stirring, until cream sauce boils and is thickened.
4. In 10-inch skillet over medium heat, in hot butter or margarine, cook mushrooms until tender; gently stir into cream sauce with turkey meat, champagne and ¼ cup parsley; heat.
5. To serve: Spoon turkey mixture into chafing dish if you like. Garnish with remaining parsley and serve with Toast Flowers.

TOAST FLOWERS: Preheat oven to 450°F. Using a 3- to 4-inch flower-shaped cookie cutter, cut "flowers" from *18 white bread slices.* Place on cookie sheet. Bake flowers 3 to 5 minutes until golden.

Apricot-glazed Turkey Drumsticks

Color index page 40

Begin 2½ hrs ahead

4 servings

588 cals per serving

Good source of iron, riboflavin, niacin

4 turkey drumsticks (about 4 pounds)	*hot water*
2 celery stalks, halved	*¾ cup apricot preserves*
1 medium onion, halved	*1 8¾-ounce can apricot halves, drained, for garnish*
¾ tablespoon salt	
½ teaspoon peppercorns, crushed	

1. In 8-quart saucepot, place turkey, celery, onion, salt and peppercorns and add hot water to cover; over high heat, heat mixture to boiling. Reduce heat to medium-low; cover and simmer 1½ hours or until drumsticks are fork-tender.
2. Meanwhile, in 1-quart saucepan over medium heat, melt apricot preserves. Preheat oven to 400°F.
3. Remove turkey from broth; drain well. (Strain; cover and refrigerate broth for soup another day.) With hands protected by paper towels, pull tendons from ends of turkey drumsticks.
4. Place turkey in open roasting pan; brush with apricot preserves; add drained apricot halves to pan and brush them with preserves.
5. Bake in oven 10 minutes to glaze turkey.

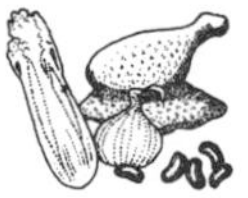

Turkey-Tamale Casserole

Color index page 40

Begin 4 hrs ahead

6 servings

299 cals per serving

Good source of iron

salad oil	*¼ teaspoon pepper*
1 1-pound frozen turkey thigh, thawed	**Tamale Topping:**
water	*¾ cup cornmeal*
½ cup chopped onion	*¼ cup all-purpose flour*
½ cup chopped celery	*1½ teaspoons double-acting baking powder*
1 16-ounce can tomatoes	*½ teaspoon salt*
1 15½- or 16-ounce can red kidney beans	*½ teaspoon ground sage*
2 teaspoons chili powder	*1 egg*
½ teaspoon salt	*½ cup milk*
	2 tablespoons salad oil

1. In 10-inch skillet over medium-high heat, in 2 tablespoons hot salad oil, cook turkey thigh until well browned. Add ½ cup water; heat to boiling. Reduce heat to low; cover and simmer 2½ hours, until turkey is fork-tender, adding more water if needed.
2. Remove turkey from skillet; cool slightly until easy to handle. Remove meat from bones; cut meat in ½-inch pieces. (Refrigerate broth for use in soup another day.)
3. In 3-quart saucepan over medium heat, in 2 tablespoons hot salad oil, cook onion and celery until tender, about 5 minutes, stirring occasionally. Add turkey, tomatoes and their liquid, kidney beans and their liquid, chili powder, salt and pepper; heat to boiling, stirring occasionally.
4. Spoon hot turkey mixture into 2-quart casserole Preheat oven to 400°F.
5. Meanwhile, prepare Tamale Topping: In medium bowl with fork, combine cornmeal, flour, baking powder, salt and sage.
6. In small bowl with fork, stir together egg, milk and salad oil until well mixed; stir into flour mixture just until batter is mixed.
7. Pour batter over hot turkey mixture in casserole; bake 20 minutes or until toothpick inserted in center of Tamale Topping comes out clean. Serve piping hot at table in casserole.

Saucy Turkey Wings

Color index page 39

Begin 2½ hrs ahead

6 servings

334 cals per serving

Good source of niacin

4 pounds turkey wings	*1 teaspoon salt*
2 tablespoons salad oil	*½ teaspoon paprika*
1 10½-ounce can condensed cream of celery soup	*¼ teaspoon pepper*
	parsley sprigs for garnish

1. Separate wings at joints. (Use wing tips for soup, if you like.)
2. In 12-inch skillet over medium-high heat, in hot salad oil, cook turkey, a few pieces at a time, until browned on all sides; arrange in 15½" by 10½" roasting pan.
3. In small bowl, combine undiluted soup, salt, paprika and pepper; spoon soup mixture over turkey. Cover roasting pan and bake in 350°F. oven 2¼ hours or until turkey wings are fork-tender; garnish.

Broiled chicken and turkey

The tender meat of most chicken and turkey makes it very suitable for broiling in the broiler or on the rotisserie. Outdoor grilling is the same cooking technique as broiling.

Unless the manufacturer's directions state otherwise, always preheat the broiler. For easier cleaning, line the broiler pan with foil and brush the rack with salad oil ahead of time.

The exact distance from the source of heat will depend on the thickness of the piece of meat, but generally, the rack should be between 7 and 9 inches away; adjust the distance if this is not close enough.

Rotisseried Chicken

Color index
page 42

Allow
¾–1 pound
uncooked
chicken
per serving

196 cals per
serving

Low in
sodium

Good source
of niacin

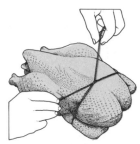

1 Remove giblets; rinse and drain chicken well. Skewer neck skin to back and tie wings to body.

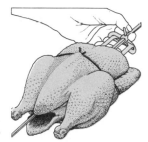

2 Insert spit through body lengthwise and tighten holding prongs. Fix bird firmly.

3 Carefully tie first the bird's tail and then its drumsticks to the spit.

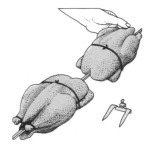

4 If cooking 2 birds, mount them on the spit in opposite directions to balance evenly. Turn spit slowly to test balance.

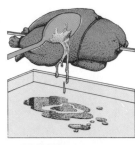

5 Following manufacturer's directions, cook, basting occasionally with *melted butter*. If using sauce, baste during last 20 minutes of cooking time.

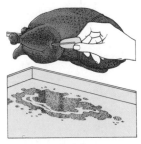

6 To test for doneness, insert meat thermometer in thigh, next to body, avoiding bone. Bird is done when it reads 180° to 185°F.

Savory Chicken

20 medium garlic cloves	**4 teaspoons dry**
1½ cups tarragon	**mustard**
vinegar	**2 teaspoons salt**
¼ cup sugar	**2 3- to 3½-pound**
2 tablespoons salad oil	**broiler-fryers,**
2 tablespoons	**quartered**
Worcestershire	

Color index
page 42

Begin 3½ hrs
ahead

8 servings

271 cals per
serving

Good source
of iron,
niacin

1. Into 13″ by 9″ baking dish, with garlic press, crush garlic cloves. Stir in next 6 ingredients.
2. Add chicken pieces; turn pieces to coat them evenly in marinade. Cover; refrigerate at least 2 hours, turning chicken often.
3. *About 1¼ hours before serving:* Prepare outdoor grill for barbecuing. Place chicken on grill over medium coals; cook 35 minutes or until chicken is fork-tender, turning chicken frequently and basting occasionally with remaining marinade.

TO BROIL IN OVEN: Marinate chicken as above. About 50 minutes before serving, preheat broiler if manufacturer directs. Place chicken, skin side down, in broiling pan. Broil 40 minutes or until chicken is fork-tender, turning once and basting occasionally with remaining marinade.

Tandoori Chicken

1 medium onion, diced	**1 teaspoon sugar**
1 garlic clove	**½ teaspoon ground**
3 tablespoons salad oil	**cumin**
2 tablespoons lemon juice	**½ teaspoon turmeric**
1 tablespoon minced,	**¼ teaspoon ground**
peeled ginger root or	**cardamom**
¾ teaspoon ground	**¼ teaspoon cayenne**
ginger	**pepper**
1 teaspoon salt	**¼ cup plain yogurt**
1½ teaspoons ground	**1 3-pound broiler-fryer,**
coriander	**quartered**

Color index
page 46

Begin day
ahead

4 servings

311 cals per
serving

Good source
of iron,
niacin

1. In blender container, place all ingredients except yogurt and chicken. Cover blender; at high speed, blend until mixture is pureed. Pour mixture into 12″ by 8″ baking dish; stir in yogurt.
2. With sharp knife, make 3 diagonal slashes in each chicken-breast half; do not cut all the way through to the bone. Make 2 diagonal slashes in each thigh. Make several small cuts in each drumstick. Add chicken to yogurt mixture. Cover; refrigerate at least 12 hours, turning chicken occasionally.
3. *About 1¼ hours before serving:* Prepare outdoor grill for barbecuing. When grill is ready, place chicken on grill over low coals. Cook 35 minutes or until chicken is fork-tender, turning chicken frequently and basting often with some yogurt mixture.

TO BROIL IN OVEN: Marinate chicken as above. About 50 minutes before serving, preheat broiler if manufacturer directs. Place chicken, skin side down, in broiling pan. Baste with some yogurt mixture. About 7 to 9 inches from source of heat (or at 450°F.), broil chicken 25 minutes or until browned. Turn; baste with remaining mixture; broil 15 minutes longer or until chicken is fork-tender.

Broiled Lemon-Chicken

Color index
page 45

Begin 50 mins
ahead

4 servings

631 cals per
serving

Good source
of iron,
vitamin A

1/2 cup butter or
margarine
1/4 cup lemon juice
1 teaspoon salt
1 teaspoon sugar
1/4 teaspoon pepper
1 2 1/2- or 3-pound
broiler-fryer,
quartered
4 medium tomatoes
2 teaspoons grated lemon
peel (optional)
2 teaspoons chopped
parsley (optional)

1 Preheat broiler if
manufacturer directs. In
1-quart saucepan over low
heat, heat butter or
margarine, lemon juice,
salt, sugar and pepper
until butter is melted.

2 Place chicken, skin side
down, on large broiling
pan; broil 20 minutes.

3 Baste with butter
mixture frequently to
moisten and add flavor to
chicken pieces.

4 Meanwhile, cut
tomatoes into 6
wedges about 3/4 way
through, gently spreading
tomato wedges apart.

5 Turn chicken pieces.
Arrange tomatoes on
same broiling pan.

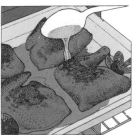

6 Broil 15 to 20 minutes
more until chicken is
fork-tender, basting
chicken and tomatoes with
butter mixture frequently.

7 Transfer to warm
platter and sprinkle
chicken with grated lemon
peel and chopped parsley
to garnish, if desired.

Chicken Marinated in Chili Sauce

Color index
page 46

Begin early
in day

4 servings

272 cals per
serving

Good source
of iron,
vitamin A,
niacin

1 12-ounce bottle chili
sauce
1/2 cup red wine
vinegar
1 tablespoon
horseradish

1 garlic clove,
quartered
3/4 teaspoon salt
1 3-pound broiler-fryer,
cut up

1. In 13" by 9" baking dish, mix all ingredients
except chicken. Place chicken in marinade; cover
and refrigerate chicken at least 2 hours, turning the
pieces occasionally.
2. *About 45 minutes before serving:* Preheat broiler
if manufacturer directs. Place chicken on rack in
broiling pan; broil 35 minutes or until fork-tender,
basting the chicken pieces with marinade and turning occasionally with tongs.

Coating with marinade:
Turn chicken occasionally
in marinade to coat the
pieces evenly.

Broiling chicken: Place
chicken on rack in broiling
pan and baste occasionally
with marinade.

OUTDOOR BARBECUE VARIATION: *About 1
hour and 10 minutes before serving:* Prepare grill
for outdoor barbecuing. Place chicken on grill
over medium coals; grill 35 minutes or until
chicken is fork-tender. Baste chicken with
marinade and turn occasionally.

MARINADES

Enhance and vary the flavor of broiled chicken by marinating it first. Refrigerate the bird in the marinade for at least 2
hours, turning it occasionally to make sure it is completely
coated. If there is any leftover marinade it can be used to
baste the chicken during the cooking time.

142 cals

LIME MARINADE: In 13" by 9" baking dish,
mix *1 tablespoon grated lime peel, 1/2 cup lime
juice, 3 tablespoons salad oil, 2 teaspoons salt* and
1/4 teaspoon cracked pepper. Use to marinate
chicken or other poultry and for basting poultry
while grilling or broiling. (Makes about 2/3 cup or
enough marinade for one broiler-fryer.)

232 cals

GREEN ONION-SOY MARINADE: In 13" by
9" baking dish, mix *1/2 cup thinly sliced green
onions, 1/2 cup soy sauce, 2 tablespoons light brown
sugar, 2 tablespoons dry sherry, 1/2 teaspoon salt*
and *1/2 teaspoon ground ginger.* Use to marinate
chicken or other poultry and for basting poultry
while grilling or broiling. (Makes about 1 cup or
enough marinade for one broiler-fryer.)

Broiled chicken and turkey

Color index page 44
Begin 1 hr ahead
6 servings

269 cals per serving
Good source of calcium, niacin

Cheese and Anchovy Broiled Chicken Breasts

1 2-ounce can anchovy fillets
2 tablespoons minced onion
1 teaspoon lemon juice

3 large whole chicken breasts, halved
1 8-ounce package mozzarella cheese, cut into 12 slices

1. Drain 1 tablespoon oil from can of anchovy fillets into 1-quart saucepan; discard all the remaining oil; mince anchovies.
2. Over medium heat, in hot anchovy oil, cook onion and anchovies about 5 minutes or until paste forms; stir in lemon juice. Remove from heat and let paste cool slightly.
3. Preheat broiler if manufacturer directs. Lift skin from each half-breast to make a small pocket; rub 1 teaspoon anchovy mixture on meat.
4. Place chicken, skin side down, on rack in broiling pan, 7 to 9 inches from source of heat (or at 450°F.); broil 20 minutes. Turn; broil 15 minutes more or until tender. Top half-breasts with cheese. Broil 5 minutes or until cheese is bubbly.

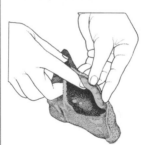

Stuffing the breast: Rub some anchovy mixture on the meat under skin.

Adding the cheese: 5 minutes before end of cooking, top with cheese.

Color index page 39
Begin 1 hr ahead
6 servings

342 cals per serving
Good source of niacin

Turkey-Sausage Kabobs

⅓ cup soy sauce
⅓ cup cooking sherry
3 tablespoons sugar
3 tablespoons salad oil
1 5- to 6-pound frozen turkey breast, slightly thawed

1 8-ounce package brown-and-serve sausages
1 8-ounce can pineapple chunks, drained
4 green onions, cut into 1½-inch pieces

1. In medium bowl, mix first 4 ingredients. With sharp knife, cut one side of turkey breast into 1-inch chunks (about 1 pound meat); use remaining turkey in other recipes. Add turkey chunks to bowl; toss lightly. Refrigerate 30 minutes. Cut each sausage crosswise in half.
2. Preheat broiler if manufacturer directs. On six 14-inch metal skewers, alternately thread turkey, sausages, pineapple and green onions. Broil 10 to 12 minutes until turkey is tender, basting frequently with marinade and turning once.

Fried chicken

Fried chicken will be juicier if first coated with flour, crushed cereal flakes or dried bread crumbs. An easy way of coating is to shake the chicken one piece at a time in a bag of flour or crumbs. Let the coated pieces dry on wire racks about 15 minutes before frying.

Chicken pieces can also be fried successfully in the oven. This method involves less handling than pan-frying, so the coating is less likely to be dislodged.

Chicken which is stir-fried is cooked quickly over very high heat in only a small amount of oil. Depending on the ingredients, at the end of cooking time you will have tender-crisp vegetables and succulent pieces of chicken.

Pan-fried Chicken with Cream Gravy

¼ cup all-purpose flour
1 2½- to 3-pound broiler-fryer, cut up
¼ cup salad oil
salt and pepper
Cream Gravy:
¼ cup all-purpose flour
2½ cups milk
1 tablespoon chopped parsley
1 tablespoon dry or medium sherry (optional)
salt and pepper

Color index page 44
Begin 1 hr ahead
4 servings 405 cals per serving

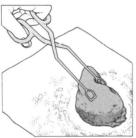
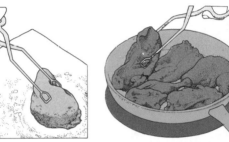

1 Put the flour on a sheet of waxed paper and coat chicken on all sides.

2 In 12-inch skillet over medium-high heat, brown chicken on all sides in hot oil, turning frequently. Sprinkle chicken lightly with salt and pepper.

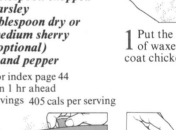
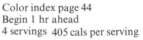

3 Reduce heat to medium-low. Cover; cook until fork-tender, about 25 minutes, removing cover for last few minutes to crisp skin. Transfer to warm platter.

4 Make gravy: Pour off all but ¼ cup drippings from skillet; blend in flour. Over medium heat, cook, stirring and scraping bits loose from skillet, until golden.

5 Gradually stir in milk and cook, stirring constantly, until mixture is smooth and thickened.

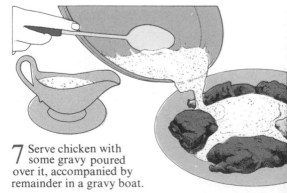

6 Stir in parsley and sherry, if used, and season to taste with salt and freshly ground pepper.

7 Serve chicken with some gravy poured over it, accompanied by remainder in a gravy boat.

Beer-Batter Chicken

Color index
page 41

Begin 55 mins
ahead

4 servings

395 cals per
serving

Good source
of niacin

⅔ cup all-purpose
  flour
1 teaspoon salt
½ teaspoon double-
  acting baking powder

⅓ cup beer
1 egg
salad oil
1 3-pound broiler-fryer,
  cut up

1. In bowl with fork, mix first 3 ingredients. In another bowl, beat together beer, egg and 2 teaspoons salad oil; stir liquid into flour mixture.
2. Coat half of chicken pieces with batter.
3. Meanwhile, in 12-inch skillet over medium heat, heat ½ inch salad oil to 370°F.
4. Fry chicken pieces until browned and tender, about 20 minutes, turning once. Drain on paper towels. Repeat with remaining chicken.

Crunchy Drumsticks

Color index
page 46

Begin early
in day or
day ahead

8 servings

286 cals per
serving

1 cup orange juice
1 tablespoon salad oil
2 teaspoons salt
¼ teaspoon pepper
3 pounds chicken
  drumsticks (about 1
  large or 2 small
  drumsticks per person)
1¼ cups quick-cooking
  oats, uncooked
¼ cup butter or
  margarine

1 In 13" by 9" baking dish, mix first 4 ingredients; add chicken, turning to coat well. Cover; refrigerate at least 4 hours, turning often.

2 *About 1 hour before serving:* On waxed paper, coat chicken drumsticks with oats.

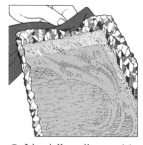

3 Line jelly-roll pan with foil; add butter and melt in 400°F. oven. Remove from oven; tilt to spread butter evenly.

4 Arrange drumsticks in one layer in pan, turning to coat with butter.

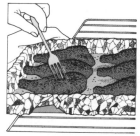

5 Bake 40 to 50 minutes until drumsticks are fork-tender, turning once.

Oven-fried Chicken

Color index
page 45

Begin 1¼ hrs
ahead

4 servings

315 cals per
serving

Good source
of vitamin A,
niacin

210 cals per
serving

278 cals per
serving

¼ cup butter or
  margarine
¾ cup cracker meal
1 teaspoon salt

⅛ teaspoon pepper
1 2½- to 3-pound
  broiler-fryer,
  cut up

1. In 13" by 9" baking dish, melt butter or margarine in 400°F. oven. On waxed paper, mix cracker meal, salt and pepper. Remove dish from oven.
2. With tongs, roll chicken in melted butter or margarine, then coat with crumbs on all sides; place in dish. Bake 40 to 50 minutes.

CORN-CRISPED: Preheat oven to 400°F. Prepare as above but omit butter or margarine; pour *⅓ cup undiluted evaporated milk* in pie plate and substitute *¾ cup corn-flake crumbs* for cracker meal; use to coat chicken.

ITALIAN-SEASONED: Prepare as above but substitute *¾ cup Italian-seasoned bread crumbs* for cracker meal; omit salt and pepper.

Lemon Chicken on Spinach Leaves

Color index
page 46

Begin 45 mins
ahead

6 servings

295 cals per
serving

Good source
of iron,
niacin

3 large whole chicken
  breasts, halved
1 cup chicken broth
⅓ cup sugar
⅓ cup lemon juice
2 tablespoons water

1 tablespoon dry sherry
1½ teaspoons soy sauce
  cornstarch
½ 10-ounce bag spinach
1 teaspoon salt
½ cup salad oil

1. Working with one half-breast at a time place it skin side up; with tip of sharp knife starting parallel and close to large end of rib bone, cut and scrape meat away from bone and rib cage, gently pulling back meat in one piece as you cut. Discard bones; remove skin and white tendon.
2. In 1-quart saucepan, mix well chicken broth, sugar, lemon juice, water, sherry, soy sauce and 2 tablespoons cornstarch. Cook over medium heat until sauce is smooth and thickened, stirring constantly. Keep warm.
3. Shred spinach coarsely and arrange on platter.
4. Sprinkle chicken with salt. Coat chicken with about ⅓ cup cornstarch. In 12-inch skillet over medium-high heat in hot salad oil, cook chicken until lightly browned and fork-tender, about 10 minutes. Arrange chicken on spinach and pour some sauce over chicken; pour remaining sauce into gravy boat and pass separately.

Boning half-breast: Cut and scrape meat away from bone in one piece.

Shredding spinach: Shred spinach coarsely and arrange on platter.

Fried chicken

Chicken Kiev

*¾ cup butter or
    margarine, softened
1 tablespoon chopped
    parsley
1 tablespoon chopped
    chives
⅛ teaspoon pepper
salt
6 medium whole
    chicken breasts,
    skinned and boned
¼ cup all-purpose
    flour*

*1 egg
1 tablespoon water
about ¾ cup dried
    bread crumbs
salad oil*

Color index page 44

Begin 3 hrs ahead

6 servings

531 cals per serving

Good source of
vitamin A, niacin

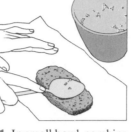

1 In small bowl, combine
butter, parsley, chives,
pepper and ½ teaspoon
salt. On waxed paper, pat
to 4½" by 3"; freeze.

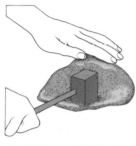

2 With smooth side of
meat mallet or dull
edge of French knife,
pound each chicken
breast until ¼ inch thick.

3 Cut firm butter mixture
into six ¾" by 3" strips.
Place one strip lengthwise
in center of one side of a
chicken breast.

4 Roll up, bringing wider
edge of breast over
butter to enclose strip.

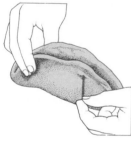

5 Secure with toothpicks.
Repeat with remaining
chicken breasts.

6 On waxed paper,
mix flour and ½ tea-
spoon salt. In pie plate,
mix egg and water. Place
crumbs on another sheet
of paper. Coat rolls with
flour, egg, then crumbs.

7 On cookie sheet, place
chicken rolls in a single
layer. Cover lightly with
waxed paper; refrigerate
1 to 2 hours to allow
crumbs to dry out.

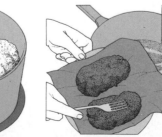

8 In 4-quart saucepan,
heat 3 inches oil to
300°F. on deep-fat thermometer. Lower in 2 breasts.

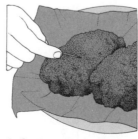

9 Fry 15 minutes or until
browned and firm when
pressed with back of fork.
Do not pierce. Drain.

10 Remove toothpicks
and keep rolls warm
in oven while frying
remaining chicken breasts.

Color index page 46

Begin 2½ hrs ahead

6 servings

546 cals per serving

Good source of
vitamin A, niacin

Crispy Chicken Rolls

*3 large whole chicken
    breasts, skinned, boned
    and halved
1¼ cups cooked, shelled
    and deveined shrimp,
    chopped
¾ cup butter or
    margarine, softened
salt*

*¼ cup chopped green
    onions
salad oil
1 cup all-purpose
    flour
1¼ teaspoons double-
    acting baking
    powder
¾ cup water*

1 With mallet or dull edge
of French knife, pound
chicken pieces to about
¼ inch thickness.

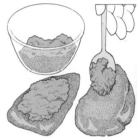

2 In medium bowl, combine shrimp with butter
or margarine, 1 tea-
spoon salt and green
onions. Spoon mixture on
to centers of breasts leaving
½ inch edge all around.

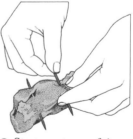

3 Starting at one of the
narrow ends, roll up
each chicken piece, jelly-
roll fashion. Fasten with
toothpicks. Cover and
refrigerate 15 minutes.

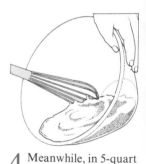

4 Meanwhile, in 5-quart
Dutch oven over me-
dium-high heat, heat 1 inch
oil to 370°F. In medium
bowl with wire whisk, blend
flour, baking powder, 1
teaspoon salt and water.

5 With tongs, roll 3
chicken rolls, one at a
time, into flour mixture
making sure all the sides
are coated evenly.

6 To fry chicken rolls:
Lower into hot salad
oil and fry until golden, 10
to 15 minutes, turning
occasionally. With a
slotted spoon, remove rolls
from oil and allow them to
drain on paper towels.
Keep warm. Repeat with
remaining rolls. Using a
fork to hold chicken rolls
steady, remove toothpicks.
Place rolls on a warm
serving platter. Serve immediately so that the chicken rolls are hot and retain
their crispness.

Stir-fried chicken

Stir-fried Chicken

Color index page 45

Begin 45 mins ahead

4 servings

603 cals per serving

Good source of calcium, iron, niacin

2 large whole chicken
  breasts, skinned, boned
  and halved
2 tablespoons salad oil
1 cup thinly sliced celery
1 medium green pepper,
  cut in thin strips
1 small onion, sliced
1/2 teaspoon salt
1/4 teaspoon ground
  ginger
1 16-ounce can bean
  sprouts, drained

1 5-ounce can water
  chestnuts, drained and
  sliced
1 envelope chicken-flavor
  bouillon or 1 teaspoon
  chicken-flavor stock
  base
1/2 cup water
2 teaspoons cornstarch
2 tablespoons soy sauce
3 cups hot cooked rice
  (optional)
3/4 cup almonds, toasted

1 On cutting board, slice chicken crosswise into 1/4-inch-wide strips. In 12-inch skillet over high heat, heat salad oil.

2 Cook celery, pepper, onion, salt and ginger, stirring quickly and frequently (stir-frying) until vegetables are tender-crisp, about 3 minutes.

3 With slotted spoon, remove vegetables to a warm plate; keep warm. To oil left in skillet, add chicken and stir-fry until chicken turns white, about 3 to 5 minutes.

4 Return vegetables to skillet. Add bean sprouts, water chestnuts, chicken bouillon or stock base and water.

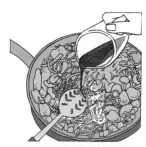

5 In cup, blend cornstarch smoothly with soy sauce. Gradually stir into hot mixture in skillet and cook, stirring constantly, until thickened.

6 Spoon stir-fried chicken and vegetables over hot cooked rice. Sprinkle toasted almonds over the top and serve immediately.

Moo Goo Gai Pan

Color index page 45

Begin 35 mins ahead

4 servings

478 cals per serving

Good source of iron, niacin

2 large whole chicken
  breasts, skinned,
  boned and halved
1 tablespoon cornstarch
2 tablespoons dry sherry
3/4 teaspoon minced,
  peeled ginger root
1/8 teaspoon monosodium
  glutamate (optional)
salt

1/3 cup salad oil
3/4 cup California
  walnuts
1 15-ounce can Chinese
  straw mushrooms,
  drained
1 8 1/2-ounce can sliced
  bamboo shoots,
  drained (about 1 cup)
1/4 pound snow peas

1. With sharp knife, slice across width of chicken breasts to make very thin pieces. In medium bowl, mix well chicken, cornstarch, sherry, ginger, monosodium glutamate and 1 1/2 teaspoons salt.
2. In 12-inch skillet over medium-high heat, in hot oil, cook walnuts about 3 minutes until lightly browned, stirring constantly. Spoon walnuts onto paper towels to drain, leaving oil in skillet.
3. In hot oil in skillet, stir-fry (stirring quickly and frequently) mushrooms, bamboo shoots, snow peas and 1/2 teaspoon salt until snow peas are tender-crisp, about 3 to 5 minutes. Spoon vegetables into a medium bowl, leaving oil in skillet.
4. In remaining oil, stir-fry chicken mixture 5 minutes or until chicken is tender; stir in vegetables. Spoon onto warm platter; sprinkle with walnuts.

Chicken with Orange Peel Szechuan Style

Color index page 45

Begin 1 hr ahead

4 servings

315 cals per serving

Good source of niacin

1 large orange
2 large whole chicken
  breasts, skinned and
  boned
1 tablespoon soy sauce
1 tablespoon dry sherry
4 green onions, cut in
  2-inch pieces
1/4 teaspoon crushed red
  pepper

1 teaspoon minced,
  peeled ginger root or
  1/4 teaspoon ground
  ginger
2 1/2 teaspoons
  cornstarch
1/2 teaspoon sugar
1/2 teaspoon salt
1/2 cup orange juice
1/4 cup salad oil

1. With vegetable peeler, cut peel from orange into 1 1/2-inch-wide pieces, being careful not to cut into white membrane. Cut pieces into 1 1/2-inch-long strips. On small cookie sheet, let peels dry slightly in 200°F. oven 30 minutes.
2. Cut chicken into 1 1/2-inch pieces. In medium bowl, mix well chicken, soy sauce, sherry, green onions, red pepper and ginger. In small bowl, mix well cornstarch, sugar, salt and orange juice. Cover and refrigerate both.
3. *About 15 minutes before serving:* In 10-inch skillet over medium heat, in hot oil, with slotted spoon, stir-fry (stirring quickly and frequently) peels until crisp and edges are slightly browned, about 2 minutes; drain on paper towels.
4. In oil remaining in skillet, over high heat, stir-fry chicken mixture until chicken loses pink color and is tender, about 4 minutes. Stir orange-juice mixture, then add to chicken and stir-fry until mixture is slightly thickened and coats chicken.
5. Spoon onto warm platter; sprinkle with peels.

Simmered chicken and turkey

Whole mature or young birds or poultry parts can be simmered or stewed in a large pan with seasonings and enough water to cover. Cook over low heat (do not boil). Cool and use meat in other recipes, if you like.

Simmered Chicken

Color index page 44

Begin 3 hrs ahead

6 servings

196 cals per serving

Good source of niacin

1 4½- to 5-pound stewing chicken, cut up
1 medium onion studded with 3 whole cloves
3 celery tops
1 carrot, sliced
2 bay leaves
1 tablespoon salt
3 cups hot water

1 In 8-quart saucepot over high heat, heat to boiling chicken, neck and giblets and remaining ingredients; reduce heat.

2 Cover; simmer 2 to 2½ hours. Discard onion, celery and bay leaves. Put chicken into serving dish or, to use later, follow step 3.

3 Place pot in cold water in sink 30 minutes. Stir broth often. Change water when warm. Refrigerate; use within 3 days.

SIMMERED CHICKEN WITH DUMPLINGS: Prepare Simmered Chicken (above). In large bowl with fork, stir *1⅓ cups all-purpose flour, 2 teaspoons double-acting baking powder, 1 teaspoon chopped parsley* and *½ teaspoon salt* until mixed. In cup, combine *⅔ cup milk* with *2 tablespoons salad oil;* slowly stir into flour until soft dough forms. Drop by heaping tablespoons onto chicken. Cook uncovered 10 minutes; cover and cook 10 minutes more. With slotted spoon, remove dumplings. Spoon chicken into serving dish; top with dumplings.

Begin 3 hrs ahead

6 servings

337 cals per serving

Cooking dumplings: Spoon dough onto simmering chicken and broth.

Serving dumplings: Spoon them over hot chicken pieces in serving dish.

Coq au Vin

Color index page 44

Begin 1½ hrs ahead

4 servings

395 cals per serving

Good source of iron, niacin

½ pound salt pork, diced
1 3- to 3½-pound broiler-fryer, cut up
½ pound small mushrooms
½ pound small white onions
¼ cup minced shallots
1 garlic clove, minced
1 cup dry red wine
¾ cup water
½ teaspoon thyme leaves
⅛ teaspoon pepper
1 bay leaf
4 parsley sprigs
2 tablespoons butter, softened
2 tablespoons all-purpose flour

1. In 8-quart Dutch oven over medium heat, cook salt pork until golden and crisp, stirring often. With slotted spoon, remove pork to paper towels to drain. In drippings, cook chicken until browned, about 20 minutes. Remove to medium bowl.
2. Spoon off all but about ¼ cup fat from Dutch oven; add mushrooms, onions, shallots and garlic. Cook until just wilted, about 5 minutes, stirring occasionally. Stir in wine, water, thyme, pepper, bay leaf and parsley. Place chicken and salt pork over vegetables. Over high heat, heat to boiling. Reduce heat to low; cover; simmer 20 minutes or until chicken is fork-tender.
3. Meanwhile, in cup, blend butter and flour.
4. Remove chicken and vegetables to platter; discard bay leaf and parsley. Blend flour mixture into pan juices. Heat to boiling, stirring. Spoon over chicken.

Turkey Molé

Color index page 39

Begin 3 hrs ahead

15 servings

305 cals per serving

Good source of iron, niacin

1 6-pound turkey breast
4 cups water
3 tablespoons sesame seed
2 tablespoons lard
1 medium onion, diced
1 garlic clove, minced
1 square semisweet chocolate
⅓ cup golden raisins
¼ cup slivered blanched almonds
1 10-ounce can mild red enchilada sauce
2 ready-to-eat taco shells, crumbled
1 slice white bread, crumbled
1 teaspoon salt
¼ teaspoon ground cinnamon
¼ teaspoon ground coriander
¼ teaspoon anise seed, crushed
⅛ teaspoon ground cloves
⅛ teaspoon pepper
1 medium avocado

1. In 8-quart Dutch oven over medium heat, simmer turkey and water about 1½ hours or until tender. Drain and reserve 1¾ cups broth. Slice meat and arrange on warm platter; keep warm.
2. Meanwhile, in 12-inch skillet over medium-high heat, cook sesame seed until lightly browned; remove to paper towel. In same skillet, in hot lard, cook onion and garlic until tender; stir in chocolate. Heat until chocolate melts. In covered blender container, blend 1 tablespoon toasted sesame seed, chocolate mixture and remaining ingredients except avocado until smooth.
3. Return mixture to skillet and stir in reserved broth. Over medium heat, heat to boiling, stirring constantly. Spoon some sauce on turkey; sprinkle with remaining sesame seed.
4. Peel, seed and slice avocado; use to garnish turkey. Pass remaining sauce separately.

Chicken Tetrazzini

2 2½- to 3-pound broiler-
  fryers
2 small onions
¼ teaspoon pepper
salt
water
1 16-ounce package
  spaghetti
½ cup butter
½ pound mushrooms,
  sliced
1 tablespoon lemon juice
½ cup all-purpose flour

¼ teaspoon ground
  nutmeg
paprika
½ cup dry sherry
  (optional)
1 cup half-and-half
1 3-ounce jar grated
  Parmesan cheese

Color index page 45
Begin 2 hrs ahead
8 servings

595 cals per serving
Good source of calcium,
iron, vitamin A, niacin

1 In 8-quart saucepot, place chickens, 1 onion, pepper and 1 tablespoon salt. Cover with water. Over high heat, heat to boiling. Reduce heat to low; cover and simmer chickens 30 minutes or until fork-tender. Remove chickens to large bowl.

2 Strain chicken broth, reserving 3½ cups (4 cups if sherry is not used). Store the remaining broth to use another day.

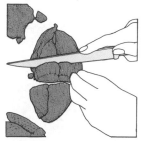

3 When chickens are cool, remove meat in large pieces and discard bones and skin. Cut chicken in large chunks; set aside.

4 After preparing spaghetti as label directs, drain in a colander. Spread it out evenly in a greased 13″ by 9″ baking dish.

5 Chop remaining onion. In 4-quart saucepan over medium heat, in 2 tablespoons hot butter, cook onion, mushrooms and lemon juice 5 minutes. Remove to medium bowl.

6 In same saucepan, melt remaining butter. When hot, stir in flour, 2 teaspoons salt, nutmeg and ½ teaspoon paprika until mixture is smooth.

7 Gradually stir in sherry and reserved chicken broth and cook, stirring, until liquid is thickened.

8 Add half-and-half, chicken chunks and mushroom mixture and over low heat, cook, stirring, just until mixture is heated through.

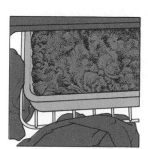

9 Spoon chicken mixture over spaghetti in baking dish. Sprinkle with grated Parmesan cheese and add a little paprika.

10 Bake in 350°F. oven 30 minutes or until spaghetti and chicken mixture are thoroughly heated and surface is golden and bubbly.

Color index page 46
Begin 2½ hrs ahead
8 servings

586 cals per serving
Good source of
calcium, iron, niacin

Chicken Pot Pie

2 2½-pound broiler-
  fryers, cut up
½ teaspoon pepper
½ teaspoon marjoram
  leaves
2 bay leaves
water
salt
2 large carrots, sliced
1 large celery stalk,
  sliced
¾ pound small white
  onions

all-purpose flour
1¾ cups half-and-half
1 10-ounce package
  frozen baby lima
  beans, thawed
½ pound small
  mushrooms, each cut
  in half
pastry for 2-crust pie
  (page 344)
1 egg yolk

1. In 5-quart Dutch oven over high heat, heat first 4 ingredients, 4 cups water and 1 tablespoon salt to boiling. Reduce heat to low; cover and simmer 35 minutes or until chicken is fork-tender.

2. When chicken is done, reserve 1 cup broth. (Use remaining broth in soup another day.) Cool chicken slightly; remove and discard bones and skin; cut meat into 1-inch pieces.

3. In 3-quart saucepan over high heat, heat carrots, celery, onions and reserved 1 cup broth to boiling. Reduce heat to low; cover and simmer 10 minutes or until vegetables are almost tender. Remove from heat. Remove vegetables to small bowl, leaving broth in saucepan.

4. In small bowl with fork, blend ⅓ cup flour with ¾ cup half-and-half; gradually stir into broth in saucepan until smooth; stir in remaining half-and-half. Over low heat, cook, stirring constantly, until sauce is thickened.

5. Stir in chicken, cooked vegetables, lima beans, mushrooms and 1¾ teaspoons salt. Spoon chicken mixture into 13″ by 9″ baking dish. Preheat oven to 350°F. Prepare pastry.

6. On lightly floured surface with lightly floured rolling pin, roll dough into 14″ by 10″ rectangle. With knife, cut out small circle in center of pastry. Place pastry loosely over filling. With kitchen shears, trim edge, leaving 1-inch overhang; fold overhang under; make a high stand-up edge.

7. In small bowl, mix well egg yolk with 1 teaspoon water. Brush pastry with egg-yolk mixture. Bake 1 hour or until crust is golden and mixture is hot.

Covering the pie: Place pastry over filling; with kitchen shears, trim edge.

Shaping pie edge: Fold overhang under and press to make stand-up edge.

Cooked turkey and chicken meat

Chicken or Turkey Salad

²/₃ cup mayonnaise
2 tablespoons cider vinegar
1 teaspoon salt
4 to 5 cups cut-up, cooked chicken or turkey
1 cup sliced celery
1 cup minced green pepper
2 teaspoons grated onion romaine or iceberg lettuce leaves

1 In large bowl with fork, combine mayonnaise, vinegar and salt.

2 Add chicken and remaining ingredients except romaine; toss well. Cover and refrigerate.

3 To serve: On chilled platter, arrange romaine leaves. Lightly pile salad on it.

HAM AND CHICKEN SALAD: Prepare as above but substitute *2 cups cooked ham chunks* for 2 cups of the chicken. Add *1 cup fresh or drained, canned pineapple chunks* to mixture. (Makes 8 servings.)

CHICKEN-WALDORF SALAD: Prepare as above but before refrigerating, add *2 cups diced unpeeled red apples* and *²/₃ cup chopped California walnuts* or pecans to mixture. (Makes 10 servings.)

TOASTED-WALNUT-CHICKEN SALAD: In 1-quart saucepan over medium heat, in *2 teaspoons hot butter* or margarine, cook *¹/₂ cup chopped California walnuts* and *¹/₈ teaspoon salt* 3 to 4 minutes until crisp. Cool toasted walnuts; add to chicken mixture. (Makes 8 servings.)

Turkey-Roquefort Salad

1 8-ounce container sour cream (1 cup)
1 3-ounce wedge or 2 1¹/₄-ounce wedges Roquefort cheese, or 1 4-ounce package blue cheese, crumbled

³/₄ teaspoon salt
3 cups cut-up, cooked turkey or chicken lettuce leaves or chicory
1 29-ounce can cling-peach halves, drained

1. In medium bowl with wire whisk or fork, mix sour cream with Roquefort and salt until well blended. Gently stir in turkey until well coated; cover and refrigerate turkey mixture.
2. To serve: Arrange lettuce leaves or chicory and 6 peach halves on chilled serving plate. Gently stir turkey mixture and spoon over peach halves, dividing equally among halves. (Refrigerate remaining peach halves to use another day.)

Chicken à la King

6 tablespoons butter
¹/₂ pound mushrooms, sliced
¹/₄ cup diced green pepper
6 tablespoons all-purpose flour
3 cups half-and-half
4 cups cubed, cooked chicken or turkey
1 4-ounce jar diced pimentos, drained
2 egg yolks
2 tablespoons medium sherry
1 teaspoon salt
8 patty shells, warmed

1 In 10-inch skillet over medium heat, in hot butter, cook mushrooms and green pepper 5 minutes or until tender.

2 Stir in flour until blended. Gradually stir in half-and-half and cook, stirring constantly, until thickened.

3 Add chicken and pimentos. Heat to boiling, stirring often. Reduce heat to low. Cover and cook 5 minutes.

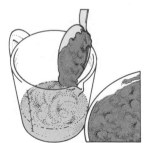

4 In cup, stir yolks until mixed. Stir in a little hot sauce; slowly pour mixture back into sauce, stirring rapidly to prevent lumping. Cook, stirring, until thickened.

5 Stir in sherry and salt and spoon the chicken mixture into patty shells.

Creamy Chicken Hash

2 tablespoons butter
1 small onion, diced
1 tablespoon all-purpose flour
1 teaspoon salt

³/₄ cup half-and-half
2 cups cubed, cooked potatoes
2 cups cubed, cooked chicken or turkey

1. In 10-inch skillet over medium heat, in hot butter, cook onion until tender, about 5 minutes. Stir in flour and salt; gradually stir in half-and-half and cook, stirring, until thickened.
2. Stir in potatoes and chicken. Cover; simmer over low heat 10 minutes until heated through.

Chicken livers

Color index page 42

Begin 1 hr ahead

6 servings

808 cals per serving

Good source of calcium, iron, vitamin A

Sour Cream Chicken Enchiladas

3¹/₂ cups sour cream
3 5-ounce cans boned chicken, cut up (about 2 cups)
2 4-ounce cans mushroom stems and pieces, drained
1 4-ounce can green chilies, drained
¹/₃ cup onion flakes
1 teaspoon chili powder
¹/₂ teaspoon salt
¹/₂ teaspoon garlic powder
¹/₄ teaspoon pepper
salad oil
12 Corn Tortillas (page 431)
¹/₃ pound Cheddar cheese, shredded

1. In 13″ by 9″ baking pan, spread 1 cup sour cream. In 2-quart saucepan with fork, flake chicken; add ¹/₂ cup sour cream, mushrooms and next 6 ingredients. Cook over low heat, stirring occasionally, just until heated through.
2. In 8-inch skillet over medium-high heat, in about ¹/₂ inch hot oil, fry 1 tortilla, a few seconds on each side, until it softens. For an enchilada, along center of tortilla, spread ¹/₄ cup chicken mixture; fold sides over filling and place, seam side down, in sour cream in pan. Repeat.
3. Preheat oven to 450°F. Spread enchiladas with remaining sour cream, then sprinkle with cheese. Bake 8 minutes or until cheese is melted.

Chicken Croquettes

Color index page 46

Begin early in day or day ahead

4 servings

754 cals per serving

Good source of calcium, iron, vitamin A, niacin

2¹/₂ cups ground, cooked chicken or turkey
1 cup Thick White Sauce (page 461)
2 tablespoons chopped parsley
1 tablespoon minced onion
¹/₂ teaspoon lemon juice
¹/₈ teaspoon rubbed sage
salt
1 egg
1 tablespoon water
¹/₄ cup all-purpose flour
¹/₂ cup dried bread crumbs
salad oil
Mushroom Sauce (page 462) or Cheese Sauce (page 461)

1. In medium bowl, blend well first 6 ingredients. Add salt to taste. Cover; chill several hours.
2. *About 30 minutes before serving:* Shape chilled mixture into 8 cones. In shallow dish with fork, beat egg with water. Place flour and bread crumbs on separate sheets of waxed paper. Coat each croquette first in flour, then in egg, then in crumbs.
3. In 4-quart saucepan over medium heat, heat 1 inch oil to 370°F. Fry croquettes until golden brown, turning frequently. Drain on paper towels; serve with Mushroom or Cheese Sauce.

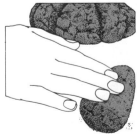
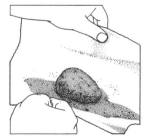

Forming the croquettes: With hands, shape chicken mixture into cones.

Coating the cones: Coat croquettes first in flour, then egg, then crumbs.

Chicken Livers Sauté

Color index page 47

Begin 30 mins ahead

6 servings

359 cals per serving

Good source of iron, vitamin A, riboflavin, niacin

6 tablespoons butter or margarine
1¹/₂ pounds chicken livers
1 small onion, coarsely chopped
¹/₄ cup all-purpose flour
2 cups water
¹/₄ cup dry or medium sherry
1¹/₂ teaspoons salt
toast or toasted split English muffins

1 In 10-inch skillet over medium heat, in butter, cook livers and onion about 10 minutes, stirring.

2 With slotted spoon, place cooked livers and onion in bowl.

3 Into drippings in skillet, add flour; with spoon, stir together until well blended.

4 Stir in water; cook over medium heat, stirring, until thickened.

5 Stir in liver mixture, sherry and salt; heat. Serve on toast.

Chicken Livers Aloha

Color index page 47

Begin 30 mins ahead

4 servings

628 cals per serving

Good source of iron, vitamin A, thiamine, riboflavin, niacin, vitamin C

¹/₄ cup butter or margarine
1 cup chopped celery
¹/₂ cup chopped onion
1 medium green pepper, sliced
1¹/₂ pounds chicken livers
1 15¹/₂-ounce can pineapple chunks, drained
2 tablespoons brown sugar
1 tablespoon cornstarch
1¹/₄ teaspoons salt
³/₄ cup water
2 tablespoons cider vinegar
3 cups hot cooked rice

1. In 12-inch skillet over medium-high heat, in hot butter, cook celery, onion and green pepper until tender-crisp, about 5 minutes. Add livers; cook 10 minutes, stirring; add pineapple.
2. In small bowl, mix sugar, cornstarch and salt. Stir in water and vinegar until smooth. Stir into chicken livers; cook, stirring, until thickened. Serve with rice.

Rock Cornish hens

Rock Cornish Hens with Red Raisin Sauce

Color index page 47

Begin 1¾ hrs ahead

4 servings

1037 cals per serving

Good source of iron, vitamin A, niacin

4 1-pound Rock Cornish hens
salt and pepper
2 cups seasoned croutons
½ cup wheat germ
½ cup finely chopped celery and leaves
½ cup chicken broth
6 tablespoons butter or margarine, melted
1 teaspoon sugar

Red Raisin Sauce:
1 10-ounce jar red currant jelly, ½ cup golden raisins, ¼ cup butter or margarine, 2 teaspoons lemon juice, ¼ teaspoon ground allspice

1 16-ounce jar spiced crabapples, drained, for garnish

1 Sprinkle body cavity of each hen with salt and pepper. Twist wing tips up and back, tucking neck skin under wings to secure it.

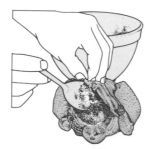

2 In large bowl, combine croutons, wheat germ, celery, broth, 2 tablespoons melted butter, sugar, ½ teaspoon salt and ⅛ teaspoon pepper; lightly spoon into body cavities.

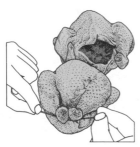

3 Tie legs and tail of each hen together. Brush with melted butter; roast, breast side up, in open roasting pan, at 425°F. 1 hour, brushing occasionally with butter.

4 Meanwhile, prepare Red Raisin Sauce: In 2-quart saucepan over medium-low heat, cook sauce ingredients, stirring occasionally, until blended, about 10 minutes.

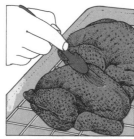

5 During last 15 minutes of roasting, cut strings around legs to allow heat to penetrate and brush hens with some Red Raisin Sauce.

6 Birds are done when leg moves easily up and down (protect hands with paper towel). Serve with sauce and garnish with drained crabapples.

Rock Cornish Hens with Dressing

Color index page 47

Begin 2¾ hrs ahead

4 servings

719 cals per serving

Good source of iron, vitamin A, niacin

1 cup regular long-grain rice
butter or margarine
¼ pound mushrooms, chopped
¼ cup chopped dry shallots
½ cup chopped celery
2 tablespoons chopped green pepper
salt and pepper
4 1-pound Rock Cornish hens
spiced apple rings and parsley for garnish

1. Prepare rice as label directs; set aside. In 10-inch skillet over medium heat, in ½ cup hot butter or margarine, cook mushrooms, shallots, celery and green pepper until vegetables are fork-tender, about 10 minutes. Add mixture to rice; stir in ½ teaspoon salt and ⅛ teaspoon pepper.
2. Remove giblets and necks from hens. Rinse and drain hens well. Lightly spoon about ½ cup of rice mixture into each hen. Spoon remainder into 1-quart greased casserole; cover; set aside. Tuck neck skin under wings to secure it. With string, tie legs and tail of each hen together.
3. Place hens, breast side up, on rack in open roasting pan; brush generously with ¼ cup melted butter; sprinkle lightly with salt. Roast, brushing occasionally with drippings in pan, in 375°F. oven 1¼ hours or until a leg can be moved easily up and down. During last 30 minutes, bake remaining rice mixture until hot.
4. Remove strings from hens. Serve hens on rice mixture; garnish with apple rings and parsley.

Stuffed Rock Cornish Hens with Rhubarb Sauce

Color index page 48

Begin 1¾ hrs ahead

4 servings

718 cals per serving

Good source of calcium, iron, niacin

4 1-pound Rock Cornish hens
salad oil
1 cup chopped onion
1 cup chopped celery
1 8-ounce package herb-seasoned stuffing mix
1 teaspoon salt

Rhubarb Sauce:
1¼ pounds rhubarb, cut up (2 cups)
½ cup water
¼ teaspoon salt
¼ teaspoon ground cinnamon
½ cup sugar

1. Remove giblets and necks from hens. Rinse and drain hens well. Tuck neck skin of each hen under wings to secure it.
2. In 10-inch skillet over medium heat, in ¼ cup hot salad oil, cook onion and celery until golden, about 10 minutes. Meanwhile, prepare stuffing mix as label directs; stir into onion mixture. Lightly spoon mixture into hens. Tie legs and tail of each hen together.
3. Brush hens generously with oil; sprinkle with salt. Place, breast side up, on rack in open roasting pan. Roast at 375°F. 1¼ hours or until a leg can be moved easily up and down.
4. Meanwhile, prepare Rhubarb Sauce: In 2-quart saucepan over medium heat, heat rhubarb, water, salt and cinnamon to boiling; cover. Reduce heat to low; cook 5 to 8 minutes or until rhubarb is tender, stirring frequently. Stir in sugar. Baste hens frequently with sauce during last 30 minutes of roasting. Remove strings. Serve with remaining sauce.

Rock Cornish Hens with Mincemeat Dressing

Color index page 47

Begin 2 hrs ahead

4 servings

450 cals per serving

Good source of iron, niacin

2 1½- to 2-pound frozen Rock Cornish hens, thawed
¼ cup butter, melted
4 slices whole-wheat bread, cubed
¾ cup orange juice
¼ cup diced celery
½ cup prepared mincemeat, drained
½ teaspoon salt
2 tablespoons light corn syrup
2 teaspoons medium sherry

1. Remove giblets and necks from hens. Rinse and drain hens. Tuck neck skin under wings of each hen to secure it. On rack in open roasting pan, place hens, breast side up. Roast, brushing occasionally with melted butter, in 350°F. oven about 1¼ hours or until a leg can be moved easily up and down.
2. Meanwhile, for stuffing, in 1-quart casserole, combine bread cubes, orange juice, celery, prepared mincemeat and salt; toss lightly. Bake along with hens for last 30 minutes of roasting.
3. In small bowl, mix corn syrup and sherry; during last 10 minutes roasting time, brush over hens to glaze them. Serve stuffing with hens.

Lemon-glazed Rock Cornish Hens

Color index page 47

Begin 1½ hrs ahead

4 servings

327 cals per serving

Good source of niacin

2 1½- to 2-pound frozen Rock Cornish hens, thawed
2 tablespoons salad oil
1 teaspoon salt
¼ teaspoon pepper
Lemon-Apple Glaze (below)

1. Remove giblets and necks from inside hens. Place hens on rotisserie skewer as manufacturer directs. Or, fold neck skin to back of hens; skewer hens on rotisserie skewer through meaty part of birds so they will balance evenly and turn without slipping. With string, tie wings close to bodies of hens and bring string down to secure legs and tail close together. Brush hens with oil; sprinkle with salt and pepper.
2. Position skewer as close to heating element as possible without birds touching it as they turn. Roast 1¼ hours until fork-tender. Meanwhile, prepare Lemon-Apple Glaze. During last 20 minutes, brush frequently with glaze.
3. Remove skewer from hens and discard strings.

LEMON-APPLE GLAZE: In small bowl, mix well ⅓ cup light corn syrup, 2 tablespoons apple juice, 1 tablespoon grated lemon peel and ¼ teaspoon salt.

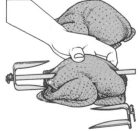

Positioning hens on skewer: To balance birds and prevent slipping, skewer through meaty part.

Tying birds: Tie wings close to bodies then bring string down, securing legs and tail close to bodies.

Honeyed Rock Cornish Hens

Color index page 48

Begin early in day or day ahead

8 servings

263 cals per serving

Low in sodium

Good source of iron, niacin

4 1½-pound frozen Rock Cornish hens, thawed
¾ cup soy sauce
⅓ cup dry sherry
½ teaspoon ground ginger
4 green onions, minced
salad oil
¼ cup honey
1 small head iceberg lettuce, shredded

1. Remove giblets and necks from inside of hens. Rinse hens with running cold water; pat dry with paper towels. Cut each hen into quarters.
2. In 13″ by 9″ baking dish mix soy sauce, sherry, ginger and green onions. Add hen quarters to soy sauce mixture and turn to coat well. Cover and refrigerate at least 6 hours, turning occasionally.
3. *About 40 minutes before serving:* In 12-inch skillet over medium-high heat, in ¼ inch salad oil, fry half of hen quarters until tender and well-browned on all sides, about 20 minutes. Remove to platter; keep warm. Repeat with remaining pieces.
4. To serve: Brush hen quarters with honey. Arrange on platter lined with lettuce.

Broiled Rock Cornish Hen

Color index page 47

Begin 50 mins ahead

2 servings

566 cals per serving

Good source of iron, vitamin A, niacin

1 1½- to 1¾-pound frozen Rock Cornish hen, thawed
¾ teaspoon salt
⅛ teaspoon pepper
2 tablespoons butter or margarine
2 tablespoons lemon juice
1 8-ounce can pineapple slices, drained
1 tablespoon light brown sugar
hot cooked rice for 2 servings
1 tablespoon chopped parsley

1. Preheat broiler, if manufacturer directs. Remove giblets and neck. Rinse hen in running cold water; pat dry with paper towels. Cut hen in half.
2. Sprinkle with salt and pepper. Place halves, skin side down, in small broiling pan or 13″ by 9″ baking pan. Place 1 tablespoon butter or margarine in each cavity; pour lemon juice over halves. About 7 inches from source of heat (or at 450°F.) broil hen 5 minutes, brushing with melted butter from cavity; broil 15 minutes longer. Turn hen and broil about 15 to 20 minutes until drumstick moves easily up and down, brushing with pan drippings occasionally.
3. During last 5 minutes of cooking time, arrange pineapple around hen, sprinkle pineapple with brown sugar and broil until slices are golden.
4. Combine rice with parsley. Serve hen with rice and pineapple slices. Spoon pan drippings over hen.

Arranging the pineapple: Place slices around hen.

Adding the sugar: Sprinkle pineapple slices with sugar.

Ducklings and geese

Ducklings and geese have more fat than other poultry, and the meat is much richer and darker.

Most ducklings and geese are sold frozen. Thaw the bird as usual; pull out clusters of excess fat from the body cavity and rinse and drain. For duckling, remove any pinfeathers. With a sharp, two-tined fork, prick the skin all over so that as the fat melts, it will escape, basting the bird as it rolls down its sides.

Always use a rack when roasting a duckling or goose. Roast duckling in a 325°F. oven until the thermometer registers a temperature of 185° to 190°F. Roast goose in a 350°F. oven, to an internal temperature of 190°F.

Because their bone structures are unlike those of chicken or turkey, ducklings and geese have a different proportion of meat to bone. Allow about 1 pound duckling per serving, 1 to 1½ pounds goose per serving.

Duckling with Sausage-Rice Stuffing

1 4- to 5-pound frozen
duckling, thawed
1 small stalk celery,
cut up
1 small onion, peeled
salt
water
Sausage-Rice Stuffing
(page 252)
¼ teaspoon paprika
⅛ teaspoon pepper

Color index page 49
Begin 4¼ hrs ahead
4 servings

1100 cals per serving

Good source of iron, vitamin A, niacin

1 Remove giblets and neck. Discard fat from cavity; rinse duckling with cold running water; drain well. Pat dry; remove pinfeathers; refrigerate.

2 In 2-quart saucepan, heat to boiling giblets, neck, celery, onion, ½ teaspoon salt and water to cover. Reduce heat; cover; simmer until tender; drain. Prepare the stuffing.

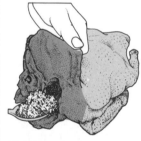

3 Discard celery and onion. Chop giblets; remove neck meat from bone; add both to stuffing. Rub cavity with ½ teaspoon salt. Spoon stuffing into neck.

4 Fold neck skin over stuffing; skewer to back. With duckling breast side up, lift wings toward neck; fold under back. Spoon stuffing into body cavity; skewer closed.

5 Place duckling, breast side up, on rack in open roasting pan. Rub mixture of paprika, pepper and 1 teaspoon salt over bird. Tie legs with string.

6 Prick skin in several places. Insert thermometer into thickest part of meat between breast and thigh. Do not touch bone. Roast at 325°F. 2¼ to 2½ hours.

7 Start checking for doneness during last 30 minutes. Bird is done when thermometer reads 185°F. to 190°F. and leg feels soft when pinched (protect hand with paper towel).

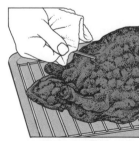

8 When duckling is done, remove skewers and strings; place on warm platter; let duckling stand at room temperature 15 minutes for easier carving.

Color index page 48   1027 cals per serving
Begin 4 hrs ahead   Good source of
8 servings   calcium, iron,
                        riboflavin, niacin

Roast Goose with Mixed-Fruit Stuffing

1 10-pound goose
Mixed-Fruit Stuffing
(page 252)
1 13¾-ounce can chicken
broth

2 tablespoons all-purpose
flour
¼ cup cold water
parsley sprigs
for garnish

1. Remove neck and giblets from goose; discard fat from body cavity; rinse; drain. Prepare stuffing.
2. Stuff bird lightly. Skewer neck skin to back. Tie legs and tail together. With two-tined fork, prick skin. Insert meat thermometer into thickest part of meat between breast and thigh, avoiding bone.
3. Place goose, breast side up, on wire rack in open roasting pan.
4. Roast at 350°F. 3½ hours or until thermometer reads 190°F. When goose is done, remove to platter; remove string from around legs and tail; garnish.
5. To make gravy, spoon fat from drippings in pan, leaving juice and browned bits; stir in broth. Over medium heat, heat to boiling. In cup, blend flour and water; gradually stir into hot mixture and cook, stirring, until thickened. Serve with goose.

Color index page 48   643 cals per serving
Begin 4¼ hrs ahead   Good source of iron
10 servings

Bohemian Roast Goose

1 9- to 11-pound frozen
goose, thawed
4 cups sauerkraut (about
2 16-ounce cans)
2 cups peeled, cubed apples

1 teaspoon salt
½ teaspoon caraway
seed

1. Remove giblets and neck from goose; rinse goose. (Use giblets and neck for broth, if you like.) With two-tined fork, prick skin.
2. In large bowl, toss sauerkraut with apples, salt and caraway seed; lightly spoon into goose. Skewer neck skin to back (or, hold in place with wings). Tie legs and tail together. Insert meat thermometer into center of thigh next to body, avoiding bone. Place, breast side up, on rack in open roasting pan.
3. Roast at 350°F. 3¼ to 4 hours or until thermometer reads 190°F. and thigh is tender when pierced with a fork. Allow goose to stand at room temperature 15 minutes for easier carving.

Shanghai Duckling with Leeks

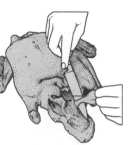

Color index
page 48

Begin 2½ hrs
ahead

4 servings

785 cals per
serving

Good source
of calcium,
iron,
vitamin A,
niacin

8 medium leeks
1 4½- to 5-pound frozen
  duckling, thawed
½ cup dry sherry
½ cup soy sauce
½ teaspoon sugar
¼ teaspoon ground
  ginger
1¼ cups water
3 small carrots, each cut
  lengthwise into
  4 strips

1 Prepare leeks: Trim roots and discard tough leaves; cut each crosswise in half. Rinse halves with running cold water to remove sand. Cover and refrigerate root halves; cut remaining halves crosswise into ½-inch slices and place in 6-quart cook-and-serve Dutch oven.

2 Remove giblets and neck from bird; trim as much fatty skin from around neck and body cavity as possible. Rinse duckling, giblets and neck with cold water.

3 Place duckling, breast side down, on leeks in Dutch oven and tuck giblets and neck around it.

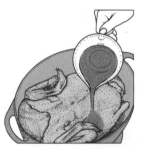

4 Add sherry, soy sauce, sugar, ginger and water. Over high heat, heat to boiling. Reduce heat to low; cover and simmer for 30 minutes.

5 With large spoon, turn duckling over; cover; cook 1 hour more, spooning pan liquid over duckling to baste occasionally.

6 Skim and discard fat from pan liquid, then place carrot strips and reserved leeks around duckling; increase heat to high and heat mixture to boiling.

7 Reduce heat to low; cover; cook 20 minutes more or until bird and vegetables are fork-tender, basting occasionally with pan liquid. Serve at once.

Elegant Duckling à l'Orange

Color index
page 49

Begin 2½ hrs
ahead

4 servings

716 cals per
serving

Good source
of iron,
niacin

1 4- to 5-pound frozen
  duckling, thawed
⅛ teaspoon pepper
salt
2 oranges
water
2 teaspoons cornstarch
¼ cup sugar
1 chicken-flavor bouillon
  cube
2 tablespoons brandy

1. Remove giblets and neck from duckling. Rinse bird under running cold water; pat dry.
2. Remove excess fat from inside of cavity; cut off and discard neck skin. Cut duckling into quarters; sprinkle with pepper and ½ teaspoon salt.
3. Place pieces, skin side down, on rack in 13″ by 9″ open roasting pan. Roast at 350°F. 1 hour; turn; roast 45 minutes more or until thickest part of drumstick feels soft when pinched with fingers protected with paper towels.
4. *About 30 minutes before duckling is done, prepare sauce:* Into 1-cup measuring cup, squeeze juice from 1 orange; add water to make 1 cup. Stir in cornstarch and ¼ teaspoon salt until cornstarch is completely dissolved; set aside.
5. In 2-quart saucepan over medium heat, heat sugar until melted and a light caramel color, stirring constantly with wooden spoon. Remove from heat and let cool 10 minutes. Add orange-juice mixture and bouillon (sugar will harden). Return to heat; cook 5 minutes more or until reduced by half and sugar is completely dissolved, stirring constantly. Stir in brandy; keep warm.
6. Slice remaining orange. Arrange duckling pieces on warm platter and pour on orange sauce. Garnish the duckling with orange slices.

Roast Duckling Montmorency

Color index
page 49

Begin 2½ hrs
ahead

4 servings

745 cals per
serving

Good source
of iron,
vitamin A,
niacin

1 4- to 5-pound fresh or
  thawed frozen
  duckling, quartered
¾ teaspoon salt
¼ teaspoon pepper
1 17-ounce can pitted
  dark sweet cherries,
  drained
½ cup claret
2 tablespoons currant
  jelly
1 teaspoon cornstarch
¼ cup water
1 tablespoon butter or
  margarine

1. With two-tined fork, prick skin of duckling in several places; sprinkle with salt and pepper. Place duckling, skin side up, on rack in open roasting pan. Roast in 350°F. oven 1¾ to 2 hours or until duckling pieces are fork-tender.
2. Meanwhile, in medium bowl, stir cherries with claret; set aside.
3. Place duckling on warm platter; keep warm. Remove rack; pour all fat from roasting pan.
4. Into roasting pan over medium heat, drain wine from cherries; scrape to loosen browned bits from pan. Pour mixture into 1-quart saucepan; add jelly. In cup, blend cornstarch and water until smooth; gradually stir into wine mixture; cook over medium heat, stirring, until smooth and slightly thickened.
5. Add cherries and butter; heat, stirring, until cherries are hot and butter is melted and blended. Serve duckling with hot cherry sauce.

Ducklings

Peking Duck

5 quarts boiling water
1 5-pound fresh or thawed frozen duckling, cleaned and with giblets and fat removed
1 tablespoon salt
1 tablespoon dry or cooking sherry
Thin Pancakes (right)
¼ cup maple-flavored syrup
½ cup canned hoisin sauce
4 green onions, cut into 2-inch pieces
coriander for garnish

Color index page 48
Begin day ahead
4 main-dish servings
1187 cals per serving
Good source of calcium, iron, vitamin A, niacin

1 Pour boiling water slowly, in a fine stream, over both sides of duckling, so its skin becomes almost white; drain thoroughly.

2 With paper towels, gently pat skin and body cavity dry. Then rub body cavity with salt and sherry.

3 On large wire rack across top of a medium open roasting pan, place duckling, breast side down. Refrigerate, uncovered, until early in evening. Make Thin Pancakes.

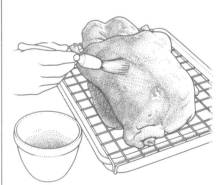

4 *Early in evening:* Generously brush duckling skin with maple syrup; refrigerate, breast side up, uncovered, until needed next day.

5 *Next day, about 5 hours before serving:* Transfer duckling, rack and pan to 175°F. oven; roast 1½ hours. Turn oven control to 325°F.; roast duckling, breast side down, 1½ hours, then breast side up, 1 to 1½ hours, until skin is crisp. 15 minutes before duckling is done, heat Thin Pancakes.

To serve: Place hoisin sauce in small bowl, and green onions on a small plate. When duckling is done, thinly slice duckling skin and meat into about 2" by 1" pieces; arrange on warm plate. Pass duckling, hoisin sauce and green onions along with heated Thin Pancakes. Let each person assemble his portion as shown (right).

Thin Pancakes

2½ cups all-purpose flour
½ teaspoon salt

1 cup boiling water
salad oil
83 cals each
Low in cholesterol

1. In large bowl, combine flour and salt; gradually add water, blending with fork, until mixture is size of peas. Press into a ball; on lightly floured surface, knead to a soft, smooth dough, about 5 minutes.
2. Shape into a roll 16 inches long; cut crosswise, into 16 slices. Cover slices with damp cloth.
3. Place 2 slices on lightly floured surface; with fingers, flatten each into 3-inch circle. Brush tops generously with oil; place one on top of another with oiled tops together. With lightly floured rolling pin, roll from center to form 8-inch circle, turning it over several times to roll evenly.
4. In ungreased 8-inch skillet over medium heat, cook each side of circle 2 to 3 minutes or until light brown; remove to 8-inch pie plate and with fingers, carefully separate its 2 warm layers, making 2 thin pancakes. Stack these, one on top of the other, browned side up; cover with foil.
5. Repeat, making 16 pancakes in all. Wrap pie plate and refrigerate until required.
6. *To reheat pancakes:* In large saucepot, in ¾ inch water, place 3 inverted 6-ounce custard cups. Remove wrap from pie plate; place plate on top of custard cups. Cover saucepot; over medium heat, heat water to boiling. Reduce heat to low; simmer 10 minutes or until pancakes are soft and hot.

Forming the pancake: Place oiled sides of two 3-inch circles together then roll to 8-inch circle.

Separating pancakes: Separate the warm layers of each cooked pancake, making 2 thin pancakes.

ASSEMBLING A PORTION

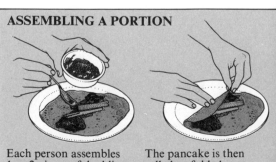

Each person assembles 1 or 2 pieces of duckling, a dab of hoisin sauce and a piece of green onion on the center of each soft, hot pancake.

The pancake is then rolled or folded over twice into a neat package. Eat sandwich-style.

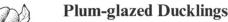

Plum-glazed Ducklings

**2 4- to 5-pound fresh or
thawed frozen
ducklings, quartered**
garlic salt
**¼ cup butter or
margarine**
1 medium onion, chopped
**1 17-ounce can purple
plums**
**½ cup packed light
brown sugar**

⅓ cup chili sauce
¼ cup soy sauce
¼ cup lemon juice
½ teaspoon salt
**1 teaspoon ground
ginger**
**2 teaspoons prepared
mustard**
**1 teaspoon
Worcestershire**

1. With two-tined fork, prick skin of ducklings in several places; sprinkle with garlic salt.
2. Place ducklings, skin side up, on racks in 2 open roasting pans. Roast in 350°F. oven 2 hours or until ducklings are tender.
3. Meanwhile, in 2-quart saucepan over medium heat, in hot butter or margarine, cook onion, stirring occasionally, 5 minutes or until tender.
4. Into blender container, drain liquid from plums; pit plums and add to container. Add onion mixture, brown sugar and remaining ingredients. Cover and blend at high speed until smooth.
5. Pour plum mixture into saucepan. Over medium heat, simmer plum mixture 25 minutes, stirring the mixture occasionally.
6. When ducklings are done, remove pans from oven; turn oven control to 400°F. Remove ducklings and racks from pans; pour off fat; discard. Return racks and ducklings to pans and brush with some of sauce. Roast ducklings 15 minutes longer, brushing occasionally with sauce. Serve ducklings with remaining plum sauce.

GLAZES FOR POULTRY

Allow about ½ cup glaze for 4- to 10-pound birds; for larger birds, double the recipe. During the last 10 to 20 minutes of roasting time, brush the bird several times with one of these glazes.

QUINCE: In 1-quart saucepan over low heat, stir *½ cup quince jelly, 1 tablespoon butter or margarine, 1 teaspoon ground cinnamon* and *½ teaspoon ground cloves* until blended. (Makes ½ cup.)

WINE-JELLY: In 1-quart saucepan over low heat, stir *½ cup wine jelly* with *¼ teaspoon salt* until blended. (Makes ½ cup.)

NUTTY: In 1-quart saucepan over medium heat, melt *½ cup apple jelly;* stir in *½ cup orange juice* and *½ cup chopped California walnuts.* (Makes 1⅓ cups.)

HONEY-BARBECUE: In small bowl, mix *½ cup honey, 1 tablespoon soy sauce* and *½ teaspoon ground ginger,* until well blended. (Makes ½ cup.)

ORANGE-WALNUT: In 1-quart saucepan over medium heat, heat *1 cup orange marmalade, ½ cup finely chopped California walnuts, 3 tablespoons lemon juice, 1 tablespoon instant minced onion* and *1½ teaspoons salt* until marmalade is melted. (Makes 1⅔ cups.)

Sauces for poultry

Either sweet or savory sauces go well with all types of poultry, particularly with roast birds. Provide 1 cup of sauce for every 4 to 5 servings of poultry.

Cranberry-Orange Sauce

2 tablespoons cornstarch
**1 teaspoon grated lemon
peel**
**½ teaspoon ground
cloves**

¼ teaspoon salt
1½ cups orange juice
1 teaspoon lemon juice
**1 16-ounce can whole-
cranberry sauce**

1. In 2-quart saucepan, combine cornstarch with lemon peel, cloves and salt; stir in orange and lemon juice until smooth.
2. Over high heat, cook, stirring constantly, until sauce is smooth and thickened.
3. Stir in cranberry sauce and heat through, stirring occasionally. Serve hot or cold.

Lemon Sauce

¼ cup sugar
¼ cup lemon juice
4 teaspoons cornstarch
**1 tablespoon grated
lemon peel**

½ teaspoon salt
**⅛ teaspoon ground
ginger**
1 drop yellow food color
1 cup water

1. In 1-quart saucepan, mix well first 7 ingredients; stir in water to blend smoothly.
2. Cook over medium heat, stirring constantly, until mixture is slightly thickened. Serve hot.

Watercress Sauce

**1 13¾-ounce can chicken
broth (about 1¾ cups)**
**3 tablespoons all-purpose
flour**
⅓ cup cold water

**2½ cups coarsely
chopped watercress**
½ teaspoon salt
⅛ teaspoon pepper

1. In 1½-quart saucepan over high heat, heat chicken broth to boiling.
2. Meanwhile, in cup with fork, blend flour and water until smooth. Reduce heat to medium; gradually stir mixture into hot broth.
3. Cook, stirring constantly, until sauce is smooth and thickened. Stir in remaining ingredients; simmer 2 minutes. Serve hot with hot poultry.

Currant-Mint Sauce

**1 10-ounce jar red
currant jelly (1 cup)**
**2 tablespoons shredded
orange peel**

**2 tablespoons chopped
mint leaves**

In small bowl with fork, stir all ingredients until well mixed. Serve with roast chicken or turkey.

Curried Pineapple Sauce

**1 8¼-ounce can crushed
pineapple**

2 tablespoons butter
1 teaspoon curry powder

In 1-quart saucepan over medium-high heat, heat to boiling all ingredients, stirring occasionally. Reduce heat to low; cover; simmer 5 minutes. Serve hot.

VEGETABLES

Vegetables are becoming an increasingly important part of our diet. They are a good source of vitamins and minerals and many are high in fiber. Furthermore, most vegetables are low in calories. Canned, frozen and dried vegetables assure a year-round supply of varieties.

Whatever the method, keep cooking to a minimum. When boiling vegetables, use as little water as possible, then save the nutrient-rich liquid for use in stocks and sauces. Serve vegetables as accompaniments to main dishes or in stews and casseroles.

The servings specified in the recipes in this chapter are accompaniment servings unless otherwise indicated. Directions for buying and using individual vegetables are given in the following pages.

Artichokes

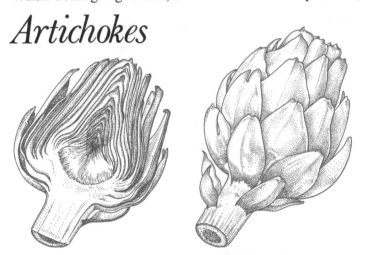

Also known as French or globe artichokes.
Season: All year. Best supplies of artichokes are in March, April and May.
Look for: Compact, plump heads, heavy in relation to their size, with tightly closed, thick green leaves. Size is not an indication of quality. Avoid over-mature ones with hard-tipped, blemished or spreading leaves.
To store: Refrigerate in a plastic bag with a few drops of water. Use within a few days.
To prepare: Cut off stem and top, trim thorny tips of leaves and pull loose leaves from around bottom of artichoke as shown right.
To cook: In large saucepot over medium heat, in 1 inch boiling, salted water, place artichokes on their stem ends. Add a few lemon slices, heat to boiling, cover saucepot, reduce heat to low and cook about 30 minutes or until leaf can be pulled out easily.
Seasonings: Cook with bay leaf, garlic, oregano.
To serve: Serve artichokes as hot or cold appetizer or salad, and in recipes. Eat with melted butter, Lemon Butter, Hollandaise or Bearnaise Sauce (all on page 463). Allow 1 artichoke per person.

Preparing artichokes: With sharp knife, cut stem from artichoke and 1 inch straight across the top.

With scissors, trim thorny tips of leaves; brush cut edges with lemon juice to prevent discoloration. Pull loose leaves from around bottom.

Eating artichokes: Pull out a leaf and dip base in melted butter or sauce on side of plate; pull through teeth, scraping out pulp. Discard leaves on plate.

Cut out fuzzy "choke" in center of artichoke; cut solid heart into chunks and dip in sauce.

ARTICHOKES BEARNAISE

With spoon, scoop out choke from *cooked artichoke*. Fill center with *Bearnaise Sauce* (page 463). Serve warm. (Color index, page 55.)

Asparagus

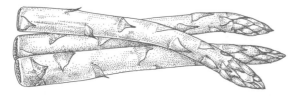

Season: March to July; sometimes in fall.
Look for: Straight stalks with closed, compact tips, good green color almost entire length (the white area at the end is tough and must be discarded).
To store: Refrigerate in crisper or wrapped in plastic bags. Use within 1 to 2 days.
To prepare: See below.
To cook: In large skillet over medium heat, in ½ inch boiling, salted water, heat stalks to boiling; reduce heat to low; cover and simmer until tender-crisp; whole asparagus take about 5 minutes, cut-up stalks about 3 to 5 minutes. Or, steam or stir-fry or use in recipes for soups, main dishes, salads, appetizers.
Seasonings: Cook with allspice, mustard, coriander, lemon, seasoned salt and pepper.
To serve: Eat hot or cold, with or without sauce.

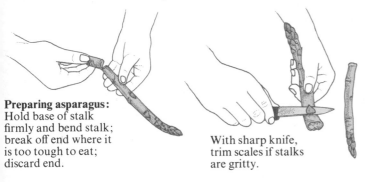

Preparing asparagus: Hold base of stalk firmly and bend stalk; break off end where it is too tough to eat; discard end.

With sharp knife, trim scales if stalks are gritty.

Steamed Asparagus

Color index page 21

Begin 15 mins ahead

8 servings

144 cals per serving

Good source of vitamin A

water
1 pound asparagus
salt

Hollandaise Sauce
(page 463) or Lemon
Butter (page 463)

1. In asparagus steamer or 3-quart saucepan with rack, heat ½ inch water to boiling.
2. Add asparagus. Cover; steam asparagus 8 to 10 minutes until tender.
3. Salt to taste. Serve with Hollandaise Sauce or Lemon Butter.

STEAMED CUT ASPARAGUS: Cut asparagus diagonally into 2-inch pieces and steam as above, cooking 6 to 8 minutes until tender-crisp.

Stir-fried Asparagus

Color index page 70

Begin 10 mins ahead

6 servings

55 cals per serving

Low in cholesterol

1½ pounds asparagus
2 tablespoons salad oil

½ teaspoon salt

1. Cut asparagus diagonally into 3-inch pieces.
2. In 10-inch skillet or 5-quart Dutch oven over high heat, in very hot salad oil, cook asparagus, stirring quickly and frequently (stir-frying) until well coated. Sprinkle with salt; continue stir-frying about 3 minutes more or until tender-crisp.

Beans, dry

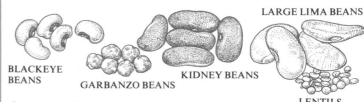

LARGE LIMA BEANS

BLACKEYE BEANS

GARBANZO BEANS

KIDNEY BEANS

LENTILS

Season: All year.
Look for: Packages.
To store: Keep in packages or in covered containers.
To prepare: Rinse well; discard any stones or shriveled beans. Dry beans and whole peas require soaking before cooking, split peas and lentils do not. *Overnight soaking:* Cover each cup beans or whole peas with 3 cups water; let stand 12 hours or overnight. *Quicker soaking:* Add beans or whole peas to boiling water, allowing 3 cups water for each cup beans or whole peas. Over high heat, heat to boiling; boil 2 minutes. Remove from heat; cover and leave for 1 hour; then cook in same water.
To cook: After soaking, add 1 teaspoon salt for each cup dry beans or peas. Over medium-low heat, simmer, covered, until tender following timetable below. One cup dry beans or peas yields 2 to 2½ cups cooked.
Seasonings: Cook with onion, garlic or bay leaf.
To serve: Serve hot; serve cold in salads; use in recipes.

1 CUP SOAKED	COOKING TIMES
Black beans	2 hours
Blackeye beans (peas or cowpeas)	25 to 30 minutes
Garbanzo beans (chick-peas)	2 to 2¼ hours
Great Northern beans	1 to 1½ hours
Kidney beans	1½ hours
Lentils (*no soaking required*)	25 to 30 minutes
Large lima beans	1 hour
Pea beans (navy beans)	1½ hours
Peas, split (*no soaking required*)	45 minutes
Peas, whole	1 hour
Pink beans	2 hours
Pinto beans	2 hours
Red beans	2 hours
Soy beans	1½ hours

Boston Baked Beans

Color index page 68

Begin early in day or day ahead

12 servings

356 cals per serving

Low in cholesterol

High in fiber

Good source of calcium, iron

2 16-ounce packages dry
  pea (navy) beans
water
4 teaspoons salt
¾ cup dark molasses
½ cup packed dark
  brown sugar

1 tablespoon dry mustard
1 teaspoon pepper
1 large onion, studded
  with 4 whole cloves
1 8-ounce piece salt pork,
  with rind slashed

1. Soak beans in water in 5-quart Dutch oven following quick soak method above; heat to boiling. Reduce heat to low; add salt; cover; simmer 1 hour.
2. Stir in molasses and next 3 ingredients. Tuck onion and salt pork into beans. Cover; bake in 250°F. oven 7 hours, adding more water if needed to keep beans moist but not too wet. Discard cloves.

Beans, dry

Beans, green and wax

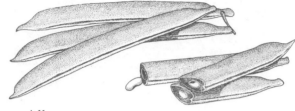

Blackeye Beans

1 16-ounce package dry   *¼ pound salt pork, sliced*
   blackeye beans   *or cut into chunks*
water   *salt and pepper*

Color index
page 68
Begin day
ahead
6 servings
278 cals per
serving
Low in
cholesterol
High in fiber

1. Soak beans in water to cover overnight.
2. *About 2 hours before serving:* Drain beans. In 5-quart Dutch oven over medium-high heat, heat beans, salt pork and 2 quarts water to boiling. Reduce heat to low; cover and simmer 1¼ hours or until beans are tender, stirring occasionally. Season to taste with salt and pepper.

Bean Relish

6 cups cooked dry red   *2 teaspoons salt*
   kidney or red beans   *2 teaspoons mustard seed*
2 12-ounce cans   *1 teaspoon cracked*
   vacuum-packed corn   *pepper*
1½ cups cider vinegar   *1 cup water*
1 cup sugar   *3 tablespoons cornstarch*
3 medium onions, sliced

Color index
page 68

Begin 4½ hrs
or up to
1 wk ahead

9 cups relish

33 cals per
tablespoon

Low in fat,
cholesterol,
sodium

1. In large bowl, combine the red kidney or red beans, corn and its liquid; set aside.
2. In 2-quart saucepan over medium heat, heat vinegar, sugar, onions, salt, mustard seed and cracked pepper to boiling. Cover and cook until onions are tender, about 5 minutes.
3. Meanwhile, combine water and cornstarch until blended. Gradually add cornstarch mixture to vinegar mixture and cook, stirring constantly, until mixture boils. Boil 1 minute; remove from heat. Pour vinegar and cornstarch mixture over bean mixture and stir to mix well.
4. Cover and refrigerate about 4 hours or overnight, stirring occasionally.

Puerto Rican Beans and Rice

1 16-ounce package dry   *1 8-ounce can tomato*
   pink beans   *sauce*
6 cups water   *½ teaspoon oregano*
1½ teaspoons salt   *leaves*
½ cup diced salt pork   *¼ teaspoon garlic*
1 large onion, diced   *powder*
1 large green pepper,   *¼ teaspoon pepper*
   diced   *4 cups hot cooked rice*

Color index
page 33

Begin 3 hrs
ahead

6 main-dish
servings

482 cals per
serving

Low in
cholesterol

High in fiber

Good source
of calcium,
iron

1. Rinse beans under running cold water and discard any stones or shriveled beans. In 5-quart Dutch oven over medium-high heat, heat beans and water to boiling; boil 2 minutes. Remove from heat; cover and let stand 1 hour.
2. Do not drain beans; add salt. Over high heat, heat beans to boiling. Reduce heat to low; cover Dutch oven and simmer 40 minutes, stirring occasionally.
3. Meanwhile, in 10-inch skillet over medium heat, cook salt pork until well browned, about 10 minutes. Add onion and green pepper; cook until tender, stirring occasionally. Stir onion mixture, tomato sauce, oregano leaves, garlic powder and pepper into beans; cook 40 to 50 minutes until beans are tender and mixture is thickened. Serve spooned over the hot cooked rice.

Season: All year.
Look for: Crisp tender beans without scars. Well-shaped pods with small seeds are most desirable. Length is unimportant.
To store: Refrigerate in crisper or plastic bags; use within 1 or 2 days.
To prepare: See below.
To cook: In saucepan over medium heat, in 1 inch boiling, salted water, heat beans to boiling. Reduce heat to low; cover and simmer whole or cut-up beans 10 minutes, French-cut beans 5 minutes, or until tender-crisp. Beans are also good used in recipes for stews, pot roasts, main dishes and cold salads.
Seasonings: Cook with chili powder, chives, dill, lemon, mustard, onion, sage, parsley, seasoned salt and seasoned pepper, or try adding a few tablespoons of bacon or ham drippings.
To serve: Eat hot, with or without sauce.

Preparing beans: Rinse beans in cold water, then snap off ends; the string will come off with the stem end.

Leave whole, or snap or cut into bite-size pieces.

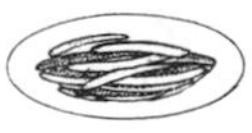

Whole Green and Wax Beans with Parsley Sauce

water   *1½ teaspoons salt*
1 pound green beans   *⅛ teaspoon pepper*
1 pound wax beans   *1 cup chicken broth*
2 tablespoons butter or   *2 egg yolks*
   margarine   *½ cup milk*
2 tablespoons all-purpose   *1 cup chopped parsley*
   flour

Color index
page 68

Begin 30 mins
ahead

8 servings

82 cals per
serving

1. In 12-inch skillet over medium heat, in 1 inch boiling water, heat beans to boiling; reduce heat to low; cover and simmer 10 minutes or until tender-crisp. Drain.
2. Meanwhile, prepare sauce: In 2-quart saucepan over medium heat, into hot butter, stir flour, salt and pepper until blended. Gradually stir in chicken broth; cook, stirring constantly, until sauce is thickened. Reduce heat to low.
3. In small bowl, beat egg yolks with milk; stir in small amount of hot sauce. Slowly pour egg mixture into sauce stirring rapidly to prevent lumping; cook, stirring constantly, until thickened (do not boil). Stir in the beans and the chopped parsley.

Beans, lima

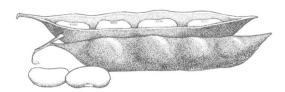

Season: All year. Best supplies of lima beans are in August and September.

Look for: Well-filled, tender, green pods. Avoid dried, spotty or yellowing, wilted ones. Shelled lima beans should be plump, with green to greenish-white skins.

To store: Refrigerate in crisper or in plastic bags. Use within 1 to 2 days.

To prepare: See below.

To cook: In saucepan over medium heat, in 1 inch boiling, salted water, heat beans to boiling. Reduce heat to low; cover and simmer 20 to 30 minutes until beans are tender. Lima beans may also be added to stews, pot roasts and soups.

Seasonings: Cook with garlic, onion, parsley.

To serve: Eat hot or cold, with or without sauce. Good topped with White or Cheese Sauce (page 461) or Mushroom Sauce (page 462).

Preparing lima beans: Snap off one end of pod and open to remove beans.

Or, with knife, cut off thin strip from the inner edge of the pod and push out beans

Lima Beans Smitane

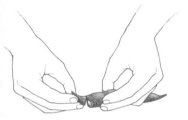

Color index page 68
Begin 25 mins ahead
4 servings
133 cals per serving
Low in cholesterol, sodium
Good source of iron, vitamin C

1½ pounds lima beans, shelled, or 1 10-ounce package frozen baby lima beans
1 pimento, diced
½ cup sour cream
3 tablespoons chopped chives
¼ teaspoon garlic salt
¼ teaspoon salt
¼ teaspoon pepper

1. Cook shelled lima beans as above, or cook frozen beans as label directs; drain.
2. Lightly toss beans, pimento, sour cream, chives, garlic salt, salt and pepper.

Zesty Lima Beans

Color index page 68
Begin 2 hrs ahead
4 servings
164 cals per serving

1 10-ounce package frozen lima beans
½ cup sliced canned water chestnuts
¼ cup Italian dressing
¾ teaspoon dill weed

1. Cook lima beans as label directs; drain.
2. Add chestnuts, Italian dressing and dill weed to lima beans and toss to combine well. Cover mixture and refrigerate to chill.

Beets

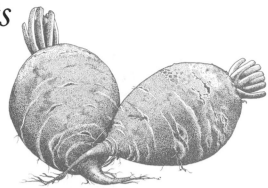

Season: All year. Best supplies of beets are from June to November.

Look for: Smooth, firm, rich red beets of uniform size, with no ridges, blemishes or soft spots, and with fresh green tops, if any.

To store: Cut off stems and tops. Refrigerate tops and beets in crisper or plastic bags. Use beets within a week or so, preferably sooner. Use tops as soon as possible (see Lettuce and other greens, page 287).

To prepare: See below.

To cook: In saucepan over medium heat, in 1 inch boiling, salted water, heat whole beets to boiling. Reduce heat to low. Cover and simmer 30 minutes to 1 hour until fork-tender (depending on maturity and size of beets). Drain and peel (see below). Or, peel beets before cooking, slice or dice, and cook over medium heat 15 to 20 minutes until tender. Or, use in soups and salads.

Seasonings: Cook with allspice, celery seed, cloves, dill, nutmeg, orange, lemon.

To serve: Serve hot or cold, with or without sauce.

Preparing beets: Cut off stem ends. Scrub raw beets under running cold water being careful not to damage the skins.

Peeling cooked beets: First cool beets in cold water, then remove skins with a sharp knife.

Harvard Beets

Color index page 68
Begin 20 mins ahead
6 servings
102 cals per serving
Low in cholesterol, sodium

¼ cup sugar
1 tablespoon cornstarch
½ teaspoon salt
⅓ cup vinegar
1 tablespoon butter or margarine
1 teaspoon minced onion
3 cups cooked, sliced beets or 2 16-ounce cans sliced beets, drained

1. In 1-quart saucepan, combine sugar, cornstarch and salt; slowly stir in vinegar; add butter or margarine and minced onion; over medium heat, cook until thickened, stirring constantly.
2. Reduce heat to low; add beets and cook just until heated through, stirring occasionally.

BEETS IN ORANGE SAUCE: Prepare as above but use ½ cup orange juice instead of vinegar and 1 teaspoon grated orange peel instead of onion.

Broccoli

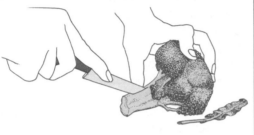

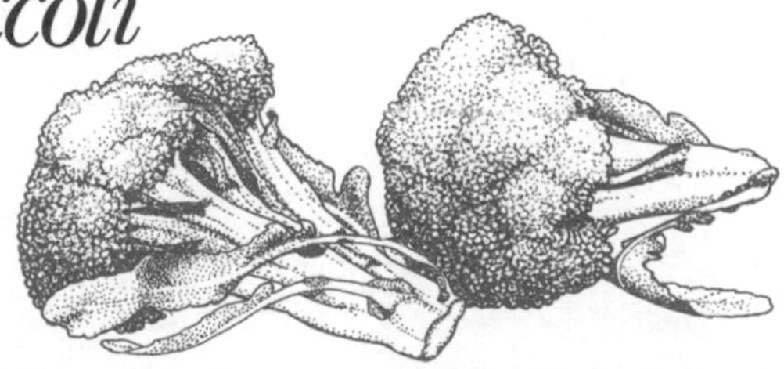

Season: All year. Lowest supplies in June, July, August.
Look for: Tender, firm stalks and tightly closed, dark-green flowerets.
To store: Refrigerate in crisper or plastic bag. Use within 1 or 2 days.
To prepare: See below.
To cook: In skillet over medium heat, in 1 inch boiling, salted water, heat broccoli to boiling. Reduce heat to low; cover and simmer about 10 minutes until tender-crisp. Or, use in poultry dishes, casseroles, soups.
Seasonings: Cook broccoli with coriander, dill, mustard, nutmeg, oregano.
To serve: Eat hot, with or without sauce.

Preparing broccoli:
Remove any large leaves and cut off any woody stalk ends. Split stalks lengthwise 2 or 3 times to speed cooking. Rinse well.

Color index page 72
Begin 15 mins ahead
6 servings
86 cals per serving
Low in cholesterol, sodium
Good source of vitamin C

Stir-fried Broccoli

3 tablespoons salad oil	*¼ cup water*
1 bunch broccoli, cut in 2″ by ½″ pieces	*½ teaspoon salt*
	¼ teaspoon sugar

1. In 12-inch skillet or 5-quart Dutch oven over high heat, in very hot oil, cook broccoli, stirring quickly and frequently (stir-frying) until well coated.
2. Add water, salt and sugar. Reduce heat to medium-high; cover and cook 2 minutes; uncover and stir-fry 5 to 6 minutes more until tender-crisp.

Color index page 72
Begin 1 hr ahead
8 servings
208 cals per serving
Good source of calcium, vitamin A, vitamin C

Swiss-Cheese Broccoli

water	*3 tablespoons chopped onion*
1 pound broccoli, coarsely chopped	*1¼ cups milk*
salt	*2 cups shredded natural Swiss cheese*
3 tablespoons butter	*2 eggs, beaten*
2 tablespoons all-purpose flour	

1. Grease a 10″ by 6″ baking dish. In 2-quart saucepan over high heat, in 1 inch boiling water, heat broccoli and ½ teaspoon salt to boiling; cover and cook 10 minutes; drain; set aside.
2. Meanwhile, in 2-quart saucepan over medium heat, melt butter; stir in flour and 1½ teaspoons salt until smooth. Add onion and cook 1 minute. Preheat oven to 325°F. Slowly stir in milk; cook, stirring constantly, until mixture thickens and begins to boil; remove from heat.
3. Stir in cheese and broccoli until cheese melts slightly; stir in eggs. Pour into baking dish; bake 30 minutes or until firm to the touch.

Brussels sprouts

Season: September to May.
Look for: Firm, fresh, bright green sprouts with tight-fitting outer leaves free from black spots. Puffy or soft sprouts are usually poor in quality.
To store: Refrigerate in crisper or wrapped in plastic bag. Use within 1 or 2 days.
To prepare: See below.
To cook: In saucepan over medium heat, in 1 inch boiling, salted water, heat sprouts to boiling. Reduce heat to low; cover and simmer about 10 minutes or until tender-crisp. Or, bake or use in recipes.
Seasonings: Cook Brussels sprouts with caraway, dill, mustard, ground nutmeg.
To serve: Eat hot, with or without sauce. Often served combined with carrots, squash or chestnuts.

Preparing Brussels sprouts:
Remove any yellow leaves and trim the stems.

With a sharp knife, cut an X into stem end to speed cooking time. Rinse sprouts.

Color index page 71
Begin 1 hr ahead
6 servings
83 cals per serving
Low in cholesterol

Baked Brussels Sprouts

½ cup dried bread crumbs	*¾ teaspoon salt*
2 tablespoons butter or margarine, melted	*2 10-ounce packages frozen Brussels sprouts, partially thawed and drained*
¼ teaspoon cracked pepper	

1. Preheat oven to 350°F. In 2-quart casserole, stir all the ingredients, except Brussels sprouts, until thoroughly blended.
2. Add Brussels sprouts; toss to mix well; cover and bake 45 minutes until sprouts are tender-crisp.

Color index page 71
Begin 30 mins ahead
10 servings
72 cals per serving
Low in cholesterol

Sweet-and-Sour Brussels Sprouts

½ 8-ounce package sliced bacon, diced	*½ medium onion, minced*
3 10-ounce containers Brussels sprouts or 3 10-ounce packages frozen Brussels sprouts, thawed	*2 tablespoons cider vinegar*
	1 tablespoon sugar
	½ teaspoon salt
	¼ teaspoon dry mustard
	⅛ teaspoon pepper

1. In 5-quart Dutch oven or 4-quart saucepan over medium-low heat, cook diced bacon until browned. With slotted spoon, remove the bacon pieces to drain on paper towels.
2. In same Dutch oven, in bacon drippings, cook Brussels sprouts with onion, vinegar, sugar, salt, mustard and pepper until tender-crisp, about 10 minutes, stirring occasionally.
3. Stir bacon into Brussels sprouts mixture.

Cabbage

SAVOY CABBAGE   GREEN CABBAGE

Season: All year.

Look for: Firm heads, heavy for their size, with fresh, crisp leaves. Most popular green varieties include Danish, pointed and domestic. Savoy-type cabbage has crinkled green leaves, loosely formed heads. Red varieties have distinctive reddish-purple color.

To store: Refrigerate cabbage in crisper or wrapped in plastic bag. Use within 1 or 2 weeks.

To prepare: See below.

To cook: In saucepan over medium heat, in 1 inch boiling, salted water, heat cabbage to boiling. Reduce heat; cover and simmer 10 to 15 minutes for wedges, 3 to 10 minutes for shredded cabbage. Or, steam, stir-fry or cook in recipes.

Seasonings: Cook with allspice, caraway seed, cloves, curry, mustard, tarragon.

To serve: Eat cabbage raw in salads or serve hot, with or without seasonings.

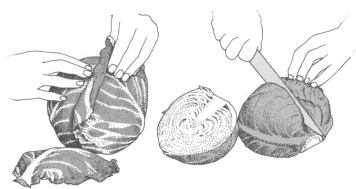

Preparing cabbage: Discard any wilted or discolored outer leaves. Rinse in cold water.

With a large sharp knife, cut the cabbage in half and then into quarters.

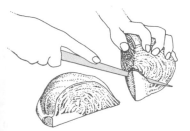

Cut core off each wedge, leaving just enough to retain shape of wedge.

Or, shred the cabbage, using a large sharp knife or shredder; discard core.

Skillet Cabbage

Color index page 69
Begin 30 mins ahead
8 servings
148 cals per serving
Low in cholesterol

8 bacon slices, diced	**1 medium cabbage,**
½ cup minced	**shredded**
onion	**1 teaspoon salt**

1. In 12-inch skillet over medium heat, fry diced bacon together with the minced onion until onion is tender, about 5 minutes.
2. Add shredded cabbage and salt and cook mixture, stirring occasionally with slotted spoon, until cabbage is tender, about 10 minutes.

Red Cabbage and Apples

Color index page 69
Begin 1 hr ahead
8 servings
123 cals per serving
Low in cholesterol
Good source of vitamin C

¼ cup butter or	**1 cup water**
margarine	**½ cup red wine**
2 medium cooking apples,	**vinegar**
peeled, cored and	**⅓ cup sugar**
thinly sliced	**1½ teaspoons salt**
1 medium onion,	**⅛ teaspoon pepper**
diced	**1 bay leaf**
1 medium head red	
cabbage, shredded	
(about 8 cups)	

1. In 4-quart saucepan over medium heat, in hot butter or margarine, cook apples and onion until tender, about 10 minutes.
2. Add cabbage, water, red wine vinegar, sugar, salt, pepper and bay leaf; heat mixture to boiling. Reduce heat to low; cover and simmer 40 minutes or until cabbage is very tender, stirring occasionally.
3. To serve, discard bay leaf.

Sautéed Caraway-Cabbage

Color index page 69
Begin 15 mins ahead
6 servings
86 cals per serving
Low in cholesterol

1 small green cabbage	**1 teaspoon caraway**
3 tablespoons salad	**seed**
oil	**¾ teaspoon salt**

1. With knife, coarsely shred cabbage.
2. In 5-quart Dutch oven over high heat, in hot salad oil, cook cabbage, caraway seed and salt, stirring quickly and frequently (stir-frying) until cabbage is tender-crisp, about 10 minutes.

Cabbage Relish

Color index page 69
Begin 3 hrs ahead
8 servings
68 cals per serving
Low in fat, cholesterol
Good source of vitamin C

¾ cup white vinegar	**1 cup cut-up green pepper**
¾ cup water	**(¾-inch cubes)**
1½ teaspoons salt	**2 4-ounce cans**
⅓ cup sugar	**pimentos, cut into**
1 tablespoon mustard	**¾-inch cubes**
seed	**1 red onion, thinly**
6 cups shredded green	**sliced**
cabbage	

1. In 3-quart saucepan, combine vinegar with water, salt, sugar and mustard seed. Over high heat, heat this marinade to boiling. Reduce heat to low; simmer 5 minutes; cool until warm.
2. In large bowl, combine cabbage, green pepper, pimentos, onion; pour marinade over vegetables, then toss to coat well.
3. Refrigerate relish, covered, 2 hours, tossing occasionally. Toss again before serving. Eat chilled, with cold sliced ham or pork.

Carrots

Season: All year.
Look for: Firm, well-formed, bright-orange-red carrots. Avoid flabby or shriveled ones.
To store: Refrigerate in crisper or in plastic bags. If carrots have tops, cut them off. Use within 1 or 2 weeks.
To prepare: See below.
To cook: In saucepan over medium heat, in 1 inch boiling, salted water, heat carrots to boiling. Reduce heat to low; cover and simmer until tender-crisp. Whole carrots will take about 20 minutes, cut-up carrots, 10 to 20 minutes. Or, use in stews, soups and casseroles.
Seasonings: Cook with cloves, curry, dill, ginger, mace, marjoram, mint, nutmeg.
To serve: Eat fresh in salads, for snacks; serve hot, with or without seasonings.

Preparing carrots: In cold water with a vegetable brush, scrub carrots or scrape with vegetable peeler. Cut off ends. Leave whole or cut in slices or chunks, slice into julienne strips or shred.

Glazed Carrots

Color index page 68

Begin 25 mins ahead

4 servings

96 cals per serving

water
1 pound carrots, cut in large chunks
salt
2 tablespoons butter
1 tablespoon sugar
¼ teaspoon ground nutmeg

1. In 2-quart saucepan over medium heat, in 1 inch boiling water, heat carrots and ¼ teaspoon salt to boiling. Reduce heat to low; cover and simmer 15 minutes or until tender-crisp; drain.
2. Add butter, sugar, nutmeg and ¼ teaspoon salt. Return mixture to heat and cook, stirring constantly, until carrots are glazed.

Spiced Carrots

Color index page 68

Begin 45 mins ahead

12 servings

149 cals per serving

¾ cup water
3 1-pound bags carrots, sliced ¼ inch thick
1 cup dark seedless raisins
½ cup butter or margarine
⅓ cup finely chopped onion
2 teaspoons ground cinnamon
1½ teaspoons salt
¼ cup packed brown sugar

1. In covered 4-quart saucepan over low heat, cook all ingredients except brown sugar 15 minutes or until the carrots are fork-tender, stirring the mixture occasionally.
2. Add brown sugar; cook until sugar is dissolved.

Cauliflower

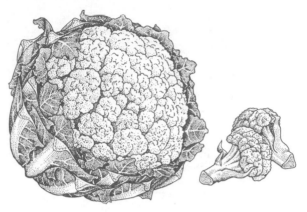

Season: All year. Best supplies in October, November.
Look for: Creamy-white, compact, tightly packed flowerets with a granular appearance. Leaves around base should be fresh and green.
To store: Refrigerate in crisper or wrapped; use quickly, within 3 to 5 days.
To prepare: See below.
To cook: In saucepan over medium heat, in 1 inch boiling, salted water, heat cauliflower to boiling. Reduce heat to low; cover and simmer 10 to 15 minutes for whole cauliflower, 8 minutes for flowerets, until tender-crisp; or, steam or use in recipes.
Seasonings: Cook with chives, paprika, cloves, nutmeg, dill, rosemary or thyme.
To serve: Eat fresh in salads or for snacks. Or, serve hot or cold, with or without sauce.

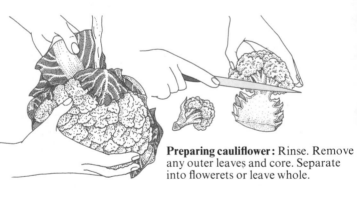

Preparing cauliflower: Rinse. Remove any outer leaves and core. Separate into flowerets or leave whole.

Cauliflower Polonaise

Color index page 67

Begin 20 mins ahead

6 servings

75 cals per serving

Good source of vitamin C

water
1 medium head cauliflower
salt
2 tablespoons butter
½ cup fresh bread crumbs
1 hard-cooked egg, chopped
1 tablespoon chopped parsley
1 tablespoon lemon juice

1. In 5-quart saucepot over medium heat, in 1 inch boiling water, heat cauliflower and ½ teaspoon salt to boiling. Reduce heat to low; cover and simmer 10 to 15 minutes until cauliflower is fork-tender; drain well. Place whole cauliflower in serving dish.
2. Meanwhile, in 1-quart saucepan over medium heat, melt butter; stir in crumbs; cook, tossing lightly, until golden. Stir in egg, parsley, juice and ¼ teaspoon salt. Sprinkle mixture over cauliflower.

Celery

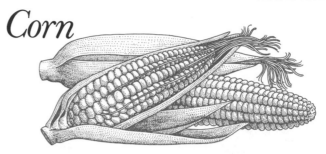

Corn

Season: All year.
Look for: Fresh, crisp, clean, medium-sized celery, pale green in color. Thin, dark-green stalks may be stringy.
To store: Refrigerate in crisper or wrapped in plastic bags; use within a week.
To prepare: See below.
To cook: In saucepan over medium heat, in 1 inch boiling, salted water, heat celery to boiling. Reduce heat to low; cover and simmer 4 to 6 minutes for whole stalks, 3 to 4 minutes for cut-up stalks, until tender-crisp. Or, use in recipes.
Seasonings: Serve celery with basil, chives, dill, mustard or tarragon.
To serve: Eat fresh for snacks, in salads; or serve hot or cold, with or without sauce.

Season: All year. Best supplies May to September.
Look for: Medium-size ears of corn with bright, plump, milky kernels just firm enough to offer slight resistance to pressure. Tiny kernels indicate immaturity; very large, deep yellow kernels may be tough.
To store: Refrigerate ears of corn in crisper. Use as soon as possible.
To prepare: See below.
To cook: In large saucepot over medium heat, in 1 inch boiling, salted water, heat corn to boiling. Reduce heat to low; cover and simmer medium-size ears of corn 5 to 6 minutes. Or, use in recipes.
Seasonings: Cook with basil, chili powder, chives, onions, oregano, garlic.
To serve: Spread corn-on-cob with butter, margarine or flavored butters (below), sprinkle with salt and eat in hands. Or, with sharp knife, cut cooked corn from cob and serve as a vegetable.

Preparing celery: Cut off leaves (use leaves as seasoning in soups or stews); trim root.

Brush celery stalks well under running cold water; drain well.

Preparing corn: Just before cooking, remove any outer husks and silk from corn.

Use a small vegetable brush to remove any remaining silk.

Color index page 71

Begin 20 mins ahead

6 servings
51 cals per serving
Low in cholesterol

Sautéed Celery

1 small bunch celery	*³/₄ teaspoon thyme leaves*
2 tablespoons salad oil	*¹/₂ teaspoon salt*
2 bay leaves	*¹/₄ teaspoon pepper*

1. With sharp knife, cut celery diagonally into thin even-sized slices.
2. In 12-inch skillet over medium heat, in hot salad oil, cook celery and remaining ingredients until celery is tender-crisp, about 5 minutes, stirring the mixture occasionally.
3. Discard bay leaves and serve immediately.

Begin 30 mins ahead
6 servings
76 cals per serving
Low in cholesterol

SAUTEED CELERY WITH GREEN ONIONS:
In 4-quart saucepan over medium heat, in *3 tablespoons hot salad oil*, cook *1 bunch green onions*, cut into 3-inch pieces, *1 small bunch celery*, cut into 3-inch-long matchstick-thin strips, *2 bay leaves, 1 teaspoon thyme leaves, ¹/₂ teaspoon salt* and *¹/₄ teaspoon pepper* until vegetables are tender-crisp, about 5 minutes, stirring occasionally. Discard bay leaves and serve immediately.

Cut cooked corn from the cob and use in recipes for main dishes, salads, relishes and vegetable casseroles.

Color index page 70

FLAVORED BUTTERS FOR CORN

CHILI BUTTER: In small bowl with wooden spoon, beat *¹/₂ cup butter* or margarine, softened, *1 teaspoon salt, 1 teaspoon chili powder* and *¹/₄ teaspoon pepper* until well blended. (Makes ¹/₂ cup.)

CHIVE BUTTER: Prepare butter as above but substitute *2 teaspoons chopped chives* for chili powder.

DILL BUTTER: Prepare butter as above but substitute *1 teaspoon dill weed* for chili powder.

Cucumbers

Season: All year. Best supplies from May to August.

Look for: Firm, well-shaped cucumbers with good, green color. Overmature ones are dull or yellow and look overgrown and puffy. Smaller varieties of cucumber are ideal for pickling.

To store: Refrigerate; use within 3 to 5 days.

To prepare: Rinse in cold water. Trim ends and cut cucumber into desired shapes. It is not necessary to peel cucumber unless called for in recipe.

To cook: Halve cucumber lengthwise. In saucepan over medium heat, in 1 inch boiling, salted water, heat cucumber to boiling. Reduce heat to low; cover and simmer 5 to 10 minutes, until tender-crisp. Or use in recipes for pickles or cold soup.

Seasonings: Sprinkle pepper, dill, tarragon, parsley or chives over sliced fresh cucumber.

To serve: Eat raw, in salads, or as cooked vegetable.

Sautéed Cucumber Rings

Color index
page 70

Begin 30 mins
ahead

4 servings

71 cals per
serving

3 medium cucumbers	1/2 teaspoon salt
2 tablespoons butter	1/8 teaspoon pepper

1. Peel cucumbers. Cut each cucumber crosswise into thirds; with spoon, remove seeds. Cut cucumbers crosswise into 1/4-inch-thick slices to form rings.

2. In 12-inch skillet over medium-high heat, melt butter; add cucumber rings, salt and pepper; cook 10 minutes or until cucumbers are just tender-crisp, stirring occasionally.

CUCUMBER GARNISHES

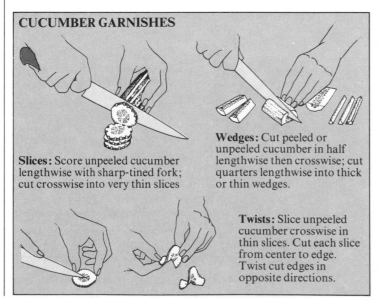

Slices: Score unpeeled cucumber lengthwise with sharp-tined fork; cut crosswise into very thin slices

Wedges: Cut peeled or unpeeled cucumber in half lengthwise then crosswise; cut quarters lengthwise into thick or thin wedges.

Twists: Slice unpeeled cucumber crosswise in thin slices. Cut each slice from center to edge. Twist cut edges in opposite directions.

Eggplant

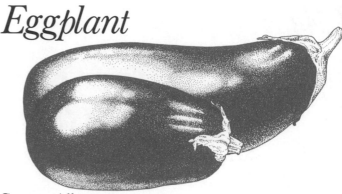

Season: All year.

Look for: Firm, heavy eggplant free from blemishes with a uniformly dark, rich purple color and a bright green cap. Avoid wrinkled or flabby eggplant which are usually bitter-tasting.

To store: Refrigerate. Use within 1 or 2 days.

To prepare: See below.

To cook: In large saucepan over medium heat, in 1 inch boiling, salted water, heat eggplant to boiling. Reduce heat to low; cover and simmer about 5 minutes or until tender. Or, sauté or use in recipes for main dishes or with other vegetables.

Seasonings: Cook with oregano, sage, garlic.

To serve: Eat as cooked vegetable.

Preparing eggplant: With knife, trim stem end and slice or cut unpeeled eggplant into desired shape just before cooking; eggplant discolors quickly.

Eggplant with Caraway Seed

Color index
page 69

Begin 25 mins
ahead

4 servings

324 cals per
serving

2 tablespoons salad oil	1 teaspoon caraway seed
3/4 cup chopped bacon slices	2 teaspoons vinegar
	3/4 teaspoon salt
1 medium onion, sliced	1 small eggplant, cubed

1. In 10-inch skillet over medium-high heat, in hot salad oil, cook all ingredients but eggplant 5 minutes or until bacon and onion are light brown.

2. Reduce heat to medium; add eggplant and cook, covered, 5 to 7 minutes until eggplant is tender, stirring occasionally.

Sautéed Eggplant Slices

Color index
page 69

Begin 15 mins
ahead

4 servings

217 cals per
serving

1 medium eggplant (about 1 pound)	3/4 cup water
	3/4 teaspoon salt
1/3 cup olive or salad oil	1/8 teaspoon pepper
2 tablespoons butter or margarine	chopped parsley

1. With knife, cut eggplant crosswise into 1/2-inch-thick slices; cut each slice in half. In 12-inch skillet over medium-high heat, in hot oil and butter or margarine, cook eggplant, stirring constantly, until well coated with oil mixture.

2. Add water, salt and pepper; cook, stirring frequently, until eggplant slices are tender, about 5 minutes more. To serve, garnish with parsley.

Endives, Belgian

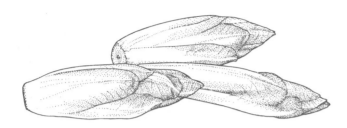

Also known as French endives.
Season: September to June.
Look for: Small, compact endives with white leaves edged with pale green. Avoid any with wilted outer leaves. (For curly endives, see Lettuce and other greens, page 287.)
To store: Refrigerate in crisper or wrapped in plastic bags. Use within 1 or 2 days.
To prepare: See below.
To cook: In saucepan over medium heat, in ½ inch boiling, salted water, heat endives to boiling. Reduce heat to low; cover and simmer about 15 minutes, until endives are tender-crisp.
Seasonings: Cook with lemon, ground nutmeg.
To serve: Eat raw, with dressing as salad or appetizer. Or serve hot as vegetable.

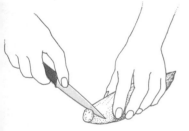

Preparing endives: Rinse in cold water, then with a small sharp knife, cut root ends from endives.

With hands, remove any wilted or bruised outer leaves.

Color index page 69

Begin 1 hr ahead

6 servings

232 cals per serving

Good source of calcium, vitamin A

Endives with Swiss Cheese

water	¼ cup butter or
12 small Belgian endives	margarine
salt	pepper
½ pound natural Swiss	⅓ cup half-and-half
cheese, shredded	

1. In 4-quart saucepan over medium heat, in 1 inch boiling water, heat endives and 1 teaspoon salt to boiling. Reduce heat to low; cover and simmer 10 minutes; drain. Preheat oven to 350°F.
2. Arrange 6 endives in metal 12″ by 8″ baking dish; sprinkle with half of cheese and dot with half of butter or margarine; sprinkle lightly with salt and pepper. Repeat.
3. Pour half-and-half over all. Bake 10 to 15 minutes until cheese is melted.
4. Turn heat control to broil; place baking dish under broiler for about 3 minutes until the cheese is golden brown and bubbling.

Fennel

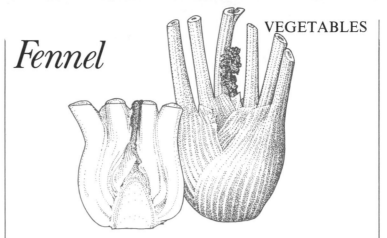

Also known as anise, sweet anise or finocchio.
Season: October to March.
Look for: Well-shaped white bulbs with green, feather-like leaves.
To store: Refrigerate fennel in crisper or wrapped in plastic bags. Use within 3 to 5 days.
To prepare: See below.
To cook: In saucepan over medium heat, in ½ inch boiling, salted water, heat cut-up fennel to boiling. Reduce heat to low; cover and simmer 10 to 20 minutes or until tender. Or use in recipes for tomato sauce or fish soups. Flavor is pungent, so use sparingly as seasoning.
To serve: Serve raw as a snack or use in salads as celery. Use cooked pieces as vegetable with melted butter or margarine and lemon juice.

Preparing fennel: Rinse in cold water. Cut off root ends and leaves from bulb.

Cut bulb lengthwise in half then slice into sticks or pieces.

Color index page 68

Begin 30 mins ahead

4 servings

82 cals per serving

Braised Fennel

2 large bunches fennel	2 tablespoons butter or
1¾ cups water	margarine, softened
2 chicken-flavor bouillon	1 tablespoon all-purpose
cubes or envelopes	flour

1. With knife, cut top off each bulb of fennel just below leaves, leaving stalks and bulb about 6 inches long. Cut bulb lengthwise in half. Chop enough fennel leaves to measure 2 tablespoons; set aside. Refrigerate leftover leaves for garnish another day.
2. In 12-inch skillet over medium heat, heat fennel, water and bouillon to boiling. Reduce heat to low; cover and simmer 15 minutes or until fennel bulbs are tender.
3. Meanwhile, in small bowl with spoon, blend butter or margarine and flour until smooth. With slotted pancake turner, remove fennel to serving dish; keep warm. With wire whisk, stir butter mixture into liquid remaining in skillet. Over medium heat, cook, stirring, until mixture is slightly thickened and boils. Spoon sauce over fennel. Garnish with chopped fennel leaves.

VEGETABLES
Kohlrabi

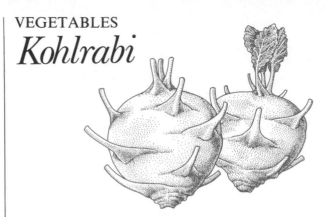

Season: May to November. Best supplies of kohlrabi are in June and July.

Look for: Small or medium-size bulbs with fresh tops and tender rind.

To store: Cut off tops and discard. Refrigerate and use within 2 or 3 days.

To prepare: See below.

To cook: In a saucepan over medium heat, in 1 inch boiling, salted water, heat cut-up kohlrabi to boiling. Reduce heat to low; cover and simmer 15 to 30 minutes or until kohlrabi is tender.

Seasonings: Cook with mustard, tarragon.

To serve: Eat peeled raw strips as snack or appetizer. Use cooked pieces as a vegetable; use in recipes.

Preparing kohlrabi: Rinse in cold water, then with a small sharp knife, peel kohlrabi thinly and slice or cut up.

Cheesy Kohlrabi

Color index page 71

Begin 45 mins ahead

6 servings

130 cals per serving

Good source of vitamin C

water
8 medium kohlrabi, peeled and sliced into ¼-inch slices
½ teaspoon salt
3 tablespoons butter
¼ cup all-purpose flour
1 10½-ounce can condensed chicken broth
¼ cup shredded American cheese
⅛ teaspoon ground allspice
2 tablespoons chopped parsley for garnish

1. In 2-quart saucepan over medium heat, in 1 inch boiling water, heat kohlrabi and salt to boiling. Reduce heat to low; cover and simmer 30 minutes or until tender; drain.
2. Meanwhile, in 3-quart saucepan over low heat, into hot butter, stir flour until smooth. Gradually add undiluted chicken broth and cook, stirring constantly, until mixture is thickened.
3. Remove from heat and stir in cheese until melted and smooth. Add kohlrabi and cook until heated through. Sprinkle the mixture with allspice, then garnish with the chopped parsley.

Leeks

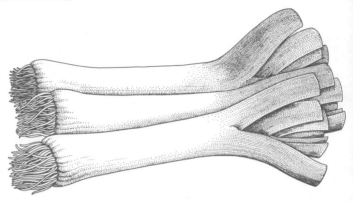

Season: All year. Best supplies September to November.

Look for: Leeks with white bulb base and fresh green tops, usually trimmed.

To store: Refrigerate, wrapped. Use within 3 to 5 days.

To prepare: See below.

To cook: In saucepan over medium heat, in 1 inch boiling, salted water, heat leeks to boiling. Reduce heat to low; cover and simmer 10 to 15 minutes or until tender; drain. Or use in recipes for soups or main dishes.

Seasonings: Cook with ginger, rosemary or sage.

To serve: Eat raw, finely shredded, in salads. Or use leeks as cooked vegetable.

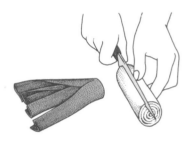

Preparing leeks: Cut off roots and trim leaf end. Cut leeks crosswise in half, then cut root ends lengthwise in half.

Rinse under running cold water to remove sand. Use halved or cut up.

To cook a large amount, tie leeks loosely with string into bundles; cook 30 minutes; when done, remove strings.

Leeks au Gratin

Color index page 70

Begin 45 mins ahead

4 servings

340 cals per serving

Good source of calcium, iron, vitamin A

8 medium leeks
3 tablespoons butter
3 tablespoons all-purpose flour
½ teaspoon dry mustard
½ teaspoon salt
1 cup milk
1 cup shredded Cheddar cheese
1 cup fresh bread crumbs

1. Cook leeks; place in broilersafe 9″ by 9″ baking pan. Preheat broiler if manufacturer directs.
2. In 1-quart saucepan over low heat, melt butter; stir in flour, mustard and salt till smooth. Gradually stir in milk; cook, stirring, until thickened; stir in cheese till melted; pour mixture over leeks.
3. Sprinkle with crumbs. Broil to brown crumbs.

Lettuce and other greens

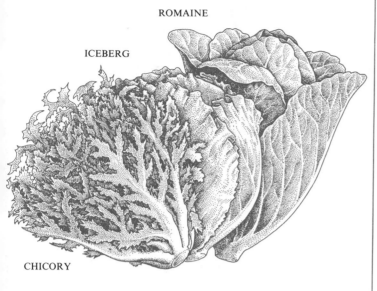

ROMAINE

ICEBERG

CHICORY

Season: All year.
Look for: Clean, crisp, tender leaves, free from decay or dirt. Crisphead varieties of lettuce (including Iceberg) have solid heads and are heavy for their size. Butterhead lettuces (including Boston and Bibb) have soft leaves with lighter-color inside leaves; Cos or Romaine lettuce have crisp coarse leaves with heavy midribs; looseleaf lettuces (including Bunching) have soft textured leaves, and are available either in long bunches or loose. Stem lettuce (Celtuce) has an enlarged stem (leaves are peeled and stem is eaten fresh or in Chinese recipes). Other greens include beet or turnip tops, cilantro (Mexican or Chinese parsley), Swiss chard, dandelion, Belgian endive (see page 285), escarole, kale, collards, leafy broccoli, mustard greens, parsley, rape, sorrel, chicory (curly endive), rapini, spinach (see page 293) and watercress. All these other greens should have fresh tender green leaves and be free from excessive sand or dirt; injured, dried or yellow leaves and coarse stems usually indicate poor quality and may cause waste.
To store: All greens which are to be served raw should be refrigerated in a crisper or plastic bag. Use Crisphead lettuce within 3 to 5 days. Use looser, leafier kinds of lettuce and other greens within 1 or 2 days.
To prepare: See pages 316 to 317.
To cook: In deep skillet or Dutch oven over medium heat, in ¼ inch boiling, salted water, cook tender leafy greens 1 to 3 minutes, until wilted, stirring occasionally; cook other greens 5 to 10 minutes or until tender-crisp. Lettuce is also good stir-fried, braised or used in recipes for vegetable dishes, soups and "wilted" salads.
Seasonings: Cook with allspice, bacon drippings, lemon, onion, nutmeg, vinegar.
To serve: Eat lettuce and other greens fresh in salads with dressings; use as cooked vegetable; in sandwiches or to garnish salads and main dishes.

Mushrooms

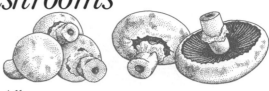

Season: All year.
Look for: Firm, plump, cream-colored mushrooms with short, clean-cut stems and caps that are either closed around the stems or slightly open, and with pink or light-tan gills. Buy only cultivated mushrooms. Wild varieties may be poisonous.
To store: Refrigerate, covered. Use within 1 or 2 days.
To prepare: See below.
To cook: Brush with melted butter or margarine and broil 4 to 5 minutes until fork-tender, or sauté (below) or use in recipes for soups and main dishes.
Seasonings: Cook with garlic, lemon, onion, nutmeg.
To serve: Eat raw in salads or serve hot as a vegetable.

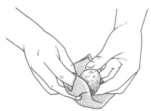 

Preparing mushrooms: Do not peel or soak; rinse in cold water; drain well. Pat dry with paper towels. Cut thin slice from stem.

Leave whole; or cut mushrooms in thin slices parallel to the stem; or cook as recipe directs.

Sautéed Mushrooms

Color index page 69

Begin 20 mins ahead

4 servings

214 cals per serving

Good source of vitamin A

¼ cup butter or margarine
2 tablespoons minced onion
1 pound mushrooms, sliced

1 teaspoon lemon juice
½ teaspoon salt
⅛ teaspoon pepper
4 white bread slices, toasted and buttered

1. In 10-inch skillet over medium heat, in hot butter or margarine, cook onion until tender, about 5 minutes. Add mushrooms; cook, covered, stirring occasionally, about 10 minutes.
2. Stir in lemon juice, salt and pepper. Serve mixture on hot buttered toast, or as is.

244 cals per serving
Good source of vitamin A

MUSHROOMS IN CREAM: Prepare as for Sautéed Mushrooms but omit lemon juice and stir in *2 tablespoons dry sherry* and *⅓ cup half-and-half*.

Mushrooms in Sour Cream

Color index page 69

Begin 30 mins ahead

12 servings

99 cals per serving

½ cup butter or margarine
2 pounds mushrooms, sliced
½ cup minced green onions

1 teaspoon salt
½ teaspoon pepper
½ cup sour cream

1. In 12-inch skillet over medium-high heat, melt butter. Add mushrooms, green onions, salt and pepper and cook, stirring frequently, until mushrooms are tender, about 10 minutes.
2. Stir in sour cream; heat through (do not boil). Spoon mushroom mixture into medium bowl. Serve warm or refrigerate to serve cold later.

Okra

Season: All year. Best supplies from May to October.
Look for: Young, tender green pods 4 to 8 inches long.
To store: Refrigerate. Use within 1 to 2 days.
To prepare: See below.
To cook: In saucepan over medium heat, in 1 inch boiling, salted water, heat okra to boiling. Reduce heat to low; cover and simmer whole okra 5 to 10 minutes or cut-up okra 3 to 5 minutes. Use in recipes.
Seasonings: Cook with cayenne or onions.
To serve: Eat okra as a cooked vegetable, hot or cold.

Preparing okra: Wash in cold water. Cut off stems. Leave okra whole or cut into pieces.

Okra Vinaigrette

Color index page 69

Begin 4½ hrs or day ahead

6 servings

181 cals per serving

Low in cholesterol

Good source of vitamin A

water
2 pounds okra
salt
½ cup olive or salad oil
⅓ cup white vinegar
½ teaspoon dry mustard
½ teaspoon thyme leaves

¼ teaspoon sugar
⅛ teaspoon pepper
1 large garlic clove, crushed
¼ cup chopped pimento
Boston lettuce leaves

1 In 12-inch skillet over medium heat, in 1 inch boiling water, heat okra and ½ teaspoon salt to boiling. Cover and cook 5 minutes or until tender.

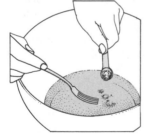

2 In large bowl with fork, mix well 1¼ teaspoons salt with oil and remaining ingredients except pimento and Boston lettuce.

3 Add okra and pimento; toss to coat mixture thoroughly. Cover and refrigerate at least 4 hours or overnight, tossing occasionally.

4 *Just before serving:* Line 6 individual salad plates with Boston lettuce leaves, then arrange chilled okra mixture on top of lettuce.

Onions

Season: All year.
Look for: Clean, firm onions, with dry, brittle, papery skins. Avoid onions which have begun sprouting.
To store: Store in refrigerator or cool room temperature (60°F. or below) in container allowing good circulation of air. Keep dry. Onions may be stored several months.
To prepare: See below.
To cook: In saucepan over medium heat, in 1 inch boiling, salted water, heat whole onions to boiling. Reduce heat to low; cover and simmer 15 to 20 minutes until tender. Or, use in recipes.
Seasonings: Cook with cloves, dill, nutmeg or paprika.
To serve: Eat raw in sandwiches and salads. Or serve hot or cold, with or without sauce.

Preparing onions: With a small sharp knife, cut off stem and roots; pull off dry, outer skin.

Slice, chop or dice. To dice: Cut onion in half; place half on cut side; cut lengthwise into ¼-inch slices; hold together and cut crosswise into ¼-inch slices.

Baked Onions

Color index page 67

Begin 1 hr ahead

8 servings

127 cals per serving

⅓ cup honey
¼ cup butter

½ teaspoon salt
6 large onions, sliced

1. Preheat oven to 425°F. In 1-quart saucepan over medium heat, heat honey, butter and salt.
2. In greased 13″ by 9″ baking dish, arrange onions; pour honey-butter mixture evenly over onions. Bake 45 minutes or until onions are fork-tender and golden brown in color.

Glazed Onions

Color index page 67

Begin 30 mins ahead

4 servings

161 cals per serving

water
1½ pounds medium onions
⅓ cup sugar

2 tablespoons butter or margarine
¼ teaspoon salt

1. In 2-quart saucepan over medium heat, in 1 inch boiling water, heat onions to boiling. Reduce heat to low; cover and simmer 15 to 20 minutes; drain.
2. In 10-inch skillet over low heat, stir sugar, butter, 2 teaspoons water and salt until mixed.
3. Add onions; cook until golden and glazed, about 5 minutes, stirring occasionally.

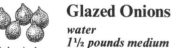

Parsnips

Season: All year.
Look for: Smooth, firm, well-shaped parsnips of medium size. Avoid any large, coarse roots or ones with gray or soft spots.
To store: Refrigerate. Use within 2 weeks.
To prepare: See below.
To cook: In saucepan over medium heat, in 1 inch boiling, salted water, heat parsnips to boiling. Reduce heat to low; cover and simmer 20 to 30 minutes for whole vegetables, 8 to 15 minutes for cut-up parsnips or until tender. Use in recipes for soups, stews, pot roasts. Or, mash and season as potatoes.
Seasonings: Serve parsnips with cinnamon, ginger, orange or tarragon.
To serve: Eat as cooked vegetable. Serve with Hollandaise Sauce or White Sauce (page 461).

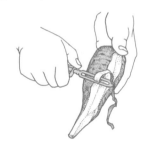

Preparing parsnips: Scrub the parsnips in cold water; cut off stem ends and tails.

Remove skin of parsnips with a vegetable peeler.

Leave parsnips whole; or halve, slice or cut them into quarters as shown, right.

Pan-fried Onions

Color index page 67
Begin 15 mins ahead
4 servings
132 cals per serving
Good source of vitamin A

¼ cup butter or margarine	1 teaspoon salt
4 to 5 medium onions, thinly sliced	¼ teaspoon thyme leaves
	⅛ teaspoon pepper

1. In 10-inch skillet over medium heat, in hot butter, cook onions, covered, 5 minutes.
2. Add salt, thyme and pepper; cook, uncovered, until onions are tender, about 8 minutes, stirring onion mixture occasionally.

French-fried Onions

Color index page 67
Begin 30 mins ahead
8 servings
147 cals per serving
Low in cholesterol, sodium

3 large onions, sliced ¼ inch thick	½ cup milk
salad oil	1 cup all-purpose flour
	½ teaspoon salt

1. Separate onion slices into rings. In electric skillet, heat ¾ inch salad oil to 370°F.
2. In small dish, place milk. In small bowl, stir flour and salt until mixed. Dip rings in milk, then in flour mixture. Repeat to coat twice.
3. In hot salad oil, cook onions 3 minutes or until lightly browned. Drain thoroughly on paper towels. Serve immediately.

Creamed Onions

Color index page 67
Begin 30 mins ahead
10 servings
126 cals per serving
Good source of vitamin A

water	3 tablespoons all-purpose flour
salt	
2 pounds small white onions	1½ cups milk
6 tablespoons butter or margarine	paprika

1. In 2-quart saucepan over medium heat, in 1 inch boiling, salted water, heat onions to boiling. Reduce heat to low; cover and simmer 10 to 15 minutes or until the onions are tender.
2. Meanwhile, in 1-quart saucepan over medium heat, melt butter; stir in flour until smooth; slowly stir in milk and ¼ teaspoon salt and cook, stirring constantly, until thickened.
3. Drain onions and place in serving dish; pour on sauce and sprinkle lightly with paprika.

GREEN ONIONS, SCALLIONS AND SHALLOTS

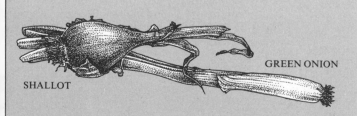

GREEN ONION

SHALLOT

Green onions, shoots of any onion harvested before the bulb forms, are available all year. Eat fresh or use in recipes. *Scallions* technically are shoots of white onions only; in a few places in the United States, the word scallion is used to mean green onions. *Shallots* have distinctive bulbs made up of cloves like garlic. Green shallots are available in summer, dry bulbs are available year round. Use in recipes.

Parsley Creamed Parsnips

Color index page 68
Begin 30 mins ahead
6 servings
56 cals per serving
Low in fat, cholesterol

1 pound parsnips	½ cup milk
1 cup water	⅛ teaspoon pepper
salt	1 teaspoon grated orange peel
2 tablespoons all-purpose flour	chopped parsley

1. Peel parsnips, then slice in ⅛-inch slices. In 2-quart saucepan over medium heat, heat parsnips, water and ½ teaspoon salt to boiling. Reduce heat to low; cover and simmer about 10 minutes until parsnips are fork-tender. Drain parsnips, reserving ½ cup liquid.
2. In 1-quart saucepan over medium heat, stir flour with milk until well mixed. Add reserved liquid, pepper and ½ teaspoon salt; cook, stirring constantly, until thickened and smooth. Stir in grated orange peel. Stir sauce with parsnips. Sprinkle mixture lightly with chopped parsley.

Peas

Season: All year. Best supplies January to August.
Look for: Fresh, young pods, light-green in color, slightly velvety to the touch and well filled with well-developed peas. Pods with immature peas are usually flat, dark green, wilted; overmature pods are swollen, light, wrinkled and yellowish, flecked with gray.
To store: Refrigerate in pods. Use within 2 days.
To prepare: See below.
To cook: In saucepan over medium heat, in 1 inch boiling, salted water, heat peas to boiling. Reduce heat to low; cover and simmer 5 to 8 minutes, until tender.
Seasonings: Cook with chives, lettuce leaves, marjoram, mint, nutmeg, oregano, onion, savory, rosemary, tarragon, thyme.
To serve: Eat as cooked vegetable.

Preparing peas: Press pods between thumb and forefinger to open; push peas out with thumb. Rinse peas in colander under running cold water. Discard pods.

Peas Amandine

Color index
page 70

Begin 40 mins
ahead

4 servings
484 cals per
serving

Good source
of iron

2 pounds peas
water
salt
2/3 cup chopped bacon
*   slices*

1/4 cup minced onion
1/2 cup slivered almonds
1/2 cup heavy or whipping
*   cream*

1. Shell peas (yield should be about 1 2/3 cups).
2. In 2-quart saucepan over medium heat, in 1 inch boiling water, heat peas and 1 teaspoon salt to boiling. Reduce heat to low; cover pan and simmer 5 minutes; drain.
3. In 10-inch skillet over medium heat, fry bacon and onion until light brown. Add peas, almonds and salt to taste; heat through. Stir in cream. Serve in individual dishes.

SNOW PEAS

Snow peas, also known as Chinese peas, are in season from May to September. Look for delicate fresh green, thin pea pods. Refrigerate and use within a day or two. To prepare, just rinse in cold water, carefully stem and string the pods (do not shell). Cook as for ordinary peas and eat pod and all, as a cooked vegetable or in recipes for Chinese dishes.

Peppers

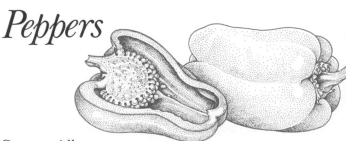

Season: All year.
Look for: Peppers that are firm, shiny and thick-fleshed, medium to dark green. When mature, peppers turn red. Pimentos are a mild, sweet pepper.
To store: Refrigerate. Use within 3 to 5 days.
To prepare: See below.
To cook: Cook in recipes for main dishes or casseroles and as a seasoning for meat, in Creole, Spanish and Italian dishes. For stuffed peppers, parboil before stuffing: In large saucepan over high heat, in boiling water to cover, cook peppers 3 to 5 minutes; drain.
To serve: Eat fresh in salads; as cooked vegetable.

Preparing peppers: Rinse in cold water. Cut around stem; remove core, seeds and white membrane.

Use whole, to stuff. Or, cut into rings, strips or halves, dice or slivers.

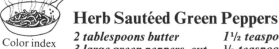

Herb Sautéed Green Peppers

Color index
page 70

Begin 15 mins
ahead

4 servings
73 cals per
serving

Good source
of vitamin C

2 tablespoons butter
3 large green peppers, cut
*   into 1/2-inch strips*

1 1/2 teaspoons marjoram
1/2 teaspoon salt

In 12-inch skillet over medium heat, in hot butter, cook all ingredients until peppers are tender, about 10 minutes, stirring occasionally.

Marinated Peppers

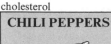

Color index
page 70

Begin early
in day or
day ahead

6 servings
108 cals per
serving

Low in
cholesterol

6 large green peppers
1/3 cup mayonnaise
1/4 cup white wine vinegar

2 teaspoons sugar
1 teaspoon salt
1/4 teaspoon white pepper

1. Preheat oven to 450°F. On cookie sheet, place peppers; bake 15 minutes or until skin puckers. Peel skin while warm; core; cut into 1/4-inch strips.
2. In medium bowl, combine remaining ingredients until smooth. Add pepper strips; toss until strips are well coated; cover and refrigerate.
3. *To serve:* Drain sauce from pepper strips.

CHILI PEPPERS

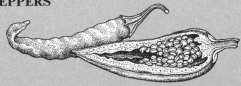

Chili peppers, the hot varieties of pepper, are smaller than sweet peppers and can be red, green or yellow. Use in salads, main dishes; prepare with care, washing hands after handling.

Potatoes

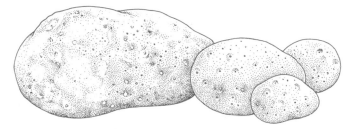

Season: All year.

Look for: Smooth, well-shaped, firm potatoes free of blemishes or sprouts.

To store: Store in dark, dry place at coolest room temperature (don't refrigerate) for about 1 week.

To prepare: See below.

To cook: Boiled potatoes: In saucepan over high heat, heat potatoes and enough salted water to cover to boiling. Reduce heat to low; cover and simmer new potatoes 15 to 20 minutes, general-purpose potatoes about 30 minutes, or until tender. Potatoes are also good baked or fried or used in recipes.

Seasonings: Sprinkle cooked potato with basil, caraway seed, celery seed, chives, dill, onion, thyme.

To serve: Eat as cooked vegetable in recipes for main dishes, casseroles; or eat in hot or cold salads.

Preparing potatoes:
Scrub in cold water. Remove skin with vegetable peeler. Use quickly to avoid discoloration and loss of food value. When possible, cook without peeling to save nutrients.

Baked Potatoes

Color index page 71
Begin 1 hr ahead
6 servings
149 cals each (without topping)
Low in cholesterol, sodium

6 medium baking potatoes, unpeeled
shortening or salad oil

Toppings: *sour cream, butter or margarine, shredded Cheddar cheese*

Preheat oven to 450°F. Wash and dry potatoes; rub with shortening. If you like a steamed texture, wrap potatoes in foil. Place in shallow pan. Bake 45 minutes or until fork-tender. Serve with choice of toppings. If desired, slash top.

Mashed Potatoes

Color index page 71
Begin 50 mins ahead
6 servings
195 cals per serving

6 medium potatoes, peeled
salt
water

¼ cup butter or margarine
¼ teaspoon pepper
¼ to ½ cup hot milk

1. In 3-quart saucepan over high heat, heat potatoes, 1 teaspoon salt and water to cover to boiling. Reduce heat to low; cover potatoes and simmer 30 minutes or until fork tender; drain.
2. In large bowl with mixer at low speed, beat potatoes, butter, 1 teaspoon salt and pepper until fluffy. Beating at medium speed, slowly add milk until mixture is moist; continue beating 2 minutes or until mixture is smooth.

French-fried Potatoes

Color index page 71
Begin 30 mins ahead
8 servings
225 cals per serving

salad oil   **salt**
8 medium potatoes

1. In deep-fat fryer, heat about 2 inches oil to 400°F.
2. Meanwhile, peel potatoes; cut potatoes into ¼-inch slices; cut slices into ¼-inch lengthwise strips. Or, use crinkle cutter to cut strips. Rinse in cold water; drain; dry well with paper towels.
3. Cover bottom of fryer basket with even layer of potatoes; gently lower into hot oil and fry 5 minutes or until golden brown; drain on paper towels. Repeat with remaining potatoes. Sprinkle lightly with salt to taste; serve immediately.

Cutting potato strips: Cut ¼-inch-thick slices; cut slices into ¼-inch strips.

Using crinkle cutter: Cut slices or strips with cutter for special effect.

Pan-roasted Potatoes

Color index page 71
Begin 1¼ hrs ahead
6 servings
181 cals per serving

6 medium potatoes, peeled
1 teaspoon salt
water

paprika, parsley or thyme leaves

1. In 3-quart saucepan over high heat, heat potatoes, salt and water to cover potatoes to boiling. Reduce heat to low; cover and simmer 10 minutes.
2. Drain potatoes; arrange around beef or pork roast in roasting pan; turn to coat with drippings in pan. Bake 40 to 60 minutes at 325°F. along with roast, turning occasionally, just until tender and evenly browned all over.
3. To serve: Sprinkle potatoes with paprika, parsley or thyme. Arrange around roast on platter.

VARIATION: When not roasting with meat, boil potatoes as above. Meanwhile, preheat oven to 400°F. In shallow baking pan, melt *½ cup butter* or margarine. Add boiled potatoes to melted butter or margarine, turning to coat evenly. Bake, turning often, 40 minutes or until tender.

Home-fried Potatoes

Color index page 71
Begin 25 mins ahead
4 servings
206 cals per serving

3 tablespoons bacon drippings
4 medium potatoes, cooked, peeled and thinly sliced

salt and pepper
paprika

In 10-inch skillet over medium-high heat, in hot drippings, fry potato slices 10 minutes or until browned, occasionally turning with pancake turner. Sprinkle with salt, pepper and paprika to taste.

Potatoes

Hash Brown Potatoes

Color index
page 71

Begin 45 mins
ahead

6 servings

247 cals per
serving

Good source
of vitamin A

½ cup butter
5 or 6 medium potatoes,
  peeled and finely diced
  or coarsely shredded
  (about 6 cups)
1 teaspoon salt
½ teaspoon paprika
  (optional)
¼ teaspoon pepper

1. In 10-inch skillet (preferably with a non-stick finish) over medium heat, in hot butter, cook potatoes, covered, 10 minutes.
2. Uncover and sprinkle potatoes with salt, paprika and pepper.
3. Continue cooking 15 minutes or until the potatoes are tender and brown, occasionally turning with a pancake turner.

Potatoes au Gratin

Color index
page 71

Begin 55 mins
ahead

6 servings

251 cals per
serving

Good source
of vitamin A

3 tablespoons butter or
  margarine
5 or 6 medium potatoes,
  peeled and thinly sliced
  (about 6 cups)
1½ teaspoons salt
1 4-ounce package
  shredded Cheddar
  cheese (1 cup)
½ cup fresh bread
  crumbs

1. Preheat oven to 425°F. In 12″ by 8″ baking pan in oven, melt butter. Remove from oven. Add potatoes and salt; toss together and arrange potatoes in even layer in baking pan.
2. Sprinkle with cheese and bread crumbs. Cover with foil. Bake 20 minutes; uncover and bake 15 minutes more or until potatoes are tender.

Potatoes Anna

Color index
page 71

Begin 1½ hrs
ahead

4 servings

185 cals per
serving

2 tablespoons butter or
  margarine
1 teaspoon salt
3 large potatoes, peeled
  (about 4 cups)

1. In 1-quart saucepan over low heat, melt butter with salt. Preheat oven to 425°F.
2. With knife, slice potatoes about ¼ inch thick.
3. In greased 8-inch pie plate, arrange potato slices, overlapping them; drizzle butter mixture on top. Cover plate tightly with foil; bake 20 minutes.
4. Uncover and bake about 55 minutes more or until potatoes are very tender and crusty.
5. Let stand at room temperature 5 minutes. With metal spatula, carefully loosen potatoes from pie plate. Place inverted plate over potatoes; holding both plates, invert and unmold. Cut into wedges.

Adding butter mixture:
Slowly pour melted butter mixture over sliced potatoes to cover evenly.

Serving potatoes: Carefully loosen cooked sliced potatoes from plate; invert onto serving plate.

Pumpkin

Season: October.
Look for: Firm, bright pumpkins, free from blemishes.
To store: Store in cool, dry place. Use within 1 month.
To prepare: See below.
To cook: In a saucepan over medium heat, in 1 inch boiling, salted water, heat cut-up pumpkin to boiling. Reduce heat to low; cover and simmer 25 to 30 minutes or until tender, depending on size of chunks. Drain; cool slightly. Remove peel.
Seasonings: Cook with allspice, cinnamon, cloves, ginger, nutmeg.
To serve: Eat hot as vegetable or in pies or bread.

 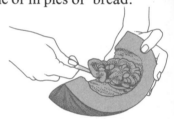

Preparing pumpkin: With large knife, halve or quarter pumpkin.

With a spoon, scoop out the seeds and stringy portions.

Cut the pumpkin flesh into large chunks.

Honeyed Pumpkin

Color index
page 72

Begin 45 mins
ahead

4 servings

133 cals per
serving

Good source
of calcium

1 4-pound pumpkin
4 cups water
1 teaspoon salt
2 tablespoons butter or
  margarine
2 tablespoons honey
½ teaspoon ground
  allspice (optional)

1. With sharp knife, cut pumpkin into quarters. Remove seeds and stringy portions.
2. In 4-quart saucepan over high heat, heat pumpkin, water and salt to boiling; reduce heat to low; cover and simmer 25 to 30 minutes until the pumpkin is fork-tender.
3. Drain pumpkin. Cool slightly and scoop flesh from peel into same saucepan. With potato masher or slotted spoon, mash pumpkin; drain well.
4. Over low heat, heat pumpkin about 3 minutes, shaking pan occasionally to evaporate excess liquid. Stir in butter, honey and allspice; mix well.

Radishes

Season: All year.
Look for: Uniformly shaped radishes that are free of blemishes, firm and bright, red or white, depending upon variety.
To store: Refrigerate in crisper or in plastic bag. Use radishes within a week.
To prepare: See below.
To serve: Eat radishes fresh as a snack or relish, sliced or cut up in salads.

Preparing radishes: Rinse in cold water. With small sharp knife, cut off stems and tails. Slice for salads. If using as garnish or relish, see below or Salad Garnishes (page 327). (If radishes have leafy tops, leave some tops on for garnish.)

Radish Spread

Color index page 18
Begin 15 mins ahead
2 cups
58 cals per tablespoon
Low in sodium

1 cup mayonnaise
1 cup minced radishes
1/4 cup sour cream
1/2 teaspoon salt
thin radish slices for garnish

1. In medium bowl with spoon, mix well mayonnaise, minced radishes, sour cream and salt.
2. Use mixture to spread on rye bread for appetizers. Garnish with radish slices.

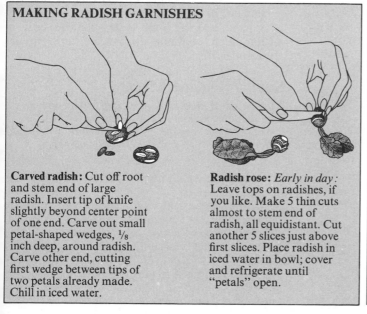

MAKING RADISH GARNISHES

Carved radish: Cut off root and stem end of large radish. Insert tip of knife slightly beyond center point of one end. Carve out small petal-shaped wedges, 1/8 inch deep, around radish. Carve other end, cutting first wedge between tips of two petals already made. Chill in iced water.

Radish rose: *Early in day:* Leave tops on radishes, if you like. Make 5 thin cuts almost to stem end of radish, all equidistant. Cut another 5 slices just above first slices. Place radish in iced water in bowl; cover and refrigerate until "petals" open.

Spinach

Season: All year.
Look for: Bright green, fresh tender leaves. Avoid spinach that is yellowish and wilted or gritty.
To store: Refrigerate spinach in crisper or wrapped. Use within 1 or 2 days.
To prepare: See below.
To cook: In saucepan over medium heat, in 1/4 inch boiling, salted water, heat spinach to boiling. Reduce heat to low; cover and simmer 1 to 3 minutes until wilted, stirring occasionally. Or use in recipes.
Seasonings: Cook spinach with allspice, bacon drippings, lemon, onion or nutmeg.
To serve: Eat raw in salads. Or use leaves to garnish other salads. Serve hot, with or without a sauce.

Preparing spinach: Wash leaves well under running cold water.

Trim any tough ribs or stems; drain; pat dry on paper towels.

Baked Creamed Spinach

Color index page 67
Begin 1 hr ahead
8 servings
100 cals per serving
Good source of calcium, iron

2 tablespoons butter or margarine
1 small onion, finely chopped
2 tablespoons all-purpose flour
1 teaspoon salt
1/8 teaspoon pepper
1 cup milk
2 eggs, separated
2 10-ounce bags spinach, finely chopped, cooked as above and well drained

1. Grease 8" by 8" baking dish. In 2-quart saucepan over medium heat, in hot butter, cook onion until tender, about 5 minutes. Stir in flour, salt and pepper until blended. Gradually stir in milk; cook, stirring, until sauce boils and is slightly thickened.
2. Preheat oven to 350°F. In small bowl with fork, beat egg yolks slightly. Into yolks, stir small amount of hot sauce; slowly pour yolk mixture into sauce, stirring rapidly to prevent lumping. Cook, stirring constantly, until thickened (do not boil). Remove from heat; stir in spinach.
3. In small bowl with mixer at high speed, beat egg whites until stiff peaks form. With wire whisk, gently fold egg whites into spinach mixture. Pour into baking dish; bake 20 to 25 minutes until a knife inserted in center comes out clean.

293

VEGETABLES
Squash, hard-skinned

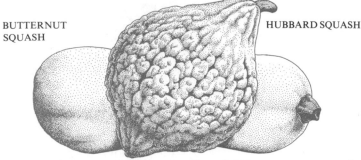

BUTTERNUT SQUASH HUBBARD SQUASH

Acorn, banana, butternut, Des Moines, green and golden delicious, green and blue Hubbard.
Season: All year. Best supplies are in fall.
Look for: Squash heavy for its size, with a hard skin. Tender skin indicates immaturity or poor quality.
To store: Refrigerate or store at cool room temperature. Use within a few weeks.
To prepare: See below.
To cook: *Boiled squash:* In saucepan over medium heat, in 1 inch boiling, salted water, heat squash, cut side down, to boiling. Reduce heat to low; cover and simmer about 15 minutes or until pulp is tender. Drain; cool slightly and eat from shell, or scoop out pulp and use in recipes for vegetables, pies or desserts. *Baked squash:* Bake squash in jelly-roll pan in 325° to 375°F. oven 45 minutes to 1½ hours till fork-tender. Or use in recipes.
Seasonings: Basil, cloves, ginger, mustard seed, nutmeg.
To serve: Eat as cooked vegetable.

Preparing squash: Rinse the squash in cold water. Cut in half lengthwise; remove the seeds. If large squash, cut in wedges or medium-sized chunks.

Mashed Butternut Squash

Color index page 72
Begin 45 mins ahead
6 servings
102 cals per serving
Good source of vitamin A

2 small butternut squash
water
salt
¼ cup packed brown sugar
2 tablespoons butter

1. Halve squash lengthwise; remove seeds.
2. In 10-inch skillet over medium heat, in 1 inch boiling water, heat squash, cut side down, and ½ teaspoon salt to boiling. Reduce heat to low; cover; simmer 15 minutes or until fork-tender.
3. Drain; cool slightly. Scoop out pulp into large bowl; with mixer at low speed, beat squash, ½ teaspoon salt and remaining ingredients till smooth.

Baked Acorn Squash

Color index page 72
Begin 1 hr ahead
2 servings
321 cals per serving

1 medium acorn squash
4 tablespoons butter
2 tablespoons brown sugar or maple syrup

1. Preheat oven to 350°F. Halve squash lengthwise; remove seeds; place, cut side up, in roasting pan.
2. Spoon butter and brown sugar equally into halves. Bake 45 minutes or until fork-tender.

Squash, soft-skinned

ZUCCHINI
YELLOW STRAIGHTNECK SQUASH

Varieties include Italian marrow, yellow straightneck, pattypan, zucchini.
Season: All year.
Look for: Small young squash, heavy for their size, with skin tender enough to yield easily to thumb pressure.
To store: Refrigerate. Use within a few days.
To prepare: See below.
To cook: In saucepan over medium heat, in 1 inch boiling, salted water, heat squash to boiling. Reduce heat to low; cover and simmer halved squash about 5 minutes and sliced squash, 3 minutes.
Seasonings: Garlic, onion, sesame seed, salt and pepper.
To serve: Serve hot; eat fresh as a snack, in salads.

Preparing squash: Scrub gently with vegetable brush in cold water. Cut slice off stem and blossom ends.

Without removing the skin or seeds, cut into slices or chunks. Cut pattypan in wedges.

Stir-fried Zucchini

Color index page 67
Begin 15 mins ahead
4 servings
48 cals per serving
Low in cholesterol

3 medium zucchini
1 tablespoon salad oil
¼ cup water
1 teaspoon salt
½ teaspoon sugar

1. Cut zucchini into ¼-inch pieces.
2. In 5-quart Dutch oven over high heat, in very hot salad oil, cook zucchini, stirring quickly and frequently (stir-frying) until well coated.
3. Add water, salt and sugar. Reduce heat to medium-high; continue stir-frying 7 to 8 minutes until tender-crisp.

Summer Squash Medley

Color index page 67
Begin 15 mins ahead
6 servings
95 cals per serving

1 pound small zucchini
1 pound small yellow straightneck squash
water
salt
½ cup chopped parsley
¼ cup butter
2 tablespoons lemon juice
¼ teaspoon pepper

1. Cut zucchini and straightneck squash into strips about 2 inches long.
2. In 3-quart saucepan over medium heat, in 1 inch boiling water, heat zucchini, squash and 1 teaspoon salt to boiling. Reduce heat to low; cover and simmer 3 minutes or until vegetables are tender-crisp; drain.
3. Return vegetables to saucepan; over low heat, stir in 1 teaspoon salt, chopped parsley, butter, lemon juice and pepper until butter is melted.

Sweet potatoes

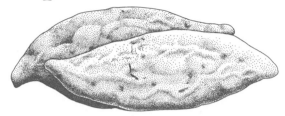

Season: All year. Best supplies are in November.

Look for: Firm, uniformly shaped sweet potatoes, free of blemishes. Yams are not botanically related to sweet potatoes, but in the United States, canned sweet potatoes are often labeled yams; use in recipes in the same way as sweet potatoes.

To store: Store sweet potatoes in a cool, dry place. Use within a week or so.

To prepare: Scrub. When possible, do not peel before cooking (to save nutrients).

To cook: *Boiled sweet potatoes:* In saucepan over high heat, heat unpeeled sweet potatoes and enough salted water to cover to boiling. Reduce heat to low; cover and simmer 30 to 40 minutes or until fork-tender. Drain and peel. *Baked sweet potatoes:* Bake unpeeled medium sweet potatoes in 450°F. oven about 1 hour until fork-tender. Or use in recipes.

Seasonings: Cinnamon, cloves, nutmeg, allspice.

To serve: Eat as cooked vegetable.

Sherried Sweet Potatoes

Color index page 67

Begin 50 mins ahead

6 servings

285 cals per serving

3 pounds sweet potatoes (about 6 medium)
salt
water
¼ cup butter or margarine

¼ cup packed brown sugar
2 tablespoons cream sherry
⅛ teaspoon pepper

1. In 4-quart saucepan over high heat, heat sweet potatoes, 1 teaspoon salt and water to cover potatoes to boiling. Reduce heat to low; cover; simmer 30 to 40 minutes until fork-tender; drain. Peel.
2. In large bowl with mixer at low speed, beat sweet potatoes and butter until smooth, scraping bowl constantly with rubber spatula. Add remaining ingredients and ¾ teaspoon salt. At medium speed, beat 2 minutes longer or until sweet potato mixture is light and fluffy.

Candied Sweet Potatoes

Color index page 67

Begin 30 mins ahead

6 servings

386 cals per serving

Good source of iron

6 medium sweet potatoes, cooked and halved lengthwise or 2 16-ounce cans whole sweet potatoes, drained

½ cup packed brown sugar
½ cup dark corn syrup
¼ cup butter or margarine

1. Preheat oven to 350°F. Arrange sweet potatoes in cook-and-serve baking dish.
2. In 1-quart saucepan over medium heat, combine brown sugar, corn syrup and butter; heat to boiling. Reduce heat to low; simmer, stirring occasionally, 5 minutes. Pour syrup over sweet potatoes.
3. Bake 20 minutes or until potatoes are well glazed, basting often with syrup.
4. To serve: Spoon syrup over potatoes.

Tomatoes

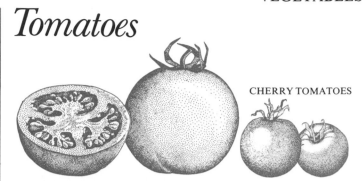

CHERRY TOMATOES

Season: All year.

Look for: Firm, unblemished tomatoes with good red color. Size does not indicate quality.

To store: If not fully ripe, leave them, stem end up, at room temperature out of sunlight until they turn red. Then refrigerate and use within 1 or 2 days.

To prepare: It is not necessary to peel tomatoes before using them. Simply rinse in cold water. If you wish to peel them, see below.

To cook: Use tomatoes in recipes for vegetables, or in soups and main dishes.

Seasonings: Basil, celery seed, chives, parsley, oregano, tarragon, thyme, coarsely ground black pepper.

To serve: Eat fresh in salads, as sandwich filling or as a cooked vegetable.

Peeling tomatoes: Dip tomato in boiling water for a minute, then into cold water. Or, with long-handled fork, rotate tomato over flame until skin pops.

With sharp knife, pull away loosened skin. Cut out stem end.

Fried Green Tomatoes

Color index page 72

Begin 30 mins ahead

10 servings

157 cals per serving

Low in cholesterol

⅔ cup all-purpose flour
2 teaspoons salt
⅛ teaspoon pepper

3 pounds green tomatoes, cut in ½-inch slices
salad oil

1. In pie plate, combine flour, salt and pepper. Dip in tomato slices to coat both sides.
2. In 12-inch skillet over medium heat, in ¼ cup hot salad oil, fry slices, a few at a time, until golden on both sides and heated through. Drain on paper towels. Repeat, adding more oil as needed.

Stewed Fresh Tomatoes

Color index page 72

Begin 30 mins ahead

6 servings

60 cals per serving

2 pounds tomatoes, peeled
2 tablespoons butter or margarine
4 green onions, chopped

1½ teaspoons sugar
1 teaspoon garlic salt
¼ teaspoon seasoned pepper

1. Cut tomatoes into wedges.
2. In 10-inch skillet over medium heat, in hot butter or margarine, cook green onions 1 minute. Add tomatoes and remaining ingredients; cook about 10 minutes, stirring occasionally.

Tomatoes

Baked Herbed Tomatoes

2 medium tomatoes
¼ teaspoon salt
¼ teaspoon rosemary
¼ teaspoon basil
2 teaspoons butter or
margarine

Color index
page 72

Begin 25 mins
ahead

4 servings

29 cals per
serving

Low in
sodium

1. Preheat oven to 350°F. Cut tomatoes horizontally in half into sawtooth pattern.
2. In cup, mix salt, rosemary and basil. Sprinkle each tomato half with some herb mixture and dot with butter or margarine.
3. Place tomato halves in 9-inch round cake pan. Bake 15 minutes or until heated through.

Scalloped Tomatoes

¼ cup butter or
margarine
1 small onion, chopped
2 cups fresh bread
crumbs
1 teaspoon salt
½ teaspoon basil
¼ teaspoon pepper
5 medium tomatoes,
sliced
4 teaspoons sugar

Color index
page 72

Begin 45 mins
ahead

6 servings

145 cals per
serving

1 Preheat oven to 375°F. In 2-quart saucepan over medium heat, in hot butter, cook onion until tender, then stir in crumbs, salt, basil and pepper.

2 Into 1½-quart shallow casserole, place ¼ of tomato slices; sprinkle with 1 teaspoon sugar and ¼ of bread-crumb mixture. Repeat, ending with bread-crumb mixture.

3 Cover casserole and bake 30 minutes or until hot and bubbly. Uncover casserole and bake 5 minutes longer or until crumbs are golden.

CHERRY TOMATOES

Cherry tomatoes are small, red tomatoes sold by the box in many markets. Although too small to peel they can be used like other tomatoes in recipes.

Sautéed Cherry Tomatoes

1 tablespoon salad
oil
1 pint cherry tomatoes
salt
pepper

Color index
page 72

Begin 10 mins
ahead

4 servings

50 cals per
serving

In 3-quart saucepan over medium heat, in hot oil, cook cherry tomatoes 5 minutes or until heated through, shaking saucepan occasionally. To serve, sprinkle with salt and pepper to taste.

Turnips

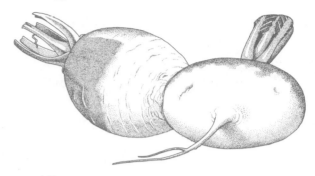

Season: All year.
Look for: Firm, unblemished turnips, heavy for their size, with fresh tops.
To store: Remove tops, if any. Refrigerate tops and turnips in crisper or wrapped. Use turnips within a week or so. Use tops as soon as possible (see Lettuce and other greens, page 287).
To prepare: Rinse in cold water. Peel thinly. Leave whole or cut into slices or pieces.
To cook: In saucepan over medium heat, in 1 inch boiling, salted water, heat turnips to boiling. Reduce heat to low; cover and simmer whole turnips 20 to 30 minutes, cut-up turnips, 10 to 20 minutes. Or, use in recipes for soups, stews, main dishes.
Seasonings: Cook with bay leaf, cloves.
To serve: Eat as cooked vegetable.

Mashed Turnips

water
2½ pounds turnips,
peeled and diced
¼ cup butter or
margarine
2 teaspoons salt
1 teaspoon sugar
¼ teaspoon pepper
parsley for garnish

Color index
page 68

Begin 40 mins
ahead

8 servings

64 cals per
serving

1. In 4-quart saucepan over high heat, in 1 inch boiling water, heat turnips to boiling. Reduce heat to low; cover and simmer 15 minutes or until tender. Remove from heat; drain.
2. Mash. Add butter, salt, sugar and pepper; stir until well mixed. Serve garnished with parsley.

RUTABAGA

The rutabaga, a yellow-fleshed relative of the turnip, is also in season the year round, but is most plentiful from September to May. Look for rutabagas free of decay and heavy for their size. Store them at cool room temperature and keep dry for use within a week or so. Prepare and cook as for turnips and serve as a cooked vegetable with White Sauce (page 461) or Cheese Sauce (page 461) or in recipes for soups, stews and casseroles.

Combination dishes

Ratatouille

Color index page 67

Begin 45 mins ahead or early in day

8 servings

160 cals per serving

Low in cholesterol

½ cup olive or salad oil
1 large onion, diced
1 large garlic clove, cut in half
1 medium eggplant, cut in 1-inch chunks
1 large green pepper, cut in 1-inch pieces
3 medium zucchini, cut in 1-inch-thick slices
½ cup water
1 tablespoon salt
2 teaspoons oregano leaves
1 teaspoon sugar
2 large tomatoes, cut in wedges

1 In 6-quart Dutch oven or saucepot over medium heat, in hot olive oil, cook onion and garlic until tender, about 10 minutes, stirring occasionally; discard garlic.

2 Add eggplant and the green pepper; cook for 5 minutes, stirring the mixture frequently.

3 Stir in zucchini, water, salt, oregano and sugar; heat to boiling. Reduce heat to medium-low; cook 30 minutes or until vegetables are tender, stirring occasionally.

4 Stir in tomato wedges; heat through; serve hot or follow step 5.

5 Cover vegetable mixture and refrigerate to serve cold later.

Confetti Vegetables

Color index page 71

Begin 30 mins ahead

12 servings

100 cals per serving

¾ cup water
⅓ cup butter or margarine
1 tablespoon sugar
2 teaspoons salt
4½ cups shredded zucchini (about 1½ pounds)

3 cups coarsely shredded carrots (about 1½ pounds)
3 cups shredded parsnips or turnips (about 1½ pounds)

In 5-quart Dutch oven or large saucepot, in boiling water, heat all ingredients to boiling. Cover and simmer about 5 minutes until vegetables are tender-crisp, stirring occasionally.

Summer Vegetable Bowl

Color index page 69

Begin 1 hr ahead

8 servings

209 cals per serving

Good source of iron

4 bacon slices
12 small white onions
1 small green pepper, diced
2 cups hot water
1 pound green beans
6 ears corn, broken in thirds
2 teaspoons salt

2 teaspoons sugar
¼ teaspoon white pepper
6 small zucchini, cut in 1-inch chunks
2 large celery stalks, cut in 1-inch slices
1 large tomato, cut in wedges

1. In 6-quart Dutch oven over medium heat, fry bacon until crisp; drain on paper towels.
2. To drippings in Dutch oven, add onions and green pepper; cook until golden; add hot water and next 5 ingredients. Heat to boiling; reduce heat to low; cover; simmer 10 minutes.
3. Add zucchini and celery; cover and cook 8 to 10 minutes until all vegetables are tender.
4. With slotted spoon, arrange vegetables on large platter or in large, shallow bowl; crumble bacon and sprinkle over top. Arrange tomato wedges on top.

Serving the vegetables: Sprinkle over bacon then garnish the dish with tomato wedges.

Carrots and Celery

Color index page 70

Begin 30 mins ahead

8 servings

51 cals per serving

Low in cholesterol

2 tablespoons salad oil
1 16-ounce bag carrots, diagonally sliced
1¼ teaspoons salt

¼ teaspoon sugar
¼ cup water
1 small bunch celery, diagonally sliced

1. In 5-quart Dutch oven or 12-inch skillet over high heat, in hot salad oil, heat carrots, salt, sugar and water to boiling. Reduce heat to medium; cover and cook 7 minutes.
2. Uncover; add celery; cook 5 to 7 minutes until vegetables are tender-crisp, stirring frequently.

Vegetable Trio

Color index page 69

Begin 25 mins ahead

5 servings

82 cals per serving

½ pound carrots (about 4 large carrots), cut in matchstick-thin strips
½ pound green beans, cut in 1-inch pieces
¼ pound mushrooms, sliced

1 teaspoon salt
½ teaspoon thyme leaves
3 tablespoons butter or margarine

In 2-quart saucepan over medium heat, place all ingredients. Cover and cook 15 minutes or until vegetables are tender-crisp, stirring occasionally.

Combination dishes

Stir-fried Cabbage and Zucchini

¼ cup salad oil
1 large garlic clove, sliced
6 cups packed sliced cabbage
2 medium zucchini (about 1 pound), thinly sliced
2 teaspoons salt
1 teaspoon sugar

Color index page 69

Begin 15 mins ahead

8 servings

85 cals per serving

Low in cholesterol

1 In 5-quart Dutch oven over high heat, in hot oil, cook garlic until browned; discard garlic.

2 Add cabbage and zucchini, stir-frying (stirring quickly and frequently) until they are well coated with oil.

3 Add salt and sugar; reduce heat to medium-high; continue stir-frying 7 to 8 minutes until vegetables are tender-crisp.

Green Beans with Zucchini

Color index page 67

Begin 30 mins ahead

6 servings

142 cals per serving

1 9-ounce package frozen cut green beans
4 bacon slices
¼ cup butter or margarine
1 small onion, minced
2 medium zucchini, sliced ¼ inch thick
¼ teaspoon salt
⅛ teaspoon pepper

1. Prepare beans as label directs, but halve cooking time; drain. In 12-inch skillet over medium heat, fry bacon until crisp; drain; crumble. Pour off fat.
2. Wipe skillet clean. In skillet, in butter, cook onion until tender, about 3 minutes. Increase heat to medium-high; cook zucchini, stirring quickly and frequently, until tender-crisp, about 4 minutes.
3. Stir in bacon, green beans, salt and pepper and cook just until beans are hot.

Stir-fried Vegetable Mix

Color index page 70

Begin 25 mins ahead

6 servings

90 cals per serving

Low in cholesterol

3 tablespoons salad oil
2 medium carrots, cut in matchstick-thin strips
1 medium onion, thinly sliced
1 small bunch broccoli, cut in 2″ by ½″ pieces
¾ teaspoon salt
½ teaspoon sugar
1 4-ounce can whole mushrooms

1. In 12-inch skillet over high heat, in hot oil, cook carrots, onion and broccoli, stirring quickly and frequently, about 3 to 4 minutes.
2. Add salt, sugar and mushrooms with their liquid; cover and cook 5 to 6 minutes until vegetables are tender-crisp, stirring occasionally.

Pepper-and-Tomato Sauté

Color index page 70

Begin 30 mins ahead

10 servings

83 cals per serving

Low in cholesterol

Good source of vitamin C

¼ cup salad oil
6 large green peppers, cut into large chunks
2 medium onions, chopped
5 large tomatoes, peeled and cut into large chunks
2 teaspoons salt
1¼ teaspoons basil

1. In 12-inch skillet over medium heat, in hot salad oil, cook green pepper chunks and chopped onions 10 minutes.
2. Add the peeled tomato chunks together with the salt and basil; cover and simmer until the vegetables are fork-tender, stirring the mixture occasionally, about 15 minutes.

Eggplant Parmigiana

Color index page 33

Begin 1½ hrs ahead

6 main-dish servings

430 cals per serving

Good source of calcium, iron, vitamin A

olive oil
1 garlic clove, minced
1 large onion, chopped
2 16-ounce cans tomatoes
2 teaspoons sugar
½ teaspoon oregano leaves
½ teaspoon basil
½ teaspoon salt
1 cup dried bread crumbs

2 eggs
2 tablespoons water
1 large eggplant, cut into ½-inch slices
½ cup grated Parmesan cheese
1 8-ounce package mozzarella cheese, cut into ¼-inch slices

1 In 9-inch skillet over medium heat, in 2 tablespoons hot oil, cook garlic and onion until tender, then add next 5 ingredients. Reduce heat; cook, covered, 30 minutes.

2 On waxed paper, place bread crumbs; in small dish with fork, beat eggs and water. Dip eggplant slices in egg then in bread crumbs. Repeat to coat slices twice.

3 Grease 13″ by 9″ baking dish. In 12-inch skillet over medium heat, in 2 tablespoons hot oil, cook a few eggplant slices at a time till golden brown. Add more oil as needed.

4 Preheat oven to 350°F. Arrange ½ eggplant slices in baking dish; cover with ½ tomato mixture; sprinkle with ½ Parmesan top with ½ mozzarella; repeat. Bake 25 minutes.

Sauces and toppings

Caponata

Color index
page 20

Begin 4 hrs
or up to
1 wk ahead

12 first-course
or accompani-
ment servings

191 cals per
serving

Low in
cholesterol

3/4 cup olive or salad oil
1 large eggplant, cut into
bite-size pieces
(2 pounds)
6 medium zucchini, cut
into bite-size pieces
(2 pounds)
1/2 pound mushrooms,
thickly sliced
1 1/2 cups chopped
onions
1 cup sliced celery
1 garlic clove,
crushed
1/2 cup red wine
vinegar

1/4 cup capers,
drained
2 tablespoons sugar
2 teaspoons salt
1/4 teaspoon pepper
3 large tomatoes,
cut into bite-size
chunks
1 4 1/2-ounce jar pimento-
stuffed olives,
drained and halved
crosswise

1. In 8-quart Dutch oven or large saucepot over high heat, in hot olive oil, cook eggplant, zucchini, mushrooms, onions, celery and garlic 10 minutes, stirring occasionally.
2. Stir red wine vinegar, capers, sugar, salt and pepper into mixture in Dutch oven. Reduce heat to low; cover and simmer 5 to 10 minutes until vegetables are fork-tender.
3. Stir in tomato chunks and halved olives; over high heat, heat to boiling.
4. Spoon vegetable mixture into large bowl; cover and refrigerate at least 3 hours or until mixture is well chilled.
5. Serve cold as a first-course or as an accompaniment for cold, sliced meats.

Vegetable-stuffed Green Peppers

Color index
page 70

Begin 15 mins
ahead

4 servings

47 cals per
serving

Low in fat,
cholesterol

Good source
of vitamin C

2 large green peppers
salt
water

2 cups seasoned hot
cooked corn or mixed
vegetables

1. Cut peppers in half lengthwise; remove stem, seeds and membrane.
2. In 3-quart saucepan over medium heat, in 1 inch boiling, salted water, heat green peppers to boiling; cover and simmer for 5 minutes or until peppers are tender-crisp. Drain.
3. Spoon seasoned hot cooked corn or a selection of cooked and chopped mixed vegetables into the pepper halves. Serve hot.

Preparing the peppers:
With sharp knife, cut peppers in half lengthwise; remove stem, seeds and white membrane.

Stuffing the peppers: Fill pepper halves with seasoned hot cooked corn or with chopped and diced mixed vegetables.

Butter Sauce

Begin 5 mins
ahead

1/2 cup

81 cals per
1/4 cup

liquid from cooked
vegetables
water
1 tablespoon butter or
margarine, softened

1 tablespoon all-purpose
flour
salt
pepper

1. Into measuring cup, pour liquid from cooked vegetables; add water to make 1/2 cup liquid, if necessary. Return liquid to vegetables in pan. In cup, stir butter or margarine and flour to make smooth paste.
2. Stir mixture into vegetables and liquid; over medium heat, cook, stirring gently, until sauce is thickened and smooth. Add salt and pepper to taste.

Vinaigrette Sauce

Begin 10 mins
ahead

1 1/4 cups

331 cals per
1/4 cup

Low in
cholesterol

3/4 cup salad oil
1/3 cup cider or red wine
vinegar
3 tablespoons sweet
pickle relish

2 tablespoons chopped
parsley
1 teaspoon salt
3/4 teaspoon sugar

1. In covered blender container at low speed, blend all ingredients 1 minute. (Or, in medium bowl, combine vinegar with next 4 ingredients; slowly pour in oil, beating with fork until well mixed.) Just before serving beat with fork.
2. Serve on chilled fresh or cooked vegetables. Any leftover sauce may be refrigerated, covered.

Sour Cream-Mustard Sauce

Begin 10 mins
ahead

1 cup

129 cals per
1/4 cup

Low in
sodium

1 cup sour cream
1 tablespoon minced
onion
1 tablespoon prepared
mustard

1/4 teaspoon salt
1/8 teaspoon pepper
1 tablespoon chopped
parsley

1. In 1-quart saucepan over very low heat, heat sour cream, onion, prepared mustard, salt and pepper just until hot.
2. Sprinkle sauce with chopped parsley.

Buttered Crumbs

Begin 10 mins
ahead

Topping for
4 servings

71 cals per
serving

Low in
sodium

2 tablespoons butter or
margarine
1/2 cup fresh bread crumbs
1/8 teaspoon thyme or
basil

1 tablespoon lemon juice
or 1/2 cup shredded
Cheddar or grated
Parmesan cheese
(optional)

1. In 1-quart saucepan over medium heat, melt butter or margarine.
2. Add fresh bread crumbs; cook, tossing lightly, until crumbs are golden. Stir in thyme or basil until well mixed.
3. If you like, add lemon juice or Cheddar cheese.
4. Sprinkle Buttered Crumbs over drained, hot cooked vegetables.

POLONAISE SAUCE: Prepare Buttered Crumbs with lemon juice as above. Stir in *1 hard-cooked egg*, chopped, *1 tablespoon chopped parsley* and *1/4 teaspoon salt* until thoroughly mixed together.

FRUIT

Fruit makes the perfect finale to the most sophisticated dinner, but it can also be included in every course of any meal, from soup to dessert. Or fruit can be eaten as a satisfying, healthy snack, at any time.

All unripe fresh fruit should be stored in a cool, dark place (avoid direct sunlight) and allowed to ripen at room temperature. Citrus fruit never needs further ripening but other fruits do, so buy them ahead of time. But remember that, in general, fresh fruit is highly perishable and requires refrigeration once it is ripe.

Specific directions for buying and using fruit are given in the following pages.

Apples

Season: All year. Best supplies are in October, lowest in June, July and August.

Look for: Firm, crisp, well-colored fruit, the color depending on variety: Avoid any apples which have brown spots or any fruit which is shriveled or soft. Select apples according to their use (see below).

To store: Refrigerate. Use within 2 weeks.

To prepare: Wash, peel and core, depending on use. To prevent browning, if apples are sliced and are to stand, sprinkle with lemon juice or ascorbic-acid mixture.

To serve: Eat out of hand, peeled or unpeeled; use in pies, salads, sauces, desserts and coffeecakes.

BEST WAYS OF USING APPLES

	York Imperial	Winesap	Stayman	Rome Beauty	Red Delicious	Northern Spy	Newtown Pippin	McIntosh	Jonathan	Gravenstein	Golden Delicious	Cortland
Eating		●	●	●	●		●	●	●		●	●
Baking	●	●	●	●		●	●		●		●	●
Cooking	●	●	●	●		●	●	●	●	●	●	●
Sauces	●	●	●	●		●	●	●	●	●	●	●
Salads		●	●		●		●	●	●	●	●	●
Pies	●	●	●	●		●	●	●	●	●	●	●

Color index page 101

Begin 30 mins ahead

4 cups

46 cals per ¼ cup

Low in fat, cholesterol, sodium

Applesauce

½ cup boiling water
2 pounds cooking apples, peeled, cored and sliced
⅛ teaspoon ground cinnamon
⅛ teaspoon ground cloves
½ cup sugar

1. In 2-quart saucepan over medium heat, heat first 4 ingredients to boiling.
2. Reduce heat to low; cover and simmer 8 to 10 minutes until the apples are tender for chunky applesauce, 12 to 15 minutes for smoother applesauce. During last minutes of cooking time, stir sugar into applesauce mixture.

Color index page 101

Begin 1 hr ahead or early in day

6 servings

216 cals per serving

Low in fat, cholesterol, sodium

Baked Apples

6 medium cooking apples
1 cup light corn syrup
cream or ice cream (optional)

1. Preheat oven to 350°F. Core apples and starting from stem end, peel them ⅓ of the way down. Arrange in a shallow baking dish, peeled end up, and pour corn syrup over them.
2. Bake apples 45 minutes or until fork-tender, spooning syrup from pan over them occasionally. Serve hot or cold with cream or ice cream.

Color index page 72

Begin 15 mins ahead

4 servings

186 cals per serving

Low in sodium

Pan-fried Apple Wedges

2 red cooking apples, cored
2 tablespoons butter or margarine
½ cup apple jelly

1. Cut apples into ½-inch-thick wedges.
2. In 12-inch skillet over medium heat, in hot butter or margarine, cook apple wedges about 5 to 7 minutes until apples are tender-crisp; with pancake turner, turn wedges once during cooking.
3. Stir in apple jelly; heat through. Serve with baked ham or with breakfast pancakes.

Apples

Candy Apples

8 wooden ice-cream-bar sticks
8 small Red Delicious apples, washed and dried
1 cup water
3 cups sugar
½ cup light corn syrup
¼ cup red-hot candies
½ teaspoon red food color

Color index page 106

Begin 2 hrs ahead or early in day

8 candy apples

411 cals each

Low in fat, cholesterol, sodium

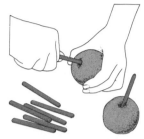

1 Insert a wooden stick part way through stem end of apples. Grease large cookie sheet; set aside.

2 In 2-quart saucepan, combine remaining ingredients. Over medium heat, heat mixture to boiling, without stirring.

3 Boil, without stirring, until candy thermometer reads 290°F., or when a little of mixture dropped into cold water separates into thin hard threads, about 20 minutes.

4 With brush dipped in hot water, occasionally brush sugar from side of pan as mixture cooks.

5 When cooked, remove syrup from heat. Tip saucepan; swirl each apple in mixture to coat.

6 Lift apple out of syrup mixture and swirl it over the saucepan a few more seconds to allow any drips to fall back into saucepan.

7 Place apples on cookie sheet to cool. Work quickly before syrup hardens. To soften, place over very low heat. Cool at least 1 hour before serving.

Apricots

Season: June and July.
Look for: Plump, juicy, orange-yellow apricots. Ripe fruit yield to gentle pressure on the skin. Avoid dull-looking, shriveled or soft fruit.
To store: Refrigerate. Use within 2 to 3 days.
To prepare: Wash, cut in half and remove seed; peel if desired. To prevent browning, if cut apricots are not eaten immediately, sprinkle with lemon juice or ascorbic-acid mixture for fruit.
To serve: Eat out of hand, peeled or unpeeled. Use in recipes for salads, desserts.

Cinnamon Apricots in Cream

1 pound apricots, unpeeled
⅓ cup sugar
⅓ cup water
½ teaspoon ground cinnamon
¼ cup heavy or whipping cream

Color index page 100

Begin 35 mins ahead

4 servings

152 cals per serving

Low in sodium

1. Preheat oven to 375°F. Halve and remove seeds from apricots. Place in 1-quart casserole.
2. In small bowl, combine sugar, water and cinnamon; pour over fruit. Bake 20 minutes or until apricots are tender.
3. Pour on cream and bake 5 minutes longer.

DRIED FRUITS

Packaged dried fruits come in 8-, 11-, 12- or 16-ounce packages depending on variety. Store tightly wrapped, at room temperature, for up to 6 months. After opening, transfer to tightly closed container.

Eat out of hand or use in recipes for sauces, coffeecakes, breads and desserts or stews, according to label directions. Or, cook following the chart below, adding sugar during last minutes of cooking.

STEWING DRIED FRUITS*

Fruit	Package size (in ounces)	Water (in cups)	Sugar (in cups)	Cooking time (in minutes)
Apples	8	3½ + ⅛ teaspoon salt	¼	25
Apricots	8 11 or 12	2½ 3	¼ ½	15 15
Figs	12	3 + 1 tablespoon lemon juice		35
Mixed fruit	11 or 12	4	½	25
Peaches	11 or 12	4	¼	25
Pears	11	3	¼	25
Prunes	16	4	0	20

Makes 4 to 6 servings

Avocados

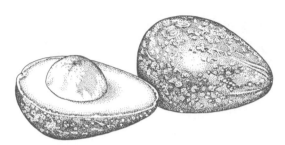

Season: All year.
Look for: Pear-shaped, round or egg-shaped fruit, green or purplish-black, depending on variety. Avoid any with dark spots or broken skin. Avocados yield to gentle pressure when ripe.
To store: Refrigerate avocados after ripening and use within 3 to 5 days.
To prepare: See below. To prevent browning, if sliced avocados are not to be served immediately, sprinkle with lemon juice or ascorbic-acid mixture for fruit.
To serve: Use in dips, appetizers (below). Serve slices with French dressing, or toss with green or fruit salads.

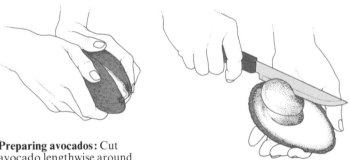

Preparing avocados: Cut avocado lengthwise around the seed; twist gently to separate halves.

To remove seed, strike it with blade of sharp knife so blade lodges in seed; twist knife gently to lift out seed.

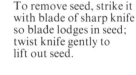

Peel and slice or cut up, depending on use. Or use unpeeled as shell for salads or filling.

Appetizer Avocados

Color index page 21

Begin 35 mins ahead

6 first-course servings

376 cals per serving

Low in cholesterol

Good source of iron

2 tablespoons water
2 tablespoons sugar
2 tablespoons white vinegar
2 tablespoons Worcestershire
¼ cup chili sauce

2 tablespoons butter or margarine
3 medium avocados, peeled and sliced
4 bacon slices, cooked and crumbled

1. In 1-quart saucepan over medium heat, heat first 6 ingredients to boiling. Reduce heat to low; simmer 15 minutes, stirring occasionally.
2. Arrange avocado slices on 6 appetizer or salad plates; spoon hot sauce over avocados and sprinkle with the crumbled bacon slices.

Bananas

Season: All year.
Look for: For immediate use, solid yellow bananas lightly flecked with brown. Fruit with some green will ripen in a few days at room temperature. Brown skins usually indicate overripened fruit.
To store: Refrigerate ripe fruit; use within 3 days.
To prepare: Peel skin from top. Slice or cut up fruit as required. To prevent browning, if cut bananas are not eaten immediately, sprinkle with a little lemon juice or ascorbic-acid mixture.
To serve: Eat out of hand or use in recipes.

Baked Bananas

Color index page 72

Begin 25 mins ahead

4 servings

166 cals per serving

3 tablespoons butter
4 slightly unripe medium bananas, peeled

salt to taste

1. Preheat oven to 450°F. In oven, in pie plate or baking dish, melt butter.
2. Remove plate from oven and roll bananas in melted butter; sprinkle lightly with salt.
3. Bake 10 to 12 minutes or until bananas are fork-tender. Serve hot as a vegetable.

Banana Pops

Color index page 101

Begin 2 hrs ahead or early in day

12 banana pops

184 cals each

Low in cholesterol, sodium

3 tablespoons water
2 teaspoons ascorbic-acid mixture for fruit
4 large bananas, peeled and sliced crosswise into thirds
1 package wooden ice-cream-bar sticks

½ cup shredded coconut
½ cup toasted shredded coconut
1 6-ounce package semisweet-chocolate pieces
2 tablespoons salad oil

1. In large bowl, in water, stir ascorbic-acid mixture until dissolved; gently toss bananas in mixture until coated. Insert a stick about 1 inch deep into end of each banana piece. Place on cookie sheet; freeze until firm, about 45 minutes.
2. Meanwhile, place each kind of coconut on a small plate. In double boiler, over hot, not boiling, water, melt chocolate pieces with salad oil, stirring occasionally. Pour into pie plate.
3. Remove bananas from freezer and quickly roll each in chocolate; roll some bananas in shredded coconut and some in toasted shredded coconut.
4. Return banana pops to cookie sheet and freeze for at least 30 minutes before serving.

Berries

BLUEBERRIES

GOOSEBERRIES   RASPBERRIES   BLACKBERRIES   STRAWBERRIES

Blackberries, Blueberries, Boysenberries, Dewberries, Gooseberries, Loganberries, Raspberries, Strawberries, Youngberries. (See also Cranberries, page 305.)
Season: Summer months, mostly June and July. Strawberries are available all year round, best supplies from April to July.
Look for: Plump, fresh, uniformly colored fruit, free of stems or leaves. Avoid fruit that is moldy, crushed or bruised, or that has leaked moisture through carton.
To store: Refrigerate. Use within 1 or 2 days.
To prepare: See below.
To serve: Serve with sugar and milk or over cereal. Eat out of hand. Use in recipes for salads, pies, muffins, coffeecakes, desserts, jams and sauces.

Preparing berries: Wash berries under running cold water, discarding any crushed or bruised ones. Drain well in a colander or strainer.

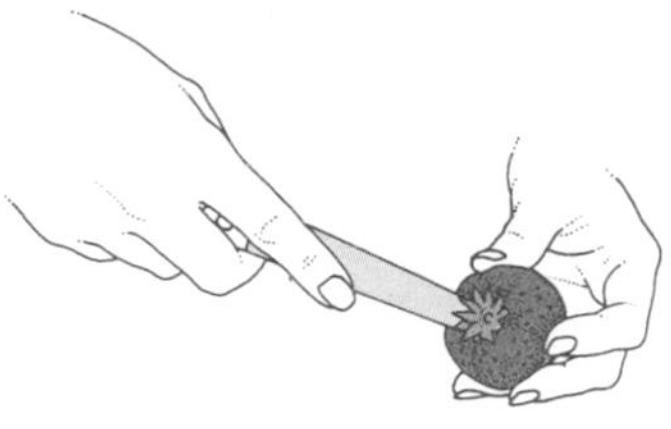

Remove stems (hulls) from berries such as strawberries.

Using kitchen scissors, cut top and tail from gooseberries.

Sugaring perfect berries for garnish: Wash and drain; roll in sugar while still wet.

Very-Berry Compote

Color index page 100 Begin 2½ hrs ahead 10 servings 211 cals per serving Low in sodium Good source of calcium, vitamin C

3 pints strawberries, halved	*1½ pints vanilla ice cream, softened*
½ cup sugar	*2 tablespoons grated orange peel*
1 cup raspberries	
1 cup blueberries	

1. In large bowl, gently toss strawberries with sugar; cover and refrigerate about 2 hours, tossing occasionally.
2. *Just before serving:* Alternately spoon strawberries, raspberries and blueberries into large glass serving bowl.
3. In medium bowl, combine ice cream with orange peel; spoon some on top of berries to garnish. Pass remainder in small bowl. Serve immediately.

Color index page 100 Begin 20 mins ahead 2¾ cups 83 cals per ¼ cup Low in fat, cholesterol, sodium

Blueberry Sauce

1 cup water	*1 tablespoon cornstarch*
1 pint blueberries	*⅛ teaspoon salt*
¾ cup sugar	*1 teaspoon lemon juice*

1. In 2-quart saucepan over medium heat, heat water to boiling; add blueberries; return to boiling.
2. Meanwhile, in a small bowl, combine sugar, cornstarch and salt; stir into blueberries and cook, stirring constantly, until thick. Add lemon juice.

Begin early in day 2⅔ cups 70 cals per ⅓ cup Low in fat, cholesterol, sodium

Blackberry Sauce

1 20-ounce bag frozen unsweetened blackberries	*2 tablespoons lemon juice*
	½ teaspoon ground cinnamon
½ cup packed light brown sugar	

In 2-quart saucepan over medium heat, heat berries, sugar, lemon juice and cinnamon, stirring occasionally, until hot and bubbly. Cover; chill. Serve over ice cream, cake and other fruits.

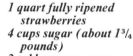

Color index page 100 Begin 2 days or up to 1 year ahead Six 8-ounce jars 594 cals per jar Low in fat, cholesterol, sodium Good source of vitamin C

Freezer Strawberry Topping

1 quart fully ripened strawberries	*1 1¾-ounce package powdered fruit pectin*
4 cups sugar (about 1¾ pounds)	*¾ cup water*
2 tablespoons orange juice	*about 6 8-ounce freezer-proof containers*

1. In large bowl with potato masher or slotted spoon, thoroughly crush berries, one layer at a time. Stir in sugar and orange juice until thoroughly mixed; let stand 10 minutes.
2. In 1-quart saucepan over medium heat, heat fruit pectin with water until boiling; boil 1 minute, stirring constantly. Stir pectin mixture into fruit; continue stirring 3 minutes to blend well (a few sugar crystals will remain).
3. Ladle mixture into containers to ½ inch from top; cover with lids. Let stand at room temperature for 24 hours or until set. Freeze to use within 1 year. For use within 3 weeks, store in refrigerator. Use to top plain or toasted slices of poundcake, angel cake; serve on rice pudding or ice cream; spoon over cheesecake; stir into plain yogurt.

Color index page 100 Begin 1½ hrs ahead 4 servings 215 cals per serving Low in sodium Good source of vitamin C

Strawberries Romanoff

¼ cup orange-flavored liqueur	*½ cup heavy or whipping cream*
¼ cup orange juice	*1½ tablespoons confectioners' sugar*
2 tablespoons brandy	
1 pint strawberries	

1. In small bowl, combine liqueur, juice and brandy. Cut strawberries in halves; add to mixture and chill at least 1 hour, spooning liquid over berries occasionally.
2. In another small bowl with mixer at high speed, whip cream until frothy; add sugar and beat until soft peaks form. Spoon strawberries into sherbet dishes and top with whipped cream.

Cherries

Season: May to August.
Look for: Plump, bright-looking cherries ranging in color from light to bright red to purplish-black, depending on variety. Tart or sour cherries are best for cooking. Sweet cherries may be eaten fresh or used in cooking. Avoid fruit which is too soft or shriveled in appearance.
To store: Refrigerate; use within 2 or 3 days.
To prepare: Remove any stems; wash and drain well. Remove pits as shown below.
To serve: Eat out of hand. Use in recipes for salads, pies, desserts, jams and sauces.

Pitting cherries: Cut into the center of the cherry with a sharp knife and remove the pit.

Or, you can remove the pit using a cherry or olive pitter.

Brandied Cherry Sauce

Color index page 100
Begin 30 mins or up to 3 days ahead
2 cups
108 cals per ¼ cup
Low in fat, cholesterol, sodium

1 pound sweet cherries, pitted
½ cup brandy
½ cup sugar

2 teaspoons cornstarch
¼ teaspoon almond extract

1. In 2-quart saucepan combine first 4 ingredients. Over medium heat, cook, stirring constantly, until mixture is thickened and boils; remove from heat. Stir in almond extract.
2. Serve warm or cover and refrigerate. Serve over vanilla ice cream, crêpes, bread pudding, or pound or sponge cake.

MAKING A MARASCHINO CHERRY BLOSSOM

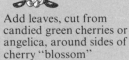

Cut canned red maraschino cherries into 6 or 8 sections, cutting about ¾ of the way through; with hand, spread open petals.

Add leaves, cut from candied green cherries or angelica, around sides of cherry "blossom"

Coconuts

Season: All year. Best supplies are from October to December.
Look for: Coconuts that are heavy for their size, filled with juice that sloshes around when coconut is shaken. Avoid fruit with moldy or wet eyes.
To store: Refrigerate and use within a week. (Fresh shredded coconut will keep in refrigerator 1 to 2 days.)
To prepare: See below.
To serve: Use coconut juice in beverages, salad dressings. Eat the coconut meat out of hand or shred it (see below) for use in recipes for salads, pies, pastries and cakes, and in desserts.

Preparing coconuts: With a skewer and hammer, puncture eyes of the coconut.

Drain the coconut juice into measuring cup (it may take some time for all the juice to drain through); reserve the juice and drink as is; or use in recipes for salads.

Open the shell by cracking very hard with a hammer at the widest part. Hit firmly all around middle.

Pry out coconut meat in pieces from the shell with a small sharp knife.

Shredding coconut: Use a small sharp knife to peel the brown skin from coconut meat (left); shred meat with a coarse grater. For *toasted shredded coconut,* preheat oven to 350°F. and spread coconut in shallow pan. Bake 20 to 30 minutes, stirring occasionally.

Autumn Buffet Supper

Harvest time ensures that markets are filled with pattypan, yellow straightneck and zucchini squashes, cauliflowers, Belgian endives, leeks, pumpkins, apples, pears, plums and grapes. Persimmons and pomegranates are also available, and thoughts turn to preserving or freezing the many fruits and vegetables at our disposal.

A buffet supper is a good way to share nature's bounty. Start with Hot Mulled Wine that is served with Homemade Pâté and Pepper-Herb Cheese with vegetables and crackers. As a main-dish choice, Châteaubriand garnished with watercress is elegant yet simple. For accompaniments, serve Dill Butter, Shrimp Cocktail with Tangy Dip, a pasta salad, Ratatouille and Italian bread slices. All tastes can be catered for with an array of desserts including Black Forest Cherry Torte and Fruit Cream Tarts.

Clockwise from left: cranberries; black grapes, persimmons; Red Delicious apples; pear (on plate); apples; pecans; walnuts; green seedless grapes; pumpkin; turban squash

Autumn Buffet
Supper

Menu

Autumn Buffet Supper
12 people

* * *

Hot Mulled Wine
page 471

* * *

Chicken Liver Pâté
page 122
Homemade Pepper-Herb Cheese
page 123

* * *

Châteaubriand and Dill Butter
(omit artichokes and Béarnaise Sauce)
pages 195 and
283
Shrimp Cocktail with Tangy Dip
(double recipe) page 164
Pasta Salad
(see over)
Ratatouille
page 297
Italian Bread Slices

* * *

Black Forest Cherry Torte
page 395
Fruit Cream Tarts
page 357
Apples and Pears

* * *

Coffee

Making a Pasta Salad

The many varieties of pasta provide a filling, nutritious, low-cost addition to any meal and pasta salads have become a popular accompaniment.

Short pastas such as corkscrew and elbow macaronis combine most easily with vegetables and other foods, but spaghetti and other long pastas can be used.

1 Cook *one 16-ounce package rotelle (corkscrew) macaroni* as label directs; drain. Place in large bowl. Meanwhile, trim stems from *1 bunch broccoli* and cut into 2-inch pieces.

2 Thinly slice *4 medium carrots* and *3 zucchini.* In 12-inch skillet, heat *2 tablespoons salad oil*; cook vegetables and *1/4 teaspoon salt,* stirring often, until tender-crisp. Add to pasta.

3 Cut *2 small red or yellow peppers* into 1-inch pieces and add to the pasta and vegetable mixture in the bowl.

4 Cut each olive from *1 cup pitted ripe olives* in half and add to the pasta-vegetable mixture. Shred *1/2 cup fresh basil leaves*; add to the mixture.

5 To serve: Add *1 cup Classic French Dressing* (page 326) and *1/2 teaspoon coarsely ground black pepper* to pasta salad and toss to coat well. Serve at room temperature.

Pasta Salad
A tasty accompaniment dish, a pasta salad can also make a substantial meal. Use filled pasta, such as cappelletti or tortellini, with tuna, chopped ham, chicken, or cheese and vary the salads with different vegetables and herbs.

Cranberries

Season: September to January.
Look for: Plump, firm berries with a high luster. Some varieties are rather large, bright red in color and quite tart; others are smaller, darker and sweeter. Avoid cranberries which are shriveled, discolored or moist. Cranberries are sold prepackaged by brands.
To store: Refrigerate. Use within 1 to 2 weeks.
To prepare: Wash and drain well.
To serve: Use in recipes below, and for sauces, salads, pies, sherbets and quick breads.

Cranberry Sauce

Color index page 72
Begin 10 mins or day ahead
5 cups
82 cals per ¼ cup
Low in fat, cholesterol, sodium

2 cups sugar	*1 16-ounce package*
1½ cups water	*cranberries*

1. In 2-quart saucepan over medium heat, heat sugar and water to boiling.
2. Add cranberries and return to boiling. Reduce heat to low; cover and simmer 7 minutes or until cranberries pop. Serve hot, or chill to serve cold.

Cranberry Relish

Color index page 72
Begin 3 hrs or day ahead
14 relish servings
272 cals per serving
Low in fat, cholesterol, sodium

3 15- or 16-ounce	*4½ cups packed brown*
packages fresh or	*sugar*
frozen cranberries	*¾ cup orange juice*

1. In 5-quart saucepan over high heat, heat all ingredients to boiling, stirring occasionally. Reduce heat to low; cover and simmer 30 minutes or until berries pop.
2. Spoon mixture into medium bowl, cover and refrigerate until well chilled.

CRANBERRY RELISH IN ORANGE CUPS: *About 1 hour before serving:* With sharp knife, cut each of *7 large oranges* in half. Scoop out pulp to use in salad another day. With kitchen shears, trim rim of each orange shell into sawtooth pattern. Fill orange shells with cranberry mixture.

Cranberry Chutney

Color index page 72
Begin 2 hrs or up to 1 wk ahead
7 cups
28 cals per tablespoon
Low in fat, cholesterol, sodium

1 16-ounce package	*1 cup California walnuts,*
cranberries	*chopped*
2 cups sugar	*1 cup chopped celery*
1 cup water	*1 medium apple,*
1 tablespoon grated	*chopped*
orange peel	*1 teaspoon ground ginger*
1 cup orange juice	
1 cup golden or dark	
seedless raisins	

1. In 3-quart saucepan over medium heat, heat cranberries, sugar and water to boiling, stirring the mixture frequently. Reduce heat to low and simmer 15 minutes.
2. Remove from heat; stir in remaining ingredients. Cover and refrigerate chutney.

Grapefruit

Season: All year. Best supplies October to May.
Look for: Well-shaped, firm fruit that is springy-to-touch and heavy for its size. Discolored spots on the skin rarely affect eating quality. Varieties include seedless, with seeds, pink- or white-fleshed. Avoid fruit which is soft or discolored at stem end.
To store: Refrigerate. Use within 1 to 2 weeks.
To prepare: See below.
To serve: Eat fresh, with sugar or salt, or bake with cinnamon or ginger. Use in recipes below, and for main dishes. For segments, peel like an orange.

Preparing grapefruit: Cut fruit in half between blossom and stem ends. With sharp pointed knife, cut sections from membrane, leaving them in place if serving in the shell.

Cut out the core; remove any seeds.

Broiled Grapefruit

Color index page 23
Begin 15 mins ahead
2 servings
68 cals per serving
Low in cholesterol, sodium

1 grapefruit	*butter or margarine,*
brown sugar	*softened*

1. Preheat broiler if manufacturer directs. Cut grapefruit in half, section and remove seeds.
2. Sprinkle each half with a little brown sugar; dot with softened butter or margarine. Broil 10 minutes or until golden and heated through.

BAKED GRAPEFRUIT: Prepare as above but bake in 450°F. oven for 20 minutes.

VARIATIONS: Instead of sugar, use honey, maple-flavored syrup or dark corn syrup.

Grapefruit Ambrosia

Color index page 100
Begin 5 mins ahead
4 servings
175 cals per serving

1 16-ounce can	*¼ cup honey*
grapefruit	*½ cup flaked coconut*
sections	

1. Thoroughly drain liquid from grapefruit sections; set aside for use another day.
2. In bowl, toss well grapefruit sections, honey and coconut. Serve immediately.

FRUIT
Grapes

Season: All year. Best grape supplies are available from July to November.

Look for: Plump, fresh-looking grapes with individual berries firmly attached to stems. A high color for the variety usually means good flavor. Avoid grapes with dry, brittle stems or any that are shriveled or leaking moisture and staining the carton.

To store: Refrigerate. Use within 1 to 2 weeks.

To prepare: Wash and seed fruit.

To serve: Eat out of hand. Use in recipes for salads, fish and poultry dishes, desserts, sauces, jellies and jams. Or sugar and use as a garnish (below).

Seeding grapes: With a small sharp knife, carefully cut each grape lengthwise in half.

Scoop out the seeds, either with the point of the knife or using the point of a small teaspoon.

Sugaring grapes: Dip a small bunch of grapes into egg white taking care to coat evenly. Then, dip the grapes in sugar.

Place grapes on rack until sugar coating is dry.

Color index page 101
Begin early in day
4 servings
195 cals per serving
Low in fat, cholesterol

Minted Grapes

1 bunch seedless green grapes
½ cup honey
2 tablespoons lime juice

2 tablespoons finely chopped mint

1. Stem grapes and arrange them in 4 sherbet or dessert dishes.
2. In small bowl, combine remaining ingredients; pour over grapes and refrigerate to marinate.

Kiwi Fruit

Also known as Chinese Gooseberries.

Season: June to December.

Look for: Small, slightly firm fruit with fairly fuzzy skin. When fully ripened, kiwi fruit should yield to gentle pressure on the skin.

To store: Refrigerate after the fruit has ripened and use within 1 or 2 days.

To prepare and serve: See below.

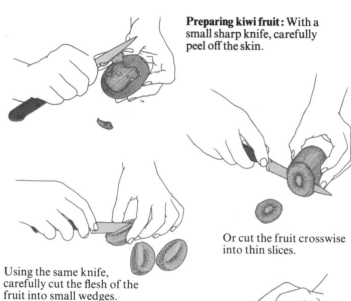

Preparing kiwi fruit: With a small sharp knife, carefully peel off the skin.

Or cut the fruit crosswise into thin slices.

Using the same knife, carefully cut the flesh of the fruit into small wedges.

Serving suggestion: Arrange slices from 1 or 2 kiwi fruit on a plate; garnish with fresh mint leaves and serve at once as a first course.

Gingered Kiwi Fruit

Color index page 101
Begin 2½ hrs ahead
4 servings
136 cals per serving
Low in fat, cholesterol, sodium
Good source of vitamin C

3 tablespoons sugar
3 tablespoons water
2 tablespoons minced crystallized ginger

¼ teaspoon vanilla extract
4 large kiwi fruit
2 medium oranges

1. In 1-quart saucepan over medium-high heat, heat sugar, water and ginger to boiling, stirring constantly. Boil until mixture reaches light syrup consistency, about 3 minutes. Remove from heat; stir in vanilla. Cool slightly.
2. Meanwhile, peel and slice kiwi fruit. With knife, peel and section oranges. In dessert dish, gently fold sliced kiwi fruit, orange sections and ginger syrup until well mixed. Cover the dish with plastic wrap; refrigerate until well chilled, about 2 hours.

Kumquats

Season: November to February.
Look for: Small, firm bright orange kumquats, with smooth, shiny skins. Avoid blemished or shriveled fruit.
To store: Keep a few days at room temperature or refrigerate and use within a week.
To prepare: See below.
To serve: Eat out of hand, peel and all. Add cut-up kumquats to fruit salads; use as a garnish or in recipes for jams and marmalades. Use canned, preserved kumquats, drained, as garnish for main dishes, especially those made with poultry or ham.

Preparing kumquats: Wash the kumquats under running cold water and remove any stems.

Serve whole, or, with a small sharp knife, cut the kumquats in half lengthwise and with the tip of the knife, remove the seeds.

Lemons and limes

Season: All year.
Look for: Bright, firm fruits that are heavy for their size. Pale or greenish-yellow lemons usually indicate fruit of higher acidity. Limes should be glossy skinned; irregular purplish-brown marks on skins do not affect quality. Avoid soft, shriveled or hard-skinned fruits.
To store: Keep a few days at room temperature. Or refrigerate and use within 2 weeks.
To prepare: See below.
To serve: Use lemon or lime juice in recipes for sauces for seafood, poultry, vegetables or fruits, and in beverages, salad dressings and desserts. Use slices or peel to garnish soups, main dishes, desserts, beverages.

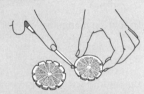

Preparing lemons and limes: For squeezing, cut in half between blossom and stem ends. Squeeze on a juice reamer. Discard seeds. Fruit at room temperature gives more juice. For garnishes, slice into rings or cut into chunky wedges. See left and below.

PREPARING CITRUS FRUIT PEEL

Lemon, lime and orange peel can all be grated, slivered or minced as illustrated here.

Grated peel: Wash fruit; dry. With grater over waxed paper, using quick downward strokes, remove outer colored layer of peel only. Measure lightly in spoon. Do not pack.

Slivered peel: Score peel of fruit into quarters; remove with fingers. With tip of spoon, scrape most of white membrane from peel. Stack 2 or 3 pieces at a time on cutting board. Cut into thinnest possible strips.

Minced peel: Prepare slivered peel, then finely chop with a sharp knife to mince.

MAKING LEMON AND LIME GARNISHES

Twists: Cut fruit crosswise in thin slices. Cut each slice once from center to edge, then twist the cut edges in opposite directions.

Cartwheels: Cut thin crosswise slices. Cut small V-shaped notches in peel around each slice.

Roses: Cut a thin crosswise slice from both ends of fruit. With a vegetable peeler, peel a continuous ½-inch-wide strip of peel.

Roll peel tightly, skin side out. Hold end in place with toothpick.

Lemon boats: Cut lemon in half lengthwise. Ream out juice; scrape clean. Edges may be notched with kitchen shears. To prevent tipping, cut small slice from bottom.

Mangoes

Season: April to September.

Look for: Oval or round, yellowish or orange fruit, sometimes with speckled skin. Ripe mangoes should yield slightly to gentle thumb pressure on the skin. (Unripe fruit are hard and have very poor flavor.) Avoid any bruised, soft or shriveled fruit.

To store: Allow to ripen at room temperature. Then refrigerate and use within 2 or 3 days.

To prepare: See below.

To serve: Eat out of hand; use sliced pieces for adding to fruit salads.

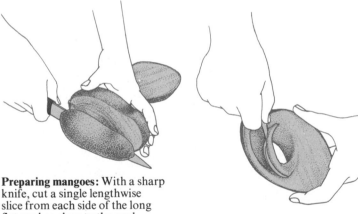

Preparing mangoes: With a sharp knife, cut a single lengthwise slice from each side of the long flat seed as close to the seed as possible; set aside the middle section of the mango containing the seed.

With a spoon, carefully scoop out the mango flesh in long curved slices for serving.

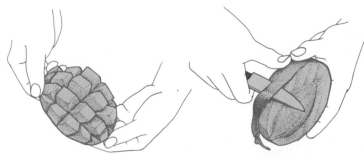

Or, for eating out of hand, score crosswise and then lengthwise the flesh of the slices without cutting through the skin. Gently push it out to eat the cubes.

Peel the skin from the inner section of the mango and either eat out of hand or carefully slice the flesh from the seed lengthwise and serve in recipes for fruit salad.

Melons

Season: April to November, depending on variety.

Look for: Fully ripened fruit for best sweetness and flavor. Avoid bruised or cracked melons. Follow these guidelines when selecting varieties:

Cantaloupe: Should be smooth at stem end, without a sign of any stem remaining. Rind around the blossom end should yield slightly to gentle thumb pressure. Cantaloupes should have a pleasant odor. The coarse, corky netting (veining) should stand out over the rind, which should not be green. Cantaloupes may be firm at store but ripen well at home.

Casaba: Gold yellow color indicates ripeness. Rind at blossom end should yield slightly to gentle thumb pressure. Casabas have no aroma.

Crenshaw: Rind should be deep golden yellow, sometimes with small areas of lighter yellow. The rind, especially around the blossom end, should yield slightly to gentle thumb pressure. Crenshaws should have a pleasant aroma.

Honey Ball: Follow tips for *honeydew,* except that honey ball is smaller and has slight, irregular netting over surface of rind.

Honeydew: Yellowish to creamy-white in color, with a soft, velvety feel. Ripeness is difficult to judge, but a honeydew should be slightly soft around the blossom end and have a faint, agreeable aroma.

Persian: Follow tips for *cantaloupe.* Persian melon is rounder and has fine netting.

Watermelon: Should be firm and symmetrically shaped (round or oblong, depending on variety). Ripeness is not always easy to judge so look for melons sold in halves or quarters. Flesh should be firm, of good red color, with dark brown or black seeds. Avoid melons with hard white streak running through flesh.

To store: Ripen at room temperature, then refrigerate and use within 2 to 3 days. Melons with strong aroma should be stored well wrapped to prevent aroma transferring to other foods in refrigerator. After cutting melons, tightly cover cut surfaces.

To prepare: See following page.

To serve: Serve melon with lemon or lime wedges as appetizer or dessert. Use in fruit and poultry salads.

Melons

Preparing melons: To serve cantaloupe or honeydew halves, cut melon in half between blossom and stem ends. Remove seeds with spoon. For decorative effect, with a knife, mark sawtooth design around melon shell (see Making a Watermelon Bowl, right).

For rings, with a sharp knife, cut crosswise into thick slices. Discard seeds.

For wedges, with a sharp knife, cut melon in half from stem to blossom end; discard seeds. Slice thickly lengthwise.

Scoop out balls of melon flesh either with a measuring half teaspoon or melon baller.

Gingered Melon Wedges

Color index page 23
Begin 2 hrs ahead
8 servings
39 cals per serving
Low in fat, cholesterol, sodium

1 large honeydew melon
2 tablespoons confectioners' sugar
½ teaspoon ground ginger

1. Cut melon in half lengthwise and remove seeds; slice each half into 4 wedges. Slash the pulp of wedges criss-cross into bite-size pieces, then cut pulp loose from rind, leaving pulp in place.
2. In cup, combine sugar and ginger; sprinkle over melon. Cover melon and refrigerate.

Cantaloupe Ice

Color index page 101
Begin day or several days ahead
5 cups
57 cals per ½ cup
Low in fat, cholesterol, sodium

2 medium cantaloupes
½ cup sugar
2 tablespoons lemon juice
½ teaspoon salt

1. Cut cantaloupes in half and remove seeds. With sharp knife, cut halves into thick slices and remove rind. Cut slices into chunks to make 6 cups.
2. In covered blender container at low speed, blend sugar, lemon juice, salt and about 1 cup of melon chunks until smooth; add remaining melon and blend a few seconds until smooth.
3. Pour into jelly-roll pan or large, shallow baking pan and place in freezer until partially frozen or mushy, about 2 hours.
4. Spoon mixture into chilled bowl; with mixer at high speed, beat until fluffy. Return to pan; freeze until firm. For easier serving, let stand at room temperature until soft enough to scoop.

Marinated Watermelon

Color index page 101
Begin 4 hrs ahead or early in day
16 servings
113 cals per serving
Low in fat, cholesterol, sodium

3 cups cranberry-juice cocktail
1 cup light corn syrup
2 tablespoons lime juice
1 small honeydew melon
1 10-pound oval-shaped watermelon

1. In large bowl, mix well first 3 ingredients. Cut honeydew in half; discard seeds; scoop pulp into balls; add to cranberry mixture.
2. Prepare watermelon bowl (see below): Cut lengthwise slice, 3 inches from top of melon; scoop out and cut pulp from both sections into 1-inch pieces; discard seeds and top rind. Add melon to cranberry mixture. Cut sawtooth edge around shell; cut thin slice off bottom.
3. Spoon melon mixture into watermelon bowl; cover. Refrigerate at least 3 hours. Serve the mixture in individual bowls.

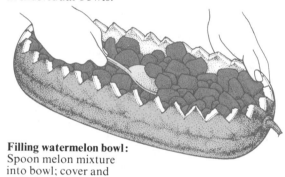

Filling watermelon bowl: Spoon melon mixture into bowl; cover and chill thoroughly.

MAKING A WATERMELON BOWL

With a large sharp knife, cut a lengthwise slice about 3 inches from the top of an oval-shaped watermelon; remove the top.

Scoop pulp into balls. Or, with a large spoon, scoop the red pulp from both sections, leaving the white. Cut up and reserve for use in recipes. Discard seeds.

With a small sharp knife, cut an even sawtooth pattern around the rim of the bottom shell. Cut a very thin slice of rind from bottom so bowl stands level. Refrigerate until serving time.

Nectarines

Oranges

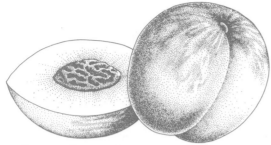

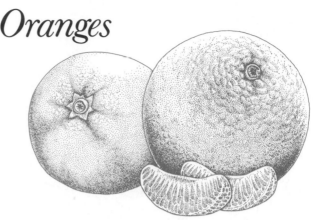

Season: June to September.
Look for: Plump, rich-colored fruit with slight softening along the seam side. Color can be reddish to yellowish, depending on variety. Slightly firm fruit ripens well at room temperature. Avoid hard, soft or shriveled fruit, or any with a large proportion of green skin.
To store: Ripen at room temperature. Refrigerate and use within 3 to 5 days.
To prepare: See below. To prevent browning, if cut nectarines are not to be eaten immediately, sprinkle with a little lemon juice or ascorbic-acid mixture for fruit.
To serve: Eat out of hand. Use in salads, desserts, relishes, pies; or use in recipes below.

Season: All year. Best in winter and early spring.
Look for: Firm oranges, heavy for their size. Strict state regulations help assure tree-ripened fruits. Slight greenish color or russeting of skin of some varieties does not affect quality. Navel and Temple oranges peel and section easily; Valencia, Parson Brown, Pineapple and Hamlin are juicy. Avoid dry, soft or spongy fruit.
To store: Keep at room temperature a few days or refrigerate and use within 2 weeks.
To prepare: Peel; slice, cut up or section (see below). See also Preparing Citrus Fruit Peel, page 307.
To serve: Eat out of hand. Use in recipes for salads, desserts, beverages, sauces, cakes.

Preparing nectarines: Wash the nectarine under running cold water; peel if you like. Cut nectarine in half; remove the seed.

Peeling and sectioning oranges: With a sharp knife, cut off peel and white portion, being sure to remove thin membrane that covers pulp.

Cut along both sides of each dividing membrane and lift out sections from center of orange.

Fresh Nectarine Relish

Color index page 72
Begin 4 hrs or up to 3 days ahead
4 cups
34 cals per tablespoon
Low in fat, cholesterol, sodium

2 pounds nectarines, seeded and diced
1 cup California walnuts, chopped
½ cup dark seedless raisins
½ cup packed dark brown sugar
¼ cup diced crystallized ginger
2 tablespoons lemon juice
½ teaspoon salt

In large bowl combine all ingredients. Cover with plastic wrap; refrigerate at least 3½ hours to blend flavors. Serve relish as accompaniment to chicken, pork, duck or ham.

Spiced Nectarine Slices

Color index page 72
Begin early in day
16 relish servings
47 cals per serving
Low in fat, cholesterol, sodium

1½ cups water
¾ teaspoon whole cloves
¼ teaspoon ground cinnamon
¼ teaspoon ground ginger
¼ teaspoon salt
4 large nectarines, peeled and thinly sliced
½ cup sugar
3 tablespoons lemon juice

1. In 10-inch skillet over medium heat, heat water with cloves, cinnamon, ginger and salt to boiling; boil 2 minutes.
2. Add nectarine slices and cook until fork-tender, about 10 minutes, stirring occasionally. During last minutes of cooking time, stir in sugar and lemon juice. Refrigerate until well chilled. Serve as accompaniment to meat or poultry.

Candied Orange Peel

Color index page 103
Begin day or up to 2 wks ahead
2 pounds
89 cals per ounce
Low in fat, cholesterol, sodium

4 cups long thin orange peel strips, lightly packed (about 3 large oranges)
water
½ cup light corn syrup
sugar
1 3-ounce package orange-flavor gelatin

1. In 5-quart saucepot over high heat, heat peel and 8 cups hot water to boiling; boil 15 minutes. Drain peel in colander and rinse. With 8 more cups of hot water, boil peel 15 minutes again; drain.
2. In same saucepot over high heat, heat corn syrup, 1¾ cups sugar and 1½ cups water until boiling and sugar is dissolved, stirring frequently. Stir in peel. Reduce heat to medium-low; cook until most of syrup has been absorbed, about 40 minutes, stirring.
3. Remove from heat; gently stir in gelatin until gelatin is dissolved; cool 10 minutes. (Mixture will be thick and sticky.)
4. Onto waxed paper, place 1 cup sugar. Lightly roll pieces of peel, a few at a time, in sugar, adding more sugar if necessary.
5. Place sugar-coated peel in single layer on wire racks; let dry overnight or about 12 hours. Store in tightly covered container.

Papayas

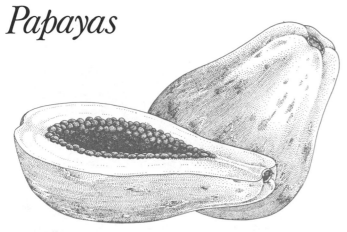

Season: All year.
Look for: Greenish-yellow to almost-yellow fruit that yields to gentle thumb pressure. Avoid shriveled or bruised fruit.
To store: Refrigerate. Use within 3 to 4 days.
To prepare: Cut in half lengthwise and scoop out seeds. Peel and slice or cut up.
To serve: Serve unpeeled halves with lemon or lime wedges for appetizer or dessert. Or fill with ice cream or sherbet, or flavored cream (see recipe below); use cut up in salads or desserts.

Papayas with Lemon Cream

Color index
page 100

Begin 1 hr
ahead

6 servings

289 cals per
serving

Low in
sodium

Good source
of vitamin A,
vitamin C

3 medium papayas
1 cup heavy or whipping
* cream*
2 egg yolks
⅓ cup sugar

3 tablespoons lemon
* juice*
⅛ teaspoon salt
lemon slices for garnish

1 Cut each papaya in half lengthwise and scoop out seeds. In small bowl with mixer at medium speed, beat the heavy or whipping cream until stiff peaks form.

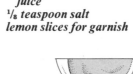

2 In another small bowl with mixer at high speed, beat egg yolks, sugar, lemon juice and salt until sugar dissolves. Gently fold mixture into whipped cream.

3 Spoon mixture into center of each papaya. Refrigerate until cream is slightly set, about 30 minutes.

4 *To serve:* Garnish papaya halves with lemon slices made into twists. (To make lemon twists, see page 308.)

Peaches

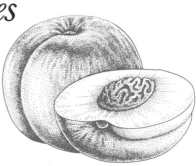

Season: May to October.
Look for: Fairly firm to slightly soft, yellow or cream-colored fruit with, depending on variety, a red blush. Avoid green, shriveled or bruised fruit. Pulp of freestone varieties is easily removed from the seed.
To store: Refrigerate. Use within 3 to 5 days.
To prepare: Peel (see below) and halve to remove seed. To prevent browning, if cut peaches are not eaten immediately, sprinkle with lemon juice or a little ascorbic-acid mixture for fruit.
To serve: Eat out of hand. Use in recipes below and for salads, desserts, pies, preserves.

Peeling peaches: To peel a peach, dip it into rapidly boiling water for about 15 seconds; dip immediately in pan of cold water.

With a small sharp knife, peel off the skin.

Stewed Peaches

Color index
page 100
Begin 20 mins
ahead
6 servings
69 cals per
serving

¼ cup sugar
¾ cup water
4 whole cloves

1½ pounds peaches,
* peeled and halved*
Low in fat, cholesterol, sodium

1. In 2-quart saucepan over medium heat, heat sugar, water and cloves to boiling.
2. Add peaches; return to boiling. Reduce heat to low; cover and simmer 10 minutes or until tender.

Buttery Baked Peaches

Color index
page 100

Begin 1 hr
ahead

6 servings or
12 garnishes

184 cals per
serving

Low in
sodium

6 peaches
½ cup sugar
2 tablespoons lemon juice
2 tablespoons butter or
* margarine*

1 cup water
mint jelly (optional)

1. Preheat oven to 350°F. Peel, halve and seed peaches. In 1-quart saucepan over medium-high heat, heat sugar, lemon juice, butter or margarine and water to boiling; simmer 5 minutes.
2. Place peaches in 3-quart casserole; add syrup. Cover and bake 30 minutes or until peaches are tender. Place a little mint jelly in center of each half, if you like. Serve, drained, as a garnish for meat dishes or warm as a dessert.

Pears

Season: All year, but best from August to December.

Look for: Well-shaped fruit which yields to soft pressure. Color depends upon variety. Avoid shriveled, discolored or bruised fruit. Bartlett, Anjou and Bosc pears can be used both for eating fresh and cooking; Comice, Seckel, Nelis and Kieffer are for eating fresh.

To store: Ripen firm pears at room temperature a few days, then refrigerate and use within 3 to 5 days.

To prepare: Wash; peel; halve and remove core and stem. For even slices, use a pear slicer (see below).

To serve: Eat out of hand; or with Roquefort, Cheddar or other cheese. Use in salads, pies, desserts.

Using a pear slicer: Press the cutter firmly down on top of the pear; slices fall away from the core, which remains intact.

Poached Pears in Sauterne

Color index page 101

Begin 4 hrs or day ahead

6 servings

81 cals per serving

Low in fat, cholesterol, sodium

3 large pears	*½ cup sauterne*
water	*¼ cup sugar*

1. Peel, halve and core each pear. In 10-inch skillet over medium-high heat, heat ½ inch water to boiling; add pears; heat to boiling. Reduce heat to low; cover and simmer 20 minutes or until tender.
2. With slotted spoon, remove pears from skillet and place in 9" by 9" baking dish.
3. To liquid in skillet, add sauterne and sugar; heat to boiling. Reduce heat to low; simmer 8 minutes; pour over pears; cover and refrigerate. Serve chilled.

Pears in Chocolate Sauce

Color index page 101

Begin 30 mins ahead or early in day

2 servings

387 cals per serving

Good source of vitamin A

2 ripe medium pears, chilled	*1 square unsweetened chocolate*
¼ cup sugar	*2 tablespoons milk*
2 tablespoons brandy	*½ cup thawed frozen whipped topping*
1 egg yolk	
⅛ teaspoon salt	

1. Remove cores from bottom of pears (do not remove stems). Stand pears on plate. In small bowl, mix well sugar, brandy, egg yolk and salt.
2. In 1-cup liquid measuring cup, place chocolate and milk. In 1-quart saucepan over low heat, in 1 inch hot, not boiling, water, place cup; heat until chocolate is melted, stirring constantly.
3. Stir in sugar mixture until slightly thickened; pour over pears. If prepared ahead, refrigerate.
4. Spoon topping on 2 dessert plates; stand pears in topping. Serve pears with knives and forks.

Pineapples

Season: All year.

Look for: Firm fruit, heavy for its size, with distinct aroma and plump, glossy eyes. Color depends on variety but green usually indicates that pineapple is unripe.

To store: Ripen pineapple at room temperature a few days; then refrigerate. Use within 1 to 2 days.

To prepare: See below.

To serve: Use as appetizer or dessert. Use in recipes for salads and pies (do not use fresh pineapple in gelatin because it prevents jelling).

Cutting rings: With a sharp knife, cut off crown and stem end; cut fruit into crosswise slices ½ to 1 inch thick, depending on recipe.

Carefully cut off the peel from the fruit.

Remove the eyes with the tip of a sharp knife.

Core with a biscuit cutter or sharp knife; serve as is or cut up in chunks.

Cutting wedges: With a sharp knife, slice pineapple in half lengthwise from bottom through crown; cut in quarters, leaving on leafy crown for decoration. Cut off core. With small sharp knife, loosen fruit by cutting close to peel. To serve in shell, cut fruit crosswise into slices and stagger slices.

Plums

Season: June to October.
Look for: Plump, well-colored fruit that yields to gentle pressure on the skin. Depending on variety, color varies from bright yellow-green to reddish-purple to purplish-black. Avoid hard, shriveled, soft or cracked fruit.
To store: Refrigerate. Use within 3 to 5 days.
To prepare: See below.
To serve: Eat out of hand. Serve sliced or cut up, with or without skins, with milk and sugar. Use in salads, desserts, sauces, jams, coffeecakes.

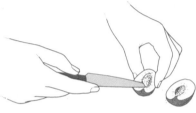

Preparing plums: Wash plums; with a small sharp knife, cut in half then remove seed.

Stewed Plums

Color index page 100
Begin 20 mins ahead
2¹/₂ cups

¹/₂ cup water
1 pound plums, halved and seeded

¹/₃ cup sugar
73 cals per ¹/₂ cup
Low in fat, cholesterol, sodium

1. In 2-quart saucepan over medium heat, heat water and plums to boiling. Reduce heat to low; cover and simmer 5 minutes.
2. During last minutes of cooking time, stir in sugar.

Creamy Plum Dressing

Color index page 100
Begin 1¹/₄ hrs ahead
1³/₄ cups
177 cals per ¹/₄ cup
Low in sodium

4 plums, seeded
¹/₂ cup confectioners' sugar

1 8-ounce package cream cheese, softened

1. In covered blender container at low speed, blend the plums and sugar until the mixture is of sauce consistency, about 1 minute.
2. Add cream cheese; blend for 30 seconds or just until smooth.
3. Refrigerate at least 1 hour. Serve well chilled over fresh fruit salad.

Plums in Port Sauce

Color index page 100

Begin day or up to 4 days ahead

6 servings

288 cals per serving

Low in fat, cholesterol, sodium

2 pounds small plums, halved and seeded
2 cups ruby port
6 whole cloves

1 cinnamon stick
1¹/₂ teaspoons grated orange peel
1 cup sugar

1. In 4-quart saucepan over high heat, heat plums, port, cloves, cinnamon and orange peel to boiling. Reduce heat to low; cover and simmer 3 to 5 minutes until plums are tender.
2. Gently stir in sugar until sugar is dissolved. Spoon plum mixture into large bowl; cover and refrigerate mixture overnight.
3. Serve the plums well chilled with their syrup or with vanilla ice cream spooned over.

Pomegranates

Season: September to December.
Look for: Fresh-looking fruit, heavy for its size. Avoid shriveled fruit or fruit with broken peel.
To store: Refrigerate. Use within 1 week.
To prepare: See below.
To serve: Use juice in beverages. Eat kernels out of hand, add them to fruit salads or use them as a garnish.

Preparing pomegranates: With sharp knife, 1 inch from and parallel to blossom end, make shallow cut all around.

With fingers, pull off top. Kernels are juicy.

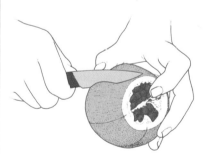

Score fruit, through peel only, in about 6 wedges.

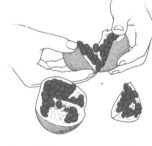

Break the pomegranate into separate sections.

Gently remove pomegranate kernels.

To extract the juice, with spoon, press kernels through sieve; discard seeds.

313

Rhubarb

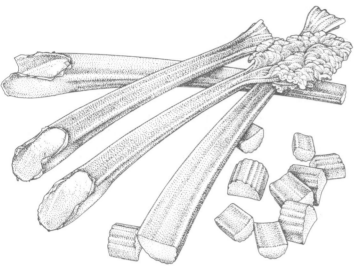

Season: January to July, but some areas may have rhubarb all year.

Look for: Firm, crisp, fairly thick stalks, either red or pink, depending on variety. Avoid limp stalks.

To store: Refrigerate. Use within 3 to 5 days.

To prepare: Cut off and discard any leaves. Trim discolored ends. With vegetable brush, scrub rhubarb under running cold water. Cut stalks into pieces for use in cooking.

To serve: Use in recipes below, and for pies, desserts, or sauces to accompany meat or poultry.

Rhubarb Sauce   Low in fat, cholesterol, sodium

1½ pounds rhubarb, cut up   *¾ cup water*
    ⅔ cup sugar

Color index page 101
Begin 20 mins ahead or early in day
2⅔ cups
70 cals per ⅓ cup

1. In 2-quart saucepan over medium heat, heat rhubarb and water to boiling. Reduce heat to low; cover and simmer 5 minutes or until rhubarb is tender, but not broken up.

2. During last minutes of cooking time, stir sugar into sauce. Serve hot or refrigerate to serve cold.

Rhubarb Crumble

1½ pounds rhubarb, cut into 1-inch pieces (about 4 cups)   *1¼ cups all-purpose flour*
¼ cup water   *½ cup butter or margarine*
1 teaspoon lemon juice   *half-and-half or vanilla ice cream*
sugar

Color index page 101
Begin 50 mins ahead
6 servings
315 cals per serving
Good source of calcium, vitamin A

1. In 4-quart saucepan over medium heat, heat rhubarb, water, lemon juice and ½ cup sugar to boiling. Reduce heat to low; cover and simmer 10 minutes or until rhubarb is tender. Pour mixture into 8″ by 8″ baking dish. Preheat oven to 425°F.

2. In medium bowl with fork, stir flour and ¼ cup sugar. With pastry blender or 2 knives used scissor-fashion, cut butter or margarine into flour mixture until mixture resembles coarse crumbs.

3. Sprinkle flour mixture over rhubarb. Bake in oven 25 minutes or until crumbs are golden. Serve warm with half-and-half or ice cream.

Tangerines and tangelos

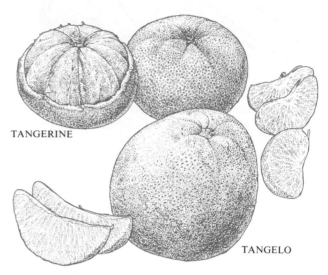

TANGERINE

TANGELO

Season: Tangelos are in season from November to February, tangerines from October to April.

Look for: Firm tangelos, heavy for their size, with good orange color. They peel and section easily (see below), are juicy and have few seeds. Tangerines are deep yellow to deep orange in color, heavy for their size, and often have loose skins which can easily be pulled away.

To store: Keep tangelos at room temperature a few days or refrigerate and use within 1 week. Refrigerate tangerines and use within 1 or 2 days.

To prepare: See below.

To serve: Eat out of hand. Use in salads.

Peeling and sectioning: Starting from the stem end, with fingers, pull off the skin.

Break the fruit into its natural sections; cut center of each section to remove seeds.

Zesty Tangelo Salad

4 large tangelos or 6 large tangerines   *2 tablespoons sliced pimento*
1 cup thinly sliced celery   *½ teaspoon salt*
¼ cup bottled Italian salad dressing   *romaine leaves*

Color index page 77
Begin 40 mins ahead
6 servings
86 cals per serving
Low in cholesterol

1. Peel tangelos; separate into sections; remove seeds, if any.

2. In large bowl combine celery, salad dressing, pimento and salt; add tangelos and gently toss to coat with dressing.

3. To serve: Line salad bowl with romaine leaves. Spoon tangelo mixture onto romaine.

More unusual fruits

Supermarkets now carry a wide range of fruit from countries worldwide. Many of these more unusual fruits have been grown in tropical climates, and have become popular for adding flavor, color and texture to a variety of recipes. Except for plantains and quinces, they can also be eaten out of hand.

Cactus pears (prickly pears)
Season: September to December.
Look for: Thorny, tough-textured fruit that have had their sharp spines removed. When ripe, the skin is red and should yield to gentle pressure.
To prepare: Peel as you would an apple, avoiding the thorns; slice or cut up to eat out of hand or use in salads.

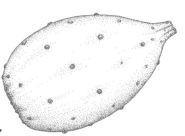

Cherimoyas (custard apples)
Season: November through May.
Look for: Large fruit, uniformly green, with rough, petallike indentations. When ripe, the skin should yield to gentle pressure.
To prepare: Cut lengthwise into halves or quarters; serve as you would melon wedges. Discard seeds when eating.

Dates
Season: All year.
Look for: Lustrous plump brown fruit, lighter in color than dried dates. Sold pitted and unpitted.
To serve: Eat out of hand. Use dates in desserts, cookies, breads and salads or as a dessert with other fruit.

Figs
Season: Summer and fall.
Look for: Slightly firm fruit, greenish-yellow to purple to black in color. When ripe, the skin should yield to gentle pressure. Avoid very soft figs or figs with sour odor.
To serve: Eat out of hand or serve with prosciutto or cheese.

Guavas
Season: September through November
Look for: Fruit with green to yellowish-red skin. Ripe guavas should yield to gentle pressure on the skin. Avoid cracked skins.
To prepare: Cut off the skin. Cut large guavas in pieces for eating out of hand.

Loquats
Season: April and early May.
Look for: Deep-colored, orange-yellow fruit that yield to gentle pressure on the skin when ripe.
To prepare: Pull off peel; remove seeds for eating out of hand, or use in salads.

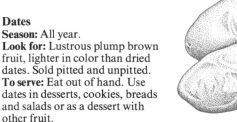

Passion fruit
Season: February through July.
Look for: Fruit with leathery, mottled, brownish-purple skin; this is wrinkled when fruit is ripe. Flesh is light orange in color, with small, numerous, dark, edible seeds; the flavor is similar to that of a sweet grapefruit.
To prepare: See opposite page 209.

Plantains (cooking bananas)
Season: All year.
Look for: Large, firm, greenish-yellow to dark-brown fruit with some black spots. The skin of very ripe plantains is black and the fruit yields to gentle pressure.
To prepare: Peel as you would a banana and use plantains cooked as a vegetable.

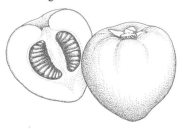

Ugli fruits
Season: December through May.
Look for: Greenish-yellow fruits with wrinkled, bumpy skin; ugli fruits are a hybrid between a tangerine and a grapefruit.
To prepare: Peel as a tangerine or cut in half and eat as a grapefruit; use in salads.

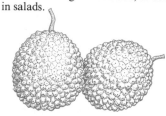

Lychees
Season: Late May through July.
Look for: Firm, rough, reddish-brown fruit with rubbery skin.
To prepare: Peel as an orange, beginning at the stem. Remove the pit for eating lychees out of hand, or use fruit in salads or in Oriental stir-fry dishes.

Persimmons
Season: October through December.
Look for: Orange, slightly firm fruit resembling a tomato, with smooth skin and stem cap attached. Oriental varieties are most common.
To prepare: See opposite page 209.

Quinces
Season: October and November.
Look for: Golden-yellow, round or pear-shaped fruit with rather fuzzy skin. Avoid bruised or small, knotty fruit.
To prepare: Quinces are usually eaten cooked and sweetened with sugar. Use as a dessert or sauce or in puddings, pies and tarts.

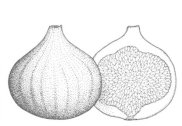

SALADS

Salads are for serving the year round, as appetizers, accompaniment dishes, substantial main dishes and desserts. Most are quick and easy to make and take little or no cooking. They can be tossed in anything from a regular salad bowl to an earthenware casserole and served from the kitchen or at the table. For variety with few calories, there's a wide range of low-calorie greens to use in salads and as garnishes.

Appetizer salads are light and tangy, to stimulate the palate for heartier foods to follow. The favorite is a simply dressed mixture of tossed greens, sometimes with vegetables or fruit added for color and flavor contrast.

Accompaniment salads may be a mixture of greens, or a heartier combination of greens and vegetables or fruit. Recipes in this chapter are for accompaniment servings, unless otherwise specified.

Main-dish salads provide the same quantity of high-quality protein to be found in hot main dishes based on meat, poultry, seafood, cheese or eggs.

Dessert salads are made of fruit, often with nuts or cheese, and a sweet dressing.

CHOOSING SALAD GREENS

Always use fresh, crisp-looking greens, free from wilted or discolored leaves, for salads. (For details of choosing and storing lettuce and other greens, see page 287.) Select firm, heavy heads of iceberg lettuce and cabbage. Besides the familiar lettuces there are many other greens from which to choose: romaine, escarole, chicory (curly endive), Belgian endive, green and red cabbage, Chinese cabbage, kale, spinach, watercress, sorrel. Young beet greens, celery and turnip tops add special flavor interest to the salad bowl, too. For tempting variety of color, texture and flavor, plan to combine tangy greens with mild-flavored ones, crisp leaves with tender ones, dark leaves with pale ones. Experiment until you find the combination of greens you like.

Greens also add good nutrition to your menus – vitamins, minerals and few calories. Don't discard outer, darker green leaves of romaine or lettuce that are not wilted or bruised. Although often less tender than the inner leaves, they are especially nutritious. Wash, dry and shred the outer leaves and add to the salad bowl, or use in sandwiches or as a garnish for cold dishes or hot clear soups or consommé.

CLEANING AND STORING SALAD GREENS

Store prepared greens in the refrigerator, in plastic bags, in covered containers, in the crisper drawer, or wrapped in plastic wrap. Use them within a day or two.

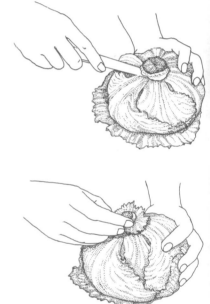

Preparing firm heads (such as iceberg lettuce, red or green cabbage): Holding lettuce firmly, insert a sharp knife alongside core and cut all the way around the core in cone shape.

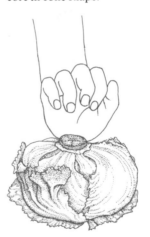

Or place lettuce, core up, on counter and with heel of hand, strike core firmly to loosen.

Then, holding lettuce firmly with one hand, twist out the loosened core with the other hand; discard core.

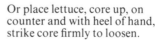

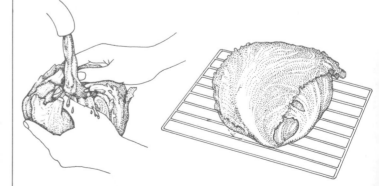

Washing a firm lettuce: Hold head, cut side up, under running cold water to clean and help separate the leaves.

Place, cored end down, on rack or in colander; allow to drain thoroughly.

Preparing loose heads (Boston lettuce, romaine): Break off individual leaves.

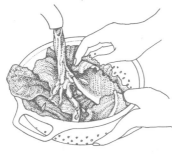

Place in a colander or French lettuce basket. Hold colander under running cold water; shake, then drain well.

PREPARING OTHER GREENS

Wash greens such as chicory, Swiss chard, kale, spinach or leafy broccoli in cold water. Drain them thoroughly, pat dry, trim tough ribs or stems.

With a small sharp knife, trim any tough ribs or stems from the washed greens.

CRISPING SALAD GREENS

Gently pat leaves dry with paper towels, taking care not to damage the leaves.

Place in plastic bags and refrigerate. Place washed and dried fresh parsley, watercress and mint, stems down, in a little water in covered jars; refrigerate.

DRESSING THE SALAD

As a general rule, light oil-and-vinegar dressings go best with tender greens such as Boston lettuce, and creamy or mayonnaise dressings with very crisp greens such as romaine or iceberg lettuce. For the weight-conscious, cut down on the quantity of salad oil used and toss the greens with freshly squeezed lemon juice, or use instead a low-calorie ingredient such as cottage cheese, sour cream or yogurt.

It's a good idea to mix the dressing ingredients well in advance to allow flavors to develop. While cooked vegetable salads absorb more flavor if part of the dressing is mixed in while they are still warm, don't dress green salads until just before serving, or the leaves will become limp and garnishes such as croutons will become soggy.

When dressing a salad, unless the recipe directs otherwise, start by adding about ⅔ of the dressing to the mixture and mix or toss gently until the dressing is well incorporated. Then, if necessary, add the rest of the dressing until the ingredients are just coated. Avoid overdressing salads – it makes them soggy.

Leftover dressings keep well in the refrigerator, and often small amounts can be combined with mayonnaise or sour cream to make enough new dressing for another meal's salad.

MOLDED SALADS

Shimmering gelatin salads, which can be shaped either individually or in a large, attractive mold, add a decorative touch to any table.

They should be prepared at least 4 hours ahead of serving, to give the gelatin time to set fully. To keep large molded mixtures from breaking, unmold them directly onto the serving platter and then surround with greens. Wet the platter first with a little cold water so the salad can be moved easily to the platter's center if needed; individual salads can simply be unmolded right onto the salad greens. Once unmolded, a gelatin salad should be taken straight to the table and served immediately.

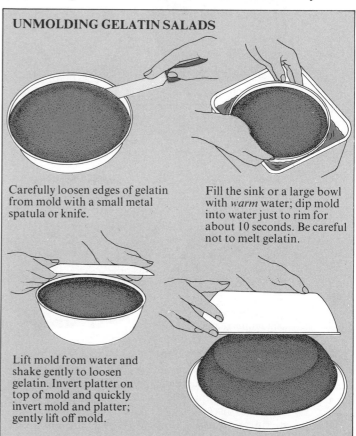

UNMOLDING GELATIN SALADS

Carefully loosen edges of gelatin from mold with a small metal spatula or knife.

Fill the sink or a large bowl with *warm* water; dip mold into water just to rim for about 10 seconds. Be careful not to melt gelatin.

Lift mold from water and shake gently to loosen gelatin. Invert platter on top of mold and quickly invert mold and platter; gently lift off mold.

Tossed salads

Caesar Salad

Color index
page 75

Begin 30 mins
ahead

6 servings

246 cals per
serving

Good source
of calcium

Garlic Croutons (below)
2 medium heads romaine
lettuce or the
equivalent in iceberg or
leaf lettuce
¹⁄₃ cup olive or salad oil
¹⁄₃ cup grated Parmesan
cheese

2 tablespoons lemon juice
¹⁄₄ teaspoon salt
¹⁄₈ teaspoon cracked
pepper
1 2-ounce can anchovy
fillets, drained
1 egg

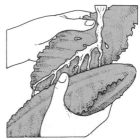

1 Prepare the Garlic Croutons; set aside. Wash romaine under running cold water; drain thoroughly in colander or French lettuce basket; pat dry with paper towels.

2 Into chilled large salad bowl, tear the romaine into bite-size pieces.

3 Add olive oil and toss together gently until the romaine leaves are thoroughly coated

4 Add Parmesan cheese, lemon juice, salt, cracked pepper, anchovies and uncooked egg; toss again gently to mix well.

5 Garnish salad with Garlic Croutons. Serve salad immediately.

GARLIC CROUTONS: Trim crusts from **3 white bread slices;** cut slices into ¹⁄₂-inch cubes. In 10-inch skillet over medium heat, heat **¹⁄₄ cup salad oil;** add **1 small garlic clove** and cook until golden, about 2 minutes; discard garlic. Add bread cubes; cook, stirring frequently, until the cubes are crisp and golden. Drain well on paper towels.

Tossed Salad with Lemony-Mustard Dressing

Color index
page 75

Begin 45 mins
ahead

10 servings

161 cals per
serving

Low in
cholesterol

Good source
of iron

2 10-ounce bags spinach
1 medium head Boston
lettuce
2 small Belgian endives
¹⁄₂ pound medium
mushrooms

Dressing:
1 large lemon

²⁄₃ cup olive or salad oil
2 teaspoons sugar
1 teaspoon salt
1 teaspoon dry mustard
1 teaspoon fresh or
frozen chopped chives
¹⁄₄ teaspoon cracked
pepper

1. Into chilled large salad bowl, tear spinach and Boston lettuce into bite-size pieces. Cut endives in half crosswise; separate top leaves; cut bottom into wedges. Thinly slice mushrooms. Add endives and mushrooms to spinach mixture.
2. Prepare the dressing: Grate 2 teaspoons peel from lemon; squeeze juice from lemon to make ¹⁄₄ cup. In small bowl with wire whisk or fork, mix lemon peel, lemon juice, olive oil and remaining ingredients.
3. Pour dressing over salad; gently toss to mix well and thoroughly coat vegetables.

Colonel's Lady's Salad Bowl

Color index
page 75

Begin 20 mins
ahead

12 servings

55 cals per
serving

Low in
cholesterol

¹⁄₂ 10-ounce package
frozen peas
boiling water
1 small head romaine
lettuce
1 small head iceberg
lettuce
1 small cucumber,
thinly sliced
3 green onions,
chopped
1 stalk celery,
sliced

Dressing:
¹⁄₄ cup salad oil
3 tablespoons white wine
vinegar
1 tablespoon sugar
1 tablespoon chopped
parsley
¹⁄₂ teaspoon garlic salt
¹⁄₂ teaspoon salt
¹⁄₄ teaspoon oregano
leaves
¹⁄₈ teaspoon seasoned
pepper

1. In medium bowl, place frozen peas; cover with boiling water and let stand 5 minutes.
2. Meanwhile, in large bowl, tear lettuce into bite-size pieces; drain peas and add to bowl with remaining salad ingredients.
3. Prepare the dressing: In cup, combine dressing ingredients; stir with fork to mix well.
4. Toss salad gently with dressing to coat lettuce.

California Salad

Color index
page 75

Begin 30 mins
ahead

8 servings

291 cals per
serving

Low in
cholesterol

Good source
of iron

¹⁄₄ cup salad oil
1 tablespoon sugar
2 tablespoons white wine
vinegar
2 teaspoons minced
parsley
¹⁄₂ teaspoon garlic salt
¹⁄₂ teaspoon seasoned salt
¹⁄₄ teaspoon oregano
leaves

¹⁄₈ teaspoon seasoned
pepper
¹⁄₂ large head iceberg
lettuce
¹⁄₂ large head Boston
lettuce
2 large avocados, peeled
and sliced
¹⁄₂ cup California walnuts

1. To make the dressing, in large salad bowl, mix thoroughly first 8 ingredients.
2. Into dressing, tear iceberg and Boston lettuce into bite-size pieces. Add avocados; gently toss to coat avocados and lettuce. Garnish with walnuts.

Vegetable salads

Deluxe Coleslaw

Color index page 76

Begin 1½ hrs ahead or early in day

8 servings

112 cals per serving

Low in sodium

Dressing:
½ cup mayonnaise or cooked salad dressing
1 tablespoon milk
1 tablespoon vinegar or lemon juice
½ teaspoon sugar
¼ teaspoon salt
⅛ teaspoon paprika
⅛ teaspoon pepper

1 medium head cabbage
1 small green pepper
1 large celery stalk
1 large carrot
2 tablespoons minced onion

1 Prepare dressing: Into cup, measure all dressing ingredients; with fork or wire whisk, stir until well blended. Set aside.

2 With sharp knife, shred cabbage and thinly slice green pepper.

3 With a sharp knife, first cut the celery stalk into ¼-inch-wide pieces. Then, using a grater, finely shred the carrot.

4 In large bowl, gently toss prepared cabbage, green pepper, celery, carrot, onion and dressing. Cover and refrigerate.

COLESLAW BOWL

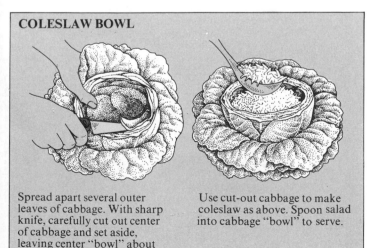

Spread apart several outer leaves of cabbage. With sharp knife, carefully cut out center of cabbage and set aside, leaving center "bowl" about ¾ inch thick.

Use cut-out cabbage to make coleslaw as above. Spoon salad into cabbage "bowl" to serve.

Cucumbers in Sour Cream

Color index page 75

Begin 20 mins ahead or early in day

6 servings

102 cals per serving

1 cup sour cream
3 tablespoons minced chives or onion
2 tablespoons lemon juice

1 teaspoon salt
⅛ teaspoon pepper
3 large cucumbers

1. In large bowl, combine sour cream, minced chives, lemon juice, salt and pepper.
2. Peel and thinly slice cucumbers; add and mix well. Cover and refrigerate.

Danish Cucumber Salad

Color index page 75

Begin 5 hrs ahead or early in day

8 servings

40 cals per serving

Low in fat, cholesterol

4 medium cucumbers
salt
½ cup white vinegar
¼ cup sugar

2 tablespoons chopped fresh dill
¼ teaspoon white pepper

1. With sharp knife, cut cucumbers into paper-thin slices. In large bowl, mix slices with 2 teaspoons salt. Let stand at room temperature 1 hour.
2. Drain liquid from cucumbers. Stir in vinegar, sugar, chopped dill, pepper and 1 teaspoon salt until thoroughly mixed.
3. Cover with plastic wrap and refrigerate salad at least 3 hours before serving.

Tomatoes Vinaigrette

Color index page 75

Begin 2 hrs ahead

6 servings

68 cals per serving

Low in cholesterol

6 medium tomatoes
2 tablespoons salad oil
1 teaspoon wine vinegar
½ teaspoon sugar
½ teaspoon dried basil leaves

½ teaspoon salt
½ teaspoon pepper
fresh basil leaves for garnish (optional)

1. Slice tomatoes and arrange in serving dish in overlapping slices.
2. In small bowl, combine salad oil, wine vinegar, sugar, dried basil leaves, salt and pepper. Stir thoroughly to blend and sprinkle over tomatoes. Cover and refrigerate until serving time.
3. *To serve:* Garnish Tomatoes Vinaigrette with fresh basil leaves, if you like.

Marinated Artichoke Hearts and Mushrooms

Color index page 20

Begin early in day or day ahead

8 first-course servings

226 cals per serving

Low in cholesterol

2 9-ounce packages frozen artichoke hearts
¾ cup salad oil
½ cup lemon juice
1 tablespoon sugar
1½ teaspoons salt
1 teaspoon dry mustard

½ teaspoon pepper
½ teaspoon basil
1 small garlic clove, crushed
1 pound mushrooms, sliced
1 tablespoon diced pimento

1. Prepare artichoke hearts as the labels direct; drain them thoroughly.
2. In large bowl, mix salad oil with lemon juice, sugar, salt, mustard, pepper, basil and garlic until well blended.
3. Stir in artichoke hearts, sliced mushrooms and diced pimento. Cover with plastic wrap and refrigerate, tossing mixture occasionally.

Vegetable salads

Greek Salad

1 medium head chicory
1 medium head iceberg
lettuce
2 medium cucumbers
2 large tomatoes
1 5½-ounce jar Greek
olives or 1 6-ounce can
pitted ripe olives,
drained
1 2-ounce can anchovy
fillets, drained
(optional)

2 green onions, chopped
2 tablespoons capers
½ pound feta cheese,
crumbled
½ cup olive or salad oil
3 tablespoons red wine
vinegar
1 teaspoon oregano
leaves
½ teaspoon salt
⅛ teaspoon pepper

Color index
page 77

Begin 30 mins
ahead

10 servings

169 cals per
serving

Low in
cholesterol

Good source
of calcium

1. Into chilled large salad bowl, tear chicory and iceberg lettuce into bite-size pieces.
2. Peel lengthwise strips of skin from cucumbers, to give striped effect; slice the cucumbers thinly; cut tomatoes into wedges.
3. Add cucumbers and tomatoes to lettuce mixture with olives, anchovy fillets; if you are using them, green onions, capers and feta cheese.
4. In cup, combine olive oil with the remaining ingredients; pour over salad; toss to mix well.

Preparing cucumber: Peel strips of skin from cucumbers, then slice cucumbers thinly.

Adding feta cheese: Add coarsely crumbled cheese to salad ingredients then add dressing and mix well.

Potato-Vegetable Salad

8 medium potatoes,
unpeeled
water
2 10-ounce packages
frozen peas and carrots
2 small cucumbers

salt
1 cup mayonnaise
⅓ cup milk
¼ teaspoon pepper
leaf lettuce

Color index
page 75

Begin 1 hr
ahead

8 servings

365 cals per
serving

Good source
of iron

1. In 4-quart saucepan over high heat, heat potatoes and enough water to cover to boiling. Reduce heat to medium-low; cover; cook 20 to 30 minutes until tender; drain.
2. Cool potatoes slightly; with a sharp knife, peel and cut into ½-inch cubes.
3. Meanwhile, prepare peas and carrots as labels direct. Cut cucumbers into paper-thin slices. In medium bowl, gently toss cucumbers with ¼ teaspoon salt; set aside.
4. In large bowl with rubber spatula, gently toss potatoes, peas and carrots, mayonnaise, milk, pepper and 1 teaspoon salt until well mixed.
5. To serve: Line large platter with lettuce leaves; spoon salad onto center of platter. Arrange cucumbers, overlapping, on top of salad.

German Hot-Potato Salad

6 medium potatoes,
unpeeled (2 pounds)
water
6 slices bacon, cut into
½-inch pieces
½ cup chopped onion
2 teaspoons sugar
1½ teaspoons salt
1 teaspoon all-purpose
flour
⅛ teaspoon pepper
3 tablespoons red wine
vinegar
minced parsley for
garnish

Color index
page 75

Begin 45 mins
ahead

6 servings

227 cals per
serving

1 In 4-quart saucepan over high heat, heat potatoes and water to cover to boiling. Reduce heat to low; cover; simmer 20 to 30 minutes until fork-tender.

2 Drain potatoes and allow to cool slightly. With sharp knife, peel and dice potatoes.

3 Meanwhile, in 10-inch skillet over medium heat, cook bacon until crisp; remove bacon to paper towels to drain.

4 Spoon off all but 2 tablespoons bacon fat from skillet. Add onion; cook until tender, about 5 minutes, stirring often.

5 Stir in sugar, salt, flour and pepper until mixture is well blended.

6 Gradually stir in red wine vinegar and ½ cup water. Cook, stirring the mixture constantly, until it is slightly thickened and boiling.

7 Gently stir in potatoes and bacon; heat through then transfer salad to warm bowl or platter. Garnish with minced parsley.

Celery Hearts Vinaigrette

4 medium bunches celery
water
1 chicken-flavor bouillon
cube or envelope
1 4-ounce jar pimentos,
drained and minced
⅔ cup white vinegar
⅓ cup salad oil

3 tablespoons minced
green pepper
1 teaspoon sugar
1 teaspoon salt
1 teaspoon dry mustard
¾ teaspoon seasoned
pepper
romaine lettuce leaves

Color index
page 20

Begin 6 hrs
or day ahead

8 first-course
servings

96 cals per
serving

Low in
cholesterol

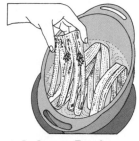

1 Remove outer rows of celery ribs; trim root ends. Cut tops and leaves from celery 6 to 8 inches from root ends; discard. Halve bunches lengthwise.

2 In 5-quart Dutch oven over medium heat, in 1 inch boiling water, heat celery and bouillon to boiling. Cover and cook 15 minutes until tender.

3 Meanwhile, in 13″ by 9″ baking dish, combine pimentos with the remaining ingredients except lettuce.

4 Drain celery; arrange in baking dish, turning to coat with marinade. Cover and refrigerate at least 4 hours or overnight, turning occasionally.

5 To serve: Line 8 salad plates with romaine leaves and arrange celery on top. Spoon some marinade over salad.

VARIATION: Prepare and cook *celery* as in steps 1 and 2 above. In 13″ by 9″ baking dish, combine *pimentos* with *Classic French Dressing* or *Mixed Herb Dressing* (page 326); omit remaining ingredients except romaine lettuce leaves. Drain and marinate celery; serve on lettuce leaves as above.

Color index
page 76

Begin 6 hrs
ahead

8 servings

108 cals per
serving

BRAISED LEEKS VINAIGRETTE: Cut off roots and trim leaf end of **8 medium leeks** (about 3 pounds). Cut each leek crosswise in half; then cut root end of each leek lengthwise in half. Rinse leeks well under running cold water to remove all sand. Divide leeks into 4 portions; tie loosely with string into 4 bundles. Cook leeks in **chicken broth** about 30 minutes until tender. Untie bundles; marinate and serve as for Celery Hearts Vinaigrette.

Three-Bean Salad

Color index
page 76

Begin early
in day or
several days
ahead

8 servings

178 cals per
serving

Low in
cholesterol

½ cup sugar
½ cup salad oil
½ cup cider vinegar
1 teaspoon salt
1 16-ounce can cut green
beans, drained

1 16-ounce can cut wax
beans, drained
1 16-ounce can red
kidney beans, drained
½ cup chopped onion

1. In large bowl, stir sugar with salad oil, vinegar and salt until blended. Add beans and onion; toss to coat beans and onion thoroughly.
2. Cover and refrigerate at least 6 hours before serving to blend flavors.

Turkish Bean Salad

Color index
page 76

Begin 5 hrs
or day ahead

10 servings

242 cals per
serving

Low in
cholesterol

Good source
of iron

1 16-ounce package dry
Great Northern, navy
or pea beans
6 cups water
3 chicken-flavor bouillon
cubes or envelopes
1 bay leaf
1 6-ounce can pitted ripe
olives, drained and
halved
2 large tomatoes,
chopped

½ cup olive or salad oil
½ cup lemon juice
2 tablespoons crumbled
dried mint or ⅓ cup
chopped fresh mint
1 tablespoon salt
1 tablespoon sugar
¼ teaspoon white pepper
mint leaves
for garnish

1. Rinse beans under running cold water and discard any stones or shriveled beans.
2. In 7-quart Dutch oven over high heat, heat beans, water, bouillon and bay leaf to boiling; boil 2 minutes. Remove from heat; cover and allow to stand 1 hour.
3. Over high heat, return beans to boiling. Reduce heat to low; cover and simmer beans 1 hour or until tender but firm, stirring occasionally. Drain beans; discard bay leaf.
4. In large bowl with rubber spatula, gently combine beans, olives and remaining ingredients except mint leaves. Cover; refrigerate until well chilled.
5. *To serve:* Spoon into salad dish and garnish.

German Sauerkraut Salad

Color index
page 76

Begin 1½
hrs or up to
3 days ahead

8 servings

101 cals per
serving

Low in
cholesterol

1 27-ounce can
sauerkraut (4 cups)
2 red eating apples
⅓ cup olive oil

2 teaspoons sugar
½ teaspoon cracked
pepper

1. Drain sauerkraut; set aside. With grater, grate eating apples, including the peel.
2. In large bowl, combine sauerkraut, grated apples, olive oil, sugar and pepper.
3. Cover and refrigerate salad at least 1 hour.

321

Fruit salads

Waldorf Salad

1 cup mayonnaise
¼ cup lemon juice
1 pound red eating
*   apples*
2 cups thinly sliced celery
1 cup California walnuts,
*   chopped*
1 cup dark seedless
*   raisins*
lettuce leaves

Color index
page 77

Begin 20 mins
ahead

8 servings

381 cals per
serving

1 In medium bowl with
fork, mix mayonnaise
with lemon juice.

2 With small sharp knife,
dice eating apples (do
not peel them); discard
cores and stems.

3 Add diced apples to
mayonnaise and lemon
juice mixture and with
spoon, stir to coat well.

4 Add sliced celery, wal-
nuts and raisins; toss
gently to mix well.

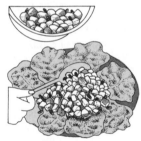

5 Arrange lettuce leaves
on serving platter and
spoon salad into center.

Hawaiian Fruit Salad

Color index
page 21

Begin 20 mins
ahead

8 first-course
servings

136 cals per
serving

Low in fat,
cholesterol,
sodium

Good source
of vitamin C

preserved ginger in
*   syrup*
¼ cup lime juice
¼ cup light corn syrup
¼ teaspoon salt

4 medium papayas
4 medium bananas
¼ cup shredded
*   coconut*

1. Mince enough drained, preserved ginger to make
¼ cup; set aside.
2. In small bowl, combine lime juice, corn syrup, salt
and ¼ cup syrup from preserved ginger; set aside.
3. With sharp knife, cut papayas lengthwise in half
and scoop out seeds. Slice off thin piece from
rounded side of each papaya half, so that each will
stand evenly. With paring knife, score flesh.
4. With small sharp knife, slice bananas crosswise;
arrange on papaya halves.
5. Spoon syrup mixture over bananas and papayas,
then sprinkle with shredded coconut; top mixture
with the drained minced preserved ginger.

Sacramento Fruit Bowl

2 cups water
1½ cups sugar
3 tablespoons lemon juice
2 tablespoons anise seed
½ teaspoon salt
1 small pineapple
1 small honeydew melon
1 small cantaloupe
2 oranges
2 nectarines or 4 apricots
2 purple plums
1 cup seedless green
*   grapes*
1 lime, sliced

Color index
page 101

Begin early
in day

12 first-course
or dessert
servings

161 cals per
serving

Low in fat,
cholesterol,
sodium

1 In 2-quart saucepan
over medium heat, cook
water with sugar, lemon
juice, anise seed and salt
15 minutes or until mix-
ture becomes a light syrup.
Chill syrup well.

2 Meanwhile, cut peel
from pineapple, melon,
cantaloupe and oranges
and cut pulp from all into
bite-size chunks.

3 Cut nectarines or
apricots and purple
plums into halves and
remove seeds; slice.

4 In large bowl or large
container, combine
cut-up fruits with grapes
and lime slices.

5 Pour chilled syrup
through strainer over
fruits. Cover and
refrigerate, stirring the
salad frequently.

Fresh Fruit Bowl
with Cardamom Dressing

Color index
page 101

Begin 30 mins
ahead

12 first-course
or dessert
servings

144 cals per
serving

Cardamom Dressing
*   (page 326)*
1 small honeydew melon
1 medium cantaloupe

6 medium plums
2 medium pears
3 medium peaches

1. Prepare Cardamom Dressing; set aside.
2. With a sharp knife, peel melon and cantaloupe;
cut into bite-size pieces. Slice plums and pears; peel
and slice peaches.
3. In large bowl, gently toss melon, plums, pears and
peaches. Serve fruit with Cardamom Dressing.

Molded salads

Tomato Aspic

7 medium tomatoes
2 medium celery stalks
1 medium onion
2½ teaspoons salt
1 bay leaf
2 envelopes unflavored
  gelatin
½ cup water
3 tablespoons sugar
2 tablespoons lemon juice
½ teaspoon Worcestershire
⅛ teaspoon hot pepper
  sauce

vegetable cooking spray
1 8-ounce container plain
  yogurt (1 cup)
2 tablespoons chopped
  fresh dill
1 teaspoon grated lemon
  peel
lettuce leaves for garnish

Color index page 76
Begin 4 hrs or day ahead
8 servings
74 cals per serving
Low in fat, cholesterol

1 With sharp knife, cut tomatoes into bite-size chunks. Slice celery, onion.

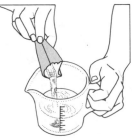

2 In 3-quart saucepan over medium heat, cook tomatoes, celery, onion, salt and bay leaf about 20 minutes until vegetables are very tender, stirring frequently.

3 In 1-cup measuring cup, mix gelatin with water; let gelatin stand 5 minutes to soften.

4 Into blender container, spoon tomato mixture; cover container; blend at high speed until pureed.

5 Into same saucepan, press tomato mixture through coarse sieve or food mill; discard seeds and skin. Stir in sugar, lemon juice, Worcestershire and pepper sauce.

6 Add gelatin mixture to tomato mixture. Over medium heat, cook, stirring frequently, until the gelatin is completely dissolved.

7 Lightly spray 6-cup mold or Bundt pan with vegetable cooking spray and pour in gelatin mixture. Cover and refrigerate until set, 3 hours.

8 Meanwhile, prepare dressing: In small bowl, mix yogurt, dill and lemon peel. Cover bowl with plastic wrap; chill.

9 Unmold gelatin mixture onto salad platter; tuck lettuce leaves under for garnish. Serve aspic with yogurt dressing.

Color index page 76
Begin 4 hrs or day ahead
8 servings
137 cals per serving
Low in fat, cholesterol

Perfection Salad

water
4 envelopes unflavored
  gelatin
1 cup sugar
1½ teaspoons salt
1 cup cider vinegar
¼ cup lemon juice

3 cups finely shredded
  cabbage
1⅓ cups diced celery
1 4-ounce jar diced
  pimentos
lettuce leaves for garnish

1. In 1-quart saucepan, heat 2 cups water to boiling. In medium bowl, mix gelatin with sugar and salt. Stir in boiling water until gelatin is dissolved. Stir in vinegar, lemon juice and 3 cups cold water. Refrigerate until mixture mounds slightly when dropped from a spoon.
2. Fold in cabbage, celery and pimentos with their liquid; pour into 2-quart bowl; cover and chill until set, about 3½ hours.
3. *To serve:* Unmold salad onto plate. Garnish with lettuce leaves.

Color index page 76
Begin 6 hrs or day ahead
10 servings
429 cals per serving
Low in sodium

Cranberry Nut Mold

1 15- or 16-ounce
  package fresh or
  frozen cranberries
1½ cups sugar
1½ cups dry red wine
water
1 envelope unflavored
  gelatin
1 6-ounce package
  lemon-flavor
  gelatin

1½ cups diced celery
¾ cup California
  walnuts, chopped

Dressing:
1 8-ounce container sour
  cream (1 cup)
¾ cup mayonnaise

orange peel for garnish

1. In 3-quart saucepan combine cranberries, sugar, wine and ½ cup water; lightly sprinkle unflavored gelatin over cranberry mixture.
2. Over medium heat, heat mixture to boiling, stirring constantly. Reduce heat to low; simmer 3 minutes, stirring constantly.
3. Stir in lemon-flavor gelatin until gelatin is completely dissolved. Remove saucepan from heat; stir in 1 cup *cold* water.
4. Refrigerate until mixture mounds slightly when dropped from a spoon, about 2 hours.
5. Gently fold celery and walnuts into gelatin mixture; pour into 8-cup mold. Cover and refrigerate until set, about 3½ hours.
6. Meanwhile, prepare dressing: In small bowl, stir sour cream and mayonnaise until blended; cover and refrigerate.
7. *To serve:* Unmold gelatin onto chilled platter. With kitchen shears, cut orange peel into flower petals to garnish top of gelatin. Serve Cranberry Nut Mold with sour-cream dressing.

Main dish salads

Chef's Salad

Color index
page 66

Begin 30 mins
ahead

6 servings

511 cals per
serving

Good source
of calcium,
iron

1 garlic clove, halved
1 large head romaine or
  iceberg lettuce
¼ pound cooked chicken
  or turkey meat
1 8-ounce package sliced
  Swiss cheese
1 6-ounce package sliced
  cooked ham

2 medium tomatoes
2 hard-cooked eggs
Classic French Dressing
  (page 326), Russian
  Dressing (page 326)
  or Thousand Island
  Dressing (page 326)

1 Rub large, shallow salad bowl well with the halved garlic clove; discard both pieces.

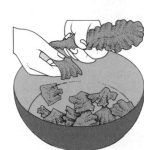

2 Into salad bowl, tear romaine lettuce into bite-size pieces.

3 With knife, cut chicken or turkey, cheese and ham into thin strips. Cut tomatoes into wedges. Peel and then quarter the hard-cooked eggs.

4 On lettuce, arrange chicken, cheese, ham, tomato and egg. Just before serving, toss together with dressing.

Herring Salad

Color index
page 66

Begin early
in day

6 servings

297 cals per
serving

Good source
of vitamin A

1 cup heavy or whipping
  cream
1½ cups diced cooked
  potatoes
1 16-ounce can sliced
  pickled beets,
  drained
1 medium apple, diced
½ cup pickled herring in
  wine sauce, drained
  and chopped

¼ cup diced dill
  pickle
¼ cup minced onion
1½ teaspoons salt
¼ teaspoon pepper
2 hard-cooked eggs,
  cut in wedges
  for garnish
parsley for garnish

1. In medium bowl with mixer at medium speed, beat cream until soft peaks form.
2. Gently fold in potatoes, pickled beets, apple, pickled herring, diced dill pickle, minced onion, salt and pepper.
3. Cover the bowl with plastic wrap and refrigerate at least 6 hours before serving.
4. *To serve:* Arrange salad on platter; garnish with wedges of hard-cooked eggs and parsley.

Salade Niçoise

Color index
page 66

Begin early
in day

4 servings

839 cals per
serving

Good source
of calcium,
iron, niacin

3 medium potatoes,
  unpeeled
3 eggs
2 medium tomatoes
1 12½- to 13-ounce can
  tuna
1 2-ounce can anchovy
  fillets
2 small heads Boston
  lettuce
1 16-ounce can French-
  style green beans,
  drained

1 5½-ounce jar Greek
  olives or 1 6-ounce
  can pitted ripe
  olives
Classic French Dressing
  (page 326) or Sauce
  Vinaigrette
  (page 326)

1 Cook potatoes until fork-tender. Hard-cook eggs. Refrigerate cooked potatoes and hard-cooked eggs until they are thoroughly chilled.

2 *About 45 minutes before serving:* Peel cooked potatoes and cut them into bite-size pieces; set aside.

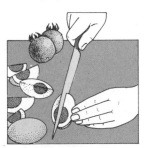

3 Peel hard-cooked eggs under running cold water (take care not to peel white away with shell); cut each egg into 4 wedges. Cut medium tomatoes into wedges.

4 Drain can of tuna; separate into bite-size pieces. Drain anchovies and carefully separate the fillets; set aside.

5 Into large salad bowl, tear lettuce into bite-size pieces. On lettuce, arrange in separate piles potatoes, tuna, eggs, tomatoes, beans, anchovies.

6 With spoon, sprinkle olives over top of salad for garnish. Let each person help himself to a portion of salad. Pass dressing separately.

Pineapple-Cheese Salad

1 large pineapple
8 ounces sharp Cheddar
* cheese*
³/₄ cup mayonnaise
2 tablespoons milk
¹/₂ teaspoon salt

¹/₂ cup sliced celery
¹/₂ medium green pepper,
* diced*
8 ounces Swiss cheese,
* cut into bite-size pieces*

Color index
page 66

Begin 30 mins
ahead

4 servings

866 cals per
serving

Good source
of calcium,
vitamin A,
vitamin C

1. With sharp knife, slice pineapple into 4 wedges from bottom through crown, leaving on leafy crown for decoration. Cut off hard core from each wedge; then with paring knife, loosen fruit by cutting close to rind, leaving ¹/₂-inch-thick shell; cover with plastic wrap and refrigerate shells. Cut fruit into bite-size pieces.
2. Shred ¹/₂ cup Cheddar cheese for garnish; set aside. Cut remaining cheese into bite-size pieces.
3. In medium bowl with fork, blend mayonnaise, milk and salt. Stir in celery, green pepper, pineapple and the Cheddar and Swiss cheese pieces. Mound mixture in the chilled pineapple shells; sprinkle shredded cheese over the top.

Crab Louis

1 cup mayonnaise
3 tablespoons catchup
2 tablespoons chopped
* green onion*
1 tablespoon
* Worcestershire*
1 tablespoon red wine
* vinegar*
2 teaspoons lemon juice
¹/₂ teaspoon salt
¹/₈ teaspoon white
* pepper*

1 pound cooked fresh
* crab or 3 6-ounce*
* packages frozen*
* Alaska King crab,*
* thawed and drained*
lettuce leaves
3 hard-cooked eggs,
* sliced*
1 cucumber, sliced
1 tomato, sliced

Color index
page 66

Begin 1 hr
ahead

4 servings

639 cals per
serving

Good source
of calcium,
iron,
vitamin A

1. In medium bowl, combine mayonnaise, catchup. onion, Worcestershire, wine vinegar, lemon juice, salt and pepper; refrigerate 30 minutes.
2. In center of salad platter, heap crab; encircle it with lettuce, egg, cucumber and tomato slices; pass the dressing separately.

Shrimp Salad

2 cups cooked, shelled
* and deveined shrimp,*
* chilled*
1¹/₂ cups sliced celery
¹/₂ cup California
* walnuts, chopped*
* (optional)*

¹/₄ cup sliced stuffed
* olives*
¹/₄ cup French dressing
¹/₄ cup mayonnaise
1 teaspoon minced onion
lettuce leaves

Color index
page 66

Begin 1 hr
ahead

4 servings

335 cals per
serving

Good source
of calcium

1. Into large bowl, cut shrimp in half lengthwise.
2. Add all ingredients except lettuce leaves; toss to mix well; cover with plastic wrap and refrigerate. Serve on lettuce leaves.

TUNA SALAD: Prepare as above but substitute *two 6¹/₂- or 7-ounce cans tuna*, flaked, for shrimp.

SALMON SALAD: Prepare as for Shrimp Salad but substitute *one 16-ounce can salmon,* drained and coarsely flaked, for shrimp; omit walnuts; add *2 cut-up hard-cooked eggs.*

Brown Rice, Western Style

1¹/₂ cups brown rice
1¹/₂ teaspoons salt
* water*
³/₄ pound cooked ham
1 medium-sized green
* pepper*

1 17-ounce can whole-
* kernel corn, drained*
¹/₂ cup salad oil
¹/₃ cup taco sauce
2 tablespoons cider vinegar
¹/₂ teaspoon sugar

Color index
page 66

Begin 1 hr
ahead or
early in day

6 servings

441 cals per
serving

Low in
cholesterol

Good source
of iron

1. In 3-quart saucepan over high heat, heat brown rice, salt, and 3³/₄ cups water to boiling. Reduce heat to low; stir rice. Cover and simmer about 45 minutes or until rice is tender and all liquid is absorbed.
2. Meanwhile, dice ham and green pepper. In large bowl, mix ham, green pepper, corn, salad oil, taco sauce, vinegar, and sugar.
3. When rice is cooked, add to bowl with ham mixture; toss to mix well. Serve salad at room temperature or cover and refrigerate to serve later. **STORING AND REHEATING LEFTOVER RICE:** To store leftover rice or rice cooked in advance, cover tightly so the grains will not dry out or absorb other food flavors, then refrigerate. Cooked rice will keep up to a week in the refrigerator. To reheat leftover rice, cover and cook with a little liquid (about 2 tablespoons) over low heat for a few minutes, until hot. Or reheat rice in a steamer or microwave oven.

Chunky Egg Salad

¹/₄ cup mayonnaise
1 tablespoon cider
* vinegar*
1 teaspoon salt
1 teaspoon minced onion
¹/₂ teaspoon
* Worcestershire*

¹/₈ teaspoon pepper
6 hard-cooked eggs
1 cup thinly sliced celery
2 tablespoons minced
* green pepper*
lettuce leaves
parsley for garnish

Color index
page 66

Begin 1 hr
ahead or
early in day

4 servings

216 cals per
serving

Good source
of iron,
vitamin A

1. In medium bowl, stir mayonnaise and next 5 ingredients until well mixed.
2. Cut eggs into big pieces; add eggs, celery and green pepper to mayonnaise mixture; mix well. Cover and refrigerate.
3. *To serve:* Spoon mixture onto lettuce leaves and garnish with parsley.

Smoked Chicken Salad

2 whole small boneless
* fully cooked smoked*
* chicken breasts (about*
* 8 ounces each)*
2 large tomatoes
1 16-ounce package
* mozzarella cheese*

¹/₂ cup salad oil
3 tablespoons Dijon
* mustard with seeds*
2 tablespoons red wine
* vinegar*
¹/₂ 10-ounce bag spinach

Color index
page 66

Begin 30 mins
ahead

8 servings

375 cals per
serving

Good source
of calcium,
iron,
vitamin A

1. Slice smoked chicken breasts, tomatoes, and mozzarella cheese.
2. In small bowl, with wire whisk or fork, mix salad oil, mustard, and vinegar; set mustard vinaigrette dressing aside.
3. Line platter with spinach leaves. Arrange smoked chicken, tomatoes, and cheese slices on spinach. Pour some mustard vinaigrette dressing over salad; pass remaining dressing to spoon on servings.

Dressings and sauces

Classic French Dressing

Begin 10 mins
or day ahead
1 cup
394 cals per
¼ cup
Low in
cholesterol

*¾ cup olive or
  salad oil
¼ cup cider or
  wine vinegar*

*½ teaspoon salt
⅛ teaspoon pepper*

Into a small bowl or a covered jar, measure all ingredients; stir with fork or cover and shake until thoroughly mixed. Cover and chill. Stir or shake the dressing just before serving.

FLAVORED FRENCH DRESSINGS

GARLIC: Prepare as for Classic French Dressing but add *1 garlic clove,* crushed. (Makes 1 cup.)

ROQUEFORT OR BLUE CHEESE: Prepare as for Classic French Dressing but add *½ cup crumbled Roquefort or blue cheese.* (Makes 1⅓ cups.)

MIXED HERB: Prepare as for Classic French Dressing but add *2 teaspoons chopped parsley* and *½ teaspoon tarragon* or basil. (Makes 1 cup.)

ANCHOVY: Prepare as above but stir in *1 tablespoon anchovy paste.* (Makes 1 cup.)

Thousand Island Dressing

Begin 10 mins
ahead
1⅓ cups
413 cals per
⅓ cup

*1 cup mayonnaise
2 tablespoons chili
  sauce
2 tablespoons minced
  green pepper*

*1 tablespoon chopped
  parsley
1 teaspoon grated
  onion*

In small bowl, stir all ingredients until well mixed. Serve on tossed greens or Chef's Salad (page 324).

Poppy-Seed Dressing

Begin early
in day
or up to
1 wk ahead
1½ cups
417 cals per
¼ cup
Low in
cholesterol

*1 cup salad oil
½ cup sugar
⅓ cup cider vinegar
1 tablespoon poppy
  seed*

*1 tablespoon grated
  onion
1 teaspoon salt
1 teaspoon dry
  mustard*

1. In covered blender container at medium speed, blend the salad oil, sugar, vinegar, poppy seed, grated onion, salt and mustard until thoroughly mixed. Dressing will be thick.
2. Store in tightly covered jar in refrigerator. Stir well before using. Serve dressing on tossed greens or fruit salad, or cottage cheese.

Green Goddess Dressing

Begin 10 mins
or day ahead
1 cup
324 cals per
¼ cup

*¾ cup mayonnaise
2 anchovy fillets,
  minced
1 tablespoon chopped
  parsley
1 tablespoon chopped
  chives*

*1 tablespoon chopped
  green onion
1 tablespoon tarragon
  vinegar
¾ teaspoon tarragon*

1. In small bowl, stir together mayonnaise, anchovies, parsley, chives, green onion, vinegar and tarragon until well mixed.
2. Cover and refrigerate. Serve on tossed greens, chilled vegetables or cold seafood or poultry.

Deluxe Garlic French Dressing

Begin 15 mins
or up to
1 wk ahead
1¾ cups
400 cals per
¼ cup
Low in
cholesterol

*1¼ cups olive or salad oil
½ cup cider vinegar or
  lemon juice
3 tablespoons chili sauce
1½ teaspoons salt
1 teaspoon sugar
1 teaspoon horseradish*

*1 teaspoon prepared
  mustard
½ teaspoon paprika
¼ teaspoon pepper
2 garlic cloves,
  crushed*

Into small bowl or covered jar, measure all ingredients; stir with fork or cover and shake until well blended. Cover and refrigerate. Stir before serving.

Blender Mayonnaise

Begin 10 mins
ahead
1¼ cups
429 cals per
¼ cup

*olive or salad oil
1 egg
2 tablespoons cider
  vinegar*

*1 teaspoon sugar
1 teaspoon dry mustard
¾ teaspoon salt
⅛ teaspoon white pepper*

1. In covered blender container at low speed, blend ¼ cup oil and remaining ingredients for 1 or 2 seconds until thoroughly mixed.
2. Remove center of cover (or cover) and, at low speed, very slowly pour ¾ cup oil in steady stream into mixture; continue blending until well mixed.

Russian Dressing

Begin 10 mins
ahead
1 cup
415 cals per
¼ cup

*1 cup mayonnaise
3 tablespoons chili
  sauce*

*1 teaspoon minced onion
  or chopped chives*

In small bowl, stir mayonnaise, chili sauce and minced onion until well mixed.

Cardamom Dressing

Begin 15 mins
ahead
1½ cups
200 cals per
¼ cup
Low in
sodium

*1 8-ounce package cream
  cheese, softened
¼ cup milk
3 tablespoons sugar*

*3 tablespoons lemon juice
¾ teaspoon ground
  cardamom*

In small bowl with mixer at low speed, beat all ingredients just until mixed. Increase speed to medium; beat until smooth.

Creamy Anise Sauce

Begin 15 mins
ahead or
early in day
1 cup
262 cals per
¼ cup
Low in
sodium

*1 8-ounce package cream
  cheese
4 to 5 tablespoons milk*

*1 teaspoon sugar
½ teaspoon anise
  seed*

In covered blender container with blender at high speed, blend all ingredients until smooth and of thick pouring consistency. If prepared early in day, sauce will thicken when refrigerated; stir in additional milk until of pouring consistency. Spoon over cut-up fruit as first course or dessert.

Sauce Vinaigrette

Begin 10 mins
ahead
1 cup
338 cals per
¼ cup

*⅔ cup olive or salad oil
¼ cup red wine vinegar
1 teaspoon salt*

*½ teaspoon chervil
½ teaspoon tarragon
⅛ teaspoon pepper*

In small bowl, mix thoroughly oil, vinegar, salt, chervil, tarragon and pepper.

Decorative ideas

GARNISHES

Cucumber slices: With sharp-tined fork, completely score peeled or unpeeled cucumber. Cut crosswise into thin slices.

Radish accordions: Cut radish crosswise into thin slices, almost all the way through. In bowl, on ice, refrigerate; drain.

Ruffled green onions: Cut off all but 3 inches green tops; shred tops down to white. Chill in ice water to curl; drain.

Melon clusters: Peel honeydew. Halve cross-wise; slice into thin rings. Cut one edge of each ring.

Roll each ring into cone shape; secure with toothpick.

Place parsley in center of each cone. Make cluster with 3 cones; secure with toothpicks.

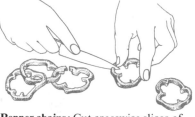

Pepper chains: Cut crosswise slices of red or green pepper. Cut one edge of each ring. Slip together to make chain.

Celery fans: Cut celery stalks into 3-inch pieces; slit each piece, almost to end, into narrow strips. Place on ice in bowl until ends curl; drain.

Cheese balls: With hands, shape softened cream cheese into balls. Roll in chopped nuts.

Vegetable cutouts: Cut peeled turnip, kohlrabi or rutabaga into thin crosswise slices. Cut shapes with canapé cutters. To make flower shapes, cut V-shaped notches around circle; cut off corners to form rounded petals. Cut thinly sliced carrots with smaller canapé cutters or knife.

CARROT FLOWER

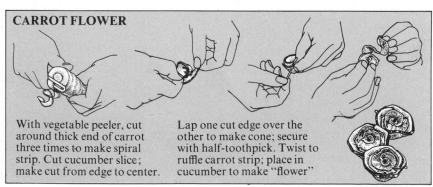

With vegetable peeler, cut around thick end of carrot three times to make spiral strip. Cut cucumber slice; make cut from edge to center.

Lap one cut edge over the other to make cone; secure with half-toothpick. Twist to ruffle carrot strip; place in cucumber to make "flower"

SHELLS FOR SALADS

These fruit and vegetable shells make attractive serving dishes for salads.

Apple cup: Cut top off apple. Scoop out inside, leaving ¼-inch-thick shell. With pointed small knife, mark petal shapes; cut along marking. Brush cut surface with lemon juice.

Avocado half: Slice avocado lengthwise in half. Remove seed. Cut thin slice from underside so avocado stays even. Brush cut surface with lemon juice.

Grapefruit or orange zig-zag: Remove flesh from grapefruit or orange half. Cut zig-zag edge for special effect.

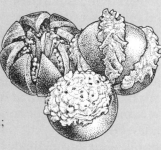

Tomato shells: Cut top off tomato and scoop out flesh. Or cut tomato into 8 wedges, being careful not to cut all the way through; spoon filling into center. Or, cut 3 slices from top almost to bottom; fill between slices.

Pepper flower: Cut top off small pepper. Remove seeds and white membrane. Cut petal shapes as for the apple cup (above).

Pineapple half: Cut pineapple lengthwise in half. Cut out core and flesh. Cut thin slice from underside so pineapple stays upright.

327

PASTA

The term pasta covers a rich variety of Italian-style noodles and dough shapes, of which macaroni and spaghetti are the best known. Spaghetti is available in various thicknesses and macaroni can be short or long, curved or straight. Noodles are usually flat. Apart from these familiar shapes, there are corkscrews, ribbons, stars, fans, rings and bow ties and shapes that are filled such as ravioli, cannelloni, shells, tortellini and manicotti. Pasta products provide hearty, delicious eating at relatively low cost. They combine readily with other foods ranging in flavor from sweet and mild to savory and highly seasoned.

All types are made from what is essentially the same flour and water dough, except noodles which also contain eggs. Although dried pasta is widely available in packaged form, many people are discovering how easy it is to make fresh pasta at home. With homemade pasta, the same dough can be rolled out into wide, flat sheets to make lasagna, or cut into pieces for cannelloni or ravioli. Our Homemade Pasta Dough (opposite), is made with eggs for a rich flavor and tender texture.

Pasta can be served plain or with a sauce. Different types of pasta are interchangeable in most recipes, but if the size or thickness is different, so will be the proportion of pasta to sauce or other ingredients. Dry pasta should be substituted by weight. Do not use a cup measure, as a cupful of one uncooked product may weigh more or less than a cupful of another kind. Different kinds of cooked pasta may be substituted cup for cup.

How much pasta you plan to serve per portion is very much a matter of personal preference. Eight ounces of spaghetti is usually sufficient for 4 to 6 servings, especially if the dish is to be served as a first course or accompaniment, but for a main dish you may well find that you need up to a pound of pasta for the same number of servings.

CHOOSING PASTA

The best pasta is made from durum (hard) wheat which has a high gluten content and makes an elastic dough which shapes easily. Look for the term "enriched" on the labels of pasta products. This tells you that they are

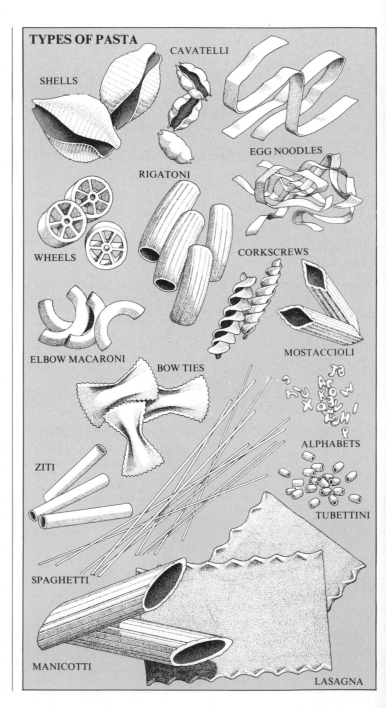

TYPES OF PASTA

SHELLS

CAVATELLI

EGG NOODLES

RIGATONI

WHEELS

CORKSCREWS

ELBOW MACARONI

BOW TIES

MOSTACCIOLI

ZITI

ALPHABETS

TUBETTINI

SPAGHETTI

MANICOTTI

LASAGNA

rich in B vitamins and iron. Other ingredients are sometimes added to change the color of the pasta: eggs will turn it golden, spinach puree makes it green.

COOKING PASTA

Use a large, deep saucepot containing at least 8 cups water and about 1 teaspoon salt for every 8 ounces pasta. Let the water come to a rolling boil, then add pasta gradually so that water does not stop boiling. Hold spaghetti vertically in the boiling water until you feel the ends begin to soften. Then press them down, coiling the strands around until they are totally submerged in the water. You can also break the spaghetti into pieces into the boiling water.

Cook pasta uncovered, stirring occasionally to separate, until tender but still firm *(al dente)*. Be guided by the cooking times suggested on the package; small pasta may take only 2 minutes while large pasta may take 15 minutes. The average cooking time is 8 to 10 minutes. Cook for a shorter time if the pasta is to be used in a casserole and cooked further.

As soon as the pasta is done to your taste, drain it thoroughly in a colander or strainer. Do not rinse. Add a tablespoon of salad oil, softened butter or margarine to prevent pasta sticking.

Adding spaghetti to water: Gradually add spaghetti to boiling water, pushing it down as the ends soften. Be sure water keeps boiling.

SERVING PASTA

A dish of pasta dressed with sauce is at its best served as soon as it is cooked. Heap drained pasta on a warm serving plate and pour the sauce over the top. For individual servings you can use a large fork and spoon to divide the pasta between the plates, then spoon a portion of sauce over each one. Another way of serving pasta with sauce is to toss the two together thoroughly. As an alternative to a topping of sauce, toss cooked pasta with one of the following: tomato chunks or halved cherry tomatoes; drained canned or cooked mushrooms; shredded raw carrot; drained canned or cooked peas and diced canned pimento; whole or diced stuffed or ripe olives.

If you are planning to serve grated cheese with the dish, sprinkle a little over the top and pass around more in a separate bowl or let each person grate some himself.

STORING PASTA

Cover and store uncooked pasta and noodles at room temperature in a cool, dry place. Spaghetti and macaroni will keep up to a year, noodles should be used within about 6 months.

Toss leftover cooked pasta with a small amount of salad oil and refrigerate in a covered container. It can be reheated in a pot of boiling water, just long enough to heat through, and then drained.

PASTA MACHINES

Although all pasta is available in packaged form, many people make their own by hand or with the help of a pasta machine.

Noodle machines knead the dough, then roll it into sheets between two smooth steel rollers. Cutters at the other end of the machine then cut the dough into strips. Most machines have two sizes of cutter for broad or fine noodles. Other shapes such as ravioli or lasagna have to be handcut out of the rolled sheet of dough.

To make ravioli, you can either use an attachment to a noodle machine or use a specially built ravioli machine. Place a rolled sheet of dough, cut to width, in the hopper. The two edges of the dough are opened and the filling added. When the handle is turned, the sealed ravioli emerges.

Pasta makers work like meat grinders with different dies for shaping the various pastas. They can make spaghetti and macaroni as well as noodles; just press the dough into the hopper and crank.

Homemade Pasta Dough

1 pound dough for recipes, pages 330 to 335

1098 cals

Good source of calcium, iron, vitamin A, thiamine

2¼ to 2½ cups all-purpose flour
⅓ cup water (if using pasta machine, follow manufacturer's directions)

2 eggs
1 egg yolk
1 tablespoon olive or salad oil
1 teaspoon salt

1. In large bowl, combine 1 cup flour and remaining ingredients. With mixer at low speed, beat 2 minutes, occasionally scraping bowl.
2. With wooden spoon, stir in enough additional flour to make a soft dough.
3. Turn dough onto lightly floured surface, knead until smooth and elastic, about 10 minutes. Cover dough and let rest 30 minutes.

Kneading the dough: On a lightly floured board with floured hands, fold furthest edge of dough toward you; then push the dough away in a rolling motion with heels of hands. Give dough a quarter turn and repeat.

Noodles

Homemade Egg Noodles

Color index
page 74

Begin 3½ hrs
ahead

6 accompani-
ment servings

201 cals per
serving

***Homemade Pasta Dough
(page 329)
3 quarts water
9 chicken- or beef-flavor
bouillon cubes or
envelopes, or 3
tablespoons beef-flavor
stock base, or 1
tablespoon salt
1 tablespoon butter or
margarine***

1 Prepare Homemade
Pasta Dough and knead
until smooth and elastic,
about 10 minutes. Wrap in
waxed paper and let stand
30 minutes as directed; cut
dough in half.

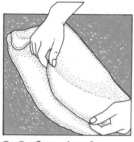

2 On floured surface
with floured rolling pin,
roll half of dough into 20″
by 14″ rectangle, then fold
in half crosswise and in
half again crosswise to
form 5″ by 14″ rectangle.

3 Cut into ⅛-inch strips
for narrow noodles,
¼-inch strips for medium
noodles or ½-inch strips
for wide noodles.

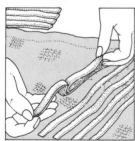

4 Open dough strips and
place them in a single
layer on clean cloth towels.
Repeat with remaining
dough. Let the strips dry
at least 2 hours before
cooking them.

5 *About 20 minutes before
serving:* In 8-quart
saucepot over high heat,
heat to boiling water,
bouillon and butter or
margarine. Break noodles in
smaller lengths, if desired,
and add to saucepot; heat
to boiling and cook 5 to 8
minutes until tender
but firm, then drain in
colander. Serve the noodles
with more butter or
margarine, if you like.

WHOLE-WHEAT PASTA DOUGH: In large
bowl, with wooden spoon, stir *1½ cups whole-
wheat flour, 2 eggs, ½ cup water, 1 teaspoon salt and
1 cup all-purpose flour* to make a stiff dough. On
well-floured surface, knead dough until smooth and
not sticky, about 20 times. Cover with plastic wrap;
let rest 30 minutes. (Or in food processor with knife
blade attached, blend ingredients 10 to 15 seconds
to form a smooth ball. Do not knead; cover and let
rest 30 minutes.) Cut dough in half; to prepare and
cook noodles, follow steps 2 to 5 above.

Homemade Spinach Noodles

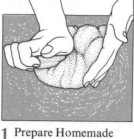

Color index
page 74

Begin 3 hrs
ahead

8 accompani-
ment servings

305 cals per
serving

Good source
of calcium,
iron,
vitamin A

***1 10-ounce bag fresh
spinach
water
salt
2 eggs***   ***2½ to 3 cups all-purpose
flour
1 tablespoon salad oil
½ cup butter or
margarine***

1. Wash spinach; trim off tough ribs and stems. In
3-quart saucepan over medium heat, heat to boiling
¼ inch water and ½ teaspoon salt. Add spinach and
return to boiling; cover; cook 3 minutes. Drain well;
blot excess moisture with paper towels. Puree
spinach with blender or food mill and place in large
bowl. Or, into large bowl press through a coarse
strainer with back of spoon or rubber spatula.
2. With fork, stir in eggs, 2½ cups flour and 1
teaspoon salt until mixture resembles coarse
crumbs. Shape dough into ball. On well-floured
surface, knead until smooth and not sticky, about 10
minutes, kneading in more flour if needed. Wrap in
waxed paper; let stand 30 minutes; cut dough in 2
equal pieces.
3. On floured surface with rolling pin, roll half of
dough into 20″ by 14″ rectangle. With knife, cut into
20″ by ½″ strips. Place in single layer on clean cloth
towels. Repeat with remaining dough. Let noodles
dry at least 2 hours.
4. *About 20 minutes before serving:* In 8-quart
saucepot over high heat, heat to boiling 4 quarts
water, 2 tablespoons salt and oil. Add noodles and
return to boiling; cook 5 minutes or until tender but
firm. In colander, drain noodles; return to pot. Add
butter; toss until melted. Serve on heated platter.

Drying spinach: Drain
cooked spinach; with
paper towels, blot excess
moisture from leaves.

Making spinach puree:
Puree the spinach in a
blender or a food mill.

Fettucini Alfredo

Color index
page 74

Begin 30mins
ahead

8 accompani-
ment servings

148 cals per
serving

Low in
cholesterol

***1 8-ounce package
fettucini or medium
egg noodles
¼ cup butter, melted
¼ cup grated Parmesan
cheese***   ***2 tablespoons half-and-
half
¼ teaspoon salt
⅛ teaspoon pepper***

1. Prepare noodles as label directs; drain noodles in
colander and keep hot.
2. Meanwhile, in warm serving dish, combine butter,
cheese, half-and-half, salt and pepper.
3. Toss hot noodles with cheese mixture to coat well.
Serve immediately. Pass more grated cheese, if you
like, to sprinkle over servings.

Spaghetti

Spaghetti and Meatballs

Color index page 32

Begin 2¼ hrs ahead

6 main-dish servings

659 cals per serving

Good source of calcium, iron, niacin, vitamin C

Spaghetti Sauce (page 337)
1½ pounds lean ground beef
1 cup fresh bread crumbs
1 egg
½ teaspoon oregano leaves
⅛ teaspoon pepper
salt
salad oil
4 quarts water
1 16-ounce package spaghetti
grated Parmesan cheese

1 Prepare Spaghetti Sauce. Prepare meatballs: In large bowl, combine ground beef, crumbs, egg, oregano, pepper and 1½ teaspoons salt.

2 With hands, shape ground-beef mixture into 1-inch balls.

3 In 12-inch skillet over medium-high heat, in 2 tablespoons oil, cook meatballs until browned. Spoon off drippings from the skillet.

4 Add Spaghetti Sauce; heat to boiling. Reduce heat to low; cover skillet and simmer sauce and meatballs for 10 minutes.

5 Meanwhile, in 8-quart saucepot, heat to boiling water and 2 teaspoons salt. Add spaghetti; cook until spaghetti is tender but firm (al dente).

6 Drain spaghetti in colander. Toss with 1 tablespoon oil to prevent spaghetti sticking.

7 Arrange on warm plate. Serve meatballs and sauce over spaghetti. Pass grated cheese.

Bacon and Eggs Spaghetti

Color index page 32

Begin 30 mins ahead

4 main-dish servings

770 cals per serving

Good source of calcium, iron, vitamin A

1 16-ounce package spaghetti
8 bacon slices, cut up
2 medium onions, coarsely chopped
4 eggs, slightly beaten
½ 8-ounce package pasteurized process cheese spread, cubed

1. Prepare spaghetti as label directs; drain well in colander and keep warm.
2. Meanwhile, in 12-inch skillet over medium heat, cook bacon until crisp; with slotted spoon, remove to paper towels; set aside.
3. In drippings in skillet, cook onions until tender, about 5 minutes. Add spaghetti and bacon to onions; toss until well mixed; stir in eggs and cheese; heat until cheese is melted.

Spaghetti with Four Cheeses

Color index page 32

Begin 45 mins ahead

4 main-dish servings

672 cals per serving

Good source of calcium, vitamin A

1 8-ounce package spaghetti
¼ cup butter or margarine
1 tablespoon all-purpose flour
1½ cups half-and-half or light cream
1 cup shredded mozzarella or scamorze cheese
1 cup shredded fontina cheese
½ cup grated provolone cheese
¼ cup grated Parmesan or Romano cheese
¼ teaspoon salt
¼ teaspoon cracked pepper
2 tablespoons chopped parsley

1. Prepare spaghetti as label directs; drain well in colander and keep hot.
2. Meanwhile, in 3-quart saucepan over medium heat, in hot butter, stir in flour until blended; cook 30 seconds. Gradually stir in half-and-half; cook, stirring, until mixture boils and slightly thickens. Stir in mozzarella, fontina, provolone and Parmesan cheeses, salt and pepper until smooth and cheeses are melted.
3. Pour hot spaghetti into warm, large bowl. Pour cheese sauce over spaghetti; sprinkle with parsley. Toss until spaghetti is well coated.

Spaghetti with Ham and Peas

Color index page 32

Begin 45 mins ahead

4 main-dish servings

670 cals per serving

Good source of calcium, iron, vitamin A

1 8-ounce package spaghetti
¼ cup butter or margarine
1 tablespoon all-purpose flour
¼ teaspoon salt
¼ teaspoon cracked pepper
1½ cups half-and-half
1 10-ounce package frozen peas, thawed
1 cup shredded fontina cheese
1 cup shredded mozzarella cheese
1 4-ounce package sliced cooked ham, cut into ⅛-inch strips

1. Prepare spaghetti as label directs. Drain spaghetti in colander and keep warm.
2. Meanwhile, in 3-quart saucepan over low heat, melt butter; stir in flour, salt and pepper; gradually stir in half-and-half; cook, stirring, until thickened. Add peas and cheeses, stirring until cheeses are melted; stir in ham; heat.
3. In large bowl, toss spaghetti and cheese mixture until spaghetti is well coated and serve immediately.

Macaroni and cavatelli

The short curved elbow macaroni is the most popular. Other types of macaroni or its special shapes such as bow ties, corkscrews and rigatoni can be substituted for elbow macaroni in recipes. All are delicious with a sauce or piping hot with a homemade cheese topping.

Baked Macaroni and Cheese

Color index page 32

Begin 45 mins ahead

4 main-dish servings

621 cals per serving

Good source of calcium, vitamin A

2 quarts water
salt
1 8-ounce package elbow macaroni
4 tablespoons butter or margarine
¾ cup fresh bread crumbs

1 small onion, minced
1 tablespoon all-purpose flour
¼ teaspoon dry mustard
⅛ teaspoon pepper
1½ cups milk
2 cups shredded Cheddar cheese

1 In 3-quart saucepan, heat to boiling water and 1 teaspoon salt. Add macaroni; cook until tender but firm; drain. Grease 2-quart baking dish. Preheat oven to 350°F.

2 In 1-quart saucepan over medium heat, melt 2 tablespoons butter or margarine; add bread crumbs and toss to coat; set aside.

3 Meanwhile, in 2-quart saucepan over medium heat, melt remaining butter; add onion and cook until tender, about 5 minutes.

4 Blend in flour, mustard, pepper and 1 teaspoon salt. Stir in milk; cook, stirring, until thickened. Remove from heat; stir in cheese.

5 Place macaroni in baking dish. Pour cheese mixture over macaroni.

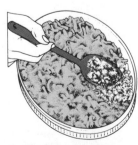

6 Sprinkle crumb mixture over top. Bake in oven 20 minutes.

Skillet Macaroni and Cheese

Color index page 32

Begin 45 mins ahead

4 main-dish servings

636 cals per serving

Good source of calcium, vitamin A

½ cup butter or margarine
2 cups elbow macaroni
¼ cup minced onion
2 tablespoons minced green pepper
1 teaspoon salt

¼ teaspoon dry mustard
2 cups water
2 cups shredded Cheddar cheese
10 medium pimento-stuffed olives, sliced

1. In 10-inch skillet over medium heat, in hot butter, cook uncooked macaroni and next 4 ingredients for 5 minutes, stirring frequently.
2. Stir in water; heat to boiling. Reduce heat to low; cover; simmer 10 to 15 minutes until macaroni is tender, stirring occasionally.
3. Remove from heat; stir in cheese and olives until cheese is melted.

Cavatelli with Meat Sauce

Color index page 32

Begin 4 hrs ahead

4 main-dish servings

656 cals per serving

Meat Sauce (page 337)
Homemade Pasta Dough (page 329)
4 quarts water
2 tablespoons salt
1 tablespoon salad oil
grated Parmesan or Romano cheese for topping

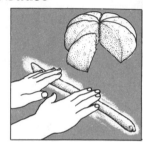

1 Prepare Meat Sauce and dough; cut dough into 8 pieces. Roll each piece into 15-inch rope.

2 Cut ropes into ½-inch pieces. Press each piece in center; draw finger toward you to flatten slightly and curl ends.

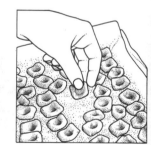

3 Place cavatelli in single layer on floured, clean cloth towels. Let dry 2 hours before cooking.

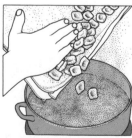

4 In 8-quart saucepot, heat to boiling water, salt and oil; add cavatelli; cook until tender but firm, about 10 minutes.

5 Drain well and arrange on heated platter. Spoon heated sauce over cavatelli; sprinkle with grated Parmesan cheese.

Stuffed pasta

Ravioli, tortellini, manicotti, shells and cannelloni are popular shapes that are stuffed with fillings. They can all be stuffed with meat, cheese or vegetable fillings. Ravioli and tortellini are usually boiled, while cannelloni, shells and manicotti are baked.

Ravioli

Color index
page 32

Begin 3 hrs
ahead

4 main-dish
servings

582 cals per
serving
(meat filling)

Good source
of calcium,
iron,
vitamin A,
vitamin C

***Cheese, Meat or Spinach
Filling (below right)
Homemade Pasta Dough
(page 329)
Marinara Sauce
(page 337)***

***6 quarts water
2 tablespoons salt
1 tablespoon salad oil
1/4 cup grated Parmesan
cheese***

1 Prepare filling and dough; cut dough into 6 pieces. On floured surface with floured rolling pin, roll 1 piece into 18″ by 4″ rectangle; cut nine 4″ by 2″ pieces.

2 Drop scant teaspoonful of filling on 2-inch side of each piece of dough to within 1/2 inch of edges. Brush dough edges lightly with water.

3 Fold dough over filling, bringing edges to-gether. With 4-tined fork dipped in flour, press edges together.

4 Place ravioli in one layer on floured, clean cloth or paper towels. Repeat, making 54 ravioli in all. Let dry 30 minutes. Make Marinara Sauce.

5 In 8-quart saucepot, heat water, salt and oil to boiling. Add ravioli; stir-ring occasionally, heat to boiling. Reduce heat; cook about 5 minutes till tender.

6 Drain well in colander. Arrange on warm plat-ter. Reheat Marinara Sauce and spoon evenly over ravioli; sprinkle with grated cheese.

Jumbo Ravioli

Color index
page 32

Begin 2 1/2 hrs
ahead

4 main-dish
servings

568 cals per
serving
(meat filling)

Good source
of calcium,
iron,
vitamin A,
vitamin C

***Cheese, Meat or Spinach
Filling (below)
Homemade Pasta Dough
(page 329)
Marinara Sauce
(page 337)***

***4 quarts water
2 tablespoons salt
1 tablespoon salad oil
1/4 cup grated Parmesan
cheese***

1. Prepare Cheese, Meat or Spinach Filling
2. Prepare dough; cut into 4 pieces. On well-floured surface with floured rolling pin, roll 1 piece into 15″ by 6″ rectangle; with sharp knife, cut rectangle crosswise into five 6″ by 3″ pieces.
3. Spread rounded tablespoonfuls of filling on 3-inch side of each piece of pasta to within 1/4 inch of edges. Fold dough over filling, bringing ends to-gether; with fork dipped in flour, firmly press edges together. Place ravioli in single layer on floured, clean cloth towels. Repeat with remaining pasta and filling making 20 ravioli in all. Let dry 30 minutes. Meanwhile, make Marinara Sauce.
4. In 8-quart saucepot over high heat, heat to boiling water, salt and oil. Cook ravioli a few at a time, 10 minutes or until tender but firm; drain. Arrange on heated platter.
5. Reheat Marinara Sauce and spoon evenly over ravioli; sprinkle with Parmesan Cheese.

Forming the shape: Fold dough over filling, bringing ends together.

Sealing edges: With fork dipped in flour, press edges together to seal.

FILLINGS FOR RAVIOLI

113 cals per
serving

CHEESE FILLING: In small bowl, combine *8 ounces ricotta cheese* (1 cup), *3 tablespoons minced parsley, 2 tablespoons grated Parmesan cheese, 1 egg white* and *1/4 teaspoon salt.* Stir ingredients until they are well mixed.

127 cals per
serving

MEAT FILLING: In 10-inch skillet over medium-high heat, cook *1/2 pound ground beef, 1/3 cup minced onion, 1 garlic clove,* minced, until meat is browned; remove from heat; spoon off juices. Stir in *1 egg, 1/4 cup minced parsley, 2 tablespoons grated Parmesan cheese* and *1/2 teaspoon salt.* Stir ingredients until well mixed.

126 cals per
serving

SPINACH FILLING: In small bowl, combine *one 10-ounce package frozen chopped spinach,* thawed and well drained, *1/3 cup grated Parmesan cheese, 2 egg yolks, 1 tablespoon butter,* softened, *1/4 tea-spoon salt, 1/8 teaspoon pepper, 1/8 teaspoon ground nutmeg.* Stir ingredients until well mixed.

Stuffed pasta

Manicotti

Spaghetti Sauce
(page 337)

Pancakes:
1 cup all-purpose
flour
4 eggs
1 tablespoon salad oil
1 teaspoon salt
1 cup water

Manicotti Sauce:
2 tablespoons butter
1 pound ground veal or
ground uncooked
turkey

Filling:
2 cups ricotta or creamed
cottage cheese
2 tablespoons grated
Parmesan cheese
¾ teaspoon salt
¼ teaspoon pepper
2 eggs
1 8-ounce package
mozzarella cheese,
coarsely shredded

Color index page 33
Begin 3 hrs ahead
8 main-dish servings
467 cals per serving
Good source of calcium,
iron, vitamin A, vitamin C

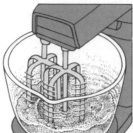

1 Prepare Spaghetti Sauce. For pancakes: In small bowl with mixer at low speed, blend pancake ingredients; at medium speed, beat 1 minute.

2 Lightly brush 7-inch skillet with salad oil. Over medium-high heat, heat skillet.

3 Pour in about 2 tablespoons pancake batter; tip pan to coat bottom evenly with batter.

4 Cook until top is set and dry and underside lightly browned, about 30 seconds. Lift pancake onto waxed paper. Repeat.

5 Prepare sauce: In 10-inch skillet over medium-high heat, in hot butter, cook ground veal until well browned then add Spaghetti Sauce.

6 Heat sauce through then spoon ⅓ of hot sauce evenly into a 15½" by 10½" roasting pan.

7 Prepare filling: In medium bowl, mix ricotta cheese, Parmesan cheese, salt, pepper and eggs until well blended. Preheat oven to 375°F.

8 Spoon heaping tablespoon of cheese mixture down center of each pancake; top with some shredded mozzarella.

9 Fold pancake edges over cheese. Arrange filled pancakes, seam side down, in roasting pan.

10 Spoon remaining sauce over pancakes. Bake 30 minutes or until sauce is hot and bubbly.

Color index page 33
Begin 2½ hrs ahead
10 main-dish servings
472 cals per serving
Good source of calcium, iron, vitamin A, vitamin C

Stuffed Shells

Spaghetti Sauce
(page 337)
1 16-ounce package
jumbo shell macaroni
(about 40)
4 cups ricotta or cottage
cheese
1 8-ounce package
mozzarella cheese,
shredded

2 eggs
⅓ cup dried bread
crumbs
¼ cup chopped
parsley
1 teaspoon salt
¼ teaspoon pepper
½ cup grated Parmesan
cheese

1. Prepare Spaghetti Sauce.
2. Prepare shells as label directs; drain well in colander. Preheat oven to 350°F. In large bowl, combine ricotta and next 6 ingredients. Stuff rounded tablespoonful of cheese mixture into each shell.
3. Spoon ¾ cup sauce into each of two 13" by 9" baking dishes. Place shells, seam side down, over sauce in one layer. Spoon over remaining sauce; sprinkle with Parmesan. Bake 30 minutes.

Color index page 33
Begin 2½ hrs ahead
8 main-dish servings
692 cals per serving
Good source of calcium, iron, vitamin A

Hearty Manicotti

water
1 pound Italian sweet
sausage links
1 pound ground beef
1 medium onion, chopped
2 16-ounce cans tomato
puree
1 6-ounce can tomato
paste
1 teaspoon sugar
½ teaspoon pepper

basil
salt
1 8-ounce package
manicotti shells (16)
4 cups ricotta cheese
1 8-ounce package
mozzarella cheese,
diced
2 tablespoons chopped
parsley
grated Parmesan cheese

1. In covered 5-quart Dutch oven over medium heat, in ¼ cup water, cook sausage links 5 minutes. Uncover; brown well; drain on paper towels.
2. Spoon fat from Dutch oven; over medium heat, brown ground beef and onion well; stir in tomato puree, tomato paste, sugar, pepper, 1 teaspoon basil, 1 teaspoon salt and 1 cup water; simmer, covered, 45 minutes.
3. Cut sausage into bite-size pieces; add to mixture; cook 15 minutes, stirring occasionally. Meanwhile, cook manicotti as label directs; drain in colander. Preheat oven to 375°F.
4. In large bowl, combine ricotta and mozzarella cheeses, parsley, ¾ teaspoon basil and ½ teaspoon salt; stuff into shells.
5. Spoon half of meat sauce into one 13" by 9" baking dish. Place half of shells over sauce in one layer. Spoon remaining sauce except ¾ cup over shells; top with remaining shells in one layer. Spoon reserved meat sauce over top. Sprinkle with Parmesan. Bake 30 minutes.

FILLING PASTA SHELLS

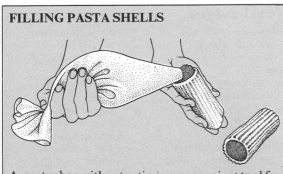

A pastry bag without a tip is a convenient tool for filling pasta shapes. Use it to stuff manicotti and jumbo shells if you are cooking in large quantities.

Color index page 23
Begin 3 hrs ahead
12 first-course servings   349 cals per serving
Good source of calcium, vitamin A

Tortellini in White Cream Sauce

Homemade Pasta Dough (page 329)
2 ounces prosciutto
1/2 pound boneless, skinless chicken breast
1/3 cup dried bread crumbs
1/2 teaspoon salt
1/8 teaspoon pepper
water
1/8 teaspoon ground nutmeg
1/2 cup butter or margarine
1 cup heavy or whipping cream
1 cup grated Parmesan cheese

1. Prepare Homemade Pasta Dough.
2. While pasta dough is resting, finely chop prosciutto and chicken breast. In bowl, mix chicken mixture with bread crumbs, salt, pepper, nutmeg and 1/3 cup water. (Or, cut prosciutto into 1-inch pieces; in food processor with knife blade attached, finely chop prosciutto. Cut chicken into 1-inch pieces and drop through feed tube while processor is running. Gradually add remaining ingredients. Process until smooth.)
3. Cut pasta dough into 4 pieces. On floured surface, with floured rolling pin, roll 1 piece (keep remaining dough in plastic wrap) into 12″ by 12″ square. With 2-inch round cookie cutter, cut out as many rounds as possible. Remove trimmings; reserve.
4. Place 1/2 teaspoon chicken filling in center of each round. Brush edges with water; fold in half with edges not quite meeting; press to seal. Place straight edge of half-round at right angle to an index finger; bend around finger until two ends meet to form a fan shape; press to seal ends.
5. Place tortellini in single layer on paper towels. Repeat with remaining pasta and filling; reroll trimmings and cut as above. (Makes about 125 tortellini.)
6. In 8-quart saucepot over high heat, heat 6 quarts water to boiling. Add tortellini; stir gently to separate pieces; heat to boiling. Reduce heat to medium; cook 5 minutes or until tender but firm and filling is cooked through. Drain.
7. In same saucepot over low heat, melt butter. Add pasta and cream; heat to boiling. Stir gently until cream thickens slightly. Sprinkle with Parmesan cheese; toss.

Cannelloni

Homemade Pasta Dough (page 329)
2 tablespoons butter or margarine
1 tablespoon chopped green onion
1 10-ounce package frozen chopped spinach, cooked and drained
1 cup finely chopped cooked chicken
1/2 cup finely chopped cooked ham
1/2 cup grated Parmesan cheese
1 egg, beaten
1 tablespoon dry sherry
1/4 teaspoon ground ginger
salt
salad oil
5 quarts water
Parmesan-Cheese Sauce (page 463)
chopped parsley for garnish
Color index page 33
Begin 2 hrs ahead
8 main-dish servings,
411 cals per serving
Good source of calcium iron, vitamin A

1 Prepare dough; cut into 3 pieces. On well-floured surface with floured rolling pin, roll 1 piece into 16″ by 8″ rectangle.

2 With knife, cut the dough rectangle into eight 4-inch squares.

3 Place squares on floured, clean cloth towel. Repeat with remaining dough, making 24 squares in all. Cover; let stand 30 minutes.

4 In 2-quart saucepan over medium heat, in butter, cook onion until tender. Stir in next 7 ingredients and 1/4 teaspoon salt; heat; set aside.

5 Preheat oven to 350°F. Grease 13″ by 9″ metal pan or broiler-safe baking dish.

6 In 8-quart saucepot, heat to boiling water, 2 tablespoons salt and 1 tablespoon oil. Cook squares a few at a time, 5 minutes.

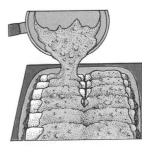
7 Remove pasta with slotted spoon; drain in colander and assemble while warm.

8 To assemble cannelloni: With spoon, spread rounded tablespoon of meat mixture across center of warm pasta square.

9 Roll jelly-roll fashion. Place, seam side down, in pan. Repeat with remaining pasta squares and meat mixture.

10 Prepare cheese sauce; pour over cannelloni; sprinkle with parsley. Bake in oven 20 minutes then broil 5 minutes.

Lasagna

Lasagna

Color index
page 33

Begin 2½ hrs
ahead

8 main-dish
servings

450 cals per
serving

Good source
of calcium,
iron,
vitamin A,
vitamin C

1 pound ground beef
1 small onion, diced
1 28-ounce can tomatoes
1 12-ounce can tomato
 paste
1 tablespoon sugar
1½ teaspoons salt
½ teaspoon oregano
 leaves
½ teaspoon thyme
 leaves
½ teaspoon crushed red
 pepper

¼ teaspoon garlic
 salt
1 bay leaf
⅔ 16-ounce package
 lasagna noodles (about
 14 noodles)
2 eggs
1 15-ounce container
 ricotta cheese
1 16-ounce package
 mozzarella cheese,
 diced

1 In 5-quart Dutch oven over high heat, cook ground beef and onion until pan juices evaporate and beef is browned. Add tomatoes, their liquid, and next 8 ingredients.

2 Heat mixture to boiling, stirring to break up tomatoes. Reduce heat to low; cover and simmer 30 minutes, stirring mixture occasionally.

3 Discard bay leaf. Tilt pan and spoon off any fat which accumulates on top of sauce. Cook lasagna noodles as label directs; drain well in colander.

4 In 13″ by 9″ baking dish, arrange half of drained lasagna noodles, overlapping to fit. Preheat oven to 375°F.

5 In a small bowl with spoon, combine eggs and ricotta cheese and spoon one-half of this mixture over lasagna noodles in baking dish.

6 Sprinkle with one-half mozzarella; top with one-half sauce. Repeat layers. Bake in oven 45 minutes. Remove from oven and let stand 10 minutes before serving.

Veal Lasagna

Color index
page 33

Begin 2½ hrs
ahead

10 main-dish
servings

429 cals per
serving

Good source
of calcium,
iron,
vitamin A,
niacin

1 3-pound rolled veal
 shoulder roast
 boneless
salad oil
½ 16-ounce package
 lasagna noodles
 (12 noodles)
⅓ cup butter or
 margarine
2 large onions, minced
⅓ cup all-purpose flour
4 cups milk

⅓ cup medium sherry
2 teaspoons salt
¼ teaspoon white
 pepper
¼ teaspoon ground
 nutmeg
1 3-ounce can grated
 Parmesan and
 Romano cheese
chopped parsley for
 garnish

1. Cut veal into ½-inch cubes, discarding fat. In 12-inch skillet over medium-high heat, in 2 tablespoons hot oil, cook veal until lightly browned, stirring occasionally. Reduce heat to low; cover; simmer 30 minutes or until tender, stirring occasionally.

2. Meanwhile, cook lasagna noodles as label directs, adding 1 tablespoon salad oil to cooking water; drain well in colander.

3. In heavy 3-quart saucepan over medium heat, in hot butter, cook onions until tender, about 5 minutes, stirring occasionally. Stir in flour until blended. Stir in milk; cook, stirring, until thickened. Drain meat; add to mixture; stir in sherry, salt, pepper and nutmeg.

4. Arrange 4 noodles lengthwise in baking dish; spoon ½ of meat mixture evenly over noodles. Repeat layers, ending with noodles Cover dish tightly with foil.

5. Preheat oven to 350°F. Bake lasagna, covered, 30 minutes. Remove cover; sprinkle with grated cheese. Continue baking 15 minutes or until lasagna mixture is lightly browned. Sprinkle with chopped parsley. Let stand 10 minutes before serving.

Eggplant Lasagna

Color index
page 33

Begin 2¼ hrs
ahead

8 main-dish
servings

460 cals per
serving

Good source
of calcium,
iron,
vitamin A,
vitamin C

Spaghetti Sauce
 (page 337)
½ 16-ounce package
 lasagna noodles
 (12 noodles)
1 cup dried bread
 crumbs
⅛ teaspoon pepper
salt
2 eggs

2 tablespoons water
1 medium eggplant, cut in
 ½-inch slices
salad oil
1 16-ounce package
 mozzarella cheese,
 thinly sliced
¼ cup grated Parmesan
 cheese

1. Prepare Spaghetti Sauce. Cook lasagna noodles as label directs; drain.

2. On waxed paper, combine crumbs, pepper and ½ teaspoon salt. In small dish with fork, beat eggs with water. Dip eggplant into egg mixture, then crumb mixture.

3. In 12-inch skillet over medium heat, in 2 tablespoons hot salad oil, cook eggplant slices, a few at a time, until tender, adding more oil when necessary. Drain on paper towels. Preheat oven to 350°F.

4. In 13″ by 9″ baking pan layer half of noodles, eggplant slices, mozzarella and Spaghetti Sauce; repeat. Sprinkle with Parmesan cheese. Bake 30 minutes or until hot.

Sauces for pasta

Spaghetti Sauce

To make 1 hr
ahead

4 cups

42 cals per
1/4 cup

Low in fat,
cholesterol

2 tablespoons salad oil
1 medium onion, diced
1 medium garlic clove,
  minced
2 15-ounce cans tomato
  sauce
1 12-ounce can tomato
  paste
2 teaspoons brown sugar

2 tablespoons chopped
  parsley
1 teaspoon oregano
  leaves
1 teaspoon salt
1/4 teaspoon cracked
  pepper
1 bay leaf

1. In 3-quart saucepan over medium heat, in hot salad oil, cook onion and garlic until tender, stirring frequently, about 10 minutes.
2. Add tomato sauce and remaining ingredients; over high heat, heat to boiling.
3. Reduce heat to medium-low, partially cover and cook 30 minutes. Discard bay leaf.

Meat Sauce

To make 1 1/2 hrs
ahead

4 cups

72 cals per
1/4 cup

Good source
of iron

2 tablespoons olive or
  salad oil
1 pound ground beef
1 medium onion, chopped
1 garlic clove, minced
1 16-ounce can tomatoes
1 12-ounce can tomato
  paste

4 teaspoons sugar
2 teaspoons oregano
  leaves
1 1/2 teaspoons salt
1/8 teaspoon cayenne
  pepper
1 bay leaf, crumbled

1. In 5-quart Dutch oven over medium heat, in hot olive oil, cook ground beef, onion and garlic until meat is well browned; spoon off excess fat.
2. Stir in tomatoes, their liquid, and remaining ingredients. Reduce heat to low; partially cover and simmer tomato meat mixture 35 minutes or until very thick, stirring occasionally.

White Clam Sauce

Begin 20 mins
ahead

3 cups

63 cals per
1/4 cup

Low in
cholesterol

Good source
of iron

3 8-ounce cans minced
  clams
1/4 cup olive or salad oil
1 garlic clove, minced
3/4 cup chopped parsley

2 tablespoons white wine
  (optional)
1 teaspoon basil
1/2 teaspoon salt

1. Drain juice from clams, reserving juice.
2. In 2-quart saucepan over medium heat, in hot oil, cook garlic until tender. Stir in reserved clam juice and remaining ingredients except clams; cook 10 minutes, stirring occasionally.
3. Stir in drained clams; cook sauce just until clams are heated through.

Anchovy Sauce

Begin about
20 mins
ahead

1/2 cup

343 cals per
1/4 cup

Low in
cholesterol
Good source
of calcium,
iron

1/4 cup olive or salad oil
1 small garlic clove,
  halved
1 2-ounce can anchovy
  fillets, drained and
  chopped

2 tablespoons minced
  parsley
2 tablespoons grated
  Parmesan cheese
1 teaspoon lemon juice

1. In 1-quart saucepan over medium-high heat, in hot olive oil, brown garlic. Remove from heat; discard garlic.
2. Stir in remaining ingredients until well mixed.

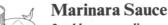

Marinara Sauce

Begin 30 mins
ahead

2 cups

22 cals per
1/4 cup

Low in fat,
cholesterol

2 tablespoons olive or
  salad oil
2 garlic cloves, minced
1 small onion, chopped
1 16-ounce can
  tomatoes

1 6-ounce can tomato
  paste
1 tablespoon sugar
2 teaspoons oregano
1 1/4 teaspoons salt

1. In 2-quart saucepan over medium heat, cook garlic and onion until tender, 5 minutes.
2. Stir in tomatoes, their liquid, and remaining ingredients. Reduce heat to low; cover and cook minutes or until thickened, stirring occasionally.

Shrimp Marinara Sauce

Begin 30 mins
ahead

4 cups

54 cals per
1/4 cup

Low in fat

1 tablespoon olive oil
1 garlic clove, minced
1 15-ounce can tomato
  sauce
1 6-ounce can tomato
  paste
2 tablespoons chopped
  parsley

1 tablespoon sugar
3/4 teaspoon salt
1/2 teaspoon oregano
  leaves
1/8 teaspoon pepper
1 pound frozen shrimp,
  and deveined

1. In 10-inch skillet over medium-high heat, in olive oil, lightly brown garlic.
2. Add tomato sauce and next 6 ingredients; heat to boiling. Reduce heat to low; cover and simmer sauce mixture over low heat 10 minutes.
3. Add frozen shrimp and cook until shrimp are tender, about 8 minutes, stirring occasionally.

Spinach Sauce

Begin 15 mins
ahead

2 1/2 cups

93 cals per
1/4 cup

Low in
cholesterol

Good source
of calcium,
iron

1/4 cup butter or
  margarine
1 10-ounce package
  frozen chopped spinach
1 teaspoon salt
1 cup ricotta cheese

1/4 cup grated Parmesan
  cheese
1/4 cup milk
1/8 teaspoon ground
  nutmeg

1. In 2-quart saucepan over medium heat, in hot butter, cook spinach and salt 10 minutes.
2. Reduce heat to low; add remaining ingredients; mix sauce well; cook sauce until just heated through (do not boil).

Walnut Sauce

Begin 15 mins
ahead

1 1/3 cups

291 cals per
1/3 cup

Low in
cholesterol
Good source
of vitamin A

1/4 cup butter or
  margarine
1 cup California walnuts,
  coarsely chopped

1/2 cup milk
2 tablespoons minced
  parsley
3/4 teaspoon salt

In 9-inch skillet over medium heat, in hot butter, lightly brown walnuts, about 5 minutes, stirring occasionally. Stir in remaining ingredients; heat.

Pesto

Begin 5 mins
ahead

1/2 cup

349 cals per
1/4 cup

Low in
cholesterol
Good source
of calcium

1/3 cup olive or salad oil
1/4 cup grated Parmesan
  cheese
1/4 cup chopped parsley
1 small garlic clove,
  quartered

2 tablespoons basil
  or 1/2 cup fresh
  basil
1/2 teaspoon salt
1/4 teaspoon ground
  nutmeg

In blender container, place all ingredients; cover and blend at medium speed until well mixed.

RICE

The delicate flavor of rice combines readily with foods ranging in taste from sweet and mild to highly seasoned. Cook rice, tightly covered, in a measured amount of liquid, so all liquid is absorbed. Check for doneness by tasting a grain: it should be tender throughout.

For different flavors, prepare your favorite kind of rice, but vary the liquid. Substitute chicken or beef broth for all of the water; or use half water and half tomato juice or cocktail vegetable juice; or substitute ½ cup orange or apple juice for ½ cup water.

Hot Fluffy Rice

Color index page 73

Begin 20 mins ahead

3 cups or 4 servings

158 cals per serving

Low in fat, cholesterol

2 cups water
1 cup regular long- or medium-grain rice
1 teaspoon salt

1 tablespoon butter or margarine (optional)

1 In 3-quart saucepan with tight-fitting lid, over high heat, heat water, rice, salt and butter or margarine, if you wish, to boiling.

2 Reduce heat until mixture just simmers; with fork, stir once or twice.

3 Cover pan and simmer without stirring or lifting lid, about 14 minutes or until rice is tender and all liquid is absorbed. Check tenderness by tasting a grain.

4 For drier rice, remove pan from heat; fluff with fork; cover and let stand 5 to 10 minutes. Or, spoon cooked rice into warm serving dish and fluff with fork before serving.

104 cals per serving

Low in fat, cholesterol

BROWN RICE: *About 50 minutes ahead:* Prepare as above but use *2½ cups water, 1 cup brown rice* and *1 teaspoon salt* and simmer mixture about 45 minutes. Or, prepare brown rice as the label directs. (Makes 4 cups or 6 servings.)

Oven Dinner Rice

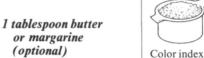

Color index page 73

Begin 35 mins ahead

3 cups or 4 servings

213 cals per serving

2 cups boiling water
1 cup regular long-grain rice or ¾ cup parboiled rice

2 tablespoons butter or margarine
1 teaspoon salt

1. Preheat oven to 350°F. Grease a 1½-quart casserole. In casserole, combine boiling water, rice, butter or margarine and salt.
2. Cover and bake mixture 30 minutes or until rice is tender and all liquid is absorbed. Fluff rice with fork just before serving.

Red-and-Green Rice

Color index page 73

Begin 30 mins ahead

6 servings

204 cals per serving

4 cups hot cooked rice
¼ cup chopped green pepper
¼ cup sliced green onions
1 canned pimento, chopped

2 tablespoons butter or margarine
½ teaspoon seasoned salt

In warm serving bowl, toss hot cooked rice with all ingredients until butter or margarine is melted. Serve rice immediately.

Herbed Orange Rice

Color index page 74

Begin 45 mins ahead

6 servings

190 cals per serving

¼ cup butter or margarine
⅔ cup chopped celery (with leaves)
2 tablespoons minced onion
1½ cups water
1 tablespoon grated orange peel

1 cup orange juice
¾ teaspoon salt
⅛ teaspoon thyme leaves
1 cup regular long-grain rice or ¾ cup parboiled rice

1. In 2-quart saucepan over medium heat, in hot butter or margarine, cook celery and onion until tender, about 5 minutes.
2. Add water, grated orange peel, orange juice, salt and thyme leaves. Heat to boiling; stir in rice. Reduce heat to low; cover and simmer mixture 15 to 20 minutes until rice is tender and all liquid is absorbed. Fluff lightly with fork before serving.

338

Accompaniment dishes

Rice Pilaf with Peas

Color index
page 73

Begin 40 mins
ahead

12 servings

187 cals per
serving

8 bacon slices, diced
1 medium onion, finely
chopped
2 cups regular long-grain
rice
2 10-ounce packages
frozen green peas
2 cups water
1 13 ³/₄-ounce can
chicken broth
1¹/₂ teaspoons salt
¹/₄ teaspoon pepper

1 In 12-inch skillet
over medium heat,
cook bacon until crisp.
With slotted spoon,
remove bacon to paper
towels; set aside.

2 Pour off all but ¹/₄ cup
bacon drippings from
the skillet.

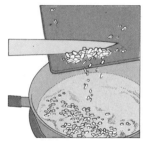

3 Add chopped onion to
skillet and cook until
tender, about 5 minutes,
stirring occasionally.

4 Stir rice, frozen peas,
water, chicken broth,
salt and pepper into mix-
ture; heat to boiling.
Reduce heat to low; cover
and simmer about 20 min-
utes until rice is tender.

5 To serve, toss rice mixture together with the
reserved bacon until well
mixed. Transfer mixture to
warm serving dish and
serve immediately.

Curried Rice and Onions

Color index
page 74

Begin 35 mins
ahead

4 servings

222 cals per
serving

2 tablespoons butter or
margarine
2 small onions, sliced
¹/₄ inch thick
¹/₂ teaspoon curry
powder

¹/₂ teaspoon salt
¹/₈ teaspoon ground
nutmeg
2 cups hot cooked rice
¹/₂ cup half-and-half

1. In 2-quart saucepan over low heat, in hot butter or
margarine, cook onions, curry, salt and nutmeg,
stirring mixture often, until onions are tender, about
7 minutes.
2. Stir in cooked rice and half-and-half; then heat
the curried mixture through to serve.

Risotto alla Milanese

Color index
page 74

Begin 45 mins
ahead

6 servings

272 cals per
serving

¹/₄ cup butter
¹/₃ cup minced onion
1¹/₂ cups regular long-
grain rice
2 13 ³/₄-ounce cans
chicken broth, heated

³/₄ teaspoon salt
¹/₈ teaspoon saffron
¹/₈ teaspoon pepper
¹/₃ cup grated Parmesan
cheese

1 In 3-quart ovensafe
saucepan over medium
heat, in hot butter, cook
onion until golden.

2 Add rice, stirring until
butter is absorbed.
Preheat oven to 350°F.

3 Stir in broth, salt,
saffron and pepper and
heat, stirring, to boiling.
Bake 30 minutes or until
liquid is absorbed and
rice is tender.

4 Stir in Parmesan
cheese until well blen-
ded. Serve in heated dish as
first course or as an accompaniment to veal.

TYPES OF RICE

REGULAR WHITE RICE: Milled to remove outer coating of bran
and sometimes polished; available as long-, medium- or short-
grain. Long-grain rice is best in curries, stews, salads and main
dishes. Medium- and short-grain rice is preferred for puddings
and rice rings. May be nutrient-enriched; check label. One cup
uncooked regular rice yields about 3 cups cooked.

PRECOOKED RICE: Fully cooked and dehydrated, milled, long-
grain rice with short preparation time. Follow label directions
for preparation and yield.

PARBOILED RICE: A long-grain rice subjected to a special
process before milling so it retains vitamins and minerals. It
requires slightly longer cooking than regular rice. One cup
uncooked parboiled rice yields about 4 cups cooked.

BROWN RICE: Unmilled so grains retain most of their food
value. Brown absorbs more liquid and takes longer to cook
than white rice. Nutty in flavor. One cup uncooked brown rice
yields about 4 cups cooked.

WILD RICE: Not a true rice but served as an accompaniment
like rice. Cook as label directs. One cup uncooked wild rice
yields about 3 cups cooked.

Accompaniment dishes

Rice-and-Mushroom Casserole

Color index
page 73

Begin 1 hr
ahead

4 servings

201 cals per
serving

Good source
of vitamin A

½ cup regular long-grain
  rice
4 tablespoons butter or
  margarine
¼ pound mushrooms,
  sliced
½ cup chopped onion

½ cup chopped celery
1¼ cups water
1 beef-flavor bouillon
  cube or envelope
½ teaspoon salt
⅛ teaspoon thyme leaves

1 Preheat oven to 350°F.
In 10-inch skillet over
medium heat, cook rice,
stirring constantly, until
rice is golden, about
5 minutes. Pour into
1-quart casserole.

2 In same skillet, in 2
tablespoons hot butter,
cook mushrooms, onion
and celery until tender,
about 5 minutes. Add re-
maining ingredients; heat
to boiling.

3 Over rice in casserole,
pour mixture from skil-
let. Cover and bake 35
minutes or until all liquid
is absorbed.

4 With fork, lightly toss
2 tablespoons butter
into rice mixture until
butter is melted and
mixture is fluffy.

Party Rice and Noodles

Color index
page 73

Begin 1¼ hrs
ahead

12 servings

224 cals per
serving

butter or margarine
2 medium onions,
  chopped
2 cups regular
  long-grain
  or 1½ cups
  parboiled rice
½ pound mushrooms,
  sliced

½ teaspoon curry powder
⅛ teaspoon pepper
4 cups chicken broth
1½ teaspoons salt
½ 8-ounce package
  medium noodles
  (2 heaping cups)

1. In 5-quart Dutch oven over medium heat, in ¼
cup butter, cook onions until tender, about 5 minutes. Preheat oven to 350°F.
2. Add rice, mushrooms, curry and pepper and cook
5 minutes, stirring frequently. Stir in broth, ¼ cup
butter and salt and heat to boiling. Gently stir in
uncooked noodles.
3. Pour mixture into 3-quart casserole; cover and
bake 35 to 40 minutes until rice and noodles are
tender and all liquid is absorbed. Just before serving,
fluff rice and noodle mixture with fork.

Baked Spanish Rice

Color index
page 73

Begin 1 hr
ahead

6 servings

269 cals per
serving

4 bacon slices
1 cup chopped onions
½ cup diced green pepper
1 16-ounce can tomatoes
water
1 8-ounce can tomato
  sauce
2 teaspoons sugar
½ teaspoon salt
1⅓ cups regular long-
  grain rice
½ cup shredded Cheddar
  cheese

1 Preheat oven to 350°F.
In 12-inch skillet over
medium heat, fry bacon
crisp; drain on paper
towels; crumble and set
aside. Pour off all but 2
tablespoons drippings.

2 In hot drippings, cook
onions and green pep-
per until tender, stirring
often, about 5 minutes.

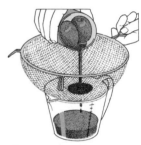

3 Into measuring cup,
drain tomatoes; add
enough water to tomato
liquid to make 1¾ cups.
Cut up tomatoes.

4 To onion mixture, add
liquid, tomatoes, to-
mato sauce, sugar and salt;
heat to boiling. Grease
1½-quart casserole.

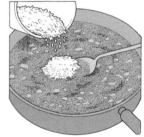

5 Remove from heat and
stir in rice; pour into
casserole. Cover; bake 35
minutes or until rice is
tender and liquid absorbed.

6 Fluff rice with fork;
sprinkle with cheese
and bake 5 minutes.
Garnish with bacon.

Rice pudding

Boiled Wild Rice

Color index page 73

Begin 1 hr ahead

6 servings

170 cals per serving

1⅓ cups wild rice (8 ounces)
2⅔ cups water

1½ teaspoons salt
2 tablespoons butter or margarine

1. Wash wild rice well; drain thoroughly.
2. In 2-quart saucepan over high heat, heat water to boiling. Stir in wild rice and salt. Reduce heat; cover and simmer 45 to 50 minutes until rice is tender and all liquid is absorbed.
3. With fork, lightly toss butter or margarine into rice until butter is melted.

Rice Ring

Color index page 73

Begin 25 mins ahead

6 servings

301 cals per serving

Low in sodium

6 cups hot cooked rice
¼ cup chopped parsley

3 tablespoons butter or margarine

1. Thoroughly grease a 5½-cup ring mold.
2. In large bowl, toss hot cooked rice, chopped parsley and butter or margarine; lightly pack in ring mold; let stand 1 minute.
3. Loosen edges; invert plate on top of mold; holding mold and plate, quickly invert rice ring onto plate. Lift off mold.

Packing in rice: Lightly pack hot cooked rice into greased ring mold.

Turning out rice ring: Invert rice ring onto warm serving plate.

Chinese Fried Rice

Color index page 74

Begin 2½ hrs ahead

6 servings

356 cals per serving

1 cup regular long-grain rice (or 3 cups cold, cooked rice)
6 eggs
¼ teaspoon salt
salad oil

1 8-ounce package sliced bacon, cooked and crumbled
1 tablespoon soy sauce
2 tablespoons chopped green onions

1. Prepare rice as label directs. Refrigerate cooked rice until well chilled.
2. In medium bowl with fork, beat eggs and salt lightly. In 12-inch skillet over high heat, heat 3 tablespoons salad oil until very hot. Pour in egg mixture; cook, stirring quickly and constantly with spoon, until eggs are the size of peas and leave side of pan. Reduce heat to low.
3. Push eggs to one side of skillet. In same skillet, gently stir rice and 2 tablespoons salad oil until rice is well coated with oil. Add bacon and soy sauce; gently stir to mix all ingredients in skillet; heat mixture through.
4. To serve, spoon fried rice into warm bowl and sprinkle with chopped green onions.

Rice Pudding

Color index page 98

Begin 4½ hrs ahead

8 servings

277 cals per serving

Good source of calcium, vitamin A

6 cups milk
1 cup regular medium-grain rice
½ cup sugar
2 tablespoons butter or margarine

¼ teaspoon salt
2 teaspoons vanilla extract
¼ teaspoon ground nutmeg

1 Add milk, rice, sugar, butter or margarine and salt to 3-quart saucepan.

2 Over medium heat, heat milk mixture until tiny bubbles form around the edge, stirring mixture frequently.

3 Reduce heat to low; cover; simmer 1 hour or until rice is very tender, stirring occasionally.

4 Stir in vanilla. Cover and refrigerate until well chilled, about 3 hours.

5 *To serve:* Spoon rice pudding into dessert dishes; sprinkle each serving with nutmeg.

322 cals per serving

CREAMY RICE PUDDING: Prepare as above but omit butter. Refrigerate. In small bowl with mixer at medium speed, beat *1 cup heavy or whipping cream* into soft peaks. With rubber spatula, fold cream into pudding; spoon into dessert dish; sprinkle with nutmeg. (Makes 10 servings.)

331 cals per serving

FRUIT RICE PUDDING: Prepare Rice Pudding as above but omit nutmeg. On top of each serving, place *canned peach half*, cut side down, then over each peach half pour some *Melba Sauce* (page 465). (Makes 8 servings.)

341

PIES

Pies lend themselves to infinite variation. You can make baked or unbaked pastry or crumb crusts filled with fruit, custard or cream, chiffon, even ice cream.

The best pie plates to use are those made of anodized aluminum, tin-coated or enamel-coated steel, porcelain-coated aluminum with a non-stick finish or glass; these materials all absorb heat and help the piecrusts to brown. Crusts baked in shiny, heat-reflecting metal pans tend to be pale; place these on cookie sheets to help the crust to brown. For a golden glaze, brush the top crust (not the edge) with milk, half-and-half, undiluted evaporated milk or slightly beaten egg white and sprinkle the crust with sugar, if you like. If the top crust seems to be browning too much cover the pie loosely with foil for the last 15 minutes of baking time.

Make sure your pie plates are the diameter specified in the recipe. Pie plates which are of the same diameter may be of different capacity. Our recipes fill those which are of a larger capacity. Any leftover filling can be baked in a custard cup, covered with foil if the pie has a top crust, for about a third of the pie baking time.

Don't grease the pie plate unless specifically directed to do so, for the crust will not stick to the plate. To loosen an unbaked crumb crust, wrap a cloth wrung out in hot water around the plate for a minute or two before cutting the pie. A pie with an ice cream or frozen filling will not only be easier to cut, but also have more flavor, if allowed to stand at room temperature for 15 minutes after removal from the freezer.

MAKING PASTRY

For best results, use cold water; if the water from the cold tap feels rather lukewarm, first chill it with an ice cube. If using lard instead of shortening, use it from the refrigerator also.

Handle pastry as little as possible. Cut in shortening with a pastry blender or two knives used scissor-fashion. Stir in water with a fork, stopping as soon as the ingredients hold together. Then, with hands, gently press the pastry into a ball. If, on a hot day, the pastry becomes too soft to handle, wrap it in waxed paper and refrigerate for 30 minutes, or until firm again.

If making a 1-crust pie, prepare enough pastry for 2 crusts (or more). Refrigerate or freeze unused pastry.

ROLLING PASTRY

Pastry should be rolled with a stockinette-covered rolling pin on a lightly floured surface. First roll the pin over the floured surface so that the stockinette cover absorbs some of the flour. Then slightly flatten the ball of pastry and roll it out as shown below.

Rolling the pastry: Roll it out from the center to the edges, keeping it circular. Push the sides in occasionally by hand, if necessary, and lift the rolling pin slightly as you near the edges to avoid making them too thin.

Lift the pastry from time to time to make sure that it is not sticking. If it does stick, loosen it with a spatula and sprinkle a little more flour on the surface underneath. Mend any cracks or breaks as they appear, patching tears with a strip of pastry cut from the edge. Moisten the torn edges, lay the patch over the tear and press it carefully into position.

LINING THE PIE PLATE

If you are making a 2-crust pie, divide your pastry into 2 pieces, one slightly larger than the other. Use the larger piece for the bottom crust. For 2 bottom crusts, divide the dough evenly in half.

Roll the pastry into a circle about ⅛ inch thick and 2 inches larger all around than the pie plate. Roll half of the circle loosely around the rolling pin and lift the pastry on to the pie plate, centering it over the plate. Unroll the pastry and ease it into the pie plate, pressing it lightly onto the bottom and side with your fingertips. Do not stretch the pastry at any point; it will just shrink back while baking. Make a decorative edge (opposite) and fill the pie, or make a top crust.

MAKING A TOP CRUST

Use a smaller ball of pastry to make the top crust. Roll it out into a circle like the bottom crust. Then, with a sharp knife, cut a few short slashes or a design in the center. Roll the pastry around a rolling pin as above and transfer it to the pie, centering it over the filling. Make one of the decorative edges shown opposite.

DECORATIVE PIE EDGES

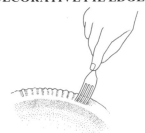

Old-fashioned fork edge: Trim pastry even with plate rim. With floured 4-tined fork, press pastry to rim all around pie edge.

Fluted edge: Trim pastry, leaving a 1-inch overhang. Fold overhang under to make a stand-up edge. Place one index finger on inside edge and with index finger and thumb of other hand, pinch pastry to make a curved flute. Repeat, leaving ¼ inch between flutes.

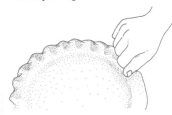

Rope edge: Make a stand-up edge as for fluted edge then press thumb into pastry at an angle and pinch pastry between this thumb and knuckle of index finger. Place thumb in groove left by index finger and repeat all around edge.

Modified fluted edge: Make as fluted edge but leave ½ inch between flutes; flatten each flute with a floured 4-tined fork.

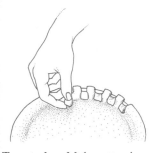

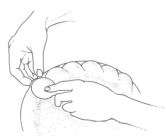

Turret edge: Make a stand-up edge as for fluted edge. With knife, cut through pastry to pie plate rim at ½-inch intervals. Press alternate strips of pastry flat around edge.

Scalloped edge: Make a stand-up edge as for fluted edge. Put thumb and index finger of one hand about 1¼ inches apart on outside of pie edge; with a floured round-bowl measuring tablespoon, press pastry outward to make scallops. Pinch points in between.

DECORATIVE TOPS FOR 2-CRUST PIES

Lattice top: Fill bottom crust and trim edge, leaving a 1-inch overhang. Roll pastry for top crust into a circle and cut it into ½-inch strips. Moisten edge of bottom crust with water. Place strips about 1¼ inches apart across filling. Trim strips even with overhang. Press ends of each strip to overhang to seal them. Lay an equal number of pastry strips at right angles to first layer. Turn overhang up over strips. Pinch edges to seal and make a high, stand-up edge. Make a fluted edge.

Twisted lattice top: Make as above but twist strips.

Diamond lattice top: Make a lattice top but attach cross-strips diagonally to make a diamond pattern.

WOVEN LATTICE TOP

Cut pastry strips as for lattice top. Place layer of strips on filling; fold every other strip back. Place center cross-strip on pie and replace folded strips. Fold back alternate strips; position second cross-strip. Repeat to weave lattice. Seal ends. Make a fluted edge.

STORING PIES AND PASTRY

Keep pies with cream, custard, whipped cream or chiffon fillings in the refrigerator; use within a day or so. Store fruit pies at room temperature and use within 2 or 3 days. Balls of unbaked pastry, wrapped in plastic wrap or foil, may be stored in the refrigerator for a day or two.

FREEZING PIES AND PASTRY

Pastry: Freeze balls of uncooked pastry, freezer-wrapped, up to 2 months. Thaw, wrapped, at room temperature 2 to 4 hours. Or roll pastry into circles 3 inches larger all around than pie plates, stack with 2 sheets of waxed paper between each, wrap and freeze. To use, place circle on pie plate; thaw 10 to 15 minutes before shaping.

Piecrusts: Freeze baked or unbaked piecrusts in their pie plates. Wrap, then stack with crumpled waxed paper between each. Store baked piecrusts 4 to 6 months; thaw, unwrapped, at room temperature 15 minutes. Store unbaked crusts 2 to 3 months; bake without thawing either unfilled, for about 20 minutes in a 425°F. oven, or filled and baked as directed in the recipe.

Fruit pies: Freeze baked or unbaked fruit pies 3 to 4 months. To freeze unbaked fruit pies, if fruit is very juicy, add 1 to 2 tablespoons extra thickening per pie. Do not cut slits in top crust. Freezer-wrap and freeze. Or, if pie is fragile, first freeze until firm, then cover top with a paper plate for protection, freezer-wrap and store. To use an unbaked fruit pie, unwrap, cut slits in top crust and bake still frozen, allowing 15 to 20 minutes additional baking time or until fruit is bubbling. Thaw baked pies at room temperature 30 minutes, then bake in a 350°F. oven 30 minutes or until warm.

Pumpkin pies: Bake pumpkin pies before freezing, or the crust may become soggy. Use within 4 to 6 months. Thaw as for fruit pies. Or freeze filling and unbaked crust separately; thaw and complete pie as recipe directs.

Chiffon pies: Freeze until firm, wrap and store. Use within 1 month. To thaw, unwrap and let stand at room temperature 2 to 4 hours, or in refrigerator overnight.

Don't freeze cream and custard pies, fillings may separate; or meringue topping, it may shrink.

Pie crusts

Pastry for 2-Crust Pie

2 cups all-purpose flour
1 teaspoon salt
¾ cup shortening
5 to 6 tablespoons cold
*   water*

Pastry for one 2-crust pie
or two 8- or 9-inch piecrusts
2570 total cals

1 In medium bowl with fork, lightly stir together flour and salt.

2 With pastry blender or 2 knives used scissor-fashion, cut in shortening until mixture resembles coarse crumbs.

3 Sprinkle in cold water, a tablespoon at a time, mixing lightly with a fork after each addition until pastry just holds together.

4 With hands, shape pastry into a ball. (If it is a hot day, wrap in waxed paper and refrigerate 30 minutes.)

5 For a 2-crust pie, divide pastry into 2 pieces, one slightly larger, and then gently shape each piece into a ball.

6 On lightly floured surface with lightly floured stockinette-covered rolling pin, roll larger ball into a ⅛-inch-thick circle, 2 inches larger all around than pie plate.

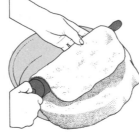

7 Roll half of circle onto rolling pin; transfer pastry to pie plate and unroll, easing into bottom and side of plate. Fill as recipe directs.

8 For top crust, roll smaller ball as for bottom crust; with sharp knife, cut a few slashes or a design in center of circle; center over filling in the bottom crust.

9 With scissors or a sharp knife, trim the pastry edges, leaving 1-inch overhang all around the pie plate rim.

10 Fold overhang under; pinch a high edge; make a decorative edge (page 343). Bake pie as recipe directs.

Making 2 piecrusts:
Prepare pastry as directed in steps 1 to 4 then divide pastry evenly in half, shaping each half into a ball. On a lightly floured surface with a lightly floured stockinette-covered rolling pin, roll out each ball and line 2 pie plates as directed in steps 6 and 7. Trim pastry edge and make a decorative edge as in steps 9 and 10. Fill and bake or bake and fill as recipe directs.

UNBAKED PIECRUST: Prepare as steps 1 to 3 of Pastry (left) but use only *1 cup all-purpose flour, ½ teaspoon salt, ¼ cup plus 2 tablespoons shortening* and *2 to 3 tablespoons water.* Shape all of pastry into one ball. On lightly floured surface with lightly floured stockinette-covered rolling pin, roll pastry into circle ⅛ inch thick and about 2 inches larger all around than pie plate. Roll pastry circle gently onto rolling pin; transfer to pie plate and unroll, easing into bottom and side of plate. With kitchen scissors or sharp knife, trim pastry edges, leaving a 1-inch overhang. Fold overhang under; pinch to form a high edge, then make a decorative edge. Fill and bake as directed in recipe. (Makes one 8- or 9-inch piecrust.) 1294 cals

BAKED PIECRUST: Preheat oven to 425°F. Prepare as above for Unbaked Piecrust. With 4-tined fork, prick bottom and side of crust in many places to prevent puffing during baking. Bake for 15 minutes or until golden. Cool. (Makes one 8- or 9-inch piecrust.)

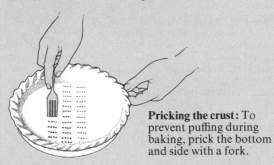

Pricking the crust: To prevent puffing during baking, prick the bottom and side with a fork.

COBBLER OR TOP CRUST: Prepare pastry for one Unbaked Piecrust (above). Roll 2 inches larger all around than 9½" by 1½" deep pie plate; place over filling; trim edges leaving a 1-inch overhang; pinch to form a high edge and make a decorative edge. Cut a 4-inch "X" in center of crust; fold back points from center of "X" to make a square opening. Bake as directed in recipe.

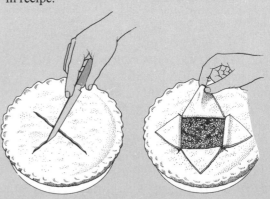

Making a cobbler crust: First cut a 4-inch "X" in center of top crust.

Fold back the 4 points to make a square opening and reveal the filling.

Baked Graham-Cracker Crumb Crust

Begin 1½ hrs ahead

One 9-inch piecrust

1181 cals

about 18 graham crackers (1½ cups graham-cracker crumbs)
¼ cup sugar
⅓ cup melted butter or margarine

1 In covered blender container, blend crackers, ¼ at a time, until finely crumbed; or place crackers in strong bag and roll fine with rolling pin.

2 Preheat oven to 375°F. In medium bowl, mix well crumbs, sugar and melted butter. If you like, set aside 3 tablespoons mixture for garnish.

3 With back of spoon, press rest of mixture to bottom and side of 9-inch pie plate, making a small rim.

4 Bake 8 minutes then remove crumb crust to wire rack to cool.

5 Fill as recipe directs; garnish with reserved crumb mixture or as recipe directs.

1034 cals

8-INCH GRAHAM-CRACKER: Prepare as above but use *14 graham crackers* (1¼ cups crumbs), *3 tablespoons sugar* and *¼ cup melted butter.*

844 cals

VANILLA- OR CHOCOLATE-WAFER: Prepare as above but for 8-inch crust use about *24 vanilla or 14 chocolate wafers* (1¼ cups crumbs) and *¼ cup melted butter;* for 9-inch crust use about *35 vanilla or 18 chocolate wafers* (1½ cups crumbs) and *⅓ cup melted butter.*

843 cals

GINGERSNAP: Prepare as above but for 8-inch crust use about *18 gingersnaps* (1¼ cups crumbs) and *¼ cup melted butter;* for 9-inch crumb crust use about *24 gingersnaps* (1½ cups crumbs) and *⅓ cup melted butter.*

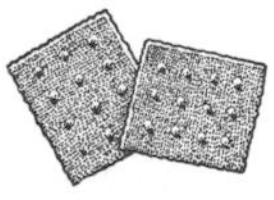

Unbaked Crumb Crust

Begin 1½ hrs ahead

One 9-inch piecrust

830 cals

1½ cups graham-cracker crumbs
⅓ cup packed brown sugar
½ teaspoon ground cinnamon
⅓ cup melted butter or margarine

Prepare as Baked Graham-Cracker Crumb Crust (left) but do not make rim and do not bake. Chill well; fill as recipe directs or with chilled filling; top with reserved crumb mixture. Refrigerate.

8-INCH CRUST: Prepare as above but decrease quantities. Use *1⅓ cups graham-cracker crumbs, ¼ cup packed brown sugar, ¼ teaspoon ground cinnamon* and *¼ cup melted butter.*

Baked Tart Shells

Begin 1¾ hrs ahead

12 tart shells

126 cals each

1½ cups all-purpose flour
1 tablespoon sugar
¼ teaspoon salt
⅓ cup shortening
3 to 4 tablespoons cold water

1. In medium bowl with fork, mix flour, sugar and salt. With pastry blender or 2 knives used scissor-fashion, cut in shortening.
2. Sprinkle in cold water, a tablespoon at a time, mixing lightly with fork after each addition, until pastry just holds together.
3. Shape dough into a ball; divide into 12 equal pieces; carefully shape each into a ball. Preheat the oven to 425°F.

4 Roll each ball into circle, ⅛ inch thick and 5 inches in diameter.

5 Press pastry circles into 3¼" by 1¼" deep fluted tart pans.

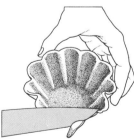

6 With knife, trim each pastry shell even with top of tart pan.

7 With 4-tined fork, prick the bottom of each tart shell.

8. Bake 10 to 12 minutes until light golden. Turn shells out of pans onto wire rack; cool completely. Fill with chilled filling.

UNBAKED: Prepare dough and line pans as above; do not prick. Fill and bake as recipe directs.

Fruit pies

Fruit pie is always in season and if fresh fruit is unavailable, canned and frozen products can be substituted. Follow the guidelines below.

The best apples for pies are York Imperial, Winesap, Stayman, Rome Beauty, Northern Spy, Newtown Pippin, McIntosh, Jonathan, Gravenstein, Golden Delicious and Cortland. One pound of apples is equal to 3 medium apples or 3 cups sliced.

Tart or sour cherries are used most for pies. Two cups pitted cherries equal one 16-ounce can or 20 ounces frozen cherries. One pint blackberries, blueberries or cranberries is equal to 1¾ cups.

Use Bartlett, Anjou or Bosc pears for cooking. One 29-ounce can of pears equals 3 fresh ones or about 2 cups peeled and sliced. Two 29-ounce cans of sliced cling peaches equals 5 cups sliced fresh peaches or about 2½ pounds whole.

Apple Pie

Pastry for 2-Crust Pie (page 344)
⅔ to ¾ cup sugar
2 tablespoons all-purpose flour
½ teaspoon ground cinnamon
¼ teaspoon ground nutmeg
½ teaspoon grated lemon peel
1 to 2 teaspoons lemon juice

6 to 7 cups thinly sliced, peeled and cored cooking apples (2 pounds)
1 tablespoon butter or margarine
milk

Color index page 86

Begin 2 hrs ahead or early in day

6 servings

608 cals per serving

1 Prepare pastry. Roll out half of pastry and line 9-inch pie plate.

2 In small bowl, combine sugar (amount depends on tartness of apples) and next 5 ingredients.

3 Place half of thinly sliced apples in piecrust; sprinkle with half of sugar mixture. Top with rest of apples, then rest of sugar mixture.

4 Dot the filling with butter or margarine. Preheat oven to 425°F.

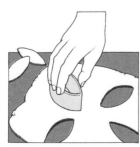

5 Roll out remaining pastry for top crust and using a floured leaf-shaped cookie cutter, cut out design. Place crust over pie; trim edges.

6 Fold pastry overhang under then bring up over pie-plate rim. Pinch to form a high edge then make your choice of decorative edge.

7 For a golden glaze, brush the top crust (not the edge) lightly with some milk. Bake pie for 40 to 50 minutes or until crust is golden.

Color index page 86

Begin 2 hrs ahead

6 servings

679 cals per serving

Cherry Pie

Pastry for 2-Crust Pie (page 344)
1 cup sugar
¼ cup cornstarch
½ teaspoon salt

5 cups pitted fresh tart cherries
1 tablespoon butter or margarine

1. Prepare pastry. Roll out half of pastry and line 9-inch pie plate. Preheat oven to 425°F.
2. For filling, combine sugar, cornstarch, salt and pitted cherries. Place filling in piecrust; dot with butter or margarine.
3. Roll out remaining pastry for top crust and cut a few slashes; cover with slashed top crust; flute edge. Bake 50 to 60 minutes until golden.

Color index page 87

Begin 2 hrs ahead

8 servings

337 cals per serving

Blueberry Cobbler

Cobbler or Top Crust (page 344)
⅔ cup sugar
¼ cup all-purpose flour
½ teaspoon ground cinnamon
¼ teaspoon ground nutmeg

½ teaspoon grated lemon peel
2 teaspoons lemon juice
⅛ teaspoon salt
6 cups blueberries
1 tablespoon butter or margarine

1. Prepare Cobbler or Top Crust as directed. Preheat oven to 425°F.
2. For filling, toss together sugar, flour, cinnamon, nutmeg, lemon peel, lemon juice, salt and blueberries. Place filling in 9½" by 1½" deep pie plate; dot with butter or margarine. Top with crust. Bake 50 minutes or until golden brown.

Color index page 86

Begin 2 hrs ahead

6 servings

602 cals per serving

Blackberry Pie

Pastry for 2-Crust Pie (page 344)
⅔ to ¾ cup sugar
¼ cup all-purpose flour
½ teaspoon ground cinnamon
¼ teaspoon ground nutmeg

½ teaspoon grated lemon peel
⅛ teaspoon salt
5 cups blackberries
1 tablespoon butter

1. Prepare pastry. Roll out half of pastry and line 9-inch pie plate. Preheat oven to 425°F.
2. For filling, toss together sugar, flour, cinnamon, nutmeg, lemon peel and salt with blackberries. Place filling in piecrust; dot with butter.
3. Roll out remaining pastry for top crust; cut a few slashes and cover filling with slashed top crust; make a decorative edge. Bake 50 minutes or until the piecrust is golden brown.

Peach Pie

Color index
page 88

Begin 2 hrs
ahead or
early in day

6 servings
631 cals per
serving

Pastry for 2-Crust Pie
 (page 344)
6 cups peeled, sliced
 peaches
³/₄ to 1 cup sugar
¹/₃ cup all-purpose
 flour
1 tablespoon lemon juice

¹/₂ teaspoon grated lemon
 peel
¹/₂ teaspoon ground
 cinnamon
milk

1 Prepare pastry. Roll out half of pastry and line 9-inch pie plate.

2 Toss sliced peaches in large bowl with remaining ingredients except milk then spoon peach mixture into piecrust.

3 Roll remaining pastry into 11-inch-diameter circle and cut into 6 strips of equal width. Preheat oven to 425°F

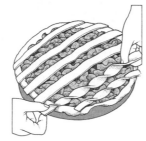

4 Place pastry strips parallel across pie; twist, then fasten ends to the piecrust.

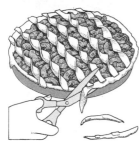

5 Trim the pastry edges. Fold overhang over strip ends; pinch to form a high edge, then make a decorative edge.

6 Brush strips with milk. Bake 45 to 50 minutes or until crust is golden. Serve pie warm or cold.

Begin 2 hrs
ahead or
early in day

6 servings
652 cals per
serving

PEAR PIE: Prepare as Peach Pie (above) but for filling combine **6 pears**, peeled, cored and sliced, **³/₄ cup sugar, 3 tablespoons quick-cooking tapioca, 2 tablespoons lemon juice, 2 tablespoons butter** or margarine, **1 teaspoon grated lemon peel, ¹/₂ teaspoon ground nutmeg, ¹/₂ teaspoon ground cinnamon** and **¹/₄ teaspoon salt.** Bake in preheated 425°F. oven 50 to 60 minutes until pears are tender.

Streusel-topped Pear Pie

Color index
page 88

Begin 2 hrs
ahead or
early in day

8 servings
517 cals per
serving

2¹/₄ cups all-purpose flour
salt
1 cup butter or margarine
2¹/₂ to 3 tablespoons
 cold water
5 medium pears
¹/₂ cup sugar
2 tablespoons lemon
 juice
¹/₂ cup packed light
 brown sugar

1 teaspoon ground
 cinnamon
¹/₄ teaspoon ground
 nutmeg
¹/₄ teaspoon ground
 cloves
¹/₂ cup shredded Cheddar
 cheese

1. In medium bowl with fork, stir 2 cups flour and 1 teaspoon salt. With pastry blender or 2 knives used scissor-fashion, cut in ³/₄ cup butter until mixture resembles coarse crumbs. Measure 1 cup mixture into medium bowl; reserve.
2. To remaining flour mixture, add cold water, 1 tablespoon at a time, mixing lightly with a fork after each addition until moist enough to hold together. With hands, shape pastry into a ball.
3. On lightly floured surface with lightly floured rolling pin, roll pastry into an 11-inch circle; use to line 9-inch pie plate. Trim pastry edges, leaving 1-inch overhang. Fold overhang under; bring up over pie-plate rim; pinch to form a high edge; make a fluted edge.
4. Peel, core and cut pears into thick slices to measure about 4¹/₂ cups. In large bowl, toss pears with sugar, lemon juice, ¹/₄ cup flour and ¹/₄ teaspoon salt; put in crust. Preheat oven to 425°F.
5. In medium bowl, combine reserved flour mixture, brown sugar and next 3 ingredients. With pastry blender or 2 knives used scissor-fashion, cut in cheese and ¹/₄ cup butter until mixture resembles coarse crumbs and ingredients are well blended. Sprinkle over pears. Bake 40 minutes; cover with foil and bake 20 minutes more. Serve warm or refrigerate to serve cold.

Prune and Apricot Pie

Color index
page 86

Begin early
in day or
day ahead

8 servings
339 cals per
serving

1 9-inch Baked Piecrust
 (page 344)
water
1 12-ounce package
 pitted prunes (about
 2 cups)
1 cup dried apricots
¹/₄ cup chopped
 California walnuts

3 tablespoons cornstarch
¹/₄ cup sugar
1 tablespoon finely
 grated lemon
 peel
1 teaspoon ground
 cinnamon
¹/₈ teaspoon salt

1. Prepare piecrust; cool. Preheat oven to 375°F.
2. In 2-quart saucepan over medium-high heat, heat 3 cups water, prunes and apricots to boiling; reduce heat to low and simmer 15 minutes or until fruits are tender.
3. Meanwhile, spread walnuts on cookie sheet; toast in oven 8 to 10 minutes until lightly browned.
4. In cup, blend cornstarch and ¹/₂ cup water; gradually stir into simmering fruit and cook, stirring constantly, until thickened. Stir in sugar, lemon peel, cinnamon and salt. Pour mixture into piecrust. Sprinkle with walnuts. Cool.

Fruit pies

Color index page 86

Begin early in day or day ahead

10 servings 462 cals per serving

Deep-Dish Peach Pie

1 cup sugar	*Pastry for 2-Crust Pie*
¼ cup cornstarch	*(page 344)*
½ teaspoon ground	*10 cups sliced peaches*
cinnamon	*(about 5 pounds)*
⅛ teaspoon salt	*3 tablespoons butter*

1. In medium bowl, combine sugar, cornstarch, cinnamon and salt; set aside. Prepare pastry; cut off one-fourth; set aside.

2. Roll three-fourths of pastry into 17″ by 13″ rectangle. Use to line 12″ by 8″ baking dish. Add peaches to dish; dot with butter; sprinkle with sugar mixture. Preheat oven to 425°F.

3. Roll remaining pastry into 10″ by 6″ rectangle; cut into six 1-inch-wide strips; place the strips crosswise over the peach filling, twisting them. Make a high, fluted edge.

4. Bake 50 minutes or until filling is bubbly and crust is golden brown.

5. Let stand 15 minutes, then serve warm. Or cool to serve cold.

Color index page 87

Begin 2 hrs ahead or early in day

10 servings 493 cals per serving

Deep-Dish Plum Pie

Pastry for 2-Crust Pie	*4 tablespoons butter or*
(page 344)	*margarine*
4 pounds plums, halved	*1½ cups sugar*
and pitted	*6 tablespoons all-purpose*
½ teaspoon almond	*flour*
extract	*1 egg white or milk*

1. Prepare pastry. Roll three-fourths of pastry into 18″ by 14″ rectangle; use to line 13″ by 9″ baking dish. Arrange the plums in pastry lining; sprinkle with almond extract and dot with butter.

2. In small bowl, combine sugar and flour; sprinkle over plums. Preheat oven to 425°F.

3. Roll remaining pastry into 15″ by 5″ rectangle; cut into ten ½-inch-wide strips; use to make a lattice top (page 343); make a rope edge. Brush pastry with egg white or milk. Bake 45 to 50 minutes until filling is bubbly and crust is golden brown. Serve the pie warm or cool to serve cold later.

PREVENTING OVERBROWNING

If the piecrust edges begin to brown too much during baking, cover them with strips of foil to prevent burning.

Deluxe Apple Tart

1 cup all-purpose flour
5 tablespoons butter,
softened
⅛ teaspoon salt
sugar
water
9 medium Golden
Delicious apples
(3 pounds)
1 teaspoon lemon juice
1 10- or 12-ounce jar
apricot preserves

Color index page 88

Begin early in day or day ahead

8 servings

390 cals per serving

1 In medium bowl, knead flour, butter, salt, 2 tablespoons sugar and 2 tablespoons water until dough forms a ball, adding a little more water if it is needed.

2 Pat pastry into bottom and up side of 9-inch tart pan with removable bottom, or in 9″ by 3″ springform pan to within 2 inches from top of pan; refrigerate piecrust.

3 Quarter 3 apples; with sharp knife, peel, core and cut in ⅛-inch-thick slices to make 3 cups.

4 In medium bowl with spoon, toss apples with lemon juice and 2 tablespoons sugar.

5 Make applesauce: Peel and core remaining apples; cut into chunks. In blender, puree ¼ cup water and ⅓ of apple chunks. Add remaining chunks, ⅓ at a time; blend until smooth. In 3-quart pan, heat puree, ⅓ cup apricot preserves and ¼ cup sugar to boiling. Reduce heat; cook, uncovered, 20 minutes or until very thick, stirring frequently.

6 Spread applesauce (about 1½ cups) evenly over piecrust. Preheat oven to 400°F.

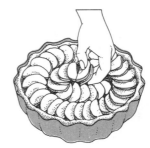

7 Place apple slices, closely overlapping, in concentric circles on pie. Bake 45 minutes or until apple is tender and lightly browned. Remove to rack.

8 Strain remaining apricot preserves through sieve into 1-quart saucepan and stir in 1 tablespoon sugar.

9 Over medium-high heat, heat to boiling; cook 2 minutes more or until mixture coats spoon.

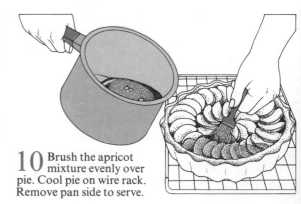

10 Brush the apricot mixture evenly over pie. Cool pie on wire rack. Remove pan side to serve.

Custard pies

Unbaked custard pie fillings are very thin mixtures and it is advisable to rub the crust of our Custard Pie with butter or margarine before adding the filling to prevent the unbaked piecrust from becoming soggy. Avoid spilling any mixture by placing the pie on the oven rack before pouring in the filling, then carefully push the rack back in place. Bake a custard pie until the filling has set and a knife inserted into filling comes out clean. Garnish with chocolate curls, chopped nuts, whipped cream or shredded or flaked coconut.

Custard Pie

Color index
page 88

Begin early
in day

6 servings

422 cals per
serving

1 9-inch Unbaked
Piecrust (page 344)
1 tablespoon butter or
margarine, softened
2¹/₂ cups milk
¹/₂ cup sugar
3 eggs
1 teaspoon vanilla
extract
¹/₂ teaspoon salt
¹/₄ teaspoon ground
nutmeg
chopped nuts, ground
nutmeg or whipped
cream for garnish

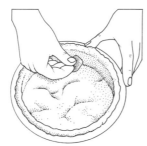

1 Prepare piecrust. Rub unbaked piecrust with softened butter or margarine; refrigerate. Preheat oven to 425°F.

2 In medium bowl with wire whisk or hand beater, beat remaining ingredients except garnish.

3 Place pie plate on oven rack and pour milk mixture into piecrust.

4 Bake 20 to 25 minutes until knife inserted about 1 inch from edge comes out clean. Cool.

5 Garnish cooled pie with chopped nuts, ground nutmeg or whipped cream to serve.

452 cals per
serving

COCONUT-CUSTARD PIE: Prepare pie as above but sprinkle *¹/₂ cup shredded or flaked coconut* over the bottom of the prepared piecrust before pouring in the milk mixture.

Pumpkin Pie

Color index
page 86

Begin early
in day or
day ahead

6 servings

458 cals per
serving

1 9-inch Unbaked
Piecrust (page 344)
3 eggs, separated
1 16-ounce can pumpkin
(2 cups)
1 cup evaporated milk
1 cup sugar
1 teaspoon ground
cinnamon

¹/₂ teaspoon ground
ginger
¹/₄ teaspoon ground
nutmeg
¹/₄ teaspoon ground
cloves
¹/₄ teaspoon salt
Brandy Hard Sauce
(below)

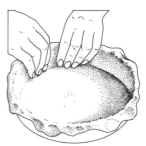

1 Prepare unbaked piecrust with your choice of decorative edge. Preheat oven to 375°F.

2 In small bowl with mixer at high speed, beat egg whites just until soft peaks form.

3 In large bowl with same beaters and with mixer at low speed, beat together egg yolks, pumpkin and next 7 ingredients until well blended.

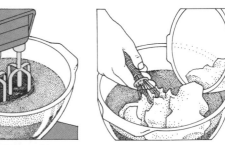

4 With wire whisk or rubber spatula, gently fold beaten egg whites into pumpkin mixture.

5 To avoid spilling pumpkin mixture, place pie plate on oven rack and pour filling into crust; carefully push rack back.

6 Bake 45 minutes until filling is set and knife inserted 1 inch from edge comes out clean; refrigerate. Serve with sauce.

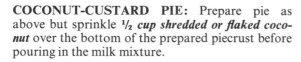

369 cals per
¹/₄ cup

BRANDY HARD SAUCE: In small bowl with mixer at medium speed, beat *¹/₄ cup butter* or margarine, softened, until light and fluffy. Gradually beat in *³/₄ cup confectioners' sugar, 1 tablespoon brandy* and *¹/₄ teaspoon vanilla extract* until creamy. Refrigerate. (Makes ¹/₂ cup.)

349

Cream pies

Cream pie fillings are usually cooked separately and then added to a baked pastry or crumb crust. If the recipe calls for the filling to be chilled, press plastic wrap or waxed paper to the surface of the cream filling to prevent a skin forming; be sure to remove the covering before adding a topping.

Whipped cream and meringue are the most popular toppings for cream pies. Remember that meringue toppings require special care to keep them from shrinking. Spread the meringue over the pie, making sure it touches the crust at all points and after baking, be sure to allow the pie to cool away from any drafts.

Chocolate Cream Pie

1 9-inch Baked Piecrust (page 344) or 9-inch Baked Vanilla or Chocolate-Wafer Crumb Crust (page 345)
½ cup sugar
⅓ cup all-purpose flour
¼ teaspoon salt
2 cups milk
2 squares unsweetened chocolate, coarsely chopped
3 egg yolks

3 tablespoons butter or margarine
1 teaspoon vanilla extract
1 cup heavy or whipping cream

Color index page 86
Begin 5½ hrs ahead or early in day
8 servings
497 cals per serving

1 Prepare piecrust; cool. In 2-quart saucepan with spoon, mix together sugar, flour and salt; stir in milk.

2 Stir in chocolate and over low heat, cook mixture, stirring constantly, until chocolate is completely melted.

3 With wire whisk, beat until chocolate is blended; increase heat to medium: cook, stirring till mixture is thickened and boils (about 10 minutes); remove at once from heat.

4 In cup with wire whisk, beat egg yolks with small amount of hot chocolate mixture.

5 Slowly pour egg mixture into saucepan, stirring rapidly. Over low heat, cook, stirring, until *very* thick (do not boil) and mixture mounds when dropped from spoon.

6 Remove from heat; stir in butter and vanilla then pour into piecrust. Cover surface with plastic wrap to prevent skin forming. Refrigerate until set, about 4 hours.

7 *Just before serving:* In small bowl with mixer at medium speed, beat cream until stiff peaks form. Discard plastic wrap on filling. Spread whipped cream on top of pie.

MERINGUE-TOPPED CHOCOLATE CREAM PIE: Prepare as Chocolate Cream Pie (left) but omit whipped cream. Do not cool pie. Top with *3-Egg-White Meringue Topping* (opposite); bake as directed. Cool; refrigerate. (Makes 8 servings.)

Color index page 89
Begin 5½ hrs ahead or early in day
8 servings   452 cals per serving

Vanilla Cream Pie

1 9-inch Baked Piecrust (page 344) or 9-inch Baked Graham-Cracker Crumb Crust (page 345)
½ cup sugar
⅓ cup all-purpose flour

¼ teaspoon salt
2¼ cups milk
4 egg yolks
1 tablespoon butter
2 teaspoons vanilla extract
1 cup heavy cream

1. Prepare piecrust or crumb crust; cool.
2. In 2-quart saucepan with spoon, mix sugar, flour and salt. Stir in milk until smooth. Over medium heat, cook mixture, stirring constantly, until mixture is thickened and begins to boil (about 10 minutes). Boil 1 minute. Remove immediately from heat and set aside.
3. In cup with wire whisk, beat egg yolks with small amount of hot milk mixture. Slowly pour egg mixture into saucepan, stirring rapidly to prevent lumping. Over low heat, cook, stirring constantly, until *very* thick (do not boil) and mixture mounds when dropped from spoon.
4. Remove from heat; stir in butter and vanilla; pour into piecrust. Cover surface of mixture with plastic wrap to prevent skin forming. Refrigerate until set, about 4 hours.
5. *Just before serving:* In small bowl with mixer at medium speed, beat cream until stiff peaks form. Discard plastic wrap. Spread cream on pie.

BANANA CREAM PIE: Prepare piecrust and filling as above but do not pour filling into crust. Cover surface of filling with plastic wrap; refrigerate until cool, about 2 hours. Peel and slice *3 medium bananas* over bottom of piecrust; top with filling; chill until set, about 2 hours. Spread whipped cream evenly on top. To garnish, grate peel of *1 lemon*; sprinkle around top edge of pie. Cut lemon in half and squeeze juice into bowl. Into juice, peel and slice *1 large banana*; toss to coat; drain on paper towels. Arrange banana slices in center of top of pie. In 1-quart saucepan over low heat, heat *⅓ cup apple jelly* until just melted; brush over banana slices. Chill.

LEMON CREAM PIE: Prepare piecrust and filling as above but increase sugar to ⅔ cup and reduce milk to 1¾ cups. Omit vanilla but stir in *¼ cup lemon juice* and *1 teaspoon grated lemon peel.* Fill and top pie with whipped cream as above.

BUTTERSCOTCH CREAM PIE: Prepare crust and filling as above but substitute *¾ cup packed light brown sugar* for sugar; reduce milk to 2 cups and increase butter to 3 tablespoons. Fill and top pie with whipped cream as above.

Lemon Meringue Pie

Color index page 89

Begin 6 hrs ahead or early in day

6 servings

511 cals per serving

*1 9-inch Baked Piecrust
(page 344)*
⅓ cup cornstarch
sugar
salt
1½ cups warm water
grated peel of 1 lemon
½ cup lemon juice
4 eggs, separated
*1 tablespoon butter
or margarine*
*4-Egg-White
Meringue Topping
(right)*

1 Prepare piecrust. Into 2-quart saucepan, measure cornstarch, 1 cup sugar and ⅛ teaspoon salt; stir together.

2 Stir in water, lemon peel and juice; cook over medium heat, stirring, until mixture boils; remove from heat.

3 In small bowl with wire whisk or spoon, beat egg yolks; then stir in small amount of hot sauce.

4 Slowly pour egg mixture into sauce, stirring rapidly to prevent lumping. Return to heat; cook, stirring, until mixture is thick (do not boil).

5 Add butter or margarine to thickened mixture and stir until melted and thoroughly blended.

6 Pour mixture into piecrust. Preheat oven to 400°F. Make 4-Egg-White Meringue Topping (right) with egg whites.

7 Spread meringue over filling, touching piecrust all around. Bake as directed; cool and refrigerate pie.

MAKING A MERINGUE TOPPING

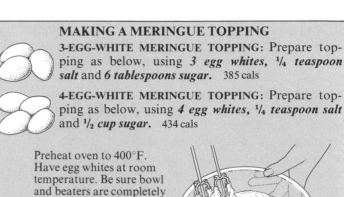

3-EGG-WHITE MERINGUE TOPPING: Prepare topping as below, using *3 egg whites,* *¼ teaspoon salt* and *6 tablespoons sugar.*   385 cals

4-EGG-WHITE MERINGUE TOPPING: Prepare topping as below, using *4 egg whites,* *¼ teaspoon salt* and *½ cup sugar.*   434 cals

Preheat oven to 400°F. Have egg whites at room temperature. Be sure bowl and beaters are completely free of fat. In small bowl with mixer at high speed, beat egg whites and salt until soft peaks form.

At high speed, sprinkle in sugar, 2 tablespoons at a time, beating after each addition until sugar is dissolved. Rub a bit of meringue between fingers; if it doesn't feel grainy, sugar is dissolved. Whites should stand in stiff, glossy peaks.

With back of spoon, spread meringue over filling; seal to piecrust all around edge. Swirl up points to make attractive top. Bake 10 minutes or until golden. Cool away from drafts.

460 cals per serving

8-INCH LEMON MERINGUE PIE: Prepare as Lemon Meringue Pie but use ¾ cup sugar, ¼ cup cornstarch, ⅛ teaspoon salt, 1¼ cups water, grated peel of 1 lemon, ⅓ cup lemon juice, 3 eggs, separated, and 1 tablespoon butter or margarine for filling; turn into 8-inch Baked Piecrust. Make 3-Egg-White Meringue Topping.

419 cals per serving

LEMON SNOW PIE: Prepare as Lemon Meringue Pie but fold meringue into hot filling; pour into piecrust; don't bake. Refrigerate until set.

ORANGE MERINGUE PIE: Prepare as Lemon Meringue Pie but reduce sugar to ⅓ cup, water to ½ cup, lemon juice to 2 tablespoons; substitute *grated peel of 1 orange* for lemon peel; add *1 cup orange juice* with water.

461 cals per serving

PINEAPPLE MERINGUE PIE: Drain *one 8-ounce can crushed pineapple,* reserving liquid. To liquid, add water to make 1½ cups; use as liquid in filling. Prepare as Lemon Meringue Pie but reduce sugar to ½ cup, lemon juice to 1 tablespoon; add drained pineapple to the hot filling.

Chiffon pies

Chiffon pies depend upon both gelatin and beaten egg whites for their lightness and height. Some also have whipped cream folded into their fillings. They are always served cold and are made in baked pastry or crumb crusts or unbaked crumb crusts. Store them in the refrigerator. Because they can be made a day ahead they are an ideal choice for a party dessert.

In most of our recipes, sugar is mixed with the gelatin or cornstarch before the liquid is added. This helps to separate the granules and prevent clumps forming. Remember to cook egg mixtures over medium-low heat, stirring constantly to prevent curdling. The whites should be beaten until soft peaks form

and then gently folded into the gelatin mixture. If stirred too much the egg whites will lose volume and may even become runny again. For further tips on using egg whites, see page 139.

Garnish chiffon pies with shredded lemon, lime or orange peel, whipped cream, small amounts of fresh berries or orange sections, angelica, chocolate curls or shaped chocolate and candied fruits.

For easy serving of pies with unbaked crumb crusts, dip a dish cloth in warm water, wring it out and wrap it around the pie plate for a minute or two. Then cut the pie and serve straight away. The heat will loosen the crust so that the pieces come out easily.

Lemon Chiffon Pie

1 9-inch Baked Piecrust (page 344) or 9-inch Baked Vanilla-Wafer or Graham-Cracker Crumb Crust (page 345)
1 envelope unflavored gelatin
¼ teaspoon salt
sugar
4 eggs, separated
⅓ cup water
1 tablespoon grated lemon peel
¼ cup lemon juice

½ cup heavy or whipping cream, whipped
shredded lemon peel for garnish

Color index page 87
Begin early in day or day ahead
8 servings
347 cals per serving

1 Prepare piecrust. In 1-quart saucepan, mix well gelatin, salt and ⅓ cup sugar.

2 In small bowl with wire whisk, beat egg yolks with water, lemon peel and lemon juice, then stir this mixture into the gelatin mixture.

3 Cook over medium-low heat, stirring, until mixture is thickened and coats spoon; remove saucepan from heat.

4 In large bowl with mixer at high speed, beat whites until soft peaks form; gradually sprinkle in ½ cup sugar, beating until sugar is completely dissolved.

5 With rubber spatula, gently fold lemon mixture into egg whites just until blended.

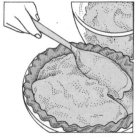
6 Spoon mixture into piecrust; refrigerate pie until lemon chiffon filling is set.

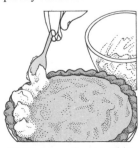
7 *To serve:* Spoon whipped cream in mounds around pie edge. Sprinkle with shredded lemon peel.

LIME-SWIRL PIE: Prepare as Lemon Chiffon Pie (left) but omit the ⅓ cup sugar; substitute *1 teaspoon grated lime peel* for lemon peel, and *lime juice* for lemon juice. Swirl whipped cream through filling in shell; top pie with *shredded lime peel*. (Makes 8 servings.)   314 cals per serving

Color index page 88
Begin early in day or day ahead
8 servings   482 cals per serving

Orange Chiffon Pie

1 9-inch Baked Piecrust (page 344) or Unbaked Crumb Crust (page 345)
1 envelope unflavored gelatin
¼ teaspoon salt
sugar
3 eggs, separated

1 teaspoon grated orange peel
1 cup orange juice
2 tablespoons lemon juice
few drops yellow food color
1½ cups heavy cream
orange sections, drained, for garnish

1. Prepare piecrust; cool crust if baked.
2. In 1-quart saucepan, stir gelatin with salt and ½ cup sugar until well mixed. In small bowl with wire whisk or hand beater, beat egg yolks with orange peel, orange juice and lemon juice until mixed; stir into gelatin mixture.
3. Cook over medium-low heat, stirring constantly, until mixture is thickened and coats spoon; remove from heat. Stir in food color; refrigerate, stirring occasionally, until mixture mounds when dropped from spoon, about 45 minutes.
4. In large bowl with mixer at high speed, beat egg whites until soft peaks form; beating at high speed, gradually sprinkle in ¼ cup sugar; beat until sugar is completely dissolved. With wire whisk or rubber spatula, gently fold gelatin mixture into whites.
5. In small bowl with same beaters and with mixer at medium speed, beat ½ cup heavy cream until soft peaks form; fold into gelatin mixture. Spoon mixture into crust; refrigerate pie until set, about 30 minutes.
6. *To serve:* In small bowl with mixer at medium speed, beat remaining heavy cream with 2 tablespoons sugar until stiff peaks form. Spoon on pie; garnish with orange sections.

Rich Bavarian Pie

Color index
page 87

Begin early
in day or
day ahead

8 servings

344 cals per
serving

*1 9-inch Baked Piecrust
(page 344)*
*1 envelope unflavored
gelatin*
⅛ teaspoon salt
sugar
3 eggs, separated
1¼ cups milk
*1 teaspoon vanilla
extract*
*½ to 1 cup heavy cream,
whipped*
*¼ teaspoon ground
nutmeg*
*shaved unsweetened
chocolate for garnish*

1 Prepare piecrust; cool. Into 1-quart saucepan, measure gelatin, salt and ¼ cup sugar and stir thoroughly until they are well mixed.

2 In small bowl with wire whisk, beat egg yolks with milk until mixed, then with spoon, stir into gelatin mixture.

3 Cook over medium-low heat, stirring, until mixture is thickened and coats spoon. Remove from heat and stir in vanilla.

4 Refrigerate until mixture mounds when dropped from spoon, about 40 minutes. With hand beater, beat the mixture smooth.

5 In large bowl with mixer at high speed, beat egg whites into soft peaks; gradually sprinkle in ¼ cup sugar; beat until sugar is dissolved.

6 With rubber spatula, fold whipped cream and gelatin mixture into beaten egg whites.

7 Spoon into crust; sprinkle with nutmeg. Chill. To serve, garnish with chocolate shavings.

RICH BAVARIAN PIE VARIATIONS

COFFEE: Prepare Rich Bavarian Pie as left but add *2 tablespoons instant coffee powder* to egg whites before beating. Omit whipped cream and shaved chocolate. For topping melt *¾ cup semisweet-chocolate pieces* over hot, *not boiling,* water; stir in *¼ cup water* until smooth; drizzle over top of pie.

STRAWBERRY: Prepare pie as left but fold *1 cup sliced strawberries* into filling. Omit chocolate; garnish top of pie with *whole strawberries.*

EGGNOG: Prepare pie as left but omit vanilla extract; add *½ teaspoon rum extract* and increase ground nutmeg to 1 teaspoon.

COCONUT: Prepare pie as left but omit nutmeg; add *½ cup flaked or grated fresh coconut* with gelatin mixture. If fresh coconut, add *¼ teaspoon almond extract* with vanilla.

CRANBERRY-TOPPED: Prepare the pie as left but substitute *almond extract* for vanilla; use only ½ cup heavy cream; omit nutmeg and chocolate. For topping, in 2-quart saucepan over medium heat, cook *one 16-ounce can whole-cranberry sauce* with *1 tablespoon cornstarch* until clear and thickened; cool; spread on pie when filling is set.

Chocolate Chiffon Pie

Color index
page 87

Begin 4 hrs
ahead

8 servings

238 cals per
serving

*1 9-inch Baked
Chocolate-Wafer
Crumb Crust
(page 345)*
3 eggs, separated
½ teaspoon salt
1 cup water
sugar
*2 squares unsweetened
chocolate*

*1 envelope unflavored
gelatin*
*½ teaspoon vanilla
extract*
*¼ teaspoon cream of
tartar*
*whipped cream for
garnish*

1. Prepare crust; set aside. In heavy 2-quart saucepan with fork, mix well egg yolks, salt, water and ¾ cup sugar; add chocolate and sprinkle gelatin over mixture. Cook over medium heat, stirring, until gelatin is dissolved and chocolate melts. Remove from heat; stir in vanilla.
2. Pour mixture into large bowl. With mixer at high speed, beat 1 minute (the mixture may look slightly speckled). Refrigerate until mixture is cold and mounds when dropped from a spoon, stirring occasionally, about 45 minutes.
3. In small bowl with mixer at high speed, beat egg whites and cream of tartar into soft peaks; beating at high speed, gradually sprinkle in ¼ cup sugar. Whites should stand in stiff peaks. Do not scrape side of bowl during beating.
4. Using same beaters, beat chocolate mixture until fluffy, about 2 minutes. With wire whisk, fold in beaten egg whites until well blended.
5. Carefully pour mixture into piecrust so mixture does not run over edge of piecrust; refrigerate at least 2 hours or until set. Garnish the edge of the pie with dollops of whipped cream.

Chiffon pies

Raspberry Ribbon Pie

Color index page 89

Begin early in day or day ahead

8 servings

414 cals per serving

1 9-inch Baked Piecrust (page 344)
1 3-ounce package raspberry-flavor gelatin
¼ cup sugar
1¼ cups boiling water
1 10-ounce package frozen raspberries
1 tablespoon lemon juice

1 3-ounce package cream cheese or Neufchâtel cheese, softened
⅓ cup confectioners' sugar
1 teaspoon vanilla extract
⅛ teaspoon salt
1 cup heavy cream fresh raspberries or whipped cream for garnish

1 Prepare piecrust. In medium bowl, stir gelatin and sugar with boiling water until gelatin and sugar are dissolved; then add frozen raspberries and lemon juice.

2 Stir mixture until berries thaw. Cover and refrigerate, stirring frequently, until mixture mounds when dropped from a spoon.

3 In small bowl with wire whisk, mix cream cheese with confectioners' sugar, vanilla extract and salt until smooth.

4 In second small bowl with mixer at medium speed, beat heavy cream into soft peaks; then with wire whisk or rubber spatula, gradually fold cream-cheese mixture into cream.

5 Spread half of the whipped-cream mixture in the prepared piecrust then spoon half of raspberry mixture over it.

6 Repeat with rest of cream mixture and berries. Refrigerate until set then garnish with raspberries or whipped cream.

Coffee Cordial Pie

Color index page 89

Begin 4½ hrs or day ahead

8 servings

386 cals per serving

1 9-inch Baked Chocolate-Wafer Crumb Crust (page 345)
1 envelope unflavored gelatin
⅛ teaspoon salt
sugar
3 eggs, separated

½ cup water
½ cup coffee-flavor liqueur
1 tablespoon instant coffee
2 teaspoons vanilla extract
1½ cups heavy cream

1. Prepare crust; cool. In 2-quart saucepan, mix gelatin, salt and ¼ cup sugar. With wire whisk, beat in egg yolks and water until well mixed. Cook over low heat, stirring, until gelatin is dissolved and mixture is slightly thickened, about 10 minutes (do not boil). Remove from heat; stir in liqueur, coffee and vanilla extract.
2. Refrigerate, stirring often, until mixture is consistency of unbeaten egg white, about 20 minutes.
3. In large bowl with mixer at high speed, beat egg whites into soft peaks; gradually sprinkle in ¼ cup sugar, beating until sugar is dissolved and whites stand in stiff peaks. With wire whisk, gently fold in gelatin mixture.
4. In small bowl at medium-high speed, beat cream into stiff peaks; fold 2 cups into gelatin mixture. Spoon into crust. Chill until set. Decorate with remaining cream.

Pumpkin Chiffon Pie

Color index page 88

Begin early in day or day ahead

10 servings

263 cals per serving

1 3½-ounce can flaked coconut
¼ cup finely crushed graham-cracker crumbs
⅓ cup melted butter or margarine
sugar
1 envelope unflavored gelatin
¾ teaspoon ground cinnamon

½ teaspoon ground ginger
½ teaspoon ground nutmeg
½ teaspoon salt
3 eggs, separated
½ cup milk
1¼ cups canned pumpkin whipped heavy or whipping cream, for garnish

1. Preheat oven to 375°F. Spread coconut on cookie sheet; bake 8 to 10 minutes until lightly browned; reserve 2 tablespoons for garnish. In 9-inch pie plate, mix remaining coconut, crumbs, butter and 2 tablespoons sugar; press firmly to bottom and side of pie plate. Bake crust for 6 to 8 minutes until golden; cool.
2. In double-boiler top, mix well gelatin, cinnamon, ginger, nutmeg, salt and ½ cup sugar. In small bowl with wire whisk, beat egg yolks with milk until well mixed; stir into gelatin mixture; stir in pumpkin. Cook over boiling water 20 minutes or until thickened, stirring frequently. Refrigerate the mixture until cool but not set.
3. In large bowl with mixer at high speed, beat egg whites into soft peaks; gradually sprinkle in ¼ cup sugar beating at high speed. With wire whisk, gently fold pumpkin mixture into whites. Pour into crust; refrigerate until set. To serve, top with whipped cream; sprinkle cream with reserved coconut.

Nesselrode Pie

Color index page 89

Begin early in day or day ahead

8 servings

426 cals per serving

1 9-inch Baked Graham-Cracker Crumb Crust (page 345)
1 envelope unflavored gelatin
¼ teaspoon salt sugar
4 eggs, separated
1¼ cups milk
1 tablespoon rum
1 teaspoon grated lemon peel
1 4-ounce jar diced mixed candied fruit (about ½ cup)
1 cup heavy or whipping cream, whipped
red and green candied pineapple, cut in slivers, for garnish

1. Prepare crust. In 2-quart saucepan, mix well gelatin, salt and 3 tablespoons sugar. In small bowl with wire whisk, beat egg yolks with milk until mixed; stir into gelatin mixture.
2. Cook mixture over medium-low heat, stirring, until thickened and it coats spoon. Remove from heat; stir in rum and lemon peel. Refrigerate until cold but not firm, about 40 minutes.
3. In large bowl with mixer at high speed, beat egg whites into soft peaks; gradually sprinkle in ¼ cup sugar, beating until sugar is dissolved and whites stand in stiff peaks. Gently fold gelatin mixture into whites with mixed candied fruit. Spoon into piecrust; refrigerate about 1 hour or until set.
4. *To serve:* Top with whipped cream. Garnish with candied pineapple.

Black Bottom Pie

Color index page 89

Begin early in day or day ahead

8 servings

346 cals per serving

1 9-inch Baked Gingersnap Crumb Crust (page 345)
2 squares unsweetened chocolate
1 envelope unflavored gelatin
2¼ teaspoons cornstarch
sugar
3 eggs, separated
1¼ cups milk
1 teaspoon vanilla extract
1 tablespoon light rum
½ cup heavy or whipping cream, whipped

1. Prepare crust; cool. In 1-quart saucepan over very low heat, melt 1½ squares of the unsweetened chocolate; set aside.
2. In second 1-quart saucepan, mix gelatin, cornstarch and ¼ cup sugar. In small bowl with fork, beat egg yolks with milk; stir into gelatin mixture. Cook over medium-low heat, stirring, until mixture is thickened and coats the back of a spoon. Remove from heat.
3. Divide custard in half. Into one half, stir melted chocolate and vanilla; with spoon, beat smooth; refrigerate until it mounds when dropped from spoon. Pour into crust; refrigerate. Chill remaining custard until it mounds when dropped from spoon.
4. In small bowl with mixer at high speed, beat egg whites into soft peaks; gradually sprinkle in ¼ cup sugar, beating until sugar is dissolved. Gently fold whites and rum into chilled custard.
5. Pour as much custard mixture as crust will hold into crust. Refrigerate pie a few minutes, then pour rest of mixture on top. Refrigerate until set.
6. *To serve:* Garnish pie with whipped cream. Shave the remaining half square of chocolate and sprinkle over the whipped cream.

Cherry Cream Tart

Color index page 88

Begin early in day

8 servings

535 cals per serving

1¼ cups all-purpose flour
¾ cup butter, softened
¾ cup sugar
4 egg yolks
1 envelope unflavored gelatin
2 cups half-and-half
¼ cup cherry-flavor liqueur
½ cup heavy or whipping cream, whipped
1 pound sweet cherries, pitted

1 In small bowl with mixer at low speed, beat flour, butter, ¼ cup sugar and 1 egg yolk until well mixed; cover and refrigerate 1 hour. Preheat oven to 400°F. Press dough onto bottom and 1 inch up side of 10-inch round quiche pan with removable bottom or 10-inch springform pan. Bake 10 minutes or until lightly browned. Cool completely on wire rack.

2 In 2-quart saucepan, combine gelatin and ½ cup sugar; stir in half-and-half. Over medium heat, cook, stirring constantly, until the gelatin is completely dissolved.

3 In small bowl with wire whisk or fork, beat remaining 3 egg yolks, then stir in a small amount of hot gelatin mixture.

4 Slowly pour egg mixture into sauce, stirring rapidly to prevent lumping; cook, stirring constantly, until thickened (do not boil).

5 Remove from heat and stir in liqueur, then refrigerate until custard mounds slightly when dropped from a spoon, about 1 hour, stirring frequently.

6 Gently fold whipped cream into custard then pour filling into the cooled piecrust.

7 Arrange cherries on top. Refrigerate until set, about 1 hour. Remove side of pan to serve.

Nut pies

Pecans, peanuts and California walnuts are the most popular nuts for fillings. The nut crusts below are good with the filling from any of the following: Rich Bavarian Pie or Chocolate Chiffon Pie (page 353); Vanilla or Chocolate Cream Pie (page 350).

Allow nut pies to cool on a wire rack before serving them garnished with your choice of either ice cream or whipped cream.

For further information about the preparation of nuts and cooking with nuts, see the Index.

Pecan Pie

Color index page 86

Begin early in day

10 servings

433 cals per serving

1 9-inch Unbaked Piecrust (page 344)
3 eggs
1 cup dark corn syrup
½ cup sugar

¼ cup butter or margarine, melted
1 teaspoon vanilla extract
1 cup pecan halves

1 Prepare piecrust with your choice of decorative edge, then preheat oven to 350°F.

2 In medium bowl with wire whisk or hand beater, beat eggs well.

3 Beat in corn syrup, sugar, butter or margarine and vanilla extract until well blended.

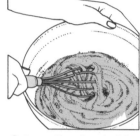

4 Arrange pecan halves in single layer in bottom of piecrust.

5 Pour egg mixture over the pecans in piecrust being careful not to disturb the nuts.

6 Bake pie 1 hour or until knife inserted about 1 inch from edge comes out clean. Cool.

Double Peanut Pie

Color index page 88

Begin early in day

12 servings

372 cals per serving

1 9-inch Unbaked Piecrust (page 344)
3 eggs
1 cup dark corn syrup
½ cup sugar
½ cup creamy peanut butter

½ teaspoon vanilla extract
1 cup salted peanuts whipped cream for garnish

1. Prepare piecrust. Preheat oven to 350°F.
2. In large bowl with mixer at medium speed, beat eggs with corn syrup, sugar, peanut butter and vanilla until smooth. Stir in peanuts.
3. Place pie plate on oven rack; pour mixture into crust. Bake 55 to 60 minutes or until knife inserted about 1 inch from edge comes out clean. Cool. Garnish servings with whipped cream.

Fudge-Nut Pie

Color index page 88

Begin early in day

8 servings

553 cals per serving

1 9-inch Unbaked Piecrust (page 344)
2 squares unsweetened chocolate
¼ cup butter or margarine
¾ cup sugar
½ cup packed light brown sugar
½ cup milk
¼ cup corn syrup or maple-flavor syrup

1 teaspoon vanilla extract
¼ teaspoon salt
3 eggs
1 cup finely chopped California walnuts coffee, vanilla or chocolate ice cream for garnish

1. Prepare piecrust. Preheat oven to 350°F.
2. In 2-quart saucepan over low heat, heat chocolate with butter or margarine just until melted; remove saucepan from heat.
3. Add sugar and brown sugar, milk, corn syrup, vanilla, salt and eggs; with hand beater or wire whisk, beat until well mixed. Stir in the chopped California walnuts.
4. Pour mixture into piecrust. Bake 45 to 55 minutes until filling is puffed. Cool. To serve, top each serving with a small scoop of ice cream.

NO-ROLL NUT CRUSTS

928 cals

WALNUT PASTRY CRUST: Preheat oven to 400°F. In 9-inch pie plate with hands, mix *1 cup all-purpose flour, ½ cup butter* or margarine, softened, *¼ cup confectioners' sugar* and *¼ cup finely chopped California walnuts* until soft and pliable. Press against bottom and side of pie plate. With fork, prick bottom of crust well. Bake 12 minutes or until golden; then cool crust on wire rack. (Makes one 9-inch piecrust.)

1325 cals

GROUND NUT CRUST: Preheat oven to 400°F. In small bowl with spoon, mix *1½ cups finely ground Brazil nuts,* pecans, California walnuts, blanched almonds or peanuts with *3 tablespoons sugar* and *2 tablespoons butter* or margarine, softened. With back of spoon, press to bottom and side of pie plate; do not spread on rim. Bake about 8 minutes, just until golden. Cool on wire rack. (Makes one 9-inch piecrust.)

Tarts

Fruit Cream Tarts

Color index
page 87

Begin early
in day or
day ahead

12 tarts

214 cals each

**Baked Tart Shells
(page 345)**
¼ cup sugar
2 tablespoons cornstarch
¼ teaspoon salt
1 cup milk
1 egg
**1 teaspoon vanilla
extract**
**½ cup heavy or whipping
cream, whipped**

Garnish: *whole or sliced
strawberries, blueberries,
raspberries, peach slices,
apricot halves or
mandarin-orange
sections, drained*

**1 cup currant jelly
(optional)**
**1 tablespoon water
(optional)**

1 Prepare tart shells. In 2-quart saucepan, mix sugar, cornstarch and salt; stir in milk until smooth. Over medium heat, cook, stirring, until mixture boils; boil 1 minute.

2 In 1-cup measure with fork, beat egg slightly, then slowly stir in small amount of the hot sauce.

3 Slowly pour egg mixture into sauce, stirring rapidly to prevent lumping. Cook, stirring, until thickened (do not boil).

4 Cover with waxed paper and refrigerate. When the custard is cold (after about 40 minutes), stir in vanilla extract; then, with wire whisk, fold in whipped cream.

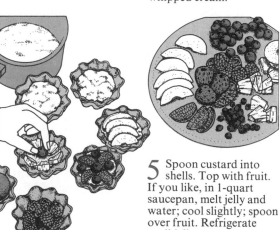

5 Spoon custard into shells. Top with fruit. If you like, in 1-quart saucepan, melt jelly and water; cool slightly; spoon over fruit. Refrigerate until jelly sets.

Color index
page 87

Begin early
in day

12 tarts

437 cals each

Walnut Tarts

**Unbaked Tart Shells
(page 345)**
3 eggs
1 cup dark corn syrup
½ cup sugar
**¼ cup butter or
margarine, melted**

**1 teaspoon vanilla
extract**
**1 cup coarsely chopped
California walnuts**
**whipped cream for
garnish**

1. Prepare tart shells. Preheat oven to 350°F. In medium bowl with wire whisk, beat eggs well. Beat in next 4 ingredients until well blended.
2. Distribute chopped walnuts evenly among tart shells; carefully pour filling over walnuts.
3. Bake 25 to 30 minutes. Cool 10 minutes; remove from pans and cool on wire rack. Serve topped with whipped cream.

Color index
page 89

Begin day
ahead

12 tarts

385 cals each
(without
sauce)

Mince Tarts

**1 18-ounce jar prepared
mincemeat (2 cups)**
**1½ cups coarsely broken
California walnuts**
**2 large apples, cored and
diced**
**½ cup packed brown
sugar**

**¼ cup brandy or rum
(optional)**
1 tablespoon lemon juice
**Unbaked Tart Shells
(page 345)**
**Brandy Hard Sauce
(page 349)**

1. In medium bowl, stir first 6 ingredients until well mixed; cover and refrigerate overnight to allow flavors to blend.
2. *About 3 hours before serving:* Prepare tart shells. Preheat oven to 425°F. Fill shells with undrained mincemeat mixture. Bake 20 to 25 minutes until golden. Serve warm, each topped with some sauce.

Begin day
ahead

8 servings

578 cals per
serving

MINCE PIE: Prepare as above but use Pastry for 2-Crust Pie (page 344). Roll out half of pastry to line 9-inch pie plate. Fill crust and use remaining pastry to make a lattice top (page 343). Bake in preheated 425°F. oven 30 to 40 minutes until crust is golden. Serve warm with Brandy Hard Sauce.

Color index
page 89

Begin 3 hrs
ahead

12 tarts

170 cals each

Peach Meringue Tarts

**4 cups sliced ripe peaches
(about 2 pounds)**
3 tablespoons quick-cooking tapioca
2 tablespoons lemon juice
**¼ teaspoon almond
extract**

sugar
**Unbaked Tart Shells
(page 345)**
2 egg whites

1. In medium bowl with rubber spatula, gently stir peaches, tapioca, lemon juice, almond extract and ½ cup sugar; let stand 20 minutes. Meanwhile, prepare tart shells. Preheat oven to 425°F.
2. Gently stir peach mixture again; spoon into tart shells; place on cookie sheet. Bake 30 to 35 minutes until juices are bubbly.
3. Beat egg whites until foamy; gradually beat in 2 tablespoons sugar, until stiff peaks form. Remove tarts from oven; spoon dollop of meringue on top of each; bake about 4 minutes longer, just until tarts are lightly browned.

DESSERTS

Our recipes for desserts fall into the following categories: Custards, Bavarian Cream, Cold Soufflés, Mousse, Hot Soufflés, Meringues, Crêpes and Blintzes, Cream Puffs and Eclairs and Other Desserts. The recipes range from simple everyday desserts to internationally popular ones calling for special techniques.

THICKENING WITH EGGS
Many desserts and sauces call for using eggs as a thickening agent. The key to successful custard preparation is low heat; high heat causes the eggs to curdle, resulting in lumpy, thin mixtures. Either cook custard in a double boiler or if cooking over direct heat, always use a heavy saucepan. Stir the mixture constantly with a whisk until it thickens and coats a metal spoon (do not boil). Check thickness by lifting the spoon from custard and holding it up for 15 to 20 seconds; if the spoon does not show through mixture the custard has thickened to the correct consistency.

Testing consistency: Hold up spoon for 15 to 20 seconds; spoon should not show through mixture.

USING GELATIN
Many desserts – fruit molds, Bavarian creams, cold soufflés – call for gelatin, both flavored and unflavored.
Dissolving gelatin: For properly set jelled mixtures, the gelatin must be dissolved completely; no granules of gelatin should remain in the mixture. Stirring is essential to dissolve gelatin. To prevent granules from splashing up the side of the bowl or saucepan, always be sure to stir steadily but not too vigorously.

Checking dissolving: Run a rubber spatula through the mixture, next to the side of the pan, to see if the granules are all dissolved.

Flavored gelatins are stirred with hot or boiling water, depending on the package directions. Recipes using unflavored gelatin vary slightly in the dissolving technique, depending on the other ingredients used. The rule of thumb is this: never add unflavored gelatin directly to hot liquid because the gelatin will become lumpy and will not dissolve completely. Usually, unflavored gelatin is sprinkled over a small amount of cold liquid, left to stand a minute to soften, then stirred with hot liquid or cooked over low heat to dissolve. In recipes with more than a cup of liquid, as for many sauces, unflavored gelatin is sprinkled over cold liquid; cook it without standing, stirring until the gelatin is completely dissolved. In recipes which call for sugar, the sugar is sometimes mixed with the gelatin and then at least a cup of boiling liquid is stirred in.

Gelatin consistency: Allow gelatin to partially set before adding fruits, whipped cream or other solids. A partially set mixture holds them in suspension, keeps them uniformly distributed throughout. Some recipes, especially ones with cut-up fruit added, call for mixtures jelled to the consistency of "an unbeaten egg white." Other recipes, especially ones with whipped cream or whipped egg whites added, call for mixtures jelled until "mixture mounds when dropped from a spoon." Then the whipped cream or whipped egg whites are folded in.

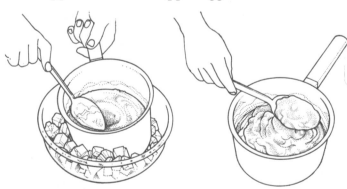

Hastening setting: Put the saucepan or bowl of gelatin mixture into a bowl of ice and stir to hasten setting.

Testing consistency: Take up a spoonful of mixture and drop it back on top. It should "mound," not disappear.

As an alternative to the method explained and illustrated above, if you want to hasten the setting of a gelatin mixture, you can put the bowl of gelatin mixture in the freezer, and stir occasionally until partially set. Do not try to freeze the mixture until it has set, as ice crystals may form, making the gelatin watery.

Custards

Egg custards are really quite simple to prepare, provided you follow recipe directions. Avoid using excessive heat which will ruin the texture of the dish. If cooking over direct heat, stir the custard constantly and watch the mixture carefully as it thickens.

Crème Brûlée

Color index page 97

Begin early in day or day ahead

10 servings

444 cals per serving (without fruit)

3 cups heavy or whipping cream
6 egg yolks
⅓ cup sugar
1 teaspoon vanilla extract
⅓ cup packed brown sugar

sliced strawberries, bananas, fresh or canned pineapple chunks and canned mandarin-orange sections

1 In 1-quart saucepan over medium heat, heat cream until tiny bubbles form around edge of pan.

2 Meanwhile, in 2-quart saucepan with wire whisk, blend yolks with sugar. Slowly stir in cream.

3 Over medium-low heat, cook the mixture, stirring constantly, until it just coats back of metal spoon, about 15 minutes (do not boil). Stir in vanilla.

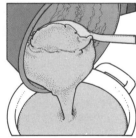

4 Pour mixture into 1½-quart broilersafe casserole; refrigerate until well chilled, about 6 hours.

5 Preheat broiler if manufacturer directs. Sift brown sugar over chilled cream mixture; broil 3 to 4 minutes until sugar melts. Refrigerate.

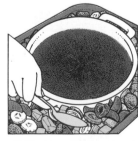

6 *To serve:* Place casserole in center of large tray; surround with fruit. Serve portions of mixed fruit with Crème Brûlée spooned over.

Crème Caramel

Color index page 96

Begin early in day or day ahead

8 servings

210 cals per serving

sugar
5 eggs
¼ teaspoon salt
3 cups milk
1½ teaspoons vanilla extract

1 Butter eight 6-ounce custard cups. In small skillet over medium heat, melt ½ cup sugar, stirring, till it is a light brown syrup.

2 Pour syrup into buttered cups. Place cups in shallow baking pan for easy handling. Preheat oven to 300°F.

3 In large bowl with mixer at low speed, beat eggs, salt and ½ cup sugar until lemon-colored. Gradually beat in milk and vanilla extract.

4 Pour mixture in cups; put hot water in pan to within 1 inch of top of cups; bake 1 hour until knife inserted in center comes out clean.

5 Cool on wire racks; refrigerate; with knife, loosen custard from cups and invert onto dessert dishes, letting syrup run down sides onto dish.

BAKED CUSTARD: Prepare as for Crème Caramel (above) but omit making syrup in steps 1 and 2. Before baking, sprinkle with *ground nutmeg*.

Custard Sauce

Begin early in day

1½ cups

142 cals per ¼ cup

3 tablespoons sugar
1¾ cups half-and-half
1 egg yolk
1 tablespoon cornstarch

⅛ teaspoon salt
½ teaspoon vanilla extract

In heavy, 2-quart saucepan, combine all ingredients except vanilla. Cook over medium heat, stirring, until mixture coats back of spoon, about 15 minutes. Remove from heat; stir in vanilla. Chill.

Custards

Bavarian cream

Apricot-Cream Flan

Color index
page 95

Begin 5 hrs
ahead or
early in day

8 servings

512 cals per
serving

1 cup all-purpose flour
*¾ cup California
walnuts, finely ground*
*6 tablespoons butter or
margarine, softened*
*¼ teaspoon ground
cinnamon*
sugar
salt
8 egg yolks

2 cups milk
¼ cup cornstarch
*¾ teaspoon almond
extract*
*1 17-ounce can apricot
halves, drained or
7 large apricots,
halved and pitted*
¼ cup apple jelly

1. In large bowl with mixer at low speed, beat flour, walnuts, butter or margarine, cinnamon, 3 table-spoons sugar, ¼ teaspoon salt and 2 egg yolks until well mixed.
2. Preheat oven to 400°F. Pat mixture evenly onto bottom and side of fluted 10-inch tart pan with removable bottom or into 10-inch springform pan (pat mixture only 1 inch up side of pan). With fork, prick bottom of crust well. Bake 20 minutes or till golden brown. Cool on wire rack.
3. Meanwhile, in 2-quart saucepan, stir milk, corn-starch, ⅓ cup sugar and ¼ teaspoon salt until smooth. Cook over medium heat, stirring con-stantly, until mixture is thickened and boils, about 5 minutes; remove pan from heat. In small bowl with wire whisk, beat remaining 6 egg yolks; stir in small amount of hot milk mixture. Slowly pour yolk mixture into milk mixture, stirring rapidly to pre-vent lumping.
4. Return the saucepan to the heat; cook, stirring constantly with whisk, until mixture thickens and coats a spoon (do not boil). (To check thickness, lift metal spoon from custard and hold up 15 to 20 seconds; spoon should not show through mixture when it is the correct consistency.)
5. Stir in almond extract; cover the custard sur-face with waxed paper; refrigerate 30 minutes until mixture is cool but not set. Pour cooled custard mixture into cooled crust; refrigerate until custard is completely set, about 4 hours.
6. *To serve:* Remove side from pan; transfer flan to large flat serving dish. Arrange apricot halves on custard. In 1-quart saucepan, melt apple jelly; brush melted jelly over apricots.

Zabaglione

Color index
page 97

Begin 20 mins
ahead

6 servings

152 cals per
serving

6 egg yolks
¼ cup sugar

*½ cup dry or sweet
Marsala*

1. In double-boiler top, not over water, with port-able mixer at high speed, beat egg yolks and sugar until of a thick consistency and light colored, about 5 minutes. Reduce the speed to medium and beat in the Marsala.
2. Place mixture over simmering water in double-boiler bottom; cook, beating constantly at medium speed, until mixture is fluffy, warm and mounds slightly on the surface when the beater is lifted, about 10 minutes.
3. Serve at once as dessert or spoon over fresh berries or sliced fruit as a sauce.

A light mixture of gelatin, custard, egg whites and cream, classic Bavarian Cream is an elegant molded dessert, often served with sliced fruit such as peaches, strawberries or canned pineapple. Sometimes the fruit is folded into the flavored cream mixture before jelling.

Bavarian Cream

Color index
page 95

Begin early
in day or
day ahead

8 servings

216 cals per
serving

*1 envelope unflavored
gelatin*
½ teaspoon salt
sugar
2 eggs, separated
1¼ cups milk

*1 cup heavy or whipping
cream*
*1½ teaspoons vanilla
extract*
*sliced strawberries and
nectarines*

1 In 3-quart saucepan, stir gelatin, salt and 2 table-spoons sugar until well mixed. In small bowl with wire whisk, mix together egg yolks and milk.

2 Stir milk mixture into gelatin mixture; over low heat, cook, stirring constantly, until mixture coats spoon. Refrigerate until mixture mounds when dropped from spoon.

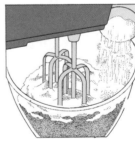

3 In small bowl at high speed, beat egg whites until soft peaks form; at high speed, gradually beat in ¼ cup sugar until dissolved.

4 Spoon whites over gelatin mixture. In same bowl, beat cream with vanilla until soft peaks form; add to gelatin mixture in pan.

5 With wire whisk, gently fold whites and cream into gelatin; pour into 6-cup mold; refrigerate till set, about 3 hours.

6 *To serve:* Carefully un-mold Bavarian Cream onto chilled serving plate. Serve with sliced straw-berries and nectarines.

Cold soufflés

Raised high with beaten egg whites and whipped cream, light, fluffy dessert soufflés can be made in almost any deep serving dish. To make a cold soufflé look like a hot soufflé which rises above the top of its dish, add a collar of foil which extends beyond the top of the dish to support the soufflé mixture during the setting process; remove the collar just before the soufflé is served.

Unlike hot soufflés, cold soufflés can be made well ahead of time and kept in the refrigerator ready to be brought to the table; add the decorative garnish, such as slivered citrus peel, whipped cream or chocolate curls, just before serving.

Color index page 96
Begin early in day
12 servings   372 cals per serving

Chocolate-Cherry Soufflé

2 16½- to 17-ounce cans pitted dark sweet cherries, drained	sugar
6 tablespoons Kirsch (cherry-flavor brandy)	4 squares semisweet chocolate
3 eggs, separated	2 envelopes unflavored gelatin
2 cups milk	2 cups heavy or whipping cream

1. Prepare foil collar for 1½-quart soufflé dish (see instructions below).

2. Reserve 3 cherries; cut remaining cherries in half. In medium bowl, mix cherry halves and 3 tablespoons Kirsch; set aside.

3. In 2-quart saucepan with wire whisk, beat egg yolks, milk and ½ cup sugar until well mixed. Add chocolate; sprinkle gelatin evenly over mixture. Over low heat, cook, stirring constantly, until gelatin is completely dissolved, chocolate is melted and mixture coats a spoon, about 15 minutes. Stir in remaining 3 tablespoons Kirsch; cover and refrigerate until mixture mounds when dropped from a spoon, about 1 hour.

4. In small bowl with mixer at high speed, beat egg whites until stiff peaks form. Beating at high speed, gradually sprinkle in ¼ cup sugar, beating mixture until sugar is completely dissolved.

5. In large bowl, using same beaters, beat 1¾ cups heavy cream until soft peaks form. With rubber spatula, fold chocolate mixture, egg whites and cherry halves into whipped cream until blended. Pour the mixture into the prepared soufflé dish. Cover with plastic wrap and refrigerate until it has set, about 4 hours.

6. *To serve:* Remove collar from soufflé dish. In small bowl with mixer at medium speed, beat remaining ¼ cup heavy cream until stiff peaks form. Garnish top of soufflé with whipped cream and reserved cherries.

Strawberry Soufflé

2 pints strawberries
2 envelopes unflavored gelatin
sugar
4 teaspoons lemon juice
6 egg whites
¼ teaspoon salt
2 cups heavy or whipping cream

Color index page 94
Begin 6 hrs or day ahead
12 servings
237 cals per serving

1 Reserve 6 strawberries for garnish. Wash and hull remainder. Place in covered blender container; puree them at medium speed.

2 In 2-quart saucepan, stir gelatin with 3 tablespoons sugar; gradually stir in one third of pureed strawberries. Cook over low heat, stirring, till gelatin dissolves.

3 Remove from heat; stir in remaining puree and lemon juice; pour into bowl. Chill in freezer, about 20 minutes, until mixture mounds when dropped from spoon.

4 Prepare foil collar for 2-quart soufflé dish or casserole (right). In large bowl with mixer at high speed, beat egg whites and salt until soft peaks form; beating at high speed, gradually sprinkle in ⅓ cup sugar, 2 tablespoons at a time, until the whites form stiff glossy peaks. (Do not scrape side of bowl during beating.)

5 Beat chilled strawberry mixture until fluffy, about 2 minutes. In another small bowl at medium speed, using same beaters, beat cream until stiff peaks form.

6 With rubber spatula, gently fold the strawberry mixture and whipped cream into the beaten egg whites.

7 Spoon folded mixture into prepared soufflé dish. Refrigerate the mixture until it has set, about 2 hours.

8 Remove foil collar from dish. Wash and hull 6 reserved strawberries and use whole or halved to garnish top of soufflé.

MAKING A FOIL COLLAR

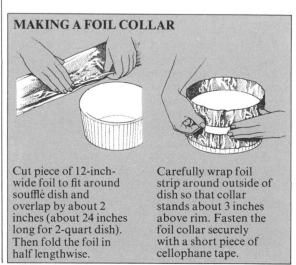

Cut piece of 12-inch-wide foil to fit around soufflé dish and overlap by about 2 inches (about 24 inches long for 2-quart dish). Then fold the foil in half lengthwise.

Carefully wrap foil strip around outside of dish so that collar stands about 3 inches above rim. Fasten the foil collar securely with a short piece of cellophane tape.

Cold soufflés

Color index page 97

Begin early in day

8 servings

247 cals per serving

Frosty Lime Soufflé

1 envelope unflavored gelatin
sugar
½ teaspoon salt
4 eggs, separated
½ cup cold water

⅓ cup lime juice
grated peel of 1 lime
⅛ teaspoon green food color
1 cup heavy or whipping cream

1. In double boiler, stir gelatin with ¼ cup sugar and salt until well mixed.

2. In small bowl with wire whisk, beat egg yolks with cold water and lime juice until mixed; stir into gelatin mixture. Cook over hot, *not boiling,* water, stirring constantly, until mixture thickens and coats a spoon. Remove from heat; stir in 1 teaspoon of grated peel and food color; pour into large bowl and cool to room temperature, stirring occasionally. Meanwhile, prepare collar for a 1-quart soufflé dish (page 361).

3. In small bowl with mixer at high speed, beat egg whites until soft peaks form; beating at high speed, gradually sprinkle in ½ cup sugar; beat until sugar is completely dissolved. Whites should stand in stiff peaks. Spoon into bowl with lime mixture.

4. In small bowl with mixer at medium speed, whip cream; gently fold with beaten egg whites into lime mixture. Pour into prepared soufflé dish; chill until firm, at least 3 hours. Carefully remove foil collar and garnish with remaining peel.

Color index page 98

Begin early in day

10 servings

173 cals per serving

Cranberry Soufflé

2 cups cranberries
1½ cups cranberry juice
sugar
3 envelopes unflavored gelatin
Sugared Cranberries (below)

4 egg whites, at room temperature
¼ teaspoon salt
1 cup heavy or whipping cream

1. Into 2-quart saucepan, measure cranberries, cranberry juice and 1 cup sugar; evenly sprinkle with gelatin. Cook over medium-high heat, stirring constantly, until gelatin is completely dissolved and cranberries pop, about 7 minutes. Refrigerate until mixture mounds slightly when dropped from a spoon, about 45 minutes.

2. Meanwhile, make collar for a 1-quart soufflé dish (page 361). Prepare Sugared Cranberries.

3. In large bowl with mixer at high speed, beat egg whites and salt until soft peaks form. Beating at high speed, gradually sprinkle in ½ cup sugar, 2 tablespoons at a time, beating until each addition is dissolved. Whites should stand in stiff peaks.

4. In small bowl with same beaters and with mixer at medium speed, beat cream until soft peaks form. With rubber spatula, gently fold cranberry mixture and whipped cream into beaten whites until well blended. Pour into soufflé dish; cover and refrigerate until set, about 4 hours. Carefully remove the foil collar; top with Sugared Cranberries.

SUGARED CRANBERRIES: In cup, beat *1 egg white* till frothy. Dip *18 whole cranberries* into egg white; roll in *sugar* to coat; dry on rack.

Mousse

Many people judge restaurants or cooks by the quality of their chocolate mousse, that rich, light, whipped cream dessert. This all-time favorite, served in little cups, is called, literally, "pots of cream."

Color index page 94

Begin 5 hrs or day ahead

6 servings

363 cals per serving

Pots de Crème au Chocolat

2 cups half-and-half (1 pint)
4 squares semisweet chocolate
6 egg yolks
¼ cup sugar

½ teaspoon salt
vanilla extract
¼ cup heavy or whipping cream
2 tablespoons confectioners' sugar

1 In 1-quart saucepan over medium heat, heat half-and-half until tiny bubbles form around edge of saucepan (do not allow half-and-half to boil). Set saucepan aside. In double boiler over hot, *not boiling*, water, melt semisweet chocolate squares, stirring occasionally with rubber spatula.

2 Remove double-boiler top to work surface and, with rubber spatula, beat egg yolks into the melted chocolate until smooth; then stir in sugar and salt.

3 Gradually stir half-and-half into the chocolate mixture until thoroughly blended. Replace double-boiler top over simmering (not boiling) water.

4 Cook, stirring constantly, until mixture coats back of a spoon, about 15 minutes. Stir in 2 teaspoons vanilla extract.

5 Pour mixture into six 6-ounce *pots de crème* cups or stemmed glasses. Refrigerate for about 4 hours or just until the mixture is set.

6 In small bowl with mixer at low speed, beat cream, confectioners' sugar and ¼ teaspoon vanilla until stiff; use to top *pots de crème*.

Hot soufflés

Timing is the key to success when making hot soufflés and since they tend to collapse if left to stand for more than a few minutes, they should always be served as soon as they come from the oven. It helps to avoid a lot of last-minute work when preparing the meal and this is easy to arrange with hot soufflés because both the basic sauce and the soufflé dish itself can be prepared well in advance; let the egg whites stand in the mixer bowl, at room temperature, ready to be beaten and folded with the sauce just before baking. Do not open the oven door before the end of baking time; cold air could cause the soufflé to fall.

Chocolate Soufflé

⅓ *cup all-purpose flour*
sugar
1½ cups milk
3 squares unsweetened chocolate, coarsely chopped or grated
6 eggs, separated
¼ teaspoon salt
2 teaspoons vanilla extract

Color index page 95
Begin 2 hrs ahead
8 servings
210 cals per serving

1 In 2-quart saucepan, into flour and ¼ cup sugar, slowly stir milk. Cook over medium heat, stirring constantly, until the mixture thickens and starts to boil.

2 Cook mixture 1 minute more. Remove pan from heat and stir in chocolate until melted.

3 With wooden spoon, rapidly beat in egg yolks, all at once, beating until thoroughly blended; refrigerate to cool the mixture to lukewarm, stirring occasionally.

4 Grease 2-quart soufflé dish or round casserole with butter or margarine and lightly sprinkle dish with sugar. Preheat the oven to 375°F.

5 In large bowl with mixer at high speed, beat egg whites and salt until soft peaks form.

6 With the mixer at high speed, gradually sprinkle in ¼ cup sugar; beat well until the sugar is completely dissolved. The whites should stand in stiff glossy peaks.

7 With wire whisk or rubber spatula, gently fold chocolate mixture, one third at a time, and vanilla into egg whites, until blended. Pour mixture into soufflé dish.

8 With back of spoon, 1 inch from edge of dish, make 1-inch indentation all around soufflé. Bake 35 to 40 minutes until knife inserted under "top hat" comes out clean.

Color index page 95
Begin 1 hr ahead
6 servings   435 cals per serving

Individual Chocolate Soufflés

sugar
¼ cup all-purpose flour
1¼ cups milk
3 squares unsweetened chocolate
5 eggs, separated
¼ teaspoon salt
2 teaspoons vanilla extract
½ cup heavy or whipping cream, whipped
½ cup chocolate syrup

1. Grease six 10-ounce soufflé dishes or custard cups with butter or margarine and then lightly sprinkle them with sugar.
2. In 2-quart saucepan, combine flour and ¼ cup sugar; gradually add milk, stirring constantly until mixture is smooth. Cook mixture over medium heat, stirring constantly, until mixture is thickened; remove from heat.
3. Stir chocolate into mixture until melted. Rapidly beat in egg yolks all at once, until well mixed; set aside and allow to cool to lukewarm.
4. Preheat oven to 375°F. In large bowl with mixer at high speed, beat egg whites, salt and vanilla until soft peaks form; beating at high speed, gradually add ½ cup sugar, 2 tablespoons at a time. Whites should stand in stiff peaks. With rubber spatula, gently fold chocolate mixture into beaten egg whites until blended; spoon into the prepared soufflé dishes or custard cups.
5. Place filled cups in 15½″ by 10½″ jelly-roll pan for easier handling. Bake soufflés 30 to 35 minutes until puffy and brown.
6. Serve soufflés immediately. Pass whipped cream and chocolate syrup to spoon over top.

CHOCOLATE TIPS

Melting chocolate: Use any of these ways: Place in top of double boiler and melt over hot, *not boiling*, water. Or place in custard cup and set in pan of hot water. Or place in heavy, 1-quart saucepan; melt over low heat – if the pan is too thin, it will transfer heat too fast and burn the chocolate.

To speed melting: Break up chocolate into smaller pieces; stir frequently. If you are melting the chocolate in a double boiler or in a custard cup set in a pan of water, do not boil the water to speed melting as this will only thicken or curdle the chocolate.

If chocolate thickens or curdles, add vegetable shortening (not butter or margarine) a little at a time and stir until of the desired consistency.

In an emergency you can substitute cocoa for unsweetened chocolate in recipes. The proportions to use are 3 tablespoons cocoa plus 1 tablespoon shortening or salad oil (not butter or margarine) for each square of chocolate called for in the recipe.

Do not substitute semisweet or milk chocolate in recipes calling for unsweetened.

Hot soufflés

Color index
page 97

Begin 1¼ hrs
ahead

6 servings

439 cals per
serving

Orange Liqueur Soufflé

¼ cup butter or margarine	1 tablespoon grated orange peel
⅓ cup all-purpose flour	6 egg whites, at room temperature
⅛ teaspoon salt	¼ teaspoon cream of tartar
1½ cups milk sugar	1 cup heavy or whipping cream, whipped
4 egg yolks	
⅓ cup orange-flavor liqueur	

1. In 3-quart saucepan over low heat, melt butter. Stir in flour and salt until well blended; gradually stir in milk; cook, stirring, until mixture is thickened. Remove pan from heat.
2. With wire whisk, beat 3 tablespoons sugar into milk mixture. Rapidly beat in egg yolks, all at once. Stir in liqueur and orange peel; set aside.
3. Preheat oven to 375°F. Grease 2-quart soufflé dish or round casserole with butter or margarine and sprinkle lightly with sugar.
4. In large bowl with mixer at high speed, beat egg whites and cream of tartar until stiff peaks form. With rubber spatula or wire whisk, gently fold egg-yolk mixture, one third at a time, into egg whites until blended.
5. Pour the mixture into the prepared soufflé dish; with back of spoon, about 1 inch from edge of dish, make 1-inch indentation all around. Bake 30 to 35 minutes until knife inserted under "top hat" comes out clean.
6. Serve soufflé immediately and pass bowl of whipped cream separately to spoon over top.

Banana Soufflé

Color index
page 95

Begin 1 hr
ahead

8 servings

275 cals per
serving

3 large bananas	¾ cup milk
1 tablespoon lemon juice	3 large eggs, separated
⅓ cup sugar	2 tablespoons melted butter or margarine
1 tablespoon cornstarch	1½ teaspoons vanilla extract
½ teaspoon ground nutmeg	1 cup heavy or whipping cream, whipped
¼ teaspoon grated lemon peel	
⅛ teaspoon salt	

1. Grease bottom of 1½-quart soufflé dish. Peel and slice bananas. In covered blender container at medium speed, blend bananas and lemon juice until well mixed and creamy.
2. In 3-quart saucepan, mix sugar, cornstarch, nutmeg, lemon peel and salt. Stir in milk until blended. Over medium heat, cook milk mixture until thickened, stirring constantly. Remove from heat.
3. Preheat oven to 375°F. In small bowl with fork, beat egg yolks well. Add a little of hot-milk mixture; mix together well. Mix egg-yolk mixture well with remaining hot-milk mixture. Stir in butter or margarine, vanilla extract and banana mixture.
4. In small bowl with mixer at high speed, beat egg whites until stiff peaks form. Carefully fold into banana mixture; pour into soufflé dish. Bake 35 minutes or until golden brown. Serve immediately with whipped cream to spoon over the top.

Meringues

Meringue, a mixture of stiffly beaten egg whites and sugar, is baked into small or large shells to be served with either ice cream or another filling. Soft meringue, which is beaten with less sugar, is baked on top of pies or can be poached for Floating Island.

Meringue Shells

Begin early
in day or
up to 5 days
ahead

6 shells

105 cals each

3 egg whites, at room temperature	¾ cup sugar
⅛ teaspoon cream of tartar	½ teaspoon vanilla extract

1. Preheat oven to 275°F. In small bowl with mixer at high speed, beat egg whites and cream of tartar until soft peaks form.
2. Gradually sprinkle in sugar, 2 tablespoons at a time, beating after each addition for about 2 minutes or until sugar is completely dissolved, about 15 minutes. To test, rub meringue between fingers; if grainy, continue beating. Add vanilla, beating at high speed until mixture stands in stiff, glossy peaks.
3. Onto large greased cookie sheet, spoon mixture into 6 mounds. Spread each mound into a 4-inch circle, heaping mixture to form a nest shape.
4. Bake 45 minutes until meringues are crisp and very lightly browned. Turn off oven; let meringues stand in oven 45 minutes longer to dry. Cool completely on cookie sheet. Store loosely wrapped in waxed paper; keep at room temperature.

Shaping meringue: Spoon on cookie sheet; spread into 4-inch circles.

Forming nests: Heap mixture at edge of each circle to form nest shape.

MAKING A MERINGUE PIE SHELL
Preheat oven to 275°F. Prepare steps 1 and 2 of Meringue Shells (above) then shape as shown below. Bake 1 hour. Turn off oven; let stand in oven 1 hour.

Into greased 9-inch pie plate, spoon mixture, smoothing it at center.

Pile meringue high on the sides to form a pie "shell."

Surprise Angel Pecan Pie

Color index
page 95

Begin 4 hrs or
day ahead

8 servings

393 cals per
serving

*3 egg whites, at room
temperature*
⅛ teaspoon salt
sugar
vanilla extract
¾ cup chopped pecans

*¾ cup crushed soda
crackers*
*1 teaspoon double-acting
baking powder*
*1 cup heavy or whipping
cream*

1. Preheat oven to 350°F. Grease 9-inch pie plate;
line with foil; grease foil.
2. In small bowl with mixer at high speed, beat egg
whites and salt until soft peaks form. Gradually
sprinkle in 1 cup sugar, 2 tablespoons at a time,
beating well after each addition. Whites should
stand in stiff glossy peaks. Lightly beat in 1 teaspoon
vanilla extract.
3. Into egg-white mixture, fold pecans, crackers and
baking powder. Spread evenly in pie plate. Bake 35
minutes or until light golden but not brown. Cool on
wire rack 2 hours. Using foil, lift pie from plate;
refrigerate until pie is thoroughly chilled, at least
1 hour or overnight.
4. *To serve:* Remove foil; place pie on plate. In small
bowl with hand beater or mixer at medium speed,
beat cream with 2 tablespoons sugar and 1 teaspoon
vanilla extract until stiff peaks form. Spread
whipped cream mixture over pie.

Strawberry Meringues

Color index
page 97

Begin early
in day

6 servings

363 cals per
serving

*Meringue Shells
(opposite)*
*1½ pints vanilla ice
cream*

1½ pints strawberries
⅓ cup sugar

1. Prepare Meringue Shells.
2. Using ice-cream scoop or large spoon, scoop ice
cream into 6 balls onto cookie sheet; freeze.
3. Thinly slice strawberries; place in medium bowl.
Stir sugar into berries; refrigerate.
4. *To serve:* Top each meringue shell with ice-cream
ball and spoon on strawberries and juice.

Chocolate Angel Pie

Color index
page 97

Begin early
in day

10 servings

292 cals per
serving

*1 Meringue Pie Shell
(opposite)*
*2 squares unsweetened
chocolate*
3 tablespoons water
3 egg yolks

¼ cup sugar
⅛ teaspoon salt
*1½ cups heavy or
whipping cream*
*1 teaspoon vanilla
extract*

1. Prepare Meringue Pie Shell.
2. Meanwhile, in double boiler over hot, *not boiling*,
water, combine chocolate, water, egg yolks, sugar
and salt. Cook until chocolate melts and mixture is
very thick and mounds when dropped from a spoon,
about 5 minutes, stirring constantly. Remove from
heat and set aside.
3. In large bowl with mixer at medium speed, beat
heavy cream and vanilla extract until soft peaks
form. With wire whisk, gently fold chocolate mixture into whipped-cream mixture.
4. Spoon mixture into meringue shell. Refrigerate
until filling is set, about 4 hours.

Floating Island

Color index
page 94

Begin 1½ hrs
ahead

4 servings

370 cals per
serving

5 egg yolks
2 cups milk
¼ teaspoon salt
sugar
*½ teaspoon vanilla
extract*
*1 egg white, at room
temperature*
water

1 In double boiler over
hot, *not boiling*, water,
combine egg yolks, milk,
salt and ¾ cup sugar.
Cook, stirring constantly,
until mixture thickens and
coats spoon, about 15
minutes. (To test
consistency, lift metal
spoon; hold up 15 to 20
seconds; spoon should not
show through mixture.)
Stir in vanilla extract.

2 Pour custard into
4 wine goblets or into
dessert dishes. Cover;
refrigerate until well
chilled, about 1 hour.

3 Meanwhile, in small
bowl with mixer at high
speed, beat egg white until
soft peaks form. Gradually
sprinkle in 2 tablespoons
sugar, beating till
completely dissolved.

4 Preheat oven to 350°F.
Onto ½ inch cold
water in 8″ by 8″ baking
dish, drop beaten egg
white in 4 mounds. Bake
7 to 10 minutes until
lightly browned.

5 With slotted spoon, remove each light brown
meringue from water;
drain on spoon over paper
towels. Slip onto custard
in wine goblet.

6 In heavy, 1-quart
saucepan over high
heat, heat 3 tablespoons
sugar, stirring constantly,
until smooth and amber,
about 3 minutes.

7 Remove saucepan from
heat; let stand 2
minutes then, with spoon,
quickly drizzle the sugar
syrup over each dessert in
thin strands.

Cream puffs and éclairs

Based on *choux* paste, a butter, egg and flour mixture, cream puffs and éclairs have a lightly browned, crisp and tender shell with a slightly moist hollow interior.

Cream Puffs

Choux paste:
½ cup butter or
  margarine
1 cup water
¼ teaspoon salt
1 cup all-purpose flour
4 eggs

Vanilla or Almond
Pastry Cream (right)
confectioners' sugar

Color index
page 95

Begin early
in day or
day ahead

12 servings
402 cals per
serving

1 Grease 2 large cookie sheets. Prepare *choux* paste: In 2-quart saucepan over medium heat, heat butter, water and salt until butter mixture boils. Remove from heat.

2 Add flour all at once. With wooden spoon, vigorously stir until mixture forms a ball and leaves side of pan. Preheat oven to 375°F.

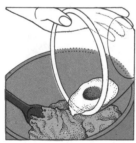

3 Add eggs to flour mixture, one at a time, beating well after each addition, until smooth. Cool mixture slightly.

4 Using large spoon and rubber spatula, drop batter onto cookie sheets in 12 large mounds, 3 inches apart, swirling top of each. Bake 50 minutes.

5 Remove from oven; cut slit in side of each puff. Return to oven; bake 10 minutes. Turn off oven; dry puffs in oven 10 minutes. Cool. Prepare filling; cover and chill.

6 When puffs are cool, slice top off each. Fill each shell with the chilled Vanilla Pastry Cream; replace top. Sprinkle tops of cream puffs with some confectioners' sugar.

FILLINGS AND GLAZE

VANILLA PASTRY CREAM: In 2-quart saucepan, combine **¾ cup sugar, ¼ cup all-purpose flour** and **¼ teaspoon salt;** stir in **1½ cups milk.** Over medium heat, cook, stirring, until mixture thickens and boils, about 10 minutes; boil 1 minute. In small bowl with fork, beat **6 egg yolks** slightly; beat small amount of milk mixture into yolks; slowly pour egg mixture back into milk mixture, stirring. Cook over medium-low heat, stirring until mixture thickens and coats spoon well, about 8 minutes (do not boil). (To check thickness, lift metal spoon from mixture and hold up 15 seconds; spoon should not show through mixture.) Remove from heat; stir in **1½ teaspoons vanilla extract.** Cover surface with plastic wrap; chill well, about 2 hours. In small bowl with mixer at medium speed, beat **1½ cups heavy or whipping cream** until stiff peaks form. With rubber spatula, gently fold cream into custard. (Makes 4⅔ cups.)

 ALMOND PASTRY CREAM: Prepare as above but substitute **1 teaspoon almond extract** for vanilla.

 SEMISWEET CHOCOLATE GLAZE: In 1-quart saucepan over low heat, melt **2 squares semisweet chocolate** and **2 tablespoons butter,** stirring constantly. Stir in **1 cup confectioners' sugar** and **3 tablespoons milk** until smooth. (Makes 1 cup.)

Eclairs

choux paste from Cream
  Puffs (left)
Vanilla Pastry Cream
  (above)

Semisweet Chocolate
  Glaze (above)

Color index
page 97

Begin early
in day or
day ahead

10 éclairs
539 cals each

1. Preheat oven to 375°F. Make *choux* paste as for Cream Puffs in steps 1 to 3; drop by ¼ cupfuls onto cookie sheet 2 inches apart, and in rows 6 inches apart, to make 10. Spread each mound into rectangle, rounding edges. (Or use pastry bag as below.) Bake 40 minutes or until lightly browned. Cut slit in side of each shell and bake 10 minutes longer. Turn off oven; dry shells in oven 10 minutes. Cool on rack.
2. Meanwhile, prepare Vanilla Pastry Cream and Semisweet Chocolate Glaze.
3. Slice about ⅓ from top of each shell and fill bottom of shells with cream filling; replace tops and spread with glaze. Refrigerate until serving time.

Shaping *choux* paste:
With a small spatula, spread paste in 5″ by ¾″ rectangles.

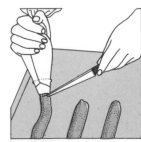

Piping *choux* paste: Or, use a pastry bag with plain round tube to form éclairs.

Cream Puff Ring

choux paste from Cream
Puffs (opposite)
Almond Pastry Cream
(opposite)
Semisweet Chocolate
Glaze (opposite)
1 pint strawberries,
hulled and washed

Color index
page 94

Begin early
in day or
day ahead

10 servings

577 cals per
serving

1 On greased, lightly floured cookie sheet, using a 7-inch plate as a guide, trace a circle. Preheat oven to 400°F. Prepare *choux* paste as in Cream Puffs, steps 1 to 3.

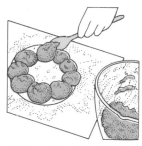

2 Drop heaping table-spoonfuls of *choux* paste just inside circle to form ring. Bake 40 minutes or until golden and firm. Turn off heat; leave in oven 15 minutes; cool.

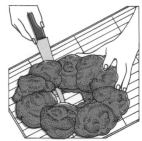

3 With sharp knife, care-fully cut puff ring in half horizontally.

4 With spoon, remove soft interior; discard, leaving hollow ring shell.

5 Prepare Almond Pastry Cream; fill bottom shell with cream; replace top shell; refrigerate.

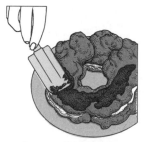

6 Prepare Semisweet Chocolate Glaze; spread on top of ring. Refrigerate ring.

7 *To serve:* Fill center of Cream Puff Ring with fresh strawberries. Serve immediately.

Swans

choux paste from Cream   *Vanilla Filling (below)*
Puffs (opposite)

Color index
page 95

Begin early
in day

36 pastries

104 cals each

1. Grease large cookie sheet. Preheat oven to 375°F. Make *choux* paste as for Cream Puffs in steps 1 to 3. Spoon scant ¾ cupful mixture into pastry bag with ⅛″ round tube. Onto sheet, pipe thirty-six 2-inch long "question marks" for swans' necks, making a small dollop at end of each for head.

2. Spoon remaining mixture into large pastry bag with ½″ round tube. Pipe thirty-six 1½″ by 1″ teardrops for swans' bodies, about 1 inch apart. Bake 10 minutes until swans' necks are golden; remove to rack; cool. Continue baking bodies 20 to 25 minutes longer until golden. Remove to wire racks to cool. Prepare Vanilla Filling.

3. Cut off top third of swans' bodies; set aside. Spoon filling into pastry bag with large fluted tube. Pipe some filling mixture into bottom pieces. Cut top pieces of swans' bodies lengthwise in half; set into filling for wings. Place necks into filling. Chill.

VANILLA FILLING: In 3-quart saucepan, mix well *1 envelope unflavored gelatin* with ½ cup sugar and *2 tablespoons all-purpose flour.* In small bowl with wire whisk, beat *4 egg yolks* with *1 cup milk* until well mixed; stir into gelatin mixture. Cook over medium-low heat, stirring constantly, until mixture is very thick and coats a spoon well, about 10 minutes (do not boil). Remove pan from heat; stir in *1 teaspoon vanilla extract.* Cover and refrigerate until mixture is cold but not set, about 45 minutes. In small bowl with mixer at medium speed, beat *1 cup heavy cream* into soft peaks; fold into custard.

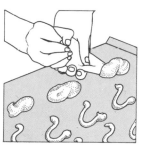

Piping *choux* paste: Pipe necks then teardrop shapes for bodies.

Adding filling: Cut off top third of bodies then pipe in filling. Cut top pieces lengthwise in half.

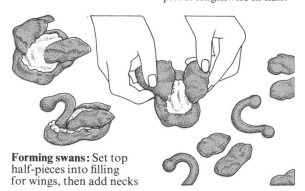

Forming swans: Set top half-pieces into filling for wings, then add necks

Crêpes and blintzes

Crêpes Suzette

Color index
page 94

Begin early
in day

12 crêpes or
6 servings

155 cals each

Crêpes:
*butter or margarine,
  melted*
1½ cups milk
⅔ cup all-purpose flour
½ teaspoon salt
3 eggs

Suzette Sauce (below)
*¼ cup orange-flavor
  liqueur*

1. In medium bowl with wire whisk, beat 2 tablespoons butter and remaining crêpe ingredients until smooth. Cover; chill 2 hours.
2. Brush bottom of 7-inch crêpe pan and 10-inch skillet with melted butter. Over medium heat, heat pans; pour scant ¼ cup batter into crêpe pan, tip pan to coat bottom; cook 2 minutes till top is set, underside slightly browned.
3. Loosen crêpe; invert into hot 10-inch skillet; cook other side 30 seconds. Slip crêpe onto waxed paper. Meanwhile, start cooking another crêpe. Stack crêpes between waxed paper. Use immediately or wrap in foil and refrigerate.
4. *About 30 minutes before serving:* Prepare Suzette Sauce. Fold crêpes in quarters; arrange in Suzette Sauce. Simmer over medium-low heat 10 minutes; pour liqueur in center (do not stir). Heat liqueur a minute or two; light with a long match and flame. Or, in 1-quart saucepan over low heat, heat liqueur just until warm. Carefully light the warm liqueur with a long match and pour over crêpes in chafing dish. Serve the crêpes immediately.

SUZETTE SAUCE: In chafing dish or 10-inch skillet over low heat, heat *⅓ cup orange juice, ¼ cup butter* or margarine, *2 tablespoons sugar* and *¼ teaspoon grated orange peel* until butter melts.

SERVING CREPES SUZETTE

Fold crêpes in quarters; arrange in sauce in chafing dish. Simmer 10 minutes.

Pour the liqueur in center of chafing dish over the crêpes (do not stir).

Heat liqueur a minute or two, then light with a long match. Let liqueur flame. Or, heat liqueur in 1-quart saucepan; ignite; pour over crêpes. Serve crêpes and sauce immediately.

Dessert Crêpes with Orange Sauce

Color index
page 94

Begin 1 hr
ahead

6 servings

481 cals per
serving

Orange Sauce (below)
1½ cups milk
¾ cup all-purpose flour
*½ teaspoon double-
  acting baking powder*
½ teaspoon salt
6 eggs, separated

salad oil
*1 8-ounce container sour
  cream (1 cup)*
*2 medium oranges,
  peeled, seeded and
  diced*

1. Prepare Orange Sauce; keep warm.
2. In large bowl with wire whisk or fork, mix milk, flour, baking powder, salt and egg yolks until smoothly blended.
3. In small bowl with mixer at high speed, beat egg whites until stiff peaks form. With wire whisk or rubber spatula, gently fold the beaten egg whites into the flour mixture.
4. Heat 12-inch skillet over medium heat; lightly brush with salad oil. Making 3 crêpes at a time, pour batter by ½ cupfuls into hot skillet; spread batter into 4-inch circles. Cook crêpes until golden on both sides, about 3 minutes, turning once. With pancake turner, remove crêpes to cookie sheet; keep warm. Repeat, making 12 crêpes in all, brushing skillet with more salad oil if it becomes too dry.
5. To serve, spread some sour cream over each crêpe. Roll each crêpe, jelly-roll fashion; arrange on warm large platter. Spoon Orange Sauce over crêpes; top with diced oranges.

ORANGE SAUCE: In 1-quart saucepan over low heat, melt *¼ cup butter* or margarine. Stir in *1½ cups confectioners' sugar, ⅓ cup orange juice* and *2 tablespoons grated orange peel.* Cook over low heat, stirring frequently, until heated through.

Cheese Blintzes

Color index
page 98

Begin early
in day

6 servings

383 cals per
serving

*12 crêpes from
  Crêpes Suzette (left)*
*1 8-ounce container
  creamed cottage
  cheese (1 cup)*
*1 3-ounce package cream
  cheese, softened*
¼ cup sugar

*½ teaspoon vanilla
  extract*
*2 tablespoons butter or
  margarine*
*1 10-ounce package
  frozen strawberries,
  thawed*

1. Prepare crêpes as in steps 1 to 3 of Crêpes Suzette.
2. *About 30 minutes before serving:* In a small bowl with mixer at medium speed, beat cottage cheese, cream cheese, sugar and vanilla extract until smooth. Spread about a tablespoon of mixture on each crêpe to within ½ inch of edge; fold two sides of each crêpe slightly toward the center then roll in opposite direction, jelly-roll fashion.
3. Preheat oven to 350°F. In 15½" by 10½" jelly-roll pan in the oven, melt butter or margarine. Remove from oven. Arrange blintzes in one layer in pan. Bake 10 minutes until heated through. Serve topped with strawberries.

435 cals per
serving

CHERRY BLINTZES: Prepare Cheese Blintzes but omit strawberries. Prepare Cherry Sauce (page 464) in cook-and-serve skillet; add filled crêpes. Over low heat, simmer 10 minutes to heat through.

Winter Brunch

Wonderful hardy winter produce topped up with citrus fruits from Florida and California and a myriad of imported tropical fruits make certain our dining tables are always warm and welcoming. Widely available vegetables include root vegetables like parsnips, turnips, and rutabagas as well as fennel, Brussels sprouts, cabbages, and winter squashes.

Shut out all thoughts of cold on a winter weekend by treating guests to a hearty brunch. Offer generous slices of Pineapple-glazed Baked Half Ham garnished with watercress and grapes and serve them with Honeyed Pumpkin, Zesty Tangelo Salad and Cranberry Chutney. Reserve leftover ham for supper. For the less hearty eaters Quiche Lorraine, fresh fruit, biscuits and muffins form an alternative choice. No one will resist, however, your homemade Apple Pie.

Clockwise from left: kumquats; limes; oranges; grapefruit; satsumas (with leaves); ugli fruit; tangelos; lemon; pomelo; ortanique (a flatish orange); pink grapefruit; satsuma (on plate)

Decorating a Pie Top

Decorating the top of a two-crust pie can give a simple dessert a special look, especially if you use decorations that suit the season or occasion.

Reroll any pastry trimmings and use a cookie cutter, knife or pastry wheel to make leaves and berries, lattice strips or shapes such as hearts or diamonds.

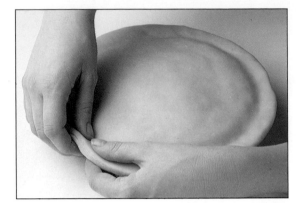

1 Prepare Apple Pie (page 346, steps 1 to 4). Roll out remaining pastry. Place over pie and trim edge. Fold under, then bring pastry up over rim; pinch to form stand up edge.

2 Make fluted edge: Place one index finger on the inside edge of pastry and, with index finger and thumb of other hand, pinch pastry to make flute. Repeat around edge.

3 Reroll pastry trimmings. With leaf-shaped cutter, cut leaves and roll small pieces of dough into balls. Arrange on pie top.

4 Alternatively, with sharp knife, cut leaf shapes from pastry trimmings; with knife tip, slash pastry to form veins on leaves. Arrange on pie top.

5 Arrange cut out pieces on pie top. Lightly brush top of pie with *milk*. In a small bowl, mix *1 tablespoon sugar* with *¹/₈ teaspoon cinnamon*. Sprinkle over pie and bake as directed.

Apple Pie
A two-crust pie makes a hearty, warming, winter-time dessert. Before baking Apple Pie (or any other two-crust pie) with a decorative pastry top, cut two holes in pie top to allow steam to escape. Or, if you like, slash pie top with a knife before placing over pie.

Other desserts

Strawberry Shortcake

Color index
page 97

Begin 45 mins
ahead

8 servings

471 cals per
serving

sugar
1¾ cups all-purpose
    flour
½ cup shortening
⅓ cup milk
1 egg
1 tablespoon double-
    acting baking
    powder

1 teaspoon grated lemon
    peel
¾ teaspoon salt
2 pints strawberries
butter or margarine,
    softened
1 cup heavy or whipping
    cream, whipped

1. Preheat oven to 450°F. Prepare shortcake: Grease 9-inch round cake pan. Into medium bowl, measure ¼ cup sugar and next 7 ingredients. With mixer at medium speed, beat mixture until well combined and a soft dough forms. Pat the dough evenly into the prepared cake pan. Bake 15 minutes or until golden on top.

2. Wash and hull strawberries, reserving a few for garnish. Sprinkle the remainder with ⅓ cup sugar; mash slightly.

3. Invert the shortcake onto platter; with long, sharp knife, carefully split hot shortcake horizontally. Spread both cut surfaces evenly with softened butter or margarine.

4. Onto bottom half, spoon half of strawberries; top with other cake half; spoon remaining strawberries over top.

5. Spread the whipped cream over the mashed strawberries and then garnish with the reserved whole strawberries.

Splitting the cake: Using a long, sharp knife, halve the cake horizontally; spread both cut surfaces with softened butter or margarine.

Layering the cake: Spoon half of the mashed strawberries on cake half; top with the second layer and spoon over the rest of the strawberries.

INDIVIDUAL SHORTCAKES: Prepare as above but onto greased cookie sheet, drop dough in 8 equal mounds about 2 inches apart. Bake 10 minutes or until golden. Split and serve as above.

Syllabub

Color index
page 94

Begin 10 mins
ahead

16 servings

181 cals per
serving

5 cups half-and-half
2 cups Chablis
1 cup sugar
½ cup brandy

⅓ cup lemon juice
shredded peel of 1 lemon
    for garnish

In large bowl with mixer at low speed, beat half-and-half until frothy; gradually beat in remaining ingredients except lemon peel until well mixed; pour into chilled stemmed glasses. Lightly sprinkle the shredded lemon peel over the top.

Deluxe Strawberry Shortcake

Color index
page 94

Begin 4 hrs
ahead or early
in day

12 servings

309 cals per
serving

4 eggs, separated, at
    room temperature
¼ teaspoon cream of
    tartar
sugar
1 cup all-purpose flour
⅓ cup water
¼ cup salad oil
1½ teaspoons double-
    acting baking powder

½ teaspoon vanilla
    extract
2 pints strawberries,
    hulled
1½ cups heavy or
    whipping cream,
    whipped

1. In large bowl with mixer at high speed, beat egg whites and cream of tartar until soft peaks form. Beating at high speed, sprinkle in ¼ cup sugar, 2 tablespoons at a time, beating well after each addition until sugar is completely dissolved. Whites should stand in stiff peaks.

2. Preheat oven to 325°F. In small bowl with mixer at medium speed, beat yolks, flour, water, oil, baking powder, vanilla and ½ cup sugar until well mixed. With wire whisk, fold flour mixture into beaten egg whites, just until blended. Pour mixture into ungreased 9-inch tube pan.

3. Bake 1 hour or until top of cake springs back when lightly touched with finger. Invert cake in pan on bottle; cool completely.

4. Cut strawberries lengthwise in half. Remove cake from pan; with serrated knife, slice in two horizontally. Place bottom layer on platter; spread with half whipped cream; top with one third berries; top with second layer. Spread remaining cream on top of cake; garnish with remaining berries.

YOGURT DESSERTS

Yogurt is a versatile ingredient for all kinds of cooking, especially for desserts. Try some of these ideas for serving light, refreshing desserts.

Combine plain yogurt with honey (below left) or fresh berries or other fruit (below right).

Coffee flavored yogurt is delicious with chocolate syrup on top, and layered with chopped nuts, cake or cookie crumbs (above).

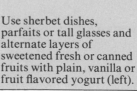

Use sherbet dishes, parfaits or tall glasses and alternate layers of sweetened fresh or canned fruits with plain, vanilla or fruit flavored yogurt (left).

Other desserts

Color index page 95

Begin 2 hrs ahead or early in day

8 servings   285 cals per serving

Chocolate Cups with Strawberry Cream

1 6-ounce package semi -
*   sweet-chocolate pieces*
1 tablespoon shortening
1 pint strawberries

1 cup heavy or whipping
*   cream*
⅓ cup confectioners'
*   sugar*

1. Place a fluted paper baking cup in each of eight 3-inch cups of muffin pan; set aside.

2. In double boiler over hot, *not boiling*, water (or in heavy, 1-quart saucepan over low heat), heat the chocolate pieces together with shortening until melted and smooth, about 5 minutes, stirring chocolate mixture occasionally.

3. Lift one paper cup and tilt slightly; drizzle chocolate, 1 heaping teaspoonful at a time, down side of cup to cover sides evenly. About 3 of these teaspoonfuls will cover the entire inside of each cup. Repeat with remaining paper cups. Refrigerate the chocolate-coated cups until chocolate is firm, about 30 minutes.

4. *About 30 minutes before serving:* With cool hands, remove 1 cup at a time from refrigerator; gently but quickly peel paper from each, leaving a chocolate cup. Set the chocolate cups on chilled dessert platter and refrigerate.

5. Wash and hull strawberries; pat dry with paper towels. Cut berries into ⅛-inch-thick slices. Reserve ½ cup sliced strawberries for garnish.

6. In small bowl with mixer at medium speed, beat heavy or whipping cream and confectioners' sugar until stiff peaks form. With rubber spatula, gently fold strawberries into whipped-cream mixture; spoon into chocolate cups. Arrange a few reserved strawberry slices on each.

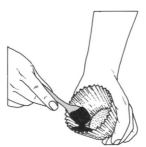 

Making cups: Lift cup, tilting slightly, and drizzle chocolate over cup to cover inside.

Filling cups: Spoon strawberry and cream mixture into cups; top with strawberry slices.

Begin 2 hrs ahead or early in day

8 servings

CHOCOLATE CUPS WITH COCOA CREAM: Prepare Chocolate Cups as above. For filling, omit strawberries; instead, beat **¼ cup cocoa** and **¼ teaspoon vanilla extract** with the heavy or whipping cream and confectioners' sugar.   280 cals per serving

Apple Strudel

2 pounds tart
*   cooking apples,*
*   thinly sliced*
*   (about 6 cups)*
½ cup dark
*   seedless raisins*
*   or currants*
½ cup chopped
*   California walnuts*
*   or pecans*
⅓ cup sugar
½ teaspoon ground
*   cinnamon*
¼ teaspoon ground
*   nutmeg*
¼ teaspoon salt

about 1 cup dry bread
*   crumbs*
½ pound phyllo (strudel
*   leaves)*
½ cup butter or
*   margarine, melted*

Color index page 94

Begin 3 hrs ahead or early in day

10 servings

340 cals per serving

1 Grease 15½" by 10½" jelly-roll pan. In large bowl, mix first 7 ingredients and ½ cup bread crumbs; set apple mixture aside.

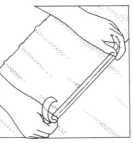

2 Cut two 25-inch lengths of waxed paper; overlap two long sides about ½ inch; fasten with cellophane tape.

3 On waxed paper, place one sheet of phyllo; brush with some butter then sprinkle with scant tablespoon of remaining bread crumbs.

4 Preheat oven to 375°F. Layer remaining sheets of phyllo to make an 18-inch square, brushing each sheet with butter and sprinkling with crumbs.

5 About 3 inches from one edge of phyllo, evenly spoon apple mixture in a 12" by 4" row, leaving 3 inches of phyllo at each end.

6 Fold ends over apples. Starting with edge by apples, roll phyllo jelly-roll fashion, lifting waxed paper as you roll.

7 Place roll in jelly-roll pan seam side down. Brush with melted butter. Bake 40 minutes or just until golden brown.

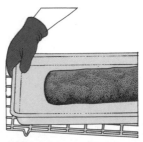

8 Remove cooked strudel from oven and allow to cool in jelly-roll pan on wire rack about 30 minutes.

9 With sharp knife, cut strudel crosswise into individual serving pieces; serve warm or cold.

Baklava

4½ cups California walnuts (1 16-ounce package), finely chopped
½ cup sugar
1 teaspoon ground cinnamon
1 pound phyllo (strudel leaves)
1 cup butter or margarine, melted
1 cup honey

Color index page 96

Begin 3 hrs or up to 1 wk ahead

24 servings

279 cals per serving

1. Grease 13″ by 9″ baking pan. In large bowl, mix walnuts, sugar and cinnamon; set aside.

2. In baking pan, place 1 sheet of phyllo, allowing it to extend up sides of pan; brush with butter or margarine. Repeat to make 5 more layers; sprinkle with 1 cup walnut mixture. Cut remaining phyllo into approximately 13″ by 9″ rectangles. Preheat oven to 300°F.

3. Place one phyllo rectangle in pan; brush with butter or margarine. Repeat to make at least 6 layers, overlapping small strips of phyllo to make rectangles, if necessary. Sprinkle with 1 cup of the walnut mixture.

4. Repeat step 3 three more times. Place remaining phyllo on top of last walnut layer. Trim any phyllo that extends over top of pan. With sharp knife, cut just halfway through all layers in a diamond pattern to make 24 servings. Bake 1¼ hours or until top is golden brown.

5. Meanwhile, in 1-quart saucepan over medium-low heat, heat honey until hot, not boiling. Spoon hot honey evenly over baklava. Cool in pan on wire rack at least 1 hour, then cover and leave at room temperature until serving time.

6. *To serve:* Finish cutting through layers.

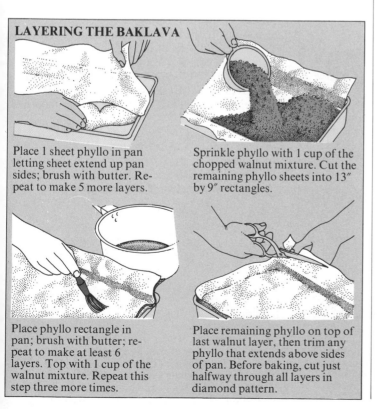

LAYERING THE BAKLAVA

Place 1 sheet phyllo in pan letting sheet extend up pan sides; brush with butter. Repeat to make 5 more layers.

Sprinkle phyllo with 1 cup of the chopped walnut mixture. Cut the remaining phyllo sheets into 13″ by 9″ rectangles.

Place phyllo rectangle in pan; brush with butter; repeat to make at least 6 layers. Top with 1 cup of the walnut mixture. Repeat this step three more times.

Place remaining phyllo on top of last walnut layer, then trim any phyllo that extends above sides of pan. Before baking, cut just halfway through all layers in diamond pattern.

Galatoboureko

4 cups milk
2 cups heavy or whipping cream
½ cup plus 1 tablespoon quick enriched farina
½ cup sugar
6 egg yolks
1 tablespoon vanilla extract
½ pound phyllo (strudel leaves)
¾ cup butter or margarine, melted
Syrup (below)

Color index page 96

Begin 2½ hrs or up to 2 days ahead

24 servings

259 cals per serving

1. Grease a 13″ by 9″ baking pan. In 3-quart saucepan over medium-high heat, heat milk and heavy cream just until boiling. In small bowl, mix together the farina and sugar; gradually sprinkle into milk and cream, stirring with wire whisk or spoon; heat to boiling. Reduce heat to medium-low; continue cooking, stirring constantly, until mixture is slightly thickened, 5 to 10 minutes; remove the saucepan from the heat.

2. In large bowl with mixer at high speed, beat the egg yolks with the vanilla extract until thoroughly blended. Reduce speed to medium and gradually beat in the farina mixture to blend well. Preheat oven to 375°F.

3. In baking pan, place 1 sheet of phyllo, allowing it to extend up the sides of the pan; brush with butter or margarine. Repeat to make about 5 more layers; pour the farina and egg-yolk mixture into phyllo-lined baking pan.

4. Cut remaining phyllo into approximately 13″ by 9″ rectangles. Place one sheet of phyllo on farina mixture; brush with butter or margarine. Repeat with remaining phyllo and butter. (If necessary, overlap small strips of phyllo to make rectangles.) With sharp knife, cut the top phyllo layer into 2¼-inch squares.

5. Bake 35 minutes or until top is golden brown and puffy. Pour the hot, lemon-flavored Syrup over the top. Let Galatoboureko cool on wire rack at least 1 hour before serving.

6. *To serve:* Finish cutting through the layers. Galatoboureko may be served either warm or cold. Refrigerate to serve cold.

SYRUP: In 1-quart saucepan over medium heat, heat **¾ cup sugar** and **⅓ cup water** to boiling, stirring occasionally. Reduce heat to low; simmer for about 8 minutes or until the syrup is thickened then stir in *1 tablespoon lemon juice.*

Making phyllo rectangles: Using a sharp knife, carefully cut 13″ by 9″ sheets of phyllo.

Cutting dessert: Before baking, cut the top phyllo layer into 2¼-inch squares.

Other desserts

Sherry Trifle

6 tablespoons all-purpose flour
½ teaspoon double-acting baking powder
¼ teaspoon salt
2 egg whites
sugar
6 egg yolks
vanilla extract
½ cup raspberry jam
¼ cup cream sherry
½ cup crushed macaroons (about 6)
2 cups milk

1 cup heavy or whipping cream, whipped
candied red cherries (optional)
toasted slivered almonds (optional)

Color index page 97

Begin early in day or day ahead

8 servings

377 cals per serving

1 Grease bottom of 9-inch round cake pan; line with waxed paper. In cup with fork, mix flour, baking powder and salt. In small bowl with mixer at high speed, beat egg whites until soft peaks form; gradually sprinkle in 3 tablespoons sugar, beating until sugar is dissolved and whites stand in stiff glossy peaks. In medium bowl at high speed, beat 2 egg yolks, ¼ cup sugar and ¼ teaspoon vanilla extract just until thick.

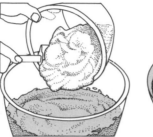

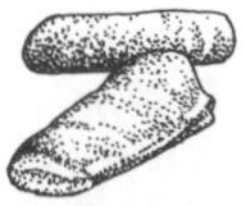

2 Preheat oven to 375°F. Sprinkle flour mixture over beaten yolk mixture in medium bowl.

3 Add beaten egg whites to mixtures in medium bowl, then with rubber spatula, gently fold until blended. Spread batter evenly in pan.

4 Bake 15 minutes until top springs back when touched with finger. Cool in pan on wire rack 10 minutes; remove from pan and cool on wire rack.

5 With knife, cut cake horizontally in half; spread lower half with jam. Replace top.

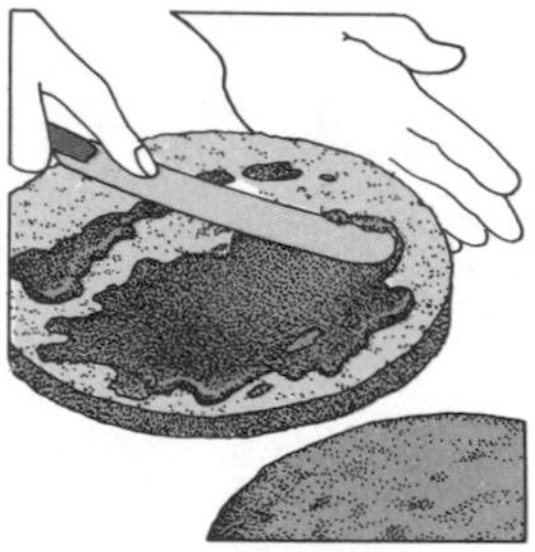

6 Cut layers into bite-size pieces and place randomly in bottom of deep, 1½-quart glass bowl.

7 Sprinkle with sherry. Reserve 2 tablespoons macaroons; sprinkle remainder over cake; set aside.

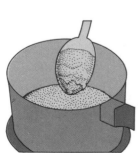

8 In 2-quart saucepan over low heat, cook milk, 4 egg yolks and 3 tablespoons sugar, stirring, until thickened. Remove from heat; add ½ teaspoon vanilla extract.

9 Pour custard over cake pieces in bowl. Cover surface with plastic wrap; refrigerate about 2 hours. Sprinkle the reserved crushed macaroons over custard surface.

10 Spoon whipped cream into pastry bag with large rosette tube; use to decorate custard. Garnish with candied red cherries and the toasted slivered almonds.

Color index page 98

Begin 5 hrs ahead or early in day

8 turnovers   444 cals each

Apple Turnovers

2 cups all-purpose flour
1 teaspoon salt
1 cup butter or margarine
½ cup iced water
2 apples, peeled, cored and sliced
½ cup sugar
1 tablespoon cornstarch

1 teaspoon lemon juice
¼ teaspoon ground cinnamon
1 egg
water
½ cup confectioners' sugar

1. In medium bowl with pastry blender, combine flour and salt. Cut in ½ cup butter until mixture resembles coarse crumbs. Sprinkle with iced water. With fork, mix well. Shape dough into a ball; with lightly floured rolling pin on lightly floured surface, roll into an 18″ by 8″ rectangle. Cut ¼ cup butter into thin slices. Starting at one of the 8-inch sides, place butter slices over ⅔ of rectangle to within ½ inch of edges.

2. Fold unbuttered ⅓ of pastry over middle ⅓; fold opposite end over to make an 8″ by 6″ rectangle. Roll dough into an 18″ by 8″ rectangle.

3. Slice remaining ¼ cup butter; place slices on dough and fold as in steps 1 and 2; wrap in plastic wrap. Chill 15 minutes. Roll folded dough into an 18″ by 8″ rectangle. Fold lengthwise then crosswise; wrap and chill 1 hour.

4. Prepare filling: In saucepan with spoon, mix apples, sugar, cornstarch, lemon juice and cinnamon. Cook over low heat, stirring frequently, until apples are tender. Chill.

5. Preheat oven to 450°F. Cut dough crosswise in half; roll one half into a 12-inch square (keep rest chilled); cut into four 6-inch squares. In cup, beat egg with 1 tablespoon water. Brush mixture over squares. Spoon ⅛ of apple mixture in center of each and fold in half; press edges to seal. Place on ungreased cookie sheet. Chill while preparing other half of pastry.

6. Brush turnovers with egg mixture. Cut a few slashes on each. Bake 20 minutes or until golden. Cool on wire rack.

7. In bowl, combine confectioners' sugar and 1 tablespoon water; drizzle over turnovers.

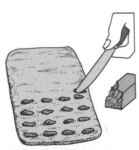

Adding butter to dough: Dot slices of butter over ⅔ of the dough rectangle to within no more than ½ inch of the edges.

Folding dough: Fold unbuttered ⅓ of pastry over middle ⅓; fold opposite end over top making a rectangle.

Color index
page 96

Begin up to
3 days ahead

16 servings

647 cals per
serving

Chocolate-Cinnamon Torte

2 cups sugar
1½ cups butter, softened
2 eggs
2 tablespoons ground
   cinnamon
2⅔ cups all-purpose
   flour

3 squares semisweet
   chocolate
4 cups heavy or whipping
   cream
¾ cup cocoa

1. Tear 14 sheets of waxed paper, each about 9½ inches long. On one sheet, trace bottom of 9-inch round cake pan. Evenly stack all sheets with pattern on top. With kitchen shears, cut out circles.

2. Into large bowl, measure sugar, butter, eggs, cinnamon and 2 cups flour. With mixer at low speed, beat ingredients until well mixed, constantly scraping bowl with rubber spatula. Increase speed to medium; beat mixture 3 minutes or until very light and fluffy, occasionally scraping bowl. With spoon, stir in remaining flour to make a soft dough.

3. Preheat oven to 375°F. With damp cloth, moisten 1 large or 2 small cookie sheets. Place 2 waxed-paper circles onto large cookie sheet or 1 on each small cookie sheet. With metal spatula, spread a scant ⅓ cup dough in a very thin layer onto each circle. Bake layers 8 to 12 minutes or until lightly browned around the edges.

4. Remove cookie sheet to wire rack; cool 5 minutes. With pancake turner, carefully remove cookie still on waxed paper to wire rack to cool completely. (Allow cookie sheet to cool before spreading waxed-paper circles with more dough. The more sheets you have the faster you can bake the cookies.) Repeat until all dough is baked. Carefully stack cooled cookies on a flat plate; cover with plastic wrap and store in a cool, dry place.

5. *Early in day or day ahead:* Coarsely grate chocolate squares; set aside. In large bowl with mixer at medium speed, beat cream and cocoa until soft peaks form.

6. Carefully peel off paper from one cookie; place on flat cake plate; spread with about ½ cup whipped mixture. Repeat layering until all cookies are used, ending with whipped mixture on top.

7. Pile grated chocolate on top of cake; refrigerate until serving time or at least 3 hours before serving so cookies soften for easier cutting.

Shaping cookies: With metal spatula, spread dough in very thin layer on each of the waxed-paper circles.

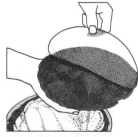

Assembling torte: Peel off paper and layer cookies spread with whipped mixture, ending with mixture on top.

GARNISHES FOR DESSERTS

Chocolate Leaves: Prepare chocolate sheet from Chocolate Leaves (below). Using leaf as guide or with chilled leaf-shaped cookie cutter, cut leaves from chocolate sheet.

With chilled, small metal spatula, carefully lift chocolate leaves from sheet. Arrange around dish of dessert or Almond-Cream Bombe (page 375), on cakes, pies or tortes.

Glazed Orange Peel: To prepare, see below. Use to top cold soufflés, cheesecake or ice cream.

Chopped nuts: Use favorite kind to top creamy and frozen desserts, cakes and tortes.

GLAZED ORANGE PEEL: With vegetable peeler, cut peel from *2 medium oranges* in 1-inch-wide strips. With knife, cut peel crosswise in ⅛-inch-wide strips. In 1-quart saucepan over high heat, heat peel and *½ cup water* to boiling; reduce heat to low; simmer 5 minutes, stirring often. Drain. To peel, add *½ cup light corn syrup;* over medium heat, heat to boiling; reduce heat to low and simmer 5 minutes, stirring often. With fork, lift peel onto waxed paper; cool 10 minutes. (Use syrup on pancakes.)

WHIPPED CREAM: With hand beater or mixer at medium speed, beat well-chilled *heavy or whipping cream* just until soft or stiff peaks form, depending on use. (Overbeating causes cream to turn to butter.) On hot days, chill bowl and beaters. Cream doubles in volume when beaten.

SWEETENED WHIPPED CREAM: For *each cup heavy or whipping cream,* add *1 to 2 tablespoons sugar* and *1 teaspoon vanilla extract* or ¼ teaspoon almond extract or dry sherry to taste. Beat as above.

CHOCOLATE WHIPPED CREAM: Place *2 tablespoons instant-cocoa mix* (or 2 tablespoons sugar and 2 tablespoons cocoa) in small bowl; add *1 cup heavy or whipping cream.* With hand beater or mixer at low speed, beat just until soft peaks form.

CHOCOLATE LEAVES: In double boiler over hot, *not boiling,* water, heat *one 6-ounce package semisweet-chocolate pieces* (1 cup) and *1 tablespoon shortening* until smooth, stirring occasionally. With small metal spatula, spread a thin layer of chocolate mixture on sheet of waxed paper. Place chocolate-coated sheet on cookie sheet; refrigerate 20 minutes or until firm. Cut into leaf shapes as directed above.

Other desserts

Chocolate Fancy

Color index page 96

Begin early in day or day ahead

16 servings

481 cals per serving

Strawberry-Almond Cream:
2 pints strawberries, hulled
4 envelopes unflavored gelatin
1/2 teaspoon salt
sugar
6 eggs, separated
3 1/2 cups milk
2 teaspoons almond extract
1 cup heavy or whipping cream

Chocolate Cake:
1 cup cake flour
3/4 cup sugar

1 1/2 teaspoons double-acting baking powder
1/2 teaspoon salt
1/4 cup salad oil
3 eggs, separated
1 square unsweetened chocolate, melted
1/4 cup water
1/4 teaspoon cream of tartar

Chocolate Coating (right)

1. Prepare Strawberry-Almond Cream: In covered blender container, blend 1 pint strawberries until pureed. Dice remaining strawberries.
2. In heavy, 3-quart saucepan, combine gelatin, salt and 1/2 cup sugar. In small bowl with wire whisk, beat egg yolks and milk; gradually stir into gelatin mixture until blended. Cook over medium-low heat, stirring, until mixture thickens and coats a spoon, about 20 minutes. Stir in almond extract, strawberry puree and diced strawberries. Remove pan from heat; cool slightly; place in large bowl; fill bowl with ice cubes and cold water to come halfway up side. (Add more ice if needed to keep water *very* cold.) Stir mixture often until mixture mounds from spoon, about 30 minutes.
3. Meanwhile, line 2 1/2-quart bowl (about 9 inches in diameter) with plastic wrap, leaving overhang.
4. In large bowl with mixer at high speed, beat egg whites until soft peaks form. Beating at high speed, sprinkle in 3/4 cup sugar, beating until sugar is dissolved. Using same beaters, in small bowl with mixer at medium speed, beat half the heavy cream until soft peaks form. With wire whisk, gently fold whipped cream and strawberry mixture into egg-white mixture. Spoon into prepared bowl; cover and refrigerate until firm, about 2 hours.
5. Prepare Chocolate Cake: Preheat oven to 350°F. In large bowl with spoon, stir flour, sugar, baking powder and salt until blended. Stir in salad oil, egg yolks, chocolate and water until smooth.
6. In large bowl with mixer at high speed, beat egg whites and cream of tartar until stiff peaks form; fold in chocolate mixture. Pour batter into an ungreased 9-inch round cake pan. Bake 30 minutes or until cake springs back when lightly touched. Invert cake *with pan* on rack; cool 1 hour. Meanwhile, prepare Chocolate Coating (right).
7. Remove cake from pan; place on cake plate. In small bowl with mixer at medium speed, beat remaining cream until soft peaks form; spread over top of cake. Assemble dessert (right) and chill.
8. *To serve:* Remove dessert from refrigerator; let stand about 20 minutes to soften chocolate slightly for easier slicing. Dip sharp knife in hot water then carefully cut cake into even-sized wedges.

CHOCOLATE COATING: Cut waxed paper into five 8″ by 7″ sheets and one 17″ by 5″ sheet. Place sheets on 3 large cookie sheets; set aside. In double boiler over hot, *not boiling*, water (or in heavy, 1-quart saucepan over low heat), heat *one 12-ounce package semisweet-chocolate pieces*, *1/4 cup butter* or margarine, *1/4 cup light corn syrup* until chocolate is melted and mixture is smooth, about 5 minutes. Remove double boiler from heat. On each 8″ by 7″ waxed paper sheet, with metal spatula, spread about 1/4 cup chocolate mixture. Spread remaining chocolate mixture on 17″ by 5″ sheet. Chill 2 hours.

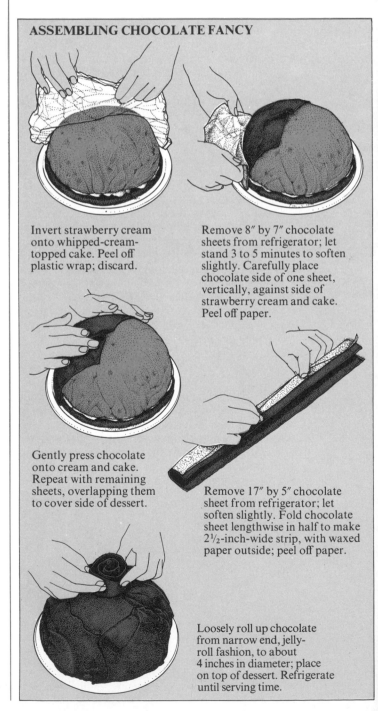

ASSEMBLING CHOCOLATE FANCY

Invert strawberry cream onto whipped-cream-topped cake. Peel off plastic wrap; discard.

Remove 8″ by 7″ chocolate sheets from refrigerator; let stand 3 to 5 minutes to soften slightly. Carefully place chocolate side of one sheet, vertically, against side of strawberry cream and cake. Peel off paper.

Gently press chocolate onto cream and cake. Repeat with remaining sheets, overlapping them to cover side of dessert.

Remove 17″ by 5″ chocolate sheet from refrigerator; let soften slightly. Fold chocolate sheet lengthwise in half to make 2 1/2-inch-wide strip, with waxed paper outside; peel off paper.

Loosely roll up chocolate from narrow end, jelly-roll fashion, to about 4 inches in diameter; place on top of dessert. Refrigerate until serving time.

Steamed Pudding

2¼ cups all-purpose
flour
1 cup sugar
1 cup fresh bread crumbs
1 teaspoon double-acting
baking powder
1 teaspoon salt
½ teaspoon ground
cinnamon
½ teaspoon ground
cloves
butter or margarine
1 cup chopped pitted
dates
1 cup peeled chopped
apple

½ cup chopped
California walnuts
1 cup buttermilk
½ cup dark molasses
2 eggs
1 cup confectioners'
sugar
½ teaspoon vanilla
extract
½ cup brandy or liqueur
holly leaves for garnish

Color index page 96
Begin 4 hrs ahead
12 servings
541 cals per serving

1 Heavily grease a 2½-quart bowl; cut foil with 1-inch overhang to cover bowl. Grease well one side of foil circle. Set aside.

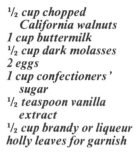

2 In large bowl, combine flour, sugar, bread crumbs, baking powder, salt, cinnamon and cloves.

3 With pastry blender, cut in 1 cup butter until mixture resembles coarse crumbs; add dates.

4 Add apple and nuts, then stir in buttermilk, molasses and eggs. Pour into prepared bowl.

5 With foil, greased side down, cover mixture in bowl. Tie foil to bowl tightly with string.

6 Place metal trivet in 12-quart saucepot. Set bowl on trivet. Pour water into pot to about 1 inch below rim of foil. Cover pot. (If needed, add more water during cooking.)

7 Over high heat, heat water to boiling. Reduce heat to low; simmer 3½ hours or until toothpick inserted through foil comes out clean.

8 For sauce, in small bowl with mixer at medium speed, beat ⅓ cup butter, confectioners' sugar and vanilla until creamy.

9 Cool pudding in bowl on rack 5 minutes. In 1-quart pan, heat brandy to lukewarm. Invert pudding onto warm platter.

10 Top with holly; pour brandy over and ignite; when alcohol burns off, serve Steamed Pudding with sauce.

Color index page 96
Begin day ahead
8 servings   586 cals per serving

Almond-Cream Bombe

1 4-ounce can blanched
whole almonds
(about ¾ cup)
1 10¾- or 12-ounce
ready-to-serve frozen
pound cake,
thawed
¼ cup almond-flavor
liqueur

½ 6-ounce package
semisweet-chocolate
pieces (½ cup)
2 cups heavy or whipping
cream
⅔ cup confectioners'
sugar
⅛ teaspoon salt

1. In 9″ by 9″ baking pan, toast the blanched whole almonds in 375°F. oven until golden, about 10 minutes, stirring occasionally; cool thoroughly; with a sharp knife, chop almonds coarsely.
2. Meanwhile, line 1½-quart round-bottom bowl with plastic wrap; set aside. Cut pound cake into ¼-inch-thick slices; cut each slice diagonally in half to make 2 triangles. Sprinkle with almond-flavor liqueur. Use triangles with top brown cake crust first to line bowl, with narrow points at bottom of bowl, so that brown crusts form a pinwheel design. Complete lining bowl by placing more cake triangles around inside of bowl, making sure there are no spaces between triangles. Reserve any remaining cake triangles.
3. In heavy, 1-quart saucepan over low heat, place chocolate pieces; stir occasionally until chocolate is melted; cool slightly.
4. In large bowl with mixer at medium speed, beat heavy or whipping cream, confectioners' sugar and salt until the mixture stands in soft peaks. Fold in the toasted chopped almonds.
5. Spread ⅔ whipped cream evenly over cake in bowl. Fold melted chocolate into remaining whipped-cream mixture; use to fill center of dessert. Top the dessert with the remaining cake triangles. Cover the dish with plastic wrap and leave in the refrigerator overnight.
6. *To serve:* Remove top sheet of plastic wrap. Invert bowl onto chilled serving plate; remove and discard plastic wrap. With a sharp knife, carefully cut dessert into wedges.

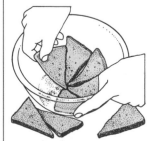

Lining the bowl: Arrange cake triangles in pinwheel design then completely line bowl with triangles making sure that there are no spaces.

Covering the filling: Top dessert with remaining cake triangles. Cover the bowl with plastic wrap and leave to chill overnight.

ICE CREAM AND SHERBET

Ice cream, ice milk and sherbet are all favorite frozen desserts. Commercial *ice cream* and *ice milk* are basically mixtures of milk fat, non-fat milk solids, sweeteners and flavorings. Ice cream has the highest butterfat content of all frozen desserts. Ice milk has about half the butterfat of ice cream but contains more sweetener. *Sherbet* is virtually fat-free while *fruit ices* are a fat-free mixture of water, sugar and fruit. *Frozen, low-fat yogurts* are made with skim milk, non-fat milk solids, yogurt cultures, fruit, fruit flavorings and jelling agents or emulsifiers and stabilizers.

Frozen desserts are easy to make at home. When using a churn-type ice-cream freezer, fill the freezer can only as full as the manufacturer directs, to allow for expansion—any excess mixture may be frozen in an ice-cube tray. After freezing, transfer the mixture from the ice-cream freezer to a chilled container and place in home freezer a few hours to harden or pack in ice-cream freezer as directed in recipe. If using an ice-cube tray, about 1 hour before serving, remove mixture to a bowl and beat at medium speed until smooth; return to tray; keep frozen until serving time. To serve, stand at room temperature 10 minutes for easier scooping.

Keep some trays specially for desserts since ice cubes tend to stick in trays previously used for freezing desserts. You can tell when a mixture is partially frozen because it will be frozen firm to 1 inch in from the edge, with a soft, mushy center.

Ice cream

Homemade Vanilla Ice Cream

2 cups sugar
6 tablespoons all-purpose flour
1 teaspoon salt
5 cups milk
6 eggs
4 cups half-and-half
3 tablespoons vanilla extract
20 pounds cracked ice
2 to 3 pounds rock salt

Color index page 102

Begin early in day or up to 1 month ahead

3 quarts or 12 servings

358 cals per serving

1 In heavy, 3-quart saucepan with spoon, combine sugar, flour and salt. In medium bowl with hand beater or wire whisk, beat milk and eggs together until well blended; stir into sugar mixture until smooth. Cook over low heat, stirring constantly, until the mixture thickens and coats a spoon, about 30 to 45 minutes, being sure custard does not boil or it will curdle. Remove saucepan from the heat.

2 Cover the surface of the thickened mixture with waxed paper and refrigerate until thoroughly cooled, approximately 2 hours.

3 Pour the half-and-half, vanilla extract and cooled custard mixture into 4-quart ice-cream freezer can.

4 Place dasher in the ice-cream freezer can; put lid on can and place can in bucket; attach motor or hand crank to the freezer can.

5 Fill bucket half full with ice; sprinkle with ¼ cup rock salt. Add 1 inch ice and ¼ cup salt; repeat to 1 inch below can lid.

6 Freeze according to manufacturer's directions, adding more ice and salt as needed. Freezing will take 35 to 45 minutes.

7 Remove motor or hand crank; wipe can lid and remove; remove dasher. With spoon, pack down the soft ice cream.

8 Cover opening of the freezer can with waxed paper and then replace the can lid; put cork in the hole in center.

9 Add more ice and salt to cover can lid. Let stand to harden ice cream, 2 to 3 hours, adding more ice and salt as needed.

Ice cream

ICE CREAM VARIATIONS

598 cals per serving

HOME-FREEZER METHOD: Prepare egg mixture as in step 1 of Homemade Vanilla Ice Cream, but use *1 cup sugar, 3 tablespoons all-purpose flour, ½ teaspoon salt, 2½ cups milk* and *3 eggs;* cook about 15 minutes; cool. Stir in *2 cups heavy or whipping cream* and *5 teaspoons vanilla extract.* Pour into 9″ by 9″ pan; cover; freeze until frozen but still soft, 3 to 4 hours; spoon into large bowl. Beat at medium speed until smooth but still frozen; return to pan; cover; freeze until firm. (Makes 6 cups or 6 servings.)

Color index page 102
384 cals per serving

CHOCOLATE: Prepare egg mixture as in step 1 of Homemade Vanilla Ice Cream, but omit 1 cup milk. While mixture is cooling, in 1-quart saucepan over low heat, melt *8 squares unsweetened chocolate;* stir in *¾ cup sugar* and *1 cup hot water* until blended; chill. In 4-quart freezer can, combine egg mixture, chocolate mixture, half-and-half and vanilla; freeze. (Makes 3 quarts or 12 servings.)

Color index page 102
331 cals per serving

PEACH: Prepare egg mixture as in step 1 of Homemade Vanilla Ice Cream; while mixture is cooling, in covered blender container at low speed, blend *10 to 12 ripe peaches,* peeled and cut up, and *½ cup sugar* until smooth. In 4-quart freezer can, stir peaches, egg mixture, only *2 cups half-and-half* and *¾ teaspoon almond extract* instead of vanilla; freeze. (Makes 7 pints or 14 servings.)

Color index page 102
255 cals per serving

STRAWBERRY: Prepare as for Homemade Vanilla Ice Cream but, while egg mixture is cooling, in medium bowl with potato masher, crush *1½ pints strawberries,* hulled, *1 cup sugar* and *2 tablespoons lemon juice;* let stand about 1 hour. In 4-quart freezer can, stir well egg mixture, half-and-half, strawberries and *¼ teaspoon red food color;* freeze. (Makes 4 quarts or 16 servings.)

Color index page 102
490 cals per serving

PISTACHIO: Prepare egg mixture as in step 1 of Homemade Vanilla Ice Cream, but use *1 cup sugar, 3 tablespoons all-purpose flour, ½ teaspoon salt, 2½ cups milk* and *3 eggs* and cook about 15 minutes. In step 3, use only *2 cups half-and-half* and, for vanilla, substitute *⅛ teaspoon green food color* and *¼ teaspoon almond extract;* freeze about 20 minutes. While mixture is freezing, coarsely chop *1½ cups salted pistachio nuts.* Remove dasher. With long-handled spoon, stir in nuts. Cover can and harden. (Makes 3 pints or 6 servings.)

Color index page 102
292 cals per serving

SPICED BANANA: Prepare egg mixture as in step 1 of Homemade Vanilla Ice Cream, but use *1 cup sugar, 3 tablespoons all-purpose flour, ½ teaspoon salt, 2½ cups milk* and *3 eggs;* cook about 15 minutes. While mixture is cooling, in blender container, dissolve *1 tablespoon ascorbic-acid mixture for fruit* in *¼ cup water;* add *6 ripe, firm, medium bananas,* cut up, to mixture. (Too-ripe bananas will over-flavor and color ice cream.) Add *⅓ cup sugar* and *1½ teaspoons ground cinnamon;* cover and blend until smooth. In 4- to 6-quart freezer can, stir egg and banana mixtures, only *2 cups half-and-half;* omit vanilla. Freeze 20 minutes. (Makes 5 pints or 10 servings.)

Color index page 102
Begin 6 hrs or up to 1 month ahead
6 quarts or 24 servings
311 cals per serving

Peppermint-Candy Ice Cream

6 cups half-and-half
3 14-ounce cans sweetened condensed milk
2 cups milk

3 tablespoons vanilla extract
1 cup water
2 cups coarsely crushed peppermint candies

1. In 6-quart ice-cream freezer can, stir first 5 ingredients with 1 cup peppermint candies; refrigerate 1 hour or until thoroughly chilled.
2. Remove can from refrigerator and prepare as in steps 4 to 9 of Homemade Vanilla Ice Cream but in step 7, with spoon, stir in remaining candies.

HOME-FREEZER METHOD: In large bowl, stir *one 14-ounce can sweetened condensed milk, 1 cup water, 1 tablespoon vanilla extract* and half of *⅔ cup coarsely crushed peppermint candies;* fold in *2 cups heavy or whipping cream,* whipped. Pour into 12″ by 8″ pan; cover; freeze 1 hour. Spoon into large bowl. With mixer at medium speed, beat until smooth; fold in remaining candies. Refreeze until firm. (Makes 6 cups or 6 servings.)

PARFAIT IDEAS

Parfaits are layers of ice cream and dessert sauce, fruit, jelly or candy; serve them in parfait, sherbet or small iced-tea glasses.

For chocolate parfaits, alternate layers of vanilla ice cream with Chocolate Sauce (page 464). Garnish with whipped cream and shaved chocolate.

For fruit-cocktail parfaits, alternate layers of vanilla ice cream with chilled canned fruit cocktail mixed with seedless grapes and grated orange peel.

For raspberry-macaroon parfaits, layer vanilla ice cream and thawed frozen raspberries. Top each individual serving with crumbled macaroons.

Ice milk

Strawberry Ice Milk

1 quart milk
1 envelope unflavored
gelatin
3/4 cup sugar
2 teaspoons vanilla
extract

1/4 teaspoon salt
1 pint strawberries,
hulled
6 drops red food color
(optional)

Color index
page 102

Begin early
in day or
day ahead

2 quarts or
12 servings

112 cals per
serving

1 In 3-quart saucepan,
over 1 cup milk, evenly
sprinkle gelatin. Cook over
medium-low heat, stirring,
until gelatin is dissolved.

2 Remove saucepan from
heat; stir in remaining
milk, sugar, vanilla extract
and salt.

3 Pour into 13″ by 9″
baking pan; cover with
foil and freeze about
3 hours until partially
frozen. Crush straw-
berries; set aside.

4 In covered blender
container at medium
speed, blend half of milk
mixture until smooth but
still frozen. Pour into chilled bowl; repeat.

5 Fold crushed straw-
berries and red food
color into milk mixture
just until mixed.

6 Return mixture to baking pan; cover; freeze 2
hours until firm, stirring
occasionally. *To serve:*
Let stand 10 minutes
before scooping.

130 cals per
serving

PEACH ICE MILK: Prepare milk mixture as above
but use *1/2 teaspoon almond extract* for vanilla; omit
berries and food color. In blender, blend *4 cups
peeled, diced peaches* and *1/4 cup lemon juice*. Stir into
milk mixture; pour into pan; freeze 3 hours. Spoon
into large bowl; with mixer at medium speed, beat
until smooth. Freeze 2 hours. Beat again and freeze.
Serve as above.

Ice-cream desserts

Baked Alaska Pie

18 ladyfingers, split
1/3 cup orange-flavor
liqueur
1 10-ounce package
frozen raspberries,
slightly thawed
3 pints vanilla ice cream,
slightly softened
4 egg whites, at room
temperature
1/4 teaspoon salt
1/8 teaspoon cream of
tartar
2/3 cup sugar

Color index
page 102

Begin 5 hrs
or up to
2 wks ahead

12 servings

339 cals per
serving

1 Line 9-inch pie plate
with about 2/3 of lady-
fingers, allowing ends to
extend over rim; sprinkle
with half of liqueur.

2 In medium bowl with
potato masher, crush
raspberries to make a
paste consistency.

3 In large bowl, stir ice
cream slightly. Spoon
on berries; cut through
mixture to create "ripple"

4 Keeping ripples, spoon
1/2 mixture into plate.
Layer remaining fingers on
top; sprinkle with remaining liqueur. Spoon on re-
maining ice cream. Freeze
until firm, 4 hours.

5 *About 20 minutes before
serving:* Preheat oven
to 500°F. In large bowl
with mixer at high speed,
beat egg whites, salt and
cream of tartar until soft
peaks form.

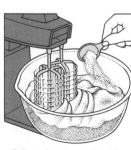

6 Beat in sugar, 2 tablespoons at a time, beat-
ing at high speed till sugar
is dissolved and whites
stand in stiff peaks.

7 Quickly spread meringue over top of pie, sealing to edge; swirl up points.
Bake 3 to 4 minutes till light
brown. Serve at once.

Ice-Cream Bombe Les Dames d'Escoffier

3 pints vanilla or coffee
ice cream
2 pints strawberry ice
cream or raspberry
sherbet
1/2 7.8-ounce bag almond
brickle chips for
baking
1 cup heavy or whipping
cream
1/4 teaspoon vanilla
extract
2 tablespoons
confectioners' sugar
strawberries for
garnish

Chocolate Sauce:
3/4 cup sugar
1/2 cup cocoa
1/2 cup heavy or whipping
cream
1/4 cup butter or
margarine
1 1/2 teaspoons vanilla
extract

Color index page 103
Begin early in day or up to
2 wks ahead
12 servings
574 cals per serving

1 Remove vanilla ice cream from freezer; let stand in refrigerator until softened; then, spread the ice cream evenly to line deep, 2 1/2-quart mold or bowl.

2 Cover and freeze about 30 minutes or until ice cream is firm. Meanwhile, soften strawberry ice cream in same way.

3 Spread strawberry ice cream evenly over vanilla ice cream, leaving a well in center of mold; freeze until firm.

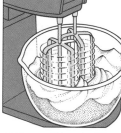

4 Spoon almond brickle chips into the well in center of mold.

5 In sink of warm water, quickly dip mold to loosen ice-cream bombe.

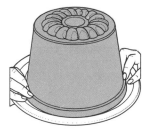

6 Invert large, chilled platter on top of mold; invert mold and platter; gently lift off mold; freeze.

7 In small bowl with mixer at medium speed, beat cream, vanilla and sugar till stiff peaks form.

8 Spoon whipped-cream mixture into pastry bag fitted with large rosette tube; use to decorate bombe; freeze.

9 About 10 minutes before serving: Remove bombe from freezer; garnish top of bombe with strawberries; let stand 10 minutes for easier slicing. Prepare Chocolate Sauce: In heavy, 2-quart saucepan over medium heat, cook sugar, cocoa, cream and butter or margarine until the mixture is smooth and boils. Remove from heat; stir in vanilla extract. Keep the Chocolate Sauce warm until ready to serve bombe.

10 To serve: Cut a wedge; place on a dessert plate. Spoon over some candy from center of bombe. Serve with sauce.

Color index page 102
Begin day or up to 2 wks ahead
10 servings   349 cals per serving

Nesselrode Ice Cream Mold

1/3 cup diced candied
orange peel
1/3 cup candied cherries,
chopped
1/3 cup golden raisins,
chopped
1/3 cup black walnuts,
chopped

3 pints French vanilla ice
cream, slightly
softened
1 3-ounce package
ladyfingers
6 tablespoons brandy or
orange-flavor
liqueur

1. In large bowl, stir first 5 ingredients until just mixed. Spoon 1/3 of ice-cream mixture into 7-cup mold. Split 1/3 of ladyfingers and press lightly into ice-cream mixture, overlapping slightly if necessary; drizzle with 2 tablespoons brandy. Repeat layering twice. Cover and freeze.

2. About 1 hour before serving: With metal spatula, loosen edges of frozen mixture from mold. In large bowl of hot water, quickly dip mold almost to top to loosen; dry mold with towel. Unmold onto freezer-safe platter. Return to freezer.

OTHER COMBINATIONS: Instead of candied orange peel, cherries and golden raisins, use *two 4-ounce jars mixed candied fruit*. Substitute *California walnuts,* almonds or pecans for black walnuts; use *rum* instead of brandy.

Color index page 103
Begin early in day or up to 1 month ahead
12 servings   597 cals per serving

Rainbow Ice-Cream Torte

2 pints chocolate ice
cream
2 pints chocolate-chip-
mint ice cream
2 pints strawberry ice
cream
2 pints vanilla ice cream
2 1/2 cups gingersnap
crumbs

1/2 cup butter or
margarine, melted
2 17-ounce cans pitted
dark sweet cherries,
drained
1/2 cup chopped
California walnuts

1. Soften ice cream in refrigerator about 30 minutes. Meanwhile, in 10-inch springform pan, combine gingersnap crumbs and butter or margarine. With hands, firmly press crumb mixture into bottom of springform pan; chill in freezer 10 minutes or until mixture is firm.

2. On top of crumb mixture, evenly spread the chocolate ice cream, then the chocolate-chip-mint ice cream, drained sweet cherries, strawberry ice cream and end with the vanilla ice cream. Sprinkle the top evenly with chopped California walnuts. Cover the torte and freeze until firm.

3. To serve: Run knife or metal spatula, dipped in hot water, around edge of pan to loosen ice cream. Remove side of springform pan. Allow the ice cream torte to stand at room temperature 10 minutes for easier slicing.

Sherbet

Pineapple Sherbet

³/₄ cup sugar
¹/₂ cup water
1 large pineapple
3 tablespoons lemon juice
2 egg whites, at room temperature

Color index page 102

Begin early in day or day ahead

5 cups or 8 servings

128 cals per serving

1 In 1-quart saucepan over medium heat, heat sugar and water to boiling, stirring the mixture constantly. Remove saucepan from heat.

2 With sharp knife, cut crown and stem end off pineapple; cut off rind; remove eyes. Cut pineapple in half; remove core. Cut pineapple into small chunks.

3 In covered blender container at medium speed, blend pineapple until smooth. Strain into large bowl; with spoon, press out all juice and discard fibers.

4 Stir sugar mixture and lemon juice into pineapple. In small bowl with mixer at high speed, beat egg whites into stiff peaks.

5 Fold beaten egg whites into pineapple mixture. Pour into 13″ by 9″ baking pan. Cover with foil and freeze until firm, 3 hours.

6 Spoon pineapple mixture into chilled large bowl; with mixer at low speed, beat until softened. Increase speed to medium and beat until fluffy but still frozen; return to baking pan. Cover with foil. Freeze 2 hours until partially frozen. Spoon into chilled large bowl and beat again as above. Return mixture to baking pan; cover again with foil and freeze until firm.

7 *To serve:* Let sherbet stand at room temperature 10 minutes. Scoop into serving dishes.

Cantaloupe Sherbet

1 small very ripe cantaloupe
1 quart milk
2 envelopes unflavored gelatin
³/₄ cup light corn syrup

¹/₂ cup sugar
³/₄ teaspoon salt
3 drops yellow food color
1 drop red food color

Color index page 102

Begin early in day or up to 1 month ahead

2 quarts or 12 servings

150 cals per serving

1. Cut cantaloupe in half; discard seeds and peel. Cut cantaloupe into bite-size chunks. In covered blender container at medium speed, blend cantaloupe and 1 cup milk until smooth; set aside.
2. In 3-quart saucepan over 1 cup milk, evenly sprinkle gelatin. Cook over medium-low heat, stirring, until gelatin is dissolved. Remove from heat; stir in cantaloupe mixture, remaining milk and remaining ingredients (mixture may look curdled). Pour mixture into 13″ by 9″ baking pan. Cover and freeze until partially frozen, about 3 hours, stirring mixture occasionally.
3. Spoon cantaloupe mixture into chilled large bowl; with mixer at medium speed, beat until smooth but still frozen; return to pan. Cover; freeze until firm, about 3 hours.
4. *To serve:* Let sherbet stand at room temperature 10 minutes for easier scooping.

Minted Sherbet Ring with Berries

3 pints lemon sherbet, slightly softened
¹/₃ cup green crème de menthe

2 pints strawberries, hulled
shredded coconut for garnish

Color index page 103

Begin early in day or day ahead

10 servings

230 cals per serving

1. In large bowl with mixer at medium speed, beat sherbet with crème de menthe until smooth; spoon into a 5¹/₂-cup ring mold; freezer-wrap; freeze.
2. *To serve:* With metal spatula, loosen edges of frozen mixture from mold. In sink of hot water, quickly dip frozen mixture almost to top to loosen; dry mold with towel. Invert mold onto platter; remove mold. Fill center of ring with strawberries; sprinkle with coconut.

Orange Milk Sherbet

5 cups milk
1 envelope unflavored gelatin
1¹/₂ cups sugar
1 cup orange juice
¹/₄ cup grated orange peel

¹/₄ cup lemon juice
³/₄ teaspoon salt
¹/₄ teaspoon yellow food color
¹/₈ teaspoon red food color

Color index page 102

Begin early in day or up to 1 month ahead

2 quarts or 12 servings

171 cals per serving

1. In 3-quart saucepan over 1 cup milk, evenly sprinkle gelatin. Cook over medium-low heat, stirring, until gelatin is dissolved. Remove pan from heat; stir in remaining ingredients and milk (mixture may look curdled). Pour mixture into 13″ by 9″ baking pan. Cover; freeze until partially frozen, about 3 hours, stirring occasionally.
2. Spoon mixture into chilled large bowl; with mixer at medium speed, beat until smooth but still frozen; return to pan. Cover; freeze until firm.
3. *To serve:* Let sherbet stand at room temperature 10 minutes for easier scooping.

Fruit ices

Lemon Ice in Lemon Cups

6 large lemons
1 envelope unflavored
gelatin
1 cup sugar
2¼ cups water
mint sprigs
for garnish

Color index page 103

Begin early in day or
day ahead

1 quart or 6 servings

155 cals per serving

1 With sharp knife, cut off ⅓ of each lemon from one end. Grate peel from top ⅓ pieces.

2 Squeeze juice from all pieces of lemon to make approximately ¾ cup. Discard tops.

3 Remove all crushed pulp and membrane from lemon cups; cut a thin slice off bottom of each so they can stand. Place in plastic bag; refrigerate cups.

4 In 1-quart saucepan over low heat, cook gelatin, sugar and water, stirring constantly, until gelatin is dissolved.

5 Remove saucepan from heat; stir in lemon juice and grated lemon peel.

6 Pour mixture into 9" by 9" baking pan; cover with foil or plastic wrap; freeze about 3 hours until partially frozen.

7 Spoon lemon mixture into chilled large bowl; with mixer at medium speed, beat until smooth but still frozen.

8 Return lemon mixture to baking pan; cover; freeze about 2 hours until partially frozen.

9 Spoon mixture into chilled large bowl and with mixer at medium speed, beat again as in step 7. Freeze until firm.

10 *To serve:* Let ice stand at room temperature 10 minutes. Scoop into lemon cups; garnish with mint sprigs.

Begin early in day or day ahead

1 quart or 6 servings

103 cals per serving

ORANGE ICE: In 1-quart saucepan, combine *1 envelope unflavored gelatin* and *½ cup sugar*; stir in *1 cup water*. Over medium heat, heat until gelatin is completely dissolved, stirring constantly. Remove saucepan from heat; stir in *2 cups orange juice, 1 teaspoon grated lemon peel* and *1 tablespoon lemon juice*. Pour into 9" by 9" baking pan and freeze. Spoon orange and lemon mixture into chilled large bowl; beat and serve as Lemon Ice, left, but omit lemon cups and mint sprigs.

Color index page 103

Begin early in day or up to 1 month ahead

10 cups or 20 servings   110 cals per serving

Strawberry-Orange Ice

1½ cups orange juice
½ cup lemon juice
¼ cup orange-flavor
liqueur

3 pints strawberries,
hulled
2 cups sugar

1. In covered blender container at high speed, blend all ingredients until smooth, blending about half at a time; pour mixture into a 9" by 9" baking pan and mix well. Cover with foil or plastic wrap and freeze until partially frozen, about 4 hours.
2. Spoon strawberry-orange mixture into chilled large bowl and, with mixer at medium speed, beat until smooth but still frozen; return mixture to baking pan. Cover with foil or plastic wrap and freeze mixture until firm.
3. *To serve:* Remove mixture from freezer and allow it to stand at room temperature about 10 minutes for easier scooping.

Color index page 103

Begin early in day or up to 1 month ahead

5 cups or 10 servings   40 cals per serving

Watermelon Ice

½ small watermelon,
peeled, seeded and
cut into 1-inch
chunks (about 6 cups)

3 tablespoons
confectioners' sugar
1 tablespoon lemon juice
¼ teaspoon salt

1. In covered blender container at low speed, blend 1 cup watermelon chunks with confectioners' sugar, lemon juice and salt until the mixture is smooth; add remaining watermelon chunks and blend a few seconds longer until smooth. Pour into 9" by 9" baking pan; cover with foil or plastic wrap and freeze until partially frozen, about 2 hours.
2. Into chilled large bowl, spoon watermelon mixture. With mixer at high speed, beat until fluffy. Return mixture to baking pan and freeze until firm, about 1½ hours.
3. *To serve:* Remove Watermelon Ice from freezer and let it stand at room temperature 10 minutes for easier scooping.

CAKES

The cakes in this chapter all follow one of two basic methods. Most of our layer cakes, loaves and cupcakes contain solid shortening, butter or margarine and are mixed and beaten in one bowl. Others, such as angelfood, chiffon and sponge cakes, depend on beaten egg whites or eggs to make them high, light and fluffy. Whichever type you bake, if you follow directions carefully you can be assured of success.

BEFORE MAKING CAKES

Before you start, read the recipe carefully and assemble all ingredients and equipment. Prepare pans, set oven racks in position and preheat the oven. Have all ingredients at room temperature.

Ingredients: Don't substitute; different ingredients give different results. We use Large eggs and double-acting baking powder in our recipes in this book.

Measuring: Measure dry and liquid ingredients in the same way as for Quick Breads (page 421).

Pans: Use shiny metal pans or pans with a non-stick finish. Avoid dull, dark or enamel pans which can cause uneven and excessive browning. If using glass or porcelain-coated aluminum pans with non-stick finish, reduce the oven temperature 25°F. Be sure your pans are the size called for and prepare them as directed. If to be greased and floured, grease bottom and sides generously with solid shortening, using crumpled waxed paper or with melted shortening, using a pastry brush. Then sprinkle the pan with a little flour, shake it until coated, invert it and tap it to remove excess flour. Don't grease pans for angel, chiffon and sponge cakes.

Oven space: Set your oven rack so the center of cake or layers is close to the center of the oven. If using two racks, arrange them so they divide the oven into thirds. Make sure the pans do not touch each other or the sides of the oven and if using more than one rack, stagger the pans so that one is not directly underneath another.

MIXING CAKES

Shortening cakes: Beat ingredients with a mixer for the time and at the speed specified, scraping the bowl often so ingredients are mixed well. If you beat with a wooden spoon, use *150 vigorous strokes for every minute of beating time*. Before baking, cut through batter in pan with knife to remove air bubbles.

Angel, chiffon and sponge cakes: Be sure the bowl for egg whites is free from grease and no traces of yolk are present in the whites. With a rubber spatula, fold ingredients into the beaten egg whites by cutting down through the whites, across the bottom and up the side of the bowl. Give the bowl a quarter turn and repeat just until dry ingredients are no longer visible. Don't overfold or egg whites will break down. Before baking, cut through the batter in the pan with a rubber spatula several times to remove any large air bubbles.

Fruitcake: Toss about ½ cup of the flour with fruits and nuts to coat them so they won't sink in the batter.

TESTING FOR DONENESS

Do not open the oven door to test a cake until the minimum baking time has passed, or the cake might fall.

Test shortening cakes and fruitcakes by inserting a toothpick into the center. It should come out clean and dry. Test angel, chiffon and sponge cakes by pressing the top lightly with a finger. Top should spring back and any cracks on surface should look dry.

COOLING CAKES

Shortening cakes: Leave in the pan on a wire rack for 10 minutes, then run a spatula around the edges to loosen them from the pan and turn the cake out as below.

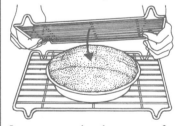

Invert a second rack over top of cake in pan on rack.

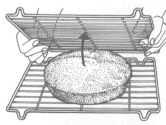

Turn two racks upside down. Remove upper rack; lift off pan.

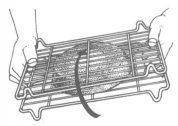

Replace rack; turn two racks over again so cake rests top up.

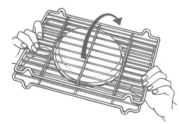

Remove top rack; let cake cool before frosting or storing.

382

Angel, chiffon and sponge cakes: If baked in tube pan, invert pan on a bottle or funnel, so top of cake does not touch counter. Cool completely in pan, then gently cut around pan side and tube with a knife. Invert and shake the cake onto a plate.

Fruitcakes: Cool completely in the pan on a wire rack.

FROSTING CAKES

Allow your cake to cool completely. Before frosting, trim off any crisp edges with kitchen scissors and brush away all loose crumbs. Keep the cake plate clean by covering the edges with strips of waxed paper arranged in a square. Lay the cake on the paper strips, centering it on the plate. After frosting the cake, carefully slide out the paper strips.

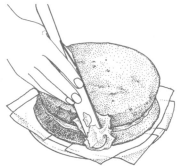

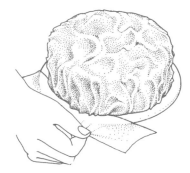

Keeping plate clean: Lay cake on waxed paper strips arranged in square, and frost.

After frosting, carefully slide out strips. If needed, touch up base with a little more frosting.

It's easier to frost a cake evenly if you can turn it as you work. Place cake on a plate on a turntable, lazy Susan or top of a large bowl. Spread frosting with a broad-bladed knife or spatula.

Cutting a cake in layers: With a ruler and toothpicks, mark the cutting line(s) all around a layer or tube cake. With a long, sharp knife, using toothpicks as a guide, cut the layers. Remove toothpicks. If you make a shallow vertical cut in one side of the cake before splitting it, it will be easier to reassemble the layers in their original position; just align the marks when putting the cake together again.

Frosting a layer cake: Place one layer, top side down, on the plate. Spread the layer with filling or frosting almost to edge. If the filling is soft, spread it only to within an inch of the edge – the weight of the top layer will push it to the edge. Place the second layer, top side up, on the filling, so that the flat bottoms of the two layers face each other, keeping the top layer from cracking or sliding off. Frost sides of cake thinly to set any loose crumbs, then apply a second, generous layer of frosting, swirling it up to make a ½-inch ridge above rim of cake. Finally, frost the top of the cake, swirling the frosting or leaving it smooth, as you like. Decorate if desired.

Frosting an oblong cake: Frost top and sides as layer cake; or, leave in pan and frost top only.

Frosting a tube or ring cake: Frost sides then top and inside center of cake as layer cake.

Glazing a cake: Brush crumbs from top only, then drizzle glaze over top with spoon, so it runs down sides.

Frosting cupcakes: Dip the top of each cupcake in frosting, turning it slightly to coat it evenly.

CUTTING CAKES

Use a long, thin, sharp knife with a sawing motion to cut layer cakes and loaves. Fruitcakes are easier to slice thinly if first chilled. For angel, chiffon and sponge cakes, use a serrated knife or cake breaker.

STORING CAKES

Cakes left in the pan, frosted or unfrosted, should be covered tightly with a lid, plastic wrap or foil.

Layer cakes and frosted tube cakes are best stored in a cake keeper or under a large, inverted bowl. However, a cake with fluffy frosting should be frosted and served on the same day, as the frosting gradually disintegrates during storage. Leftovers may be put in a cake keeper or under an inverted bowl with a spoon or knife handle inserted under the top to hold it open, so that air will be able to circulate freely and help keep the frosting fluffy. Store cakes with whipped-cream frosting or cream filling in the refrigerator. Most cakes are best eaten within 1 or 2 days.

Wrap fruitcakes closely in plastic wrap or foil; if you like, sprinkle them first with brandy or wine, or wrap them in a wine- or brandy-dampened cloth, then over-wrap with foil and store for up to 2 months. Redampen the cloth weekly. Glaze or decorate just before serving.

FREEZING CAKES

Unfrosted cakes should be wrapped in freezer wrap, plastic wrap or foil, and sealed with tape. They will keep from 4 to 6 months, fruitcake up to 12 months.

Freeze frosted cakes, unwrapped, on a sheet of cardboard covered with foil until frosting hardens. Then wrap and seal as above, and return to freezer. Frosted cakes can be kept frozen for 2 to 3 months.

Don't freeze cakes which have a custard or fruit filling; they may become soggy when thawed. Never freeze uncooked batter.

THAWING CAKES

Thaw unfrosted cakes and cakes with butter-cream or with fudge frosting, wrapped, at room temperature. Unfrosted cakes will take about 1 hour; frosted tube cakes and layer cakes, 2 to 3 hours; cupcakes will thaw in about 30 minutes.

Cakes with a whipped-cream topping or filling, or a fluffy frosting, should be unwrapped before they are thawed. Thaw cakes with whipped-cream topping or filling in the refrigerator for 3 to 4 hours. Thaw cakes with fluffy frosting at room temperature.

Shortening cakes

Yellow Cake

**2¼ cups cake flour
1½ cups sugar
¾ cup shortening
¾ cup milk
3 eggs
2½ teaspoons double-acting baking powder
1 teaspoon salt
1 teaspoon vanilla extract
½ teaspoon almond extract
Butter-Cream Frosting (page 400)**

Color index page 92

Begin early in day

10 servings

631 cals per serving

1 Preheat oven to 375°F. Prepare pans: First grease and then flour two 9-inch round cake pans.

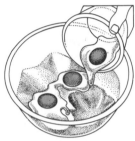

2 Into large bowl, measure all ingredients except frosting.

3 With mixer at low speed, beat until well mixed, constantly scraping bowl with rubber spatula. Increase speed to medium; beat 5 minutes, occasionally scraping bowl.

4 Pour batter into prepared cake pans, smoothing top with rubber spatula. Cut through batter with knife to remove any air bubbles.

5 Bake layers 25 minutes or until toothpick inserted deep into center comes out clean.

6 Cool in pans on wire racks 10 minutes then remove from pans and cool completely on racks.

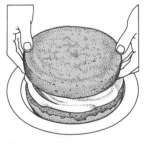

7 Meanwhile, prepare frosting. When layers are completely cooled, fill and frost cake.

Pineapple-Upside-Down Cake

**½ cup butter or margarine
2 cups packed brown sugar
1 15½-ounce can pineapple chunks**

**maraschino cherries, drained
Yellow Cake batter (left)
cream, whipped cream or vanilla ice cream**

Color index page 92

Begin early in day

12 servings

554 cals per serving

1. Preheat oven to 375°F. Before making cake batter, prepare topping: In 13″ by 9″ baking pan, place butter or margarine; place pan in oven until butter melts. Sprinkle brown sugar over butter. Meanwhile, drain pineapple chunks; use pineapple to form "flowers" in sugar mixture. Use a cherry for center of each flower.

2. Prepare cake batter as recipe directs but carefully spoon over design in baking pan.

3. Bake 35 to 40 minutes until toothpick inserted in center comes out clean. Cool in pan on wire rack 10 minutes. Then loosen cake from sides of pan; place platter on top of pan and invert both; lift off pan. (If fruit sticks to pan, lift off with spatula and replace in design on cake.) Serve topped with cream, whipped cream or vanilla ice cream.

Making sugar mixture: Sprinkle the brown sugar over melted butter in the baking pan.

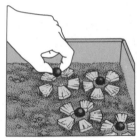

Arranging pineapple: Form flowers with pineapple chunks. Place cherry in center of each.

Devil's Food Cake

**2 cups cake flour
1½ cups sugar
1¼ cups buttermilk
½ cup shortening
3 eggs
3 squares unsweetened chocolate, melted
1½ teaspoons baking soda
1 teaspoon salt**

**1 teaspoon vanilla extract
½ teaspoon double-acting baking powder
Quick Fudge Frosting (page 400), Snow Peak Frosting (page 401) or Mocha Butter-Cream Frosting (page 400)**

Color index page 90

Begin early in day

10 servings

706 cals per serving

1. Preheat oven to 350°F. Grease and flour two 9-inch round cake pans.

2. Into large bowl, measure all ingredients except frosting. With mixer at low speed, beat until well mixed, constantly scraping bowl with rubber spatula. Increase speed to high; beat 5 minutes, occasionally scraping bowl.

3. Pour batter into pans. Bake 25 to 30 minutes until toothpick inserted in center comes out clean. Cool on wire racks 10 minutes then remove from pans; cool completely on racks.

4. Prepare chosen frosting. Fill and frost cake.

Silver-White Cake

Color index page 90

Begin early in day

8 servings

722 cals per serving

4 egg whites
1½ cups sugar
2¼ cups cake flour
1 cup milk
½ cup shortening
1 tablespoon double-acting baking powder
1 teaspoon salt
1 teaspoon vanilla extract

¼ teaspoon almond extract
Mocha Butter-Cream Frosting (page 400), or Fresh Lemon Filling (page 401) and Snow Peak Frosting (page 401)

1. Preheat oven to 375°F. Grease and flour two 8-inch round cake pans; line pans with waxed paper.

2 In small bowl with mixer at high speed, beat egg whites until soft peaks form.

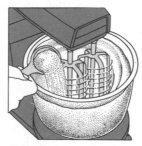

3 Beating at high speed, sprinkle in ½ cup sugar, 2 tablespoons at a time; beat until sugar is dissolved and whites stand in stiff peaks (do not scrape bowl). Set aside.

4 In large bowl at low speed, beat 1 cup sugar and remaining ingredients except frosting, constantly scraping bowl. At medium speed, beat 3 minutes longer.

5 At low speed, beat in whites. Pour into pans; bake 25 minutes. Cool in pans on wire racks 10 minutes; remove from pans and cool completely on wire racks.

6. Meanwhile, prepare chosen frosting and filling. Fill and frost with Mocha Butter-Cream Frosting or alternatively, fill with Fresh Lemon Filling and frost with Snow Peak Frosting.

Begin early in day

10 servings

597 cals per serving

LADY BALTIMORE CAKE: Prepare and cool *Silver-White Cake* as above. With sharp knife, cut each cake layer horizontally in half. In small bowl, combine ½ *cup candied cherries,* chopped, ⅓ *cup dried figs,* chopped, ⅓ *cup raisins,* chopped, and ¼ *cup chopped pecans*; set fruit mixture aside. Prepare *2 packages fluffy white-frosting mix* as label directs; stir fruit mixture into 3 cups of frosting; use this mixture to fill cake layers. Spread remaining frosting on top and sides of cake.

Chocolate Cupcakes

Color index page 93

Begin early in day

24 cupcakes

287 cals each

2 cups cake flour
1 ¾ cups sugar
¾ cup cocoa
1¼ cups milk
¾ cup shortening
3 eggs
1¼ teaspoons baking soda
1 teaspoon salt

1 teaspoon vanilla extract
½ teaspoon double-acting baking powder
Coffee Cream-Cheese Frosting (page 400)

1 Preheat oven to 350°F. Place liners in 2 dozen 3-inch muffin-pan cups or grease and flour cups.

2 Into large bowl, measure all cupcake ingredients except frosting.

3 With mixer at low speed, beat until well mixed, constantly scraping bowl; at high speed, beat 5 minutes, scraping the bowl occasionally.

4 Spoon into muffin-pan cups, filling each half full. Bake 20 minutes or until toothpick inserted in center of one comes out clean and dry.

5 Cool in pans on wire racks 10 minutes, then remove from pans and cool completely on racks.

6 Prepare frosting then dip tops of cupcakes into frosting and turn slightly to coat.

Color index page 93

Begin early in day

10 servings

528 cals per serving

CHOCOLATE CAKE: Preheat oven to 350°F. Grease and flour two 9-inch round cake pans. Prepare batter as above but pour into pans; bake 30 to 35 minutes. Cool layers in pans on wire racks 10 minutes; remove from pans and cool completely on racks. Fill and frost the chocolate cake layers with your choice of either *Coffee Cream-Cheese Frosting (page 400)* or *Fluffy Boiled Frosting (page 400)*.

Shortening cakes

Deluxe Marble Cake

Color index
page 90

Begin early
in day

12 servings

312 cals per
serving

**2 squares unsweetened
chocolate
1¼ cups sugar
¼ cup water
1 teaspoon vanilla extract
½ cup butter, softened
2 cups all-purpose flour
¾ cup evaporated milk
3 eggs
2 teaspoons double-acting
baking powder
1 teaspoon orange extract
½ teaspoon salt
½ teaspoon baking soda
confectioners' sugar**

1 Preheat oven to 350°F.
Grease well a 9-inch
springform pan. In 1-quart
saucepan over very low
heat, melt chocolate and ¼
cup sugar with water, stirring. Stir in vanilla; cool.

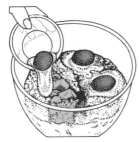

2 Into large bowl,
measure 1 cup sugar
and all ingredients except
chocolate mixture and confectioners' sugar.

3 With mixer at low
speed, beat until well
mixed, constantly scraping
bowl; at high speed, beat 5
minutes, scraping the bowl
occasionally. Remove 2½
cups batter.

4 Beat chocolate mixture
into remaining batter;
alternately spoon plain and
chocolate batters into pan.

5 With knife, cut through
batter a few times, then
bake 55 to 60 minutes (top
will be cracked).

6 Cool in pan on rack 10
minutes; remove sides of
pan and cool cake on rack.

7 Sprinkle top of cooled
cake lightly with some
confectioners' sugar.

Fresh Coconut Cake

Color index
page 92

Begin 3 hrs
or day ahead

16 servings

458 cals per
serving

**2¼ cups cake flour
1½ cups sugar
¾ cup shortening
¾ cup milk
3 eggs
2½ teaspoons double-
acting baking powder
1 teaspoon salt
1 teaspoon vanilla
extract**

**Custard Filling (below)
meat from 1 medium
coconut, shredded
(3 to 4 cups; to extract
meat, see page 304)
Snow Peak Frosting
(page 401)
candied orange slices for
garnish**

1. Preheat oven to 375°F. Grease and flour two 9-
inch round cake pans.
2. In large bowl with mixer at low speed, beat first 8
ingredients until well mixed, constantly scraping
bowl. Beat at medium speed 5 minutes, occasionally
scraping bowl.
3. Pour into pans; bake 25 to 30 minutes until
toothpick inserted in center of cakes comes out
clean. Cool in pans on wire racks 10 minutes;
remove from pans and cool completely on racks.
4. Meanwhile, prepare Custard Filling. Stir 1 cup
shredded coconut into chilled Custard Filling.
Prepare Snow Peak Frosting.
5. With sharp knife, cut each cake horizontally in
half. Place first layer on cake plate, cut side up;
spread cake with ⅓ of filling. Repeat layering,
ending with a cake layer, top side up.
6. Frost side and top of cake with frosting. Sprinkle
side and top of cake with about 2 cups shredded
coconut. Garnish top with candied orange slices.
Refrigerate until serving time.

CUSTARD FILLING: In heavy, 2-quart saucepan
with wire whisk, mix well **4 egg yolks, 2 cups milk, ½
cup sugar, ⅓ cup cornstarch** and **3 tablespoons
orange-flavor liqueur** until well blended; then, over
medium heat, cook, stirring constantly, until mixture thickens, about 10 minutes. Cover custard
surface with waxed paper; refrigerate until well
chilled, about 1½ hours.

German Gold Poundcake

Color index
page 90

Begin early
in day

16 servings

324 cals per
serving

**2 cups sugar
1 cup butter,
softened
3½ cups cake flour
1 cup milk
6 egg yolks**

**1½ teaspoons double-
acting baking powder
2 teaspoons vanilla
extract
⅛ teaspoon salt**

1. Preheat oven to 350°F. Grease and flour 10-inch
Bundt pan or two 9″ by 5″ loaf pans.
2. In large bowl with mixer at high speed, beat sugar
and butter until light and fluffy.
3. Add flour and rest of ingredients; at low speed,
beat until well mixed, constantly scraping bowl with
rubber spatula. Beat at high speed 4 minutes, occasionally scraping bowl.
4. Pour batter into Bundt pan and bake 1 hour or, if
using loaf pans, 45 to 50 minutes until toothpick
inserted in center comes out clean. Cool cake in pan
on wire rack 10 minutes; remove from pan; cool
completely on rack.

Spicy Gingerbread

Color index
page 90

Begin early
in day

9 servings

401 cals per
serving

2¹/₂ cups all-purpose flour
1 cup molasses
¹/₂ cup sugar
¹/₂ cup shortening
1 egg
1¹/₂ teaspoons baking soda
1 teaspoon ground
* cinnamon*
1 teaspoon ground ginger
³/₄ teaspoon salt
¹/₂ teaspoon ground
* cloves*
1 cup boiling water
whipped cream for
topping

1 Preheat oven to 350°F. Grease one 9-inch square cake pan then sprinkle with flour.

2 In large bowl with mixer at low speed, mix well all ingredients except cream; then beat at medium speed 3 minutes.

3 Pour gingerbread batter into greased and floured cake pan.

4 Bake 55 to 60 minutes until toothpick inserted in cake comes out clean.

5 Cool cake in pan on wire rack then top cake with whipped cream.

Merryfield Apple Cake

Color index
page 91

Begin early
in day

18 servings

382 cals per
serving

3 cups all-purpose flour
2 cups sugar
1 cup salad oil
1 teaspoon baking soda
1 teaspoon salt
2 teaspoons vanilla
* extract*
3 eggs
3 cups diced, peeled
* cooking apples*
1 cup chopped California
* walnuts*
¹/₂ cup chopped raisins
confectioners' sugar

1. Preheat oven to 325°F. Grease well and flour two 8-inch square cake pans.
2. In large bowl with mixer at low speed, mix well first 7 ingredients, constantly scraping bowl. Beat 3 minutes more, occasionally scraping bowl. Stir in apples, nuts and raisins.
3. Spread in pans. Bake 1 hour. Cool on wire racks. Place paper doily on each cake; sprinkle with confectioners' sugar; remove doilies.

Spice Cake

Color index
page 91

Begin early
in day

8 servings

669 cals per
serving

2 cups cake flour
³/₄ cup sugar
³/₄ cup milk
¹/₂ cup packed brown
* sugar*
¹/₂ cup shortening
2 eggs
2¹/₂ teaspoons double-
* acting baking powder*
1 teaspoon salt
1 teaspoon ground
* cinnamon*
1 teaspoon ground
* allspice*
¹/₂ teaspoon ground
* cloves*
¹/₂ teaspoon ground
* nutmeg*
1 teaspoon vanilla
* extract*
Whipped-Cream
Frosting (page 400) or
Buttermilk Icing
(page 401)

1. Preheat oven to 350°F. Grease and flour two 8-inch round cake pans.
2. In large bowl with mixer at low speed, beat all ingredients except frosting just until blended. Beat 3 minutes at high speed.
3. Pour batter into pans. Bake 25 to 30 minutes. Cool on racks. Prepare frosting; fill and frost cake.

Lane Cake

Color index
page 90

Begin early
in day

16 servings

600 cals per
serving

8 eggs, at room
* temperature*
2 cups sugar
2³/₄ cups cake flour
1 cup milk
1 cup butter or
* margarine*
3 teaspoons double-
* acting baking powder*
1 teaspoon salt
1 teaspoon vanilla
* extract*
Filling (below)
Frosting (below)

1. Preheat oven to 375°F. Separate eggs, placing 6 whites in large bowl, 2 whites in small bowl and all the yolks in 2-quart saucepan. Grease two 9-inch round cake pans; line bottoms of cake pans with waxed paper; grease.
2. In large bowl with mixer at high speed, beat egg whites until soft peaks form. Beating at high speed, sprinkle in 1 cup sugar, 2 tablespoons at a time. Beat until stiff peaks form.
3. In another large bowl at low speed, mix flour, next 5 ingredients and 1 cup sugar. At medium speed, beat 4 minutes; fold in whites.
4. Pour into pans; bake 35 minutes. Cool in pans on wire racks 10 minutes; remove from pans; discard paper; cool. Prepare Filling. Cut each layer in half horizontally; assemble 4-layer cake with filling. Prepare Frosting; frost cake.

FILLING: Into 8 yolks, stir *1¹/₄ cups sugar* and *¹/₂ cup butter.* Over medium heat, cook, stirring until slightly thickened, about 5 minutes. Stir in *one 4-ounce can shredded coconut, 1 cup pecan halves,* chopped, *1 cup candied red cherries,* chopped, *1 cup dark seedless raisins,* chopped and *¹/₃ cup bourbon.*

FROSTING: In 1-quart saucepan over medium heat, heat *1¹/₂ cups sugar, 1 tablespoon dark corn syrup, ¹/₃ cup water* and *¹/₂ teaspoon salt* to boiling. Boil, without stirring, to 240°F. on candy thermometer. Remove from heat. With mixer at high speed, beat reserved 2 egg whites until soft peaks form. Pour syrup in thin stream into whites, beating constantly. Add *1 teaspoon vanilla extract* and continue beating until very thick.

Shortening cakes

Banana Cake

Color index page 92

Begin early in day

10 servings

536 cals per serving

2¼ cups cake flour
1¼ cups sugar
1½ cups well-mashed
  ripe bananas (3 to 4)
½ cup shortening
2 eggs
2½ teaspoons double-
  acting baking powder
1 teaspoon vanilla
  extract
½ teaspoon baking soda
½ teaspoon salt
Whipped-Cream
  Frosting (page 400)
banana slices for garnish
lemon juice

1 Preheat oven to 375°F. Prepare two 8-inch round cake pans: First grease and then flour the bottom and sides of the cake pans.

2 Into large bowl, measure all ingredients except frosting, banana slices and lemon juice.

3 With mixer at low speed, beat until well mixed, constantly scraping bowl, then beat at high speed 5 minutes, occasionally scraping bowl.

4 Pour batter into pans and bake 25 minutes or until toothpick inserted deep into center of cake comes out clean.

5 Cool layers in pans on wire racks 10 minutes, then remove from pans and cool completely on racks before filling and frosting cake.

6 Prepare Whipped-Cream Frosting then, with metal spatula, fill and frost cake layers.

7 Just before serving, dip banana slices in lemon juice; use to garnish top of Banana Cake.

Walnut-Fudge Cake

Color index page 92

Begin early in day or day ahead

16 servings

548 cals per serving

8 eggs, separated
1½ cups confectioners'
  sugar
1 cup unsalted butter,
  softened
2 cups California
  walnuts, finely
  chopped
6 squares semisweet
  chocolate, melted

3 tablespoons all-purpose
  flour
1½ teaspoons vanilla
  extract
Chocolate-Walnut
  Filling (below)
Thin Chocolate Glaze
  (below)
California walnut halves
  for garnish

1. Preheat oven to 325°F. Grease and flour three 9-inch round cake pans.
2. In large bowl with mixer at high speed, beat egg whites until soft peaks form; beating at high speed, sprinkle in ½ cup sugar, 2 tablespoons at a time; beat until sugar is completely dissolved and whites stand in stiff, glossy peaks.
3. In another large bowl at low speed, mix well yolks, remaining sugar, butter, chopped walnuts, chocolate, flour and vanilla, constantly scraping bowl. Beat 4 minutes at medium speed, occasionally scraping bowl. With rubber spatula, gently fold in egg whites until just blended.
4. Pour batter into pans; bake 35 minutes or until toothpick inserted in center comes out clean. Cool in pans on wire racks 10 minutes; remove from pans and cool completely on racks.
5. Prepare Chocolate-Walnut Filling and fill between layers; place cake on cake plate. Prepare glaze; spread over top and sides of cake. Garnish with walnut halves; refrigerate. Cut cake into wedges to serve

CHOCOLATE-WALNUT FILLING: In double boiler, over hot, *not boiling*, water, melt *2 squares semisweet chocolate.* Stir in *⅓ cup sugar, 2 cups California walnuts,* chopped, and *½ cup milk.* Cook over boiling water 5 minutes until sugar is completely dissolved. Remove from heat; with spoon, beat in *¼ cup butter* or margarine, softened, and *1 teaspoon vanilla extract* just until blended. Refrigerate just until cool.

THIN CHOCOLATE GLAZE: In double boiler over hot, *not boiling*, water, melt *one 6-ounce package semisweet-chocolate pieces* with *2 tablespoons shortening*; remove from heat. Beat in *2 tablespoons light corn syrup* and *3 tablespoons milk* until smooth; spread while still warm.

Adding glaze: Spread glaze over top and down sides of filled cake.

Chiffon cakes

Orange Chiffon Cake

Color index
page 90

Begin early
in day

16 servings

278 cals per
serving

*1 cup egg whites, at room
temperature*
*½ teaspoon cream of
tartar*
sugar
2¼ cups cake flour
¾ cup orange juice
½ cup salad oil

5 egg yolks
*1 tablespoon double-
acting baking powder*
*3 tablespoons grated
orange peel*
1 teaspoon salt
*Fluffy Orange Frosting
(below)*

1 Preheat oven to 325°F.
In large bowl with mixer
at high speed, beat egg
whites and cream of tartar
into soft peaks.

2 At high speed, beat in
½ cup sugar, 2 table-
spoons at a time, until dissolved and whites stand in
stiff, glossy peaks. Do not
scrape the bowl.

3 In another large bowl
at low speed, beat
1 cup sugar and remaining
ingredients except frosting.

4 With rubber spatula,
gently fold mixture
into beaten whites. Pour
batter into ungreased
10-inch tube pan.

5 Bake 1¼ hours or until
top springs back when
lightly touched. Invert in
pan on funnel; cool.

6 Meanwhile, prepare
frosting. Remove cake
from pan; frost top and
sides. Keep refrigerated.

FLUFFY ORANGE FROSTING: In 1-quart
saucepan over medium heat, heat *one 12-ounce jar
sweet orange marmalade* to boiling. In large bowl
with mixer at high speed, beat *2 egg whites,
½ teaspoon vanilla extract, 10 drops yellow food
color* and *⅛ teaspoon salt* until soft peaks form.
Slowly pour in hot marmalade, beating 6 to 8
minutes until peaks form.

Sugar Bush Walnut Cake

Color index
page 90

Begin early
in day

12 servings

376 cals per
serving

*1 cup egg whites, at room
temperature (7 or 8
egg whites)*
*½ teaspoon cream of
tartar*
1½ cups sugar
*2¼ cups all-purpose
flour*
¾ cup water

7 egg yolks
*⅔ cup California
walnuts, finely chopped*
½ cup salad oil
*1 tablespoon double-
acting baking powder*
*1 teaspoon vanilla
extract*
1 teaspoon maple extract

1. Preheat oven to 325°F. In large bowl with mixer at
high speed, beat egg whites and cream of tartar until
soft peaks form; beating at high speed, sprinkle in ½
cup sugar, 2 tablespoons at a time; beat until sugar is
dissolved and whites stand in stiff peaks. Do not
scrape bowl during beating.
2. In another large bowl with mixer at medium
speed, beat flour with water, 1 cup sugar, egg yolks,
finely chopped California walnuts, salad oil, baking
powder, vanilla extract and maple extract until
thoroughly blended.
3. Pour flour mixture over whites and, with rubber
spatula, gently fold until just blended.
4. Pour batter into ungreased 10-inch tube pan and
bake 1¼ hours or until top springs back when
lightly touched with finger.
5. Invert cake in pan on funnel or bottle; cool
completely in the pan.
6. With metal spatula, carefully loosen cake from
tube pan; place on cake plate.

Chocolate Chiffon Cake

Color index
page 92

Begin early
in day or
day ahead

12 servings

235 cals per
serving

2 cups cake flour
½ cup cocoa
*1 tablespoon double-
acting baking powder*
1 teaspoon salt
sugar
¾ cup water
½ cup salad oil

*1 teaspoon vanilla
extract*
*6 eggs, separated, at
room temperature*
*½ teaspoon cream of
tartar*
confectioners' sugar

1. In medium bowl with wire whisk or spoon, stir
flour, cocoa, baking powder, salt and 1¼ cups sugar
until thoroughly blended. With same wire whisk or
spoon stir in water, salad oil, vanilla and egg yolks
until smooth.
2. Preheat oven to 350°F. In large bowl with mixer at
high speed, beat egg whites and cream of tartar until
soft peaks form; beating at high speed, gradually
sprinkle in ½ cup sugar, 2 tablespoons at a time;
beat until sugar is completely dissolved and whites
stand in stiff peaks. Do not scrape side of bowl
during beating.
3. With rubber spatula, gently fold flour mixture
into beaten egg whites until just blended.
4. Pour batter into ungreased 10-inch tube pan.
Bake 60 to 65 minutes until top springs back when
lightly touched with finger.
5. Invert cake in pan on funnel or bottle; cool
completely in the pan.
6. With spatula, loosen cake from pan; place on cake
plate. Sprinkle cake with confectioners' sugar.

Angel-food cake

Sponge cakes

Angel-Food Cake

*1¼ cups confectioners'
 sugar*
1 cup cake flour
*1½ cups egg whites, at
 room temperature
 (12 to 14 egg whites)*
*1½ teaspoons cream of
 tartar*
*1½ teaspoons vanilla
 extract*
¼ teaspoon salt
*¼ teaspoon almond
 extract*
1 cup sugar

Color index
page 91

Begin early
in day

12 servings

146 cals per
serving

1 Preheat oven to 375°F.
In small bowl, stir confectioners' sugar and cake flour; set aside.

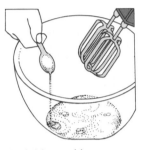

2 Add egg whites, cream of tartar, vanilla extract, salt and almond extract to large bowl and, with mixer at high speed, beat until well mixed.

3 Beating at high speed, sprinkle in sugar, 2 tablespoons at a time; beat just until sugar dissolves and whites form stiff peaks. Do not scrape bowl during beating.

4 With rubber spatula, fold in flour mixture, about ¼ at a time, just until flour disappears.

5 Pour mixture into ungreased 10-inch tube pan and with spatula, cut through batter to break any large air bubbles.

6 Bake 35 minutes or until top of cake springs back when lightly touched with finger. Any cracks on surface should look dry.

7 Invert cake in pan on funnel; cool completely. With spatula, loosen cake from pan and remove to plate.

Daffodil Cake

1¼ cups egg whites
*1½ teaspoons cream of
 tartar*
*1 teaspoon vanilla
 extract*
¼ teaspoon salt
1½ cups sugar
1 cup cake flour

4 egg yolks
*1 tablespoon grated
 orange peel*
*2 teaspoons grated lemon
 peel*
*Orange-Lemon Icing
 (below)*
orange sections

Color index
page 93

Begin early
in day or
day ahead

12 servings

348 cals per
serving

1 Preheat oven to 375°F. Into large bowl, measure egg whites, cream of tartar, vanilla and salt. With mixer at high speed, beat until soft peaks form.

2 Sprinkle in sugar, 2 tablespoons at a time, beating at high speed until sugar dissolves and whites stand in stiff glossy peaks. Do not scrape bowl.

3 Reduce mixer speed to low; gradually beat in flour until just blended.

4 In another large bowl at high speed, beat yolks until thick and lemon-colored; fold in half of egg-white mixture and orange and lemon peel.

5 In 10-inch tube pan, drop heaping tablespoons of white and yellow batters to form a checkerboard pattern; bake 35 to 40 minutes.

6 Invert cake and cool in pan for 1 hour. Meanwhile, prepare icing. Remove cake from pan and frost; garnish with orange sections; refrigerate.

ORANGE-LEMON ICING: In small bowl with mixer at medium speed, beat *1½ cups confectioners' sugar* with *¾ cup butter*, softened, *3 egg yolks* and *⅛ teaspoon salt* until fluffy; stir in *2 tablespoons grated orange peel* and *4 teaspoons grated lemon peel*.

Jelly Roll

Color index page 91

Begin early in day

10 servings

231 cals per serving

³/₄ cup all-purpose flour
1 teaspoon double-acting baking powder
¹/₂ teaspoon salt
4 eggs, separated, at room temperature sugar

¹/₂ teaspoon vanilla extract
confectioners' sugar
1 10-ounce jar favorite jam or jelly

1 Preheat oven to 375°F. Grease 15¹/₂" by 10¹/₂" jelly-roll pan; line with waxed paper. In small bowl, combine flour, baking powder and salt. In another small bowl with mixer at high speed, beat whites into soft peaks; gradually sprinkle in ¹/₃ cup sugar, beating until sugar is completely dissolved and stiff peaks form.

2 In large bowl at high speed, beat egg yolks until thick and lemon-colored; at same speed, gradually sprinkle in ¹/₂ cup sugar then vanilla extract. Sprinkle flour mixture over yolks; add beaten whites; with rubber spatula, gently fold mixture to blend thoroughly.

3 Spread batter in pan; bake 15 minutes or until top springs back when lightly touched with finger.

4 Meanwhile, sprinkle cloth towel with ¹/₃ cup confectioners' sugar.

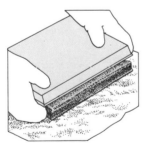

5 Immediately invert hot cake onto towel; gently remove waxed paper and cut off crisp edges of cake, if you like.

6 While still warm, carefully roll up cake and towel from narrow end.

7 Cool cake completely on rack, then unroll and spread with jam.

8 Reroll without towel and sprinkle roll with confectioners' sugar.

Mocha-Cream Roll

Color index page 91

Begin 2 hrs or day ahead

10 servings

350 cals per serving

5 eggs, separated, at room temperature
1 cup confectioners' sugar
¹/₈ teaspoon salt

cocoa
Mocha-Cream Filling (below)
Chocolate Icing (below)
Confectioners' Sugar Glaze (below)

1. Preheat oven to 400°F. Grease 15¹/₂" by 10¹/₂" jelly-roll pan; line bottom of pan with waxed paper; grease and flour paper.

2. In large bowl with mixer at high speed, beat egg whites until soft peaks form. Beating at high speed, gradually sprinkle in ¹/₂ cup confectioners' sugar, beating thoroughly after each addition. Continue beating until the egg whites stand in stiff, glossy peaks. Set aside.

3. In small bowl with same beaters and with mixer at high speed, beat egg yolks until thick and lemon-colored. Reduce speed to low; beat in salt, ¹/₂ cup confectioners' sugar and 3 tablespoons cocoa, occasionally scraping bowl with rubber spatula. With wire whisk or rubber spatula, gently fold yolk mixture into beaten whites just until the mixture is blended.

4. Spread batter evenly in pan and bake 15 minutes or until top springs back when lightly touched with finger. Prepare a clean cloth towel by sprinkling it with cocoa.

5. When cake is done, with small spatula, immediately loosen edges from side of pan; invert cake onto prepared towel. Gently peel waxed paper from bottom of cake. Roll towel with cake from narrow end, jelly-roll fashion. Cool completely, placing it seam side down, on wire rack. Meanwhile, prepare Mocha-Cream Filling.

6. When cake is cool, unroll from towel. Evenly spread Mocha-Cream Filling on cake almost to edges. Starting at same narrow end, roll up cake without the towel this time. Place the cake, seam side down, on platter.

7. Prepare Chocolate Icing. Spread icing over top and down sides of roll.

8. Prepare Confectioners' Sugar Glaze; use to drizzle over top of the roll to make a decorative design. Keep the roll in the refrigerator until you are ready to serve it.

MOCHA-CREAM FILLING: In medium bowl with mixer at medium speed, beat *1¹/₂ cups heavy or whipping cream, ¹/₂ cup cocoa, ¹/₄ cup confectioners' sugar* and *2 tablespoons coffee-flavor liqueur* until stiff peaks form.

CHOCOLATE ICING: In double boiler, over hot, *not boiling*, water, melt *one-half 6-ounce package semisweet-chocolate pieces* with *1 tablespoon butter* or margarine; remove from heat; then beat in *1 tablespoon light corn syrup* and *3 tablespoons milk* until smooth.

CONFECTIONERS' SUGAR GLAZE: In small bowl, stir *¹/₂ cup confectioners' sugar* and *2 to 3 teaspoons water* until smooth.

Sponge cakes

Holiday Petits Fours

Cake:
4 eggs
¾ cup sugar
¾ cup all-purpose flour
1 teaspoon double-acting baking powder
½ teaspoon salt
½ teaspoon almond extract
1 10-ounce jar apple jelly (1 cup)
Almond Paste (right)

Sugar Icing:
1 16-ounce package confectioners' sugar

5 tablespoons water
1 teaspoon almond extract
2 drops red food color

Decorations: *red candied cherries, dragées, candied flowers, nonpareils*

Color index page 91

Begin early in day

30 petits fours

164 cals each

1 Grease 15½″ by 10½″ jelly-roll pan; line with waxed paper and grease paper. Preheat oven to 350°F. Prepare cake: In large bowl with mixer at high speed, beat eggs until foamy. Gradually sprinkle in sugar, beating until mixture is fluffy and very pale yellow, about 7 minutes. At low speed, beat in flour, baking powder, salt and almond extract. Spread evenly in pan.

2 Bake 20 minutes or until cake springs back when lightly touched. Cool on rack 10 minutes; invert from pan onto rack; peel off paper; cool completely.

3 In 1-quart saucepan over low heat, melt jelly, then with pastry brush, glaze cake with some jelly. Cut cake crosswise in half into two 10½″ by 7¾″ rectangles.

4 Between 2 sheets of waxed paper, roll Almond Paste to about 10½″ by 7¾″ rectangle. Peel off top sheet.

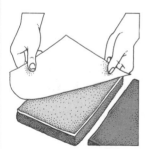

5 Invert bottom sheet with Almond Paste onto one cake rectangle and peel off paper.

6 Top with second cake rectangle, glazed side down, pressing layers together firmly.

7 Cut lengthwise into six 1¼-inch-wide strips. Then cut each strip crosswise into five pieces.

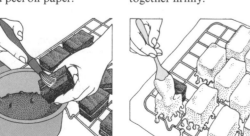

8 Brush cut surfaces of pieces with remaining jelly; place 1 inch apart on racks over waxed paper. Combine icing ingredients.

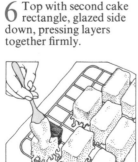

9 Drizzle icing over pieces. Return dripped icing to bowl; beat smooth to re-use, adding ½ teaspoon water if needed.

10 When icing is dry, decorate petits fours with your choice of candied cherries, candied flowers, dragées and nonpareils.

Begin 20 mins ahead

1 cup

264 cals per ¼ cup

Almond Paste

1 cup ground almonds
1 cup confectioners' sugar
1 egg yolk

2 teaspoons lemon juice
½ teaspoon almond extract

1. In small bowl, mix well the ground almonds, confectioners' sugar, egg yolk, lemon juice and almond extract.
2. Sprinkle work surface generously with confectioners' sugar; with sugared hands, knead mixture until smooth and not sticky.

Color index page 92

Begin early in day

12 servings   330 cals per serving

Coffee Cloud Cake

¾ cup egg whites, at room temperature
½ teaspoon cream of tartar
2 cups sugar
6 egg yolks
2 cups all-purpose flour
1 cup cold coffee

1 tablespoon double-acting baking powder
1 teaspoon vanilla extract
½ teaspoon salt
1 cup California walnuts, finely chopped

1. Preheat oven to 350°F. In large bowl with mixer at high speed, beat egg whites and cream of tartar until soft peaks form; beating at high speed, gradually sprinkle in ½ cup sugar, 2 tablespoons at a time; beat until sugar is completely dissolved and whites stand in stiff peaks. Do not scrape side of bowl during beating. Set aside.
2. In another large bowl with mixer at medium speed, beat 1½ cups sugar, egg yolks, flour, coffee, baking powder, vanilla and salt until light and fluffy.
3. Sprinkle egg whites with nuts; with rubber spatula, gently fold flour mixture into whites, just until blended.
4. Pour batter into ungreased 10-inch tube pan and bake 60 to 70 minutes until top springs back when lightly touched with finger. Invert cake in pan on bottle; cool completely. Loosen cake in pan and turn out as shown below.

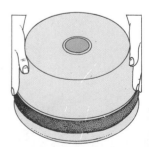

Loosening cake in pan: Gently cut around pan side and tube with knife.

Turning out cake: Invert pan and shake cake out onto a plate.

Fruitcakes

Golden Fruitcake

2 cups golden raisins
1½ cups chopped dried figs
1 cup diced candied citron
1 cup diced candied lemon peel
1 cup diced candied orange peel
1 cup chopped pitted dates
1 cup slivered blanched almonds or pecans
½ cup diced candied pineapple

½ cup candied cherries, halved
½ cup dried currants
all-purpose flour
1 cup butter, softened
2 cups sugar
2 teaspoons double-acting baking powder
½ teaspoon salt
6 eggs
1 teaspoon lemon or orange extract
1 cup dry sherry or orange juice

¼ cup apple jelly candied cherries and blanched whole almonds for garnish

Color index page 93
Begin day or several wks ahead
One 7-pound fruitcake
189 cals per 2-ounce serving

1 Preheat oven to 300°F. Line 10-inch tube pan with aluminum foil.

2 In large bowl, combine first 10 ingredients; toss lightly with ¾ cup flour until fruits and nuts are well coated to prevent them sinking in batter.

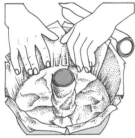

3 In another large bowl with mixer at medium speed, beat butter with sugar until light and fluffy.

4 Add 3 cups flour, baking powder, salt, eggs, extract and sherry or orange juice and beat at low speed until well mixed, constantly scraping bowl.

5 Increase speed to medium and beat 4 minutes longer, occasionally scraping bowl.

6 With spoon, stir fruit mixture into batter until well mixed.

7 Spoon batter evenly into foil-lined tube pan then bake fruitcake 3 hours or until toothpick inserted in center of cake comes out clean.

8 Cool completely in pan on rack; remove from pan; peel off foil. Flavor improves on storing. To wrap and store fruitcake, see page 383.

9 Before serving: In small saucepan over low heat, melt jelly; brush on cake. Press in cherries and almonds in flower design. Let glaze set.

Color index page 91
Begin several wks ahead
One 5-pound fruitcake   249 cals per 2-ounce serving

Dark Christmas Fruitcake

3 cups dark seedless raisins
1½ cups diced candied citron
1 cup candied cherries, halved
1 cup diced candied pineapple
1 cup pecan halves
1 cup slivered blanched almonds
1 cup dried currants
½ cup diced candied orange peel
½ cup diced candied lemon peel

all-purpose flour
6 eggs, separated, at room temperature
sugar
1½ teaspoons ground cinnamon
1½ teaspoons ground cloves
1 teaspoon ground nutmeg
½ teaspoon baking soda
1 cup shortening
½ square unsweetened chocolate, melted
¼ cup lemon juice
¼ cup orange juice
¼ cup apple jelly

1. Preheat oven to 300°F. Line 10-inch tube pan with foil. In large bowl, combine first 9 ingredients; toss fruit and nuts with 1 cup flour to coat well.
2. In another large bowl with mixer at high speed, beat egg whites until soft peaks form; at high speed, beat in ½ cup sugar, 1 tablespoon at a time, until sugar is dissolved and whites stand in stiff peaks.
3. In medium bowl at low speed, mix well 1 cup flour, ½ cup sugar, yolks and rest of ingredients except apple jelly, constantly scraping bowl. Beat at high speed 5 minutes, occasionally scraping bowl.
4. Stir batter into fruit mixture. Fold in whites.
5. Pour batter into pan; bake 2 hours 10 minutes or until toothpick inserted in center comes out clean. Cool cake completely in pan on wire rack; remove from pan; peel off foil. Wrap and store.
6. *Before serving:* Melt jelly; brush on cake; let set.

Color index page 92
Begin several wks ahead   205 cals per 2-ounce
One 3-pound fruitcake   serving

Brazil-Nut Sensation Fruitcake

3 cups Brazil nuts
2 cups whole pitted dates
1 cup maraschino cherries, well drained
¾ cup all-purpose flour
¾ cup sugar

½ teaspoon double-acting baking powder
½ teaspoon salt
3 eggs
1 teaspoon vanilla extract

1. Preheat oven to 300°F. Grease 9″ by 5″ loaf pan; line with foil. In large bowl, stir nuts, dates and cherries. Add flour, sugar, baking powder and salt; mix to coat nuts and fruits.
2. In small bowl with mixer at medium speed, beat eggs and vanilla until foamy; stir into nut mixture; mix well. Pour into pan; level top.
3. Bake 2½ hours or until toothpick inserted in center comes out clean. Cool in pan on wire rack 15 minutes. Turn out cake; peel off foil; allow to cool completely on wire rack. Wrap well; refrigerate.

Very special cakes

Sachertorte

Color index
page 90

Begin 6 hrs
ahead

12 servings

486 cals per
serving

5 squares semisweet
chocolate
½ cup butter, softened
1 teaspoon vanilla
extract
¼ teaspoon salt
6 eggs, separated, at
room temperature

¾ cup sugar
1 cup cake flour
1 10- or 12-ounce jar
apricot preserves
Chocolate Glaze (below)
1 cup heavy cream,
whipped

1. In double boiler over hot, *not boiling*, water, melt
chocolate; remove from heat. Stir in butter, vanilla
and salt until mixture is smooth and cool. Add egg
yolks; stir until blended.
2. Lightly grease and flour 9″ by 3″ springform pan.
Preheat oven to 350°F. In large bowl with mixer at
high speed, beat egg whites until soft peaks form.
Beating at high speed, sprinkle in sugar, 2 tablespoons at·a time, beating until sugar is dissolved and
whites stand in stiff, glossy peaks.
3. Gently fold chocolate mixture into beaten whites.
While folding, sprinkle in flour, about ⅓ at a time;
fold gently until blended. Pour batter into pan; with
spatula, cut through batter a few times to break any
air bubbles. Bake 45 minutes or until cake springs
back when lightly touched with finger. Cool cake in
pan on wire rack 10 minutes; remove side of pan;
cool completely.
4. Assemble torte as shown below, then refrigerate
torte until chocolate is firm.
5. *To serve:* With 2 pancake turners, transfer torte
to cake plate; let stand about 30 minutes. Serve torte
with whipped cream.

CHOCOLATE GLAZE: In double boiler over hot,
not boiling, water, melt *1 cup semisweet chocolate*
pieces and *2 tablespoons butter;* stir in *1 tablespoon*
milk and *1 tablespoon light corn syrup* until smooth.

ASSEMBLING THE SACHERTORTE

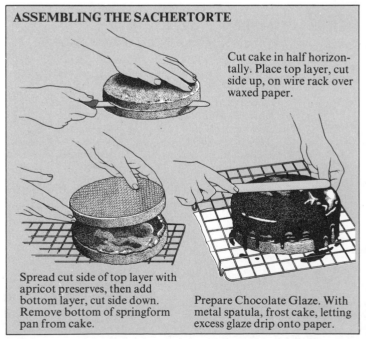

Cut cake in half horizon-
tally. Place top layer, cut
side up, on wire rack over
waxed paper.

Spread cut side of top layer with
apricot preserves, then add
bottom layer, cut side down.
Remove bottom of springform
pan from cake.

Prepare Chocolate Glaze. With
metal spatula, frost cake, letting
excess glaze drip onto paper.

MAKING CHOCOLATE CURLS
Make chocolate curls as shown below and use them to garnish
frosted cakes, pies or whipped-cream desserts.

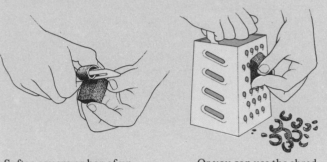

Soften square or bar of unsweetened or semisweet chocolate
with heat of your hands or in
just-warm oven. Slowly and
firmly pull vegetable peeler across
wide side of chocolate for wide
curls, thin side for thin curls.

Or you can use the shred-
der side of a grater to
make curly shreds.

Six-Layer Eggnog Cake

Color index
page 93

Begin 4 hrs
or day ahead

12 servings

638 cals per
serving

2 cups all-purpose flour
2 teaspoons double-
acting baking powder
½ teaspoon ground
nutmeg
½ teaspoon salt
1½ cups heavy or
whipping cream
½ teaspoon rum
extract

4 eggs
1¼ cups sugar
Buttery Chocolate
Frosting (page 401)
4 squares semisweet
chocolate made into
chocolate curls
(above)

1. Preheat oven to 350°F. Grease and flour three 9-
inch round cake pans.
2. In small bowl with fork, combine first 4 ingredients; set aside. In another small bowl with
mixer at medium speed, beat heavy or whipping
cream and rum extract until stiff peaks form.
3. In large bowl using same beaters, with mixer at
high speed, beat eggs and sugar until thick and
lemon-colored, about 5 minutes. With wire whisk or
rubber spatula, gently fold flour mixture and whipped heavy cream into egg mixture until blended;
pour batter into cake pans.
4. Stagger pans on 2 oven racks so no pan is
directly above another. Bake 20 to 25 minutes until
toothpick inserted in center of cakes comes out
clean. Cool cake layers on wire racks 10 minutes;
carefully remove cakes from pans and cool completely, about 1 hour.
5. Prepare Buttery Chocolate Frosting. With sharp
knife, cut each cake layer horizontally in half. Place
first layer on cake plate, cut side up; spread with a
scant ½ cup frosting. Repeat until 4 more frosted
layers are stacked on top. Top with last layer, top
side up. Frost side and top of cake with remaining
chocolate frosting.
6. Garnish top of cake with chocolate curls, transferring them to cake with toothpick to avoid breaking
them. Refrigerate until serving time.

Black Forest Cherry Torte

2 15- or 16-ounce cans
pitted tart cherries,
drained
about ½ cup kirsch
(cherry-flavor
brandy)
Chocolate Cake layers
(page 385)
2 cups heavy or whipping
cream
½ cup confectioners'
sugar
1 square semisweet
chocolate, grated

12 maraschino cherries,
well drained
2 squares semisweet
chocolate made into
chocolate curls
(opposite)

Color index page 92
Begin 4 hrs ahead
12 servings
633 cals per serving

1 In medium bowl, place cherries and ⅓ cup kirsch; leave at room temperature for 2½ hours, stirring occasionally.

2 Meanwhile, preheat oven to 350°F. Prepare cake layers as recipe directs but pour batter into 3 greased and floured 9-inch round cake pans. Stagger pans on 2 oven racks so no pan is directly above another. Bake cake layers 20 to 25 minutes until toothpick inserted in center comes out clean. Cool on wire racks 10 minutes; remove layers from pans and cool them completely on wire racks, about 2 hours.

3 With fork, prick well top of each cake, then drain cherries well and sprinkle cherry liquid over cake layers.

4 In small bowl with mixer at medium speed, beat heavy or whipping cream, confectioners' sugar and 2 tablespoons kirsch until the cream stands in stiff peaks.

5 Place one cake layer on cake platter. Spread with one-fourth whipped-cream mixture; top with half of cherries.

6 Repeat with the second layer and then top with the third one.

7 Frost side of cake with half of remaining whipped-cream mixture.

8 With spoon, gently press grated semisweet chocolate onto whipped-cream mixture all around the side of the cake.

9 Garnish with dollops of remaining whipped-cream mixture; top each dollop with a drained maraschino cherry.

10 Pile chocolate curls in center; keep refrigerated. (Chocolate curls may turn slightly gray in color.)

Color index page 91
Begin 3 hrs ahead
12 servings   331 cals per serving

Filbert Torte

6 eggs, separated
sugar
⅓ cup dried bread
crumbs
¼ cup all-purpose flour

1 cup ground filberts
2 cups heavy or whipping
cream
1 teaspoon vanilla
extract

1. Preheat oven to 325°F. In large bowl with mixer at high speed, beat egg whites until soft peaks form. Beating at high speed, gradually sprinkle in ¼ cup sugar, beating well after each addition. Whites should stand in stiff peaks.
2. In small bowl with mixer at medium speed, beat egg yolks until thick and lemon-colored. Gradually beat in ½ cup sugar until blended. Stir in bread crumbs, flour and ⅔ cup ground nuts; with wire whisk or rubber spatula, fold into beaten egg whites. Pour batter into 10″ by 3″ springform pan and spread evenly.
3. Bake 40 minutes or until cake springs back when lightly touched with finger. Invert cake in pan on wire rack; cool completely.
4. In small bowl with mixer at medium speed, beat heavy or whipping cream, vanilla extract and 2 tablespoons sugar until stiff peaks form.
5. Remove cake from pan; with a long sharp knife, slice cake horizontally into 2 layers. Place bottom layer on cake platter; spread with one-fourth whipped-cream mixture; top with second layer. Frost side of cake with half of remaining whipped-cream mixture. With hand, gently press remaining ⅓ cup ground nuts onto cream.
6. Spoon remaining cream mixture into a pastry bag with a large star tube; use to decorate top of cake.

DECORATING THE FILBERT TORTE

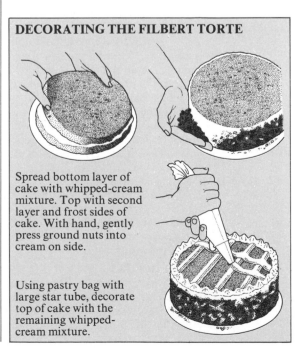

Spread bottom layer of cake with whipped-cream mixture. Top with second layer and frost sides of cake. With hand, gently press ground nuts into cream on side.

Using pastry bag with large star tube, decorate top of cake with the remaining whipped-cream mixture.

Very special cakes

Party Cake

12 eggs, at room temperature	1 tablespoon vanilla extract
5 cups sugar	2 teaspoons salt
6 cups cake flour	Lemon Butter-Cream Filling (below)
2½ cups milk	Pink Butter-Cream Frosting (below right)
1½ cups butter or margarine, softened	Vanilla Butter-Cream Frosting (below right)
2 tablespoons double-acting baking powder	Decorations (opposite)

Color index page 93

Begin day or up to 1 wk ahead

62 servings

356 cals per serving

1. Generously grease and flour 14-inch, 10-inch and 6-inch round cake pans. Separate eggs, placing whites in a large bowl and yolks in another large bowl. Be sure to have wire racks large enough to cool cake layers. If necessary, use a refrigerator wire rack or several racks taped together for the 14-inch layer. Also have large cookie sheets on hand for handling the layers.

2. In large bowl with mixer at high speed, beat egg whites until soft peaks form. Beating at high speed, sprinkle in 1 cup sugar, 2 tablespoons at a time. Beat until stiff peaks form; set aside.

3. Into second large bowl with yolks, measure cake flour, milk, butter, baking powder, vanilla, salt and remaining 4 cups sugar. With mixer at low speed, beat until well mixed, constantly scraping bowl. Beat at medium speed 10 to 15 minutes or until mixture is fluffy.

4. Place upper oven rack one-third from top and lower rack two-thirds down from top, then preheat oven to 375°F.

5. Pour yolk mixture into 8-quart bowl or saucepot; fold in beaten egg whites. Pour batter evenly into the three pans. Place 14-inch layer on lower oven rack and the other two on the upper rack with the 6-inch layer in front. Bake 6-inch layer 40 minutes or until toothpick inserted in center comes out clean. Quickly remove from oven to wire rack; cool 10 minutes; remove from pan; cool completely. Bake 10-inch layer 15 minutes longer than small layer or 55 minutes in all. Quickly remove from oven; cool on wire rack 10 minutes; remove from pan; cool completely. Bake 14-inch layer 20 minutes longer than the second layer or 1¼ hours in all. Cool in pan on wire rack 10 minutes; remove from pan; cool completely. If cakes are made 1 week ahead, freeze layers on cookie sheets; wrap with plastic wrap. To thaw cake layers, unwrap and leave them to stand 2 hours at room temperature.

6. *Early in day:* Prepare filling and assemble layers in three tiers (right). Prepare Pink Butter-Cream Frosting and Vanilla Butter-Cream Frosting and frost cake (opposite). Make decorations and decorate cake (opposite).

LEMON BUTTER-CREAM FILLING: In large bowl with mixer at medium-low speed, beat *two 16-ounce packages confectioners' sugar, ¾ cup butter* or margarine, softened, and *6 to 8 tablespoons lemon juice* until the filling is smooth and of a good spreading consistency.

ASSEMBLING THE LAYERS

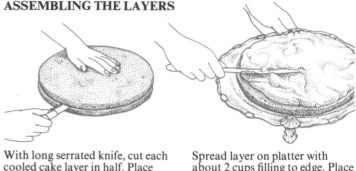

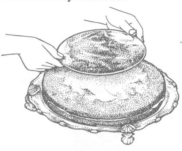

With long serrated knife, cut each cooled cake layer in half. Place top half of 14-inch layer upside down on large platter or foil-covered heavy cardboard.

Spread layer on platter with about 2 cups filling to edge. Place second half of layer, cut side down, over filled layer.

Spread filling thinly in center of 14-inch tier to about 2 inches from edge; then, for easier cutting, place 10½-inch foil-covered round cardboard in center.

Place half of 10-inch layer in center of 14-inch tier, on foil-covered cardboard. Fill and top with other half.

Spread filling thinly in center of 10-inch layer; place 6½-inch foil-covered cardboard on top.

Place half of 6-inch layer on 10-inch tier, on cardboard. Fill and top with other half.

FROSTINGS

PINK BUTTER-CREAM FROSTING: In large bowl with mixer at medium-low speed, beat *two 16-ounce packages confectioners' sugar, ¾ cup butter* or margarine, softened, *6 to 8 tablespoons milk, 1 tablespoon vanilla extract, ¼ teaspoon salt* and enough *red food color* until the frosting is tinted a pretty pale pink color.

VANILLA BUTTER-CREAM FROSTING: In medium bowl with mixer at medium-low speed, beat *one 16-ounce package confectioners' sugar, 6 tablespoons butter* or margarine, softened, *3 to 4 tablespoons milk, 1½ teaspoons vanilla extract* and *⅛ teaspoon salt* until the frosting is smooth and of easy spreading consistency.

FROSTING THE CAKE

With pink frosting, frost sides of cake tiers smoothly.

Next, frost the tops of the cake layers with pink frosting.

Spoon vanilla frosting into bag with round tube (No. 5). String icing around top of tiers: Attach icing then pull tube straight away letting string drop; move along; reattach icing; repeat.

Unscrew retainer ring and change to small star tube (No. 17). Using same white frosting, make borders around both top and bottom edges of cake tiers. Allow frosting to harden.

ADDING DECORATIONS

With small round tube and green frosting, pipe stems onto cake then press on roses. Change to leaf tube and make leaves on stems.

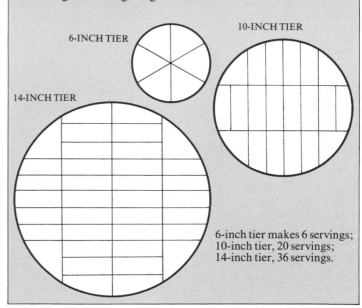

MAKING DECORATIONS: In small bowl with mixer at low speed, beat *one 16-ounce package confectioners' sugar, 1/2 teaspoon cream of tartar* and *3 egg whites,* at room temperature, until just mixed. Increase speed to high and beat until mixture is very stiff and knife drawn through mixture leaves a clean-cut path. Remove about one-fourth to small bowl; with *green food color,* tint green; cover with plastic wrap. Into remaining three-fourths of mixture, beat enough *red food color* to tint a rose-pink color. With rose-pink frosting in decorating bag fitted with small petal tube (No. 103), make a small rose (page 399); let dry at least 30 minutes. Repeat to make more. Spoon green frosting in to decorating bag fitted with small round tube (No. 5); pipe stems onto cake. Arrange roses on stems. Change round tube to leaf tube (No. 70); make leaves on stems.

CUTTING THE CAKE

Using a long, thin knife with a sawing motion, cut the cake into 62 servings following the guide below.

6-INCH TIER

10-INCH TIER

14-INCH TIER

6-inch tier makes 6 servings; 10-inch tier, 20 servings; 14-inch tier, 36 servings.

Cake decorating

With a decorating bag fitted with a coupler, and a selection of tubes and flower nails, you can make a wide range of shapes and designs. Each tube is numbered to indicate the design it makes. Except for shapes which require flower nails, practice on an inverted jelly-roll pan, scraping up the icing to re-use. Butter-Cream, Fluffy Boiled and Ornamental Frostings are the best to use.

The consistency of the icing is very important. Use a stiff icing for flowers, a medium-stiff icing for borders, and a thinner icing for leaves and writing; if necessary, thin icing by adding a few drops of water or milk. Keep the bowl covered with a damp cloth while working to prevent the icing from drying out.

Make flowers ahead by piping them onto waxed paper. Freeze Butter-Cream flowers 24 hours ahead; they'll keep a week in the freezer. Air-dry flowers made of Fluffy Boiled or Ornamental Frosting; they'll keep for months in a tightly covered container.

Our instructions are for right-handed cooks. If you are left-handed, read "left" for "right" and vice versa.

BASIC EQUIPMENT

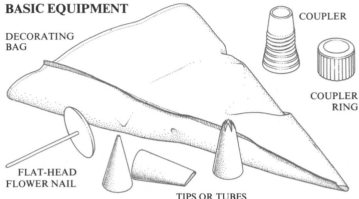

DECORATING BAG

COUPLER

COUPLER RING

FLAT-HEAD FLOWER NAIL

TIPS OR TUBES

HOLDING THE BAG

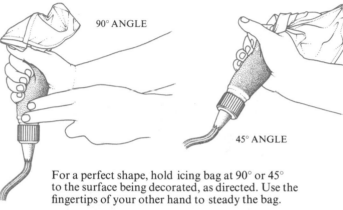

90° ANGLE

45° ANGLE

For a perfect shape, hold icing bag at 90° or 45° to the surface being decorated, as directed. Use the fingertips of your other hand to steady the bag.

FITTING AND FILLING THE BAG

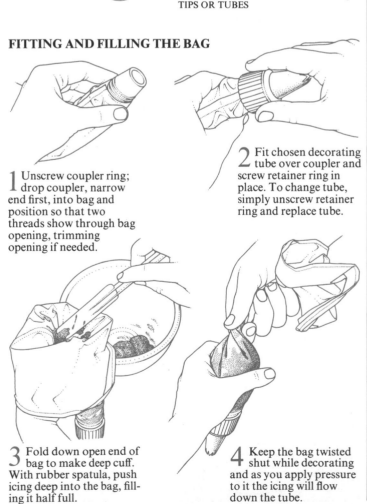

1 Unscrew coupler ring; drop coupler, narrow end first, into bag and position so that two threads show through bag opening, trimming opening if needed.

2 Fit chosen decorating tube over coupler and screw retainer ring in place. To change tube, simply unscrew retainer ring and replace tube.

3 Fold down open end of bag to make deep cuff. With rubber spatula, push icing deep into the bag, filling it half full.

4 Keep the bag twisted shut while decorating and as you apply pressure to it the icing will flow down the tube.

TYPES OF TUBE

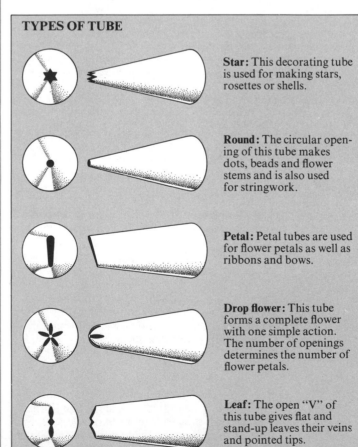

Star: This decorating tube is used for making stars, rosettes or shells.

Round: The circular opening of this tube makes dots, beads and flower stems and is also used for stringwork.

Petal: Petal tubes are used for flower petals as well as ribbons and bows.

Drop flower: This tube forms a complete flower with one simple action. The number of openings determines the number of flower petals.

Leaf: The open "V" of this tube gives flat and stand-up leaves their veins and pointed tips.

MAKING STARS, ROSETTES AND SHELLS

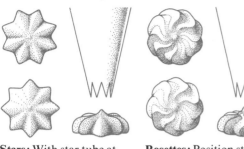

Stars: With star tube at 90° and almost touching surface, squeeze to form star, then lift slightly keeping tip in icing. Stop pressure and lift tube.

Rosettes: Position star tube as for stars, but as you squeeze move tube up and to left in a circular motion. Stop pressure and lift tube away from icing.

Shells: With star tube at 45° and touching surface, squeeze, lifting slightly as icing fans out. Then relax pressure, bringing tube down and toward you.

MAKING DOTS AND BEADS

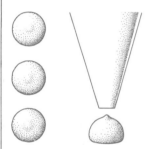

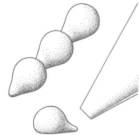

Dots: With round tube at 90° and almost touching surface, squeeze to form dot, then lift tube slightly keeping tip in icing. Stop pressure and lift tube.

Beads: With round tube, follow the technique for making shells. Slightly overlap beads, starting each bead on the point of the preceding one.

WRITING MESSAGES

Use a round tube and thinned icing which will flow smoothly. With tube at 45°, touch surface to secure icing then slightly lift tube as it moves to form letters. Use even pressure and guide tube with your entire arm. To finish a letter or word, just stop pressure and lift tube.

MAKING RIBBONS, SWAGS AND BOWS

Ribbon: With petal tube at 45°, place wide end of opening at surface of cake, narrow end slightly up. Squeeze, while making a series of curves.

Ribbon swag: Follow the ribbon technique, as shown above, but as you complete each curve, move the tube up and down in 3 short strokes.

Bow: Work with bag pointing toward you. Hold petal tube at 45° with wide end of opening on surface and narrow end straight up. Squeezing evenly, make loop to left. Stop pressure as you cross starting point. Squeeze again to make loop to right, stopping at starting point. From center, make 2 streamers.

MAKING A ROSE

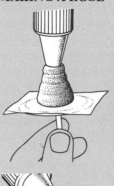

Attach 2-inch square of waxed paper to flat-head flower nail with dab of frosting; hold nail between thumb and forefinger of left hand. With round tube at 90°, pipe mound of icing. Now use nail as turntable, always turning nail to left (counterclockwise) as you form petals to right.

With petal tube at 45°, touch wide end to just below top of mound with narrow end straight up; turn nail to left as you pipe band of icing up, around and back down to starting point to make bud.

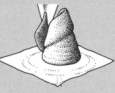

Touch wide end to base, narrow end up; move tube up and down in arc. Make two more petals.

With narrow end pointing out a little, pipe row of 4 petals under the first row.

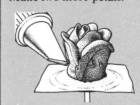

With narrow end of tube pointing out, pipe final row of 5 to 7 petals under previous row. Slip finished rose off nail to dry.

MAKING LEAVES

Plain leaf: Hold leaf tube at 45°. Squeeze until icing fans out, then relax pressure and draw leaf to a point. Stop pressure and pull tube away.

Stand-up leaf: Hold leaf tube at 90°. Squeeze until icing fans out, then relax pressure as you raise tube, drawing leaf up to a point. Stop pressure and lift tube.

Frostings and fillings

Fluffy frostings should be made just before use but most uncooked creamy frostings can be made in advance and stored until needed in a tightly covered container to prevent a crust forming on top. If creamy frostings are refrigerated and as a result become too firm to spread easily, let them stand at room temperature or stir well to soften to spreading consistency. Each of the frosting recipes that follows makes enough frosting to frost a 13″ by 9″ cake, tube cake or 24 cupcakes, or to fill and frost a 2-layer cake. Each of the filling recipes makes enough filling for a 2-layer cake.

Butter-Cream Frosting

Begin 15 mins ahead

205 cals per one-twelfth

1 16-ounce package confectioners' sugar
6 tablespoons butter or margarine, softened
3 to 4 tablespoons milk or half-and-half
1½ teaspoons vanilla extract
⅛ teaspoon salt

In large bowl with spoon or with mixer at medium speed, beat all ingredients until very smooth, adding more milk if necessary to make the icing of good spreading consistency.

LEMON: Prepare as above but substitute *lemon juice* for milk and omit vanilla.

MOCHA: Prepare as above but add *½ cup cocoa;* substitute *⅓ cup hot coffee* for milk and reduce vanilla to ½ teaspoon.

ORANGE: Prepare as above but add *2 egg yolks* and *1 teaspoon grated orange peel* and use only about 2 tablespoons milk.

CHOCOLATE: Increase butter to ½ cup. Melt, then cool, *3 squares unsweetened chocolate*; add with *2 egg yolks* to rest of above ingredients.

Whipped-Cream Frosting

Begin 15 mins ahead

176 cals per one-twelfth

2 cups heavy or whipping cream
¼ cup confectioners' sugar
⅛ teaspoon salt
1 teaspoon vanilla extract

In small bowl with mixer at medium speed, beat cream with sugar and salt until stiff peaks form; fold in vanilla extract. Keep frosted cake refrigerated until serving time.

CHOCOLATE: Over hot, *not boiling*, water, melt *one 6-ounce package semisweet-chocolate pieces* (1 cup); cool completely. Prepare frosting as above but fold in cooled chocolate.

COFFEE: Prepare as above but add *1 teaspoon instant coffee* with sugar.

ORANGE: Prepare as above but add *1 teaspoon shredded orange peel* with vanilla.

PEPPERMINT: Beat cream and salt together (no sugar) as above and fold in *¼ cup crushed peppermint candy*; omit vanilla extract.

Quick Fudge Frosting

Begin 30 mins ahead

299 cals per one-twelfth

1 12-ounce package semisweet-chocolate pieces (2 cups)
¼ cup shortening
3 cups confectioners' sugar
½ cup milk

1. In double boiler, over hot, *not boiling*, water, melt chocolate pieces with shortening.
2. Stir in sugar and milk; remove from heat. With spoon, beat until smooth.

Cream-Cheese Frosting

Begin 15 mins ahead

217 cals per one-twelfth

2 3-ounce packages cream cheese, softened
2 tablespoons evaporated milk
1 teaspoon vanilla extract
⅛ teaspoon salt
1 16-ounce package confectioners' sugar

1. In small bowl with mixer at medium speed, beat together the softened cream cheese and evaporated milk just until smooth.
2. Beat in vanilla, salt and sugar until blended.

COFFEE: Prepare as above but, with sugar, add *4 teaspoons instant coffee.*

Ornamental Frosting

Begin 30 mins ahead

150 cals per one-twelfth

1 16-ounce package confectioners' sugar
½ teaspoon cream of tartar
3 egg whites, at room temperature
½ teaspoon vanilla or almond extract

1. Into large bowl, sift sugar and cream of tartar.
2. With mixer at low speed, beat in egg whites and vanilla; at high speed, beat until knife drawn through mixture leaves clean-cut path. On humid days it may be necessary to beat in more confectioners' sugar.
3. Cover bowl with damp cloth. Use to make cake and cookie decorations with decorating bag fitted with tubes. To tint, in small bowl, place some of frosting; stir in food color a drop at a time.

Fluffy Boiled Frosting

Begin 45 mins ahead

85 cals per one-twelfth

1¼ cups sugar
⅛ teaspoon cream of tartar
⅛ teaspoon salt
6 tablespoons water
3 egg whites, at room temperature
1 teaspoon vanilla extract

1. In 1-quart saucepan over medium heat, heat sugar, cream of tartar, salt and water to boiling; set candy thermometer in place and boil, without stirring, until temperature reaches 260°F. or until a little mixture dropped in cold water forms hard ball. Remove from heat.
2. In small bowl with mixer at high speed, beat egg whites until soft peaks form.
3. Pour syrup in thin stream into whites, beating constantly; add vanilla and continue beating until mixture forms stiff peaks.

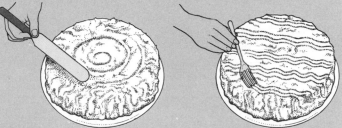

EASY DECORATIVE TOUCHES
With back of spoon, swirl circles, S-shapes or wavy lines in frosting, or pull frosting up in peaks. Or make patterns below.

For spiral, place cake on turntable or lazy Susan. Press tip of spatula into center of frosting and, turning cake in one direction, slowly move spatula outward.

On creamy-frosted cake, draw tines of fork across top in parallel rows; repeat rows at right angles.

Buttery Chocolate Frosting

Begin 20 mins ahead

335 cals per one-twelfth

1 cup egg whites (7 or 8 egg whites)	*1/2 teaspoon rum extract*
1 cup sugar	*1 3/4 cups butter*
	3/4 cup cocoa

1. In heavy, 1-quart saucepan over medium heat, heat whites, sugar and rum extract until sugar is dissolved, about 2 minutes, stirring constantly (over-heating will cause egg whites to coagulate).
2. In large bowl with mixer at medium speed, beat butter until light and fluffy, about 4 minutes (if butter becomes too warm, frosting will separate).
3. *Gradually* beat egg-white mixture into butter; beat in cocoa. At high speed, beat until the mixture is light and fluffy, about 2 minutes.

"Seven-Minute" Frosting

Begin 20 mins ahead

104 cals per one-twelfth

1 1/2 cups sugar	*1 tablespoon light corn syrup*
1/2 cup water (for crusty surface, use only 1/3 cup water)	*1 teaspoon vanilla extract*
2 egg whites	*1/2 teaspoon salt*

1. In top of double boiler with mixer at high speed, beat all ingredients about 1 minute.
2. Place over rapidly boiling water; beat at high speed until the mixture forms soft peaks (this may take longer than 7 minutes).
3. Pour into large bowl; beat until the mixture is thick enough to spread.

Snow Peak Frosting

Begin 20 mins ahead

95 cals per one-twelfth

1 1/4 cups light corn syrup	*1/8 teaspoon salt*
2 egg whites, at room temperature	*1 teaspoon vanilla extract*

1. In 1-quart saucepan over medium heat, heat corn syrup to boiling; remove from heat.
2. In large bowl with mixer at high speed, beat egg whites until foamy; add salt and continue beating just until soft peaks form.
3. Slowly pour in hot syrup, beating 6 to 8 minutes until the mixture is fluffy and peaks form when beater is raised. Beat in vanilla extract.

Buttermilk Icing

Begin 30 mins ahead

458 cals per one-twelfth

3 cups sugar	*1 teaspoon baking soda*
1 cup butter	*1 cup finely chopped pecans*
1 cup buttermilk	
2 tablespoons light corn syrup	

1. In 4-quart saucepan over medium heat, heat first 5 ingredients to boiling, stirring constantly. Set candy thermometer in place; cook, stirring occasionally, until temperature reaches 238°F. or until a little of the mixture dropped in a cup of cold water forms a soft ball.
2. Pour mixture into large bowl; with mixer at high speed, beat to spreading consistency, about 7 minutes, occasionally scraping bowl with a rubber spatula. Fold in chopped pecans.

Fresh Lemon Filling

Begin 1 1/2 hrs ahead

32 cals per one-twelfth

1/2 cup water	*4 teaspoons cornstarch*
1/4 cup sugar	*1/4 teaspoon salt*
1 tablespoon grated lemon peel	*1 tablespoon butter*
1/4 cup lemon juice	

1. In 1-quart saucepan, stir first 6 ingredients until blended. Over medium heat, cook until very thick and boiling briskly, stirring constantly. Reduce heat; simmer 1 minute, stirring occasionally.
2. Remove from heat; stir in butter. Cool mixture at room temperature.

Creamy Mocha Filling

Begin 20 mins ahead

221 cals per one-twelfth

2 eggs, separated, at room temperature	*2 squares unsweetened chocolate, melted*
confectioners' sugar	*2 teaspoons instant coffee*
1/3 cup water	*1 teaspoon vanilla extract*
1 cup butter or margarine, softened	

1. In small bowl with mixer at high speed, beat egg whites until soft peaks form; gradually sprinkle in 1/4 cup confectioners' sugar, beating until sugar is dissolved and whites stand in stiff peaks. Do not scrape bowl during beating.
2. In large bowl with same beaters and at medium speed, mix well 1 1/4 cups confectioners' sugar with yolks, water and remaining ingredients.
3. With rubber spatula, fold in egg whites.

Pineapple Filling

Begin 1 1/2 hrs ahead

56 cals per one-twelfth

1/4 cup sugar	*1 tablespoon lemon juice*
3 tablespoons cornstarch	*1 teaspoon grated lemon peel*
1/8 teaspoon salt	
3/4 cup canned pineapple juice	
2 tablespoons butter or margarine	

In 1-quart saucepan, mix sugar, cornstarch and salt; stir in juice; add remaining ingredients. Over low heat, heat to boiling, stirring constantly; boil 1 minute until smooth and thickened; cool.

COOKIES

Cookies are quick and easy to make, and are an excellent introduction to the more complicated techniques of cake and bread making. All cookies are made from basically the same ingredients – flour, sugar, shortening, possibly eggs and leavening, plus liquid and flavoring – they vary in texture and taste according to the proportions and flavorings used.

Measure ingredients carefully so dough is the right consistency. Most cookie doughs can be whipped up in the mixer in minutes with our one-bowl method. Use low or medium speed as directed and beat only as long as the recipe indicates. For mixing by hand, use a long-handled wooden spoon so you can mix, stir and beat the ingredients easily. Don't overmix; this could make cookies tough or hard. When rolling dough, use as little extra flour as possible so cookies won't look floury and rerolled trimmings won't be tough. Be sure that the cookies you place on a cookie sheet are of the same size and thickness so they will be uniformly cooked and browned and ready at the same time.

BAKING COOKIES

For best results, use clean, shiny aluminum cookie sheets 2 inches smaller all around than the oven so that the heat will be able to circulate evenly. If baking one sheet of cookies at a time, place it in the center of the oven; when baking 2 sheets, stagger the oven racks so that they divide the oven into thirds, switching the sheets once, about half-way through baking time, to make certain that cookies brown evenly. Don't grease cookie sheets unless indicated in the recipe, or cookies will tend to spread too much.

When baking several batches in succession, plan ahead so that while the first sheet is in the oven, you are preparing the second one. Let sheets cool before placing more dough on them, or the dough will soften and spread, and finished cookies will be misshapen If you don't have enough spare cookie sheets, use inverted baking pans. Or, place unbaked cookies on a sheet of heavy-duty foil and, as soon as baked cookies have been transferred to wire racks, place the foil on the cookie sheet and return it to the oven.

Cookies bake quickly, so test them for doneness at the end of the minimum baking time given; correctly baked, the cookies will feel set and dry to the touch.

TYPES OF COOKIE

There are six types of cookie, made from doughs of varying degrees of stiffness. Bar and drop cookies are made from soft unchilled dough. For pressed cookies, dough should be moderately stiff; for refrigerator, molded and rolled cookies, dough must be stiff, chilled if necessary to make it easy to handle.

 Bar cookies are simplest of all to make. Just spread the dough evenly in a well-greased shallow pan, bake, then cut the slab into bars or squares with a sharp, thin-bladed knife once it has cooled slightly.

 Drop cookies are formed by scooping up teaspoonfuls of soft dough and dropping them about 2 inches apart onto a cookie sheet; use a small spatula to shape them.

 Refrigerator cookie dough can be made a week or more ahead, shaped into a smooth roll, wrapped in waxed paper and refrigerated until needed. To bake, slice the roll thinly and evenly with a sharp knife, and arrange slices slightly apart on cookie sheet.

 Molded cookie dough should always be firm enough for shaping in a mold or by hand into balls, crescents and wreaths.Chill dough just until easy to handle.

 Pressed cookies are forced through a cookie press or decorating bag. Dough should be soft enough to go through the press but firm enough to hold its shape. Chill only if directed.

 Rolled cookie dough should be stiff, chilled if necessary, then rolled out and cut into shapes with lightly floured cookie cutters, a pastry wheel, or knife and a pattern. Or, dough can be rolled out directly onto a cookie sheet, and the cookies cut and trimmings removed. Cut cookies as close together as possible, so that you reduce the amount of rerolling that is necessary.

COOLING COOKIES

Unless the recipe directs otherwise, empty cookie sheets as soon as they come out of the oven, or the cookies will continue to bake on the hot sheet. Loosen cookies carefully with a pancake turner, transfer them to wire racks, and let cool in a single layer; don't overlap them or they will soften. Wait until they are quite cold before decorating or storing them. Cool bar cookies in the pan.

STORING AND FREEZING COOKIES

Crisp cookies and soft cookies must be stored separately in containers with tight-fitting lids. To keep soft cookies moist, add a piece of apple to the storage jar and replace it often. Crisp cookies which have turned soft can be re-crisped by heating them for 3 to 5 minutes in a 300°F. oven. Bar cookies can be stored in the pan. Allow the slab to cool slightly before cutting it into bars (otherwise the edges tend to crumble), and leave until quite cold. Then cover the whole pan tightly with foil or plastic wrap and store at room temperature.

Cookies can be stored in the freezer for up to 6 months, either baked, or as unbaked dough. Pack unbaked dough in freezer containers or, for refrigerator cookies, shape it into rolls or bars and wrap tightly in foil or plastic wrap.

Baked cookies should be quite cold before they are packed for the freezer. Use sturdy containers, and cushion fragile cookies with crumpled foil or waxed paper. If the cookies have been decorated or have a soft frosting, lay them out on cookie sheets and freeze them hard, then pack them. Thaw baked cookies, unwrapped, at room temperature for about 10 minutes. When you are ready to bake frozen cookie dough, thaw it until it is soft enough to handle, then shape the cookies and bake as usual. Frozen refrigerator cookie dough should be left in the refrigerator to soften until it slices easily.

DECORATING COOKIES

To decorate cookies you can use homemade ornamental or butter cream frosting; canned, ready-to-spread frostings; and decorating icings sold in tubes to which different tips are attached. Colored decorating gels in tubes are also attractive. To use homemade frosting in a decorating bag, see Cake Decorating, pages 398 to 399

Assemble all frostings and tools before starting to decorate cookies. Useful items include a soft pastry brush to brush crumbs from cookies; a decorating bag and tubes; a small cutting board for chopping nuts or candied fruit; small, sharp knives and metal spatulas; custard cups to keep decorations separate, and wire racks on which to decorate cookies.

DECORATIVE IDEAS

It is easy to transform the plainest cookies into something special. Everything you need can be found in the supermarket – frostings, icings, nuts, candies, multicolored sugar decorations, chocolate for melting, chocolate sprinkles or chips, candied fruit and decorative cereals. Here are some basic decorated cookies you can adapt as required.

Double star: Frost 2 star-shaped cookies with white icing; press together so all points show. Decorate top with multicolored sprinkles.

Chessboard: Frost oblong cookie with white icing. With round tube attached to decorating bag, crosshatch with dark frosting; fill in alternate squares with dark frosting.

Love kiss: Frost heart-shaped cookie with white icing. Decorate the 2 halves of the heart with contrasting colored sugar flowerets, sprinkles or dragées.

Pine cone: Frost oval cookie and press unblanched sliced nuts into the frosting to resemble a pine cone.

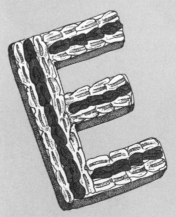

Letter cookie: Using a decorating bag with star tube cover letter with rippled lines of frosting; fill in with contrasting gel.

Doughnut sprinkle: Frost top of doughnut-shaped cookie; toss in multicolored sprinkles; press well to coat cookie completely in sprinkles.

Bar cookies

Fudgy Brownies

Color index
page 104

Begin early
in day

24 brownies

274 cals each

1 cup butter or margarine
4 squares unsweetened
chocolate
2 cups sugar
4 eggs
1 cup all-purpose flour
1 teaspoon vanilla
extract
½ teaspoon salt
2 cups coarsely chopped
nuts

1 Preheat oven to 350°F. Grease 13″ by 9″ baking pan. In 3-quart saucepan over very low heat, melt butter or margarine and chocolate, stirring the mixture constantly.

2 Remove pan from heat and with a spoon, stir the sugar into the chocolate. Allow the mixture to cool slightly.

3 Add eggs, one at a time, beating until well blended after the addition of each egg.

4 Add the flour, vanilla and salt to the mixture and stir in well.

5 Add the chopped nuts to the mixture and stir to blend well.

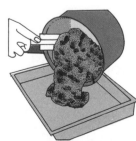

6 Pour chocolate-nut mixture into greased baking pan, scraping the side of saucepan with a rubber spatula; bake in oven 30 to 35 minutes.

7 Brownies are done when toothpick inserted in center comes out clean. Cool in pan on wire rack; with a sharp knife, cut brownies into pieces.

Backpacking Bars

Color index
page 104

Begin 3 hrs
or up to
1 wk ahead

12 cookies

263 cals each

¾ cup all-purpose flour
½ cup uncooked quick-
cooking oats
½ cup butter, softened
¼ cup toasted wheat
germ
1 tablespoon grated
orange peel

brown sugar
2 eggs
1 4¼-ounce can
blanched whole
almonds
½ cup shredded
coconut

1. Preheat oven to 350°F. In large bowl with mixer at low speed, beat first 5 ingredients and ½ cup packed brown sugar until just mixed; at medium speed, beat 2 minutes (mixture will look dry).
2. With lightly floured hands, shape mixture into a ball, then pat into 8″ by 8″ baking pan.
3. In small bowl with hand beater, beat eggs with ¼ cup packed brown sugar; stir in almonds and coconut. Pour evenly over mixture in pan.
4. Bake 35 minutes or until toothpick comes out clean. Cool in pan on rack. Cut into 12 pieces.

Luscious Apricot Squares

Color index
page 105

Begin 3 hrs
ahead

16 cookies

209 cals each

water
⅔ cup dried apricots
½ cup butter, softened
¼ cup sugar
all-purpose flour
1 cup packed light brown
sugar
2 eggs

½ cup chopped
California walnuts
½ teaspoon double-
acting baking powder
½ teaspoon vanilla
extract
¼ teaspoon salt
confectioners' sugar

1. In covered 1-quart saucepan over low heat, in enough water to cover apricots, cook apricots 15 minutes; drain and finely chop.
2. Preheat oven to 350°F. Grease 8″ by 8″ baking pan. In large bowl with mixer at medium speed, beat butter, sugar and 1 cup flour until well mixed and crumbly; pat into pan. Bake 25 minutes or just until layer is golden.
3. Meanwhile, in same bowl at medium speed, mix well apricots, brown sugar, ⅓ cup flour and remaining ingredients except confectioners' sugar.
4. Pour over baked layer; bake 25 minutes longer.
5. Cool in pan; cut into squares. Sprinkle with confectioners' sugar.

Toffee Bars

Color index
page 105

Begin 3 to 5
days ahead

50 cookies

76 cals each

1¾ cups all-purpose flour
1 cup sugar
1 cup butter or
margarine, softened

1 teaspoon vanilla extract
1 egg, separated
½ cup finely chopped
California walnuts

1. Preheat oven to 275°F. Grease 15½″ by 10½″ jelly-roll pan. In large bowl with mixer at medium speed, beat all ingredients except egg white and walnuts until well mixed; pat evenly into pan.
2. In cup with fork, beat egg white slightly; brush over top of dough and sprinkle with nuts.
3. Bake 1 hour and 10 minutes or until golden. Immediately cut into 50 bars and remove from pan to cool on wire racks. Store in tightly covered container for at least 3 days before serving.

Shortbread

2 cups all-purpose flour
1 cup butter or
margarine, softened
¹/₂ cup confectioners'
sugar
¹/₄ teaspoon salt

¹/₄ teaspoon double-
acting baking powder
1 teaspoon vanilla
extract
2 tablespoons sugar

Color index
page 104

Begin early
in day

14 cookies

215 cals each

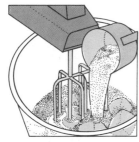

1 Preheat oven to 350°F.
In large bowl with
mixer at medium speed,
beat first 6 ingredients until
well mixed, occasionally
scraping the bowl.

2 Pat dough into 9-inch
round cake pan and
with fork, prick well.

3 With spoon, sprinkle
sugar over dough.
Bake 30 to 35 minutes.

4 Cut into wedges while
warm. Cool on wire
rack; separate cookies.

Marbled Fudge Bars

Color index
page 104

Begin 2 hrs
or up to
1 wk ahead

36 cookies

188 cals each

1 cup butter or margarine
4 squares unsweetened
chocolate
sugar
4 eggs
1 cup all-purpose flour

¹/₂ teaspoon salt
1 cup chopped California
walnuts
vanilla extract
1 8-ounce package cream
cheese, softened

1. Grease a 13″ by 9″ baking pan. In 2-quart heavy
saucepan over low heat, melt butter and chocolate.
With wire whisk or spoon, beat in 2 cups sugar and 3
eggs until well blended. With wooden spoon, stir in
flour, salt, nuts and 1 teaspoon vanilla extract.
Spread evenly in pan.
2. Preheat oven to 350°F. In small bowl with mixer
at low speed, beat cream cheese, ¹/₂ cup sugar, 1 egg
and 1 teaspoon vanilla extract until just mixed; at
medium speed, beat 2 minutes, occasionally scraping bowl with rubber spatula.
3. With large spoon, drop mixture in dollops on top
of batter. Using tip of knife, lightly score top surface
in a crisscross pattern.
4. Bake 40 to 45 minutes until toothpick comes out
clean. Cool on rack. Cut into bars. Refrigerate.

Prune-Ribbon Cookies

Color index
page 105

Begin 3 hrs
or up to
2 wks ahead

27 cookies

155 cals each

1 12-ounce package
pitted prunes (2 cups)
1 cup water
¹/₄ cup honey
¹/₄ large lemon, unpeeled
2 cups all-purpose flour
1¹/₄ cups packed light
brown sugar

³/₄ cup butter or
margarine, softened
1 teaspoon double-acting
baking powder
1 teaspoon vanilla
extract
¹/₂ teaspoon salt
1 egg

1. In 2-quart saucepan over medium-high heat, heat
prunes and water to boiling. Reduce heat to low;
cover saucepan and simmer 3 minutes; drain prunes
well. In covered blender container at high speed,
blend prunes, honey and lemon until smooth.
2. Meanwhile, preheat oven to 350°F. Grease 9″ by
9″ baking pan. Into large bowl, measure remaining
ingredients; with mixer at low speed, beat until just
mixed. At medium speed, beat until smooth.
3. Divide dough into thirds. With greased fingers,
pat one piece into bottom of baking pan. With
spoon, spread half of prune mixture on dough;
repeat layering, ending with dough.
4. Bake 1 hour or until browned and cookie pulls
away from side of pan. Cool in pan on wire rack.
With sharp knife, cut into 3″ by 1″ bars.

Linzer Cookies

Color index
page 105

Begin 4 hrs
or up to
3 days ahead

30 cookies

140 cals each

1 3¹/₂- to 4-ounce can
blanched slivered
almonds, ground
1 egg
2 cups all-purpose flour
1 cup sugar
³/₄ cup butter, softened

1 teaspoon cinnamon
1 teaspoon grated lemon
peel
¹/₈ teaspoon ground
cloves
¹/₂ 12-ounce jar raspberry
preserves

1. In large bowl with mixer at low speed, beat all
ingredients except preserves until well mixed, occasionally scraping bowl. (Mixture will be crumbly.)
Shape dough into ball; wrap; chill until easy to
handle, about 2 hours.
2. Preheat oven to 350°F. Grease 11″ by 7″ baking
pan. Press half of dough into pan (keep remainder
chilled). Spread preserves over dough in pan.
3. Roll half of remaining dough into six 11-inch-long
ropes; arrange lengthwise, one inch apart on preserves. Roll remaining dough into eight 7-inch-long
ropes; arrange crosswise over preserves.
4. Bake 40 minutes or until top is golden. Cool in
pan on wire rack. Cut into 2″ by 1″ bars.

Making ropes: With hands,
roll chilled dough into
ropes on countertop.

Arranging ropes: Position
11-inch ropes lengthwise,
then 7-inch ropes crosswise.

405

Drop cookies

Chocolate Chip Cookies

Color index
page 104

Begin 2¼ hrs
ahead

48 cookies

72 cals each

1¼ cups all-purpose flour
*½ cup packed light
brown sugar*
½ cup butter, softened
¼ cup sugar
1 egg
*1 teaspoon vanilla
extract*
½ teaspoon baking soda
½ teaspoon salt
*1 6-ounce package
semisweet-chocolate
pieces*
*½ cup chopped
California walnuts*

1 Preheat oven to 375°F.
Grease cookie sheets.
Into large bowl, measure
all ingredients except
chocolate pieces and nuts.

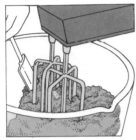

2 With mixer at medium
speed, beat until well
mixed, scraping bowl.

3 Add the chocolate
pieces and chopped
nuts. Stir in well.

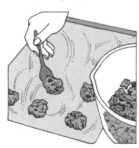

4 Drop by rounded
teaspoonfuls, 2 inches
apart, on sheets. Bake 10
to 12 minutes until cookies
are lightly browned.

5 With pancake turner or
spatula, remove
cookies to wire racks; cool.

Soft Molasses Cookies

Color index
page 105

Begin 2 hrs
ahead

30 cookies

109 cals each

2 cups all-purpose flour
½ cup sugar
½ cup shortening
½ cup light molasses
1 egg
2 teaspoons baking soda

1 teaspoon ground ginger
*1 teaspoon ground
cinnamon*
¼ teaspoon salt
*⅓ cup cold water
raisins for garnish*

1. Preheat oven to 400°F. Grease cookie sheets. In
large bowl with mixer at medium speed, beat all
ingredients except raisins until well mixed.
2. Drop mixture by rounded tablespoonfuls, at least
2 inches apart, onto cookie sheets; place 4 or 5
raisins on top of each cookie.
3. Bake 8 minutes or until top springs back when
lightly pressed with finger. With pancake turner,
remove cookies to wire racks; cool.

Double Chocolate Drops

Color index
page 104

Begin 2½ hrs
or up to
1 wk ahead

48 cookies

105 cals each

1¾ cups all-purpose flour
¾ cup sugar
½ cup milk
*½ cup butter or
margarine, softened*
*1 teaspoon vanilla
extract*
½ teaspoon salt

½ teaspoon baking soda
1 egg
*2 squares unsweetened
chocolate, melted*
*Chocolate Butter-Cream
Frosting (below)*
1 cup pecan halves

1. Preheat oven to 400°F. Into large bowl, measure
all ingredients except Frosting and pecans; with
mixer at low speed, beat just until blended, scraping
bowl constantly with rubber spatula. Increase mixer
speed to medium; beat 3 minutes, scraping bowl
occasionally, until well blended.
2. Drop batter by heaping teaspoonfuls onto cookie
sheets, about 1 inch apart. Bake 8 to 10 minutes until
cookies are puffy and slightly cracked on top. Cool.
3. Top cookies with frosting; garnish with pecans.

CHOCOLATE BUTTER-CREAM FROSTING:
In small bowl with mixer at medium speed, beat
together *1½ cups sifted confectioners' sugar*, *¼ cup
butter* or margarine, softened, and *⅛ teaspoon salt*
until light and fluffy. Add *1½ squares unsweetened
chocolate*, melted, *1 to 2 tablespoons milk* and *1
teaspoon vanilla extract*, beating until well blended.
(Makes 1¼ cups.)

Raisin-Granola Cookies

Color index
page 105

Begin 1¾ hrs
or up to
1 wk ahead

48 cookies

110 cals each

*1¾ cups regular
granola*
*1½ cups all-purpose
flour*
*1 cup butter or
margarine,
softened*
⅜ cup sugar
*¾ cup packed dark
brown sugar*

*1 teaspoon baking
soda*
1 teaspoon salt
*1 teaspoon vanilla
extract*
1 egg
*1 cup dark seedless
raisins*
*½ cup unsalted peanuts,
coarsely chopped*

1. Preheat oven to 375°F. Grease cookie sheets. Into
large bowl, measure all ingredients except raisins
and peanuts. With mixer at low speed, beat ingredients just until mixed; increase speed to medium
and beat 2 minutes, occasionally scraping bowl with
rubber spatula. Stir in raisins and peanuts until
mixture is well blended.
2. Drop dough by heaping teaspoonfuls, about 2
inches apart, on cookie sheets.
3. Bake 12 to 15 minutes until cookies are lightly
browned around edges.
4. With pancake turner, remove cookies to wire
racks and allow to cool completely. Store cookies in
a tightly covered container up to 1 week.

120 cals each

CHOCOLATE-GRANOLA COOKIES: Prepare
dough as for Raisin-Granola Cookies, above, but
substitute *one 6-ounce package semisweet-chocolate
pieces* for seedless raisins.

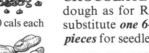

109 cals each

DATE-GRANOLA COOKIES: Prepare dough as
for Raisin-Granola Cookies, above, but substitute
1 cup chopped, pitted dates for seedless raisins.

Almond Lace Rolls

Color index
page 105

Begin 1¾ hrs
ahead

30 cookies

62 cals each

*⅔ cup blanched almonds,
   ground*
½ cup sugar
*½ cup butter or
   margarine*
*1 tablespoon all-purpose
   flour*
2 tablespoons milk

1 Preheat oven to 350°F.
Grease and flour cookie
sheet. In 10-inch skillet
over low heat, cook all
ingredients, stirring just
until mixture is blended.

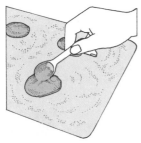

2 Keeping mixture warm
over very low heat,
drop 4 heaping teaspoon-
fuls, 2 inches apart, on
sheet. Bake 5 minutes.

3 When cookies are
golden, remove cookie
sheet from oven and, with
pancake turner, loosen and
lift cookies one by one.

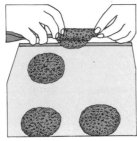

4 Roll each cookie
around handle of
wooden spoon and cool.
If cookies get too hard
quickly reheat in oven.

5 Finish cooling on rack.
Repeat steps 2–5,
greasing and flouring
cookie sheet each time.

Oatmeal Cookies

Color index
page 104

Begin 1¾ hrs
ahead

48 cookies

58 cals each

*1 cup uncooked quick-
   cooking oats*
¾ cup all-purpose flour
*½ cup packed brown
   sugar*
*½ cup chopped
   California walnuts*

½ cup shortening
¼ cup sugar
1 egg
½ teaspoon salt
½ teaspoon baking soda
*½ teaspoon vanilla
   extract*

1. Preheat oven to 375°F. In large bowl with mixer
at medium speed, beat all ingredients until well
mixed, occasionally scraping bowl.
2. Drop by teaspoonfuls, 1 inch apart, on sheet.
3. Bake for 12 minutes or until lightly browned.
Immediately remove cookies to wire racks; cool.

Walnut Clusters

Color index
page 104

Begin 2 hrs
ahead

36 cookies

84 cals each

*1½ squares unsweetened
   chocolate, melted*
½ cup all-purpose flour
½ cup sugar
*¼ cup butter or
   margarine, softened*
1 egg
½ teaspoon salt

*1½ teaspoons vanilla
   extract*
*¼ teaspoon double-
   acting baking powder*
*2 cups chopped
   California walnuts*
confectioners' sugar

1. Preheat oven to 350°F. Grease cookie sheets. In
large bowl with mixer at medium speed, beat all
ingredients except walnuts and confectioners' sugar
until well mixed, occasionally scraping bowl with
rubber spatula. Stir in walnuts.
2. Drop mixture by rounded teaspoonfuls, ½ inch
apart, onto cookie sheets.
3. Bake 10 minutes. Remove cookies to wire racks;
cool. Sprinkle with confectioners' sugar.

Choco-Peanut Drops

Color index
page 104

Begin 2 hrs
ahead

48 cookies

71 cals each

all-purpose flour
*2 squares unsweetened
   chocolate, melted*
½ cup sugar
½ cup shortening
1 egg
1 teaspoon salt

*1 teaspoon vanilla
   extract*
*½ cup packed light
   brown sugar*
¼ cup peanut butter
*2 tablespoons butter or
   margarine, softened*

1. Preheat oven to 325°F. In large bowl with mixer
at medium speed, beat 1 cup flour and next 6
ingredients until well mixed, occasionally scraping
bowl with rubber spatula. Wash beaters.
2. In small bowl with mixer at medium speed, beat 3
tablespoons flour and remaining ingredients until
well mixed (mixture will be crumbly).
3. Drop chocolate dough by teaspoonfuls, 1 inch
apart, onto cookie sheet; top each with ½ teaspoon
peanut-butter dough. Dip a fork into flour and press
gently across top of each cookie.
4. Bake 12 minutes or until firm. With pancake
turner, remove cookies to racks; cool.

Raisin-Orange Cookies

Color index
page 104

Begin 1½ hrs
or up to
2 wks ahead

30 cookies

163 cals each

*2¼ cups all-purpose
   flour*
1½ cups sugar
*1 cup butter or
   margarine, softened*
3 eggs
*1 teaspoon double-acting
   baking powder*

1 teaspoon salt
*1 teaspoon vanilla
   extract*
*1½ cups dark seedless
   raisins*
*2 tablespoons grated
   orange peel*

1. Preheat oven to 375°F. Grease 2 large cookie
sheets. Into large bowl, measure all ingredients
except raisins and orange peel. With mixer at low
speed, beat ingredients until just mixed. Increase
speed to medium and beat 2 minutes, occasionally
scraping bowl with rubber spatula. Stir in raisins
and orange peel.
2. Drop batter by heaping tablespoonfuls, about 2
inches apart, on cookie sheets.
3. Bake 15 minutes or until cookies are golden
brown. Remove cookies to wire racks to cool.

Drop cookies

Almond Macaroons

2 cups sliced blanched almonds (about 9 ounces)
3/4 cup sugar
2 teaspoons almond extract
2 egg whites, at room temperature

Color index page 105

Begin 1 hr or up to 2 wks ahead

36 cookies
56 cals each

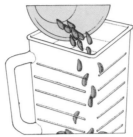

1 In covered blender container, blend almonds half at a time until finely ground.

2 Line cookie sheet with heavy-duty foil. Preheat oven to 350°F.

3 In medium bowl, combine all ingredients until well mixed and stiff.

4 Drop in 1-inch mounds, 1 inch apart, on sheet. Bake 20 minutes or until firm at edges but soft in center and golden.

5 Remove from oven and lift foil with macaroons to wire rack to cool. When cool, peel off foil. Store in tightly covered container.

Coconut Meringues

2 egg whites, at room temperature
1/8 teaspoon cream of tartar
3/4 cup confectioners' sugar

1/4 cup shredded coconut
1/4 teaspoon almond extract

Color index page 104

Begin 1 1/2 hrs or up to 3 wks ahead

24 cookies
17 cals each

1. Preheat oven to 250°F. In small bowl with mixer at high speed, beat egg whites and cream of tartar until soft peaks form. Beating at high speed, gradually sprinkle in sugar, 2 tablespoons at a time, beating until sugar is completely dissolved. (Whites should stand in stiff glossy peaks.) With rubber spatula, fold in coconut and extract until mixed.
2. Drop mixture by rounded teaspoonfuls onto large cookie sheet, about 1 inch apart.
3. Bake 1 hour or until dry. Remove to rack to cool.

Molded cookies

Peanut-Butter Cookies

2 1/4 cups all-purpose flour
1 cup creamy peanut butter
2/3 cup honey
1/2 cup sugar

1/2 cup butter or margarine, softened
2 eggs
1/2 teaspoon double-acting baking powder

Color index page 105

Begin 2 1/4 hrs or up to 2 wks ahead

36 cookies
126 cals each

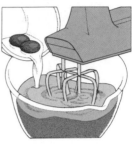

1 Preheat oven to 350°F. Into large bowl, measure all ingredients. With mixer at medium speed, beat until well mixed, occasionally scraping bowl.

2 With hands, shape dough into 1 1/2-inch balls; place 3 inches apart on cookie sheets.

3 Dip a fork into flour and press deeply across top of each cookie; repeat in opposite direction. Bake in oven 15 minutes or just until cookies are lightly browned.

4 With pancake turner, immediately remove cookies to wire racks; allow to cool. Store in tightly covered container.

Filbert Drops

1 cup all-purpose flour
1/2 cup shortening
1/4 cup sugar
1 tablespoon water
1 teaspoon grated orange peel

1/2 teaspoon grated lemon or lime peel
1/4 teaspoon salt
1 egg, separated
2/3 cup finely ground filberts

Color index page 105

Begin 3 hrs ahead or early in day

24 cookies
94 cals each

1. Into large bowl, measure all ingredients except egg white and filberts. With mixer at medium speed, beat ingredients until well mixed, occasionally scraping bowl with rubber spatula. Refrigerate dough until easy to handle.
2. Preheat oven to 350°F. Put egg white in saucer; put nuts on waxed paper. With hands, shape dough into 1-inch balls; roll in egg white, then in ground nuts. Place 1 inch apart on cookie sheets.
3. Bake 18 to 20 minutes until cookies are firm. Immediately remove to wire racks; cool completely. Store cookies in tightly covered container.

Danish Almond Cakes

Color index
page 104

Begin 4 hrs
ahead

42 cookies
95 cals each

1²/₃ cups all-purpose flour
½ cup sugar
*½ cup diced toasted
 almonds*
*½ cup butter or
 margarine, softened*
½ cup shortening
1 egg
*1 tablespoon ground
 cinnamon*

*½ teaspoon double-
 acting baking
 powder*
*½ teaspoon ground
 cardamom*
1 egg yolk, beaten
*1 tablespoon water
 blanched almonds,
 halved*

1. Into large bowl, measure all ingredients except 1 egg yolk, water and almonds. With mixer at medium speed, beat ingredients until well mixed, occasionally scraping bowl with rubber spatula. Cover; refrigerate 2 hours.
2. Preheat oven to 375°F. With hands, shape dough into 1-inch balls; place 2 inches apart on cookie sheets. Cover the bottom of a flat-bottomed glass with a damp cloth and use to flatten slightly each ball of dough.
3. In cup, blend remaining egg yolk with water; brush egg yolk glaze on tops of cookies and top with an almond half.
4. Bake 10 minutes or until golden. With pancake turner, immediately remove cookies to wire racks and allow to cool. Store in tightly covered container.

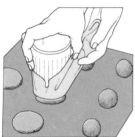

Shaping the dough: Use a flat-bottomed glass covered with a damp cloth to flatten slightly each ball.

Decorating the cakes: Brush on egg yolk glaze and top each cookie with half a blanched almond.

Cardamom Cookies

Color index
page 105

Begin 3 hrs
or up to
2 wks ahead

72 cookies
92 cals each

*3³/₄ cups all-purpose
 flour*
*2 cups butter or
 margarine, softened*
*1 cup chopped
 California walnuts*

*1½ teaspoons almond
 extract*
*1 teaspoon ground
 cardamom*
*⅛ teaspoon salt
 confectioners' sugar*

1. Preheat oven to 350°F. Into large bowl, measure flour, butter, walnuts, almond extract, cardamom, salt and 1½ cups confectioners' sugar.
2. With hand, knead until well blended; shape dough into 1-inch balls. Place balls of dough, 2 inches apart, on cookie sheets.
3. Bake cookies 20 minutes or until lightly browned. With pancake turner, immediately remove cookies to wire racks; cool.
4. If you like, just before serving, roll cookies in confectioners' sugar. Store tightly covered.

Madeleines

Color index
page 105

Begin 1 hr
or up to
3 days ahead

30 cookies
97 cals each

2 eggs
⅓ cup sugar
*½ teaspoon vanilla
 extract*
*1 teaspoon grated lemon
 peel*

1 cup all-purpose flour
*¾ cup butter or
 margarine, melted and
 cooled*
3 tablespoons salad oil

1. Grease and flour well each 3³/₈″ by 2″ shell of one 12-shell Madeleine pan to prevent dough sticking. Preheat oven to 425°F.
2. In small bowl with mixer at high speed, beat eggs, sugar and vanilla; beating at high speed, beat until mixture becomes thick and lemon-colored, about 5 minutes, occasionally scraping the bowl with a rubber spatula.
3. With rubber spatula, fold in lemon peel. Sprinkle flour, about 2 tablespoons at a time, over egg mixture and gently fold into mixture. Fold in butter and salad oil, about 1 tablespoon at a time.
4. Fill shells about three-fourths full. Bake 8 minutes or until golden. Immediately remove from shells to wire rack; allow cookies to cool completely. Repeat until all the Madeleine batter is used.

Christmas Wreaths

Color index
page 104

Begin 2½ hrs
or up to
2 wks ahead

54 cookies
69 cals each

sugar
*2½ cups all-purpose
 flour*
*1 cup butter or
 margarine, softened*
*2 teaspoons grated
 orange peel*

2 egg yolks
¼ teaspoon salt
*1 egg white,
 beaten*
*red and green candied
 cherries, chopped*

1. In large bowl, measure ½ cup sugar and next 5 ingredients. With mixer at low speed, beat ingredients until just mixed; increase speed to medium and beat 4 minutes, occasionally scraping bowl with rubber spatula. (Mixture may look dry.)
2. Preheat oven to 400°F. Take a heaping teaspoonful of dough at a time and roll it into a 6-inch rope. Place each dough rope on cookie sheet in a circle, crossing ends over.
3. Brush cookies with egg white and sprinkle on some sugar. Decorate with red and green cherries.
4. Bake 10 to 12 minutes until light golden. Allow wreaths to cool on cookie sheet. Store cookies in a tightly covered container.

Shaping the wreaths: Arrange dough rope in a circle but cross one end over the other with ½ inch extending at each end .

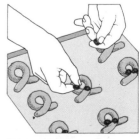

Decorating the cookies: Press pieces of red and green candied cherries into cookies before baking to make a pretty decoration.

Molded and Pressed cookies

Spritz

3¾ cups all-purpose flour
1⅓ cups butter or margarine, softened
¾ cup sugar
¼ cup orange juice
1 egg yolk

Color index page 106

Begin 3½ hrs ahead or early in day

108 cookies

45 cals each

1 Into large bowl, measure flour, butter, sugar, orange juice and egg yolk. With mixer at medium speed, beat ingredients until well mixed, occasionally scraping bowl with rubber spatula. Cover; refrigerate about 1 hour. Preheat oven to 375°F. Use part of dough at a time; keep rest of dough refrigerated.

2 Using cookie press fitted with bar-plate tip, press dough in long strips, about 1 inch apart, down length of cookie sheets.

3 With sharp knife, cut each strip into 2½-inch pieces. Leave pieces in place. Bake 8 minutes or until light golden, being careful not to overbake.

4 Remove from oven and immediately cut again between cookies to separate any cookies which are still joined together.

5 With pancake turner, immediately remove cookies to wire racks. Allow cookies to cool completely. Store tightly covered.

Color index page 106
Begin 4 hrs or up to 2 wks ahead
120 cookies
70 cals each

Chocolate-dipped Butter Cookies

4⅓ cups all-purpose flour
1½ cups butter or margarine, softened
1 cup sugar
½ cup sour cream
2 egg yolks
½ teaspoon almond extract
¼ teaspoon salt

Chocolate Glaze:
1½ cups sugar
¼ cup light corn syrup
2 tablespoons butter or margarine
½ cup water
1 6-ounce package semisweet-chocolate pieces

1. Preheat oven to 375°F. Into large bowl, measure all ingredients except glaze; with mixer at low speed, beat until just mixed. Increase speed to medium; beat 2 minutes, occasionally scraping bowl with rubber spatula.

2. With cookie press fitted with 1½-inch Christmas tree plate, fill cookie press cylinder with dough. Refrigerate remaining dough. Press dough shapes onto cookie sheets, about ½ inch apart.

3. Bake 12 to 15 minutes until lightly browned around edges.

4. With pancake turner, immediately remove to wire racks and allow to cool completely. (Wash and cool cookie sheets completely before reusing, or cookies will not have a nice shape.)

5. Prepare Chocolate Glaze: In a 2-quart heavy saucepan over high heat, heat sugar, light corn syrup, butter or margarine and water to a full rolling boil; boil mixture for 2 minutes then remove saucepan from heat. Into mixture in saucepan stir semisweet-chocolate pieces until pieces are melted and glaze is smooth. Keep glaze warm over low heat while dipping cooled cookies.

6. With fork, gently lower one cookie at a time, flat side down, into Chocolate Glaze, to allow mixture to coat back and approximately ⅛ inch up sides of each of the cookies.

7. Carefully lift cookie out and allow excess glaze to drain off. Place cookies chocolate side up on wire racks to allow glaze to cool and harden. Store in a tightly covered container.

Dipping in chocolate: With fork, lower cookie flat side down into glaze to coat one side; lift out; allow excess to drain off.

Hardening the glaze: Carefully place each cookie, chocolate side up, on a wire rack. Leave until glaze is completely hard.

RASPBERRY THUMBPRINTS

Use ½ *of chilled Spritz dough* (above). Shape rounded teaspoonfuls of dough into balls. Place 1 inch apart on cookie sheets.

Press thumb into centers of cookies, making deep indentations. Bake 10 minutes.

Remove from oven and with ⅓ *cup red raspberry preserves* fill indentations. Bake 5 minutes more; immediately remove and cool cookies on racks. (72 cookies.)

RINGLETS

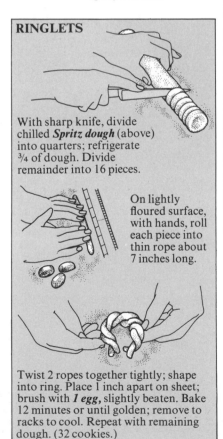

With sharp knife, divide chilled *Spritz dough* (above) into quarters; refrigerate ¾ of dough. Divide remainder into 16 pieces.

On lightly floured surface, with hands, roll each piece into thin rope about 7 inches long.

Twist 2 ropes together tightly; shape into ring. Place 1 inch apart on sheet; brush with *1 egg,* slightly beaten. Bake 12 minutes or until golden; remove to racks to cool. Repeat with remaining dough. (32 cookies.)

Refrigerator cookies

Color index
page 103

Begin 6 hrs
or up to
1 wk ahead

96 cookies

44 cals each

Refrigerator Cookies

2½ cups all-purpose flour
1½ cups sugar
1 cup butter or
margarine, softened
1 egg

1½ teaspoons double-
acting baking powder
1 teaspoon vanilla
extract
½ teaspoon salt

1. With mixer at low speed, beat all ingredients until just mixed. At medium speed, beat 3 minutes.
2. Shape dough into rolls about 1½ inches in diameter. Wrap in waxed paper; refrigerate until firm, at least 4 hours or up to 1 week.
3. Preheat oven to 375°F. Cut rolls into ¼-inch-thick slices; rewrap and refrigerate rest of roll.
4. Place slices 1 inch apart on cookie sheet. Bake 8 minutes or until lightly browned. Immediately remove cookies to wire racks; cool.

Color index
page 105

Begin 6 hrs
ahead

96 cookies

46 cals each

Citrus Pinwheels

Refrigerator Cookies
dough (above)
1 teaspoon milk
(optional)
confectioners' sugar
¼ teaspoon lemon
extract

½ teaspoon yellow food
color
½ teaspoon orange
extract
10 drops red food
color

1. Prepare Refrigerator Cookies dough as directed in step 1. If dough is too dry, add milk. Divide dough into 4 equal portions. On waxed paper covered with confectioners' sugar, with lightly sugared rolling pin, roll one dough portion into 12″ by 6″ rectangle.
2. Into small bowl, spoon another dough portion; stir in lemon extract and ¼ teaspoon yellow food color; mix well. On another sheet of sugared paper, roll lemon dough to 12″ by 6″ rectangle.
3. Invert lemon dough on to basic dough; peel off top paper. Trim doughs to same size.
4. Starting with a long end, roll doughs jelly-roll fashion, peeling back waxed paper while rolling. Wrap and refrigerate until firm, about 4 hours.
5. Repeat steps 1–4 using remaining 2 portions of dough. For step 2, flavor and color portion of dough with orange extract, remaining yellow food color and red food color.
6. Preheat oven to 350°F. Unwrap rolls and cut each roll crosswise into ¼-inch-thick slices.
7. Place slices, cut side up, on cookie sheets, 1 inch apart. Bake 12 to 15 minutes until light brown. Remove cookies to wire racks to cool.

Inverting the dough: Invert lemon-flavored dough on top of basic dough.

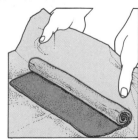

Rolling the dough: Peel back waxed paper while rolling jelly-roll fashion.

Color index
page 105

Begin 6 hrs
ahead

72 cookies

66 cals each

Neapolitan Cookies

Refrigerator Cookies
dough (left)
½ teaspoon almond
extract
5 drops red food
color
1 square unsweetened
chocolate
½ cup chopped
California
walnuts

1 Prepare dough and divide among 3 small bowls. Add almond extract and red food color to one portion; stir until thoroughly mixed.

2 In 1-quart saucepan over low heat, melt chocolate. Mix chocolate into second portion; mix California walnuts with remainder.

3 Line 9″ by 5″ loaf pan with waxed paper and spread almond dough evenly in pan. Then spread walnut dough and finally, chocolate dough.

4 Cover layered dough in pan with waxed paper and place it in the refrigerator until firm, about 4 hours.

5 Preheat oven to 350°F. Invert pan over board to turn out chilled dough and peel off waxed paper.

6 With sharp knife, cut dough lengthwise in half. Slice each half of dough crosswise into ¼-inch slices.

7 Place slices on cookie sheet, 1 inch apart. Bake 10 to 12 minutes until light brown. Remove to wire racks to cool.

Rolled cookies

Sugar Cookies

3¼ cups all-purpose flour
1½ cups sugar
⅔ cup shortening
2 eggs
2½ teaspoons double-acting baking powder
2 tablespoons milk
1 teaspoon vanilla extract
½ teaspoon salt

heavy or whipping cream or 1 egg white slightly beaten with 1 tablespoon water

Decorative toppings:
nonpareils, sugar, chopped nuts, shredded coconut, cut-up gumdrops or butterscotch pieces

Color index page 105

Begin 6 hrs ahead

72 cookies

68 cals each

1 Into large bowl, measure first 8 ingredients. With mixer at medium speed, beat until well mixed, occasionally scraping bowl.

2 Shape dough into ball; wrap with waxed paper; refrigerate 2 to 3 hours until easy to handle. Preheat oven to 400°F. Lightly grease cookie sheets.

3 On lightly floured surface, roll half of dough at a time, keeping rest refrigerated. For crisp cookies, roll paper thin. For softer cookies, roll ⅛ inch to ¼ inch thick.

4 With floured cookie cutters, cut dough into various shapes. Reroll dough trimmings and continue to cut shapes.

5 Place cookies ½ inch apart on greased cookie sheets. To glaze: Brush tops of cookies with heavy or whipping cream or with the beaten egg white and water mixture.

6 Sprinkle cookies with your choice of toppings; bake 8 minutes or until very light brown. With pancake turner remove cookies to racks; cool completely.

Sandwich Cookies

2 egg yolks
2 tablespoons milk
2¼ cups all-purpose flour
¾ cup sugar
¾ cup butter or margarine, softened
1 teaspoon vanilla extract
¼ teaspoon salt

Butter-Cream Frosting (page 400)
4 drops green food color
3 drops red food color
3 drops yellow food color

Color index page 106

Begin 3 hrs or up to 2 wks ahead

42 cookies

135 cals each

1. Preheat oven to 375°F. In large bowl with mixer at low speed, beat egg yolks and milk until well blended. Add flour, sugar, butter or margarine, vanilla and salt; beat ingredients until just mixed; increase speed to medium and beat 2 minutes, occasionally scraping bowl. Divide dough in half.
2. On floured pastry cloth, with lightly floured, stockinette-covered rolling pin, roll one dough half ⅛ inch thick. With 2¼-inch fluted-edged cookie cutter, cut dough into rounds; with ½-inch round cutter, cut out centers from half of rounds. Reserve the dough scraps.
3. Place rounds about ½ inch apart on cookie sheets; bake 8 to 10 minutes until lightly browned. With pancake turner, remove cookies to wire racks to cool completely. Repeat steps 2 and 3 with remaining dough, rerolling scraps.
4. Prepare frosting as recipe directs; divide mixture into thirds; place portions in separate bowls. Tint portions with food color.
5. On bottom side of a cookie without a hole, spread teaspoonful of either green, pink or yellow frosting; top with a cookie with a hole in it, top side up, to make a "sandwich". Repeat with remaining cookies and frosting. (Use any leftover frosting for graham crackers or cupcakes.)

Almond Butter Cookies

1¾ cups all-purpose flour
¾ cup butter or margarine, softened
1 teaspoon almond extract
⅛ teaspoon salt
sugar

1 egg white, slightly beaten
⅛ teaspoon ground cinnamon
⅓ cup toasted diced and buttered almonds

Color index page 105

Begin 1¾ hrs or day ahead

36 cookies

78 cals each

1. Into large bowl, measure flour, butter or margarine, almond extract, salt and ¼ cup sugar. With mixer at medium speed, beat ingredients until well mixed, occasionally scraping bowl with rubber spatula. (Mixture will be crumbly.)
2. With hands, shape into ball. (If dough is too soft to roll, cover and refrigerate until firm.)
3. Preheat oven to 325°F. On lightly floured surface, with floured rolling pin, roll dough into 12″ by 8″ rectangle. With pastry wheel or knife, cut into 3″ by 1″ strips; place on cookie sheets; brush with slightly beaten egg white.
4. In small bowl, mix a scant ¼ cup sugar with cinnamon and almonds; sprinkle on cookies. Bake 15 minutes or until golden. With pancake turner, remove cookies to wire racks; allow to cool.

Gingerbread-Men Cookies

2¼ cups all-purpose
flour
½ cup sugar
½ cup shortening
½ cup light molasses
1 egg
1½ teaspoons ground
cinnamon
1 teaspoon double-acting
baking powder
1 teaspoon ground
ginger
1 teaspoon ground
cloves

½ teaspoon ground
nutmeg
½ teaspoon baking
soda
½ teaspoon salt
dried currants
Ornamental Cookie
Frosting (right)

Color index page 104

Begin 6 hrs ahead

24 cookies

157 cals each

1 Into large bowl measure all ingredients except currants and frosting. With mixer at medium speed, beat ingredients until well mixed. Cover and refrigerate 1 hour.

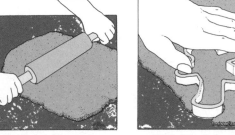

2 On lightly floured surface, with floured rolling pin, roll chilled dough ⅛ inch thick. Preheat oven to 350°F.

3 With 5-inch long cutter, cut out men. Reroll trimmings and cut more cookies. With pancake turner, place ½ inch apart on cookie sheets.

4 On each cut out, place currants to represent buttons, eyes and mouth. (Or, omit currants and mark with frosting after cookies have been baked.)

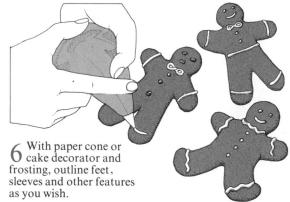

5 Bake 8 minutes or until browned, then, with pancake turner, remove cookies to racks. Cool before decorating.

6 With paper cone or cake decorator and frosting, outline feet, sleeves and other features as you wish.

MAKING A PATTERN

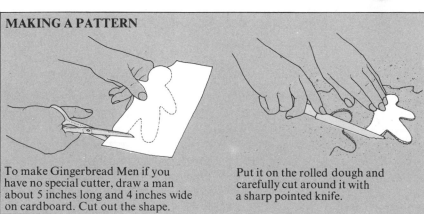

To make Gingerbread Men if you have no special cutter, draw a man about 5 inches long and 4 inches wide on cardboard. Cut out the shape.

Put it on the rolled dough and carefully cut around it with a sharp pointed knife.

ORNAMENTAL COOKIE FROSTING: Into small bowl, sift *1¼ cups confectioners' sugar* and *⅛ teaspoon cream of tartar* through very fine sieve; add *1 egg white.* With mixer at high speed, beat mixture so stiff that knife drawn through leaves clean path. (On humid days you may need to beat in more confectioners' sugar.)

Color index page 105
Begin day ahead
108 cookies
50 cals each

Spice Cookies

sugar
3⅔ cups all-purpose flour
1 cup butter or
margarine, softened
2 eggs
1 tablespoon milk
1½ teaspoons baking
soda

1½ teaspoons ground
cinnamon
½ teaspoon ground
nutmeg
¼ teaspoon ground
cloves
1 cup dried currants

1. Into large bowl, measure 1½ cups sugar and remaining ingredients except currants. With mixer at medium speed, beat ingredients until well mixed, occasionally scraping bowl with rubber spatula. Stir in currants. Cover; refrigerate overnight.
2. Preheat oven to 375°F. On lightly floured board, with floured rolling pin, roll dough as thin as possible; lightly sprinkle with sugar.
3. With pastry wheel or knife, cut dough into 2-inch diamond; place on cookie sheets.
4. Bake 8 minutes or until very lightly browned.
5. With pancake turner, remove cookies to wire racks and allow to cool completely.

Color index page 104
Begin 4 hrs or up to 2 wks ahead
72 cookies 42 cals each

Cinnamon Cookies

2 cups all-purpose flour
1 cup sugar
½ cup butter or
margarine, softened
3 egg yolks
2 tablespoons milk

2 teaspoons ground
cinnamon
½ teaspoon double-
acting baking powder
½ teaspoon salt

1. Into large bowl, measure all ingredients. With mixer at medium speed, beat ingredients until well mixed, about 3 minutes, occasionally scraping bowl.
2. Wrap the dough in plastic wrap then put it in the refrigerator for 2½ hours or until easy to handle.
3. With lightly floured rolling pin, directly onto *cold* cookie sheet, roll half of dough to ⅛-inch thickness. Keep remaining dough refrigerated.
4. With floured 2¼-inch cookie cutters, cut cookies, spacing 1 inch apart. Chill about 1 hour; remove dough from between cookies. Meanwhile, preheat oven to 350°F.
5. Bake 15 minutes or until lightly browned. Immediately remove cookies to wire racks; cool. Repeat with remaining dough and trimmings.

CANDY

Homemade candies are family favorites at any time; if you are afraid that they will dull the appetite for meals, you can always serve them as an alternative to dessert.

COOKING CANDY
Use a heavy saucepan for candies, one large enough to allow the mixture to boil freely without running over; stir with a long wooden spoon – a metal one would become too hot to handle.

Undissolved sugar crystals will make a candy grainy. You can either grease the sides of the saucepan first to prevent crystals clinging to them, or keep brushing down any crystals with a pastry brush dipped in hot water and shaken dry. Once the sugar has dissolved, stop stirring the mixture immediately, unless the recipe specifically directs otherwise.

USING A CANDY THERMOMETER
The most reliable way of testing a candy mixture is to check the temperature with a candy thermometer. Always cook the mixture to the exact temperatures specified. If you suspect that your thermometer is not quite accurate, stand it in boiling water for a few minutes. It should register 212°F. If it rises above (or does not reach) this temperature, add the difference to (or subtract it from) that specified in the recipe. Hold the thermometer upright, keeping the bulb totally immersed in the boiling (not foaming) mixture, yet *well clear of the bottom of the pan*. When you have finished with the thermometer, always be sure that you allow it to cool before washing it, otherwise it might break.

Reading a candy thermometer: Always read the temperature of candy mixture at eye level. Watch carefully once it reaches 220°F. as it rises rapidly from this point.

COLD-WATER TEST
If you do not own a candy thermometer, with practice you can soon learn how to recognize the different consistencies of candy by using the cold-water test. Have ready a measuring cup of very cold, not iced, water. Remove the candy from the heat and, with a clean spoon, drop about ½ teaspoon of the hot mixture into the water. Let it stand a minute then test the firmness of the mixture with your fingers. Use this chart as your guide when you make candy.

CANDY COOKING TEMPERATURES		
Stage	**Temperature**	**Consistency**
Thread	230° to 234°F.	Syrup spins 2-inch thread in the air as it falls from spoon
Soft ball	234° to 240°F.	Syrup (in cold water) forms soft ball which flattens on removal from water
Firm ball	244° to 248°F.	Syrup (in cold water) forms firm ball which does not flatten on removal from water
Hard ball	250° to 266°F.	Syrup (in cold water) forms hard, yet pliable ball
Soft crack	270° to 290°F.	Syrup (in cold water) separates into threads which are hard but not brittle
Hard crack	300° to 310°F.	Syrup (in cold water) separates into hard, brittle threads

COOLING CANDY
For recipes that call for a mixture to be cooled to lukewarm, let it stand undisturbed, off the heat, until the temperature falls to 110°F., or until the bottom of the saucepan feels lukewarm to the touch. Never move the pan or beat the mixture while it is hot or large sugar crystals will form, giving the candy a grainy texture.

When the mixture is ready for pouring out, do it quickly, holding the saucepan close to the pan. Use a rubber spatula for pushing out the mixture; always avoid scraping the saucepan since the mixture on the sides may be sugary.

Allow the candy to cool before cutting or breaking it up and do not store it until it is completely cold.

STORING CANDY
Sugar readily absorbs moisture so most candies are best stored in a cool place in tightly covered containers. Creamy candies such as fudge and penuche, chewy caramels and taffy should be individually wrapped in plastic wrap, waxed paper or foil. Refrigerated candies should always be wrapped or covered and kept well chilled until you are ready to serve them.

Fudges

Chocolate Fudge

Color index
page 106

Begin 2½ hrs
ahead

36 pieces or
1¼ pounds

111 cals each

3 cups sugar
1 cup milk
2 tablespoons light corn
syrup
2 squares unsweetened
chocolate
3 tablespoons butter or
margarine

1 teaspoon vanilla
extract
1 cup chopped
California walnuts
or pecans

1 In 3-quart saucepan over medium heat, heat sugar, milk, corn syrup and chocolate to boiling, stirring constantly. Wash crystals from pan side with damp pastry brush.

2 Set candy thermometer in place and continue cooking mixture, stirring occasionally, until temperature reaches 238°F. (soft-ball stage).

3 Remove pan from heat; add butter and vanilla. Cool, without stirring, to 110°F., or until outside of saucepan feels lukewarm.

4 Meanwhile, butter 8" by 8" pan. With spoon, beat until the mixture becomes thick and begins to lose its gloss.

5 Quickly stir in chopped walnuts or pecans until evenly mixed. Pour into pan. (Don't scrape saucepan; mixture on side may be sugary.)

6 Cool chocolate fudge in pan; when the fudge has cooled completely, cut it into small even-sized squares with a sharp knife.

114 cals each **PEANUT BUTTER FUDGE:** Prepare as above but use ¼ *cup creamy peanut butter* instead of butter or margarine and substitute *1 cup chopped salted peanuts* for the California walnuts or pecans.

Nutty Butterscotch Fudge

Color index
page 106

Begin 1½ hrs
ahead

49 pieces or
1¼ pounds

72 cals each

1 cup sugar
¼ cup butter or
margarine
¾ teaspoon salt
1 7½-ounce jar
marshmallow cream
1 5.33-ounce can
evaporated milk,
undiluted

1 12-ounce package
butterscotch-flavored
pieces
½ teaspoon vanilla
extract
½ cup salted peanuts,
pecans or cashews,
chopped

1. Grease 9" by 9" baking pan; set aside.
2. In heavy, 3-quart saucepan, combine sugar, butter or margarine, salt, marshmallow cream and undiluted milk. Over medium-high heat, heat to a rolling boil; cook 5 minutes, stirring.
3. Remove saucepan from heat. Quickly stir in butterscotch-flavored pieces and vanilla extract until butterscotch pieces are melted and well blended; stir in peanuts. Pour mixture into pan. Cool. Cut into small squares with a sharp knife.

Pecan Penuche

Color index
page 107

Begin 2½ hrs
ahead

36 pieces or
2 pounds

136 cals each

2 cups packed light
brown sugar
2 cups sugar
1 cup milk
3 tablespoons butter

1½ teaspoons vanilla
extract
1 cup coarsely chopped
pecans

1. In 3-quart saucepan over medium heat, heat sugars and milk to boiling, stirring constantly. Set candy thermometer in place and continue cooking, without stirring, until temperature reaches 238°F. or until a small amount of mixture dropped into very cold water forms a soft ball. Remove from heat; add butter and vanilla.
2. Cool mixture, without stirring, to 110°F. or until outside of saucepan feels lukewarm to hand. Meanwhile, butter 8" by 8" pan.
3. With spoon, beat until mixture becomes thick and begins to lose its gloss; quickly stir in pecans. Pour into pan. (Don't scrape saucepan; mixture on side may be sugary.) Cool in pan on wire rack; when cold, cut into squares with a sharp knife.

Maple Kisses

Color index
page 106

Begin 1½ hrs
or up to
1 wk ahead

24 pieces or
¾ pound

117 cals each

1 cup packed light brown
sugar
½ cup sugar
½ cup evaporated milk
¼ cup light corn syrup

1 tablespoon butter or
margarine
1 teaspoon maple flavor
1½ cups chopped
California walnuts

1. In 2-quart saucepan over very low heat, heat sugars, undiluted milk and corn syrup to boiling, stirring constantly. Set candy thermometer in place and continue cooking, stirring constantly, until temperature reaches 235°F. or until a small amount of mixture dropped into very cold water forms a soft ball. (This takes about 30 minutes.) Remove candy mixture from heat.
2. With spoon, beat butter, maple flavor and nuts into mixture. Quickly drop mixture by teaspoonfuls onto waxed paper; cool on wire racks.

Other candies

Molasses Taffy

1 14-ounce can sweetened condensed milk (1⅓ cups)
½ cup light molasses
⅛ teaspoon salt

Color index
page 107

Begin 2 hrs
or day ahead

50 pieces or
¾ pound

33 cals each

1 Butter an 8″ by 8″ pan or large platter. In 2-quart saucepan over medium heat, heat all ingredients to boiling, stirring occasionally.

2 Set candy thermometer in place and continue cooking the mixture, stirring constantly, until the temperature reaches 244°F. (firm-ball stage), about 20 minutes.

3 Remove saucepan from heat; pour mixture into pan. Let stand until cool enough to handle.

4 With buttered fingers, pull the candy mixture until it becomes shiny and light colored.

5 With fingers, twist taffy into continuous rope about ¾ inch thick.

6 With kitchen shears, cut rope into 1-inch pieces. Wrap each piece in plastic wrap.

Orange-Almond Caramels

Color index
page 107

Begin 1½ hrs
or up to
1 wk ahead

50 pieces or
1½ pounds

77 cals each

3 cups sugar
¼ cup boiling water
1 cup evaporated milk
⅛ teaspoon salt

2 teaspoons grated orange peel
1⅓ cups toasted slivered almonds

1. In heavy, 2-quart saucepan over medium heat, heat 1 cup sugar, stirring constantly, until entirely melted and a deep golden color. Stirring constantly, slowly add boiling water; cook until mixture is a smooth syrup. Stir in remaining 2 cups sugar, undiluted evaporated milk and salt.
2. Set candy thermometer in place and continue cooking over medium heat, stirring constantly, until temperature reaches 238°F. or soft-ball stage. Remove from heat; add orange peel and stir until mixture cools slightly; add 1 cup slivered almonds and continue stirring until a little of the mixture retains its shape and looks slightly dull when dropped on waxed paper.
3. Drop by heaping teaspoonfuls onto waxed paper; press a few more nuts on top of each piece; wrap individually in plastic wrap, waxed paper or foil.

Nougats

Color index
page 107

Begin day
or up to
2 wks ahead

2¼ pounds

473 cals per
¼ pound

½ pound hard gum candy (not sugar coated)
cornstarch
2 cups sugar
1½ cups light corn syrup
¼ teaspoon salt
¼ cup water

2 egg whites
1 teaspoon vanilla extract
¼ cup butter or margarine, softened
1 cup coarsely chopped California walnuts

1. With kitchen shears, cut gum candy into small pieces; set aside. Grease well 9″ by 9″ baking pan; sprinkle lightly with cornstarch. In 2-quart saucepan with candy thermometer in place, over medium-high heat, heat sugar, corn syrup, salt and water to boiling, stirring constantly. Continue cooking, stirring occasionally, until temperature reaches 250°F. or hard-ball stage.
2. Meanwhile, in large bowl with mixer at high speed, beat egg whites until stiff peaks form. Beating at high speed, gradually pour about one-fourth of hot syrup into egg whites. Continue beating while heating remaining syrup to 300°F. or hard-crack stage. Egg-white mixture should stand in stiff, glossy peaks; beat in vanilla extract.
3. With mixer at high speed, gradually beat remaining syrup into egg-white mixture, then beat in butter or margarine until well blended. If mixture becomes too thick for the mixer to beat, continue beating with a wooden spoon.
4. With wooden spoon, stir in walnuts and gum candy; spoon evenly into baking pan. With pastry brush, lightly brush mixture with some cornstarch.
5. Let nougat cool in pan on wire rack for about 12 hours or overnight. Remove nougat from pan; with kitchen shears or knife, cut into 1-inch squares, wiping shears as needed with damp cloth. To store, wrap each piece in plastic wrap.

Lollipops

12 8-ounce paper hot-drink cups
36 ¾-inch-long oval hard candies in assorted colors
about 2 ounces cinnamon red-hot or other small red candies
2 cups sugar
1 cup water
¾ cup light corn syrup
½ teaspoon oil of lemon
10 drops yellow food color
12 lollipop sticks

Color index
page 106

Begin 3 hrs
or up to
1 wk ahead

Twelve 3-inch
lollipops

246 cals each

1 Cut off top of each cup to make 1½-inch-deep ring mold; cut ⅛-inch-wide slit from cut edge to, but *not* through, rim.

2 Grease well molds and 2 cookie sheets; put molds, rim side down, in rows on sheets, leaving space for sticks.

3 Arrange a flower pattern of 3 hard candies and two clusters of 3 cinnamon red-hot candies in each mold; set aside.

4 In heavy, 2-quart pan, stir sugar, water and syrup until sugar dissolves. With damp pastry brush, wipe side of pan to remove sugar crystals.

5 With candy thermometer in place, over high heat, without stirring, heat mixture to 300°F. or hard-crack stage.

6 Remove from heat and stir in oil of lemon and food color then, working quickly, pour about ¼ cup mixture into each mold.

7 Press sticks through slits into candy; cool completely. With spatula, loosen lollipops from sheets; discard molds.

Divinity

3 cups sugar
½ cup light corn syrup
½ cup water

2 egg whites, at room temperature
1 teaspoon vanilla extract

Color index
page 107

Begin 1½ hrs
or up to
1 wk ahead

60 candies or
1½ pounds

45 cals each

1. Avoid making Divinity on a humid day; candy will not harden. In 2-quart saucepan over medium-high heat, heat sugar, syrup and water to boiling, stirring until sugar is dissolved. Set candy thermometer in place and continue cooking, without stirring, until temperature reaches 248°F.
2. Meanwhile, in medium bowl with mixer at high speed, beat egg whites until stiff peaks form. Beating at medium speed, slowly pour half of syrup into whites. Continue beating while heating other half of syrup to 272°F.
3. While turning bowl and continuing beating, slowly pour remaining hot syrup into mixture (mixture will be stiff). (Don't scrape saucepan; mixture on side may be sugary.) Add vanilla; beat until mixture holds stiff, glossy peaks. Working quickly, drop by heaping teaspoonfuls onto waxed paper. Cool completely before storing.

Fondant

4 cups sugar
¼ cup light corn syrup
¼ teaspoon cream of tartar
⅛ teaspoon salt

1 cup water
peppermint or favorite extract
green, red or yellow food color

Color index
page 107

Begin 5 hrs
or up to
1 wk ahead

60 pieces or
1 pound

55 cals each

1. In heavy, 2-quart saucepan with candy thermometer in place, over high heat, heat first 5 ingredients until boiling and sugar is dissolved, stirring occasionally. Reduce heat to medium; continue cooking, without stirring, until temperature reaches 238° to 240°F. or soft-ball stage, about 10 to 15 minutes. (If mixture takes too long to reach desired temperature, it will not become stiff after beating in step 3.) During cooking, wipe down sides of pan with damp pastry brush to remove sugar crystals. Remove pan from heat.
2. Set thermometer in large bowl; add mixture. (Don't scrape mixture from side of pan; it may be sugary.) Cool the mixture, *without stirring*, until temperature reaches about 125°F., about 1 hour.
3. With wooden spoon, beat mixture till white and stiff, about 10 minutes. If it does not stiffen after beating 10 minutes, it has cooled too much. Reheat in pan just to boiling; beat again.
4. Divide fondant into several portions; keep covered tightly with plastic wrap as you work with each portion in turn. Flatten one portion; add flavoring extract to taste and a drop or two of food color; knead to blend well. Repeat with remaining fondant. Shape fondant into balls and other shapes.
5. Place shapes on waxed paper and let stand 1½ hours or until a light crust has formed, then place on wire rack so light crust will form on bottom also. Cover and store or you can use the fondant for dipping into melted chocolate or for Bonbons (page 418).

Other candies

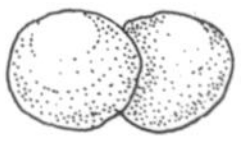

Bonbons

Color index
page 107

Begin 7 hrs
or up to
1 wk ahead

30 bonbons and
6 or 8 patties or
1 pound

111 cals each
bonbon

Fondant (page 417)
¼ teaspoon peppermint,
almond extract or
other flavoring

red, yellow or green food
color
½ to 1 teaspoon hot
water

1. Prepare Fondant as in steps 1 through 3; divide in two; tightly wrap one portion in plastic wrap. Flatten other and add peppermint extract to taste; knead until well blended. Shape into ¾-inch balls. Place on waxed paper and let stand 1½ hours or until a light crust has formed; place on wire rack about 1½ hours so crust forms on bottom also. (Crust helps prevent distortion of coating and centers when dipping.)
2. In double-boiler top over simmering water, melt reserved fondant portion with one or two drops food color to make a delicate pastel color, stirring constantly until mixture is hot and thin. A crust will begin to appear as soon as stirring stops, so work steadily to dip fondant pieces.
3. Dip one fondant piece at a time: Drop, flat side down, into melted fondant. With long-handled, 2-tined fork, quickly turn to coat rounded side; immediately lift piece, rounded side down and rap fork on rim of pan two or three times; scrape fork across rim to remove excess fondant, but do not scrape fondant from bonbon.
4. Onto waxed paper, invert fork to place bonbon rounded side up. Hold fork in contact with bonbon for a few seconds, then lift off, pulling fondant up to make a "curl." During dipping, keep stirring fondant to remove crust. Let dipped bonbons stand at least 1 hour before removing from paper.
5. To any melted fondant left in pan, add hot water, and heat over simmering water, stirring until mixture is thin and well melted. Pour mixture onto waxed paper in little patties; let dry as above.

Popcorn Balls

Color index
page 106

Begin 2 hrs or
day ahead

12 balls

189 cals each

12 cups popped corn
(about ¾ cup
popcorn)
½ pound candied
cherries, halved
1 16-ounce bottle light
corn syrup (2 cups)

1 tablespoon white
vinegar
1 teaspoon salt
2 teaspoons vanilla
extract

1. In greased 8-quart saucepot toss popped corn with cherries until well mixed. In 2-quart saucepan over medium-high heat, heat to boiling corn syrup, vinegar and salt, stirring occasionally. Set candy thermometer in place; continue cooking, without stirring, until temperature reaches 250°F. or until a small amount dropped in very cold water forms a hard but pliable ball. Remove syrup mixture from heat and stir in vanilla extract.
2. Slowly pour syrup over popped-corn mixture, tossing until kernels are coated. With greased hands, shape mixture into 3-inch balls, using as little pressure as possible, so balls will not be too compact. (If mixture hardens, place saucepot over very low heat until mixture is pliable.)

Peanut Brittle

Color index
page 106

Begin 2 hrs or
up to 2 wks
ahead

1 pound

552 cals per
¼ pound

1 cup sugar
½ cup light corn syrup
¼ teaspoon salt
¼ cup water
1 cup shelled raw
peanuts

2 tablespoons butter or
margarine,
softened
1 teaspoon baking
soda

1. Grease large cookie sheet. In heavy, 2-quart saucepan over medium heat, heat to boiling sugar, corn syrup, salt and water, stirring until sugar is dissolved. Stir in peanuts. Set candy thermometer in place and continue cooking, stirring frequently, until temperature reaches 300°F. or until a small amount of mixture dropped into very cold water separates into hard and brittle threads.
2. Remove from heat; immediately stir in butter or margarine and baking soda; pour at once onto cookie sheet.
3. With 2 forks, lift and pull peanut mixture into rectangle about 14″ by 12″; cool. With hands, snap candy into small pieces.

Walnut Crunch

Color index
page 107

Begin 3½ hrs
ahead

1½ pounds

702 cals per
¼ pound

1¼ cups sugar
¾ cup butter or
margarine
1½ teaspoons salt
¼ cup water
1½ cups coarsely
chopped California
walnuts

½ teaspoon baking soda
⅓ cup semisweet-
chocolate pieces,
melted
½ cup finely chopped
California walnuts

1. Butter 15″ by 10″ jelly-roll pan. In 2-quart saucepan over medium heat, heat sugar, butter or margarine, salt and water to boiling, stirring often. Set candy thermometer in place and continue cooking, stirring often, until temperature reaches 290°F. or until a small amount of mixture dropped into very cold water separates into threads which are hard but not brittle.
2. Remove mixture from heat; stir in coarsely chopped walnuts and soda; pour at once into pan. (Don't scrape saucepan; side may be sugary.)
3. Spread mixture with chocolate and sprinkle with finely chopped walnuts; cool. With hands, snap candy into small pieces.

Testing sugar mixture:
Cook to 290°F. or until
small amount dropped
into very cold water
separates into hard but
not brittle threads.

Adding chocolate: Use a
spatula to spread melted
chocolate over the walnut
layer, then sprinkle the top
with finely chopped
walnuts.

Color index
page 107

Begin 3 hrs
or up to
2 wks ahead

64 patties or
2½ pounds

79 cals each

Peppermint Patties

1 14-ounce can sweetened
condensed milk
2 teaspoons peppermint
extract
12 drops red food color

1½ to 2 16-ounce
packages
confectioners' sugar
1½ cups pecan halves

1. In large bowl, mix sweetened condensed milk, peppermint extract and food color. With spoon, stir in 1½ packages confectioners' sugar.
2. On cutting board generously sprinkled with confectioners' sugar, gradually knead in enough additional sugar so that mixture forms a smooth, firm ball that doesn't stick to hands or board.
3. Pat mixture into 8″ by 8″ square. With knife, cut into 1-inch squares. Shape each piece into a ball and, with fingers, flatten into 2-inch patty; top with pecan half. Repeat with remaining pieces. (Keep pieces covered with plastic wrap while preparing patties.) Let patties dry at least 1 hour.

Color index
page 107

Begin day
or up to
2 wks ahead

4¼ pounds

605 cals per
¼ pound

Marzipan Fruits

Marzipan Dough:
2 cups canned almond
paste
4 egg whites
about 12 cups
confectioners' sugar

Glossy Sugar Glaze
(below)

1. Prepare Marzipan Dough: In large bowl, knead almond paste with egg whites; slowly knead in confectioners' sugar or enough to make a stiff dough; cover to keep moist for easy handling.
2. Shape the Marzipan Dough into apples, bananas, pears, oranges or strawberries (right); make only one shape or a selection, if you wish. Allow the fruits to dry on a tray. Meanwhile, prepare glaze.
3. Place Marzipan Fruits (do not let them touch) on a rack in shallow, open pan. With spoon, carefully remove any crystallized sugar on top of glaze. To coat fruits, evenly pour on glaze with as little agitation as possible to prevent glaze crystallizing. Dry overnight.

GLOSSY SUGAR GLAZE: In 2-quart saucepan over medium heat, cook **4½ cups sugar** with **1 cup water** just until sugar dissolves and candy thermometer reads 223°F. Remove from heat very gently; do not stir. Let stand undisturbed until cool.

Preparing Marzipan Dough: Knead almond paste with egg whites, then with confectioners' sugar.

Coating Marzipan Fruits: Pour glaze over fruits on rack; be sure to avoid agitating the syrup.

SHAPING THE FRUITS

14 apples

APPLES: On waxed paper, knead about **2 drops green food color** into **1½ cups Marzipan Dough**. Divide dough into 14 pieces and shape into apples; insert knobs of **whole cloves** part way into tops of apples. Using fine brush, tint apples with **red food color** diluted with **water**. Dry on tray.

Adding stems: Insert knobs of whole cloves part way into tops of apples.

Tinting apples: Use a fine brush to apply diluted red food color.

BANANAS: On waxed paper, knead about **6 drops yellow food color** into **½ cup Marzipan Dough**. Divide dough into 7 pieces and shape into bananas. Prepare brown color as label of food color directs; using brush, paint lines. Dry on tray.

7 bananas

PEARS: On waxed paper, knead about **4 drops green and 4 drops yellow food color** into **1 cup Marzipan Dough**. Divide dough into 12 pieces and shape into pears. In top of each pear, insert a leaf of **dried rosemary** part way. Dry on tray.

12 pears

ORANGES: On waxed paper, knead about **6 drops yellow and 4 drops red food color** into **1 cup Marzipan Dough**. Divide dough into 9 pieces and shape into oranges. Roll oranges over grater to make surface texture. Insert **stems from whole cloves** into tops of oranges. Dry on tray.

9 oranges

STRAWBERRIES: Divide **¾ cup Marzipan Dough** into 20 pieces and shape into strawberries. Roll strawberries over grater to make surface texture. Using fine brush, tint berries with **red food color** diluted with **water**. On waxed paper, knead about **5 drops green food color** into **¼ cup Marzipan Dough**. Using lightly cornstarch-dusted cutting board and rolling pin, roll dough ⅛ inch thick. With 1¼-inch star-shaped canapé cutter, cut 20 stars; press a star on large end of each berry. Dry on tray.

20 berries

Making surface texture: Roll berry over grater to mark strawberry seeds.

Adding stars: Press star on large end of each berry to complete the fruit.

Chocolates

Melt-Away Chocolate Mints

*2 8-ounce packages
    semisweet chocolate
    squares
2 tablespoons shortening*

*½ cup heavy cream
1 tablespoon peppermint
    extract
cocoa*

Color index
page 107

Begin 2½ hrs
or up to
2 wks ahead

1 pound

927 cals per
¼ pound

1. Line bottom of 8″ by 8″ baking pan with waxed paper; set aside. Chop chocolate into small pieces. Place chocolate and shortening in double-boiler top (not over water). Set candy thermometer in place; set aside. Heat water to boiling in double-boiler bottom; remove from heat. Place double-boiler top over hot water; melt chocolate, stirring with rubber spatula, until temperature reaches 130°F.
2. Immediately discard water from double-boiler bottom and refill with cold water. Set top in place and cool chocolate, stirring constantly but gently, until chocolate reaches 83°F. on special 40° to 120°F. thermometer.
3. Meanwhile, in 1-quart saucepan over medium heat, heat heavy cream just to boiling; remove saucepan from heat.
4. In small bowl with mixer at low speed, beat chocolate, cream and peppermint until blended. Increase speed to medium; beat 2 minutes, occasionally scraping bowl with rubber spatula.
5. Pour mixture into prepared pan; set aside until firm, about 2 hours.
6. *To serve:* With metal spatula, loosen chocolate mixture from sides of pan. Invert pan onto cutting board; discard waxed paper. Lightly dust sharp knife with cocoa; cut chocolate mixture into diamonds or 1-inch squares.

Truffles

*1 12-ounce package
    semisweet-chocolate
    pieces
¾ cup sweetened
    condensed milk
1 teaspoon vanilla
    extract*

*⅛ teaspoon salt
½ cup cocoa or 1 cup
    chopped, flaked
    coconut for
    garnish*

Color index
page 107

Begin 2 hrs or
up to 1 wk
ahead

36 truffles or
1½ pounds

71 cals each

1. In double boiler over hot, *not boiling,* water (or in heavy, 2-quart saucepan over low heat), melt chocolate pieces. Stir in condensed milk, vanilla and salt until well mixed. Refrigerate mixture about 45 minutes or until easy to shape.
2. With buttered hands, shape mixture into 1-inch balls. Roll balls in cocoa or coconut.

Shaping balls: With buttered hands, shape mixture into balls.

Coating balls: Roll the balls in cocoa or chopped, flaked coconut.

Chocolate-dipped Fruit

*2 large oranges
2 pints large strawberries
1 cup salted peanuts*

*2 8-ounce packages
    semisweet-chocolate
    squares*

Color index
page 107

Begin 1½ hrs
ahead or early
in day

60 fruit and
12 clusters

59 cals each
fruit

1. Peel oranges and separate them into their sections; wrap sections with plastic wrap so fruits will not dry out. Rinse strawberries under running cold water but do not remove stems, being sure to pat berries completely dry with paper towels. Set fruit aside. (For dipping, fruit should be at room temperature.) In small bowl, place peanuts.
2. Into double-boiler top (not over water) grate semisweet-chocolate squares. Set candy thermometer in place; set aside. Heat water to boiling in double-boiler bottom; remove from heat. Place double-boiler top over hot water; melt chocolate, stirring chocolate constantly with rubber spatula, until temperature reaches 130°F.
3. Immediately discard hot water from double-boiler bottom and refill with cold water to come one-third way up side of double boiler. Set top in place and cool chocolate, stirring constantly, until chocolate temperature reaches 83°F. on special 40° to 120°F. thermometer.
4. Remove double-boiler top and replace cold water in bottom with warm water (about 85°F.). This will keep chocolate at dipping consistency longer.
5. With fingers, hold 1 piece of fruit at a time and dip it into chocolate, leaving part of fruit uncovered. Shake off excess chocolate or gently scrape one side of fruit across rim of double boiler being careful not to scrape too much chocolate from fruit; place on waxed paper.
6. Working quickly, stir peanuts into leftover chocolate in pan. Drop mixture by tablespoonfuls onto waxed paper. Let chocolate-covered fruit and peanut clusters stand until chocolate is set (about 10 minutes) before removing from waxed paper. Serve dipped fresh fruit same day. Store peanut clusters in tightly covered container; use within 1 week.

DIPPING THE FRUIT

Dip fruit into chocolate, leaving part uncovered. Gently scrape off excess chocolate across rim of double boiler; place fruit on waxed paper. Stir peanuts into remaining chocolate; drop by tablespoonfuls onto paper.

QUICK BREADS

Unlike yeast breads, quick breads are made with quick-acting leavening and are mixed, shaped and baked in one uninterrupted process. Some, such as muffins, loaves and soda bread, can accompany a meal like ordinary bread, while waffles and pancakes make a delicious meal in themselves. Doughnuts are a tasty snack at any time of the day.

Most quick breads are raised with baking powder, baking soda, or both. The double-acting baking powder used in all our recipes produces gas bubbles twice, first when it comes in contact with liquid and again when subjected to heat; the mixture can, therefore, be left to stand for a little while after mixing, if necessary. Baking soda is usually used in mixtures containing an acid ingredient such as buttermilk, sour cream, fruit juice, molasses or even chocolate. Baking soda starts reacting as soon as it comes in contact with liquid, so mixtures containing it should be baked immediately.

MAKING QUICK BREADS
By following our recipe directions to the letter – measuring carefully, mixing and handling doughs and batters as lightly and quickly as possible, and by baking at the temperature given – you will turn out a perfect quick bread every time.

Measuring: Ingredients should be measured accurately. For dry ingredients, use a graduated measuring cup set; for liquids, use glass or plastic measuring cups with a pouring lip. The same measuring spoons are used for both. Spoon unsifted flour into the measuring cup and level off lightly with the straight edge of a knife or metal spatula. Measure granulated white or brown sugar in the same way, but press regular brown sugar lightly into the cup so that it holds its shape when turned out.

Mixing: The secret of a perfect quick bread lies in the lightness and speed with which the ingredients are handled. To make a dough, first mix the dry ingredients well. Then cut in the shortening with a pastry blender or two knives used scissor-fashion until the mixture resembles coarse crumbs. Next, add the liquid and stir just enough to moisten dry ingredients and hold them together. When making batters, unless otherwise directed, stir in the liquid only until dry ingredients are moistened. Muffin and pancake batters will be lumpy but, if overmixed, the breads will be tough and won't

rise to full volume and muffins will have unattractive "tunnels." For some breads, however, ingredients should be well mixed. In each case, always be sure to follow the directions carefully.

Cutting in shortening: With a pastry blender or two knives used scissor-fashion, cut in shortening.

Kneading and rolling: A dough which is to be kneaded should be mixed just long enough to come away from the side of the bowl (it will still be sticky). Turn it out onto a lightly floured surface and knead it lightly – 6 to 8 strokes will be enough to make it manageable and knead ingredients. Roll it gently with a floured rolling pin. Biscuit dough doubles in height when baked; so for high biscuits, roll dough out ½ inch thick. For thin, crusty biscuits, roll it ¼ inch thick. After cutting out the first batch, press the trimmings together gently; reroll lightly. Don't knead again or the biscuits will be tough.

Testing for doneness: Biscuits are done when they are well risen and golden; muffins, when they are golden. To test loaves for doneness, pierce them deeply with a toothpick; it should come out clean and dry. For some very moist loaves, however, the recipe may describe the toothpick as "almost clean," meaning that there will be a few crumbs sticking to it when the bread is done. Turn pancakes when the little bubbles on top start to burst and the edges look dry; cook until underside is golden. If your waffle baker doesn't have a signal light, wait until it stops steaming, then lift the cover and wait a few seconds so waffles will be crisp. Using a slotted spoon, tongs or a two-tined fork, turn doughnuts as soon as they rise to the surface of the fat; don't pierce them or they will soak up fat. Fry until golden on both sides.

QUICK BREADS

BAKING EQUIPMENT

Shiny metal cookie sheets and baking pans are best for browning biscuits and muffins. For loaves, use dull metal, anodized aluminum or glass loaf pans.

Always check pan sizes and if the dimensions are different from those called for, directions will have to be adapted – the muffin cups we use are generally 2½ inches in diameter, for example. If yours are different, fill them no more than two-thirds full (only half full for popovers). Wipe muffin pans clean of any spills and if any greased cups remain empty, half-fill them with water to protect them from burning. Loaf pans that are larger than specified will result in thin loaves. If they are smaller than required, fill them no more than two-thirds full and bake remaining batter in custard cups, filling them two-thirds full; bake 20 minutes or until done.

SERVING QUICK BREADS

Most quick breads are at their best fresh from the oven. Bring them to the table in an attractive baking dish, or serve in a basket or on a napkin-lined plate. Turn muffins out of their cups as soon as they are ready, or they will steam and become soggy. If they are not to be served at once, keep them warm by leaving them in their cups, slightly tipped to allow the steam to escape. Fruit and nut loaves, on the other hand, may be hard to slice soon after they come from the oven. Allowed to cool, then wrapped and left overnight, they often develop a mellower flavor and are easier to slice.

STORING AND REHEATING LEFTOVERS

Quick breads quickly turn stale. To retain moisture, store, tightly wrapped, at room temperature. Reheat them in one of the following ways to restore their fresh-baked flavor.

Wrap biscuits in foil and reheat in a 375°F. oven about 20 minutes. Or pour 2 tablespoons water into a large skillet and arrange biscuits on a rack in skillet. Cover and heat over low heat 8 to 10 minutes until hot. Biscuits can also be toasted. Split them, spread with butter or margarine and top with any of the following: shredded cheese, celery seed, poppy seed or caraway seed, cinnamon sugar, cheese spread, garlic spread, softened plain or flavored cream cheese or jelly. Then toast the biscuits in the broiler, split sides up, until they are hot and golden.

Wrap muffins in foil and reheat in a 400°F. oven about 15 minutes. Both muffins and corn bread can be toasted in the broiler like biscuits.

Place Boston Brown Bread, out of its can, in a double boiler or a colander set over a pan of water; cover and heat. Or, slice the bread, spread with butter or margarine and toast in broiler.

Reheat coffeecake either wrapped in foil, in a 400°F. oven for 20 to 30 minutes, or in a covered skillet as directed for biscuits (above).

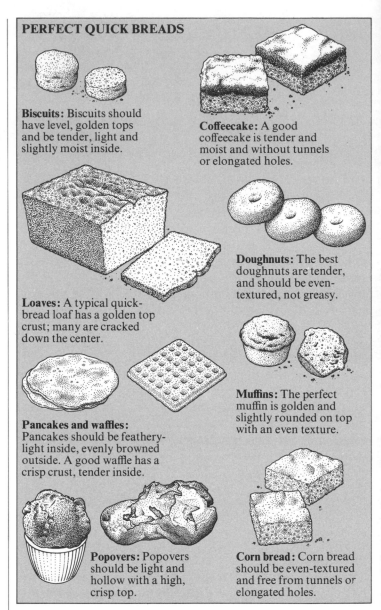

PERFECT QUICK BREADS

Biscuits: Biscuits should have level, golden tops and be tender, light and slightly moist inside.

Coffeecake: A good coffeecake is tender and moist and without tunnels or elongated holes.

Loaves: A typical quick-bread loaf has a golden top crust; many are cracked down the center.

Doughnuts: The best doughnuts are tender, and should be even-textured, not greasy.

Pancakes and waffles: Pancakes should be feathery-light inside, evenly browned outside. A good waffle has a crisp crust, tender inside.

Muffins: The perfect muffin is golden and slightly rounded on top with an even texture.

Popovers: Popovers should be light and hollow with a high, crisp top.

Corn bread: Corn bread should be even-textured and free from tunnels or elongated holes.

FREEZING QUICK BREADS

Biscuits and muffins are so quick to make that there is nothing to be gained by making them ahead for the freezer. Fruit loaves, nut loaves and coffeecakes are a different matter. To freeze them, cool completely, then wrap in foil, heavy-duty plastic wrap or freezerwrap. Freeze for up to 3 months; thaw wrapped at room temperature, about 1½ hours. If they are to be frosted, frost them after they are thawed.

If you plan to freeze waffles, bake them until only lightly browned. Cool, wrap and freeze as above; or freeze, unwrapped, on cookie sheets, then pack in heavy-duty plastic bags. Store in the freezer for 1 or 2 months. Thaw in a toaster at medium setting.

Doughnuts, packed in freezer cartons or in heavy-duty plastic bags, can be stored in the freezer for 4 to 6 months. Thaw, wrapped in foil, in a 400°F. oven.

Biscuits

Biscuits

2 cups all-purpose
  flour
1 tablespoon double-
  acting baking
  powder
1 teaspoon salt
¼ cup shortening
¾ cup milk

Color index
page 85

Begin 35 mins
ahead

18 biscuits

94 cals each

1 Preheat oven to 450°F. In large bowl with fork, mix flour, baking powder and salt. With pastry blender, cut in shortening until mixture resembles coarse crumbs.

2 Add milk and with fork, mix just until mixture forms soft dough that leaves side of bowl.

3 Turn onto lightly floured surface; knead 6 to 8 strokes to mix dough thoroughly.

4 Roll out the dough, ½ inch thick for high, fluffy biscuits, ¼ inch thick if you are making thin, crusty ones.

5 With floured 2-inch biscuit cutter, cut biscuits, using straight downward motion. Do not twist the cutter.

6 Place biscuits on ungreased cookie sheet, 1 inch apart for crusty biscuits, nearly touching for soft-sided ones.

7 Press dough trimmings together (don't knead); reroll and cut until all dough is used. Bake 12 to 15 minutes until golden.

91 cals each

86 cals each

BUTTERMILK BISCUITS: Prepare Biscuits (left) but use *buttermilk* in place of milk and use only *2 teaspoons baking powder*; add *¼ teaspoon baking soda* to flour mixture. (Makes 18 biscuits.)

SPEEDY BISCUITS: Prepare Biscuits (left) but after rolling dough, cut with knife into different shapes including squares, triangles or diamonds; bake biscuits as directed.

DROP BISCUITS: Prepare Biscuits (left) but increase milk to 1 cup. With fork, stir the dough until thoroughly mixed but do not knead it. Onto ungreased cookie sheet, drop heaping tablespoonfuls of the mixture 1 inch apart. Bake biscuits as directed. (Makes 20 biscuits.)

Mixing dough: With fork, stir the dough until it is thoroughly mixed; don't knead.

Shaping drop biscuits: Drop heaping table-spoonfuls of the mixture onto cookie sheet.

94 cals each

BLUEBERRY DROP BISCUITS: Grease cookie sheet. Make Drop Biscuits (above) but stir *1 cup fresh or frozen unsweetened blueberries* into flour mixture. Sprinkle tops of biscuits with *sugar* before placing in the oven. (Makes 20 biscuits.)

102 cals each

FRUITED DROP BISCUITS: Grease cookie sheet. Make Drop Biscuits (above) but add *¼ cup sugar* and *½ teaspoon ground cinnamon* to flour mixture. Add *one 8¾-ounce can fruit cocktail,* well drained, with milk or water. (Makes 20 biscuits.)

CUTTING OUT BISCUITS

For biscuits with level tops, press a floured cutter straight down without twisting (step 5, left). Or cut them with a sharp, floured knife, using firm, downward strokes.

To avoid distorting the shape, transfer the biscuits to cookie sheets with a pancake turner or broad spatula.

Muffins

Muffins

Color index
page 85

Begin 35 mins
ahead

12 muffins

156 cals each

*2 cups all-purpose
   flour*
2 tablespoons sugar
*1 tablespoon double-
   acting baking
   powder*
½ teaspoon salt
1 egg
1 cup milk
¼ cup salad oil

1 Preheat oven to 400°F.
With pastry brush,
grease well twelve 2½-inch
muffin-pan cups.

2 In large bowl with fork,
mix flour, sugar,
baking powder and salt.

3 In small bowl with
fork, beat egg slightly,
then stir milk and salad oil
into beaten egg.

4 Add egg mixture all at
once to flour mixture
and with spoon, stir just
until flour is moistened.
(Avoid overmixing which
causes toughness; batter
should be lumpy.)

5 Spoon batter into
greased muffin-pan
cups. Be sure to wipe pan
clean of any spills.

6 Bake muffins 20 to 25
minutes until they are
well risen and golden and
toothpick inserted in
center of one comes out
clean and dry.

7 Immediately remove
muffins from pan onto
wire rack; serve at once, or
keep warm by leaving in
cups, slightly tipped to
allow steam to escape.

161 cals each

186 cals each

148 cals each

ORANGE MUFFINS: Prepare Muffins (left) but
use ¼ cup sugar; use only ¾ cup milk. Add *¼ cup
orange juice* and *1 tablespoon finely shredded orange
peel* to the egg mixture.

BLUEBERRY MUFFINS: Prepare Muffins (left)
but use ½ cup sugar and add *¾ cup fresh or frozen
unsweetened blueberries* with egg mixture.

WHOLE-WHEAT MUFFINS: Prepare Muffins
(left) but use only ¾ cup flour; add *1 cup whole-
wheat flour*. Increase sugar to ¼ cup and baking
powder to 4 teaspoons.

Bran Muffins

Color index
page 85

Begin 45 mins
ahead

Sixteen
2½-inch
muffins

147 cals each

3 cups bran flakes
1¼ cups all-purpose flour
½ cup sugar
*1¼ teaspoons baking
   soda*

¼ teaspoon salt
1 egg
1 cup buttermilk
¼ cup salad oil

1. Preheat oven to 400°F. Grease eight 3-inch
muffin-pan cups or sixteen 2½-inch muffin-pan cups
and set them aside.
2. In bowl, mix first 5 ingredients. In small bowl with
fork, beat egg, buttermilk and salad oil until they are
thoroughly blended.
3. Stir egg mixture into flour mixture just until flour
is moistened. Spoon batter into muffin-pan cups.
Bake 25 minutes for 3-inch cups, 15 minutes for 2½-
inch cups, or until lightly browned. Immediately
remove muffins from pan.

MAKING BUTTER SHAPES
Early in day or several days ahead, make the butter or
margarine shapes below. Keep refrigerated in covered bowl of
iced water until time to use; drain shapes thoroughly and
arrange in a chilled serving dish.

Butter balls: In iced water, chill
wooden butter paddles well.
Cut firm ¼-pound bar of butter
into ½-inch-thick pats. Place a
pat between paddles; holding the
bottom paddle steady, rotate
top paddle to form ball. For
cylinders, flatten balls and roll
between paddles.

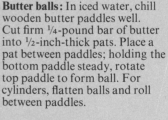

Butter curls: Let butter curler
stand in hot water 10 minutes to
heat. Pulling lightly, scrape
curler over top of a ¼-pound
bar of firm butter (if the bar is
too cold, the curls will break).
Reheat the curler briefly in hot
water each time.

Doughnuts

Doughnut dough should be soft and shaped lightly and quickly or doughnuts will be tough. After mixing, refrigerate the dough at least 1 hour to make it easier to handle and remember to cut doughnuts close together to reduce the amount of rerolling.

Doughnuts can be plain or varied by adding such ingredients as chocolate, nuts or whole-wheat flour. Try them sprinkled with sugar or coated with a glaze.

You can fry doughnuts in either an electric skillet or deep-fat fryer, or in a large saucepan or Dutch oven using a deep-fry thermometer to check the temperature.

Doughnuts are best eaten the day they are made.

Old-fashioned Doughnuts

Color index
page 85

Begin 2½ hrs
ahead

24 doughnuts

147 cals each

*3 cups all-purpose
  flour*
1 cup sugar
¾ cup buttermilk
2 eggs
2 tablespoons shortening
*2 teaspoons double-acting
  baking powder*
1 teaspoon baking soda
1 teaspoon salt
*½ teaspoon ground
  nutmeg*
salad oil
*confectioners' sugar or
  Nutmeg Sugar (right)*

1 Into large bowl, measure 1½ cups flour and remaining ingredients except salad oil and confectioners' sugar; with mixer at low speed, beat just until smooth, constantly scraping bowl. At medium speed, beat 1 minute, constantly scraping bowl. Stir in remaining flour to make soft dough. Refrigerate at least 1 hour to make it easier to handle.

2 On well-floured surface with floured rolling pin, roll dough ½ inch thick.

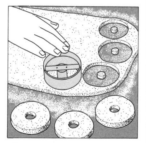

3 With floured doughnut cutter, cut out doughnuts. Reroll and cut trimmings until all the dough is used.

4 In deep-fat fryer, heat 3 or 4 inches salad oil to 370°F. Fry 4 or 5 rings at a time. Turn with a pancake turner as they rise to surface then turn often until golden brown.

5 Lift them from fat with slotted spoon and drain on paper towels. Serve as is or sprinkle with confectioners' sugar or shake in Nutmeg Sugar while still warm.

NUTMEG SUGAR: In paper bag, combine *1 cup sugar* and *¾ teaspoon ground nutmeg;* shake warm doughnuts in mixture, a few at a time, to coat well.

DOUGHNUT "HOLES": Use centers cut from doughnuts; or, using small biscuit cutter, cut all dough into small circles. Fry as directed (left). Toss in *sugar* or shake in Nutmeg Sugar (above).

160 cals each

CHOCOLATE DOUGHNUTS: In double boiler over hot, not boiling, water, melt *1½ squares unsweetened chocolate.* Prepare dough (left) but use 1¼ cups sugar and omit nutmeg; add melted chocolate and *1 teaspoon vanilla extract* with milk. Roll, cut and fry; cool. Serve doughnuts as is or, if you like, sprinkle doughnuts with confectioners' sugar.

161 cals each

NUTTED DOUGHNUTS: Prepare dough (left) but add *½ cup chopped California walnuts* with remaining flour.

166 cals each

WHOLE-WHEAT DOUGHNUTS: Prepare as left but substitute *1½ cups whole-wheat flour* for 1½ cups of the all-purpose flour, stirring it in after beating dough 1 minute. Roll dough about ⅜ inch thick. Fry. Make glaze: In small bowl with fork, stir *½ cup honey* with *⅔ cup confectioners' sugar* thoroughly until glaze is smoothly blended. Spread over warm Whole-Wheat Doughnuts.

Beignets

Color index
page 85

Begin 45 mins
ahead

8 servings

399 cals per
serving

1 cup water
*½ cup butter or
  margarine*
1 teaspoon sugar
¼ teaspoon salt
1 cup all-purpose flour
4 eggs

*1 teaspoon vanilla
  extract*
salad oil
confectioners' sugar
*Cinnamon-Maple Syrup
  (below)*

1. In 2-quart saucepan over medium heat, heat water, butter or margarine, sugar and salt until butter melts and mixture boils.
2. Remove pan from heat and add flour all at once. With wooden spoon, vigorously stir until the ingredients are thoroughly combined and mixture leaves side of pan and forms a ball.
3. Add eggs, one at a time, beating thoroughly after each addition until the mixture is smooth and glossy. Add vanilla.
4. Meanwhile, in another 2-quart saucepan over medium heat, heat about 1½ inches salad oil to 375°F. on deep-fat thermometer, or heat oil in deep-fat fryer set at 375°F. Drop heaping teaspoonfuls of dough into hot oil and fry beignets, a few at a time, until golden. Drain on paper towels; keep warm.
5. To serve: Sprinkle warm beignets lightly with some confectioners' sugar. Serve with Cinnamon-Maple Syrup poured over them or pass syrup separately in a sauce boat.

CINNAMON-MAPLE SYRUP: In 1-quart saucepan over low heat, heat *one 12-ounce bottle maple-flavored syrup* and *2 tablespoons cinnamon red hot candies* until the candies are completely melted, stirring the mixture occasionally.

Pancakes and waffles

Basic pancake and waffle recipes can be varied by adding whole-wheat flour, nuts, fruit or other ingredients. Serve with butter or margarine and your choice of syrup, honey, preserves or confectioners' sugar.

Remember that you can thin a batter which has become too thick while standing with extra milk. Refrigerate any leftover batter to use the next day.

If you are using an electric griddle, skillet or waffle baker, preheat it following manufacturer's directions. Test a non-automatic model by sprinkling with a few drops of water; drops should sizzle.

Pancakes

Color index page 84

Begin 30 mins ahead

Twelve 4-inch pancakes

123 cals each

1¼ cups all-purpose flour
2 tablespoons sugar
2 teaspoons double-acting baking powder
¾ teaspoon salt
1 egg
1⅓ cups milk (for thicker pancakes, use only 1 cup milk)
salad oil
butter or margarine
maple or maple-flavor syrup, honey, preserves, marmalade, apple butter as desired

1 In large bowl, mix first 4 ingredients. In small bowl, beat egg slightly; stir in milk and 3 tablespoons oil; add to flour mixture and stir just until flour is moistened.

2 Heat skillet or griddle over medium-high heat until drop of water sizzles. Brush lightly with oil.

3 Pour batter by scant ¼ cupfuls onto hot skillet or griddle, making a few pancakes at a time.

4 Cook until bubbly and bubbles burst; edges will look dry. With pancake turner, turn and cook until underside is golden.

5 Place on heated platter; keep warm. Repeat, brushing skillet with more oil, if needed. Serve with butter and syrup.

Potato Pancakes

Color index page 84

Begin 1¼ hrs ahead

16 pancakes

122 cals each

cold water
4 large potatoes (3 pounds), peeled and rinsed
1 small onion, peeled
2 eggs
⅓ cup all-purpose flour
2 teaspoons salt
⅛ teaspoon pepper
⅓ cup salad oil
parsley sprigs for garnish

1 Into large bowl half filled with cold water, coarsely shred potatoes and small onion.

2 In colander lined with clean towel or cheesecloth, drain shredded potatoes and onion.

3 Wrap potatoes and onion in towel; squeeze towel to remove as much water as possible.

4 In same large bowl, beat eggs; add the shredded potatoes and onion, flour, salt and pepper and toss together until well mixed.

5 In 12-inch skillet over medium heat, in hot salad oil, drop mixture by scant ¼ cupfuls into 4 mounds.

6 With pancake turner, flatten each mound to make a 4-inch pancake. Cook until golden brown on one side, about 4 minutes; turn pancake and brown other side.

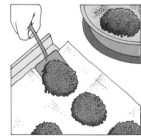

7 Remove to paper-towel-lined cookie sheet to drain; keep warm. Repeat to make about 12 more pancakes, stirring mixture occasionally; garnish with parsley sprigs.

Popovers

Buttermilk Waffles

Color index
page 84

Begin 30 mins
ahead

4 cups batter
or 5 waffles

371 cals each

1³/4 cups all-purpose flour
1 teaspoon double-acting
  baking powder
1 teaspoon baking soda
¹/2 teaspoon salt
2 cups buttermilk
¹/3 cup salad oil
2 eggs

1 Preheat waffle baker as manufacturer directs. In large bowl with whisk, mix flour, baking powder, baking soda and salt.

2 Add buttermilk, salad oil and eggs to flour mixture and beat until thoroughly blended.

3 Pour batter into center of lower half of baker until it spreads to about 1 inch from edges.

4 Cover and bake as manufacturer directs; do not lift the cover during baking time.

5 Loosen baked waffle carefully with fork. Reheat baker before pouring next waffle.

PANCAKE AND WAFFLE VARIATIONS

BUCKWHEAT PANCAKES: Prepare Pancakes (opposite) but substitute *¹/2 cup buckwheat flour* for ¹/2 cup all-purpose flour.

SILVER DOLLAR PANCAKES: Prepare Pancakes (opposite) but pour batter by measuring tablespoonfuls onto hot griddle. (Color index, page 84; makes twenty-four 2-inch pancakes.)

SWEET-MILK WAFFLES: Prepare Buttermilk Waffles (above) but substitute *regular milk* for buttermilk; use 1 tablespoon baking powder and omit the baking soda.

OTHERS: To pancake or waffle batter, add drained canned whole-kernel corn, drained canned crushed pineapple, chopped nuts, flaked coconut, raisins or currants, or fresh fruit, as desired.

Giant Popovers

Color index
page 85

Begin 1¹/2 hrs
ahead

8 popovers

320 cals each

6 eggs
2 cups milk
6 tablespoons butter or
  margarine,
  melted
2 cups all-purpose
  flour
1 teaspoon salt
Butter Curls or Balls
  (page 424)

1 Preheat oven to 375°F. Grease 8 deep 7-ounce pottery custard cups.

2 Set greased custard cups in jelly-roll pan for easier handling.

3 In large bowl with mixer at low speed, beat eggs until frothy; beat in milk and butter.

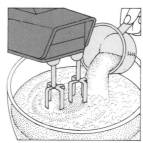

4 At low speed, beat flour and salt into egg, milk and butter mixture.

5 Pour about ³/4 cup batter into each of 8 greased custard cups.

6 Bake 1 hour; make slit in each to let out steam; bake 10 minutes more.

7 Immediately remove from cups. Serve hot with Butter Curls or Balls.

170 cals each

REGULAR POPOVERS: Prepare as above but grease eight 6-ounce custard cups and use *3 eggs, 1 cup milk, 3 tablespoons melted butter, 1 cup all-purpose flour* and *¹/2 teaspoon salt;* bake 50 minutes before cutting slit in each popover to allow steam to escape. (Makes 8 popovers.)

Loaves

Nut Bread

3 cups all-purpose flour
1½ cups coarsely chopped California walnuts
5 teaspoons double-acting baking powder
1¼ cups sugar
1½ teaspoons salt
3 eggs
1½ cups milk
⅓ cup salad oil

Color index page 84

Begin day ahead

1 loaf

4836 cals

Good source of calcium, iron, vitamin A, thiamine, riboflavin, niacin

1 Preheat oven to 350°F. Grease 9" by 5" loaf pan. In large bowl with fork, mix the flour and next 4 ingredients.

2 In small bowl, beat eggs slightly; stir in milk and salad oil; stir this mixture into flour mixture just until flour is moistened.

3 Pour batter into pan; bake 1 hour and 20 minutes or until bread pulls away from sides of pan.

4 Cool in pan on wire rack 10 minutes then remove from pan and cool completely on rack.

Lemon Loaf

Color index page 84

Begin 2 hrs or up to 3 days ahead

1 loaf

4099 cals

Good source of calcium, iron, vitamin A, thiamine, riboflavin, vitamin C

1 medium lemon
2¼ cups all-purpose flour
1½ teaspoons double-acting baking powder
¾ teaspoon salt
sugar
¾ cup butter or margarine
3 eggs
¾ cup milk

1. Preheat oven to 350°F. From lemon, grate 1 tablespoon peel and squeeze 4½ teaspoons lemon juice; set aside. Grease 9" by 5" loaf pan.
2. In large bowl with fork, mix flour, baking powder, salt and 1½ cups sugar. With pastry blender or 2 knives used scissor-fashion, cut in butter until mixture resembles coarse crumbs. Stir in peel.
3. In small bowl with fork, beat eggs slightly and stir in milk; then stir this mixture into flour mixture just until flour is moistened.
4. Spoon into pan. Bake 1¼ hours. Cool in pan on wire rack 10 minutes; remove from pan.
5. In 1-quart saucepan over medium-high heat, heat lemon juice and 2 tablespoons sugar to boiling. Cook, stirring, until slightly thickened, about 5 minutes. With pastry brush, brush sugar mixture evenly over top of bread. Serve warm; or cool loaf completely to serve later.

Corn Bread

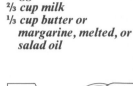

1 cup all-purpose flour
¾ cup cornmeal
2 to 4 tablespoons sugar
1 tablespoon double-acting baking powder
1 teaspoon salt
1 egg
⅔ cup milk
⅓ cup butter or margarine, melted, or salad oil

Color index page 84

Begin 35 mins ahead

9 servings

197 cals per serving

1 Preheat oven to 425°F. Grease 8" by 8" baking pan. In medium bowl with fork, mix together flour, cornmeal, sugar, baking powder and salt.

2 In small bowl with fork, beat together egg, milk and butter or margarine and pour egg mixture all at once into flour mixture.

3 Stir just until flour is moistened and quickly pour batter into the prepared baking pan.

4 Spread batter evenly and bake 25 minutes or until golden. Cut into squares to serve.

221 cals per serving

CORN-BREAD RING: Grease a 5½-cup ring mold. Prepare as above but spoon batter into ring mold. Bake about 25 minutes; invert from mold onto serving platter. Slice and serve as bread or fill center with creamed ham, chicken, shrimp or favorite curry mixture and serve as main dish for 8. (Makes 1 corn-bread ring.)

148 cals each

CORN MUFFINS: Grease twelve 2½-inch muffin-pan cups. Prepare batter as above, then spoon into greased cups, filling each cup two-thirds full. Bake muffins about 20 minutes. (Color index, page 85; makes 12 muffins.)

157 cals each

BLUEBERRY CORN MUFFINS: Grease sixteen 2½-inch muffin-pan cups. Prepare as above but, to flour mixture, add **1 cup fresh or frozen unsweetened blueberries**. Spoon batter into greased muffin-pan cups, filling each two-thirds full. Bake 20 minutes. (Makes 16 muffins.)

149 cals each

CORN STICKS: Grease 14 corn-stick molds very well with **salad oil**. Prepare batter as above; spoon batter into molds, filling each mold three-fourths full. Bake corn stick for 15 to 20 minutes. (Color index, page 84; makes 14 corn sticks.)

Chocolate Date-Nut Loaf

¾ cup boiling water
1 cup sliced pitted dates
*1 6-ounce package semi-
    sweet-chocolate
    pieces*
¼ cup butter
1 egg
¾ cup milk
*1 teaspoon vanilla
    extract*

2½ cups all-purpose flour
*1 cup coarsely chopped
    California walnuts or
    pecans*
⅓ cup sugar
1½ teaspoons salt
*1 teaspoon double-acting
    baking powder*
1 teaspoon baking soda

Color index
page 84

Begin day
ahead

1 loaf

4161 cals

High in fiber

Good source
of calcium,
iron,
vitamin A,
thiamine,
riboflavin,
niacin

1. Preheat oven to 350°F. Grease 9″ by 5″ loaf pan. In small bowl, pour boiling water over dates. In double boiler, over hot, not boiling, water, melt chocolate with butter. In small bowl with fork, beat egg, milk and vanilla just until mixed.
2. In large bowl with spoon, mix flour and next 5 ingredients; add dates and liquid, chocolate and milk mixtures; mix just until blended.
3. Pour mixture into loaf pan. Bake 1 hour and 10 minutes. Cool in pan on wire rack 10 minutes; remove from pan; cool on rack.

Irish Soda Bread

4 cups all-purpose flour
3 tablespoons sugar
*1 tablespoon double-
    acting baking powder*
1 teaspoon salt
¾ teaspoon baking soda
*6 tablespoons butter or
    margarine*

*1½ cups dark seedless
    raisins*
*1 tablespoon caraway
    seed*
2 eggs
1½ cups buttermilk

Color index
page 83

Begin 5 hrs
ahead

1 loaf

3960 cals

High in fiber

Good source
of calcium,
iron,
vitamin A,
thiamine,
riboflavin,
niacin

1. Preheat oven to 350°F. Grease 2-quart round casserole. In large bowl with fork, mix flour and next 4 ingredients. With pastry blender, cut in butter until mixture resembles coarse crumbs; stir in raisins and caraway seed.
2. In small bowl with fork, beat eggs slightly; remove 1 tablespoon and reserve. Stir buttermilk into remaining egg; stir into flour mixture just until flour is moistened (dough will be sticky).
3. Turn dough onto well-floured surface; knead about 10 strokes to mix thoroughly. Shape into a ball; place in casserole. In center of ball, cut 4-inch cross ¼ inch deep. Brush dough with reserved egg.
4. Bake about 1 hour and 20 minutes. Cool in casserole on wire rack 10 minutes; remove from casserole and cool completely on rack.

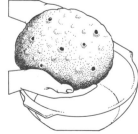

Shaping the bread: Shape dough into a ball; place in greased casserole.

Making the cross: With sharp knife, carefully cut 4-inch cross ¼ inch deep.

Boston Brown Bread

1 cup whole-wheat flour
1 cup rye flour
1 cup cornmeal
*1½ teaspoons baking
    soda*
1½ teaspoons salt
2 cups buttermilk
¾ cup dark molasses
*1 cup dark seedless
    raisins (optional)*

Color index
page 85

Begin 2½ hrs
ahead

2 small loaves

1128 cals
per loaf

Low in
cholesterol

High in fiber

Good source
of calcium,
iron,
thiamine

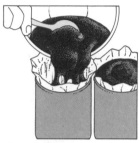

1 Line 2 tall 1-pound coffee cans with foil (it should stand 1 inch above top); cut foil for lids; grease.

2 Into large bowl, measure all ingredients; with spoon, mix well.

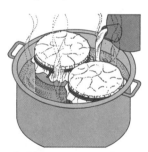

3 Pour batter into cans; cover with foil and tie foil to can with string.

4 Place cans on rack in deep saucepot; add boiling water to come halfway up sides of cans. Cover saucepot.

5 Over low heat, simmer 2 hours. When toothpick inserted in center comes out almost clean, invert onto wire rack to cool.

Zucchini Bread

3 cups all-purpose flour
1½ cups sugar
*1 cup California walnuts,
    chopped*
*4½ teaspoons double-
    acting baking powder*

1 teaspoon salt
4 eggs
⅔ cup salad oil
2 cups grated zucchini
*2 teaspoons grated lemon
    peel*

Color index
page 83

Begin 2 hrs
or up to
3 days ahead

2 loaves

2602 cals
per loaf

Good source
of calcium,
iron,
vitamin A,
thiamine

1. Preheat oven to 350°F. Grease two 8½″ by 4½″ loaf pans. In large bowl with fork, mix flour, sugar, walnuts, baking powder and salt.
2. In medium bowl with fork, beat eggs slightly; stir in salad oil, zucchini and lemon peel.
3. Stir liquid mixture into flour mixture just until flour is moistened; spread evenly in pans.
4. Bake bread 1 hour. Cool in pans on wire racks 10 minutes; remove from pans. Serve warm or cold.

Coffeecakes

Cherry Coffeecake

Color index page 85

Begin 2 hrs ahead

9 servings

372 cals per serving

all-purpose flour
sugar
1 teaspoon double-acting baking powder
¼ teaspoon baking soda
¼ teaspoon salt
10 tablespoons butter, melted
½ cup milk
1 egg
1 teaspoon vanilla extract
¼ teaspoon lemon extract
1 21- or 22-ounce can cherry-pie filling

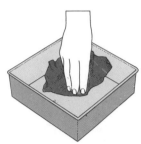

1 Preheat oven to 350°F. Grease and flour 9" by 9" baking pan. In large bowl with fork, mix 1¼ cups flour, ½ cup sugar, baking powder, baking soda and salt.

2 To flour mixture, add ½ cup melted butter, milk, egg and vanilla.

3 With spoon, beat until well mixed then pour batter evenly into greased and floured baking pan.

4 In small bowl with fork, combine ½ cup flour, ¼ cup sugar and remaining 2 tablespoons butter until mixture resembles coarse crumbs.

5 Sprinkle half of crumb mixture evenly over top of batter in pan.

6 Stir lemon extract into cherry-pie filling; then spread pie-filling mixture on crumb mixture in pan.

7 Sprinkle with rest of crumb mixture. Bake 1 hour or until top is golden. Cut into squares.

Peach-filled Coffeecake

Color index page 85

Begin 1½ hrs ahead

12 servings

485 cals per serving

1½ cups all-purpose flour
1 cup sugar
2 teaspoons double-acting baking powder
2 teaspoons grated lemon peel
⅛ teaspoon salt

1 cup butter or margarine, softened
4 eggs
1 29-ounce can sliced cling peaches, well drained
Topping (below)

1. Preheat oven to 350°F. Grease 13" by 9" baking pan. In large bowl with mixer at low speed, beat first 7 ingredients until well mixed, constantly scraping bowl. Increase speed to high; beat 4 minutes, occasionally scraping bowl.
2. Spread batter evenly in baking pan. Arrange peaches on top of batter. Sprinkle with Topping. Bake 45 to 50 minutes until light golden and toothpick inserted in center comes out clean.

TOPPING: In 1-quart saucepan over medium heat, melt *½ cup butter* or margarine; remove from heat. Stir in *1 cup all-purpose flour, ¼ cup sugar* and *1 tablespoon grated lemon peel* to form a soft dough.

Sour-Cream Coffeecake

Color index page 85

Begin 2 hrs or day ahead

10 servings

412 cals per serving

½ cup finely chopped California walnuts
1 teaspoon ground cinnamon
sugar
½ cup butter or margarine
2 cups all-purpose flour

1 cup sour cream
2 eggs
1 teaspoon double-acting baking powder
1 teaspoon baking soda
1 teaspoon vanilla extract

1. In small bowl, combine nuts, cinnamon and ½ cup sugar; set aside. Preheat oven to 350°F. Grease 9-inch tube pan.
2. In large bowl with mixer at medium speed, beat 1 cup sugar with butter until light and fluffy. Add remaining ingredients; beat at low speed until blended, constantly scraping bowl. At medium speed, beat 3 minutes, occasionally scraping bowl.
3. Spread half of batter in pan; sprinkle with half of nut mixture; repeat layers. Bake 60 to 65 minutes until cake pulls away from side of pan. Cool in pan on wire rack 10 minutes; loosen inside edge; invert from pan onto rack to cool; serve warm or cold.

Assembling batter and nut mixtures: Spread half of batter in pan; sprinkle with half of nut mixture. Repeat.

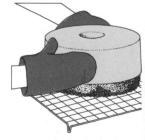

Cooling the cake: Cool in pan on rack 10 minutes then loosen inside edge and invert onto rack.

Flat breads

Corn Tortillas

Color index
page 109

Begin 45 mins
ahead

12 tortillas

85 cals each

Low in fat,
cholesterol,
sodium

**2 cups instant corn masa
(specially treated,
finely ground corn sold
in Mexican and
gourmet foodstores)**
½ teaspoon salt
about 1 cup warm water

1 In medium bowl with
fork, stir together
instant corn masa and salt.
Gradually add water to
corn masa mixture, mixing
lightly with fork until
dough is just moist enough
to hold together. If
necessary, add a little
more water, a tablespoon
at a time.

2 With hands, gather
dough into a ball;
knead a few times in bowl
until smooth.

3 Divide the dough into
12 pieces then, with
hands, shape each piece
into a small ball. Keep
dough covered with plastic
wrap while you are
shaping into tortillas.

4 To shape: Flatten one
ball to about ¼-inch
thickness; place between
sheets of waxed paper.
With rolling pin, roll into
6-inch circle. Leave in
paper until all are rolled.

5 Remove top sheet of
paper and invert
the tortilla onto hot,
ungreased 8-inch skillet
over medium heat. Peel off
bottom sheet. Cook about
30 seconds.

6 Turn; press gently with
pancake turner until
bubbles form in tortilla
(this will make a lighter
tortilla). Turn again;
cook 1 minute longer or
until bottom of tortilla has
small brown specks.

7 Remove to foil and
wrap to keep warm,
stacking tortillas as each is
made. Serve warm with
Chili con Carne (page 209);
or use in recipes for Tacos
(page 456) or Tostada
Appetizers (page 118).

Poori

Color index
page 85

Begin 1¾ hrs
ahead

20 poori
(fried Indian
bread)

61 cals each

Low in
cholesterol,
sodium

**1 cup all-purpose
flour**
**1 cup whole-wheat
flour**
1 teaspoon salt
½ cup water
salad oil

1. In medium bowl, stir flours, salt, water and 1½
teaspoons salad oil until thoroughly blended (the
mixture will be very dry).
2. In bowl, knead dough until it holds together and is
smooth, about 10 minutes. Shape into ball; place in
greased bowl, turning to grease top. Cover with
plastic wrap; let rest 10 minutes.
3. Meanwhile, in electric skillet, heat 1 inch salad oil
to 400°F. With hands, shape dough into 20 balls. On
lightly floured surface with lightly floured rolling
pin, roll each ball into paper-thin circle, 4 inches in
diameter (edges will be ragged). Keep remaining
dough and finished circles covered with plastic wrap
to keep them from drying out.
4. Drop circles, one at a time, into hot oil. With back
of slotted spoon, gently hold circle under surface of
oil until it puffs up, about 10 seconds. Fry about 20
seconds more, turning once. With slotted spoon,
remove poori to paper towels; drain. Serve warm or
store and reheat to serve later.
5. *To reheat:* Preheat oven to 325°F. Wrap poori in
foil in one layer; heat 5 minutes (they will be flat).

Onion Thins

Color index
page 85

Begin 1½ hrs
or up to
3 days ahead

32 crackers

58 cals each

Low in
sodium

2 cups all-purpose flour
½ cup cornmeal
2 tablespoons sugar
½ teaspoon baking soda
½ teaspoon salt
**¼ cup butter or
margarine**
**about ½ cup cold
water**
**2 tablespoons cider
vinegar**
**⅓ cup instant minced
onion**

1. In large bowl with fork, stir flour, cornmeal,
sugar, baking soda and salt. With pastry blender or
2 knives used scissor-fashion, cut in butter or
margarine until mixture resembles coarse crumbs.
Stir water and vinegar into mixture, mixing lightly
with fork until pastry is just moist enough to hold
together. If necessary, gradually add more water, a
tablespoon at a time.
2. Shape dough into a ball; knead a few times in
bowl until well mixed; divide into 32 pieces; shape
each into a ball. Keep dough covered with plastic
wrap while rolling each piece.
3. Preheat oven to 375°F. On floured board with
floured rolling pin, roll one piece of dough into
paper-thin 4½-inch circle (edges may be ragged).
Sprinkle circle with ½ teaspoon instant minced
onion. With rolling pin, roll again to press onion
into dough. With pancake turner, remove circle to
ungreased cookie sheet. Repeat until enough dough
pieces are rolled to fill sheet.
4. Bake circles 8 to 10 minutes until golden brown.
Cool on wire rack. Repeat with remaining dough
pieces. Store in tightly covered container or
wrapped in plastic wrap. Serve Onion Thins as an
accompaniment to salads or entrees.

YEAST BREADS

The delicious aroma of fresh bread is a pleasure many families are rediscovering. It is not difficult to make a perfect loaf, if you keep the following points in mind.

Do not add ingredients to speed up the yeast, or increase the amount of flour, sweetener or salt. These additions will make the bread heavier. All ingredients should be at room temperature.

Use baking pans of the proper size. If they are too small, the dough will spill over the sides; if they are too large, the bread will not rise sufficiently above the sides.

INGREDIENTS
Yeast: Yeast, which makes dough rise, is available in active dry granule form or as fresh (compressed) cakes. One package of active dry yeast equals one 0.6-ounce cake of fresh yeast. In our recipes only dry yeast is used. Store it in a cool, dry place and it will stay fresh and retain its leavening power until the expiration date stamped on the package. In all our recipes the yeast should be mixed with some of the dry ingredients and dissolved later when the liquid is added.

Flour: The texture of a yeast bread largely depends on the gluten in the flour. The gluten content varies from flour to flour: "hard" wheat flour is richer in gluten than "soft" flour, and will give a better rise and more open, even-textured loaf; whole-wheat flour has less gluten than white flour, and unless a proportion of white is added, the loaf will be heavy and close-textured. Some flours, such as soy, rice and corn, contain no gluten and can only be used in combination with white flour. Good Housekeeping yeast breads are made with all-purpose flour which is a blend of hard and soft wheats.

Liquid: Water or milk (whole, skimmed, evaporated or reconstituted nonfat dry), or a combination of the two are most often used for breads. Water makes the crust crisp, while milk produces a soft crust and a creamy-white crumb. The liquid must be at the correct temperature: if it is too hot, it will kill the yeast; if it is too cold, the dough will take longer to rise.

Sugar: A little sugar helps the yeast to grow and produce gas to leaven the dough but extra sugar retards the action of the yeast, so sweet doughs take longer to rise than plain ones. Sugar also adds flavor and makes the crust brown. Brown sugar, molasses and honey will give good results when used as the recipe directs.

Salt: Salt adds and enhances flavor. It also controls the growth of the yeast, making the dough or batter rise more slowly, so it is important not to add too much.

Fat: Many different kinds of fat – butter, margarine, shortening, salad oil or lard – can be added to improve flavor and make the dough stretch more easily. The resulting bread has a tender crumb and stays soft longer.

Egg: Eggs are added to a yeast dough for their flavor and color. They make it richer and more nutritious, soften the crust and give the interior a fine crumb.

Other ingredients: Small quantities of herbs, seeds, fruit and nuts may be added to a dough for their flavor and texture, and to increase its food value; however, they may slow the rising time.

MAKING A YEAST DOUGH
Dissolving dry yeast: Mix active dry yeast with some of the dry ingredients, then gradually add liquid heated to 120° to 130°F. (the temperature of very hot tap water). Beat the batter for about 2 minutes, either in an electric mixer at medium speed or with a wooden spoon.

Adding flour to make a dough: Add only enough flour to make a dough that can be handled. Additional flour will be worked in during kneading. On very humid days, the dough may need more flour than the recipe indicates.

KNEADING
Lightly sprinkle a board or countertop with flour and rub some onto your hands. If the dough remains sticky, a little more flour may be added while kneading. Follow the folding, rolling and turning instructions set out below. The duration of kneading will depend on the development of gluten during beating, the stickiness of the dough and the strength with which you knead.

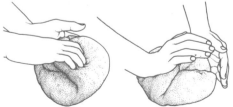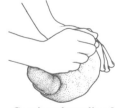

Kneading the dough: Shape the dough into a ball and, on a lightly floured surface, fold it toward you.

Using the heels of your hands, push it away with a rolling motion and give the dough a quarter turn.

Continue kneading 8 to 10 minutes until dough is smooth and elastic and doesn't stick, with little blisters under surface.

RISING.

Cover the dough with a clean cloth, while you wash, dry and lightly grease the mixing bowl. Replace dough in mixing bowl, smooth side (top) down, and turn to lightly grease the top and prevent it drying out. Cover the bowl with a towel and put in a draft-free place at a temperature of 80° to 85°F. In a cool kitchen, place bowl (1) in an unheated oven with a large pan of hot water on the shelf below, replenishing water as it cools; or (2) on a wire rack set over a large pan filled two-thirds full with hot water; or (3) in a deep pan of warm, not hot, water; or (4) near, but not on, a warm range or radiator. Let the dough rise until doubled in bulk and test as below.

Testing the rising: The dough is doubled when two fingertips pressed ½ inch into it leave dents that remain. If dents fill in quickly, let rise 15 minutes longer and test again. A batter should look light and bubbly, with an uneven, slightly rounded top.

PUNCHING OR STIRRING DOWN

When a dough has doubled in bulk it is punched down by hand; batters are stirred down. To punch down dough, push your fist deep into the center of the dough, pull edges to the center and turn the dough over.

Stir batter with a wooden spoon until it has fallen to about its original size.

RESTING

Dough is easier to handle if it is allowed to rest before shaping. Turn it out on a lightly floured surface, divide pieces as required and put it aside for 10 to 15 minutes, covered with the bowl or a towel.

SHAPING BREAD

For a round loaf, hold ball of dough and pull sides under until ball is evenly rounded and smooth on top. Place on a cookie sheet; flatten slightly. For a loaf shape, follow the directions set out below.

 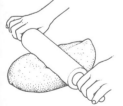 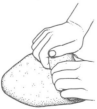 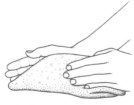

Shaping a loaf: With a lightly floured rolling pin, roll dough into a rectangle.

Starting at narrow end, roll dough up tightly and pinch the edge with your fingers to seal.

Seal ends by pressing with the sides of your hands; fold under. Place roll, seam side down, in loaf pan.

After shaping, cover the loaf with a towel and leave in a warm, draft-free place until it has redoubled and a finger pressed into it lightly leaves a dent.

BAKING

Place loaf pans on the middle shelf of a preheated oven, 2 inches apart so heat circulates. If baking on 2 shelves, stagger pans. If tops brown too quickly, cover loosely with foil. Test bread after the minimum specified baking time. If it is not ready, return it to the oven; retest the bread a few minutes later.

Testing for doneness: Tap top of loaf lightly with your fingertips. If it sounds hollow and is well browned on top, the bread is ready.

Cooling: Remove loaves from pans (or cookie sheet) immediately so bottoms don't become soggy; cool on wire racks away from drafts.

HIGH ALTITUDE BAKING

Yeast doughs rise faster and higher at high altitudes. At 5,000 feet use only half the yeast specified. Punch down the dough as soon as it tests doubled, even if it does not look as if it has doubled in size.

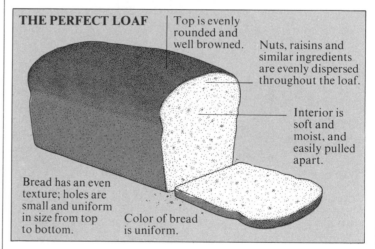

THE PERFECT LOAF

Top is evenly rounded and well browned.

Nuts, raisins and similar ingredients are evenly dispersed throughout the loaf.

Interior is soft and moist, and easily pulled apart.

Bread has an even texture; holes are small and uniform in size from top to bottom.

Color of bread is uniform.

STORING BREAD

To keep bread fresh, wrap each cooled loaf in foil or plastic wrap, or seal in a plastic bag; store in a cool, dry cupboard or bread box. Bread may be stored in the refrigerator but it goes stale more quickly.

Bread keeps in the freezer for up to 3 months if tightly wrapped in foil, heavy-duty plastic wrap or freezer wrap, or if sealed in plastic bags. Always make sure to press out as much air as possible.

Slices of frozen bread can be toasted without thawing. To thaw a loaf, leave it at room temperature for 2 to 3 hours, unwrapped for a crisp crust. Or, wrap in foil and thaw in a preheated 375°F. oven for 20 minutes. For a crisp crust, remove wrapping for last 5 minutes.

Everyday breads

In this section, we give recipes for conventional breads shaped as loaves, rounds or rolls which can be served with meals every day. Today's breadmaking techniques are easily acquired, yet thanks to modern ingredients and equipment, give the same good flavor, texture and appearance as older, more complicated methods.

All bread tastes best fresh from the oven. However, if it has gone slightly stale, you can "refresh" it by wrapping it in foil and putting it in a 375°F. oven for 15 minutes. For a crisp crust, unwrap it and put it back in the oven for 5 minutes more.

Here are ways to glaze bread before baking. For a dark, shiny glaze, brush on 1 beaten egg yolk. For a light shiny glaze, beat the whole egg or brush on melted butter or margarine. For shine with no color, brush on 1 egg white beaten with 1 tablespoon water.

To slice fresh bread, use a sharp knife or serrated knife and slice with a sawing motion.

White Bread

3 tablespoons sugar
2 teaspoons salt
1 package active dry yeast
5½ to 6½ cups all-purpose flour
2 cups milk
butter or margarine

Color index page 78

Begin 4 hrs ahead

2 loaves

1885 cals per loaf

Good source of calcium, iron, vitamin A, thiamine, niacin

1 In large bowl, combine sugar, salt, yeast and 2 cups flour. In 2-quart saucepan over low heat, heat milk and 3 tablespoons butter until very warm (120° to 130°F.).

2 With mixer at low speed, gradually beat liquid into dry ingredients, until just blended. Increase speed to medium; beat 2 minutes, occasionally scraping bowl.

3 Beat in ¾ cup flour or enough to make a thick batter; continue beating 2 minutes, scraping bowl often. With spoon, stir in enough flour (about 3 cups) to make soft dough.

4 On floured surface, knead dough until elastic, about 10 minutes. Shape into ball; turn over in greased bowl to grease top. Cover; let rise until doubled, about 1 hour.

5 Punch down dough by pushing fist into center and pulling in edges. Transfer to a lightly floured surface; cut in half; cover with bowl; let dough rest 15 minutes.

6 Grease two 9" by 5" loaf pans. Roll each dough half into 12" by 8" rectangle. Shape into loaf (page 433); place, seam side down, in loaf pan.

7 Cover with a towel; let dough rise in a warm place (80° to 85°F.), away from draft, until doubled (dough will double in about 1 hour).

8 Preheat oven to 400°F. If liked, brush loaves with 2 tablespoons melted butter. Bake 25 to 30 minutes until loaves test done. Remove from pans; cool.

Color index page 78
Begin 4½ hrs ahead
2 loaves
2410 cals per loaf
High in fiber

Good source of calcium, iron, vitamin A, thiamine, riboflavin, niacin

Whole-Wheat Bread

3 tablespoons sugar
4 teaspoons salt
2 packages active dry yeast
4 cups whole-wheat flour

3 to 3½ cups all-purpose flour
2¼ cups milk
⅓ cup butter or margarine
⅓ cup molasses

1. In large bowl, combine sugar, salt, yeast, 2 cups whole-wheat flour and 1 cup all-purpose flour. In 2-quart saucepan over low heat, heat milk, butter or margarine and molasses until very warm (120° to 130°F.). (Butter does not need to melt completely.)
2. With mixer at low speed, gradually beat liquid into dry ingredients. Increase speed to medium; beat 2 minutes, occasionally scraping bowl with rubber spatula. Beat in ½ cup whole-wheat flour and ½ cup all-purpose flour or enough to make a thick batter; continue beating 2 minutes, occasionally scraping bowl with rubber spatula.
3. With spoon, stir in 1½ cups whole-wheat and additional all-purpose flour (about 1½ cups) to make a soft dough.
4. Turn dough onto lightly floured surface and knead until smooth and elastic, about 10 minutes. Shape dough into ball and place in greased large bowl, turning dough to grease top. Cover with towel; let rise in warm, draft-free place (80° to 85°F.), until doubled, about 1 hour.
5. Punch down dough; turn onto lightly floured surface; cut in half; cover with bowl; let dough halves rest 15 minutes for easier shaping. Grease 2 9" by 5" loaf pans.
6. With lightly floured rolling pin, roll one dough half into a 12" by 8" rectangle. Starting at a narrow end, roll dough up tightly and pinch the edge with your fingers. Seal ends by pressing them with the sides of your hands and fold them under. Place the roll, seam side down, in loaf pan.
7. Repeat step 6 with remaining dough. Cover loaves with towel; let rise in warm place, away from draft, until loaves are doubled, about 1 hour.
8. Preheat oven to 400°F. Bake loaves 30 to 35 minutes or until golden and loaves sound hollow when top is tapped lightly with fingers. Remove from pans immediately so bottoms don't become soggy, and cool on wire racks.

Round Rye Bread

4 cups all-purpose flour
2 cups rye flour
2 packages active dry yeast
1½ teaspoons salt

2 tablespoons caraway seed
2 cups buttermilk
⅓ cup light molasses
butter or margarine

Color index
page 78

Begin 4½ hrs
ahead

2 loaves

2297 cals per
loaf

High in fiber

Good source
of calcium,
iron,
vitamin A,
thiamine,
riboflavin

1. In medium bowl, combine all-purpose flour and rye flour. In large bowl, combine 2 cups flour mixture, yeast, salt and caraway seed. In 2-quart saucepan over low heat, heat buttermilk, molasses and ⅓ cup butter or margarine until very warm (120° to 130°F.). (Butter or margarine does not need to melt, and mixture will appear curdled.)
2. With mixer at low speed, gradually beat liquid into dry ingredients. Increase speed to medium; beat mixture 2 minutes, occasionally scraping bowl with rubber spatula.
3. Gradually beat in ½ cup flour mixture or enough to make a thick batter; continue beating 2 minutes, occasionally scraping bowl with rubber spatula. With spoon, stir in enough additional flour mixture (about 2½ cups) to make a soft dough.
4. Turn dough onto well-floured surface and knead until smooth and elastic, about 10 minutes. Shape the dough into a ball and place it in a greased large bowl, turning dough over to grease top. Cover with towel; let rise in warm place (80° to 85°F.), away from draft, until doubled, about 1 hour. (Dough is doubled when two fingers pressed lightly into dough leave a dent.)
5. Punch down dough by pushing down the center with fist, then pushing edges of dough into center. Turn dough onto lightly floured surface; cut dough in half; cover with bowl and let rest for 15 minutes.
6. Grease large cookie sheet. Shape each dough half into a smooth round ball by pulling the sides of the dough underneath; place balls of dough on cookie sheet and flatten slightly. Cover with towel; let rise in warm place, away from draft, until the dough has doubled, about 1 hour.
7. Preheat oven to 350°F. Brush loaves with 2 tablespoons melted butter or margarine. Bake loaves 35 minutes or until loaves sound hollow when lightly tapped with fingers. Remove loaves from cookie sheet immediately so the bottoms don't become soggy and leave them to cool completely on wire racks away from draft.

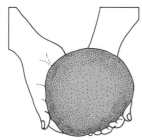

Shaping the dough: Pull sides of each dough half under to form a smooth, round ball.

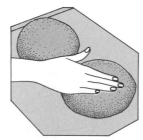

Flattening the balls: Place balls on cookie sheet and with hand, flatten each one slightly.

Marbled Loaf

Dark Dough:
2 cups whole-wheat flour
2 cups rye flour
about 3 cups all-purpose flour
1 tablespoon sugar
1 tablespoon salt
2 packages active dry yeast
2¼ cups water
¾ cup yellow cornmeal
⅓ cup dark molasses
3 tablespoons butter
1 tablespoon caraway seed

Light Dough:
3 tablespoons sugar
2½ teaspoons salt
1 package active dry yeast
about 6 cups all-purpose flour
1½ cups water
½ cup milk
3 tablespoons butter

1 egg white, beaten

Color index
page 78

Begin 4½ hrs
ahead

2 loaves

4190 cals per
loaf

High in fiber

Good source
of calcium,
iron,
vitamin A,
thiamine,
riboflavin,
niacin

1. Prepare Dark Dough: In medium bowl, combine whole-wheat flour, rye flour and 2½ cups all-purpose flour. In large bowl, combine sugar, salt, yeast and 1½ cups flour mixture. In 2-quart saucepan, combine water, cornmeal and molasses; add butter and caraway seed; over low heat, heat until very warm (120° to 130°F.).
2. With mixer at low speed, gradually beat liquid mixture into dry ingredients until just blended. Increase speed to medium; beat 2 minutes, occasionally scraping bowl. Gradually beat in 1 cup flour mixture or enough to make a thick batter. Continue beating 2 minutes, occasionally scraping bowl. Stir in enough additional flour mixture (about 3 cups) to make a soft dough.
3. On lightly floured surface, knead dough about 10 minutes, until smooth and elastic, working in remaining flour mixture while kneading. Shape into ball; place in greased large bowl, turning dough over to grease top. Cover; let rise in warm place until doubled, about 1½ hours.
4. Meanwhile, prepare Light Dough as for Dark Dough in steps 1–3, but for dry mixture combine sugar, salt, yeast and 2 cups flour and for liquid mixture, in 1-quart saucepan, combine water, milk and butter. After first 2 minutes' beating, beat in ¾ cup flour and after second 2 minutes' beating, stir in about 3 cups flour. Let dough rise in warm place until doubled, about 1 hour.
5. Punch down Dark Dough and turn onto lightly floured surface; cut into 2 equal pieces; cover with bowl and let rest 15 minutes for easier shaping. Meanwhile, repeat with Light Dough.
6. Grease 2 large cookie sheets. Carefully knead together 1 piece Dark Dough with 1 piece Light Dough about 15 times. With lightly floured rolling pin, roll into 16″ by 9″ rectangle. Starting at 16-inch end, tightly roll dough jelly-roll fashion; pinch seam to seal and tuck ends under; place, seam down, diagonally across cookie sheet. Repeat with remaining dough; place on second cookie sheet. Cover; let rise until doubled, about 1 hour.
7. Preheat oven to 400°F. Brush loaves with egg white. Bake on 2 oven racks 20 minutes; switch sheets between oven racks so loaves brown evenly; bake 20 minutes more, or until loaves sound hollow when tapped. Remove to wire racks to cool.

Everyday breads

Italian Bread

1 tablespoon sugar
2 teaspoons salt
2 packages active dry
yeast
about 5 cups all-purpose
flour

1 tablespoon butter or
margarine
water
cornmeal
salad oil
1 egg white

Color index page 79

Begin 4 hrs or day ahead

2 loaves

1471 cals per loaf

Low in cholesterol

Good source of calcium, iron, thiamine, niacin

1. In large bowl, combine sugar, salt, yeast and 2 cups flour. In 1-quart saucepan over low heat, heat butter or margarine and 1¾ cups water until very warm (120° to 130°F.). (Butter or margarine does not need to melt.)

2. With mixer at low speed, gradually beat liquid into dry ingredients until just blended. Increase speed to medium; beat 2 minutes, occasionally scraping bowl with rubber spatula.

3. Beat in ½ cup flour to make thick batter; continue beating mixture at medium speed 2 minutes, scraping bowl often with rubber spatula. With wooden spoon, stir in enough additional flour (about 1¾ cups) to make a soft dough.

4. Turn dough onto floured surface; knead until smooth and elastic, about 10 minutes, adding flour while kneading.

5. Cut dough in half; cover pieces with bowl; let dough rest 20 minutes for easier shaping.

6. Grease large cookie sheet; sprinkle cookie sheet with cornmeal.

7 On floured surface with floured rolling pin, roll each half into 15″ by 10″ rectangle. From 15-inch side, tightly roll dough, jelly-roll fashion; pinch seam to seal.

8 Place loaves, seam side down, on cookie sheet and taper ends. Brush loaves with oil; cover loosely with plastic wrap. Refrigerate 2 to 24 hours.

9 Preheat oven to 425°F. Meanwhile, remove loaves from refrigerator; uncover; let stand 10 minutes. Cut 3 or 4 diagonal slashes on top of each loaf. Bake 20 minutes.

10 In small bowl with fork, beat egg white with 1 tablespoon water. Remove loaves from oven; brush with egg-white mixture; return to oven and bake 5 minutes.

Whole-Grain Bread

2 cups rye flour
1 cup unprocessed bran
½ cup wheat germ
about 4¼ cups whole-
wheat flour
3 tablespoons sugar
4 teaspoons salt
2 packages active dry
yeast

¾ cup milk
½ cup butter or
margarine
⅓ cup dark molasses
water
2 eggs
2 tablespoons yellow
cornmeal
1 teaspoon caraway seed

Color index page 78

Begin 5 hrs ahead

1 loaf

4977 cals

High in fiber

Good source of calcium, iron, vitamin A, thiamine, riboflavin, niacin

1. In large bowl, combine rye flour, bran, wheat germ and 3 cups whole-wheat flour. In another large bowl, combine sugar, salt, yeast and 3 cups flour mixture. In 2-quart saucepan over low heat, heat milk, butter or margarine, molasses and 1 cup water until very warm (120° to 130°F.).

2. With mixer at low speed, gradually beat liquid into dry ingredients until just blended. Increase speed to medium; beat 2 minutes, occasionally scraping bowl. Reserve 1 egg white; beat in remaining eggs and 2 cups flour mixture; continue beating 2 minutes, occasionally scraping bowl. With spoon, stir in remaining flour mixture and enough additional whole-wheat flour (about ¾ cup) to make the mixture a soft dough.

3. Lightly flour surface with whole-wheat flour; turn dough onto surface; knead until smooth and elastic, about 10 minutes, adding more whole-wheat flour while kneading. Shape dough into ball; place in greased large bowl, turning dough to grease top. Cover; let rise in warm place, away from draft, until doubled, about 1 hour. (Dough is doubled when two fingers pressed lightly into dough leave a dent.)

4. Punch down dough; turn onto surface lightly floured with whole-wheat flour; cover with bowl; let dough rest for 15 minutes.

5. Sprinkle cookie sheet with cornmeal. Shape dough into oval, tapering ends; place on cookie sheet. Cover with towel; let rise in warm place until doubled, about 1 hour. (Dough is doubled when one finger very lightly pressed against it leaves a dent.)

6. Preheat oven to 350°F. Cut 3 diagonal slashes on top of loaf. In cup, mix reserved egg white with 1 tablespoon water. With pastry brush, brush bread with egg-white mixture. Sprinkle bread with caraway seed. Bake 50 to 60 minutes until loaf sounds hollow when lightly tapped with fingers. Immediately remove loaf from cookie sheet; cool.

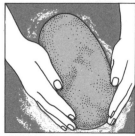

Shaping the dough: Form dough into an oval with tapering ends.

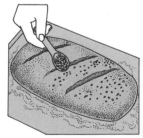

Adding caraway seed: Sprinkle seed over loaf brushed with mixture of egg white and water.

Pumpernickel and Whole-Wheat Braid

Color index page 78

Begin 4½ hrs ahead

1 loaf

4247 cals

High in fiber

Good source of calcium, iron, vitamin A, thiamine, riboflavin, niacin

Pumpernickel Dough:
4½ teaspoons sugar
1½ teaspoons salt
1 package active dry yeast
about 1¼ cups all-purpose flour
1 square unsweetened chocolate
⅓ cup molasses
2 tablespoons butter or margarine
¾ cup water
1½ cups rye flour or pumpernickel rye flour

Whole-Wheat Dough:
2¼ teaspoons sugar
2 teaspoons salt
1 package active dry yeast
about 1¾ cups whole-wheat flour
about 1½ cups all-purpose flour
⅓ cup milk
2 tablespoons honey
2 tablespoons butter
¾ cup water

Egg Glaze:
1 egg yolk
2 teaspoons water

1. Prepare Pumpernickel Dough: In large bowl, combine sugar, salt, yeast and 1 cup all-purpose flour. In heavy 1-quart saucepan over low heat, melt chocolate; stir in molasses, butter and water and heat until very warm (120° to 130°F.). (Butter does not need to melt completely.)
2. With mixer at low speed, gradually beat liquid into dry ingredients until just mixed. Increase speed to medium; beat 2 minutes, occasionally scraping bowl with rubber spatula.
3. Gradually beat in ¾ cup rye flour or enough to make a thick batter; continue beating 2 minutes occasionally scraping bowl with rubber spatula. With wooden spoon, stir in remaining rye flour and enough additional all-purpose flour (about ¼ cup) to make a soft dough.
4. Turn dough onto lightly floured surface and knead until elastic, about 7 minutes, adding as little flour as possible while kneading. (Dough will be slightly sticky.) Shape into ball; place in greased large bowl, turning to grease top. Cover bowl loosely with towel; let rise in warm place (80° to 85°F.), away from draft, until doubled, 2 hours.
5. Meanwhile, prepare Whole-Wheat Dough as for Pumpernickel Dough in steps 1–4, but for dry ingredients combine sugar, salt, yeast, ¾ cup whole-wheat flour and ½ cup all-purpose flour, and for liquid ingredients combine milk, honey, butter and water. After first 2 minutes' beating, beat in ¼ cup whole-wheat flour and ¼ cup all-purpose flour and after second 2 minutes' beating, stir in ¾ cup whole-wheat and about ½ cup all-purpose flour. Knead dough about 10 minutes. Dough will double in about 1 hour.
6. Punch down Pumpernickel Dough. Turn onto lightly floured surface; cover with towel; let rest 15 minutes. Repeat with Whole-Wheat Dough.
7. Grease a large cookie sheet. Divide Whole-Wheat Dough in half. On lightly floured surface, roll Whole-Wheat pieces and Pumpernickel Dough into 20-inch ropes and braid (right); let rise 1 hour.
8. Preheat oven to 350°F. Prepare Egg Glaze: In cup, beat egg yolk with water. Brush braid with mixture. Bake 45 minutes or until loaf sounds hollow when tapped. Let loaf cool on wire rack.

Braided Herb Bread

Color index page 78

Begin 4 hrs ahead

2 loaves

1945 cals per loaf

Good source of calcium, iron, thiamine, niacin

1 tablespoon salt
1 tablespoon rosemary leaves
2 packages active dry yeast
about 7 cups all-purpose flour
2½ cups water
1 tablespoon butter or margarine, softened
1 egg, slightly beaten

1. In large bowl, combine salt, rosemary leaves, yeast and 2½ cups flour. In 2-quart saucepan over low heat, heat water and butter until very warm (120° to 130°F.). (Butter does not need to melt.)
2. With mixer at medium speed, gradually beat liquid into dry ingredients. Beat 2 minutes, scraping bowl occasionally. Add 1 cup flour or enough to make a thick batter; beat 2 minutes at high speed, scraping bowl occasionally. With spoon, stir in 3½ cups flour to make a soft, sticky dough.
3. Place in greased bowl; cover with towel. Let dough rise in warm place, away from draft, until doubled, about 1½ hours.
4. Punch down dough and turn out onto well-floured surface. Knead until smooth and elastic, about 10 minutes. Divide dough into 6 equal pieces; roll each piece into an 18-inch rope. On one side of a large cookie sheet, braid 3 ropes (below). Repeat with remaining ropes. Cover with towel; let rise in warm place until doubled, about 30 minutes.
5. Preheat oven to 450°F. Brush tops of loaves with egg. Bake 30 minutes or until loaves sound hollow when tapped with fingers. Remove to racks to cool.

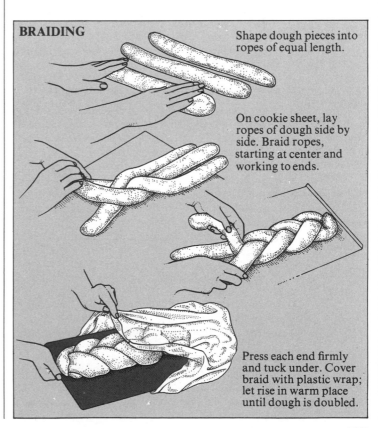

BRAIDING

Shape dough pieces into ropes of equal length.

On cookie sheet, lay ropes of dough side by side. Braid ropes, starting at center and working to ends.

Press each end firmly and tuck under. Cover braid with plastic wrap; let rise in warm place until dough is doubled.

Everyday breads and rolls

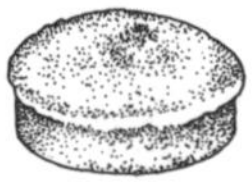

Sesame Pan Bread

Color index
page 79

Begin 3 hrs
ahead

2 loaves

2068 cals per
loaf

Good source
of calcium,
iron,
vitamin A,
thiamine,
riboflavin,
niacin

3 tablespoons sugar
1 tablespoon salt
2 packages active dry
   yeast
about 6 cups all-purpose
   flour

2 cups water
¼ cup butter or
   margarine
   milk
1 egg, slightly beaten
¼ cup sesame seed

1. In large bowl, combine sugar, salt, yeast and 2 cups flour. In 2-quart saucepan over low heat, heat water, butter and 1 cup milk until very warm (120° to 130°F.). (Butter does not need to melt.)
2. With mixer at low speed, gradually beat liquid into dry ingredients until just mixed. Increase speed to medium; beat 2 minutes, occasionally scraping bowl. Beat in egg and ½ cup flour or enough to make a thick batter; continue beating 2 minutes at medium speed, occasionally scraping bowl. With wooden spoon, stir in enough additional flour (about 3 cups) to make a soft dough.
3. Turn dough onto lightly floured surface; knead until smooth and elastic, about 10 minutes, adding more flour while kneading, if needed. Shape into ball; cover with bowl; let rest 15 minutes. Grease two 9-inch round cake pans.
4. Cut dough in half; with fingers, press into pans evenly. Cover with towel; let rise in warm place until doubled, about 40 minutes.
5. Preheat oven to 350°F. Brush loaves with milk; sprinkle with sesame seed. Bake 40 minutes or until golden and loaves sound hollow when tapped with fingers. Remove from pans; cool.

Oatmeal Batter Bread

Color index
page 79

Begin 4½ hrs
ahead

2 loaves

1712 cals per
loaf

Low in
cholesterol

High in fiber

Good source
of calcium,
iron,
thiamine,
niacin

2 teaspoons salt
2 packages active dry
   yeast
about 5 cups all-purpose
   flour

2¼ cups water
1 cup quick-cooking oats,
   uncooked
½ cup light molasses
   butter or margarine

1. In large bowl, combine salt, yeast and 2 cups flour. In 2-quart saucepan with spoon, mix water, oats and molasses; add 1 tablespoon butter; over low heat, heat until very warm (120° to 130°F.).
2. With mixer at low speed, gradually beat liquid mixture into dry ingredients until just blended. Increase speed to medium; beat 2 minutes, occasionally scraping bowl. Beat in ½ cup flour to make a thick batter; continue beating 2 minutes, scraping bowl often. Stir in enough additional flour (about 2½ cups) to make a stiff dough that leaves side of bowl.
3. Cover bowl with towel; let rise in warm place until doubled, about 1 hour.
4. Stir down dough; divide in two and turn into 2 greased 2-quart round, straight-sided, shallow casseroles. With greased fingers, turn dough over to grease top; shape into ball. Cover; let rise in warm place until doubled, about 45 minutes.
5. Preheat oven to 350°F. Bake 40 minutes or until loaves sound hollow when tapped. Remove from casseroles immediately. If you like, rub tops with softened butter; cool on racks.

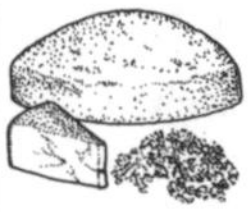

Cheese Casserole Bread

Color index
page 79

Begin 4½ hrs
ahead

1 loaf

3666 cals

Good source
of calcium,
iron,
vitamin A,
thiamine,
riboflavin,
niacin

2 tablespoons sugar
2 teaspoons salt
2 packages active dry
   yeast
about 5 cups all-purpose
   flour

2¼ cups milk
¼ pound sharp
   Cheddar cheese,
   shredded (1 cup)
1 tablespoon butter or
   margarine, melted

1. In large bowl, combine sugar, salt, yeast and 2 cups flour. In 2-quart saucepan over low heat, heat milk and cheese until very warm (120° to 130°F.). (Cheese does not need to melt.)
2. With mixer at low speed, beat liquid mixture into dry ingredients until just blended. At medium speed, beat 2 minutes, occasionally scraping bowl with rubber spatula. Beat in 1 cup flour to make a thick batter; beat 2 minutes more, scraping bowl often. Stir in enough additional flour (about 2 cups) to make a stiff dough that leaves side of bowl.
3. Cover bowl with towel; let rise in warm place until doubled, about 45 minutes.
4. Stir down dough; turn into greased 2-quart round, straight-sided, shallow casserole. Cover; let rise in warm place until doubled, about 45 minutes.
5. Preheat oven to 375°F. Brush loaf with melted butter. Bake 30 to 35 minutes until golden and loaf sounds hollow when tapped. Cool on wire rack.

Potato Bread

Color index
page 79

Begin 4½ hrs
ahead

2 loaves

2651 cals per
loaf

Good source
of calcium,
iron,
vitamin A,
thiamine,
riboflavin,
niacin

2 tablespoons sugar
4 teaspoons salt
2 packages active dry
   yeast
about 8 cups all-purpose
   flour

½ cup water
1½ cups mashed potatoes
   milk
¼ cup butter or
   margarine
2 eggs

1. In large bowl, combine sugar, salt, yeast and 1½ cups flour. In 2-quart saucepan, mix water, mashed potatoes and 1½ cups milk; add butter; over low heat, heat until very warm (120° to 130°F.), stirring often. (Butter does not need to melt.)
2. With mixer at low speed, gradually beat liquid into dry ingredients just until blended; beat in eggs. At medium speed, beat 2 minutes, occasionally scraping bowl. Beat in 1 cup flour to make a thick batter; continue beating 2 minutes, scraping bowl often. Stir in enough additional flour (about 3¼ cups) to make a soft dough.
3. On well-floured surface, knead dough about 10 minutes, until smooth and elastic, kneading in about 1½ cups flour. Shape into ball; place in greased large bowl, turning to grease top. Cover; let rise until doubled, about 1 hour.
4. Punch down dough; turn onto lightly floured surface; cut in half; cover; let rest 15 minutes.
5. Grease two 2-quart round, straight-sided, shallow casseroles. Shape 1 piece of dough into ball; place in casserole. Cut 2 parallel slashes on top. Repeat. Cover; let rise until doubled, about 1 hour.
6. Preheat oven to 400°F. Brush each loaf with milk. Bake 40 minutes or until well browned and loaves sound hollow when tapped with fingers. Remove loaves to cool on wire racks.

Old-fashioned Rolls

⅓ cup sugar
1½ teaspoons salt
2 packages active dry yeast
4½ to 5½ cups all-purpose flour
1 cup milk
¼ cup butter
2 eggs
melted butter or Egg Glaze (below)

Color index page 83

Begin 3½ hrs ahead

24 rolls

144 cals each

1 In large bowl, combine sugar, salt, yeast and 1½ cups flour. In 1-quart saucepan, heat milk and butter until very warm (120° to 130°F.). With mixer at low speed, gradually beat liquid into dry ingredients. At medium speed, beat 2 minutes, occasionally scraping bowl, with a rubber spatula.

2 Beat in eggs and about ½ cup flour to make a thick batter; continue beating 2 minutes. Stir in flour (2 to 2½ cups) to make a soft dough.

3 On lightly floured surface, knead dough until smooth and elastic, about 10 minutes. Shape dough into ball.

4 Turn in greased large bowl to grease top. Cover; let rise in warm place until doubled, 1 hour.

5 Punch down dough. Transfer to lightly floured surface; cut in half; cover; let rest 15 minutes.

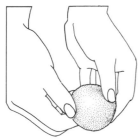

6 Cut each half into 12 pieces; shape into balls. Place 2 inches apart on greased cookie sheets. Cover; let rise until doubled, about 30 minutes.

7 Preheat oven to 400°F. Brush with melted butter or Egg Glaze. Bake 10 minutes or until golden. Cool slightly on wire racks. Serve warm.

EGG GLAZE: In small bowl with fork, beat *1 egg* with *1 tablespoon milk*.

Dinner Rolls

Old-fashioned Rolls dough (left)   melted butter or Egg Glaze (below left)

Color index page 80

Begin 3½ hrs ahead

24 rolls

1. Prepare dough as in steps 1-5 but in step 6, cut and shape dough as directed and shown below or on the next page. Brush with melted butter or glaze.
2. Preheat oven to 400°F. Bake 12 to 18 minutes or until golden, depending on the shape selected.

DINNER BUNS

Shape one half of dough into 12 oval balls, tapering ends slightly. Place 2 inches apart on greased cookie sheet. Cover; let rise until doubled.

With sharp, floured knife, slash lengthwise halfway through center of each roll.

VIENNA ROLLS

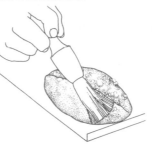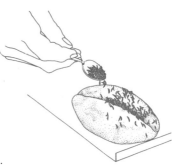

Prepare as for Dinner Buns (above). Beat *1 egg white* with *1 tablespoon water* until frothy; brush egg-white mixture over rolls.

Sprinkle with *caraway seed*.

DOUBLE TWISTS

Divide one half of dough into 12 equal pieces. Roll each piece into 6-inch-long rope. Pinch 2 ropes together at one end.

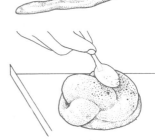

Then, carefully twist together, pinching bottom ends to seal. Overlap ends; tuck under center of twist. Place on greased cookie sheet.

Brush with Egg Glaze; sprinkle with *sesame seed*. Cover; let rise until dough is doubled.

439

Everyday breads and rolls

KNOTS

Divide one half of dough into 6 equal pieces. Roll each piece into 6-inch-long rope shape.

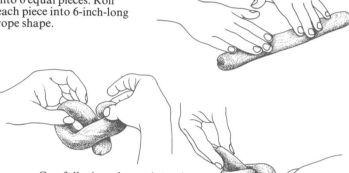

Carefully tie each rope into a knot. Arrange on greased cookie sheet. Brush with *melted butter*. Cover; let rise until doubled.

CRESCENTS

Roll one half of dough into 9-inch circle. Cut circle into 12 wedges; brush with *melted butter.*

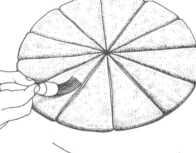

Roll up each wedge toward point; place wedges on lightly greased cookie sheet.

Curve ends. Cover with towel; let crescents rise until doubled.

PAN ROLLS

Shape one half of dough into 2-inch balls by tucking ends under.

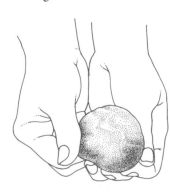

Dip balls into melted butter. In greased 8″ by 8″ baking pan, place balls letting them just touch each other. Let rise until doubled.

PINWHEELS

Roll one half of dough into 12½″ by 10″ rectangle. Cut into 2½-inch squares. Place 2 inches apart on greased cookie sheets. Cut 1½ inches deep from corners to center of each square, making 8 points (right).

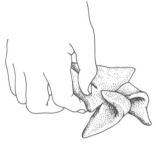

Fold every other point into center of square.

Gently press points to center to secure them in position. Brush with melted butter or Egg Glaze; let rise until doubled.

FAN-TANS

Roll one half of dough into ⅛-inch-thick rectangle. Brush with melted butter. Cut dough into 1½-inch-wide strips (right).

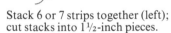

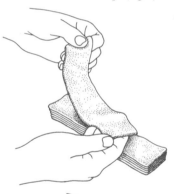

Stack 6 or 7 strips together (left); cut stacks into 1½-inch pieces.

Place, cut side up, in greased 2½- or 3-inch muffin-pan cups (left). Let rise until doubled.

POSIES

Shape one half of dough into 6 balls. Place on greased cookie sheet. Flatten slightly.

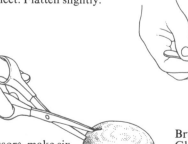

With scissors, make six ¼-inch-deep cuts in edge of each ball.

Brush lightly with Egg Glaze ; sprinkle with *poppy seed.* Let rise until dough is doubled.

440

Sourdough bread

Color index page 80

Begin 6 hrs or up to 1 wk ahead

30 rolls 159 cals each Low in cholesterol

Refrigerator Pan Rolls

½ cup sugar	2 cups water
2 teaspoons salt	butter or margarine,
2 packages active dry	softened
yeast	1 egg
6 to 6½ cups all-purpose	salad oil
flour	

1. In large bowl, combine sugar, salt, yeast and 2¼ cups flour. In 2-quart saucepan over low heat, heat water and ½ cup butter until very warm (120° to 130°F.). (Butter does not need to melt.)

2. With mixer at low speed, gradually beat liquid into dry ingredients. Add egg; increase speed to medium; beat 2 minutes, occasionally scraping bowl with rubber spatula. Beat in ¾ cup flour or enough to make a thick batter; continue beating 2 minutes, occasionally scraping bowl with rubber spatula. Stir in about 2½ cups flour to make a soft dough.

3. Turn dough onto lightly floured surface and knead until smooth and elastic, about 10 minutes. Shape into ball; place in greased large bowl, turning over to grease top. Cover with towel; let rise in warm place, until doubled, about 1½ hours.

4. Punch down dough. Turn dough over; brush with oil. Cover bowl tightly with plastic wrap and refrigerate at least 2 hours or until ready to use, punching down dough occasionally.

5. *About 2½ hours before serving:* Grease 15½" by 10½" open roasting pan. Cut dough into 30 equal pieces; shape into balls and place in pan. Cover with towel; let rise in warm place, away from draft, until doubled, about 1½ hours.

6. Preheat oven to 400°F. Bake 15 to 20 minutes until golden brown. Brush rolls with softened butter. Remove from pan and serve hot.

PARKER HOUSE ROLLS

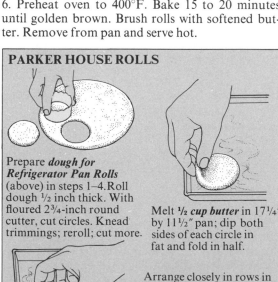

Prepare *dough for Refrigerator Pan Rolls* (above) in steps 1–4. Roll dough ½ inch thick. With floured 2¾-inch round cutter, cut circles. Knead trimmings; reroll; cut more.

Melt ½ *cup butter* in 17¼" by 11½" pan; dip both sides of each circle in fat and fold in half.

Arrange closely in rows in pan. Cover; let rolls rise until doubled. Preheat oven to 400°F. Bake 18 to 20 minutes until browned. (Makes 40 rolls.)

Sourdough Bread

Sourdough Starter:
2 cups all-purpose flour
1 package active dry yeast
2 cups warm water

Dough:
2 tablespoons sugar
1 tablespoon salt
1 teaspoon baking soda
water

6 to 8 cups all-purpose flour
3 tablespoons butter or margarine, melted

Color index page 79

Begin 4 days ahead

2 loaves

2333 cals per loaf

Low in cholesterol

Good source of calcium, iron, vitamin A, thiamine, riboflavin, niacin

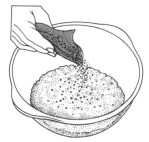

1 Make Starter: In large bowl, combine flour and yeast; stir in water; beat until smooth. Cover bowl with waxed paper.

2 Let stand 48 hours in warm place, stirring occasionally. If it does not rise, form bubbles and separate, start again. Stir well before using Starter.

3 *Day before serving, make dough:* In large bowl with mixer at medium speed, beat well sugar, salt, soda, 2 cups warm water, 1 cup Starter and 3 cups flour.

4 Cover bowl with towel; let batter rise at room temperature, away from draft, at least 18 hours.

5 *About 4½ hours before serving:* Stir in 3½ to 4 cups flour to make a soft dough. On floured surface, knead until smooth and elastic, 8 to 10 minutes.

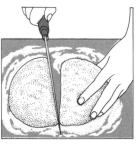

6 Cut dough in half; shape into 2 flat, round loaves, measuring about 7 inches in diameter.

7 Place loaves on well-greased cookie sheets; cover with towels and let rise in warm place until doubled, about 2 hours.

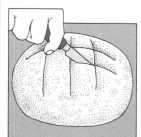

8 Preheat oven to 400°F. Brush loaves with water; with a sharp knife, cut 3 to 5 crisscross slashes across top of each loaf.

9 Bake 45 to 50 minutes until golden and loaves sound hollow when tapped. Remove to racks; brush with melted butter.

To replenish Starter:
If you plan to make Sourdough Bread regularly (at least once a week), remaining Starter may be replenished, if there is at least 1 cup of it left. Combine *1 cup all-purpose flour* with *1 cup warm water* and beat until smoothly blended. Stir into remaining Starter. Leave at room temperature a few hours until mixture begins to bubble. Cover bowl loosely; refrigerate replenished Starter until needed.

Sweet breads and rolls

A sweet dough is no more difficult to make than any plain bread. With one recipe, Sweet Dough (below), many different breads and buns can be made by adding in a few other ingredients – fruit, nuts and spices – and varying the shapes. Also included are other interesting breads, some with icing. Wait until sweet breads have cooled at least slightly before adding icing or the icing will melt and flow off. Store them as ordinary bread.

Sweet Dough

Dough for breads, pages 442 to 444

7120 cals

Good source of calcium, iron, vitamin A, thiamine, riboflavin, niacin

1 cup sugar
1 teaspoon salt
3 packages active dry yeast
8 to 9 cups all-purpose flour

2 cups milk
1 cup butter or margarine
2 eggs

1 In large bowl, combine sugar, salt, yeast and 2 cups flour. In 2-quart saucepan over low heat, slowly heat milk and butter until very warm (120° to 130°F.) (Butter does not need to melt.) With mixer at low speed, gradually beat liquid into dry ingredients. Increase speed to medium; beat 2 minutes more, occasionally scraping bowl with rubber spatula.

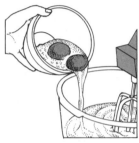

2 Beat in eggs and 2 cups flour; continue beating 2 minutes, occasionally scraping bowl.

3 With spoon, stir in enough additional flour (about 4 1/4 cups) to make a soft dough.

4 Turn dough onto lightly floured surface; knead until smooth and elastic, about 10 minutes. Shape into a ball.

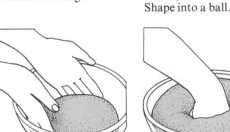

5 Turn over in greased large bowl to grease top. Cover; let rise in warm place until dough is doubled, about 1 hour.

6 Punch down dough. On lightly floured surface, divide into pieces as recipes (pages 442 to 444) direct. Cover; let rest 15 minutes.

Raisin Bread

Color index page 81

Begin 4½ hrs ahead

1 loaf

2707 cals

⅓ Sweet Dough (left)   *¾ cup raisins*

1. Prepare Sweet Dough. Grease 9″ by 5″ loaf pan. Roll dough piece into 12″ by 9″ rectangle. Sprinkle raisins on dough.
2. From 9-inch end, roll dough jelly-roll fashion; pinch seam to seal. Press ends to seal and tuck under; place, seam side down, in pan.
3. Cover; let rise until doubled, about 1½ hours. Preheat oven to 350°F. Bake 35 minutes or until loaf sounds hollow when tapped. Let cool on rack.

Turtle Bread

Color index page 81

Begin 4½ hrs ahead

1 loaf

1858 cals

Good source of calcium, iron, vitamin A, thiamine, riboflavin

¼ Sweet Dough (left)   *1 egg*
                                 water

1. Prepare Sweet Dough. Cut off ½-cup piece from dough; set aside. Shape remaining piece into 5-inch oval ball. Place on greased cookie sheet.
2. Roll reserved piece into 7-inch rope. From rope cut 2-inch piece for head; with scissors, snip eyes and mouth. Cut four 1-inch legs from rope; snip toes. Make pointed tail with remainder. Assemble body and shape shell as shown below.
3. Beat egg with a little water; brush turtle; let rise until doubled. Preheat oven to 375°F. Bake 20 to 25 minutes until browned.

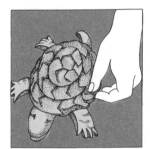

Assembling the body: Tuck head, legs and tail under oval ball and pinch to seal.

Shaping the shell: With scissors, snip design in top of body. Pinch edge to resemble shell.

Hot Cross Buns

Color index page 81

Begin 4½ hrs ahead

12 buns

368 cals each

Good source of calcium, vitamin A

½ Sweet Dough (left)
½ cup dark seedless raisins
⅓ cup chopped candied orange peel
1 egg yolk
1 teaspoon water

Sugar Icing:
¾ cup confectioners' sugar
1 tablespoon milk
1 tablespoon butter, softened
⅓ teaspoon lemon juice

1. Grease a 13″ by 9″ baking pan. Into dough knead raisins and peel. Divide dough into 12 pieces; shape into balls; place evenly in pan. Cover with towel; let rise in warm place, away from draft, until doubled, about 1 hour. Preheat oven to 350°F.
2. In small bowl, combine egg yolk with water. Brush buns with egg-yolk mixture. Bake buns 30 minutes or until brown and glazed.
3. Meanwhile, prepare icing: In small bowl with mixer at low speed, beat all ingredients until smooth. Make icing cross on buns. Serve warm.

Kolacky

¼ Sweet Dough (opposite) **Kolacky Toppings (below)**

Color index page 81

Begin 4½ hrs ahead

12 coffeecake servings

297 cals per serving

(without topping)

1. Prepare Sweet Dough. On lightly floured board with lightly floured rolling pin, roll Sweet Dough into a 12-inch circle; place the circle on a greased cookie sheet and let it rise until it has nearly *tripled* in volume, about 1½ hours.
2. Meanwhile, prepare Kolacky Toppings.
3. Preheat oven to 375°F. With hands, firmly press raised dough to within ½ inch of edges, being sure that you have pressed out all large bubbles. With back of knife, lightly mark pressed dough into 6 wedge-shaped sections.
4. Into each section, spoon one of toppings; spread evenly to fill section. Bake 20 to 25 minutes.

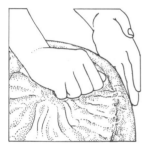 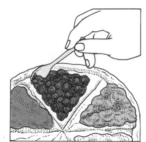

Shaping the dough: Press dough to within ½ inch of edges. With back of knife, mark 6 wedge shapes.

Adding the toppings: Evenly spoon a different topping into each of the marked sections.

KOLACKY TOPPINGS

153 cals per serving

BLUEBERRY: In small bowl, stir *⅓ cup canned blueberry-pie filling* and *¼ teaspoon grated lemon peel* until mixed. (Use leftover filling on ice cream.)

159 cals per serving

CHERRY: In small bowl, stir *½ cup canned cherry-pie filling* and *1 tablespoon shredded coconut* until mixed. (Use leftover filling on ice cream.)

185 cals per serving

CREAM CHEESE: In small bowl, stir *one 3-ounce package cream cheese,* softened, *1 tablespoon sugar, 1 tablespoon milk* and *⅛ teaspoon ground cinnamon* until mixture is smooth.

163 cals per serving

LEMON: Prepare one *3¼- to 3⅝-ounce package lemon pudding mix* as label directs. Set aside ⅓ cup lemon-pudding mixture for Kolacky. Pour remaining mixture into 3 dessert dishes and refrigerate to serve another day.

164 cals per serving
169 cals per serving

ORANGE: Use *¼ cup orange marmalade.*

PINEAPPLE: In small bowl, stir *¼ cup pineapple preserves, 1 tablespoon chopped California walnuts* and *⅛ teaspoon salt* until mixed.

Begin 4½ hrs ahead

8 servings

INDIVIDUAL KOLACKY: Cut Sweet Dough into 8 pieces; shape into balls. Place balls on 2 greased cookie sheets, 3 inches apart. Cover; let rise about 1½ hours. Meanwhile, prepare only *2 Kolacky Toppings* (above). Pat balls to make 4-inch circles with ¼-inch rim around edges; fill each with 1 tablespoon topping. Bake as above 15 minutes.

Apricot Coffeecake

¼ Sweet Dough (opposite)
1 8-ounce package dried apricots
¾ cup water
¼ cup sugar
¼ teaspoon ground cinnamon

Glaze:
½ cup confectioners' sugar
¼ teaspoon vanilla extract
2 teaspoons water

Color index page 81

Begin 4½ hrs ahead

8 coffeecake servings

323 cals per serving

Low in sodium

Good source of calcium, iron

1 Prepare Sweet Dough. In 2-quart saucepan over medium heat, heat apricots and water to boiling. Reduce heat to low; cover; simmer 30 minutes.

2 In covered blender container at high speed, blend apricots, sugar and cinnamon until smooth (if mixture is too tart, add more sugar to taste).

3 Grease large cookie sheet. On lightly floured surface with floured rolling pin, roll dough into 15″ by 12″ rectangle. Place on sheet.

4 Spread apricot mixture in 4-inch-wide strip lengthwise down center of dough rectangle.

5 With knife, cut dough on sides of mixture crosswise into 1-inch-wide strips; fold strips alternately across mixture.

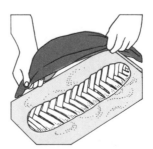 

6 Cover; let rise in warm place, away from draft, until doubled, about 1 hour. Preheat oven to 375°F. Bake cake 20 minutes or until golden.

7 Cool on sheet on wire rack 15 minutes. Meanwhile, in small bowl, combine glaze ingredients and stir until smooth. Drizzle over cake.

Sweet breads and rolls

Fruited Braid

Color index
page 81

Begin 4½ hrs
ahead

1 loaf

4653 cals

High in fiber

Good source
of calcium,
iron, vitamin A,
thiamine,
riboflavin,
niacin

½ Sweet Dough (page 442)	1 tablespoon all-purpose flour
1 cup golden raisins	1 egg yolk, slightly beaten
¾ cup finely chopped candied orange peel	½ cup confectioners' sugar
¼ cup finely chopped candied citron	1 tablespoon water

1. Prepare Sweet Dough. Grease large cookie sheet. Cut dough into 3 pieces. Roll each dough piece into a 12″ by 4″ strip.
2. In medium bowl, toss raisins, orange peel and citron with flour. Spread ⅓ of mixture lengthwise on center of each strip; brush edges with egg yolk. Fold edges of each strip over fruit and each other, forming a roll; pinch seams to seal. On greased cookie sheet, braid the 3 rolls, tucking ends under. Cover; let rise until doubled, about 1 hour. Brush braid with beaten egg yolk.
3. Preheat oven to 350°F. Bake 35 minutes or until golden and loaf sounds hollow when tapped. Remove to cool on wire rack. In small bowl, mix sugar and water; brush over braid.

Cinnamon Rolls

Color index
page 81

Begin 4½ hrs
ahead

15 rolls

395 cals each

½ Sweet Dough (page 442)	1 teaspoon ground cinnamon
½ cup packed light brown sugar	¼ cup butter or margarine, melted
½ cup pecans, chopped	Sugar Glaze (below) (optional)
½ cup dark seedless raisins	

1. Prepare Sweet Dough. Grease well 13″ by 9″ baking pan. In small bowl, combine brown sugar, pecans, raisins and cinnamon; set aside. Roll dough into 18″ by 12″ rectangle. Brush with melted butter; sprinkle with sugar mixture.
2. Starting at an 18-inch side, roll dough jelly-roll fashion. Pinch seam to seal. With roll seam side down, cut dough crosswise into 15 slices; place in pan, cut side down. Cover; let rise in warm place until doubled, about 40 minutes.
3. Preheat oven to 400°F. Bake 25 minutes or until lightly browned. Cool slightly in pan on wire rack. Spread with glaze. To serve: Pull apart with forks.

SUGAR GLAZE: In small bowl, stir **2 cups confectioners' sugar**, **½ teaspoon vanilla extract** and about **3 tablespoons water** until smooth.

 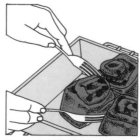

Placing rolls in pan: Arrange slices in baking pan, cut side down.

Serving rolls: Glaze rolls if you wish, then use forks to pull rolls apart.

Lemon Bubble Ring

Color index
page 81

Begin 4 hrs
ahead

1 loaf

4481 cals

Good source
of calcium,
iron,
vitamin A,
thiamine,
riboflavin,
niacin

2 packages active dry yeast	1½ cups milk
1 teaspoon salt	butter or margarine
5 to 6 cups all-purpose flour	2 eggs
sugar	grated peel from 2 lemons
	¼ teaspoon ground mace

1. In large bowl, combine yeast, salt, 2 cups flour and ½ cup sugar. In 1-quart saucepan over low heat, heat milk and ¼ cup butter until very warm (120° to 130°F.). (Butter does not need to melt.)
2. With mixer at low speed, beat liquid into dry ingredients. Add eggs; at medium speed, beat 2 minutes, occasionally scraping bowl with rubber spatula. Beat in ½ cup flour or enough to make a thick batter; continue beating 2 minutes. Stir in about 2 cups flour to make a soft dough.
3. On floured surface, knead dough until smooth and elastic, about 10 minutes. Shape into ball; place in greased large bowl, turning to grease top. Cover; let rise until doubled, about 1 hour.
4. In small bowl, combine lemon peel, mace and ½ cup sugar; set aside. In 1-quart saucepan, melt 2 tablespoons butter.
5. Punch down dough. Turn dough onto lightly floured surface; cover with bowl; let rest 15 minutes.

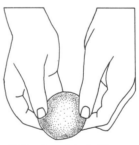 

6 Cut dough in half; cut each half into 16 pieces. Shape each piece into a ball by tucking ends under.

7 In greased 10-inch tube pan, place half of balls. Brush with half of melted butter or margarine.

8 Sprinkle balls in tube pan with half of lemon-peel mixture.

9 Put remaining balls in ring, brush with melted butter and sprinkle with lemon mixture.

10. Cover with towel; let rise in warm place until doubled, about 45 minutes. (Dough is doubled when one finger pressed lightly into dough leaves a dent.)
11. Preheat oven to 350°F. Bake 35 minutes or until golden and bread sounds hollow when tapped with fingers. Cool in pan 5 minutes; remove bread from pan to wire rack to cool.

Whole-Wheat "Sugar" Bears

1¼ cups sugar	*4 cups whole-wheat flour*
1½ teaspoons salt	*2 cups milk*
2 packages active dry	*1 cup butter or margarine*
yeast	*2 eggs*
about 4 cups all-purpose	*1 tablespoon water*
flour	

Color index
page 82

Begin 4 hrs
ahead

3 bears

2371 cals
each

High in fiber

Good source
of calcium,
iron,
vitamin A,
thiamine,
riboflavin,
niacin

1. In large bowl, combine sugar, salt, yeast, 1 cup all-purpose flour and 2 cups whole-wheat flour. In 2-quart saucepan over low heat, heat milk and butter until very warm (120° to 130°F.).
2. With mixer at low speed, beat liquid into dry ingredients until blended. At medium speed, beat 2 minutes. Reserve 1 egg white; beat in remaining eggs and 1 cup of each of flours; beat 2 minutes more. Stir in remaining whole-wheat flour and enough additional all-purpose flour (about 1½ cups) to make a soft dough.
3. On floured surface, knead dough about 10 minutes, adding all-purpose flour while kneading. Shape into ball; turn in greased large bowl to grease top. Cover; let rise until doubled, about 1 hour.
4. Punch down dough; turn onto floured surface; cover; let rest 15 minutes. Grease 2 large cookie sheets. In cup, combine egg white with water.
5. Divide dough into thirds. Cut one dough piece into one half and two quarters. Shape half-piece and one quarter-piece into balls for body and head.

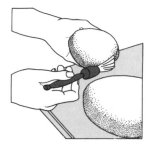

6 Slightly flatten body on cookie sheet. Brush side of head with egg white; tuck it slightly under body.

7 Roll remaining ¼-piece into 7-inch rope. Cut 2-inch snout and piece for nose. Brush with egg white. Place on head.

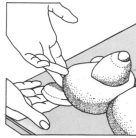

8 Cut two ½-inch pieces for ears and four 1-inch pieces for legs. Tuck under bear; pinch to seal.

9 With scissors, snip fingers, toes, eyes, mouth and belly button. Repeat for other 2 bears.

10. Cover; let rise in warm place away from draft until doubled, about 1 hour.
11. Preheat oven to 375°F. Brush bears with egg white. Bake 25 minutes until brown.

Apricot Butterfly Rolls

½ cup sugar	*1 cup milk*
1 teaspoon salt	*butter or margarine*
1 package active dry	*2 eggs*
yeast	*2 teaspoons almond*
4 to 4½ cups all-purpose	*extract*
flour	*Apricot Filling (below)*

Color index
page 82

Begin 4½ hrs
ahead

20 rolls

239 cals each

1. In large bowl, combine sugar, salt, yeast and 1 cup flour. In 1-quart saucepan over low heat, heat milk and ½ cup butter until very warm (120° to 130°F.).
2. With mixer at low speed, beat liquid mixture into dry ingredients; beat until just mixed. At medium speed, beat 2 minutes. Beat in 1 egg, almond extract and 1 cup flour or enough to make thick batter; continue beating 2 minutes. Stir in enough flour (about 2 cups) to make a soft dough.
3. On floured surface, knead dough 10 minutes until smooth and elastic, adding more flour while kneading. Shape dough into ball; place in greased large bowl, turning to grease top. Cover; let rise until doubled, about 2 hours. Prepare Apricot Filling.
4. Punch down dough; turn onto lightly floured surface; cut in half; cover for 15 minutes. With lightly floured rolling pin, roll one piece into 20" by 14" rectangle. Brush generously with melted butter; spread half of filling to within ½ inch of edges. From 20-inch edge, tightly roll dough, jelly-roll fashion; pinch edges to seal. With roll seam side down, cut into 10 wedges, each about 2½ inches at wide side, about 1 inch at short side.
5. Grease 2 large cookie sheets. Place wedges, short side up, on sheet; with finger, across top of each wedge, press to form butterfly-like wings. Repeat with remaining dough and filling. Let rise until doubled, about 30 minutes. In cup, beat remaining egg slightly; use to brush tops of rolls.
6. Preheat oven to 350°F. Bake 20 minutes or until golden. Immediately remove butterfly rolls to cool on wire racks.

APRICOT FILLING: In 2-quart saucepan over high heat, heat *one 8-ounce package dried apricots* and *2½ cups water* to boiling. Reduce heat to low; cover and simmer 15 minutes or until apricots are tender; drain. With fork or wire whisk, beat in *¾ cup sugar* until apricots are mashed; allow Apricot Filling to cool before using.

Cutting the wedges: Cut roll into 10 wedges, each 2½ inches at wide side, 1 inch at short side.

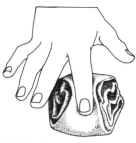

Making butterfly shape: Place wedges, short side up, on cookie sheet; press top with finger to form butterfly-like wings.

Special breads

In addition to everyday breads and rolls, there are many more fine yeast doughs to try. Some of them are served as breads for breakfast, brunch or luncheon and between meal snacking. Some special breads, like Fondue Bread, are main dishes; some, like Babas au Rhum, are served as dessert. And some, such as croissants, doughnuts and brioches, call for special techniques.

Fondue Bread

Color index
page 31

Begin 2 hrs
ahead

1 loaf or
8 main-dish
servings

838 cals per
serving

Good source
of calcium,
iron,
vitamin A

3½ teaspoons sugar
2 teaspoons salt
2 packages active dry
yeast
about 4 cups all-purpose
flour
½ cup butter or
margarine

1 cup milk
2 eggs
2 pounds Muenster
cheese, shredded
about 2 teaspoons sliced
blanched almonds for
garnish

1. In large bowl, combine sugar, salt, yeast and 1 cup flour. In 1-quart saucepan over low heat, heat butter and milk until very warm (120° to 130°F.).
2. With mixer at low speed, gradually beat liquid into dry ingredients until just mixed. Increase speed to medium; beat 2 minutes, occasionally scraping bowl. Beat in 1 cup flour or enough to make a thick batter; continue beating 2 minutes, occasionally scraping bowl. With spoon, stir in enough additional flour (about 2 cups) to make a soft dough.
3. Turn dough onto lightly floured surface and knead until smooth and elastic, about 10 minutes, adding more flour while kneading, if necessary. Shape dough into ball; cover with bowl and let dough rest 15 minutes for easier shaping.
4. Meanwhile, reserve 1 egg white. In large bowl, thoroughly combine remaining eggs with cheese; set aside. Grease 9-inch round cake pan.
5. On lightly floured surface, with lightly floured rolling pin, roll dough into a 24" by 6" rectangle.

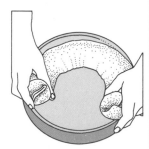

6 Lengthwise along center of dough, shape cheese mixture into cylinder. Fold dough over filling, making about 1- to 1½-inch overlap; pinch seam to seal.

7 Place roll, seam side down, in pan to make a ring, overlapping ends slightly; pinch ends together to seal. Cover with towel; let rest in warm place 10 minutes.

8. Preheat oven to 375°F. Brush loaf with reserved egg white. Garnish top with almonds. Bake 1 hour or until golden and bread sounds hollow when lightly tapped. Remove bread from pan immediately; let stand 15 minutes for easier cutting. Cut bread into wedges.

English Muffins

Color index
page 83

Begin 3½ hrs
ahead

18 muffins

204 cals each

Low in
sodium

2 tablespoons sugar
1 teaspoon salt
1 package active dry yeast
about 5 cups all-purpose
flour
1½ cups milk

butter or margarine
1 egg
2 tablespoons yellow
cornmeal
salad oil

1. In large bowl, combine sugar, salt, yeast and 1½ cups flour. In 1-quart saucepan over medium heat, heat milk and ¼ cup butter or margarine until very warm (120° to 130°F.).
2. With mixer at low speed, gradually beat liquid into dry ingredients until just blended. Increase speed to medium; beat 2 minutes, occasionally scraping bowl with rubber spatula.
3. Gradually beat in egg and 1 cup flour or enough to make a thick batter; continue beating 2 minutes, occasionally scraping bowl with rubber spatula. With spoon, stir in enough additional flour (about 2 cups) to make a stiff dough.
4. Turn dough onto lightly floured surface and knead just until well mixed, about 2 minutes. Shape dough into a ball and place in greased large bowl, turning dough over to grease top. Cover with towel; let rise in warm place, away from draft, until dough is doubled, about 1½ hours.
5. Punch down dough. Turn dough onto lightly floured surface; cover with bowl for 15 minutes and let dough rest for easier shaping. Meanwhile, place cornmeal in a pie plate.
6. With lightly floured rolling pin, roll dough about ⅜ inch thick. With 3-inch round cookie cutter, cut dough into circles; reroll scraps to make 18 circles in all.
7. Dip both sides of each circle in cornmeal; place cornmeal-coated circles about 1 inch apart on 2 small cookie sheets. Cover cookie sheets with towel; let circles rise in warm place, away from draft, until doubled, about 45 minutes.
8. Lightly brush 12-inch skillet with salad oil. Over medium heat, heat skillet until hot. Place 6 circles in skillet; cook 8 minutes on each side or until browned. Repeat with remaining circles. Cool muffins on wire rack. To store muffins for later use, wrap cooled muffins with plastic wrap or foil.
9. *Just before serving:* With tines of fork, split each muffin horizontally in half; toast the muffin halves in toaster until golden and piping hot; serve them spread with butter or margarine.

Coating circles: Dip dough circles in cornmeal in pie plate to coat well.

Splitting muffins: Use tines of fork to split each muffin in half.

Brioches

¼ cup sugar
1 teaspoon salt
2 packages active dry
*   yeast*
about 4½ cups all-
*   purpose flour*
1 cup milk
1 cup butter or margarine
5 eggs
1 teaspoon lemon extract
2 egg yolks
2 teaspoons water

Color index page 82
Begin day ahead
36 brioches
139 cals each   Low in sodium

1 In large bowl, combine sugar, salt, yeast and 1½ cups flour. In 1-quart saucepan over medium heat, heat milk and butter or margarine until very warm (120° to 130°F.).

2 With mixer at low speed, gradually beat liquid into dry ingredients until just blended. At medium speed, beat 2 minutes, occasionally scraping bowl.

3 Beat in eggs, lemon extract and 1½ cups flour to make thick batter; beat 2 minutes more. Stir in 1½ cups flour to make soft dough. Beat dough 5 minutes more.

4 Place dough in greased large bowl. Cover; let rise until doubled, about 1 hour. Stir down dough; cover tightly with foil or plastic wrap. Refrigerate overnight.

5 *About 2 hours before serving:* Punch down dough. Turn onto floured surface; cover with bowl; let rest 15 minutes. Grease 36 brioche pans.

6 Cut off ⅙ of dough; set aside. Cut rest of dough into 36 pieces. Shape each piece into a ball and place in a brioche pan.

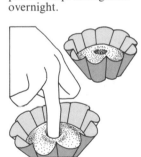

7 Cut reserved dough into 36 pieces; shape into small balls. With finger, make depression in center of each large ball.

8 Place small ball in depression. Cover; let rise in warm place until doubled, about 1 hour.

9 Preheat oven to 375°F. In small bowl, combine egg yolks with water. Brush brioches with egg mixture.

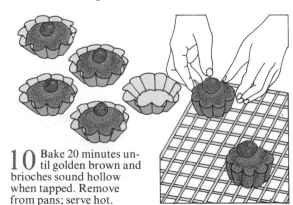

10 Bake 20 minutes until golden brown and brioches sound hollow when tapped. Remove from pans; serve hot.

Color index page 82
Begin 3 hrs ahead   238 cals each
6 pocket breads   Low in cholesterol

Pita (Pocket Bread)

3½ to 3¾ cups all-   *¼ teaspoon sugar*
*   purpose flour*   *1⅓ cups water*
1 teaspoon salt   *1 tablespoon salad oil*
1 package active dry   *cornmeal*
*   yeast*   *favorite filling*

1. In large bowl, combine 1½ cups flour, salt, yeast and sugar. In 1-quart saucepan over medium heat, heat water and salad oil until very warm (about 120° to 130°F.).

2. With mixer at low speed, beat liquid into dry ingredients; beat until just mixed. Increase speed to medium; beat 2 minutes, occasionally scraping bowl. Stir in enough additional flour (about 2 cups) to make a soft dough.

3. On floured surface, knead dough until smooth and elastic, about 5 minutes, adding more flour as needed. Shape into ball; place in greased medium bowl, turning over to grease top. Cover; let dough rise in warm place, away from draft, until doubled, about 1 hour.

4. Punch down dough; turn onto floured surface.

5 Cut dough into 6 pieces; cover; let rise 30 minutes. Meanwhile, lightly sprinkle 3 ungreased cookie sheets with cornmeal.

6 On lightly floured surface with lightly floured rolling pin, roll each piece of dough into a 7-inch circle.

7 Place 2 circles on each cookie sheet. Cover with towel; let rise in warm place 45 minutes or until doubled in height.

8 Preheat oven to 475°F. Bake 8 to 10 minutes until pitas are puffed and golden brown. Serve pitas immediately with favorite filling.

9. *To serve later:* Cool 5 minutes then place warm bread in plastic bags to keep moist and pliable. To reheat: Preheat oven to 375°F. Wrap pocket breads in foil and heat 10 minutes or until hot.

Special breads

Croissants

2 tablespoons sugar
1½ teaspoons salt
2 packages active dry yeast
about 3 cups all-purpose flour
1¼ cups milk
1 cup butter
1 egg
1 tablespoon water

Color index page 82
Begin 8 hrs or day ahead
12 croissants
305 cals each

1 In large bowl, combine sugar, salt, yeast and 1 cup flour. In 1-quart saucepan over low heat, heat milk until very warm (120° to 130°F.). With mixer at low speed, beat liquid into dry ingredients until just blended. At medium speed, beat 2 minutes, occasionally scraping bowl. Beat in ½ cup flour to make thick batter; beat 2 minutes more. Stir in about 1 cup flour to make soft dough.

2 On floured surface, knead dough until smooth and elastic, about 10 minutes, adding more flour while kneading. Shape into ball; place in greased large bowl, turning over to grease top. Cover; let rise in warm place (80° to 85°F.), away from draft, until doubled, about 1½ hours. Punch down dough; turn onto lightly floured surface; cover with a bowl; let rest 30 minutes.

3 Roll butter between 2 sheets of waxed paper to 10″ by 7″ rectangle. Turn over for even rolling; lift top sheet frequently to remove wrinkles. Chill butter with waxed paper.

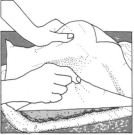

4 On floured surface, roll dough to 18″ by 9″ rectangle. Remove 1 sheet of paper from butter; invert butter on ⅔ of dough, leaving 1-inch margin on 3 sides.

5 Remove other sheet from butter. Fold unbuttered dough over butter. Fold buttered dough over center to make 9″ by 6″ rectangle.

6 Press edges to seal. Carefully roll layered dough to 18″ by 9″ rectangle; do not press edges too hard or butter may ooze out.

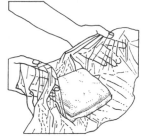

7 Fold in thirds to make a 9″ by 6″ rectangle; sprinkle with flour; wrap; chill 1 to 2 hours. Roll, fold and chill twice more (dough may be left overnight after final fold).

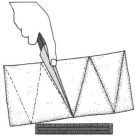

8 Cut dough in half. Roll one piece to 21″ by 10″ rectangle. (Chill other piece.) Cut triangles 7 inches wide at base; join ends for sixth triangle.

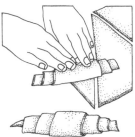

9 From 7-inch base, roll up triangles. Place, pointed tip down, on ungreased cookie sheet, 2 inches apart.

10 Bend ends around toward pointed tip to form crescent shape. Repeat with the remaining dough.

11 Cover croissants loosely with plastic wrap; let rise in warm place until doubled, about 1 hour. In hot weather, set dough in refrigerator from time to time to prevent butter oozing out. Preheat oven to 425°F. In cup with pastry brush, beat egg and water; brush over croissants. Bake 15 minutes or until puffed and browned. Immediately remove croissants to cool on wire rack 10 minutes.

Color index page 83
Begin 6 hrs ahead
2 loaves

2511 cals per loaf
Good source of calcium, iron, vitamin A, thiamine, riboflavin

Poppy-Seed Poticas

½ cup sugar
2 teaspoons grated lemon peel
½ teaspoon salt
1 package active dry yeast
3½ to 4 cups all-purpose flour
1 cup milk
½ cup butter or margarine
1 egg
Poppy-Seed Filling (below)
1 egg yolk, beaten

1. In large bowl, combine sugar, lemon peel, salt, yeast and 1 cup flour. In 1-quart saucepan over low heat, heat milk and butter until very warm (120° to 130°F.). (Butter does not need to melt.)
2. With mixer at low speed, beat liquid into dry ingredients; beat until just mixed. Increase speed to medium: beat 2 minutes, occasionally scraping bowl with rubber spatula. Beat in egg and 1 cup flour or enough to make thick batter; beat 2 minutes more, occasionally scraping bowl. With spoon, stir in enough additional flour (about 1½ cups) to make soft dough.
3. On lightly floured surface, knead dough until smooth and elastic, about 5 minutes. Shape into ball; place in greased large bowl, turning to grease top. Cover; let rise until doubled, about 1 hour.
4. Punch down dough. Turn onto lightly floured surface; cut in half; cover; let rest 15 minutes.
5. Grease 2 cookie sheets. With lightly floured rolling pin, roll one dough half into 18″ by 12″ rectangle. Spread half filling on dough, to within ½ inch of sides. From 18-inch edge, tightly roll dough, jelly-roll fashion; pinch ends to seal. Arrange dough in flat coil, seam side down, on a cookie sheet. Repeat with remaining dough. Cover with towel; let rise until doubled, about 1½ hours.
6. Preheat oven to 350°F. Brush loaves with beaten yolk. Bake 25 to 30 minutes until loaves sound hollow when tapped. Remove to wire racks to cool.

POPPY-SEED FILLING: In medium bowl, combine *one 12-ounce can poppy-seed cake-and-pastry filling, ½ cup finely chopped California walnuts, 1 tablespoon grated lemon peel* and *1 teaspoon ground cinnamon;* set aside. In small bowl with mixer at high speed, beat *1 egg white* until soft peaks form; fold into poppy-seed mixture.

Making dough roll: From 18-inch edge, tightly roll dough. Pinch ends to seal.

Forming the shape: Place roll in a flat coil, seam side down, on cookie sheet.

Jelly Doughnuts

Color index page 82

Begin 4 hrs ahead

36 doughnuts

175 cals each

5 to 6 cups all-purpose flour
⅓ cup sugar
2 teaspoons ground nutmeg
1 teaspoon salt
½ teaspoon ground cinnamon
2 packages active dry yeast

1¼ cups milk
⅓ cup butter or margarine
2 eggs
about 4 cups salad oil
2 cups apple, blackberry, grape or other jelly (2 10-ounce jars)
confectioners' sugar

1. In large bowl, combine 1½ cups flour and next 5 ingredients. In 1-quart saucepan over low heat, heat milk and butter until very warm (120° to 130°F.). (Butter does not need to melt completely.)

2. With mixer at low speed, beat liquid into dry ingredients. At medium speed, beat in eggs; beat 2 minutes more. Beat in ¾ cup flour or enough to make thick batter; beat 2 minutes more. Stir in about 1¾ cups flour to make soft dough.

3. On floured surface, knead dough until smooth and elastic, about 10 minutes. Shape into ball; place in greased large bowl; turn to grease top. Cover with towel; let rise in warm place, away from draft, until doubled, about 1 hour.

4. Punch down dough; turn onto lightly floured surface. Cut dough in half; cover with bowl; let rest 15 minutes. Grease 2 cookie sheets.

5. Roll one half of dough ¼ inch thick. Using 2¾-inch round biscuit cutter, cut circles. Repeat with remaining dough and trimmings.

6 Place circles on cookie sheets; cover with towels and let rise in warm place (80° to 85°F.), until doubled, about 1 hour.

7 In deep-fat fryer, heat 1 inch oil to 370°F. Fry 4 or 5 doughnuts at a time until golden brown, 45 seconds to 1 minute on each side, turning once with slotted spoon.

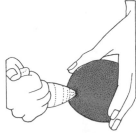

8 Drain on paper towels. With sharp, thin knife, pierce doughnuts from one side almost to other side.

9 With pastry bag with ¼-inch hole in end, press a little jelly into doughnuts through slit. Sprinkle with confectioners' sugar.

185 cals each

SUGARED DOUGHNUTS: Prepare *dough for Jelly Doughnuts* (left) as in steps 1–5 but, with lightly floured doughnut cutter, cut out doughnuts. Reroll trimmings and "holes" (or fry "holes" separately). Let rise, then fry as in steps 6 and 7. Drain. Sprinkle warm doughnuts with *sugar* or shake with sugar in a plastic bag and omit jelly. Or, spread a glaze of ½ *cup honey* and ⅔ *cup confectioners' sugar* on top.

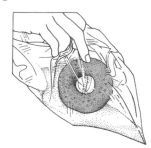

Shaping the doughnuts: Cut out the doughnuts as close together as possible.

Sugaring: Sprinkle warm doughnuts with sugar or shake with sugar in a bag.

CREAM DOUGHNUTS: Prepare as for Jelly Doughnuts but omit jelly. For filling, use *canned vanilla or chocolate pudding* or pudding prepared with regular vanilla, chocolate, butterscotch or lemon pudding mix as label directs. Store doughnuts in refrigerator.

PARTY DOUGHNUTS: Prepare *Cream Doughnuts* (above). Make glaze: In small bowl, beat *2 cups confectioners' sugar*, *½ teaspoon vanilla extract* and *3 tablespoons water* until smooth. Spread glaze over doughnuts; top with *chopped nuts,* flaked or shredded coconut, or chocolate shot or nonpareils.

Color index page 82

188 cals each

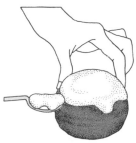

Coating with glaze: With spoon, spread glaze over tops of doughnuts.

Adding a topping: Sprinkle glazed doughnuts with toppings of your choice.

DOUGHNUT TIPS

Doughnuts can also be fried in a Dutch oven. Use medium heat and heat oil to 370°F.

Do not roll doughnut dough too many times or the last doughnuts will be tough.

Lift raised, ready-to-fry dough circles with a pancake turner so they keep their shape and do not stretch.

Use a slotted spoon to remove doughnuts from fat.

A cookie press or cake decorator can be used instead of a pastry bag to add a filling.

Special breads

Color index page 82

Begin 4 hrs or day ahead

24 babas   266 cals each

Babas au Rhum

¼ cup sugar	6 eggs
¼ teaspoon salt	1 4-ounce jar candied
2 packages active dry	citron or 1 cup dried
yeast	currants
about 3½ cups all-	Rum Sauce (below)
purpose flour	⅓ cup apricot jam
½ cup water	1 tablespoon lemon
½ cup butter or	juice
margarine	

1. Grease twenty-four 2-inch-deep, 2-inch-diameter baba molds or 3-inch muffin-pan cups; set aside. In large bowl, combine sugar, salt, yeast and ¾ cup flour. In 1-quart saucepan over low heat, heat water and butter until very warm (120° to 130°F.). (Butter does not need to melt completely.)

2. With mixer at low speed, gradually beat liquid into dry ingredients; beat just until mixed. At medium speed, beat 2 minutes, occasionally scraping bowl with rubber spatula. Beat in eggs and 1 cup flour or enough to make a thick batter; continue beating 2 minutes, occasionally scraping bowl. Stir in citron or currants and enough additional flour (about 1¾ cups) to make a soft dough.

3. Place a heaping tablespoonful of dough in each mold. Cover with towel; let rise in warm place (80° to 85°F.), until center of dough is slightly above tops of molds, about 1 hour.

4. Preheat oven to 375°F. Bake babas 15 to 20 minutes until golden brown. Meanwhile, prepare Rum Sauce. Slightly cool babas in molds on wire racks; remove from molds; place, top side up, in large, shallow roasting pan; spoon on sauce. Cover; let babas stand at least 2 hours, turning several times to absorb sauce evenly.

5. To serve: Into small bowl, press apricot jam through a sieve and stir in lemon juice until smooth. Spread over top of each baba.

RUM SAUCE: In 2-quart saucepan over medium heat, heat *3 cups water, 2¼ cups sugar, 6 thin orange slices* and *6 thin lemon slices* to boiling. Reduce heat to low; cover; simmer 5 minutes. Cool sauce to lukewarm; discard orange and lemon slices. Stir *1¼ cups light rum* into sauce.

Turning babas: During a 2-hour period, turn babas several times to absorb sauce evenly.

Making topping: With spoon, press jam through a sieve before stirring in lemon juice.

Danish Pastry Dough

¼ cup sugar

1 teaspoon salt

1 teaspoon ground cardamom

2 packages active dry yeast

about 4 cups all-purpose flour

1¼ cups milk

1 egg

1½ cups butter

Begin 5 hrs or up to 1 wk ahead

Dough for Danish Pastry (opposite)

1 In large bowl, combine sugar, salt, cardamom, yeast and 1½ cups flour. In 1-quart saucepan over low heat, heat milk until very warm (120° to 130°F.).

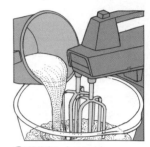

2 With mixer at low speed, beat liquid into dry ingredients until just blended; beat in egg. Increase speed to medium; beat 2 minutes.

3 Beat in ½ cup flour to make thick batter; continue beating 2 minutes. Stir in enough additional flour (about 1½ cups) to make soft dough.

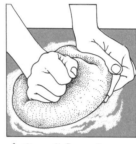

4 On well-floured surface, knead dough until smooth and elastic, about 10 minutes, adding more flour if needed. Shape into ball; cover 30 minutes.

5 Roll butter between 2 sheets of waxed paper to 12″ by 8″ rectangle; turn over for even rolling and lift top sheet frequently to remove wrinkles. Chill.

6 On floured surface with floured rolling pin, roll dough into 18″ by 9″ rectangle.

7 Remove top sheet of paper from butter; invert over ⅔ of dough, leaving ½-inch margin on 3 sides. Remove other sheet.

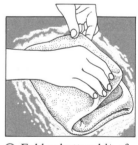

8 Fold unbuttered ⅓ of dough over middle ⅓; fold opposite end over middle to make 9″ by 6″ rectangle.

9 With rolling pin, press dough together around edges to seal in butter.

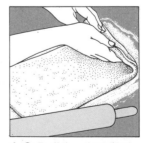

10 Roll dough to 18″ by 9″ rectangle. Fold rectangle crosswise into thirds to make 9″ by 6″ rectangle.

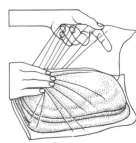

11 Wrap; chill 30 minutes. Roll, fold, wrap and chill twice more. Dough will keep 1 week. Use in recipe opposite.

Danish Pastry

Danish Pastry Dough   ***1 egg***
  (left)   ***1 tablespoon water***
Fillings (right)

Color index
page 82

Begin 5 hrs
ahead

24 pastries

1. Prepare Danish Pastry Dough. Prepare one of fillings. Cut dough into quarters; roll one piece to 12″ by 8″ rectangle (keep other pieces chilled). Cut rectangle into six 4-inch squares. In cup, beat egg with water; brush over squares. Place on ungreased cookie sheet about 2 inches apart; shape and fill as shown below. Repeat with remaining dough.
2. Cover loosely; let rise in refrigerator 1 hour.
3. Preheat oven to 400°F. Brush egg mixture over pastries. Bake 15 to 18 minutes or until puffed and golden brown. Remove to wire rack to cool. If folded portions on pastries open slightly during baking, while pastries are still hot, reshape them.

FILLINGS

JAM FILLING: *One 10- to 12-ounce jar raspberry or apricot jam* (about 1½ cups jam) will fill 24 Danish Pastries.   246 cals each

260 cals each pastry

ALMOND FILLING: In small bowl with spoon, blend well *one 8-ounce can almond paste* and *1 egg yolk.* (Makes 1¼ cups or enough for 24 pastries.)

273 cals each pastry

CREAM CHEESE FILLING: In small bowl with mixer at low speed, beat *one 8-ounce package cream cheese,* softened, *½ cup confectioners' sugar, 1 egg yolk* and *1 teaspoon grated lemon peel* until blended. Stir *¼ cup dried currants* into cream-cheese mixture. (Makes 1⅓ cups or enough filling for 24 pastries.)

PINWHEELS

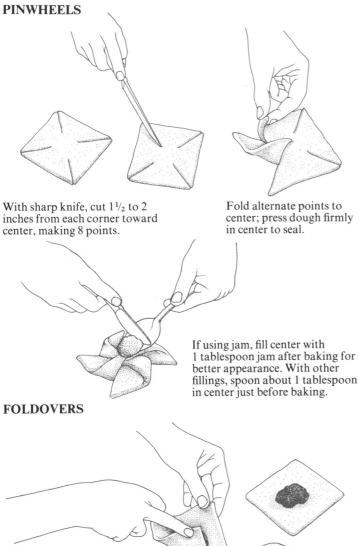

With sharp knife, cut 1½ to 2 inches from each corner toward center, making 8 points.

Fold alternate points to center; press dough firmly in center to seal.

If using jam, fill center with 1 tablespoon jam after baking for better appearance. With other fillings, spoon about 1 tablespoon in center just before baking.

FOLDOVERS

Place 1 tablespoon jam or Almond Filling in center; bring one corner over filling; bring opposite corner to center of fold; press gently to seal.

ENVELOPES

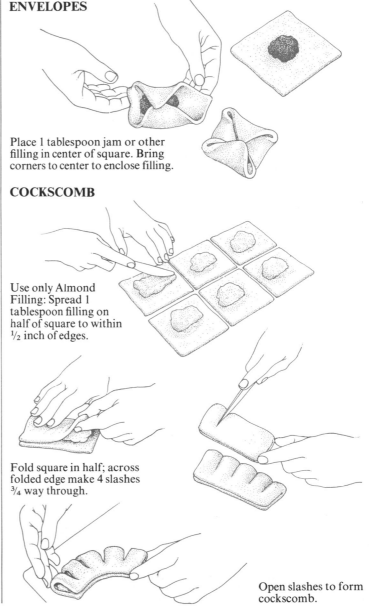

Place 1 tablespoon jam or other filling in center of square. Bring corners to center to enclose filling.

COCKSCOMB

Use only Almond Filling: Spread 1 tablespoon filling on half of square to within ½ inch of edges.

Fold square in half; across folded edge make 4 slashes ¾ way through.

Open slashes to form cockscomb.

451

Holiday breads

These breads are usually baked at a special time of year: Kulich is traditionally eaten at Easter time (see also Hot Cross Buns, page 442), and Stollen, heavy with fruit and nuts, is traditionally baked for Christmas. However, they can be enjoyed all year round, whether there is a holiday or not, so try them whenever you like.

Stollen

Color index page 83

Begin 5 hrs ahead

3 stollens

2170 cals each stollen

Good source of calcium, iron, vitamin A, thiamine, riboflavin, niacin

½ cup sugar
1½ teaspoons salt
2 packages active dry yeast
5½ to 6½ cups all-purpose flour
1¼ cups milk
⅔ cup butter or margarine

3 eggs
1 cup toasted slivered almonds
1 cup cut-up candied cherries
⅓ cup golden raisins
confectioners' sugar

1. In large bowl, combine sugar, salt, yeast and 2 cups flour. In 1-quart saucepan over low heat, heat milk and butter until very warm (120° to 130°F.). (Butter does not need to melt.)
2. With mixer at low speed, gradually beat liquid into dry ingredients. Increase speed to medium; beat 2 minutes, occasionally scraping bowl with rubber spatula. Beat in eggs and ½ cup flour or enough to make a thick batter; continue beating 2 minutes, occasionally scraping bowl. With spoon, stir in enough flour (about 2¾ cups) to make a soft dough.
3. On lightly floured surface, knead dough until smooth and elastic, about 10 minutes. Shape dough into ball; place in greased large bowl, turning to grease top. Cover with towel; let rise in warm place until doubled, about 1 hour. In small bowl, mix almonds, cherries and raisins.
4. Punch down dough. Turn onto lightly floured surface; knead nut mixture into dough. Cut dough into 3 pieces. Cover 2 pieces; refrigerate.
5. With lightly floured rolling pin, roll 1 piece into 12" by 7" oval; fold in half lengthwise. Place on large cookie sheet. Cover. Repeat with second piece of dough. Let both rise in warm place until doubled, about 1 hour. After 30 minutes of rising time, repeat with third piece of dough.
6. Preheat oven to 350°F. Bake first 2 stollens 25 to 30 minutes until they sound hollow when tapped with fingers. Remove to cool on wire racks. Bake third stollen; cool on wire rack. Sprinkle 3 stollens with confectioners' sugar.

Adding nut mixture: Knead almond, cherry and raisin mixture into dough.

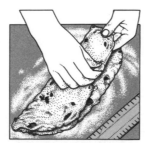

Shaping bread: Roll dough into 12" by 7" oval; fold in half lengthwise.

Kulich

Color index page 83

Begin 5 hrs ahead

3 loaves

2100 cals each loaf

Good source of calcium, iron, vitamin A, thiamine, riboflavin, niacin

½ cup sugar
½ teaspoon salt
¼ teaspoon ground cardamom
2 packages active dry yeast
about 6½ cups all-purpose flour
½ cup butter or margarine
1 teaspoon vanilla extract

milk
3 eggs
½ cup dark seedless or golden raisins
½ cup mixed candied fruit
¼ cup diced roasted almonds
1½ cups confectioners' sugar
½ teaspoon lemon juice

1. In large bowl, combine sugar, salt, cardamom, yeast and 1 cup flour. In 1-quart saucepan over low heat, heat butter, vanilla and 1 cup milk until very warm (120° to 130°F.).
2. With mixer at low speed, beat liquid into dry ingredients until just blended. At medium speed, beat 2 minutes, scraping bowl often with rubber spatula. Beat in eggs and 2 cups flour to make a thick batter; beat 2 minutes longer. Stir in about 3 cups flour to make a soft dough.
3. On floured surface, knead dough 5 minutes, adding more flour while kneading. Add raisins, candied fruit and almonds; knead until smooth and elastic, about 5 minutes. Shape into ball; place in greased large bowl, turning to grease top. Cover with towel; let rise until doubled, about 1½ hours.
4. Prepare and fill three 1-pound (5½-inch high) coffee cans, as shown below. Then cover; let rise until doubled, about 1 hour.
5. Preheat oven to 350°F. Brush each loaf with milk. Bake 50 minutes or until loaves sound hollow when tapped. (If tops brown too quickly, cover loosely with foil.) Remove loaves from cans immediately; cool them on wire racks.
6. Meanwhile prepare icing: In small bowl, with spoon, beat confectioners' sugar, 2 tablespoons milk and lemon juice until smooth.
7. Frost tops of loaves with icing, letting some drip down side of loaves.

PREPARING THE CANS

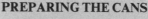

Line inside of each can with foil; grease foil. Punch down dough; divide into 3 pieces and shape to fit cans; place in cans, smooth side up.

Cut one 14-inch piece of 12-inch foil for each can; fold in fourths lengthwise; grease one side and with this side inward, wrap around outside of can leaving 2 inches extending above rim.

Challah

Color index
page 82

Begin 5½ hrs
ahead

2 loaves

2424 cals
each loaf

Good source
of calcium,
iron,
vitamin A,
thiamine,
riboflavin,
niacin

2 tablespoons sugar
1½ teaspoons salt
2 packages active dry
   yeast
6½ to 7 cups all-purpose
   flour

1½ cups water
6 tablespoons salad
   oil
6 eggs

1. In large bowl, combine sugar, salt, yeast and 2 cups flour. In 1-quart saucepan over low heat, heat water and oil until very warm (120° to 130°F.).
2. With mixer at low speed, gradually beat liquid into dry ingredients; beat until just mixed. Increase speed to medium; beat 2 minutes, occasionally scraping bowl with rubber spatula.
3. Reserve 2 egg yolks; add egg whites, remaining eggs and 1½ cups flour or enough to make a thick batter; continue beating 2 minutes, occasionally scraping bowl with rubber spatula. Stir in about 2½ cups flour to make a soft dough.
4. On lightly floured surface, knead dough until smooth and elastic, about 5 minutes, adding more flour while kneading. Shape dough into ball; place in greased large bowl, turning to grease top. Cover with towel; let rise in warm place (80° to 85°F.), until doubled, about 1 hour.
5. Punch down dough. Turn dough onto lightly floured surface; cover; let rest 15 minutes. Meanwhile, grease 1 large cookie sheet.
6. Prepare braided loaves.

Braiding loaves: Divide the dough into 3 pieces. Cut 1 piece into thirds; with hands, roll each third into a 16-inch-long rope. Place ropes side by side and braid.

Pinch ends of braid to seal. Place on cookie sheet for bottom part of loaf. Repeat with another piece for another loaf. Cut remaining dough into 6 pieces; roll each piece into 17-inch-long rope. Braid each set of 3 ropes as above; pinch ends to seal.

Place each smaller braid on top of a large braid; tuck ends of top braid under bottom braid, stretching top braid if it is necessary.

7. Arrange loaves at least 5 inches apart on cookie sheet; cover; let rise in warm place, away from draft, until doubled, about 1 hour.
8. Preheat oven to 375°F. Brush top and sides of loaf with reserved egg yolks. Bake 35 minutes or until loaves sound hollow when lightly tapped. Remove from cookie sheet and cool on wire racks.

Cardamom Christmas Wreath

Color index
page 83

Begin 4½ hrs
ahead

1 wreath

6601 cals

Good source
of calcium,
iron,
vitamin A,
thiamine,
riboflavin,
niacin

1 cup sugar
1 teaspoon salt
1 teaspoon ground
   cardamom
2 packages active dry
   yeast
about 7 cups all-purpose
   flour
1 cup butter or margarine

milk
3 eggs
1 tablespoon grated
   lemon peel
½ teaspoon almond
   extract
about 1 yard decorative
   ribbon

1. In large bowl, combine sugar, salt, cardamom, yeast and 2 cups flour. In 1-quart saucepan over low heat, heat butter or margarine and 1½ cups milk until very warm (120° to 130°F.). (Butter does not need to melt completely.)
2. With mixer at low speed, beat liquid into dry ingredients until just blended. At medium speed, beat 2 minutes. Reserve 1 egg white. Beat in remaining eggs, lemon peel, almond extract and 2 cups flour; beat 2 minutes longer. Stir in about 2½ cups flour to make a soft dough.
3. On floured surface, knead dough until smooth and elastic, about 10 minutes, adding more flour while kneading, if needed. Shape dough into ball; place in greased large bowl, turning to grease top. Cover dough with towel; let rise in warm place (80° to 85°F.), until doubled, about 1 hour.
4. Punch down dough. Turn onto lightly floured surface; cover with towel and let dough rest for 15 minutes for easier shaping.
5. Grease large cookie sheet and outside of 2-quart, straight-sided, ovensafe bowl. Invert bowl; place in center of sheet. In small bowl, combine reserved egg white and 1 tablespoon milk; set aside. Cut off about ½ cup of dough; set aside.
6. With rolling pin, roll dough into 30″ by 10″ rectangle. From 30-inch side, with hands, roll jelly-roll fashion into rope; twist slightly. Wrap rope around bowl on sheet; press ends of rope together to seal and tuck them under.
7. Roll reserved dough ⅛ inch thick. Decorate loaf:

Cutting decorations:
With floured 2½-inch leaf-shaped cookie cutter, cut about 15 leaves. Shape scraps into about fifteen ¼-inch balls.

Applying decorations:
Brush some egg-white mixture on back of leaves and balls. Place 3 leaves together and top with 3 balls as shown.

8. Cover wreath; let rise in warm place, away from draft, until doubled, about 45 minutes. Preheat oven to 350°F. Brush wreath with remaining egg-white mixture. Bake 1 hour or until golden. Remove bowl; cool wreath on wire rack. Tie ribbon around it.

Pizza

Pizza dough is as easy to make as the simplest yeast dough. Just follow the same basic techniques. By using water as the liquid ingredient, not milk as in most yeast doughs, you make the crust crisp. When the dough has risen, been punched down and allowed to rest for 15 minutes, you are ready to roll it into thin circles.

To transfer dough circles easily to pizza pans, fold them into quarters, transfer, then unfold in pans. If you don't have special pizza pans use large cookie sheets. As soon as the topping has been arranged on the dough, bake the pizza. Unlike most yeast breads, pizza does not have to rise again before being baked.

Pizza can be served as a main dish, for between-meal snacks and as party fare.

Cutting baked pizza: Use scissors to cut pizza easily into wedge-shaped slices if you don't have a straight-edge pastry wheel.

PIZZA TOPPINGS

Prepare the Cheese Pizza (right) but use only *½ pound mozzarella cheese*. Add one or more of the following to the pizzas before baking:

MUSHROOM: *½ pound mushrooms*, sliced.

PEPPERONI: *1 pound pepperoni*, thinly sliced.

ANCHOVY: *Two 2-ounce cans anchovy fillets*, well-drained.

SAUSAGE: *Two 8-ounce packages brown-and-serve sausages*, cut into ½-inch chunks; or *1 pound pork sausage*, cooked in skillet until browned, then drained well.

ITALIAN SAUSAGE: *1 pound sweet or hot Italian sausages*, cooked and cut into thin slices.

BEEF: *1 pound lean ground beef*, cooked in skillet until browned, then drained.

OLIVE: *1 cup sliced pitted ripe or pimento-stuffed green olives.*

GREEN PEPPER: *2 small green peppers*, sliced in thin strips.

ONION: *2 small onions*, minced.

PIMENTO: *½ cup chopped canned pimentos.*

Cheese Pizza

1 package active dry yeast
about 4½ cups all-purpose flour
salt
1½ cups water
olive or salad oil
1 medium onion, diced
1 garlic clove, minced
1 16-ounce can tomatoes
1 6-ounce can tomato paste
1½ teaspoons sugar

1 teaspoon Italian herb seasoning mix
¼ teaspoon crushed red pepper
1 16-ounce package mozzarella cheese, shredded

Color index page 31

Begin 2½ hrs ahead

8 main-dish servings

515 cals per serving

Good source of calcium, iron, vitamin A

1 In large bowl, combine yeast, 2 cups flour and 1 teaspoon salt. In 1-quart saucepan over low heat, heat water until very warm (120° to 130°F.). With mixer at low speed, just blend water into dry ingredients. At medium speed, beat 2 minutes, occasionally scraping bowl with rubber spatula. Beat in ½ cup flour to make a thick batter; beat 2 minutes more. Stir in about 1½ cups flour to make a soft dough.

2 On floured surface, knead dough about 8 minutes, adding more flour if needed. Shape into ball; place in greased large bowl; cover; let rise until doubled, about 1 hour.

3 In 2-quart saucepan over medium heat, in 1 tablespoon hot oil, cook onion and garlic until tender. Add tomatoes and tomato paste. Stir to break up tomatoes.

4 Add sugar, herb seasoning mix, red pepper and 1 teaspoon salt; heat to boiling, stirring. Reduce heat to low; cover partially; simmer sauce 20 minutes.

5 Punch down dough; cut in half; turn onto lightly floured surface. Cover 15 minutes. Preheat oven to 450°F. Grease 2 large cookie sheets or 12-inch pizza pans.

6 With floured rolling pin, roll each dough half into 13-inch circle.

7 Fold circles of dough into quarters; lift onto cookie sheets and unfold.

8 Pinch up edges of dough circle to form rim; brush circle with olive or salad oil.

9 Sprinkle dough circles with half of shredded mozzarella cheese. Top with tomato sauce.

10 Sprinkle with rest of cheese. Bake 20 minutes or until crust is golden. Cut into wedges.

SANDWICHES

Sandwiches can be anything from a light snack to a meal in themselves. For large quantities, use production-line techniques. Line up the bread slices in rows, two by two, and spread them with softened butter. Spread the filling on one row; top with remaining slices; cut and wrap sandwiches. When making more than one variety, cut and wrap one type before proceeding to another. Always add lettuce, tomato and similar ingredients just before serving. If added ahead, these can make the bread soggy and may moisten the filling. Many sandwiches can be prepared and frozen up to 2 weeks before serving. Always use fresh bread and the freshest filling ingredients.

Hot sandwiches

Croque Monsieur

**16 thin white-bread
  slices, crusts removed
  prepared mustard
1 8-ounce package sliced
  Swiss cheese**

**½ pound thinly sliced
  cooked ham
⅓ cup melted butter or
  margarine**

Color index
page 108

Begin 45 mins
ahead or
early in day

16 sandwiches

171 cals each

Good source
of calcium

1 Spread half of bread slices with mustard; trim cheese slices to fit and place on top.

2 Trim ham slices to fit bread; place on cheese. Top with remaining bread slices. Arrange sandwiches on cookie sheet. Wrap; refrigerate, if made ahead.

3 *About 20 minutes before serving:* Preheat oven to 450°F. Brush sandwiches with some of melted butter; toast in oven about 5 minutes until lightly browned.

4 Turn; brush other side with butter; toast 3 minutes more. Cut sandwiches into halves and serve warm wrapped individually in small paper napkins.

Mozzarella Loaf

**1 long loaf Italian bread
  with sesame seed
1 16-ounce package
  mozzarella cheese**

**½ cup olives for salad
1½ teaspoons
  oregano**

Color index
page 108

Begin 40 mins
ahead

6 servings

445 cals per
serving

Low in
cholesterol

Good source
of calcium,
iron,
vitamin A

1. Preheat oven to 400°F. Cut Italian bread crosswise into 1-inch slices, being careful not to cut through bottom crust. Cut mozzarella cheese into ¼-inch slices. Place cheese slices and olives between bread slices.
2. Place bread on cookie sheet and bake about 15 minutes or until cheese is melted and bread is heated through. Sprinkle loaf with oregano. With a sharp knife, divide loaf into slices by cutting through bottom crust. Serve Mozzarella Loaf immediately.

Barbecued Pork Sandwiches

**2½ pounds pork shoulder
  blade roast boneless,
  cut into 1½-inch
  chunks
2 medium onions,
  chopped
2 medium green peppers,
  chopped
1 6-ounce can tomato
  paste
½ cup packed brown
  sugar**

**½ cup water
¼ cup cider vinegar
3 tablespoons chili
  powder
1½ teaspoons salt
2 teaspoons
  Worcestershire
1 teaspoon dry mustard
10 6-inch-long hard rolls
lettuce leaves
1 large tomato, diced**

Color index
page 108

Begin 3½ hrs
ahead

10 sandwiches

461 cals each

Good source
of calcium,
iron,
thiamine,
niacin,
vitamin C

1. In 5-quart Dutch oven, combine first 11 ingredients. Over high heat, heat to boiling. Reduce heat to low; cover and simmer about 3 hours or until pork is *very* tender, stirring occasionally.
2. When pork is done, skim off any fat. With wire whisk, stir mixture until meat is shredded.
3. To serve, cut each roll horizontally in half but not all the way through. Line rolls with lettuce leaves; fill with pork mixture. Sprinkle with tomato.

Hot sandwiches

Reuben

Color index
page 108

Begin 45 mins
ahead

4 sandwiches

511 cals each

Good source
of calcium,
iron,
vitamin A

½ *cup mayonnaise*
1 tablespoon minced
  green pepper
1 tablespoon chili
  sauce
8 rye-bread slices
4 Swiss-cheese slices

½ *pound sliced corned*
  beef
½ *16-ounce package*
  sauerkraut, drained
  (1 cup)
butter or margarine

1. In small bowl, combine first 3 ingredients. Spread about 1 tablespoon mayonnaise mixture on each bread slice. Halve cheese slices crosswise. On each of 4 bread slices, place a cheese slice, ¼ of corned beef, ¼ of sauerkraut, another cheese slice and another bread slice, mayonnaise side down.

2. In 12-inch skillet over medium heat, in 2 tablespoons hot butter, brown sandwiches on one side. Turn and cook until bread is browned and cheese is melted, adding more butter if needed. Cut each sandwich crosswise in half.

Layering the filling: On 4 bread slices, place cheese, corned beef, sauerkraut and more cheese.

Cooking the sandwiches: Fry sandwiches in butter until bread is brown and cheese melted.

Canadian-Bacon Buns

Color index
page 108

Begin 15 mins
ahead

6 sandwiches

312 cals each

Good source
of iron

1 16-ounce package
  Canadian-bacon slices
6 hamburger buns

butter or margarine,
  softened

Preheat broiler if manufacturer directs. In 10-inch skillet over medium-high heat, fry bacon just until heated. Meanwhile, split buns and spread with butter or margarine; broil until golden brown. To serve: Place 2 or 3 slices bacon in each bun; cut in half. Serve hot.

Western Sandwiches

Color index
page 108

Begin 35 mins
ahead

4 sandwiches

385 cals each

Good source
of calcium,
iron,
vitamin A

3 tablespoons butter
1 6-ounce package sliced
  cooked ham, diced
  (about 1 cup)
½ *medium green pepper,*
  diced

½ *medium onion, diced*
6 eggs
2 tablespoons milk
¾ *teaspoon salt*
8 white-bread slices,
  toasted

1. In 10-inch skillet over medium heat, in butter, cook ham, green pepper and onion until the vegetables are tender, about 5 minutes.

2. Meanwhile, in large bowl, beat eggs, milk and salt until well mixed; stir into ham mixture. Reduce heat to low; cover and cook 12 to 15 minutes, until top is set and underside is lightly browned. Serve between the toasted white-bread slices.

Sloppy Joes

Color index
page 108

Begin 30 mins
ahead

6 sandwiches

463 cals each

Good source
of calcium,
iron

1 pound lean ground beef
1 medium green pepper,
  diced
1 medium onion, diced
1 16-ounce can pork and
  beans
½ *cup catchup*
½ *teaspoon salt*
½ *teaspoon chili*
  powder
6 8-inch-long rolls
lettuce leaves

1 In 10-inch skillet over medium-high heat, cook first 3 ingredients 10 minutes till ground beef is well browned.

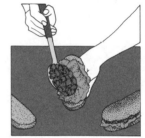

2 Stir in next 4 ingredients; heat to boiling. Reduce heat to low; simmer, uncovered, 10 minutes, stirring occasionally.

3 Halve rolls horizontally. On bottom halves arrange lettuce leaves; add ⅔ cup ground beef and pork and beans mixture; replace top halves.

Tacos

Color index
page 109

Begin 1 hr
ahead

12 sandwiches

Chicken or Beef Filling
  (below)
12 taco shells or
  Homemade Taco
  Shells (below)
shredded lettuce

2 cups shredded
  Cheddar cheese
4 medium tomatoes,
  chopped
hot red pepper sauce

Prepare filling. Stuff each shell with 2 or 3 tablespoons filling; add remaining ingredients.

120 cals each

CHICKEN FILLING: In 10-inch skillet over medium-high heat, cook *2 medium onions*, chopped, in ¼ *cup butter* until limp; add *4 cups cooked diced chicken, 4 medium tomatoes,* chopped, *2 teaspoons salt* and *1 teaspoon pepper*; heat until piping hot.

105 cals each

BEEF FILLING: In 10-inch skillet over medium-high heat, brown *2 pounds ground beef* and *2 medium onions*, chopped; spoon off any excess fat. Add *4 medium tomatoes*, chopped, *2 teaspoons oregano, 2 teaspoons salt, 1 teaspoon pepper* and *2 garlic cloves*, crushed; heat until piping hot.

141 cals each

Low in
cholesterol,
sodium

HOMEMADE TACO SHELLS: *About 1¾ hours ahead:* Prepare *Corn Tortillas* (page 431). In 10-inch skillet over medium heat, in about ½ inch hot *salad oil*, fry a tortilla just until it softens. With tongs, fold in half, holding it open about an inch. Fry one side crisp; turn and fry other side. Drain on paper towels. Repeat with rest of tortillas.

Cold sandwiches

Curried Beef in Pita

Pita (page 447)
1 pound lean ground beef
½ cup chopped onion
1 medium Delicious apple, chopped
¼ cup dark seedless raisins

1¼ teaspoons salt
1 teaspoon curry powder
1 8-ounce container plain yogurt

Color index page 108

Begin 3 hrs ahead

12 sandwiches

191 cals each

Low in cholesterol

Good source of iron

1. Prepare Pita. Prepare Curried Beef: In 10-inch skillet over medium-high heat, cook ground beef and onion until meat is browned and onion is tender; spoon off any excess fat. Add apple, raisins, salt and curry. Reduce heat to low; cover and simmer 5 minutes or until apple is tender-crisp.
2. Cut each piece of pita bread in half to make 2 "pockets." Fill each half with about ⅓ cup beef mixture. Pass the plain yogurt separately to spoon into each sandwich.

Italian Hero Sandwiches

12 sweet Italian sausages
¼ cup water
2 medium onions
5 green or red peppers

2 tablespoons olive or salad oil
4 5-inch-long hard rolls

Color index page 109

Begin 45 mins ahead

4 sandwiches

733 cals each

Good source of calcium, iron, vitamin C

1. In 12-inch skillet, place sausages; add water. Cover; simmer 5 minutes. Remove cover and continue cooking about 15 minutes longer or until sausages are browned, turning occasionally.
2. Meanwhile, cut onions into thin slices; cut peppers into ½-inch strips. In hot oil, in another 12-inch skillet, sauté onions until just limp. Add peppers and continue cooking over medium heat, stirring occasionally, until peppers are tender, about 10 minutes. Add cooked sausages.
3. Split hard rolls in half lengthwise. Layer bottom of each roll with some of pepper and onion mixture and 3 of the sausages, then add top part of roll.
4. To serve: Cut each roll crosswise into halves for easier eating.

Open-face Steak Sandwiches

4 white-bread slices
butter or margarine
4 beef cubed steaks
unseasoned meat tenderizer
1 envelope beef-flavor bouillon

¾ cup water
2 teaspoons all-purpose flour
watercress sprigs for garnish

Color index page 108

Begin 20 mins ahead

4 servings

328 cals per serving

Good source of iron, vitamin A

1. Toast bread slices; spread one side of each with butter or margarine; arrange each on a warm dinner plate; keep warm.
2. Sprinkle steaks with tenderizer as label directs. In 12-inch skillet over high heat, in 3 tablespoons hot butter or margarine, cook steaks 1 minute on each side or until of desired doneness. Place a steak on each toast slice.
3. Reduce heat to medium. In cup, blend bouillon, water and flour. Stir into drippings in skillet; cook, stirring, until thickened. Pour gravy over sandwiches. Garnish plates with watercress.

Club Sandwiches

6 bacon slices
6 white-bread slices, toasted
mayonnaise
lettuce leaves

2 large cooked turkey slices
salt
pepper
1 large tomato, sliced

Color index page 109

Begin 20 mins ahead

2 servings

682 cals per serving

Good source of calcium, iron, niacin

1 In 10-inch skillet over medium heat, cook bacon slices until crisp; drain on paper towels. Spread one side of each bread slice with mayonnaise.

2 Arrange lettuce leaves on 2 slices; top with turkey; sprinkle with salt and pepper then cover each with another bread slice, mayonnaise side up.

3 Top each sandwich with more lettuce, half of tomato slices, 3 cooked bacon slices and remaining white-bread slice, mayonnaise side down.

4 Cut sandwiches diagonally into fourths; secure each quarter with decorated toothpicks. Arrange, cut sides up, on individual plates.

VARIATIONS: Prepare as above but instead of turkey, use **2 large slices cooked ham**, corned beef, pastrami or roast beef. Instead of bacon, use **2 slices Swiss cheese** or 4 slices cooked Canadian bacon.

Poor Boy

1 1-pound long loaf unsliced French bread
¼ cup Russian dressing (page 326)
2 hard-cooked eggs, finely chopped
2 tablespoons chopped green onions
2 tablespoons mayonnaise

½ teaspoon seasoned salt
1 small cucumber, sliced
2 6-ounce packages sliced cooked ham
1 8-ounce package natural Swiss-cheese slices
1 large tomato, sliced

Color index page 109

Begin 20 mins ahead

6 servings

573 cals per serving

Good source of calcium, iron, vitamin A

1. With sharp knife, cut bread horizontally in half. In small bowl, mix Russian dressing with chopped eggs, green onions, mayonnaise and seasoned salt.
2. On bottom bread half, arrange cucumber slices and remaining ingredients in layers; evenly spread Russian-dressing mixture on top. Replace top bread half. Slice in equal pieces to serve.

Cold sandwiches

OPEN SANDWICHES

The open sandwich, originally a Scandinavian idea, is now internationally enjoyed. The most popular bread to use is pumpernickel or rye. Butter it and choose fillings and garnishes with eye appeal. Here are a few suggestions.

Top rye bread with marinated herring on lettuce; garnish with onion rings and a tomato wedge.

Rare roast beef slices on rye bread, topped with cucumber twist, tomato wedge and crumbled fried onions.

Slices of salami and cucumber twists arranged on rye bread.

Shrimp with mayonnaise on white bread, garnished with cucumber twist and lemon twist.

On white bread, slices of smoked salmon on lettuce decorated with lemon twists.

Sliced cold roast pork on white bread, decorated with orange twist and crumbled cooked bacon.

Slices of hard-cooked egg topped with black caviar and red pepper rings, served on pumpernickel.

On pumpernickel bread, slices of Danish Blue cheese topped with halved black grapes and a walnut half.

Color index page 109

Begin 30 mins ahead

4 sandwiches

236 cals each

Good source of vitamin A

Watercress-Walnut Sandwiches

½ *bunch watercress*	*1 8-ounce package*
¼ *cup California*	*Neufchâtel cheese,*
walnuts, chopped	*softened*
¼ *teaspoon seasoned*	*4 thin pumpernickel-*
salt	*bread slices*

1. Chop enough watercress to make ⅓ cup; reserve remaining watercress for garnish.
2. In medium bowl with fork, mix well walnuts, salt, cheese and chopped watercress. Spread cheese mixture on bread slices.
3. To serve: Cut each slice diagonally in half; garnish each half with 2 or 3 sprigs watercress.

Color index page 109

KEEP TRIM SANDWICHES

CRUNCHY TUNA SANDWICH: To *tuna*, add *minced celery, chopped nuts, salt* and *a bit of blended cottage cheese*. Spread on *very thin slices of date-nut bread*.

CURRIED SHRIMP SANDWICH: Mix *canned shrimp* and *chopped apple* with *low-calorie mayonnaise* and *curry powder*. Spread on *dark bread*.

CHICKEN LIVER SPECIAL SANDWICH: Chop *cooked chicken livers* with *stuffed olives*. Spread on *pumpernickel bread*.

PEPPERY SANDWICH: Make a sandwich of *thinly sliced green pepper* and *ham slices* on *dark bread*.

PEANUT-BUTTER-PLUS SANDWICHES

Make peanut-butter sandwiches varied and interesting by adding other ingredients. Use creamy or chunky-style peanut butter and spread it on pumpernickel or white bread, or try whole wheat, raisin or rye.

PEANUT-BUTTER AND BANANA SANDWICH: Spread *peanut butter* on both *bread slices*. Use *thinly sliced ripe bananas* as filling.

PEANUT-BUTTER AND CANADIAN-BACON SANDWICH: Cook *2 slices Canadian bacon* for each sandwich. Arrange bacon on a *bread slice* spread with *peanut butter*; sprinkle with *finely chopped parsley*; top with *bread slice*.

PEANUT-BUTTER AND CRANBERRY-SAUCE SANDWICH: Spread a *bread slice* with *2 tablespoons crushed jellied cranberry sauce*. Top with a tender *lettuce leaf*, then add *another bread slice* spread with *peanut butter*, butter side down.

PEANUT-BUTTER AND COLESLAW SANDWICH: In small bowl, combine *2 cups finely shredded cabbage, 2 tablespoons diced pimentos, 2 tablespoons mayonnaise, 1 teaspoon wine vinegar, ½ teaspoon salt* and *¼ teaspoon sugar*. Toss together well. Use as filling with *peanut butter*.

PEANUT-BUTTER AND DATE-NUT SANDWICH: Combine *½ cup diced pitted dates* and *¼ cup chopped pecans*. Use as filling with *peanut butter*.

Tea sandwiches

Deviled Ham Pinwheels

Color index page 109

Begin 30 mins ahead or early in day

30 tea sandwiches

33 cals each

Low in fat, cholesterol, sodium

1 4¹/₂-ounce can deviled ham
1 tablespoon grated orange peel
1 tablespoon prepared mustard

2 teaspoons horseradish
1 1-pound loaf unsliced white bread (8 inches long), crust removed

1. In bowl, combine first 4 ingredients.
2. Cut bread lengthwise into five ¹/₄-inch-thick slices. With rolling pin, lightly flatten each slice. Spread about 2 tablespoons ham mixture over surface of each slice. From short side, roll each slice jelly-roll fashion; cut each slice evenly crosswise to make 6 pinwheel sandwiches.

Spreading the mixture: Cover each bread slice with about 2 tablespoons of ham mixture.

Making the pinwheels: Roll each bread slice jelly-roll fashion; cut crosswise to make pinwheels.

Ribbon Sandwiches

Color index page 109

Begin 3¹/₂ hrs ahead or early in day

50 tea sandwiches

51 cals each

Low in sodium

¹/₂ cup butter, softened
3 tablespoons minced parsley
2 5-ounce cans chunk white chicken
¹/₃ cup mayonnaise

1 tablespoon lemon juice
¹/₄ teaspoon salt
¹/₄ teaspoon pepper
1 1-pound loaf unsliced white bread (8 inches long)

1. In small bowl, mix butter and parsley. In another bowl, mix chicken and next 4 ingredients.
2. Trim crusts from bread. Cut bread horizontally into six ¹/₂-inch slices. On first slice, spread ¹/₄ of parsley butter. Place second slice on first; spread with ¹/₂ of chicken mixture. Spread third slice with ¹/₄ of parsley butter; place, butter side down, on second slice. Wrap. Repeat. Refrigerate both loaves until well chilled.
3. Cut each loaf into ¹/₂-inch-thick slices; cut each slice crosswise in half.

Completing the layers: Add third bread slice to others, butter side down.

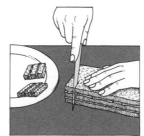

Cutting the loaves: Cut loaves into ¹/₂-inch-thick slices; halve slices.

Fillings

205 cals per ¹/₂ cup

CHEESE-AND-RAISIN: Combine *1¹/₂ 4-ounce packages shredded Cheddar cheese* (1¹/₂ cups) with *3 tablespoons raisins.* (Makes 2 cups.)

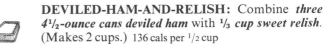

DEVILED-HAM-AND-RELISH: Combine *three 4¹/₂-ounce cans deviled ham* with *¹/₃ cup sweet relish.* (Makes 2 cups.) 136 cals per ¹/₂ cup

SALMON-AND-PARSLEY: Combine *one 15-ounce can salmon*, drained, with *3 tablespoons chopped parsley, 2 tablespoons pineapple juice* and *¹/₄ teaspoon salt.* (Makes 2 cups.) 155 cals per ¹/₂ cup

TUNA SALAD: Combine *one 6¹/₂- or 7-ounce can tuna*, drained, *¹/₂ cup diced celery, ¹/₃ cup mayonnaise, 2 tablespoons minced onion, 2 tablespoons pickle relish, ¹/₄ teaspoon salt* and *¹/₈ teaspoon pepper.* (Makes 2 cups.)

SHRIMP SALAD: Mix *1¹/₂ cups chopped, cooked shrimp, 2 chopped hard-cooked eggs, ¹/₂ cup bottled relish sandwich spread, ¹/₄ cup diced celery, 2 tablespoons milk* and *¹/₄ teaspoon salt.* (Makes 2 cups.)

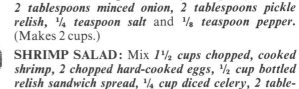
238 cals per ¹/₂ cup

EGG SALAD: Mix *6 chopped hard-cooked eggs, ¹/₄ cup minced onion, ¹/₂ cup mayonnaise, 3 tablespoons prepared mustard* and *1 teaspoon salt* until thoroughly combined. (Makes 2 cups.)

130 cals per ¹/₂ cup

TANGY PINEAPPLE: Combine *one 3-ounce package cream cheese*, softened, with *¹/₄ cup drained canned crushed pineapple* and *1 teaspoon horseradish.* (Makes ²/₃ cup.) 207 cals per ¹/₃ cup

327 cals per ¹/₂ cup

CHEESE-AND-ANCHOVY: Combine *one 8-ounce package cream cheese*, softened, *6 tablespoons half-and-half, 1 teaspoon Worcestershire, 1 tablespoon anchovy paste* and *¹/₂ cup chopped stuffed olives.* (Makes 1¹/₂ cups.)

419 cals per ¹/₂ cup

TURKEY-CHUTNEY: Mix together well *1¹/₄ cups diced cooked turkey, 1 cup thinly sliced celery, ¹/₃ cup mayonnaise, 2 tablespoons minced chutney, 1 teaspoon finely grated onion* and *³/₄ teaspoon salt.* (Makes 2¹/₃ cups.)

TONGUE SALAD: Mix well *2 cups ground cooked beef tongue, 1 cup mayonnaise, 2¹/₂ teaspoons bottled horseradish, ¹/₂ teaspoon salt* and *¹/₈ teaspoon pepper.* (Makes 2 cups.) 705 cals per ¹/₂ cup

114 cals per ¹/₃ cup

NIPPY SALMON: Mix *1 cup flaked canned salmon, 3 tablespoons mayonnaise, 1 tablespoon horseradish, 2 teaspoons bottled capers* and *2 teaspoons lemon juice.* (Makes 1 cup.) 323 cals per ¹/₂ cup

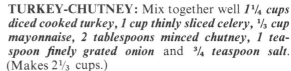

CHICKEN-CRANBERRY: Combine *2 cups diced cooked or canned chicken* with *3 tablespoons cranberry-orange relish, 1 tablespoon orange juice* and *¹/₄ teaspoon salt.* (Makes 2 cups.)

134 cals per ¹/₂ cup

CHEESE SALAD: Combine *2 cups diced natural or pasteurized process Swiss cheese, ³/₄ cup mayonnaise, ¹/₂ cup diced green pepper, 1 tablespoon chili sauce* and *¹/₈ teaspoon pepper.* (Makes 2¹/₂ cups.)

382 cals per ¹/₂ cup

DEVILED-HAM-CHEESE: Mix *one 2¹/₄-ounce can deviled ham* with *one 3-ounce package cream cheese*, softened, *¹/₂ teaspoon each lemon juice* and *horseradish.* (Makes ¹/₂ cup.) 451 cals per ¹/₂ cup

SAUCES

A repertoire of sauces is invaluable, enabling a cook to add the finishing touch to a wide variety of both sweet and savory dishes. Serve sauces with eggs, seafood, vegetables, meat, poultry and desserts.

Sauces that are especially appropriate for certain dishes, and which are traditionally associated with them, such as gravy for roast beef or meat sauce for spaghetti, are to be found in the chapters dealing with those particular foods; check the Index. More versatile sauces that can be served with a variety of dishes are given in the following pages.

INGREDIENTS

White and brown sauces usually consist of a mixture of butter or margarine, flour and liquid – either milk, half-and-half, cream, meat, fish or vegetable broth – plus seasoning. With some classic sauces, such as béarnaise or hollandaise, egg yolks act as the thickening agent.

In many recipes for sweet dessert sauces, cornstarch is used as a thickening agent because it makes a clearer sauce than flour. Sweet dessert sauces can also be thickened with beaten egg yolks.

COOKING SAUCES

When preparing sauces, always use a heavy saucepan and stir the mixture constantly. There are two ways of adding flour to the other ingredients to thicken white or brown sauces. In some recipes, the flour and butter or margarine are cooked together (this is known as the *roux* method), just until smooth for white sauces or, for brown sauces, until the mixture is evenly browned; the liquid is then added gradually while the mixture is stirred vigorously to prevent it from lumping. In other recipes, flour is combined with a small amount of liquid to make a smooth, pourable mixture; this mixture is then slowly poured into the rest of the liquid in the saucepan. The sauce must be stirred constantly to prevent lumping, then heated to boiling and cooked over medium heat until thick and smooth.

MAKING SAUCES SMOOTH

Curdled mayonnaise or lumpy white sauce are problems which beset even the most experienced cooks. By vigorous beating or stirring, lumpy sauces are quickly made smooth again, or if the lumps persist, the mixture can be blended smooth in the blender.

Mayonnaise or any other cold egg-based sauce may curdle if the oil is added too quickly, particularly in the early stages. You can save the sauce by adding the curdled mixture, just a teaspoon at a time, to a freshly beaten egg yolk; as you add the mixture, the sauce will return to a smooth consistency.

Overheating can curdle a hollandaise sauce. To rescue it, if this does happen, place a teaspoon of lemon juice and a tablespoon of curdled sauce in a bowl. With a wire whisk, beat vigorously until the mixture is creamy and thickened, then gradually beat in the remaining sauce, a tablespoon at a time, making sure that each addition has thickened before adding the next.

KEEPING SAUCES HOT

It is sometimes necessary to prepare a sauce ahead and keep it warm for serving. Sauces to be served hot can be kept in a double boiler over hot water; hollandaise and other egg-based sauces should be kept over *warm* water, otherwise they will become thin or curdled.

Preventing a skin forming: If sauce is made ahead, cover surface with waxed paper, pressing paper to surface.

Or dot surface with tiny pieces of butter. Just before serving, beat in the butter until the sauce is smooth and creamy.

FREEZING SAUCES

Many sauces freeze well, among them tomato, barbecue, mushroom, hollandaise, mornay and béarnaise. Those made with flour may separate on thawing; however, if they are thoroughly stirred during reheating they should return to the correct consistency.

To prepare sauces for the freezer, package them in meal-size amounts, in freezer containers, leaving head space for expansion. Reheat frozen sauces either in a heavy saucepan over very low heat, stirring often, or in a double boiler. Use sauces within 1 to 3 months.

Accompaniment sauces

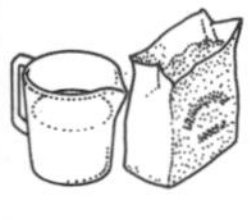

White or Cream Sauce

2 tablespoons butter or margarine
2 tablespoons all-purpose flour
½ teaspoon salt
⅛ teaspoon pepper
⅛ teaspoon paprika
1 cup milk or half-and-half

Begin 15 mins ahead

1 cup

118 cals per ¼ cup

Low in sodium

Good source of vitamin A

1 In heavy, 1-quart saucepan over low heat, melt butter or margarine.

2 Add flour, salt, pepper and paprika to melted butter or margarine. Over low heat, stir together until smooth.

3 Gradually stir in milk; cook, stirring constantly, until thickened and smooth. Serve hot on cooked vegetables, fish, poultry, seafood or hard-cooked eggs.

77 cals per ¼ cup

THIN WHITE SAUCE: Prepare as above but use 1 tablespoon butter or margarine and 1 tablespoon flour. (Makes 1 cup.)

162 cals per ¼ cup

THICK WHITE SAUCE: Prepare as above but use ¼ cup butter and ¼ cup flour. (Makes 1 cup.)

104 cals per ¼ cup

BECHAMEL SAUCE: Prepare as above but substitute **½ cup chicken broth** for ½ cup of the milk. (Makes 1 cup.)

75 cals per ¼ cup

CHEESE SAUCE: Prepare White Sauce as above but halve ingredients and, into hot sauce, stir **½ cup shredded American or Cheddar cheese** and **⅛ teaspoon dry mustard;** or half of a 5-ounce jar sharp pasteurized process cheese spread. Cook over very low heat, stirring constantly, just until the cheese is melted. (Makes 1¼ cups.)

106 cals per ¼ cup

CURRY SAUCE: When preparing White Sauce, to butter or margarine, add **¼ cup minced onion, 2 teaspoons curry powder, ¾ teaspoon sugar** and **⅛ teaspoon ground ginger.** Just before you are ready to serve the sauce, stir in **1 teaspoon lemon juice.** (Makes 1¼ cups.)

156 cals per ¼ cup

EGG SAUCE: When preparing White Sauce, use ¼ cup butter and 2 teaspoons flour; stir in **2 sliced hard-cooked eggs** and **2 teaspoons prepared mustard** or ½ teaspoon dry mustard. (Makes 1¼ cups.)

155 cals per ¼ cup

HOT THOUSAND ISLAND SAUCE: In cup, stir **¼ cup mayonnaise** with **¼ cup chili sauce;** stir into hot White Sauce. (Makes 1½ cups.)

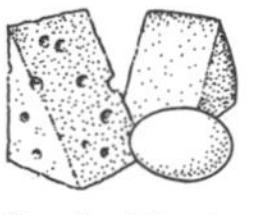

Mornay Sauce

3 tablespoons butter or margarine
2 tablespoons all-purpose flour
1 cup chicken broth
1 cup half-and-half
1 egg yolk
½ cup shredded natural Swiss cheese
¼ cup grated Parmesan cheese

Begin 20 mins ahead

2⅓ cups

164 cals per ⅓ cup

Good source of calcium, vitamin A

1 In 2-quart saucepan over medium heat, melt butter; stir flour into butter until smooth.

2 Gradually stir in broth and half-and-half and cook, stirring, until sauce is thickened; remove pan from heat.

3 In small bowl with wire whisk or fork, beat egg yolk slightly; then into egg yolk beat small amount of hot sauce.

4 Slowly pour egg mixture back into hot sauce, stirring vigorously to prevent the sauce from lumping.

5 Add cheeses and cook over low heat, stirring constantly, just until thickened (do not boil). Serve hot on cooked vegetables, fish, baked chicken or poached eggs.

Peppery Blue-Cheese Sauce

1 tablespoon butter or margarine
1 tablespoon all-purpose flour
¾ cup milk
½ cup crumbled blue cheese
½ teaspoon salt
¼ teaspoon coarsely ground pepper

Begin 15 mins ahead

1 cup

113 cals per ¼ cup

Good source of calcium, vitamin A

1. In 1-quart saucepan over medium heat, into hot butter or margarine, stir flour until blended. Gradually stir in milk and cook, stirring constantly, until mixture is thickened.

2. Remove mixture from heat; stir in cheese and remaining ingredients. Serve hot over grilled steak, lamb or beef patties or lamb chops.

Accompaniment sauces

Bordelaise Sauce

2 tablespoons butter or margarine
2 tablespoons all-purpose flour
1 tablespoon minced onion
1 tablespoon minced parsley
1 bay leaf
¼ teaspoon thyme leaves

¼ teaspoon salt
⅛ teaspoon coarsely ground or cracked black pepper
1 10½-ounce can condensed beef broth (bouillon), undiluted
¼ cup dry red wine

Begin 25 mins ahead

1⅓ cups

109 cals per ⅓ cup

Low in cholesterol

1 In heavy, 1-quart sauce-pan over low heat, in hot butter or margarine, cook the flour until it is just lightly browned, stirring often.

2 Stir in minced onion, parsley, bay leaf, thyme leaves, salt and coarsely ground pepper.

3 Slowly add undiluted beef broth and red wine. Stir the mixture to blend together well. Increase the heat to medium-high.

4 Cook, stirring constantly, until the mixture thickens. Discard bay leaf. Serve Bordelaise Sauce hot over roast or broiled beef.

Mushroom Sauce

¼ cup butter or margarine
½ pound mushrooms, sliced
¾ cup beef broth

¾ teaspoon salt
1 tablespoon cornstarch
¼ cup sauterne

Begin 20 mins ahead

2 cups

71 cals per ¼ cup

Low in cholesterol

1. In 9-inch skillet over medium heat, in hot butter or margarine, cook the sliced mushrooms until tender, about 5 minutes, stirring occasionally. Stir in beef broth and salt and heat the mixture to boiling.
2. Meanwhile, in cup, blend cornstarch and sauterne until smooth.
3. Gradually stir sauterne mixture into mushroom mixture and cook, stirring constantly, until thickened. Serve Mushroom Sauce hot over broiled beef steaks or hamburgers, chicken croquettes, hot cooked green beans or peas.

Mayonnaise

3 egg yolks
½ teaspoon salt
½ teaspoon sugar
¼ teaspoon dry mustard
1½ cups salad oil
3 tablespoons cider vinegar
1 tablespoon lemon juice

Begin 30 mins or up to 1 wk ahead

2 cups

431 cals per ¼ cup

Low in sodium

1 In small bowl with mixer at medium speed, beat egg yolks, salt, sugar and mustard 2 minutes.

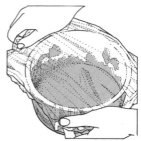

2 Continue beating and gradually add ½ cup salad oil, ½ teaspoon at a time, until mixture is smooth and thick.

3 Still beating, gradually add cider vinegar and lemon juice to mixture.

4 Beat in remaining salad oil, 1 tablespoon at a time, until all the oil is absorbed and mixture is smooth and creamy.

5 Cover and refrigerate mayonnaise. Use as ingredient in salads. Serve with cold poultry and sliced meats.

MAYONNAISE VARIATIONS: To 1 cup of mayonnaise add 1 teaspoon each **tarragon** and **minced parsley;** or **¼ cup chopped chutney;** or **1 teaspoon curry powder.**

Sauce Rémoulade

2 tablespoons chopped sour pickles
1 tablespoon chopped capers
1 cup mayonnaise

1 tablespoon chopped parsley
1 teaspoon prepared mustard
¼ teaspoon tarragon

Begin 10 mins ahead

1¼ cups

328 cals per ¼ cup

Drain well any liquid from chopped pickles and capers. In small bowl, stir mayonnaise, pickles, capers, parsley, mustard and tarragon until well mixed. Serve over chilled cooked vegetables, shrimp, scallops or lobster.

Hollandaise Sauce

3 egg yolks
2 tablespoons lemon juice
1/2 cup butter or
margarine
1/4 teaspoon salt

Begin 15 mins
ahead

2/3 cup

554 cals per
1/3 cup

Good source
of iron,
vitamin A

1 Add egg yolks and
lemon juice to double-
boiler top; with wire whisk
or slotted spoon, beat until
well mixed.

2 Place double-boiler
top over bottom
containing hot,
not boiling, water.

3 Add one third of the
butter or margarine to
the egg yolk mixture and
cook, beating constantly,
until the butter is
completely melted.

4 Add another third of
butter, beating
constantly; repeat with
remaining third, beating
until mixture thickens and
is heated through.

5 Remove from heat; stir
in salt. Keep warm.
Serve hot on hot cooked
artichoke hearts,
asparagus, broccoli,
seafood or poached eggs.

Lemon Butter

1/4 cup butter or
margarine
1 tablespoon lemon juice
1 tablespoon chopped
parsley

1/2 teaspoon salt
1/8 teaspoon cayenne or
dash hot pepper
sauce

Begin 5 mins
ahead

1/3 cup

413 cals per
1/3 cup

Good source
of vitamin A

In 1-quart saucepan over medium heat, melt butter
or margarine; stir in lemon juice, chopped parsley,
salt and cayenne. (Or, in small bowl with spoon, stir
butter or margarine until creamy. Slowly stir in
remaining ingredients.) Serve Lemon Butter hot on
hot boiled or steamed vegetables, broiled, fried or
poached fish or shellfish.

Béarnaise Sauce

2 tablespoons red wine
vinegar
1 1/2 teaspoons chopped
green onion
1 1/2 teaspoons tarragon
1/8 teaspoon cracked
black pepper

4 egg yolks
3/4 cup butter or
margarine, softened
1 tablespoon chopped
parsley

Begin 20 mins
ahead

1 cup

405 cals per
1/4 cup

Good source
of iron,
vitamin A

1. In double-boiler top, combine first 4 ingredients.
Over high heat, heat to boiling. Boil until vinegar is
reduced to about 1 tablespoon.
2. Place double-boiler top over double-boiler bottom containing hot, *not boiling*, water. Add egg
yolks and cook, beating constantly with wire whisk
until slightly thickened.
3. Add butter, about 2 tablespoons at a time, beating
constantly with whisk, until butter is melted and
mixture is thickened. Stir in parsley. Serve about 1
tablespoon hot or cold sauce over broiled beef steak
or fried, poached or baked fish.

Horseradish Sauce

1/4 cup horseradish,
drained
1 tablespoon white
vinegar
1 teaspoon sugar
1/2 teaspoon salt

1/4 teaspoon prepared
mustard
1/2 cup heavy or
whipping cream,
whipped

Begin 10 mins
ahead

1 cup

123 cals per
1/4 cup

In small bowl, mix well first 5 ingredients. Fold into
whipped cream. Serve with roast or broiled beef, hot
beef tongue, baked ham, corned beef; baked, fried
or poached fish.

Parmesan-Cheese Sauce

1/4 cup butter
1/4 cup all-purpose flour
1 1/2 cups half-and-half
1 1/2 cups water

2 chicken-flavor bouillon
cubes
1/2 cup grated Parmesan
cheese

Begin 15 mins
ahead

3 1/2 cups

88 cals per
1/4 cup

1. In 2-quart saucepan over medium heat, into hot
butter, stir flour until well blended.
2. Gradually stir in half-and-half, water and
chicken bouillon cubes. Cook, stirring constantly,
until sauce is thickened. Stir in the grated Parmesan
cheese and heat just until melted. Serve with baked
or poached fish or pasta.

Spicy Country Barbecue Sauce

2 tablespoons salad oil
1 medium onion, diced
1 8-ounce can tomato
sauce
1/2 cup packed brown
sugar
1/4 cup white vinegar

1 tablespoon
Worcestershire
4 teaspoons chili
powder
1 1/2 teaspoons salt
1/4 teaspoon dry mustard

Begin 15 mins
ahead

1 2/3 cups

161 cals per
1/3 cup

1. In 1-quart saucepan over medium heat, in hot
salad oil, cook onion until tender, about 5 minutes,
stirring occasionally.
2. Add remaining ingredients; heat to boiling, stirring constantly. Use to baste spareribs, beef or lamb
during grilling. Serve remainder with meat.

Dessert sauces

Caramel Sauce

**2 tablespoons butter or
margarine
2 tablespoons all-purpose
flour
1 1/2 cups half-and-half
3/4 cup packed light
brown sugar
3/4 cup sugar
1/4 teaspoon salt**

Begin 20 mins
ahead or
early in day

2 1/2 cups

197 cals per
1/4 cup

Low in
sodium

1 In 2-quart saucepan
over medium heat, into
hot butter or margarine,
stir flour until blended.

2 Gradually stir in
half-and-half; cook,
stirring constantly, until
the mixture is thickened
and smooth.

3 Add brown sugar,
sugar and salt; stir until
well mixed. Serve warm or
cover and refrigerate to
serve cold.

Hot Butterscotch Sauce

Begin 10 mins
ahead

1 cup

291 cals per
1/4 cup

Low in
sodium

**1 cup packed light brown
sugar
1/4 cup half-and-half
2 tablespoons butter or
margarine**

**2 tablespoons light corn
syrup**

In 1-quart saucepan over medium heat, heat brown
sugar, half-and-half, butter or margarine and corn
syrup to boiling, stirring occasionally. Serve Hot
Butterscotch Sauce warm over vanilla or chocolate
ripple ice cream, pound cake slices, peach or apple
pie, tapioca pudding, baked custard.

Hot Fudge Sauce

Begin 20 mins
ahead

1 2/3 cups

383 cals per
1/3 cup

Low in
sodium

**1 1/2 cups sugar
1/2 cup milk
1/3 cup light corn syrup
2 squares unsweetened
chocolate**

**1 tablespoon butter or
margarine
1 teaspoon vanilla
extract
1/8 teaspoon salt**

1. In 2-quart saucepan over medium heat, heat first 4
ingredients to boiling, stirring constantly. Set candy
thermometer in place and continue cooking, stirring
occasionally, until temperature reaches 228°F. or
until a small amount of mixture dropped from tip of
spoon back into mixture spins a 1/4-inch thread.
2. Remove from heat; immediately stir in butter,
vanilla and salt. Serve sauce hot over vanilla ice
cream, vanilla or butterscotch pudding, poached
pears or toasted pound cake slices.

Chocolate-Marshmallow Sauce

Begin 15 mins
ahead

1 1/2 cups

221 cals per
1/4 cup

Low in
sodium

**2 cups miniature
marshmallows
1/3 cup heavy or whipping
cream**

**1/3 cup honey
1 1/2 squares unsweetened
chocolate
1/8 teaspoon salt**

In 2-quart saucepan over low heat, cook marshmallows, cream, honey, chocolate and salt, stirring
constantly, until marshmallows and chocolate are
melted. Serve hot over gingerbread, unfrosted
yellow or chocolate cake.

Chocolate Sauce

Begin 15 mins
ahead

1 1/3 cups

352 cals per
1/3 cup

**1 6-ounce package
semisweet-chocolate
pieces (1 cup)
1/2 cup light corn syrup**

**1/4 cup half-and-half
1 tablespoon butter
1 teaspoon vanilla
extract**

1. In 1-quart saucepan over low heat, melt chocolate
with corn syrup, stirring constantly.
2. Remove from heat; stir in remaining ingredients
until mixed. Serve warm over Bavarian cream,
cream pies, éclairs, cream puffs or ice cream.

Mint Sauce

Begin 15 mins
ahead or
early in day

2/3 cup

172 cals per
1/3 cup

Low in fat,
cholesterol

**1/2 cup light corn syrup
1/2 cup packed mint leaves**

**2 tablespoons lemon juice
1/8 teaspoon salt**

In covered blender container at high speed, mix all
ingredients until well blended. If prepared early in
day, stir before serving. Spoon over cut-up fruit for
salad or dessert.

Cherry Sauce

Begin 15 mins
ahead

2 cups

48 cals per
1/4 cup

Low in fat,
cholesterol,
sodium

**2/3 cup boiling water
1 pound sweet cherries,
pitted**

1/4 cup sugar

In 2-quart saucepan over medium heat, in boiling
water, heat cherries to boiling. Reduce heat to low;
cover and simmer 5 minutes or until tender. During
last minute of cooking, add sugar. Serve over Cheese
Blintzes (page 368), waffles, pancakes.

Peach Sauce

Begin 10 mins
ahead

1 cup

26 cals per
1/4 cup

Low in fat,
cholesterol,
sodium

**1 10-ounce package
frozen peaches, thawed
1/4 teaspoon almond
extract**

**1/8 teaspoon ground
nutmeg**

In covered blender container at low speed, blend
together all ingredients until smooth.

Hot Fruit Sauce

Begin 45 mins
ahead

4 cups

47 cals per
1/4 cup

Low in fat,
cholesterol,
sodium

**3 large nectarines
3 large plums
1/2 cup orange juice**

**1/2 cup sugar
2 tablespoons brandy
(optional)**

Cut fruit into wedges. In 2-quart saucepan over low
heat, cook fruit and juice 10 minutes or until tender,
stirring occasionally. Remove from heat. Stir in
sugar and brandy until sugar is dissolved. Serve Hot
Fruit Sauce over vanilla ice cream.

Orange-Fluff Sauce

Begin early in day

2½ to 2⅔ cups

172 cals per ¼ cup

Low in sodium

½ cup sugar
½ cup frozen orange-juice concentrate, thawed

⅛ teaspoon salt
2 egg yolks
1 cup heavy or whipping cream, whipped

1 In 1-quart saucepan over low heat, cook sugar, undiluted juice concentrate and salt, stirring constantly, until sugar dissolves; set aside.

2 In small bowl with mixer at high speed, beat egg yolks until light and fluffy; at medium speed, gradually beat in orange-juice mixture.

3 Return mixture to saucepan; over low heat, cook, stirring constantly, until the mixture is slightly thickened.

4 Cool, then fold in whipped cream. Refrigerate until well chilled. Serve over cut-up fruit, dessert fruit salads.

Fluffy Sherry Sauce

Begin 15 mins ahead

1⅔ cups

170 cals per ⅓ cup

Low in sodium

2 egg yolks
¼ cup sugar
1 tablespoon medium sherry

⅛ teaspoon salt
½ cup heavy or whipping cream, whipped

1. In small bowl with mixer at low speed, beat egg yolks, sugar, sherry and salt until well mixed. Increase speed to high and continue beating for 4 minutes or until light and fluffy.
2. With wire whisk, fold in cream until well blended. Spoon over cut-up mixed fruit.

Melba Sauce

Begin early in day

2 cups

51 cals per ¼ cup

Low in fat, cholesterol, sodium

¼ cup red currant jelly
1½ 10-ounce packages frozen raspberries

2 tablespoons cornstarch
1 tablespoon cold water
red food color

1. In 2-quart saucepan over low heat, melt jelly, stirring constantly; add frozen berries and heat.
2. In measuring cup, mix cornstarch with cold water until smooth; stir into berries. Over medium heat, cook mixture, stirring occasionally until slightly thickened. Stir in a few drops red food color. Cover and refrigerate until serving time.

Eggnog Sauce

Begin 15 mins ahead

1¾ cups

147 cals per ¼ cup

Low in sodium

½ cup heavy or whipping cream
2 egg yolks

¾ cup confectioners' sugar
3 tablespoons brandy

1 In small bowl with mixer at medium speed, beat cream until stiff peaks form; set aside.

2 In another small bowl with mixer at high speed, beat egg yolks until fluffy.

3 To egg yolks, add confectioners' sugar and brandy; at high speed, beat the mixture together to blend well.

4 Add whipped cream; with rubber spatula, gently fold together. Serve over warm fruitcake slices, steamed pudding.

Brandied Strawberry Sauce

Begin 20 mins ahead or early in day

2½ cups

78 cals per ¼ cup

Low in fat, cholesterol, sodium

3 10-ounce packages frozen sliced strawberries, thawed
½ cup red currant jelly

1 tablespoon cornstarch
few drops red food color
¼ cup brandy

1. Drain strawberries, reserving ½ cup juice.
2. In 2-quart saucepan over low heat, melt currant jelly, stirring constantly.
3. In small bowl, mix reserved juice and cornstarch until smooth. Gradually stir cornstarch mixture into melted jelly, stirring constantly; increase heat to medium and cook until thickened, stirring.
4. Add food color; stir in berries and brandy. Serve hot over rolled crêpes, waffles; or cover and refrigerate to serve cold over ice cream, vanilla or tapioca pudding.

Date-Nut Sauce

Begin 10 mins ahead

2 cups

148 cals per ¼ cup

Low in cholesterol, sodium

1 7¼- or 8-ounce package pitted dates, chopped
⅛ teaspoon salt
¾ cup water

½ cup light or dark corn syrup
½ cup chopped California walnuts

In 2-quart saucepan over medium heat, heat dates, salt and water to boiling; remove from heat. Stir in corn syrup and chopped walnuts. Serve warm over apple, pear or pumpkin pie or ice cream.

BEVERAGES

A beverage can be anything from a glass of ice-cold milk to a highly complicated blend of flavors and textures. In general, winter is the time for warming hot drinks and summertime for refreshing cold ones. Some beverages, such as coffee and tea, are drunk all year round; both can be enjoyed hot or cold, plain or enhanced with other flavors. Then there are fruit-ades and milk-based drinks of all kinds; and, the alcohol-based drinks, ranging from cocktails to party punches; and, of course, wines.

However simple the beverage you make, an attractive container will do a great deal to enhance it. Rather than serving hot drinks in regular cups, use mugs, steins and demitasse cups. As well as looking more attractive in these, the drinks do stay hot. Cold drinks look better and seem to taste better if served in special glassware, such as brandy snifters or champagne glasses.

BUYING COFFEE
Most coffee sold in the United States is regular or American roast, which is light and fairly mild. Viennese or French roast is darker and stronger. Italian roast is darkest and is used for espresso.

If you grind your own coffee, try beans from supermarkets which often have quality beans priced lower than specialty-house beans or vacuum-packed coffee. Check that whole coffee beans are of uniform size and color with good coffee aroma and no trace of mustiness.

Select the grind that's right for your type of coffee maker. A percolator uses regular (coarse) grind; a drip pot generally uses drip (medium) grind; an automatic-electric drip coffee maker uses drip or the specially labeled grind; espresso pots also use specially labeled coffee grinds.

STORING COFFEE
Only fresh coffee gives good flavor. Unopened vacuum-packed ground coffee will stay fresh at room temperature for over a year. Once the can is opened, the flavor begins to dissipate immediately, so plan to use it within about a week. Replace lid quickly after using. Keep partially used cans, covered, in the refrigerator. If the vacuum-packed can contains more than a week's supply, immediately after opening it, portion weekly amounts of coffee into airtight containers and freeze them until they are needed.

Coffee beans begin to lose flavor and aroma as soon as they are roasted so plan to use them within about 3 weeks. If you don't brew a lot of coffee or can't shop often, buy beans as soon as possible after roasting and freeze in airtight containers. They will then keep fresh at least 12 months; do not refreeze them.

Unopened instant coffee will stay fresh over a year at room temperature. Once opened, use it within 2 or 3 weeks. Store opened jars at room temperature.

MAKING COFFEE
Coffee-oil residue can become rancid and give an off flavor to coffee so be sure coffee-making equipment is kept scrupulously clean. (Use a packaged coffee-pot cleaner, according to directions, to remove coffee oils and stains when necessary.) Always start with *fresh*, cold water and fresh coffee. For the best flavor, make at least three-quarters capacity of the coffee maker. Buy a smaller pot if yours is too big for daily use. Don't skimp on coffee or re-use grounds.

Coffee tastes best when freshly brewed, so try to make only what you'll serve within an hour or so. Remove wet coffee grounds as soon as brewing is completed. If you prefer to keep it hot and handy all day long, use paper coffee filters with your percolator or drip pot. Flavor keeps better when there's no sediment. If you reheat coffee, always remember to do so over low heat. Never let it boil or it will turn bitter.

When using a new coffee maker, first use the proportions of coffee to water recommended in the directions. Subsequently, if you wish to change the strength of the coffee, use more or less ground coffee. If no directions are included, use 2 level tablespoons of ground coffee to each 6 ounces (¾ cup) of cold water. (The rated capacity of most coffee makers is based on a 5-ounce cup of brewed coffee.)

COFFEE MAKERS
There are three basic ways to make coffee. All produce a good brew, but each has a distinctive taste.
Percolator: Available in automatic-electric and range-top models ranging in size from about 2 to 100 cups. Be sure water level is below the bottom of the basket. With electric model, start with cold water; with range-top, start with almost boiling water.

Coffee drinks

Drip: Drip coffee makers are available in automatic-electric and range-top models ranging in size from 2 to 12 cups. Ground coffee is placed in a filter cone or section through which almost boiling water is poured. This method of making coffee produces an exceptionally residue-free brew.

Instant coffee: This is the least expensive and quickest way to make small amounts of coffee. For best results, add boiling water to instant coffee in a cup or serving pot; stir. Use 1 teaspoon instant coffee for each ¾ cup boiling water.

BUYING TEA

There are innumerable blends of tea ranging from strong-flavored and smoky to delicate and flowery. They fall into three main types, according to how the leaves have been processed: black, green and oolong. The terms "orange pekoe" and "pekoe" do not refer to a particular variety or flavor but to the size of the leaf.

Black tea: Most of the tea sold in the United States is of this type. It is made by fermenting (oxidizing) the leaves so they turn black, producing a rich-flavored, amber brew. Well-known blends include *Assam*, a full-bodied high-quality tea; *Ceylon*, a delicate, fragrant blend; *Darjeeling*, the finest black tea from India, flavorful and aromatic; *Earl Grey*, an aromatic blend from India and Ceylon; *English Breakfast Tea*, a fragrant, mellow blend; *Keemun*, a mild yet robust Chinese tea; and *Lapsang Souchong*, a pungent tea from Taiwan, with a unique, smoky flavor.

Green tea: The leaves are not oxidized so that they retain their original green color. The resulting brew is light and greenish-yellow, with a mild, distinctive flavor. Green teas include *Basket-fired Tea*, a Japanese tea with a light flavor; *Gunpowder Tea*, which produces a delicate, pale brew; and *Hyson*, another fine Chinese tea.

Oolong tea: The leaves are only partially fermented with the result that they retain a greenish-brown color. The brew is light, with a subtle bouquet. Popular blends include *Canton Oolong*; *Formosa Oolong*, faintly wine-like in flavor; and *Jasmine Tea*, which is delicately flavored with white jasmine blossoms.

Store loose tea and tea bags in air-tight containers at room temperature and use within 6 months.

MAKING TEA

Use a teapot for brewing, and preheat it by rinsing out with hot water. Heat fresh, cold tap water to a rapid boil. Water that has been standing or reheated gives a flat taste. Also, only boiling water can extract the full flavor from the leaves. Allow ¾ measuring cup water per serving. Use 1 teaspoon loose tea or 1 tea bag per serving and pour boiling water over tea. Brew 3 to 5 minutes. Stir to make sure flavor is uniform and serve.

Café au Lait

hot coffee   *sugar*
hot milk

Color index page 110

Begin 15 mins ahead

Holding a pot of hot coffee in one hand and a pot of hot milk in the other, pour simultaneously into large cups. Serve sugar separately.

Pouring the coffee: Pour the coffee and milk from separate pots into the cup at the same time.

Caffè Espresso

8 tablespoons Italian-   *sugar*
   roast coffee   *lemon twist*
1½ cups water   22 cals per serving

Color index page 110

Begin 15 mins ahead

4 servings

Brew coffee in drip pot or *macchinetta*. Serve in demitasse cups with sugar and lemon twist. Never serve Caffè Espresso with cream.

Iced Coffee

hot double-strength   *cream (optional)*
   coffee   *sugar (optional)*
ice cubes   7 cals

Color index page 110

Begin 15 mins ahead

Brew double-strength coffee. Fill tall glasses with ice cubes and slowly pour in hot coffee. Serve with cream and sugar, if desired.

Café Brûlot

1 cup brandy   *2 small cinnamon sticks*
peel of 1 medium orange   *3 tablespoons sugar*
6 whole cloves   *3 cups hot double-*
4 whole allspice   *strength coffee*

Color index page 110

Begin 15 mins ahead

Eight ½-cup servings

86 cals per serving

1. In 1-quart saucepan over medium heat, heat first 6 ingredients until brandy is hot.
2. Pour into warmed heatsafe serving bowl. Carefully ignite brandy; flame for 1 to 2 minutes.
3. Slowly pour coffee into flaming brandy. Ladle into demitasse cups.

Irish Coffee

1½ teaspoons sugar   *hot strong black coffee*
1 jigger Irish whisky   *whipped cream*

Color index page 110

Begin 15 mins ahead

1 serving

260 cals

1. Into 6- or 8-ounce stemmed glass or coffee cup, measure sugar and Irish whisky. Add hot coffee to fill glass to within ½-inch of top; stir to dissolve sugar completely.
2. Top with a spoonful of whipped cream; do not stir. Sip coffee through cream.

Iced tea

Hot chocolate drinks

Iced Tea, Family Style

fresh cold water
⅓ cup loose tea or 15 tea bags
ice cubes
sugar
lemon slices

Color index page 111

Begin 15 mins or several hrs ahead

8 cups or eight 1-cup servings

22 cals per serving

1. In 3-quart saucepan over high heat, heat 4 cups fresh cold water to boiling. Remove from heat; stir in tea. Stir, cover and leave 5 minutes. Stir again and strain into a pitcher containing an additional 4 cups fresh cold water.
2. Cover and let stand until ready to serve. Serve over ice cubes with sugar and lemon slices.

Straining the mixture: Strain concentrated tea into pitcher containing fresh cold water.

Serving iced tea: Pour tea over ice cubes in 12-ounce glasses. Serve with sugar and lemon slices.

ICED TEA, COLD WATER METHOD: *About 6 hours or day ahead:* Into pitcher, measure **4 cups cold tap water**. Add **8 to 10 tea bags** (remove tags); cover; let stand at room temperature 6 hours or overnight; remove tea bags and stir. Serve as above. (Makes 4 cups or four 1-cup servings.)

GARNISHES FOR DRINKS

"Frost" the glass by dipping the rim first in beaten egg white and then quickly in sugar.

Serve cool drinks garnished with fruit slices, wedges or chunks; small scoops of sherbet or ice cream; mint sprigs; twists of cucumber peel.

Add flavor and color to hot milky drinks with cinnamon sticks, whipped cream or marshmallow cream; to clear drinks, add candy canes or clove-studded lime or lemon slices.

Hearty Hot Cocoa

½ cup plus 1 tablespoon cocoa
½ cup sugar
⅛ teaspoon salt
6 cups milk

½ teaspoon vanilla extract
whipped cream or 6 regular marshmallows (optional)

Color index page 111

Begin 15 mins ahead

6 cups or six 1-cup servings

275 cals per serving

1 In 3-quart saucepan, stir cocoa with sugar and salt until mixed.

2 Stir in a small amount of milk to make a smooth paste; stir in remainder. Over medium-low heat, heat, stirring occasionally, until tiny bubbles form around edge.

3 Remove from heat; add vanilla; beat with hand beater until smooth and foamy, then pour cocoa into 6 mugs.

4 Top each serving with some whipped cream or a marshmallow, if you like, then serve hot cocoa immediately.

French Hot Chocolate

4 squares semisweet chocolate
¼ cup light corn syrup
½ teaspoon vanilla extract

4 cups milk
1 cup heavy or whipping cream

Color index page 111

Begin 50 mins ahead

6 cups or 8 servings

286 cals per serving

1. In heavy 1-quart saucepan over low heat, or double boiler over hot, not boiling, water, heat chocolate and corn syrup until chocolate is melted and mixture is smooth, stirring occasionally with rubber spatula.
2. Cover and refrigerate 30 minutes or until mixture is cool. Stir in vanilla.
3. In 2-quart saucepan over medium-low heat, heat milk until very hot and small bubbles form around edge (do not boil).
4. Meanwhile, in small bowl with mixer at medium-low speed, beat heavy or whipping cream and chocolate mixture until soft peaks form.
5. To serve, pour milk into warm coffeepot. Carefully spoon whipped-cream mixture equally into 8 warmed, decorative coffee cups; gently pour hot milk mixture in cups.

Sodas and shakes

Ice Cream Soda

2 to 3 tablespoons chocolate syrup; fruit-flavored pancake syrup; light molasses; or cherry or pineapple sundae topping
¼ cup milk
scoop of ice cream
club soda, chilled
whipped cream and maraschino cherry (optional)

Color index page 110
Begin just before serving
1 serving
252 cals

1 Place your choice of syrup in a tall glass. Add milk and stir.

2 Add ice cream and pour in club soda until glass is almost filled; stir.

3 Garnish with cream and cherry. Serve with iced-tea spoon and straws.

Strawberry Sodas

Color index page 110
Begin just before serving
Five 1½-cup servings
209 cals per serving

1½ cups milk
1 10-ounce package frozen sliced strawberries, partially thawed
1 pint strawberry ice cream
1 16-ounce bottle club soda or strawberry soft drink, chilled

1. In covered blender container at high speed, blend milk and strawberries 15 seconds; pour into five 12-ounce glasses.
2. Add scoop of strawberry ice cream to each; slowly add soda or soft drink to fill almost to top.

Chocolate-Orange Sodas

Color index page 110
Begin just before serving
Eight 1½-cup servings
250 cals per serving

1 6-ounce can frozen orange-juice concentrate, thawed
1½ cups quick chocolate-flavor-milk mix
1 juice-can water
2 pints vanilla ice cream
1 28-ounce bottle club soda, chilled

1. In medium bowl, stir orange-juice concentrate with chocolate-milk mix till smooth; stir in water.
2. Pour ¼ cup chocolate-orange mixture into each of eight 12-ounce glasses. Add 1 large scoop ice cream to each. Add soda to fill almost to top.

Egg Cream

Color index page 110
Begin just before serving
1 serving
123 cals

2 tablespoons chocolate syrup
¼ cup milk
club soda

1. In 10-ounce glass, stir the chocolate syrup and milk to mix thoroughly.
2. Slowly stir in enough soda to fill glass. Serve Egg Cream with straws, if you like.

Mocha Float

Color index page 111
Begin just before serving
1 serving
160 cals

¾ teaspoon quick chocolate-flavor-milk mix
¾ teaspoon instant coffee powder
½ teaspoon sugar
club soda, chilled
2 small scoops chocolate-ripple ice cream

1. Into an 8-ounce glass, measure first 3 ingredients. Gradually add enough club soda to fill glass ¾ full; stir until sugar is dissolved.
2. Add ice cream; stir. Serve with spoon and straw.

Chocolate Milk Shakes

Color index page 111
Begin 10 mins ahead
Two 1½-cup servings
503 cals per serving

¾ cup milk
3 tablespoons chocolate syrup
1 pint chocolate ice cream

1. In covered blender container at high speed, blend all ingredients until smooth.
2. Pour mixture into chilled 12-ounce glasses; serve milk shakes with large straws.

469 cals per serving

BANANA MILK SHAKES: Prepare as above but substitute *1 large ripe banana* for chocolate syrup and *1 pint vanilla ice cream* for chocolate.

Black Cow

Color index page 111
Begin just before serving
1 serving
167 cals

½ 12-ounce can root beer, chilled
scoop of vanilla ice cream

1. Into a chilled, tall 10-ounce glass, pour the chilled root beer.
2. Top with a generous scoop of slightly softened vanilla ice cream. Serve Black Cow immediately with long straw and iced-tea spoon.

Strawberry Shakes

Color index page 111
Begin just before serving
4 cups or four 8-ounce servings
151 cals per serving

¾ cup water
1 10-ounce package frozen strawberries, thawed
1 cup instant nonfat dry milk powder
3 tablespoons sugar
1 teaspoon lemon juice
⅛ teaspoon salt
2 cups ice cubes

In blender container, place all ingredients except ice cubes; cover and blend at medium speed a few seconds until smooth. Increase speed to high; add ice cubes, one at a time, until all are finely crushed.

Party Orange Soda

Color index page 110
Begin 15 mins ahead
Sixteen ½-cup servings
61 cals per serving

4 egg whites
sugar
4 cups orange juice
1 cup milk
1 10-ounce bottle lemon-lime soda
¼ teaspoon ground nutmeg

1. In small bowl with mixer at high speed, beat egg whites until soft peaks form; beating at high speed, gradually sprinkle in ¼ cup sugar; beat until sugar is dissolved. Whites should stand in stiff peaks. Set beaten whites aside.
2. In chilled punch bowl, carefully stir orange juice, milk, lemon-lime soda, ¼ cup sugar and ground nutmeg until well mixed; stir in beaten egg whites. Serve immediately in punch cups or small glasses.

Lemonade

Cold punches

Lemonade

1½ cups sugar
1 tablespoon finely grated
lemon peel
water
1½ cups lemon juice
(8 to 10 lemons)
ice cubes
club soda (optional)

Color index
page 112

Begin 2 hrs
or up to
1 wk ahead

16 cups or
sixteen 1-cup
servings

75 cals per
serving

1 Into 1-quart jar with
tight-fitting lid, put
sugar and lemon peel; add
1½ cups very hot water.

2 With lid fitted firmly,
shake jar until sugar is
dissolved. Add lemon
juice. Refrigerate.

3 *To serve:* Into each
12-ounce glass, over ice
cubes, pour ¼ cup of the
lemon syrup.

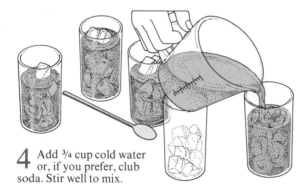

4 Add ¾ cup cold water
or, if you prefer, club
soda. Stir well to mix.

FOR 8 SERVINGS: In 2½-quart pitcher or container, combine half of the lemon syrup with 6 cups
cold water. Pour over ice cubes. Refrigerate remaining lemon syrup.

LIMEADE: Prepare Lemonade (above) but substitute *grated lime peel* for lemon peel and *lime juice*
for the lemon juice (you will need about 10 limes).
Reconstitute with water only.

Easy-Way Lemonade

2 lemons, thinly sliced   **4 cups boiling water**
½ cup sugar   **ice cubes**

Color index
page 112

Begin early
in day

Five ¾-cup
servings

87 cals per
serving

1. Into large heatsafe bowl or pitcher, place the
sliced lemons and the sugar.
2. Pour in boiling water; stir until sugar is dissolved.
Refrigerate until chilled.
3. *To serve:* Pour mixture over ice cubes in chilled 8-
ounce glasses. Serve immediately.

Eggnog

12 eggs, separated
1 cup sugar
1½ cups bourbon
½ cup brandy
6 cups milk
ground nutmeg
1 cup heavy or whipping
cream

Color index
page 110

Begin 2 hrs
ahead or
early in day

Thirty-eight
½-cup
servings

125 cals per
serving

1 In large bowl with
mixer at low speed,
beat egg yolks with sugar.
At high speed, beat until
thick and lemon-colored,
about 15 minutes, fre-
quently scraping bowl.

2 Carefully beat in
bourbon and brandy,
one tablespoon at a time
to prevent curdling
mixture. Cover and chill.

3 *About 20 minutes before
serving:* In chilled 5- to
6-quart punch bowl, stir
yolk mixture, milk and 1¼
teaspoons nutmeg.

4 In large bowl with
mixer at high speed,
beat egg whites until soft
peaks form.

5 In small bowl, using
same beaters, with
mixer at medium speed,
beat cream until stiff
peaks form.

6 With wire whisk,
gently fold egg whites
and cream into yolk
mixture until just blended.

7 To serve, sprinkle some
nutmeg over top of
eggnog; ladle into 6-ounce
punch cups.

Hot punches

Golden Punch

Color index
page 112

Begin 10 mins
ahead

Twenty
1/2-cup
servings

72 cals per
serving

*2 20-ounce cans crushed
pineapple in pineapple
juice*
*2 6-ounce cans frozen
lemonade concentrate*

1/4 cup sugar
*1 28-ounce bottle club
soda, chilled*
1 tray ice cubes

1. In covered blender container at high speed, blend crushed pineapple with its liquid, one can at a time, 15 to 20 seconds until thick.
2. In chilled punch bowl, stir blended pineapple, undiluted lemonade concentrate and sugar; stir in soda. Add ice and serve at once.

GOLDEN CHAMPAGNE PUNCH: Prepare as above but add *one 4/5-quart bottle champagne,* chilled, with club soda. (Makes 13 cups.)

Sangria

Color index
page 111

Begin just
before serving

Eight 6-ounce
servings

133 cals per
serving

1/2 cup lemon juice
1/2 cup orange juice
1/2 cup sugar
*1 4/5-quart bottle dry red
wine (3 1/4 cups)*
1/4 cup brandy

*1 7-ounce bottle club
soda, chilled*
*1 cup fruit (sliced orange,
lemon, apple, peach,
banana)*
1 tray ice cubes

Into large pitcher, pour lemon juice, orange juice and sugar; stir to dissolve sugar. Stir in remaining ingredients. To serve: Pour into glasses making sure each person gets some fruit.

Whiskey-Sour Punch

Color index
page 112

Begin 25 mins
ahead

Thirty-two
1/2-cup
servings

78 cals per
serving

1 small orange
*3 6-ounce cans frozen
lemonade concentrate,
thawed*
3 cups orange juice

*1 4/5-quart bottle rye,
bourbon or Scotch*
*1 32-ounce bottle club
soda, chilled*
2 trays ice cubes

1. Prepare garnish: Thinly slice orange; discard ends. With small sharp knife, flute edges of the orange slices; set aside.
2. In punch bowl, combine undiluted lemonade concentrate and remaining ingredients; mix well. Garnish with orange slices.

Sparkling Strawberry Punch

Color index
page 111

Begin 10 mins
ahead

Thirty-six
1/2-cup
servings

39 cals per
serving

*2 10-ounce packages
frozen sweetened
strawberries, slightly
thawed*
*1 6-ounce can frozen
lemonade concentrate,
slightly thawed*
*1 4/5-quart bottle rosé
wine, chilled*

*2 28-ounce bottles ginger
ale, chilled*
*1 28-ounce bottle club
soda, chilled*
2 trays ice cubes
1/4 cup sugar
*orange slices for
garnish*

1. In covered blender container at high speed, blend strawberries and undiluted lemonade concentrate until they are thoroughly blended.
2. Pour strawberry mixture into a chilled large punch bowl. Add wine and remaining ingredients except orange slices; stir punch until sugar is completely dissolved.
3. To serve: Garnish punch with orange slices.

Hot Mulled Wine

Color index
page 112

Begin 30 mins
ahead

Thirty-six
1/2-cup
servings

172 cals per
serving

4 cups sugar
*1 tablespoon ground
cinnamon or 6 medium
cinnamon sticks*
*1 teaspoon ground cloves
or whole cloves*

2 cups boiling water
*3 medium oranges, thinly
sliced*
*1 medium lemon, thinly
sliced*
1 gallon dry red wine

1 In 8-quart saucepot, combine sugar, cinnamon, cloves and water.

2 Add orange and lemon slices to saucepot. Over high heat, heat to boiling; boil 5 minutes, stirring occasionally.

3 Reduce heat to medium; add wine; heat till piping hot but not boiling, stirring occasionally.

4 Carefully ladle individual servings of hot wine into punch cups or heatsafe glasses.

Glögg

Color index
page 112

Begin day
ahead

Twenty
1/2-cup
servings

234 cals per
serving

*2 teaspoons dried orange
peel*
1 teaspoon whole cloves
*4 whole cardamom,
cracked*
*3 short cinnamon sticks
cheesecloth*
*1 cup dark seedless
raisins*
*1 8-ounce package dried
apricots*

*2 4/5-quart bottles
Burgundy
(6 1/2 cups)*
*1 4/5-quart bottle vodka,
gin or aquavit
(3 1/4 cups)*
3/4 cup sugar
*1 cup whole blanched
almonds*

1. Place orange peel and spices on a piece of cheesecloth; tie with string to form a bag.
2. In covered, 4-quart saucepan over medium-low heat, simmer raisins, apricots, spice bag and 1 bottle Burgundy 30 minutes.
3. Remove from heat and discard spice bag; stir in vodka, sugar and remaining Burgundy; cover mixture and let stand overnight at room temperature.
4. *To serve:* Over high heat, heat mixture until piping hot, but not boiling, stirring occasionally. Ignite mixture with long match; let burn a few seconds, then cover pan to extinguish flame. Add almonds; pour into heated punch bowl. Serve hot.

Hot punches

Wassail Bowl with Baked Apples

*3 large cooking apples,
   cored*
*1 gallon apple cider
   (16 cups)*
6 whole cloves
6 whole allspice
*2 teaspoons ground
   nutmeg*
*1 6-ounce can frozen
   lemonade concentrate*
*1 6-ounce can frozen
   orange-juice
   concentrate*
*1 cup packed brown
   sugar*
sugar
short cinnamon sticks

Color index
page 112

Begin 45 mins
ahead

Thirty-six
¹/₂-cup
servings

78 cals per
serving

1 Preheat oven to 350°F.
Cut apples in half cross-wise and place, cut side down, in 13″ by 9″ baking dish. Bake 25 minutes or until the apple halves are fork-tender.

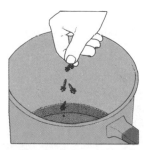

2 Meanwhile, in covered, 6-quart saucepot over low heat, simmer 2 cups apple cider, cloves, allspice and nutmeg 10 minutes.

3 Add remaining apple cider, undiluted lemonade and orange-juice concentrates and brown sugar; heat until hot, but not boiling, stirring occasionally.

4 Pour hot cider mixture from saucepot into heated large punch bowl.

5 Float apples, skin side up, in punch; sprinkle tops with a little sugar.

6 To serve, ladle about ¹/₂ cup of the hot punch into each punch cup; add a short cinnamon stick to each serving.

472

Cocktails

Cocktails are best served icy cold. If possible chill liquors, mixers and glasses. Use fresh ice for every drink and put it in the glass before other ingredients.

Serve cocktails in the appropriate glass filled ²/₃ full. Glasses most often used are: jigger, 1¹/₂ ounces; cocktail, 4 ounces; old-fashioned, 6 to 12 ounces; cordial, 1 ounce; whiskey sour, 6 ounces; highball, 8 to 12 ounces. For easy mixing, have on hand: ice bucket and tongs, mixing glass and long-handled spoon, shaker, muddler, strainer, knife and cutting board, lemon squeezer and jigger, which is the basic measure.

Frozen Daiquiris

*1 6-ounce can frozen
   limeade concentrate,
   undiluted*
*2¹/₂ cans light rum (use
   limeade can to
   measure)*
3 cans water

Color index
page 112

Begin day
ahead

5 cups or
thirteen
3-ounce
servings

90 cals per
3-ounce
serving

1 In 1¹/₂-quart freezer-safe bowl, combine limeade, rum and water; cover and freeze. (Mixture does not freeze solid.)

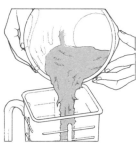

2 *Just before serving:*
Place half mixture in blender; cover and blend until slushy. Repeat.

3 Pour mixture into cocktail glasses. Serve Frozen Daiquiris with 2 short straws.

FROZEN WHISKEY SOURS: Prepare as above but substitute *one 6-ounce can frozen lemonade concentrate* for limeade and *blended whiskey* for rum. Use only 2 cans water and add *1 can orange juice.* Just before serving, garnish each drink with *maraschino cherry* and *half an orange slice.*

101 cals per
3-ounce
serving

Margarita

lime or lemon peel
salt
1 cup crushed ice
1 jigger tequila

¹/₂ jigger triple sec
*¹/₂ jigger lime or lemon
   juice*

Color index
page 112

Begin just
before serving

1 serving

118 cals

Rub rim of cocktail glass with lime peel; dip rim in salt; set aside. Over ice in cocktail shaker or large glass, pour remaining ingredients; stir; carefully pour into the prepared cocktail glass.

Company Bloody Mary

**2 18-ounce cans tomato
  juice (4½ cups)
1 cup vodka
2 teaspoons
  Worcestershire
½ teaspoon salt
¼ teaspoon coarsely
  ground pepper
few dashes hot pepper
  sauce
ice cubes
2 limes, quartered
  lengthwise**

Color index
page 112

Begin just
before serving
or early in day

5½ cups or
8 servings

88 cals per
serving

1 In large pitcher, combine first 6 ingredients. Cover and refrigerate mixture if made ahead.

2 To serve: Stir mixture, then pour over ice cubes in eight 10-ounce highball glasses.

3 Squeeze a lime wedge into each highball glass; stir Bloody Mary and serve immediately.

Bloody Mary

Color index
page 112

Begin just
before serving

1 serving
125 cals

**ice cubes
⅔ cup tomato juice
1 jigger vodka
dash Worcestershire

⅛ teaspoon salt
⅛ teaspoon pepper
dash hot pepper sauce
1 large lime wedge**

Over ice cubes in 10-ounce highball glass, measure all ingredients except lime wedge; squeeze lime wedge into mixture and stir well.

Alexander

Color index
page 112

Begin just
before serving

1 serving
232 cals

**1 cup crushed ice
1 jigger brandy or gin
½ jigger crème de
  cacao

½ jigger heavy or
  whipping cream**

Over crushed ice in cocktail shaker, pour remaining ingredients; shake together well. Strain mixture into a cocktail glass.

Old-fashioned

Color index
page 112

Begin just
before serving

1 serving
148 cals

**1 sugar cube
dash aromatic bitters
1 tablespoon water
cracked ice
1½ jiggers liquor
  (bourbon, brandy, gin,
  rum, rye or vodka)

stemmed maraschino
  cherry and slice of
  orange or lemon twist
  for garnish**

In old-fashioned glass with muddler, stir sugar with bitters and water until dissolved. Add cracked ice to fill glass; pour in liquor. Garnish with maraschino cherry and orange twist; serve with muddler.

Manhattan

Color index
page 112

Begin just
before serving

2 servings

112 cals per
serving

**1½ cups cracked ice
2 jiggers bourbon,
  blended or Canadian
  whisky

1 jigger sweet vermouth
2 dashes aromatic bitters
2 maraschino cherries**

Over ice in cocktail shaker or large glass, pour next 3 ingredients; stir. Strain mixture into 2 cocktail glasses. Garnish each with cherry.

DRY MANHATTAN: Prepare as above but substitute *dry vermouth* for sweet vermouth.

PERFECT MANHATTAN: Prepare as above but substitute *½ jigger each sweet and dry vermouth* for sweet vermouth.

Mint Julep

Color index
page 112

Begin up to
30 mins ahead

1 serving

140 cals

**4 sprigs mint
1 teaspoon sugar

finely crushed ice
1½ jiggers bourbon**

1. In 12-ounce highball glass or tankard (preferably silver or aluminum), place 3 sprigs mint and sugar. Crush mint with muddler or handle of wooden spoon until sugar is dissolved, about 5 minutes.
2. Fill glass to brim with ice; pour in bourbon; don't stir. Add more ice to fill glass. Set in freezer.
3. *Just before serving:* Garnish with mint sprig. Serve with long straw.

Tom Collins

Color index
page 112

Begin just
before serving

1 serving

145 cals

**2 tablespoons lemon
  juice
2 teaspoons sugar
1 cup cracked ice
1 jigger gin
ice cubes

club soda
maraschino cherry and
  orange slice or lime
  twist for garnish**

In covered cocktail shaker, shake lemon juice and sugar until sugar is dissolved. Add cracked ice and gin; shake well. Strain mixture over ice cubes in highball glass. Add club soda to fill glass; stir. Garnish with fruit and serve.

Martini

Color index
page 112

Begin just
before serving

2 servings

104 cals per
serving

**1½ cups cracked ice
2 jiggers gin or vodka
1 teaspoon dry
  vermouth

2 small stuffed green
  olives or lemon twists
  for garnish**

1. Over cracked ice in cocktail shaker, pour gin and vermouth; stir.
2. Strain mixture into 2 chilled cocktail glasses. Garnish each glass with an olive or a lemon twist.

Stinger

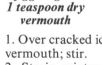

Color index
page 112

Begin just
before serving

1 serving

151 cals

**1 cup cracked ice
1 jigger brandy

½ jigger white crème de
  menthe**

Over cracked ice in cocktail shaker, pour brandy and white crème de menthe; shake well. Strain mixture into chilled cocktail glass.

CALVADOS STINGER: Prepare as above but substitute *1 jigger Calvados* for brandy.

Wines

American wines

Wine can be divided into five basic classes: appetizer wines, white table wines, red table wines, sweet dessert wines and sparkling wines. For details of characteristics of these wines, see table, opposite

SERVING WINE
Serve appetizer wines well chilled, either straight (undiluted) or over ice. All white wines should be served chilled. Depending on the type, red wines are served either cool or chilled or at room temperature. Most dessert wines may be served cool or chilled. Sparkling wines, often served for special occasions, are always served chilled and go well with any food at any occasion.

The best way to learn about wine is to experiment until you find the one you like best. Try a few of the wines in each of the five classes, and for first-time testing, buy wine in small bottles. Some wines complement certain foods more than others.

WINE WITH FOOD
Traditionally, white wines are served with white meats such as poultry, fish and seafood; red wines accompany red meats and dishes with red or brown sauces; rosé and sparkling wines are served with any food. Sweet dessert wines are served with dessert, after dinner and as a between-meal refreshment.

However, let your own taste and personal preference be your guide. Just remember to serve light wines with light foods and heavier, full-bodied wines with fuller-flavored, richer foods. That way food and wine will complement, not over-power, each other.

COOKING WITH WINE
Easy to use, and inexpensive, wine will enhance your favorite recipes for soups, broiled fish and meat, roasts and stews. Special cooking wines are lightly salted, so that you cannot drink them. Make sure to use the type of cooking wine called for in the recipe, and adjust the seasoning if necessary. Experts recommend cooking with wine of a quality you would like to drink – use some in the recipe and serve more to enjoy as a beverage with the food. Here are a few suggestions about how to cook with wine.

To flavor soups, add a tablespoon of wine for each cup of liquid; try adding sherry to consommé, chicken or vegetable soups; Burgundy or claret go well in minestrone. Add a light Rhine wine to melted butter and pour over fish before baking or broiling, or poach seafood in cooking liquid laced with sherry. A dash of sauterne will improve the flavor of gravy for roast poultry, while a dash of Burgundy or Chianti adds depth to a rich gravy for duckling or goose. Red wines add that extra flavor to beef dishes, too. Stir in Chianti or Zinfandel to gravy for roast beef, or add Chianti or Burgundy to barbecue sauce for serving with broiled beef steaks and hamburgers.

RED TABLE OR DINNER WINES	
Baco Noir	Dry, medium- to heavy-bodied, deep red wine made from French-hybrid Baco Noir grapes.
Barbera	Dry, full-bodied, heavy, deep red wine made from Barbera grapes.
Burgundy	Dry, medium- to heavy-bodied, deep ruby-red wine with pronounced flavor and bouquet, usually made from several grape varieties.
Cabernet Sauvignon	Dry, aromatic, ruby-red wine with distinctive flavor, made from Cabernet Sauvignon grapes, which are used in the production of French Bordeaux wines; one of the best Californian red-wine grapes.
Chianti (red)	Dry, fruity and slightly tart, ruby-red wine with strong flavor.
Chelois	Dry, light- to medium-bodied, light red wine made from French-hybrid Chelois grapes.
Claret	The name applied to any dry, tart, light- to medium-bodied ruby-red wine, made from one or more red grape varieties.
Concord	Medium-sweet to sweet, fruity wine, pale gold to deep red in color with a characteristic grapey flavor.
Gamay	Burgundy-type dry wine made from Gamay grapes; light-bodied; often a rosé wine.
Grignolino	Dry, claret-type wine with decided orange-red color, and distinct flavor and aroma of Grignolino grapes.
Petite Sirah	Burgundy-type dry, full-bodied wine.
Pinot Noir	Burgundy-type wine. Body and flavor vary greatly with amount of Pinot Noir grapes present (by law, as of 1983, at least 75%). Finest are velvety to taste, beautiful red color.
Rosé	Dry to slightly sweet, pink wine; lightest of red table wines.
Ruby Cabernet	Fruity, medium-bodied wine made from Ruby Cabernet grapes.
Vino Rosso	Term applied to slightly sweet to semisweet, medium- to heavy-bodied, ruby-red wines. Sometimes called "mellow red wines," they are softer in flavor than Chianti or other red dinner wines.
Zinfandel	Claret-type wine with fruity taste and aroma, made from Zinfandel grapes, produced only in California.

WHITE TABLE OR DINNER WINES

Blanc de Blancs	White wine made from white grapes.
Catawba	Dry or semisweet wine made in Eastern and Midwestern U.S.A. from Catawba grapes that give it flavor and aroma reminiscent of roses.
Chablis	Dry, fruity, pale gold wine, made from several grape varieties.
Chardonnay	Dry varietal wine with distinctive flavor and aroma of Chardonnay grapes. Sometimes called Pinot Chardonnay.
Chenin Blanc	Dry to semisweet, light-bodied, fragrant Chablis-type wine.
Chianti (white)	Dry, medium-bodied, slightly fruity and tart white wine.
Delaware	Dry to semisweet wine with flowery aroma, made from Delaware grapes grown in Eastern U.S.A.
Folle Blanche	Dry, Chablis-type wine made from Folle Blanche grapes.
Light Muscat	Dry to very sweet, light wine with characteristic Muscat grape flavor and aroma.
Niagara	Semisweet, light-bodied wine with distinctive aroma of Niagara grapes.
Pinot Blanc	Dry, tart, Chablis-type wine made from Pinot Blanc grapes.
Rhine Wine	Dry, tart, light-bodied, often flowery or fruity pale gold to green-gold white wine.
Riesling	Rhine wine made from one or a blend of Riesling grapes. Wines include Johannisberg Riesling; Grey Riesling; Franken Riesling; Emerald Riesling.
Sauterne	Dry to sweet, full-bodied, fragrant, golden wine. Three sauterne-type wines are sold in U.S.A.: Dry Sauterne, Sauterne, and Haut Sauterne.
Sauvignon Blanc	Sauterne-type wine with flavor and aroma of Sauvignon Blanc grapes. Usually dry; sometimes semisweet.
Semillon	Dry or semisweet sauterne-type wine made from Semillon grapes.
Sylvaner	Dry, sometimes tart, fruity and fragrant Rhine wine made from Sylvaner (Franken Riesling) grapes.
Traminer	Dry or slightly sweet, medium-bodied Rhine wine made from Traminer grapes. *Gewurztraminer* is a "spicy" wine from grapes of the same name.

APPETIZER WINES

Sherry	Pale to dark amber wine with characteristic nutty flavor that ranges from dry to sweet. Dry and medium sherries are preferred as appetizer and cocktail wines; they are labeled *cocktail, dry,* or *medium* sherry.
Vermouth	Wine flavored with herbs or other aromatic substances. Two main types: French-type vermouth, dry and nearly colorless; Italian-type vermouth, sweet and dark amber.
Flavored wines	Wines to which natural flavors, such as herbs and fruit, are added. *May wine* is flavored with sweet, scented woodruff; *Retsina* is white wine treated with pine resin.

DESSERT WINES

Angelica	Sweet, mild, fruity, straw-colored or amber wine resembling white Port.
Cream Sherry	Sweet, heavy, rich golden in color.
Madeira	Semisweet, deep amber wine resembling sherry but sweeter and darker. (Imported from Portugal.)
Marsala	Medium-bodied, deep amber wine resembling sherry but sweeter and darker. (Imported from Italy.)
Muscatel	Rich, robust sweet wine with typical Muscat grape flavor and aroma.
Port	Sweet, heavy-bodied, rich, deep-red to tawny wine. (Some white Port is produced.)
Tokay	Sweet, amber-colored wine with slightly nutty or sherry-like flavor, usually made by blending Angelica, Port and Sherry.

SPARKLING WINES

Champagne	Sparkling dry to sweet wine, made from one or more grape varieties. Very dry Champagne is usually labeled *nature*; dry, usually labeled *brut*; semidry, labeled *sec* or *dry*; sweet, labeled *doux*. Wine is pale gold in color. Pink champagnes are also made.
Sparkling Burgundy	Semisweet or sweet red wine made by methods used for Champagne.
Sparkling Muscat	Sweet Champagne-like wine with flavor of Muscat grapes.
Sparkling Rosé	Similar to pink Champagne. Dry to semisweet; made from grapes used for rosé dinner wine.

MICROWAVE COOKING

A popular kitchen appliance, the microwave oven can be used to simmer, steam, roast and bake, as well as to defrost and reheat foods. Its great benefit is that it normally uses much less time and energy than a conventional range to do these tasks. However, food may cook unevenly in the microwave, and special techniques, such as rotating food during cooking and allowing it to stand to complete cooking, are needed to correct this. These special microwave-cooking techniques are illustrated on pages 14 to 16 as are microwave-safe equipment and utensils. Here, we include special time-saving and preparation tips that guarantee successful microwave cooking.

The recipes on pages 478 to 495 were developed for microwave ovens rated between 600 and 700 watts, without automatic turntables. If your microwave wattage is lower, you will have to increase the cooking time or cook at a higher power than specified in the recipe; if it is higher, decrease the time or reduce the power setting.

FACTORS THAT AFFECT COOKING TIME

★ The more food cooked at the same time in the microwave oven, the longer it will take to cook. For example, one potato will bake in 4 to 5 minutes, while two potatoes take about 7 minutes.

★ A large, bulky piece of food, such as a roast, will take longer to cook in the microwave than smaller or thinner pieces, such as chops or stew meat.

★ Dense foods, such as a potato or lasagna, will cook or heat through more slowly than light, porous foods such as cakes and breads.

★ Foods high in fat or sugar, such as bacon or jelly-filled pastries, will cook faster than many other foods.

★ Foods at room temperature will take less time to cook than refrigerated or frozen foods.

★ Foods cooked in the microwave continue to cook after they are removed from the oven. Many recipes call for a standing time, which allows the food to complete cooking without overcooking.

TESTING FOR DONENESS

Food cooked in the microwave may look underdone when removed from the oven, but it will finish cooking in the standing time given in the recipe or recommended by the manufacturer. Some foods, particularly meat, poultry, breads and cakes, may appear underdone even after standing time since they do not tend to brown in the microwave; ways of improving their appearance are suggested on page 477.

Before you test for doneness, allow the food to stand as directed. Always undercook rather than overcook food; you can return food to the oven for further cooking if it is not done after the standing time but you cannot remedy overcooking. Tests for doneness depend on the food concerned and whether it is being reheated or cooked.

Thermometers For some foods, the most reliable test is a thermometer. When you think the food is done, insert an instant-read thermometer into it to check the temperature. Unless using a microwave-safe thermometer, the thermometer should be used only outside the microwave oven. As a general rule, it is advisable to remove meat from the oven before it reaches the desired degree of doneness as it will continue cooking outside the oven (see table below).

Meat	When to remove from oven	Temperature after standing time
Beef roast		
medium-rare	115° to 125°F.	125° to 140°F.
medium	130° to 140°F.	140° to 155°F.
well-done	150° to 160°F.	160° to 170°F.
Pork roast	165°F.	170°F.
Lamb		
medium-rare	130° to 140°F.	155°F.
well-done	150° to 160°F.	160° to 175°F.
Chicken	165° to 170°F.	175° to 180°F.
Duckling	170° to 175° F.	180° to 185°F.

How to test poultry Another way of checking poultry for doneness is to cut between the inner thigh and breast or next to the thigh bone; the meat should show no pink and juices should run clear. The flesh should feel soft when pinched and when the drumstick is moved up and down, the joint should give readily. Do not use an automatic temperature probe when cooking poultry in the microwave since hot melted fat runs along the probe and may turn the oven off before the bird is done.

The bottom of the dish To test whether a plate of food is heated through, feel the center of the bottom of the dish with your hand; when the food is done, the bottom of the dish will be hot. Look through the bottom of a glass dish when making foods that change texture as they cook (such as breads, custards, and cakes). The bottom should look done except for about one inch in the center. This wet spot will finish cooking during the standing time.

Other tests When cakes are done, the edges will pull away from the sides of the pan and a toothpick inserted into the center will come out clean. Any moist spots will cook on standing. Shake custards and cheesecakes gently; the edges should be set and the center thickened and slightly loose (it will set during standing). When cooked, pie shells will appear dry with tiny blisters under the surface. Remove fish from the oven when the outer edges are opaque and flake when tested with a fork; the center will be slightly transparent. Casseroles and soups are done when they are hot and bubbly.

TIPS FOR SUCCESS

Use effective dishes Ring-shaped dishes are best for cooking most foods in the microwave since microwave energy can penetrate the food from all sides and cook quickly and evenly. Round dishes also permit fairly even cooking, but the edges of food may overcook before the center is done; a glass placed in the center of the dish will help food cook more evenly.

Square or oblong dishes can produce overcooked foods in the corners before the center is done. To avoid this, shield the corners with foil before cooking or after half to two-thirds of the cooking time. Cut two 6-inch squares of foil and cut each into 2 triangles. Place a triangle diagonally across each corner and mold it over the corner and sides of the dish. When shielding the dish before cooking, check after half to two-thirds of the cooking time to see if the food underneath and in the center will finish cooking at the same time.

Always use the size and shape of dish specified in the recipe, or the timing – and the results – may be different. When thawing and reheating frozen food, use a dish that fits the size and shape of the food as closely as possible. Otherwise, the edges of the food may overcook before the center is heated through.

Many containers are suitable for microwave use, including heat-safe glassware, glass-ceramic dishes, china, and pottery – providing they do not have metal content or trim. Clay cooking pots may be used if they are presoaked according to the manufacturer's directions. Containers that should not be used include unglazed earthenware or pottery and most plastic containers that have not been developed specially for microwave use. (See Testing containers, page 14.)

Since metal can cause arcing (blue sparks), nylon twist ties or cotton string should be used instead of metal ties to close cooking bags. Small strips of foil may be used to shield food but the foil must not touch the interior surface of the oven.

Use lids and covers Casserole lids, microwave-safe large plates, and vented plastic wrap are equally effective in retaining heat and moisture in foods. Use waxed paper and paper towels for foods that need less moisture and heat retention, and to reduce splattering when cooking foods such as bacon.

Enhance the appearance Some foods that brown in the conventional oven do not brown in the microwave oven. Breads and cakes will look more tempting if you use dark-brown sugar instead of light-brown sugar. Or, sprinkle the tops of cakes with toasted coconut, sesame seeds, chopped nuts, wheat germ, a cinnamon-sugar mixture, or finely crumbled cookies. Casseroles can be sprinkled with browned bread crumbs or crumbled potato chips after the final stirring. Browning agents and glazes may be used to improve the appearance of meat and poultry:

Browning agents Brush meat or poultry with a shake-on microwave browning agent, catchup, bottled browning and seasoning sauce, barbecue sauce, Worcestershire or steak sauce, soy sauce, Angostura bitters, mustard, paprika, or chili powder. Apply the browning agent before cooking meat or poultry and again near the end of cooking time. If necessary, also apply when the food is turned over.

Glazes Ham and poultry can be glazed with orange marmalade after half the cooking time.

Shorten cooking time When water is called for in a recipe, reduce cooking time by using hot water.

Pierce skins and membranes Pierce the skin of vegetables such as potatoes, sweet potatoes, whole tomatoes, acorn squash, and the membrane of egg yolks, whole sausages, oysters, and chicken livers with a fork or knife tip. Steam builds up inside these and similar foods during microwave cooking, and they may burst during the cooking process. For the same reason, you should never attempt to cook eggs in their shell in the microwave.

Stir food Stir food such as stews from the outside edges of the dish to the center for even cooking.

Avoid boilover In the microwave oven, very hot liquid may start to boil over the top of a container when moved or stirred. For safety, use a large capacity container and carefully remove container from the microwave with a potholder. After a covered dish has been left to stand, be careful when removing the lid since steam will be released. You should never attempt to deep-fry foods in the microwave as the oil may overheat and boil over.

Appetizers

Easy Pâté

Begin early in day

10 first-course servings

270 cals per serving

2 tablespoons salad oil
1 small onion, minced
1/2 pound ground pork
1/2 pound ground veal
1/4 pound ground pork fat
1/2 cup dried bread crumbs
2 tablespoons Madeira wine
1 teaspoon salt
1/2 teaspoon pepper
1/2 teaspoon thyme leaves

1/4 teaspoon ground nutmeg
1/8 teaspoon oregano leaves
1 egg
5 medium-sized mushrooms
watercress sprigs for garnish
thin slices rye bread

1. In 2-quart bowl, place salad oil and onion; cover bowl with large plate. Cook at HIGH (100% power) 2 to 3 minutes, until onion is tender. Stir in pork, veal, pork fat, bread crumbs, Madeira wine, salt, pepper, thyme, nutmeg, oregano, and egg.
2. In 8 1/2" by 4 1/2" loaf dish, evenly spread half of meat mixture. Trim tough ends from mushroom stems. Arrange mushrooms, stem side up, in lengthwise row down center of meat mixture. Top with remaining meat mixture; pat top of meat firmly to remove any air bubbles.
3. Cover loaf dish with waxed paper. Cook at MEDIUM (50% power) 20 minutes, rotating dish a quarter turn after 10 minutes.
4. Let pâté stand 30 minutes to cool slightly. Cover loaf dish with plastic wrap and refrigerate until pâté is well chilled.
5. To serve, invert pâté in loaf dish onto chilled platter. Garnish pâté with watercress. Serve thinly sliced pâté with or on slices of rye bread.

Crab-filled Mushrooms

Begin 50 mins ahead

12 appetizers

90 cals each

1 6-ounce package frozen Alaska Snow crabmeat, thawed
1/3 cup mayonnaise
2 tablespoons minced celery
2 tablespoons minced onion
2 tablespoons dried bread crumbs
1 tablespoon lemon juice

1 tablespoon dry sherry
1/4 teaspoon salt
1/8 teaspoon hot pepper sauce
12 medium mushroom caps
2 tablespoons salad oil

1. Drain crabmeat well. In bowl, mix crabmeat with mayonnaise, celery, onion, bread crumbs, lemon juice, sherry, salt, and hot pepper sauce.
2. Lightly brush mushroom caps with salad oil. Spoon one-twelfth of crabmeat mixture into each mushroom. On waxed-paper-lined cookie sheet, freeze filled mushrooms until firm. Place in freezer container; cover, then freeze.
3. About 10 minutes before serving, on microwave-safe rack set in 12" by 8" dish, cook frozen mushrooms at HIGH (100% power) 5 to 6 minutes, until hot. If necessary, blot cooked mushrooms on paper towels before serving.

Clams Casino

Begin 55 mins ahead

12 appetizers

55 cals each

4 slices bacon
12 cherrystone clams, shucked, reserving 12 shells
1/2 cup soft bread crumbs (1 slice bread)
3 tablespoons grated Parmesan cheese

2 tablespoons minced green pepper
1 garlic clove, minced
1/2 teaspoon oregano

1. With kitchen shears, cut bacon slices into 1/2-inch pieces. In baking dish, cook bacon pieces, covered with paper towel, at HIGH (100% power) 4 to 5 minutes until browned but not crisp, stirring occasionally. Remove bacon to paper towel. Reserve 2 tablespoons bacon drippings.
2. Meanwhile, coarsely chop clams. In dish with bacon drippings, combine clams, bacon, and remaining ingredients. Spoon some of the clam mixture into each clam shell. On waxed-paper-lined cookie sheet, freeze until firm. Place in freezer container; cover; freeze.
3. About 10 minutes before serving, place clams in 10-inch round dish. Cover with waxed paper and cook at MEDIUM (50% power) 6 to 7 minutes, until heated through.

Savory Sausage Parcels

Begin 1 hr ahead

12 appetizers

65 cals each

2 tablespoons lemon juice
2 cups water
12 medium grape leaves
4 ounces hot or sweet Italian sausage links
2 tablespoons minced onion
1 garlic clove, minced

1 4-ounce jar pimientos, drained
1/4 cup shredded mozzarella cheese
2 tablespoons dried bread crumbs
salad oil

1. In 1-quart bowl, place lemon juice and water. Heat to boiling at HIGH (100% power) about 5 to 6 minutes. Add grape leaves; cover bowl with large plate and cook at HIGH 10 minutes. Drain, then cover leaves with cold water.
2. Remove casings from sausage links; crumble into 1-quart casserole; stir in onion and garlic. Cook at HIGH 2 to 3 minutes, until sausage loses its pink color, stirring to break up meat. Discard drippings.
3. From pimientos, cut 24 very thin strips, each about 2 inches long; set aside. Chop remaining pimiento; add to sausage mixture with cheese and dried bread crumbs.
4. Pat grape leaves dry with paper towels. Place scant 1 tablespoon sausage mixture in center of each leaf; fold sides over mixture, then roll up. Garnish with reserved pimiento strips. On waxed-paper-lined cookie sheet, freeze until firm. Place seam-sides down in freezer container; cover; freeze.
5. About 5 minutes before serving, place frozen stuffed leaves, seam-sides down, on rack set in 12" by 8" baking dish; brush lightly with oil. Cover and cook at HIGH 1 1/2 to 2 minutes, until hot.

Eggs

Spiced Nuts

Begin 10 mins ahead

12 appetizer servings

193 cals per serving

2 tablespoons butter
2 tablespoons ground cumin or curry powder
1 teaspoon ground cinnamon
³/₄ teaspoon chili powder
dash of garlic salt
1 12-ounce can mixed nuts

In 1-quart baking dish, melt butter at HIGH (100% power). Stir in remaining ingredients and heat at HIGH 5 minutes, stirring once. Cool and store in an airtight container.

Potato Nachos

Begin 20 mins ahead

12 appetizer servings

26 cals per serving

1 large potato (about 2 inches in diameter)
ground cumin or oregano
¹/₄ cup shredded Monterey Jack with Jalapeño Pepper cheese

1. Cut potato into 12 ¹/₄-inch-thick slices. Sprinkle lightly with ground cumin or oregano.
2. In shallow 2-quart baking dish, arrange potato slices in single layer. Cover with casserole lid or large plate and cook at HIGH (100% power) 3¹/₂ to 4 minutes. Top each potato slice with about 2 teaspoons shredded cheese. Cook at HIGH 30 seconds or just until cheese melts. Serve immediately.

Mexican Dip

Begin 10 mins ahead

1 cup

61 cals per tablespoon

1 green onion, minced
1 tablespoon butter
2 3-ounce packages cream cheese
¹/₄ cup bottled salsa (or to taste)
milk

In 2-quart bowl, cook green onion and butter at HIGH (100% power) 1 minute. Add cream cheese and heat at MEDIUM (50% power) to soften, about 1¹/₂ minutes; stir until smooth. Stir in bottled salsa and thin with about 1 tablespoon milk. Serve as a dip with vegetables, as a sandwich spread, or over a baked potato.

Designer Pizzas

Begin ¹/₂ hr ahead or early in day

12 appetizers

65 cals each

6 fresh or frozen (thawed) 2¹/₂-inch bagels
2 ounces ricotta, shredded Gruyère or goat's cheese
toppings of your choice: roasted sweet red pepper strips, sliced olives, tomatoes, fresh herbs

1. Slice bagels crosswise into halves. On cut sides of bagels, place approximately 2 teaspoons cheese. Garnish cheese with toppings of your choice. On waxed-paper-lined cookie sheet, freeze until firm. Place in freezer container; cover; freeze.
2. About 15 minutes before serving, heat 6 pizzas on paper-towel-lined plate at MEDIUM LOW (30% power) 4¹/₂ to 5 minutes, until cheese softens or melts. Repeat with remaining pizzas.

Crustless Broccoli Quiche

Begin 40 mins ahead

6 main-dish servings

240 cals per serving

Good source of vitamin C, vitamin A, calcium, iron

1 small bunch broccoli (about 1 pound)
1 small onion
¹/₂ cup half-and-half
4 eggs
¹/₂ pound Swiss cheese, shredded (2 cups)
¹/₈ teaspoon ground red pepper
tomato rose for garnish

1. Finely chop broccoli; mince onion. In 9-inch quiche dish, place broccoli and onion; cover with plastic wrap. Cook at HIGH (100% power) 5 minutes. Set aside, covered.
2. Heat half-and-half at MEDIUM (50% power) 1¹/₂ to 2 minutes, until steaming. In bowl, beat half-and-half and eggs. Stir in cheese and pepper. Pour egg mixture over vegetables in dish; stir gently.
3. Elevate dish on microwave rack or inverted plate. Cook at MEDIUM 12 to 14 minutes, until knife comes out clean, rotating dish twice. Let stand 10 minutes. Garnish with tomato rose.

Eggs in Tarragon Cream

Begin 25 mins ahead

2 main-dish servings

630 cals per serving

Good source of vitamin A, riboflavin, calcium, iron

2 tablespoons butter or margarine
1 small shallot, minced (optional)
1 tablespoon all-purpose flour
³/₄ teaspoon tarragon
¹/₂ teaspoon salt
1¹/₄ cups half-and-half
paprika
4 eggs
4 refrigerated prebaked buttermilk biscuits
¹/₄ cup finely chopped parsley for garnish

1. In 8-inch round baking dish, place butter or margarine and shallot; cover dish with waxed paper. Cook at HIGH (100% power) 2 to 2¹/₂ minutes, stirring twice, until butter or margarine melts and shallot is tender. Stir in flour, tarragon and salt. Cook mixture at HIGH 45 seconds.
2. Stir in half-and-half. Cook at HIGH 4 minutes or until mixture thickens, stirring every minute. Stir cream mixture well. Sprinkle lightly with paprika.
3. Break eggs, one at a time, into a saucer. Gently slip eggs into tarragon cream, spacing eggs evenly around dish. With toothpick, pierce each egg yolk to prevent bursting while cooking.
4. Cover dish with waxed paper. Cook at MEDIUM HIGH (70% power) 3 minutes or until eggs are of desired doneness, rotating dish a half turn halfway during cooking. Let eggs stand, still covered, while heating biscuits.
5. Place biscuits on paper towel in microwave oven. Heat as label directs, or at MEDIUM LOW (30% power) for 1¹/₂ minutes. (Do not overheat biscuits or they will be very tough.)
6. To serve, split each biscuit horizontally in half; place 4 halves on each of 2 dinner plates. Spoon 2 eggs and some tarragon cream onto biscuit halves on each plate. Sprinkle each serving with some chopped parsley.

Fish

Salmon Steaks with Watercress Sauce

Begin 35 mins ahead

4 servings

325 cals per serving

Good source of vitamin A, niacin, calcium

3 tablespoons butter or margarine
1 green onion, sliced
1/2 cup half-and-half
1 1/2 teaspoons cornstarch
1 teaspoon sugar

3/4 teaspoon salt
1 bunch watercress
1 tablespoon lemon juice
1/8 teaspoon hot-pepper sauce
4 small salmon steaks, each 1/2 inch thick

1. In 2-quart casserole or bowl, place butter or margarine and sliced onion; cover with casserole lid or large plate. Cook at HIGH (100% power) 2 to 3 minutes, stirring after 1 1/2 minutes, until the onion is tender.
2. Into mixture in casserole, stir half-and-half, then cornstarch, sugar, and salt until blended. Cook at HIGH 2 to 3 minutes, stirring after 1 1/2 minutes, until sauce thickens and boils and is smooth.
3. Rinse and drain watercress; remove tough stems to make 3 cups lightly packed watercress sprigs. To mixture in casserole, add watercress, lemon juice, and hot-pepper sauce. Cover and cook at HIGH 1 1/2 minutes or until watercress wilts.
4. Pour watercress mixture into blender container. Cover (with center part of blender cover removed) and blend at high speed until mixture is very smooth.
5. Place salmon steaks in 12" by 8" baking dish; cover with waxed paper. Cook at MEDIUM HIGH (70% power) 6 to 7 minutes just until fish flakes easily when tested with a fork, rotating dish a half turn after 4 minutes. Serve salmon steaks with watercress sauce.

ARRANGING FISH FILLETS
For best results when cooking fish fillets, arrange in shallow dish with thicker ends toward the edge. Overlap thin ends, separating them with plastic wrap or waxed paper.

Red Snapper Piquante

Begin 25 mins ahead

4 servings

275 cals per serving

Good source of vitamin C, calcium, iron

1 2 1/2-pound red snapper, dressed and head removed
2 tablespoons butter, melted
6 green onions
4 large carrots
2 large red peppers
2 celery stalks

1 garlic clove, sliced
1 tablespoon salad oil
2 tablespoons dry sherry
2 tablespoons soy sauce
1/4 teaspoon ground ginger
kiwi fruit and toasted almonds for garnish

1. Shield tail of fish; place in 13" by 9" baking dish; brush with butter. Cut green onions into 2-inch pieces; cut carrots and red peppers into thin strips; slice celery. Arrange vegetables around fish.
2. In bowl, cook garlic and oil at HIGH (100% power) 1 1/2 to 2 minutes, until garlic is golden; discard garlic. Add remaining ingredients; pour over fish and vegetables.
3. Cover baking dish and cook at HIGH 12 to 14 minutes, just until outer edges of fish are opaque, removing foil, rotating dish, and stirring vegetables halfway through cooking. Garnish with kiwi fruit and almonds.

Winter Fish Stew

Begin 1 hr ahead

4 servings

220 cals per serving

Good source of vitamin C, iron

1 16-ounce package frozen cod fillets
3 medium turnips (about 1 pound), peeled and cut into bite-sized pieces
water
2 tablespoons salad oil
1 medium onion, diced
1 large green pepper, diced

1 14 1/2- to 16-ounce can tomatoes
1 chicken-flavor bouillon cube or envelope
1/2 teaspoon oregano leaves
1/8 teaspoon ground red pepper

1. Cook unwrapped frozen fish on plate at MEDIUM LOW (30% power) 5 minutes; turn fish over once.
2. In 2-quart casserole or bowl, place turnips and 1/2 cup water; cover with casserole lid or large plate. Cook at HIGH (100% power) 14 to 16 minutes until turnips are tender; drain. Let stand, covered.
3. In 3-quart casserole or bowl, combine oil, onion, and green pepper. Cook at HIGH 6 minutes or until tender, stirring after 3 minutes.
4. To onion mixture, add turnips, tomatoes with their liquid, bouillon, oregano, ground red pepper, and 2 1/2 cups hot tap water. Cover and cook at HIGH 10 minutes, stirring once.
5. Cut fish into bite-sized chunks. Stir fish into casserole. Cover; cook at HIGH 4 minutes or until fish flakes easily when tested with fork.

Fish Steaks with Salsa

Begin 20 mins ahead

2 servings

400 cals per serving

Good source of vitamin C, iron

1 8- to 8 1/4-ounce can tomatoes
1 small green pepper, thinly sliced
1 small onion, chopped
1/2 3 1/2-ounce can pitted ripe olives, drained, each cut in half
2 tablespoons coarsely chopped cilantro or parsley

1 tablespoon salad oil
1 garlic clove, crushed
1/4 teaspoon salt
lime or lemon juice
2 6-ounce cod, salmon, or halibut steaks
1 tablespoon dry sherry
2 tablespoons mayonnaise
1/2 teaspoon cider vinegar
1/4 teaspoon chili powder

1. Prepare salsa: Drain tomatoes, reserving 2 tablespoons tomato liquid. In medium bowl, combine tomatoes and reserved liquid, green pepper, onion, olives, cilantro, oil, garlic, salt, and 1 tablespoon lime juice, stirring to break up tomatoes. Cook at HIGH (100% power) 5 to 6 minutes, until pepper is tender-crisp; stir once. Set aside, covered.
2. Lightly moisten 2 paper towels; place a fish steak on each. Combine sherry and 1 tablespoon lime juice; pour half of mixture over each steak. Twist corners of each towel together. On microwave-safe platter, cook at HIGH 2 to 2 1/2 minutes just until outer edges of fish are opaque.
3. Meanwhile, in small bowl, combine mayonnaise, vinegar, and chili powder. Set aside.
4. Discard paper towels. Spoon some mayonnaise mixture over each fish steak. Arrange salsa around fish steaks on platter.

Shellfish

Meat

Stuffed Shrimp Supreme

Begin 30 mins ahead

4 servings

350 cals per serving

Good source of vitamin A, calcium

1 pound large shrimp, shelled and deveined
salt
1 cup shredded zucchini
1/3 cup minced red pepper
1/4 cup dried bread crumbs
dash ground red pepper
1 egg

2 tablespoons butter, melted
2 tablespoons dry sherry
1 tablespoon lemon juice
1 6-ounce package goat cheese
2 tablespoons minced pecans
lettuce leaves for garnish

1. Cut each shrimp along center back, three-fourths through; spread open; pound lightly to flatten. Sprinkle lightly with salt.
2. Squeeze zucchini to remove excess moisture. Mix zucchini, red pepper, bread crumbs, ground red pepper, egg, and 1/2 teaspoon salt. Spoon some mixture along center back of each shrimp. Fold shrimp over filling; place in 13" by 9" baking dish.
3. Mix butter, sherry and lemon juice; pour over shrimp. Cover baking dish with waxed paper and cook at MEDIUM HIGH (70% power) 6 to 8 minutes just until shrimp turn pink.
4. Cut cheese into 8 slices; coat lightly with pecans. Cook at MEDIUM (50% power) 1 to 2 minutes to soften cheese slightly. Arrange shrimp and cheese on platter; pour butter mixture over shrimp; garnish.

Seafood Bake

Begin 40 mins ahead

8 servings

155 cals per serving

Good source of calcium, iron

4 ears corn
12 littleneck clams
2 8-ounce bottles clam juice
2 leeks, thinly sliced
2 tablespoons butter
1 pound medium shrimp, shelled and deveined

3/4 pound sea scallops, sliced
2 garlic cloves, minced
1 7-ounce jar roasted sweet red peppers, drained, sliced
2 tablespoons lemon juice
spinach leaves

1. Remove husks and silk from corn; cut ears crosswise into 2-inch pieces. Reassemble into ears and wrap in plastic wrap; cook at HIGH (100% power) 6 minutes, rearranging once.
2. Scrub and rinse clams. In casserole, place microwave-safe steamer or trivet; add 1/2 cup clam juice. Cover; cook at HIGH 2 minutes. Add clams; cover and cook at HIGH 3 to 3 1/2 minutes, until clams open.
3. In 3-quart casserole, place leeks and butter; cover. Cook at HIGH 3 to 4 minutes; stir in shrimp, scallops, garlic, peppers, lemon juice and remaining clam juice. Cover and cook at HIGH 6 minutes; stir twice. Add corn and clams with liquid; heat through. Add spinach leaves.

> **STEAMING FISH**
> To avoid making any mess when steaming fish in the microwave, place fish in the center of a pre-moistened paper towel (dampened quickly under running water). Then, bring all the corners of the paper towel to the center, twist to close, and put in the oven.

Freezer-to-table Pot Roast

Begin 2 1/2 hrs ahead

12 servings

340 cals per serving

Good source of vitamin A, niacin, iron

1 cup orange juice
2 teaspoons salt
1/4 teaspoon pepper
1/4 teaspoon thyme leaves
2 4" by 1" strips orange peel
1 4-pound frozen boneless beef chuck cross rib pot roast

1 small rutabaga (about 1 pound)
1 16-ounce bag carrots
3 tablespoons all-purpose flour
3 tablespoons water

1. In 5-quart casserole or bowl, combine orange juice, salt, pepper, thyme leaves, and orange peel. Add frozen chuck roast, turning to coat with orange-juice mixture. Place 2-inch-wide strip of foil over top edge of each end of meat to prevent overcooking; cover with casserole lid or large plate. Cook at MEDIUM (50% power) 1 hour, turning roast over and replacing foil strips after 30 minutes.
2. Peel rutabaga and cut into 1/4-inch-thick wedges. Peel carrots and cut into 1 1/2-inch pieces.
3. Turn meat over again and add the vegetables. Replace foil strips; cover and continue to cook at MEDIUM 1 to 1 1/4 hours, turning meat over once more, until meat and vegetables are tender.
4. With slotted spoon, remove meat and vegetables from casserole to warm platter; keep warm.
5. Skim fat from cooking liquid in casserole. In small bowl, stir flour and water until smooth. Gradually stir flour mixture into cooking liquid in casserole. Cook at HIGH (100% power) 2 to 3 minutes, until sauce thickens, stirring every minute.
6. Cut meat into slices. Pour sauce into gravy boat and pass to spoon over servings.

Steak with Mushrooms and Artichokes

Begin 25 mins ahead

4 servings

325 cals per serving

Good source of riboflavin, niacin, iron

1 9-ounce package frozen artichoke hearts
water
3/4 pound mushrooms
2 green onions, chopped
2 tablespoons butter
1 tablespoon dry red wine
3/4 teaspoon beef-flavor instant bouillon

4 beef tenderloin steaks, each cut 1 inch thick
1/2 teaspoon browning sauce
1/2 teaspoon salt
1/4 teaspoon pepper
1/4 teaspoon marjoram

1. In 1-quart casserole, place artichoke hearts and 2 tablespoons water; cover with casserole lid or large plate. Cook at HIGH (100% power) 6 to 8 minutes; stir once; drain.
2. Cook mushrooms, onions, butter, red wine, and bouillon, covered, at HIGH 3 minutes, stirring once. Add artichokes.
3. Arrange beef steaks on microwave-safe rack in baking dish. Mix browning sauce with 1 teaspoon water; brush on meat; sprinkle with salt, pepper, and marjoram. Cover with waxed paper and cook at MEDIUM HIGH (70% power) 6 to 8 minutes for medium-rare. Reheat artichoke mixture if necessary; serve with steaks.

Meat

Meat Loaf Milanese with Tomato-Basil Sauce

Begin 1 hr ahead

6 servings

370 cals per serving

Good source of iron

1 pound small red potatoes, halved
1 9-ounce package frozen Italian green beans
1/4 cup water
1 small onion, chopped
1/4 cup chopped celery
1 tablespoon lemon juice
1 1/2 pounds ground beef
1/2 cup dried bread crumbs
1 teaspoon salt

1 teaspoon browning sauce
1 egg, slightly beaten
dry red wine
basil
1 14 1/2- to 16-ounce can tomatoes, chopped
1 teaspoon sugar
1 tablespoon chopped parsley
1 teaspoon grated lemon peel

1. In large casserole or bowl, place potatoes, frozen green beans, and water; cover with casserole lid or large plate. Cook at HIGH (100% power) 12 minutes, stir once. Drain; let stand, covered.
2. In 2 1/2-quart bowl, cook onion, celery, lemon juice, covered, at HIGH 3 minutes. Stir in beef, next 4 ingredients, 1/2 cup wine, and 1/2 teaspoon basil. In 12" by 8" dish, shape into 8" by 4" loaf.
3. Cover loaf with waxed paper and cook at MEDIUM HIGH (70% power) 15 to 16 minutes, rotating the dish a half turn once. Let loaf stand, covered.
4. In bowl, place tomatoes with their liquid, sugar, 2 tablespoons wine, and 1/2 teaspoon basil; cover with large plate and cook at HIGH 5 minutes.
5. Sprinkle meat loaf with parsley and lemon peel. Serve with potatoes, beans, and sauce.

Mexican Beef Casserole

Begin 45 mins ahead

6 servings

580 cals per serving

Good source of calcium, iron

1 1/2 pounds ground beef
1 medium onion, chopped
1 garlic clove, minced
2 10-ounce cans enchilada sauce
1 10-ounce package frozen whole-kernel corn, thawed

1 6-ounce can pitted ripe olives, drained, sliced (1 cup)
6 6-inch corn tortillas, quartered
4 ounces sharp Cheddar cheese, shredded (1 cup)

1. In microwave-safe plastic colander set over bowl, place ground beef, onion, and garlic; cook at HIGH (100% power) 5 to 6 minutes; stir once. Discard drippings; place meat mixture in bowl. Stir in 1 can enchilada sauce, corn, and 3/4 cup olives.
2. In 2 1/2-quart shallow baking dish, layer half of remaining can enchilada sauce, half of tortilla pieces, half of meat mixture, and half of cheese. Repeat. Cover with casserole lid or large plate and cook at HIGH 10 to 12 minutes, until heated through. Garnish with remaining olives.

PRECOOKING FOODS
Meat as well as poultry and vegetables may be precooked in the microwave. To make barbecuing easier, partially cook meat and complete cooking on the grill; this will save 1/3 to 1/2 of the time.

Best-ever Burgers

Begin 30 mins ahead

2 servings

535 cals per serving

Good source of vitamin A, iron

1 large carrot
1 small zucchini
butter or margarine
1/2 pound ground beef
1 teaspoon cornstarch
1/2 teaspoon unseasoned meat tenderizer

1/2 teaspoon paprika
1/4 teaspoon pepper
1/2 teaspoon browning sauce
2 small onions, sliced
2 tablespoons red wine

1. Coarsely shred carrot and zucchini. Place in dish; add 1 tablespoon butter. Cover; set aside.
2. Shape ground beef into 2 oval patties, about 3/4-inch thick. On waxed paper, mix cornstarch, meat tenderizer, paprika, and pepper. In cup, melt 1 tablespoon butter with browning sauce at HIGH (100% power) 30 seconds. Brush on hamburgers; coat with cornstarch mixture.
3. Place hamburgers, onions, and 1 tablespoon butter or margarine in 8" by 8" dish. Cover with waxed paper and cook at MEDIUM HIGH (70% power) 4 to 5 minutes. Remove hamburgers to platter and cover. Stir wine into onions; cover and cook at HIGH 4 minutes.
4. Cook carrot and zucchini at HIGH 2 to 3 minutes; stir. Spoon onion mixture over hamburgers; serve with carrot and zucchini.

DEFROSTING MEAT
When using the microwave oven to defrost meat frozen in its store wrapping, remove the Styrofoam tray and its paper liner as soon as they can be separated from the meat. The tray insulates the meat, preventing the microwaves from getting through to thaw the meat; and the paper liner used to absorb meat juices will draw energy away from the meat. Place meat on a plate; cover the meat with waxed paper to hold heat around it as it defrosts.

Tostada Casserole

Begin 40 mins ahead

4 servings

520 cals per serving

Good source of vitamin C, vitamin A, niacin, calcium, iron

1 pound ground beef
1 small onion, grated
1 8-ounce can tomato sauce
1/4 cup water
2 teaspoons chili powder
1 4-ounce can diced green chilies

1/4 pound Monterey Jack or Muenster cheese, shredded (1 cup)
1 4- to 4 1/2-ounce package taco shells, coarsely broken

1. In 2-quart bowl, mix ground beef and onion; cover bowl with waxed paper. Cook at HIGH (100% power) 4 to 5 minutes, stirring and breaking up meat into small pieces every 2 minutes. Tilt bowl; skim and discard excess fat. Stir in tomato sauce, water, and chili powder. Cover and cook at HIGH 4 minutes or until meat mixture thickens, stirring after 2 minutes. Stir in undrained green chilies and cheese.
2. In shallow 1 1/2-quart casserole, place three-fourths of the coarsely broken tacos. Top with meat mixture; cover with casserole lid or large plate. Cook at MEDIUM HIGH (70% power) 12 to 14 minutes until meat mixture is hot. Let stand, still covered, 5 minutes. Sprinkle with remaining tacos.

COOKING PORK IN THE MICROWAVE

Roasts: Choose evenly shaped roasts weighing 3 to 3½ pounds. Place roast in a cooking bag (or follow the recipe directions carefully) and place in or on a microwave-safe baking dish or rack. Sprinkle roast with dried herbs or pork- or brown-gravy mix and close bag loosely. Cook at MEDIUM LOW (30% power), allowing 22 minutes per pound for a boneless roast 20 minutes per pound for a bone-in roast. Half-way through cooking, invert or turn roast over, and rotate the dish a half turn.

The roast is done when the internal temperature reaches 170°F. Use a microwave probe or instant-read thermometer to check the temperature in several places to be sure all points reach 170°F.; if any portions appear pink or red, cook roast longer. Do not let the probe or thermometer touch any fat or the dish. When roast is done, cover it (in the bag) with foil and let stand 10 minutes.

Pork spareribs: Choose closely trimmed ribs with breast bone removed, weighing 3 to 3½ pounds and cut into 3- to 4-rib pieces. Place ribs bones down in a cooking bag; add 1 cup water, tie bag loosely. Place the bag in a baking dish. (Or cook the ribs and water in a covered baking dish.) Cook the ribs at MEDIUM (50% power), allowing 14 to 16 minutes per pound. Halfway through cooking, invert ribs, rearrange them in bag, and rotate dish a half turn. No standing time is necessary.

Pork chops: Choose center-cut rib or loin or boneless top loin chops cut ¾ to 1 inch thick. Each chop should weigh 5 to 7 ounces. Place chops in a baking dish, with or without rack. Cover tightly with lid or unvented plastic wrap. Cook at MEDIUM LOW (30% power), allowing 18 minutes per pound for 4 chops, 20 minutes per pound for 1 chop. Halfway through cooking, invert chops and rotate the dish a half turn. Chops are done when the meat pulls away from the bone, loses its pink color, and the juices are clear. No standing time is necessary.

Savory Ribs

Begin 1hr ahead

4 servings

605 cals per serving

Good source of vitamin C, thiamine, niacin, iron

1 large onion, chopped
1 large green pepper, cut into thin strips
2 tablespoons salad oil
2 tablespoons paprika
1 16-ounce package sauerkraut
1 8-ounce can tomato sauce

2 tablespoons brown sugar
1 chicken-flavor bouillon envelope
½ teaspoon caraway seeds, crushed
2 pounds pork loin country ribs
sour cream (optional)

1. In 3-quart casserole, cook onion, green pepper, and oil, covered, at HIGH (100% power) 6 minutes; stir once. Add paprika; cook 1 minute.
2. Stir in undrained sauerkraut, tomato sauce, sugar, bouillon, and caraway seeds; tuck ribs into mixture. Cover and cook at HIGH 35 to 40 minutes until meat is fork-tender, turning ribs over and re-arranging after 15 minutes. Serve with sour cream.

Spicy Cranberry Pork Chops

Begin 30 mins ahead

4 servings

410 cals per serving

Good source of thiamine

4 pork loin or sirloin chops, each about ¾ inch thick
salt
pepper
1 8-ounce can whole-berry cranberry sauce
¼ cup dark seedless raisins
2 tablespoons brown sugar

2 tablespoons red-wine vinegar
2 tablespoons orange juice
½ teaspoon ground cinnamon
½ teaspoon grated orange peel

1. Sprinkle pork chops lightly with salt and pepper; place in 12″ by 8″ baking dish; cover dish with plastic wrap; do not vent. Cook at MEDIUM LOW (30% power) 16 minutes, turning chops over and rotating dish a half turn after 10 minutes.
2. Meanwhile, in small bowl, combine cranberry sauce, raisins, brown sugar, red wine vinegar, orange juice, ground cinnamon, grated orange peel, and ½ teaspoon salt.
3. Drain and discard accumulated cooking liquid from baking dish. Spoon cranberry-sauce mixture onto pork chops; cover dish with plastic wrap; do not vent. Cook at MEDIUM LOW 6 to 8 minutes until meat loses its pink color and is tender.

Bratwurst and Beer

Begin 1 hr ahead

8 servings

420 cals per serving

Good source of thiamine, niacin, iron

2 pounds fresh bratwurst or country-style sausage links
2 medium onions
1 12-ounce can beer
1 tablespoon all-purpose flour
1 tablespoon prepared mustard

½ teaspoon salt
¼ teaspoon pepper
1 pound small red potatoes
1 10-ounce package frozen whole green beans

1. Cut each bratwurst crosswise into 2 to 3 pieces. Cut each onion into 8 wedges.
2. In 3-quart casserole or bowl, combine bratwurst and onions; cover with casserole lid or large plate. Cook at HIGH (100% power) 12 minutes, stirring mixture every 4 minutes and pushing cooked pieces from edge of dish to center. Drain well; return bratwurst and onions to casserole.
3. In 2-cup glass measuring cup, stir beer, flour, mustard, salt, and pepper until smooth; pour mixture over drained bratwurst mixture.
4. Pierce the skin of each potato with fork in several places. Arrange the potatoes on top of bratwurst mixture around edge of casserole; cover with casserole lid or large plate. Cook at HIGH 10 minutes, stirring after 5 minutes.
5. Separate frozen green beans under running warm water and drain on paper towels. Stir beans into bratwurst mixture. Cover and cook at MEDIUM HIGH (70% power) 20 to 25 minutes until potatoes and beans are tender, stirring every 5 minutes.

483

Meat

Lamb Medallions with Orange

Begin 25 mins ahead

8 servings

520 cals per serving

Good source of iron

3 tablespoons butter, melted
1 teaspoon browning sauce
8 boneless lamb loin chops, each cut 1-inch thick
1/2 teaspoon rosemary
1/2 teaspoon thyme
1/3 cup mayonnaise

1/2 teaspoon grated orange peel
1/4 teaspoon cider vinegar
8 3-inch bread rounds, toasted
2 tablespoons butter, softened
1/4 cup chopped parsley
8 orange slices

1. Mix melted butter and browning sauce; brush on lamb chops. Arrange chops in 13" by 9" dish; cover with waxed paper. Cook at MEDIUM HIGH (70% power) 9 to 12 minutes for medium-rare.
2. Crush rosemary and thyme; mix with mayonnaise, orange peel, and cider vinegar.
3. Spread edges of toast rounds with softened butter. Roll edges of the toast in chopped parsley.
4. Arrange toast on platter; top each with an orange slice, lamb chop, and mayonnaise mixture.

Apricot-glazed Rack of Lamb

Begin 50 mins ahead

4 servings

530 cals per serving

Good source of iron

1/2 teaspoon browning sauce
1 teaspoon water
1 2 1/2-pound lamb rib roast*
1/2 cup apricot preserves
1 tablespoon lemon juice

1 tablespoon prepared mustard
1/2 teaspoon salt
2 16-ounce cans small whole carrots, drained
watercress sprigs for garnish

1. Mix browning sauce with water; brush on roast. Shield bone ends of ribs with strips of foil. Place roast, fat-side down, on microwave-safe rack in 12" by 8" baking dish; cover with waxed paper. Cook at MEDIUM HIGH (70% power) 8 minutes.
2. Combine apricot preserves and next 3 ingredients. Spoon 1/4 cup apricot mixture into 1 1/2-quart bowl; set aside.
3. Turn roast fat-side up; discard foil. Cook, uncovered, at MEDIUM HIGH, about 7 to 8 minutes to 145°F. for medium-rare, or until of desired doneness, brushing with apricot mixture. Let stand, tented with foil; temperature will rise to 155°F.
4. Stir carrots into bowl with apricot mixture; cover with plate and cook at HIGH (100% power) 3 to 5 minutes, until hot; stir once. Arrange lamb rib roast and carrot mixture on warm platter. Garnish with watercress sprigs. *Ask butcher to cut through backbone for easier carving.

KEEPING MICROWAVED FOOD HOT
Food cooked in the microwave oven and served in the cooked dish can cool more quickly than conventionally cooked food if the microwave cooking time is short. To keep hot food hot, choose dishes that hold heat well; or cover with casserole lid or plastic wrap to hold in steam, or with waxed paper to hold in heat without holding in steam.

Veal Roast with Sausage-Vegetable Sauce

Begin 2 hrs ahead

12 servings

300 cals per serving

Good source of vitamin A, niacin, iron

1/2 pound sweet Italian-sausage links
2 medium carrots, thinly sliced
2 medium celery stalks, thinly sliced
1 medium onion, diced
1 garlic clove, minced
1/2 cup dry white wine

1 teaspoon salt
1/2 teaspoon sugar
1 14 1/2- to 16-ounce can tomatoes
1 4-pound boneless veal shoulder roast
chopped celery leaves and grated lemon peel for garnish

1. Remove sausage meat from casings. In 4-quart casserole, break up sausage meat; cover. Cook at HIGH (100% power) 2 minutes; stir.
2. Add carrots, celery, onion, and garlic. Cover and cook at HIGH 10 to 12 minutes, stirring every 4 minutes, until vegetables are tender. Stir in wine, salt, sugar, and tomatoes with their liquid; break up tomatoes with spoon.
3. Place veal roast, fat side down, in mixture in casserole. Spoon some mixture over roast. Shield top edges of roast with 1-inch-wide strip of foil. If roast is thin at one end, cover thin end with 3-inch square of foil to prevent this from overcooking. Cover and cook roast at HIGH 10 minutes. Spoon tomato mixture over roast; cover and cook at MEDIUM (50% power) 30 minutes.
4. Turn roast fat side up; shield top edges with foil. Cover and cook at MEDIUM 30 to 40 minutes longer, spooning tomato mixture over roast every 15 minutes, until veal is tender.
5. Remove veal to cutting board; slice. Skim fat from sauce in casserole. Spoon sauce onto warm deep platter. Arrange veal slices in sauce; garnish.

Veal Ragout

Begin 1 1/4 hrs ahead

8 servings

275 cals per serving

Good source of riboflavin, niacin, iron

3 tablespoons butter or margarine
1 medium onion, minced
2 tablespoons all-purpose flour
1/4 cup dry vermouth
1 1/2 teaspoons sugar
1 teaspoon salt
1/4 teaspoon pepper
1 teaspoon chicken-flavor instant bouillon

1/2 teaspoon oregano leaves
1 14 1/2- to 16-ounce can tomatoes
2 pounds veal for stew, cut into 1-inch cubes
1/2 pound small mushrooms
1 tablespoon minced parsley

1. In 3-quart casserole or bowl, place butter or margarine and onion; cover with casserole lid or large plate. Cook at HIGH (100% power) 6 minutes, stirring every 2 minutes, until onion is tender.
2. Stir flour into mixture until smooth. Add vermouth, sugar, salt, pepper, bouillon, and oregano; mix well. Add tomatoes with their liquid; break up tomatoes coarsely with spoon. Stir in veal stew meat and mushrooms.
3. Cover and cook at HIGH 20 minutes, stirring every 5 minutes. Then cook at MEDIUM (50% power) 15 to 25 minutes, stirring after 15 minutes, until veal is tender and liquid thickens slightly. Stir in parsley.

Poultry

Roast Turkey Breast with Brown Rice

Begin 1³/₄ hrs ahead

16 servings

345 cals per serving

Good source of niacin, iron

1 small onion, finely chopped	*1 teaspoon salt*
¹/₄ pound mushrooms, sliced	*1 6-pound fresh or frozen (thawed) turkey breast*
water	*2 tablespoons butter or margarine*
1¹/₂ cups brown rice	*¹/₂ teaspoon browning and seasoning sauce*
1 teaspoon thyme leaves	

1. In 5-quart casserole or bowl, combine onion, mushrooms, and ¹/₄ cup water; cover with casserole lid or large plate. Cook at HIGH (100% power) 5 minutes, stirring after 3 minutes. Stir in brown rice, thyme, salt, and 1¹/₄ cups hot tap water. Cover and cook at HIGH 10 minutes, stirring after 5 minutes.
2. Meanwhile, if turkey breast comes with neck, giblets, and with back and rib bones attached, with kitchen shears, cut off back and rib bones.
3. Stir rice in casserole; then place turkey, skin side down, in mixture. Cover and cook at MEDIUM HIGH (70% power) 20 minutes. Remove from oven. In 1-cup glass measuring cup, place butter; cook at HIGH 45 seconds or until melted. Stir in browning and seasoning sauce.
4. Turn turkey skin side up. Add ³/₄ cup hot tap water to rice, pouring water over turkey breast to remove any rice on turkey. Brush turkey with butter mixture. Cover and cook at MEDIUM HIGH 30 to 35 minutes longer, until turkey breast reaches 160°F. when tested with a microwave-safe meat thermometer, stirring rice after 20 minutes. Remove casserole from oven. Let turkey and rice stand, still covered, 10 minutes. Turkey will continue to cook to reach 170°F. on meat thermometer. Place turkey breast on warm large platter; spoon rice around turkey.

Quick Chicken Stew

Begin 45 mins ahead

4 servings

530 cals per serving

Good source of niacin, iron

1 10³/₄-ounce can condensed chicken broth, undiluted	*1 2¹/₂-pound broiler-fryer, cut up*
3 medium potatoes (about 1 pound), cut into 1-inch chunks	*¹/₂ teaspoon thyme leaves*
	¹/₂ teaspoon salt
	¹/₄ teaspoon pepper
3 medium carrots, cut into 2-inch pieces	*3 tablespoons all-purpose flour*
1 small onion, chopped	*1 9-ounce package frozen cut green beans*

1. Reserve ¹/₃ cup chicken broth. In 4-quart casserole, combine remaining broth, potatoes, carrots, and onion; arrange chicken pieces on top of vegetables; sprinkle with thyme, salt, and pepper. Cover with casserole lid or large plate and cook at HIGH (100% power) 18 minutes, stirring occasionally.
2. Stir flour into reserved chicken broth until blended and smooth; stir into chicken mixture. Stir in frozen beans. Cover with lid or large plate and cook at HIGH 8 to 10 minutes until chicken and vegetables are tender, stirring once.

DEFROSTING A TURKEY BREAST
Unwrap the turkey breast and place it, skin side down, in a baking dish. If defrosting at MEDIUM (50% power), allow 3 to 6 minutes per pound; if defrosting at LOW (30% power), allow 7 to 9¹/₂ minutes per pound. Defrost turkey breast for half the time. Shield any warm areas with small pieces of foil and turn breast skin side up; defrost for the remaining time. Rinse breast in cool water and let stand 5 to 10 minutes until the cavity is no longer icy.

Toasted-Walnut Chicken with Dijon Mustard Sauce

Begin 35 mins ahead

4 servings

440 cals per serving (heavy cream)

375 cals per serving (half-and-half)

Good source of niacin, iron

³/₄ cup walnuts, finely chopped	*1 teaspoon chicken-flavor instant bouillon*
³/₄ teaspoon salt	*¹/₂ cup heavy or whipping cream or half-and-half*
1 egg	
¹/₈ teaspoon pepper	*1 tablespoon all-purpose flour*
water	
2 whole large chicken breasts	*2 teaspoons Dijon mustard parsley sprigs for garnish*

1. Toast walnuts: In small bowl, place walnuts. Cook at HIGH (100% power) 5 to 5¹/₂ minutes, stirring every minute, until lightly browned. Stir in salt and set aside.
2. In pie plate, beat egg, pepper, and 1 tablespoon water until blended.
3. Cut each chicken breast in half; remove skin and bones. Dip chicken-breast halves into egg mixture, then coat with toasted walnuts. Place chicken-breast halves on rack in 13″ by 9″ baking dish.
4. In cup, combine chicken bouillon and ¹/₂ cup water. Pour into baking dish around chicken; cover dish with waxed paper. Cook at HIGH 7 to 10 minutes, until chicken is firm, opaque, and fork-tender, rotating dish a half turn after 5 minutes. Remove chicken to warm platter; cover and let stand 5 minutes. Reserve cooking liquid in baking dish.
5. Meanwhile, prepare mustard sauce: In small bowl, mix cream, flour, and mustard until smooth. Stir in reserved cooking liquid from baking dish. Cook at HIGH 2 to 3 minutes, until sauce thickens and is smooth; with wire whisk, stir sauce briskly every minute. Serve sauce with chicken. Garnish with parsley sprigs.

COOKING COMPLETE MEALS
When you cook complete meals in your microwave oven, keep these points in mind:
★ Many hot desserts can be cooked at the last minute or made ahead and reheated just before serving for just-cooked flavor.
★ Prepare soups, gravies, and sauces ahead and reheat.
★ Prepare main dishes which need long standing time first, and cook vegetables while they are standing.
★ If possible, cook vegetables, fish, egg, and cheese dishes just before serving; reheating might overcook them.

Poultry

Sesame Chicken Rolls

Begin 45 mins ahead

4 servings

385 cals per serving

Good source of vitamin A, calcium, iron

$^1/_4$ cup sesame seeds
$^1/_4$ cup dried bread crumbs
2 whole large chicken breasts
salt
pepper
4 thin slices prosciutto
$^1/_2$ 10-ounce package frozen chopped spinach, thawed
1 ounce Muenster cheese, shredded ($^1/_4$ cup)
1 egg

1 tablespoon salad oil
$^1/_2$ cup water
2 tablespoons sugar
2 tablespoons lemon juice
2 teaspoons cornstarch
1 teaspoon soy sauce
1 teaspoon catchup
$^1/_4$ teaspoon grated lemon peel

1. In 1-cup glass measure, combine sesame seeds and dried bread crumbs. Cook at HIGH (100% power) $2^1/_2$ to 3 minutes, stirring after 1 minute, then every 30 seconds, until sesame seeds and bread crumbs are lightly toasted. Set aside.
2. Cut each chicken breast in half; remove skin and bones. With meat mallet or dull edge of French knife, pound each chicken-breast half until $^1/_4$ inch thick; sprinkle lightly with salt and pepper. Cover each chicken piece with 1 slice of prosciutto, folding prosciutto to fit and leaving $^1/_4$-inch border around edge of chicken.
3. Squeeze spinach to remove as much liquid as possible. Arrange spinach evenly over prosciutto layer on chicken pieces. Sprinkle lightly with salt. Top spinach on each chicken piece with 1 tablespoon shredded cheese. Starting at 1 narrow end, tightly roll each chicken piece, jelly-roll fashion.
4. In pie plate, beat egg and salad oil until smooth. Place sesame-seed mixture on sheet of waxed paper. Coat each chicken roll with egg mixture, then roll in sesame-seed mixture.
5. Place chicken rolls on microwave-safe rack set in 12" by 8" baking dish; cover with waxed paper. Cook at MEDIUM HIGH (70% power) 6 to 8 minutes just until chicken is firm and opaque, rotating dish a half turn after 4 minutes. Let dish stand, still covered, 5 minutes.
6. Meanwhile, in small bowl, with fork, mix water, sugar, lemon juice, cornstarch, soy sauce, catchup, grated lemon peel, and $^1/_8$ teaspoon salt. Cook at HIGH 2 to 3 minutes, stirring every minute, until mixture boils and thickens and is smooth. Arrange chicken rolls on warm platter; serve with sauce.

ENHANCING COLOR
Some foods brown in the conventional oven but do not brown when cooked in the microwave. To improve both the colour and flavor of chicken, brush with catchup, Angostura bitters or a browning, Worcestershire, soy, steak, barbecue, or teriyaki sauce. Or, mix butter with herbs or spices such as paprika or chili powder. Brush chicken with browning agent at the start of cooking and, if necessary, again when the food is turned over and once again near the end of cooking.

"Fried" Chicken

Begin 40 mins ahead

4 servings

440 cals per serving

Good source of niacin, iron

8 chicken thighs (about $2^1/_2$ pounds)
5 tablespoons butter or margarine
1 cup finely crushed round buttery crackers

$^1/_2$ teaspoon paprika
$^1/_2$ teaspoon salt
$^1/_4$ teaspoon rosemary, crushed

1. Remove skin and cut away any excess fat from chicken thighs.
2. Place butter or margarine in pie plate; cover with waxed paper. Cook at HIGH (100% power) 1 to $1^1/_2$ minutes until butter melts. On waxed paper, mix crumbs, paprika, salt, and rosemary.
3. Dip chicken thighs in butter or margarine; then coat with cracker-crumb mixture. Arrange coated chicken thighs on microwave-safe rack in 12" by 8" baking dish; cover dish with waxed paper. Cook at HIGH 9 minutes. Remove waxed paper and rotate dish a half turn. Cook at HIGH 5 to 7 minutes longer until thighs are tender. Let thighs stand 5 minutes before serving.

ARRANGING CHICKEN PIECES
Use this rule of thumb for best results when cooking chicken pieces. Arrange pieces with meatier portions such as breasts and thighs toward edge of cooking dish and smaller pieces like legs and wing tips toward center.

Broccoli-stuffed Chicken Breasts

Begin 30 mins ahead

6 servings

300 cals per serving

Good source of vitamin C, vitamin A, niacin, calcium, iron

1 10-ounce package frozen chopped broccoli, cooked
2 green onions, minced
1 cup shredded Monterey Jack cheese
3 whole large chicken breasts, boned, halved and skinned
3 1-ounce slices cooked ham, cut into halves

1 cup soft bread crumbs
1 tablespoon minced parsley
$^1/_2$ teaspoon paprika
butter or margarine
1 tablespoon all-purpose flour
$^1/_4$ teaspoon salt
$^1/_8$ teaspoon pepper
1 cup milk

1. Drain broccoli well; combine with green onions and $^1/_2$ cup cheese.
2. Pound each chicken-breast half to $^1/_4$-inch thickness. Top each with a piece of ham and $^1/_6$ of broccoli mixture. Fold chicken in half over filling; tuck ends under.
3. Mix bread crumbs, parsley, and paprika. Melt 1 tablespoon butter or margarine at HIGH (100% power) 45 seconds; brush over chicken, coat with crumbs. In 13" by 9" dish, place chicken; cover with waxed paper. Cook at HIGH 10 to 12 minutes, rotating once. Let stand, covered, while preparing sauce.
4. In 1-quart bowl, melt 2 tablespoons butter or margarine at HIGH 45 seconds; stir in flour, salt, and pepper. Add milk and cook at HIGH $3^1/_2$ minutes just until boiling, stirring twice. Whisk in remaining cheese. Serve with chicken.

Vegetables

Savory Stuffed Cornish Hens

Begin 40 mins ahead

2 servings

750 cals per serving

Good source of vitamin A, niacin, iron

1/4 pound small mushrooms, sliced
butter or margarine
1/2 cup shredded zucchini
2 ounces shredded Swiss cheese (1/2 cup)
1 green onion, chopped
1/4 teaspoon salt
1/8 teaspoon pepper
1 cup cooked rice
2 1 1/4-pound Cornish hens
3/4 cup herb-seasoned croutons or stuffing mix, finely crushed
1 1/2 teaspoons paprika

1. In 1 1/2-quart casserole, place mushrooms and 1 tablespoon butter; cook at HIGH (100% power) 2 to 2 1/2 minutes, stirring once. Add zucchini, cheese, green onion, salt, pepper, and cooked rice; stir.
2. Fill each Cornish-hen cavity with half of stuffing mixture. Tie legs and tail of each hen with kitchen string. Melt 1 tablespoon butter at HIGH 30 seconds; brush on hens.
3. On waxed paper, combine crushed herb-seasoned croutons and paprika; coat hens. On microwave-safe rack set in 12" by 8" baking dish, place hens; cover with waxed paper. Cook at HIGH 14 to 16 minutes, until juices run clear, rotating dish once during cooking. Let stand 5 minutes, covered. Remove string from hens.

Honey-basted Duckling

Begin 1 1/4 hrs ahead

4 servings

900 cals per serving

Good source of riboflavin, niacin, iron

1 5-pound fresh or frozen (thawed) duckling
1/4 cup honey
1/4 cup packed dark-brown sugar
2 tablespoons apricot- or apple-flavor brandy or dry sherry
2 teaspoons salt
1/4 teaspoon ground cinnamon
1/8 teaspoon ground cloves
1 tablespoon water
1 1/2 teaspoons cornstarch
1 red apple, cut into wedges, for garnish
watercress or parsley sprigs for garnish

1. Remove giblets and neck from duckling. With sharp knife and kitchen shears, cut duckling into quarters. Trim excess skin and discard fat from duckling pieces. Rinse duckling pieces with running cold water; pat dry with paper towels.
2. In 3" by 9" baking dish, combine honey, brown sugar, brandy, salt, cinnamon, and cloves. Add duckling, turning to coat well.
3. Arrange duckling pieces, skin side down, in baking dish; cover tightly with vented plastic wrap. Cook at MEDIUM HIGH (70% power) 20 minutes. Uncover; turn duckling skin side up, and spoon some honey mixture in baking dish over duckling. Cook, uncovered, at MEDIUM HIGH 20 minutes, or until fork-tender, turning duckling and spooning honey mixture over duckling every 5 minutes.
4. Arrange duckling quarters on platter. With sieve, strain honey mixture into a 4-cup glass measuring cup; spoon off fat. In small bowl, blend water and cornstarch; stir into honey mixture. Cook at HIGH (100% power) 1 1/2 to 2 minutes, stirring once, until sauce thickens and boils.
5. To serve, garnish duckling with apple wedges and watercress sprigs. Serve sauce with duckling.

Asparagus with Mushroom Sauce

Begin 50 mins ahead

6 accompaniment servings

125 cals per serving

Good source of calcium

1/8 teaspoon paprika
butter or margarine
1/3 cup fresh bread crumbs
1/2 cup sliced small mushrooms
1/4 teaspoon salt
1/2 cup milk
2 ounces Swiss cheese, shredded (1/2 cup)
1 1/2 pounds asparagus
1/2 cup water

1. In small bowl, place paprika and 1 tablespoon butter or margarine; cover with large plate. Cook at HIGH (100% power) 30 seconds or until butter melts. Stir in bread crumbs.
2. Prepare sauce: In another small bowl, place mushrooms, salt, and 2 tablespoons butter or margarine; cover with large plate. Cook at HIGH 4 minutes or until mushrooms are tender, stirring after 2 minutes. Gradually stir in milk. Cover and cook at HIGH 3 minutes or until sauce is very hot, stirring after 2 minutes. Stir in cheese until melted. Cover and keep warm.
3. In 13" by 9" baking dish, arrange asparagus, placing tips of asparagus in center of dish, overlapping if necessary, and large ends of stalks at each end of dish. Add water; cover tightly with vented plastic wrap. Cook at HIGH 10 to 12 minutes, until asparagus is tender-crisp; drain.
4. To serve, arrange asparagus on large plate; pour mushroom sauce over asparagus; top with buttered bread crumbs.

Mixed Company Vegetables

Begin 30 mins ahead

8 accompaniment servings

110 cals per serving

Low in cholesterol

Good source of vitamin C

4 green onions, cut into 1-inch pieces
3 tablespoons salad oil
1/4 teaspoon crushed red pepper
2 tablespoons soy sauce
1 pound carrots, diagonally sliced 1/4 inch thick
1/4 cup water
1 bunch broccoli, cut into 2" by 1" pieces
1/2 pound medium-sized mushrooms
1 red pepper, cut into slivers

1. In 1-quart bowl, cook green onions, oil, and crushed red pepper at HIGH (100% power) 3 minutes; stir once. Add soy sauce.
2. In 4-quart casserole, place carrots and water. Cover with casserole lid or large plate and cook at HIGH 8 to 10 minutes, until tender-crisp, stirring after 4 to 5 minutes. Add broccoli; cover and cook at HIGH 5 minutes, stirring after 2 1/2 minutes. Add mushrooms; cover and cook at HIGH 5 minutes until vegetables are tender.
3. Drain liquid from vegetables; add soy-sauce mixture and red-pepper slivers; toss.

COVERING VEGETABLES
Plastic wrap is the best choice for covering a dish of vegetables because it wraps tightly, holding in the heat and steam. Vent the wrap by turning back a small corner; this allows steam to escape, preventing the wrap from splitting.

Vegetables

SUMMER-VEGETABLE TIMETABLE

Vegetable	Quantity	Liquid	Cooking time	Power level
Beans, green or wax, whole	1/2 pound	1/4 cup water	4 to 5 mins (covered)	HIGH
Beets, sliced	1/2 pound	2 tablespoons water	6 to 7 mins (covered)	HIGH
Carrots, sliced	1/2 pound	2 tablespoons water	6 to 7 mins (covered)	HIGH
Eggplant, cut into 1/2-inch cubes	1/2 pound	2 tablespoons water	10 to 11 mins (covered; stir often)	HIGH
Kohlrabi, sliced	1/2 pound	2 tablespoons water	8 1/2 to 10 mins (covered)	HIGH
Okra, whole	1/2 pound	2 tablespoons water	4 to 5 mins (covered)	HIGH
Peppers, cut into 1/4-inch strips	2 medium	no water required	2 1/2 to 3 mins (covered)	HIGH
Potatoes, cut into 1 1/2-inch chunks	1 pound	1/4 cup water	5 mins (covered)	HIGH
Snow peas	1/2 pound	2 tablespoons water	4 to 5 mins (covered)	HIGH
Yellow summer or zucchini squash, sliced	1/2 pound	no water required	4 to 5 mins (covered)	HIGH

Eggplant Parmesan

Begin 1 hr ahead

6 main-dish servings

340 cals per serving

Good source of vitamin A, calcium, iron

1 16-ounce can tomatoes in tomato puree
1 8-ounce can tomato sauce
2 tablespoons salad oil
1 teaspoon sugar
1/2 teaspoon basil
1/2 teaspoon oregano leaves

1 16-ounce package mozzarella cheese, shredded (4 cups)
1/2 cup fresh bread crumbs (1 slice)
1/4 cup grated Parmesan cheese
1 medium eggplant (about 1 1/2 pounds)

1. In 2-quart casserole or bowl, place tomatoes with their liquid; with spoon, break tomatoes into small pieces. Stir in tomato sauce, salad oil, sugar, basil, and oregano leaves; cover with casserole lid or large plate. Cook at HIGH (100% power) 14 minutes, stirring after 7 minutes, until sauce thickens slightly.
2. Meanwhile, combine mozzarella, bread crumbs, and Parmesan. Cut eggplant crosswise into 1/4-inch-thick slices.
3. In 2 1/2- to 3-quart casserole, spoon 1/2 cup tomato mixture onto bottom of casserole. Cover mixture with one-third of eggplant slices, then one-third of remaining tomato mixture; sprinkle with one-third of cheese mixture. Repeat eggplant, tomato mixture, and cheese-mixture layers twice.
4. Cover with casserole lid or large plate. Cook at MEDIUM HIGH (70% power) 25 minutes or until eggplant is tender when pierced with a fork, rotating casserole one-quarter turn every 10 minutes.

Broccoli with Lemon

Begin 20 mins ahead

5 accompaniment servings

100 cals per serving

Low in cholesterol

Good source of vitamin C, vitamin A

1 medium bunch broccoli
3 tablespoons salad oil
1 garlic clove, cut in half
1/2 teaspoon salt
1 small lemon, cut into wedges

1. Cut broccoli into 2" by 1" pieces. In 3-quart casserole, place salad oil and garlic. Cook at HIGH (100% power) 2 minutes. Add broccoli and salt, stirring to coat broccoli with oil; cover with casserole lid or large plate. Cook at HIGH 6 to 8 minutes, stirring once, until broccoli is tender-crisp.
2. Let broccoli stand, still covered, 5 minutes. Discard garlic. Serve broccoli with lemon.

Party Brussels Sprouts

Begin 20 mins ahead

6 accompaniment servings

95 cals per serving

Good source of vitamin C

2 slices bacon
1 pound small white onions
1/4 cup water
2 10-ounce packages frozen Brussels sprouts
1 chicken-flavor bouillon cube
1/4 teaspoon salt

1. In 3-quart casserole, place bacon; cook at HIGH (100% power) 2 to 3 minutes, until browned. Drain on paper towels.
2. To drippings in casserole, add onions and water; cover with lid or large plate. Cook at HIGH 4 minutes. Add remaining ingredients; cover and cook at HIGH 10 to 12 minutes until tender, stirring occasionally. Crumble bacon and add to vegetables; toss.

Potatoes au Gratin

Begin 35 mins ahead

8 accompaniment servings

235 cals per serving

Low in cholesterol

4 tablespoons butter
1 small onion, minced
1/4 cup dried bread crumbs
3/4 teaspoon salt
1/4 teaspoon pepper
1/4 teaspoon paprika
3 pounds all-purpose potatoes, peeled if desired

1/4 cup water
1/2 cup shredded Fontina or Cheddar cheese
parsley sprigs for garnish (optional)

1. In 10-inch round dish, place butter and onion; cook at HIGH (100% power) 3 minutes until tender, stirring once. Remove onion mixture to small bowl; stir in bread crumbs, salt, pepper, and paprika.
2. Slice potatoes about 1/8 inch thick. Arrange potatoes in rows, overlapping rows if necessary, in same dish; add water. Cover and cook at HIGH 13 to 15 minutes until potatoes are tender, rotating dish once. Discard water.
3. Sprinkle potatoes evenly with cheese, then with bread-crumb mixture. Cook, uncovered, 1 1/2 minutes at HIGH or until cheese melts; garnish.

FOR FOUR SERVINGS: Prepare as above, but use half the amounts of all ingredients. In 9-inch round baking dish, cook potatoes, covered, 8 to 10 minutes. Cook topping as above.

BAKING POTATOES: Microwave-baked potatoes taste good and take very little time to cook. Pierce potato and place on a paper towel in the microwave. One medium potato takes about 4 to 5 minutes at HIGH (100% power); two take 6 to 7 minutes. When potatoes are done, remove from the oven and wrap in aluminum foil; the potatoes will stay hot for up to 30 minutes.

Green Beans and Potatoes

Begin 35 mins ahead

6 accompaniment servings

100 cals per serving

Low in cholesterol

3 tablespoons butter or margarine
1 pound green beans, cut into 2-inch pieces
2 small potatoes, peeled and cut into 1/2-inch cubes

1/4 cup water
1/2 teaspoon salt
1/4 teaspoon rubbed sage

In 2-quart casserole or bowl, place butter or margarine; cover with casserole lid or large plate. Cook at HIGH (100% power) 1 minute or until butter melts. Add green beans, potatoes, water, salt, and sage. Cover casserole and cook at HIGH 12 to 14 minutes, stirring every 5 minutes, until beans and potatoes are tender.

GARNISHING VEGETABLES
Make cooked vegetables "amandine" by topping with toasted almonds. Place 2 tablespoons sliced almonds in a 10-ounce custard cup. Cook, uncovered, at HIGH (100% power) 3 minutes or until browned, stirring once after 1 1/2 minutes. Add to vegetables.

Individual Corn Custards

Begin 35 mins ahead

4 accompaniment servings

195 cals per serving

1 8³/4-ounce can cream-style corn
3/4 cup half-and-half
1 tablespoon butter or margarine

1/2 teaspoon salt
1/8 teaspoon pepper
3 eggs
paprika

1. Grease four 6-ounce custard cups; set aside.
2. In small bowl, combine corn, half-and-half, butter or margarine, salt, and pepper. Cover bowl with large plate. Cook at MEDIUM (50% power) 6 minutes or until hot, stirring once.
3. In 4-cup glass measuring cup, beat eggs until blended. Beating eggs rapidly, gradually beat in the hot corn mixture.
4. Pour corn mixture into prepared custard cups. Place custard cups on large plate; cover with waxed paper. Cook at MEDIUM LOW (30% power) 8 to 10 minutes, just until custards are set, rotating plate a half turn after 5 minutes. Let custards stand, still covered, 5 minutes. Sprinkle with paprika.

COOKING CORN-ON-THE-COB: To cook corn-on-the-cob, pull back the husks on each ear, remove silk, then pull husks up over corn. On paper towel on oven bottom, arrange corn like spokes, placing one end in center, other end out. Cook at HIGH (100% power). Rotate ears on their side and turn so other end is at center after half this cooking time – 2 1/2 to 3 minutes for 1 ear, 4 to 6 minutes for 2 ears, 10 to 12 minutes for 4 ears, 12 to 14 minutes for 6 ears. Let stand 3 to 5 minutes before serving.
Or, husk the corn, remove the silk, and rinse and wrap each ear in plastic wrap. Cook at HIGH 3 to 4 minutes for 1 ear, 5 to 6 minutes for 2 ears and 9 to 10 minutes for 4 ears; turn once.

Mushrooms in Lemon Butter

Begin 20 mins ahead

4 accompaniment servings

140 cals per serving

Good source of riboflavin

4 tablespoons butter or margarine
1 pound small mushrooms
1/2 teaspoon salt
1/8 teaspoon pepper
1 teaspoon cornstarch or 2 teaspoons all-purpose flour

1 tablespoon half-and-half or milk
2 teaspoons chopped parsley
1 teaspoon chopped chives
1/2 teaspoon lemon juice
grated lemon peel for garnish

1. In 2-quart casserole or bowl, place butter or margarine; cover with casserole lid or large plate. Cook at HIGH (100% power) 1 1/2 minutes or until butter melts. Add mushrooms, salt, and pepper, stir to coat mushrooms with melted butter. Cover and cook at HIGH 5 to 7 minutes, stirring once until mushrooms are tender.
2. In small bowl, blend cornstarch and half-and-half until smooth; stir into mushroom mixture until blended. Cook at HIGH 1 to 2 minutes, until sauce thickens. Stir in parsley, chives, and lemon juice. Sprinkle with grated lemon peel.

Vegetables

Sauces

Gratin of Fennel

Begin 30 mins ahead

4 accompaniment servings

200 cals per serving

2 medium fennel bulbs
(about 1 pound)
1 cup water
1/2 cup heavy or whipping
cream
1/4 teaspoon salt

2 tablespoons butter or
margarine
1/3 cup coarsely crushed
saltine crackers
1/4 teaspoon paprika

1. Cut off root end and tough stalks from each fennel bulb. Cut each bulb lengthwise in half; then slice into 1/4-inch thick strips.
2. In 3-quart bowl, combine fennel and water; cover with large plate. Cook at HIGH (100% power) 10 to 12 minutes, stirring every 3 minutes, until fennel is almost tender; drain well.
3. In 1-quart casserole, combine heavy or whipping cream and salt. Stir in fennel until well coated with cream mixture.
4. In small bowl, place butter or margarine; cover bowl with waxed paper. Cook at HIGH 1 minute or until butter is melted. Stir in crushed crackers and paprika; sprinkle over fennel.
5. Cook fennel mixture at MEDIUM (50% power) 8 minutes or until fennel is tender.

Garden Vegetables and Pasta Salad

Begin 30 mins ahead

6 main-dish servings

435 cals per serving

Good source of vitamin C, calcium, iron

1/2 16-ounce package
bow-tie macaroni
1/3 cup cider vinegar
1/4 cup olive or salad oil
1 teaspoon oregano
1 teaspoon salt
1/4 teaspoon crushed
red pepper
6 green onions, minced
1/4 pound green beans
3 medium carrots, sliced
1/4 cup water

1 bunch broccoli, cut into
2" by 1 1/2" pieces
1 medium zucchini,
sliced 1/2-inch thick
1 medium yellow
straightneck squash,
sliced 1/2-inch thick
1/4 pound sharp Cheddar
cheese, cubed
1/4 pound Swiss cheese,
cubed
1/2 pint cherry tomatoes

1. Prepare macaroni conventionally as label directs; drain and set aside.
2. In large bowl, mix vinegar, oil, oregano, salt, crushed red pepper, and green onions.
3. In 12" by 8" baking dish, combine green beans, carrots, and water; cover and cook at HIGH (100% power) 6 to 8 minutes, stirring once. With slotted spoon, remove to bowl with dressing. Add broccoli to baking dish; cover and cook at HIGH 6 to 7 minutes, stirring once. Remove to bowl as above. Add zucchini and squash to baking dish; cover and cook at HIGH 3 to 4 minutes, stirring once. Remove to bowl. Add macaroni, cheese, and tomatoes to vegetable mixture in bowl; toss gently.

REHEATING PASTA
Pasta reheats successfully in the microwave, retaining its tenderness and flavor. To reheat a single serving, place on a microwave-safe dinner plate; cover with plastic wrap. Cook at MEDIUM HIGH (70% power) about 2 minutes or until bottom of plate is warm and food is steaming.

All-purpose Barbecue Sauce

Begin 25 mins or up to 3 days ahead

2 1/4 cups

80 cals per 1/4 cup

Low in cholesterol

1 small onion, minced
2 tablespoons salad oil
1 tablespoon chili powder
1 8-ounce can crushed
pineapple in juice
1 8-ounce can tomato
sauce

1/4 cup packed brown
sugar
2 tablespoons cider
vinegar
1 3/4 teaspoons salt
1/4 teaspoon hot-pepper
sauce

1. In 2-quart casserole, combine onion and salad oil; cover with casserole lid or large plate and cook at HIGH (100% power) 3 minutes or until onion is tender, stirring once. Stir in chili powder; cover and cook at HIGH 1 minute.
2. To casserole, add crushed pineapple with its juice, tomato sauce, brown sugar, vinegar, salt, and hot pepper sauce. Cover and cook at HIGH 5 minutes; stir well. Cover and cook at MEDIUM (50% power) 10 minutes or until mixture thickens slightly.

Bacon, Mushroom and Pea Sauce

Begin 25 mins ahead

4 main-dish servings

580 cals per serving

Good source of calcium, iron

8 ounces any pasta
4 slices bacon, cut into
1-inch pieces
1/2 pound mushrooms,
each cut in half
2 green onions, sliced
2 tablespoons flour
1 cup half-and-half

1 cup milk
1/2 teaspoon salt
1/4 teaspoon pepper
1 10-ounce package
frozen peas, rinsed with
hot water to thaw
1/2 cup grated Parmesan
cheese

1. Prepare pasta conventionally as label directs; drain. Keep warm.
2. Meanwhile, in 3-quart casserole, cook bacon at HIGH (100% power) 4 minutes, stirring occasionally until crisp; drain on paper towels.
3. Add mushrooms and green onions to casserole. Cook at HIGH 2 minutes. Stir in flour, then add half-and-half, milk, salt, and pepper; cover. Cook at HIGH 8 to 10 minutes until sauce thickens, stirring occasionally. Stir in peas. Cook at HIGH 1 to 2 minutes until peas and sauce are heated. Toss sauce, Parmesan cheese, and bacon with pasta.

Cranberry-Wine Sauce

Begin 15 mins ahead

2 cups

20 cals per tablespoon

Low in sodium, fat, cholesterol

1 1/4 cups cranberries
1/2 cup orange juice
3 tablespoons sugar
3 tablespoons red port wine

1/8 teaspoon salt
1 tablespoon very fine
orange-peel strips

1. In 1-quart measure, cook 1 cup cranberries, orange juice, sugar, wine, and salt at HIGH (100% power) 4 to 6 minutes until cranberries begin to pop, stirring once. In blender, blend cranberry mixture until smooth. Press mixture through sieve to remove skins and seeds.
2. Cook strained cranberry mixture, orange-peel strips, and remaining 1/4 cup cranberries at HIGH 2 to 3 minutes. Serve immediately over poultry or pork.

Microwave Hollandaise

Begin 10 mins ahead

3/4 cup

80 cals per tablespoon

1/2 cup butter or margarine
2 egg yolks
1 tablespoon milk
2 teaspoons lemon juice
1/8 teaspoon salt
dash white pepper

1. In small bowl, place butter or margarine; cover with waxed paper. Cook at HIGH (100% power) 1 1/2 to 2 minutes until butter melts and is bubbly.
2. In another small bowl, with wire whisk, beat remaining ingredients until smooth.
3. With wire whisk, gradually add hot butter to egg-yolk mixture, beating mixture constantly until smooth and thickens slightly.
4. Cook sauce at MEDIUM (50% power) 45 to 60 seconds until it thickens, stirring briskly with wire whisk every 15 seconds. Serve immediately over poached eggs, chicken, fish, or vegetables.

Baby Clam and Shrimp Sauce

Begin 25 mins ahead

4 main-dish servings

390 cals per serving

Good source of calcium, iron

8 ounces any pasta
1 10-ounce can whole baby clams
2 tablespoons olive or salad oil
2 garlic cloves, minced
1 28-ounce can tomatoes
1 tablespoon sherry
1/2 teaspoon salt
1/8 teaspoon ground red pepper
1/2 pound medium shrimp, shelled and deveined
1/4 cup chopped parsley or basil

1. Prepare pasta conventionally as label directs; drain. Keep warm. Drain clams, reserving liquid.
2. In 2 1/2-quart casserole, combine oil and garlic. Cook at HIGH (100% power) 2 minutes, stirring once. Add tomatoes with their liquid, sherry, salt, pepper, and reserved clam liquid; cook at HIGH 10 minutes, stirring twice. Add clams and shrimp; cook at HIGH 2 to 3 minutes until shrimp turn pink. Toss sauce with pasta and parsley.

Double-Cheese Sauce

Begin 20 mins ahead

4 main-dish servings

615 cals per serving

Good source of vitamin C, vitamin A, calcium, iron

8 ounces any pasta
3 medium onions, each cut in half and thinly sliced
2 large red peppers, very thinly sliced
1/4 cup olive or salad oil
4 ounces mozzarella cheese, cut into 1/4-inch cubes
4 ounces Fontina cheese, shredded (1 cup)
1 3 1/2-ounce can pitted ripe olives, drained, each cut in half
1/2 cup loosely packed basil leaves or parsley, chopped
1/2 teaspoon salt
1/4 teaspoon pepper

1. Prepare pasta conventionally as label directs; drain. Keep warm.
2. Meanwhile, in 12" by 8" baking dish, combine onions, red peppers, and oil. Cook at HIGH (100% power) 10 to 12 minutes until vegetables are tender, stirring once.
3. Toss vegetable mixture and remaining ingredients with pasta. Serve immediately.

Chunky Spaghetti Sauce

Begin 50 mins ahead

6 cups sauce or 6 main-dish servings when served over one 16-ounce package spaghetti, cooked

240 cals per cup

Good source of vitamin A, vitamin C, iron

1/2 pound hot or sweet Italian-sausage links
1/2 pound ground beef
1 medium onion, chopped
1 small green pepper, chopped
1 garlic clove, minced
1 28-ounce can tomatoes
1 6-ounce can tomato paste
1 beef-flavor bouillon cube or envelope
1/2 cup water
2 teaspoons sugar
1 1/2 teaspoons salt
1 teaspoon oregano leaves
1/2 teaspoon thyme leaves

1. Remove casing from sausage links.
2. Into 3-quart casserole or bowl, crumble sausage meat and ground beef. Stir in onion, green pepper, and garlic; cover with casserole lid or large plate. Cook at HIGH (100% power) 8 to 10 minutes, stirring to break up meat every 2 minutes, until meat is browned. Spoon off fat.
3. Into meat mixture, stir tomatoes with their liquid and remaining ingredients. Cover; cook at HIGH 15 minutes, stirring after 8 minutes. Stir well, then continue to cook at MEDIUM (50% power) 10 minutes or until sauce thickens.

Fudge Sauce

Begin 20 mins ahead

1 1/2 cups

100 cals per tablespoon

Low in sodium

1 cup sugar
1 cup heavy or whipping cream
2 tablespoons butter or margarine
1 tablespoon light corn syrup
4 squares unsweetened chocolate
1 teaspoon vanilla extract

1. In 2-quart bowl, combine sugar, heavy or whipping cream, butter, corn syrup, and unsweetened chocolate squares. Cook at HIGH (100% power), uncovered, 4 minutes; stir until smooth; continue to cook at HIGH 4 to 5 minutes until sauce thickens.
2. Add vanilla extract; stir vigorously with wire whisk until sauce is smooth and glossy.

Vanilla Custard Sauce

Begin 10 mins ahead

1 1/2 cups

131 cals per 1/4 cup

Low in sodium

1 cup half-and-half
2 tablespoons sugar
1/8 tablespoon salt
4 egg yolks
1 teaspoon vanilla extract

1. In small bowl, combine half-and-half, sugar, and salt. Cook at MEDIUM (50% power) 1 1/2 minutes or until very warm.
2. Meanwhile, in medium bowl, beat egg yolks slightly; gradually beat in half-and-half mixture.
3. Cook at MEDIUM 2 to 3 minutes, stirring briskly every 30 seconds until sauce thickens slightly. Stir in vanilla extract.

STIRRING
Remember to stir sauces and foods such as casseroles from outer edge of the dish – where food cooks first – toward the center of the dish, pushing cooler food at center toward edge.

Desserts

Raspberry-poached Pears with Chocolate-Raspberry Sauce

Begin 5 hrs ahead or early in day

6 servings

300 cals per serving

Low in sodium

1 10-ounce package frozen raspberries in syrup, thawed
1/3 cup sugar
1 tablespoon lemon juice
6 firm large pears (about 3 pounds)
1 tablespoon cornstarch

2 tablespoons water
1 square semisweet chocolate
1/2 cup heavy or whipping cream
1 tablespoon confectioners' sugar

1. In blender or food processor, puree frozen raspberries and their syrup until smooth. Set strainer over 3-quart casserole; pour blended raspberries into strainer. With rubber spatula or kitchen spoon, press raspberry juice and pulp through strainer. Discard seeds. Into raspberry puree, stir sugar and lemon juice.

2. Peel pears, leaving stems intact. With apple corer or melon baller, core pears from blossom ends.

3. Arrange pears in a circle in raspberry mixture in casserole, placing large ends of pears near edge of casserole and stem ends in center. Spoon some raspberry mixture over pears; cover casserole with lid or large plate. Cook at HIGH (100% power) 15 to 20 minutes, turning pears over once, until pears are nearly fork-tender.

4. In cup, mix cornstarch and water. Gently stir cornstarch mixture into raspberry mixture in casserole until blended. Turn pears over again. Cover casserole and continue to cook at HIGH 2 to 5 minutes until raspberry sauce thickens slightly and pears are tender. Refrigerate pears in sauce, covered, at least 3 hours to blend flavors, spooning raspberry sauce over pears occasionally.

5. Just before serving, in small bowl, place 1 cup raspberry sauce from casserole. Cook at HIGH 2 to 3 minutes, until very hot. Add chocolate; let stand a few minutes to melt. Stir sauce briskly until completely smooth.

6. Meanwhile, in small bowl, with mixer at medium speed, beat heavy or whipping cream and confectioners' sugar until soft peaks form.

7. To serve, pour chocolate mixture onto 6 dessert plates. Spoon some raspberry sauce over pears to glaze, then arrange a glazed pear on each of the plates. (Refrigerate any remaining raspberry sauce to serve over ice cream another day.) Garnish each pear with whipped cream.

CARAMELIZING SUGAR

Sugar continues to cook after it is removed from the oven, so cook only until a rich golden shade; let deeper color develop outside of the oven. An oven-safe glass measure or batter bowl with a handle is best for caramelizing sugar or cooking sugar syrups. The handle makes it easy to lift and pour while the glass can withstand the high cooking heat. To prevent boilovers, use a measure that holds double the volume of ingredients.

Caramel Pears in Strawberry Sauce

Begin 1 1/4 hrs ahead or early in day

6 servings

250 cals per serving

Low in sodium

6 large pears (about 3 pounds)
2 tablespoons lemon juice
water
1 10-ounce package frozen strawberries or raspberries in syrup, thawed

1/3 cup sugar
3 tablespoons heavy cream

1. Peel pears. With apple corer, remove cores from bottoms of pears, but do not remove stems. Cut thin slice off bottom of each pear to flatten. If desired, with stripper or tines of fork, cut spiral stripes into pears. Brush with lemon juice.

2. Arrange pears, bottoms down, in baking dish; add 1/4 cup water. Cover with plastic wrap; cook at HIGH (100% power) 12 to 14 minutes until tender, rotating dish once.

3. In blender, blend strawberries with their syrup until smooth. Press strawberry mixture through sieve to remove seeds.

4. In 1-quart glass measure, combine sugar and 1 tablespoon water. Cook at HIGH 2 to 4 minutes, without stirring, until sugar turns a light golden color. Gradually add heavy cream, stirring constantly. Cook at HIGH 1 minute; stir. Let stand 2 to 3 minutes; then stir until smooth.

5. Spoon strawberry sauce onto serving platter. Arrange pears in sauce. Spoon caramel over pears. To serve chilled, follow recipe steps 1 through 4. Refrigerate pears, sauce, and caramel. Reheat caramel; drizzle on pears just before serving.

Chocolate-Cinnamon Bread Pudding

Begin 50 mins ahead

10 servings

280 cals per serving

Low in sodium

Good source of calcium

12 slices cinnamon bread
3 squares semisweet chocolate, melted
2 cups half-and-half
1 cup milk

4 eggs
3/4 cup sugar
1 1/2 teaspoons vanilla extract

1. Remove crusts from bread. Cut each bread slice diagonally in half to form triangles. Arrange half of bread triangles in single layer, overlapping if necessary, in shallow 2-quart baking dish. Drizzle with half of chocolate. Top with remaining bread slices, arranging as above.

2. In 1-quart glass measure, combine half-and-half and milk. Cover and cook at HIGH (100% power) 4 to 6 minutes until small bubbles form at edge of cup.

3. Meanwhile, in 2-quart glass measure, beat eggs, sugar, and vanilla extract. In a thin stream, add hot liquid to egg mixture, stirring constantly. Gradually pour egg mixture over bread. Drizzle with remaining chocolate.

4. Place baking dish on microwave-safe rack; cook at MEDIUM (50% power) 14 to 16 minutes until knife inserted 1 inch from edge comes out clean, rotating dish twice. Serve warm or chilled.

Summer Fruit Tart

Begin 3 hrs ahead or early in day

8 servings

375 cals per serving

Good source of vitamin C, vitamin A, calcium

6 tablespoons butter
3 tablespoons dark brown sugar
1¼ cups vanilla-wafer crumbs
½ cup sugar
2 tablespoons cornstarch
¼ teaspoon salt
2 cups half-and-half
3 egg yolks

1½ teaspoons vanilla
¼ cup apple jelly
1 tablespoon water
1 pint strawberries
½ pint raspberries
1 kiwi fruit, peeled, sliced
½ pint blueberries

1. In 9-inch pie plate, combine butter and brown sugar; cook at HIGH (100% power) 1½ minutes until melted, stirring once. Stir in cookie crumbs; press mixture onto bottom and up side of pie plate. Cook at HIGH 1 minute; cool.
2. Meanwhile, in 1-quart bowl, combine sugar, cornstarch, and salt; whisk in half-and-half and egg yolks. Cook at HIGH 5 to 6 minutes until thickened, stirring occasionally. Add vanilla; beat until smooth. Pour into crumb-lined pie plate. Press plastic wrap directly onto surface of custard. (This will prevent a skin from forming on the surface of the custard.) Refrigerate 2 hours or until set. Discard plastic wrap.
3. In a small bowl, combine apple jelly and water; cook at HIGH 1½ to 2 minutes until melted. Arrange fruit on pie; brush with jelly mixture.

Blueberry Cobbler

Begin 25 mins ahead

4 servings

330 cals per serving

Low in sodium

¼ cup sugar
¼ cup orange juice
2 tablespoons cornstarch
⅛ teaspoon salt
1 pint blueberries
1½ cups coarsely broken pecan shortbread cookies

1 tablespoon brown sugar
1 tablespoon butter or margarine, softened
½ teaspoon ground cinnamon
1 pint vanilla ice cream (optional)

1. In 1½-quart casserole or bowl, mix sugar, orange juice, cornstarch, and salt; stir in blueberries. Cook at HIGH (100% power) 6 to 7 minutes, stirring after 3 minutes, until blueberries pop and mixture thickens slightly.
2. In small bowl, mix broken cookies, brown sugar, butter or margarine, and cinnamon. Sprinkle over blueberry mixture.
3. Cook, uncovered, at MEDIUM (50% power) 2 minutes or until topping is heated. Serve warm, topped with ice cream if you like.

MAKING CRUMB CRUSTS
In a 9-inch glass pie plate, melt 4 tablespoons butter at HIGH (100% power) 1 minute; add 1¼ cups crumbs (graham cracker, chocolate wafer, or vanilla cookie); stir to coat with butter. With a kitchen spoon or finger tips, press evenly onto plate; cook at HIGH 2 minutes. For extra special crusts, add finely ground nuts and a dash of cinnamon or nutmeg to the crumbs.

Berries in Custard Sauce

Begin 2 hrs ahead or early in day

6 servings

145 cals per serving

Low in sodium

Good source of vitamin C

1 cup half-and-half
2 tablespoons sugar
⅛ teaspoon salt
2 egg yolks
1 tablespoon orange-flavor liqueur

½ teaspoon vanilla extract
½ square semisweet chocolate, chopped (½ ounce)
2 pints strawberries

1. In 1-quart bowl, cook half-and-half, sugar, and salt at HIGH (100% power) 3 minutes just until bubbly, stirring once. In medium bowl, beat egg yolks slightly. gradually whisk in half-and-half mixture. Cook at MEDIUM (50% power) 3 minutes or until slightly thickened, whisking twice. Stir in orange-flavor liqueur and vanilla.
2. Set aside ¾ cup sauce. Add chocolate to remaining sauce; stir until melted. Refrigerate both sauces until well chilled.
3. Serve strawberries with some of each sauce.

Apple-Walnut Crisp

Begin 45 mins ahead

8 servings

225 cals per serving

Low in sodium

3 pounds cooking apples
1 tablespoon lemon juice
½ cup walnuts, chopped
½ cup flour
⅓ cup packed dark brown sugar

1 teaspoon cinnamon
½ teaspoon nutmeg
½ teaspoon ginger
4 tablespoons butter, cut into ¼-inch pieces

1. Peel, core, and cut apples into ½-inch-thick slices. Place slices in 1½-quart baking dish; toss with lemon juice to coat.
2. In bowl, mix walnuts, flour, brown sugar, cinnamon, nutmeg and ginger. Add butter; blend with fingertips until mixture resembles coarse crumbs. Sprinkle crumb mixture over apples. Cook at HIGH (100% power) 14 to 16 minutes until apples are tender and topping is crispy. Best served warm.

Fruit Compote

Begin day or up to 2 wks ahead

8 servings

455 cals per serving

Low in fat, cholesterol

Good source of vitamin A, iron

2 11-ounce packages mixed dried fruit
2½ cups hot tap water
2 3-inch-long cinnamon sticks
1 9½-ounce jar preserved kumquats

1½ cups light corn syrup
½ cup orange-flavor liqueur
vanilla ice cream (optional)

1. Remove pits from prunes in packages of mixed dried fruit. In 2½- to 3-quart casserole or bowl, place mixed dried fruit. Add hot tap water and cinnamon sticks. Cover with casserole lid or large plate. Cook at HIGH (100% power) 12 to 15 minutes, stirring every 5 minutes, until fruit is tender. Stir in kumquats with their syrup, corn syrup, and liqueur.
2. Cover casserole and refrigerate at least 24 hours before serving, to blend flavors. Store fruit in refrigerator to use up within 2 weeks.
3. Serve the fruit compote as is or use as a topping for ice cream or pound cake.

Desserts

Applesauce Spice Cake

Begin 2 hrs
ahead or
early in day

12 servings

405 cals per
serving

Good
source of
iron

2¹/₄ cups all-purpose flour	³/₄ cup salad oil
2¹/₂ teaspoons ground cinnamon	3 eggs
2 teaspoons baking soda	1 14¹/₂-ounce jar un-sweetened applesauce
1¹/₄ teaspoons salt	¹/₂ cup walnuts, chopped
¹/₄ teaspoon ground cloves	¹/₄ cup dark seedless raisins, chopped
1³/₄ cups packed brown sugar	confectioners' sugar

1. Grease a 13- to 15-cup fluted tube dish.
2. In small bowl, combine flour, ground cinnamon, baking soda, salt, and ground cloves.
3. In large bowl, with mixer at low speed, beat brown sugar, salad oil, and eggs just until blended. Increase speed to high; beat until mixture is light and fluffy, occasionally scraping bowl with rubber spatula. Reduce speed to low; beat in applesauce, then flour mixture, beating just until blended. With rubber spatula, stir in walnuts and raisins.
4. Pour batter into prepared dish; cover dish with waxed paper. Cook at MEDIUM LOW (30% power) 10 minutes, then at HIGH (100% power) 9 to 10 minutes, rotating dish a quarter turn every 5 minutes, until toothpick inserted in center of cake comes out clean.
5. Let cake stand 15 minutes, uncovered, in dish set directly on heat-safe surface. Loosen sides of cake from dish; invert cake onto cake plate. Let cake stand until cool. Sprinkle cake lightly with confectioners' sugar.

Microwave Carrot Cake

Begin 2 hrs
ahead or
early in day

12 servings

370 cals per
serving

Good
source of
vitamin A,
iron

2 cups all-purpose flour	3 eggs
1 teaspoon baking powder	1 8-ounce can crushed pineapple in juice
1 teaspoon baking soda	1¹/₂ cups shredded carrots (about 3 large carrots)
1 teaspoon ground cinnamon	¹/₂ cup walnuts, chopped
1 teaspoon salt	1 teaspoon grated orange peel
1¹/₂ cups packed brown sugar	
³/₄ cup salad oil	

1. Grease a 13- to 15-cup fluted tube dish.
2. In a small bowl, combine flour, baking powder, baking soda, ground cinnamon, and salt; set aside.
3. In large bowl, with mixer at low speed, beat brown sugar, salad oil, and eggs until blended. Increase speed to high; beat mixture until light and fluffy. Reduce speed to low; gradually beat in flour mixture just until well mixed. With rubber spatula, stir in crushed pineapple and its juice, carrots, walnuts, and orange peel just until mixed.
4. Pour batter into prepared dish; cover dish with waxed paper. Cook at MEDIUM LOW (30% power) 10 minutes, then at HIGH (100% power) 10 minutes, rotating dish a quarter turn every 5 minutes, until toothpick inserted in center of cake comes out clean.
5. Let cake stand 15 minutes, uncovered, in dish set directly on heat-safe surface or board. Loosen side of cake from dish; invert cake from dish onto cake plate. Let stand until cool.

Chocolate Mousse Torte

Begin early
in day

16 servings

290 cals per
serving

Low in
sodium

1¹/₃ cups milk	vegetable cooking spray
¹/₄ teaspoon salt	1 cup chopped nuts
1 envelope unflavored gelatin	2 tablespoons butter
sugar	2 cups heavy cream
4 eggs, separated	Chocolate Rounds (optional)
8 squares semisweet chocolate	

1. In 1-quart bowl, stir milk, salt, gelatin, and ¹/₃ cup sugar; let stand 1 minute; stir. Cook at HIGH (100% power) 3 minutes; stir once. In 4-quart bowl, whisk hot-milk mixture into egg yolks. Cook at MEDIUM (50% power) 4 minutes or until slightly thickened; stir in 6 squares chocolate until smooth; chill 20 minutes or until lukewarm.
2. Meanwhile, spray 9″ by 3″ springform pan with vegetable cooking spray. Reserve 1 tablespoon nuts. Melt 2 squares chocolate and butter at HIGH 1¹/₂ minutes; stir in remaining nuts; spread mixture on bottom of pan. Freeze 15 minutes.
3. Beat egg whites and ¹/₄ cup sugar to stiff peaks. Beat 1¹/₄ cups cream to soft peaks; fold into chocolate mixture; pour over crust in pan. Refrigerate 3 hours or until set.
4. Remove side of springform pan. Whip remaining cream; pipe onto torte; sprinkle with reserved nuts. If you like, garnish with Chocolate Rounds.

Begin 30
mins ahead
or early in
day

12 2-inch
rounds

CHOCOLATE ROUNDS: Melt *2 squares semisweet chocolate* with *1 tablespoon shortening* at HIGH 1¹/₂ minutes, stirring once. Remove from oven and stir until smooth; drop by teaspoonfuls onto waxed-paper-lined cookie sheet. Refrigerate 15 minutes or until set.

Candy

Holiday Mints

Begin early
in day or
day ahead

36 mints

70 cals each

3 cups sugar
3 tablespoons light
   corn syrup
water

1 teaspoon peppermint
   extract
red or green food color

1. Prepare fondant: In 2-quart bowl, cook sugar, corn syrup, and $^3/_4$ cup water at HIGH (100% power) 7 to 8 minutes, until sugar is completely dissolved, stirring twice. Set microwave candy thermometer in place. Without stirring, cook at HIGH 5 to 6 minutes, until temperature reaches 240°F. (or until small amount of syrup dropped into cold water forms a soft ball which flattens on removal from water).
2. Without scraping sides, pour mixture into $15^1/_2$" by $10^1/_2$" jelly-roll pan. Let stand until temperature cools to 120°F.
3. With wide stiff metal spatula (pastry scraper or clean, wide putty knife) push mixture to one end of pan, fold over, then spread out to $^1/_4$ inch thickness. Repeat pushing, folding and spreading until mixture turns white and clay-like. Knead to form a ball. Store tightly covered until ready to use. Fondant can be prepared up to 1 week ahead.
4. Crumble fondant into 2-quart bowl; add extract, 2 drops red or green food color, and 2 teaspoons water. Cook at HIGH $1^1/_2$ minutes; stir once. Stir until smooth.
5. Working quickly, spoon mixture by teaspoonfuls onto waxed paper-lined cookie sheets. If fondant becomes too hard and thick, add a few drops water, and melt at HIGH 20 to 30 seconds.

Chocolate Coconut Dessert Cups

Begin 35
mins ahead
or early in
day

6 servings

260 cals per
serving

$^1/_2$ 6-ounce package
   semisweet-chocolate
   pieces ($^1/_2$ cup)
2 teaspoons shortening
1 cup flaked coconut

1 pint ice cream
Chocolate-Dipped Fruit
   for garnish (optional)

1. Place fluted paper or foil baking cup in each of six $2^1/_2$-inch muffin-pan cups. In 1-quart bowl, place chocolate pieces and shortening. Cook at HIGH (100% power) $1^1/_2$ to 2 minutes; stir until melted and smooth. Stir in coconut. Spoon generous tablespoonful chocolate mixture into each cup; press mixture onto bottoms and up sides of paper liners. Freeze 10 minutes or until firm.
2. Peel paper from chocolate cups. Scoop some ice cream into each. If you like, top with Chocolate-Dipped Fruit (see below).

CHOCOLATE-DIPPED FRUIT
Melt $^1/_4$ cup semisweet-chocolate pieces with 1 teaspoon shortening at HIGH (100% power) $1^1/_2$ minutes. Stir until smooth and dip fruits such as strawberries, cherries, grapes, and clementine sections halfway up in chocolate. Arrange on waxed paper, refrigerate 20 minutes or until set.

Maple-Walnut Drops

Begin 2 hrs
ahead or
early in day

42 drops

60 cals each

1 cup light brown sugar
1 cup sugar
$^1/_4$ cup light corn syrup
$^1/_4$ cup water

1 cup walnuts, coarsely
   chopped
1 tablespoon butter
1 teaspoon maple extract

1. In 4-quart bowl, with microwave candy thermometer in place, cook first 4 ingredients at HIGH (100% power) $7^1/_2$ to 8 minutes, until temperature reaches 236°F. (or until small amount of syrup dropped into cold water forms a soft ball which flattens on removal from water).
2. Stir in walnuts, butter, and maple extract. Let stand 2 minutes. Drop by teaspoonfuls onto lightly greased waxed paper-lined cookie sheets. Let stand about 1 hour or until set.

Supereasy Truffles

Begin early
in day

30 truffles

60 cals each

8 squares semisweet
   chocolate
4 tablespoons butter
$^1/_4$ cup heavy or
   whipping cream

$^1/_4$ teaspoon almond
   extract
about 30 small foil candy
   cups (1 inch)

1. In 2-quart bowl, place chocolate and butter. Cook at HIGH (100% power) $1^1/_2$ to 2 minutes; stir once. Stir in cream and almond extract. Set bowl over ice water. With wire whisk, beat chocolate until mixture is fluffy and forms soft peaks.
2. Spoon into pastry bag with medium star tube. Pipe some chocolate mixture into each foil cup. Refrigerate about 1 hour or until set.

AVOIDING BOILOVER
Certain candies require that you use a large bowl for cooking since the ingredients (especially if the recipe has a milk or cream base) tend to increase in volume as they begin to boil.

Pistachio Bites

Begin early
in day

32 pieces

80 cals each

12 ounces white
   chocolate
$^1/_3$ cup heavy or
   whipping cream
1 tablespoon butter

$^3/_4$ teaspoon vanilla
   extract
green food color
2 tablespoons finely
   chopped pistachios

1. Into 2-quart bowl, break white chocolate into small pieces; cook at HIGH 3 to 4 minutes; stir until smooth. Stir in cream and butter until smooth. Divide mixture in half.
2. To one half, add vanilla and enough green food color to tint pale green; spread evenly in foil-lined $8^1/_2$" by $4^1/_2$" loaf pan. Blend nuts into remaining mixture. Spread evenly over green layer. Refrigerate 2 hours or until set.
3. Lift foil and candy from pan; discard foil. Cut candy into 2" by $^1/_2$" pieces. Keep refrigerated until ready to serve.

USEFUL INFORMATION

Healthy eating

Eating a variety of foods in moderation can help you stay healthy. To ensure your diet is well balanced, you should choose foods from the Basic Four Food Groups: *Meat and protein-rich foods*, which include meats, fish, poultry, shellfish, eggs or cheese, dry or canned beans, dry peas and lentils, nuts and peanut butter; *Fruits and vegetables*; *Breads, cereals and pasta* and *Milk and milk products,* which include cheese and yogurt.

Include two servings a day from the Meat group, four a day from Fruits and vegetables. Try to include one serving of citrus fruit or tomatoes and a serving of dark-green leafy or orange vegetable and fruit every other day.

Provide four servings from Bread, cereal or pasta. A serving equals either 1 slice bread, 1 medium potato, 1/2 cup starchy vegetable such as corn or 1/2 cup pasta or rice, or 1/2 cup cooked cereal.

From the Milk group, plan on two servings for adults, three to four for children. One serving equals either an 8-ounce glass of milk, 1 ounce of cheese, 1/2 cup cottage cheese or 1 cup plain yogurt.

Nutritionists also recommend the following guidelines: **Weight** Maintain the ideal weight for your sex, height and age. **Fat** Avoid too much fat, especially saturated fat and cholesterol. Eat eggs and organ meats such as liver in moderation. Limit your intake of butter, cream, hydrogenated margarines, shortenings, coconut or palm oil, and foods containing such products; read labels carefully to check the kinds and amounts of fat contained in foods. Eat lean meat, fish, poultry, and dry beans to obtain enough protein. Trim excess fat from meats and skin from poultry. **Starch and fiber** Eat foods containing adequate amounts of these substances. Fresh fruits, vegetables, beans, peas, whole grain breads, cereals, nuts, and seeds contain many essential nutrients and provide fiber and starch. Substitute starches, such as pasta, for fats and sugars. **Sugar** Avoid too much sugar. Use less of all sugars (including brown and raw sugars, honey and syrups) and cut down on foods containing sugars such as candy, soft drinks, ice cream, cakes, and cookies. Use fruit to satisfy your sweet tooth. **Sodium** Avoid too much sodium. Use only small amounts of salt in cooking, and cut down on table salt. **Alcohol** If you drink alcoholic beverages, do so in moderation since these tend to be high in calories and low in nutrients.

NUTRITION GUIDE

Supplying nutrients and energy are the chief jobs of food. Energy, measured as calories, is supplied by the carbohydrates, proteins and fats in the food you eat. Foods with a high fat content are the richest in calories, whereas foods such as vegetables and fruits, which contain a high percentage of water, are relatively low in calories. Below is a table comparing the calorie, fat, cholesterol and sodium content of a selection of foods from the major food groups.

Food	Amount in ounces (unless otherwise shown)	Cals	Fat (g)	Cholesterol (mg)	Sodium (mg)
MEAT AND POULTRY					
Meat					
Beef (roast rump, lean)	3	177	7.9	82	51
Lamb (roast leg, lean)	3	158	6.0	110	70
Pork (roast leg, lean)	3	189	9.4	80	54
Veal (broiled)	3	184	9.4	90	80
Poultry					
Chicken (roast dark meat, skin removed)	3	151	7.4	64	81
Chicken (roast light meat, skin removed)	3	130	3.5	64	43
Duck (roast, with skin)	3	286	24.1	71	50
Turkey (roast, skin removed)	3	128	2.2	83	57
FISH					
Cod (steamed)	3	71	0.8	60	85
Salmon (steamed)	3	167	11.0	80	94
Scallops (steamed)	3	89	1.2	34	230
Shrimp (boiled)	3	99	0.9	170	1350
DAIRY PRODUCTS					
Butter (1 tablespoon)	1/2	100	11.3	31	116
Cheese					
Brie	2	187	15.5	56	352
Cheddar	2	226	18.6	59	347
cottage, creamed	2	58	2.5	8	227
cream	2	195	19.5	62	166
Edam	2	200	15.6	50	540
Cream, half-and-half	2/3 cup	195	17.3	56	62
Egg (boiled)	1 large	87	6.1	76	301
Milk, whole	2/3 cup	92	5.0	21	74
FRUITS AND VEGETABLES					
Fruits					
Apple (1 medium)	5	80	0.8	0	1.4
Avocado	5	234	23.0	0	5.6
Banana (1 medium)	5	120	0.3	0	1.4
Pineapple (1 slice)	5	73	0.3	0	1.4
Strawberries	5	52	0.7	0	1.4
Vegetables					
Broccoli (boiled)	4	33	0.3	0	12
Cabbage (boiled)	4	24	0.3	0	21
Potato (boiled)	4	97	0.1	0	6
Sweet potato (boiled)	4	119	0.3	0	15
BREAD, PULSES, PASTA AND RICE					
Bread					
white (1 slice)	1	67	0.8	0	127
whole wheat (1 slice)	1	61	0.8	0	132
Lima beans (boiled)	5	172	0.5	0	19
Pasta (boiled)	5	155	0.6	0	1.4
Rice (boiled)	5	153	0.1	0	8.4

Figures taken from *McCance and Widdowson's Composition of Foods* by A.A. Paul and D.A.T. Southgate; *Composition of Foods*, Agricultural Handbook no. 8, U.S. Department of Agriculture

Equivalent amounts

How many cups make a quart? Are three bananas enough to make one cup of mashed? For two table-spoons of grated orange peel, will you need more than one orange? How many cups are there in a pound of flour? These questions are answered below.

EQUIVALENT MEASURES

Dash	2 to 3 drops or less than $\frac{1}{8}$ teaspoon
1 tablespoon	3 teaspoons
$\frac{1}{4}$ cup	4 tablespoons
$\frac{1}{3}$ cup	5 tablespoons plus 1 teaspoon
$\frac{1}{2}$ cup	8 tablespoons
1 cup	16 tablespoons
1 pint	2 cups
1 quart	4 cups
1 gallon	4 quarts
1 peck	8 quarts
1 bushel	4 pecks
1 pound	16 ounces

FOOD EQUIVALENTS

Apples *1 pound*	3 medium (3 cups sliced)
Bananas *1 pound*	3 medium ($1\frac{1}{3}$ cups mashed)
Berries *1 pint*	$1\frac{3}{4}$ cups
Bread *1 1-pound loaf*	14 to 20 slices
Bread crumbs, fresh *1 slice bread with crust*	$\frac{1}{2}$ cup bread crumbs
Broth, chicken or beef *1 cup*	1 bouillon cube or 1 envelope bouillon or 1 teaspoon instant bouillon dissolved in 1 cup boiling water
Butter or margarine *$\frac{1}{4}$-pound stick*	$\frac{1}{2}$ cup
Cheese *$\frac{1}{4}$ pound*	1 cup shredded
Cheese, cottage *8 ounces*	1 cup
Cheese, cream *3 ounces*	6 tablespoons
Chocolate, unsweetened *1 ounce*	1 square
Chocolate, semisweet pieces *1 6-ounce package*	1 cup
Coconut flaked, $3\frac{1}{2}$-ounce can	$1\frac{1}{3}$ cups
shredded, 4-ounce can	$1\frac{1}{3}$ cups
Cream, heavy or whipping *1 cup*	2 cups whipped cream

FOOD EQUIVALENTS (*continued*)

Cream, sour *8 ounces*	1 cup
Egg whites, large *1 cup*	8 to 10 whites
Egg yolks, large *1 cup*	12 to 14 yolks
Flour *1 pound* all-purpose	about $3\frac{1}{2}$ cups
cake	about 4 cups
Gelatin, unflavored *1 envelope*	1 tablespoon
Lemon *1 medium*	3 tablespoons juice, about 1 tablespoon grated peel
Lime *1 medium*	2 tablespoons juice
Milk, evaporated $5\frac{1}{3}$- or 6-ounce can	$\frac{2}{3}$ cup
13- or $14\frac{1}{2}$-ounce can	$1\frac{2}{3}$ cups
Milk, sweetened condensed 14-ounce can	$1\frac{1}{4}$ cups
Nuts *1 pound*	
Almonds, *in shell*	1 to $1\frac{1}{4}$ cups nutmeats
shelled	3 cups
Brazil nuts, *in shell*	$1\frac{1}{2}$ cups nutmeats
shelled	$3\frac{1}{4}$ cups
Filberts, *in shell*	$1\frac{1}{2}$ cups nutmeats
shelled	$3\frac{1}{2}$ cups
Peanuts, *in shell*	2 to $2\frac{1}{2}$ cups nutmeats
shelled	3 cups
Pecans, *in shell*	$2\frac{1}{4}$ cups nutmeats
shelled	4 cups
Walnuts, *in shell*	2 cups nutmeats
shelled	4 cups
Onion *1 large*	$\frac{3}{4}$ to 1 cup chopped
Orange *1 medium*	$\frac{1}{3}$ to $\frac{1}{2}$ cup juice 2 tablespoons grated peel
Potatoes *1 pound* white	3 medium ($2\frac{1}{4}$ cups diced)
sweet	3 medium
Raisins *1 pound*	3 cups, loosely packed
Rice, regular long-grain *1 cup*	3 cups cooked
Salad oil *16 ounces*	2 cups
Sugar *1 pound* granulated	$2\frac{1}{4}$ to $2\frac{1}{2}$ cups
brown	$2\frac{1}{4}$ cups packed
confectioners'	4 to $4\frac{1}{2}$ cups
Syrup corn 16 ounces	2 cups
maple 12 ounces	$1\frac{1}{2}$ cups
Tomatoes *1 pound*	3 medium

Storage guide

CUPBOARD STORAGE

Store foods in your coolest kitchen cabinets – not over the range or near the refrigerator's exhaust. Dry foods do best in airtight containers, which also keep out insects. Choose fresh-looking packages; avoid cans with swollen ends or dents and keep all foods in their original package or in a tightly closed container in a dry spot, unless indicated otherwise. With longer storage than the times recommended here, the flavors will gradually fade and nutrients are eventually lost.

Food	Time	Special Handling
Baking powder, soda	18 months	
Barbecue sauce, catchup, chili sauce	1 month	
Bouillon cubes, powder	1 year	
Cake mixes	1 year	
Canned foods fish fruits, vegetables gravies, sauces meat, poultry milk (both kinds) soups	 1 year 1 year 1 year 1 year 1 year 1 year	Refrigerate after opening. See Refrigerator Storage.
Casserole mixes	18 months	
Cereals ready-to-eat ready-to-cook	 check date on package 6 months	
Chocolate, cooking	1 year	
Coconut	1 year	Refrigerate after opening.
Coffee, vacuum pack	1 year	Refrigerate after opening vacuum pack.
Coffee, instant	6 months	Keep 2 weeks after opening.
Flour all-purpose, cake rye, whole-wheat	 1 year	Keep refrigerated.
Frosting, cans, mixes	8 months	
Fruit, dried	6 months	
Gelatin (both kinds)	18 months	
Herbs, spices whole ground	 1 year 6 months	Keep in cool spot. Replace if aroma fades. Refrigerate red spices.
Honey	1 year	
Jam, jelly	1 year	
Macaroni, spaghetti, pasta	1 year	After opening, transfer to airtight container.

Food	Time	Special Handling
Molasses	2 years	
Nonfat dry milk	6 months	
Olive oil	1 month	For longer storage, refrigerate.
Olives, pickles	1 year	Refrigerate after opening.
Pancake mixes	6 months	
Peanut butter	6 months	Keeps 2 months once open
Piecrust mixes	6 months	
Potato mixes, instant	18 months	
Pudding mixes	1 year	
Rice brown, wild white	 1 year 2 years	
Salad dressings	6 months	Refrigerate after opening.
Salad Oil	3 months	Refrigerate after opening.
Sauce, gravy, soup mixes	6 months	
Shortening, solid	8 months	
Sugar brown, confectioners granulated	 4 months 2 years	
Syrups, corn, maple-flavor, maple	1 year	Refrigerate after opening. Keep maple syrup 1 month after opening.
Tea, bags, loose	6 months	
Tea, instant	1 year	
Vegetables onions, potatoes, rutabagas, squash (hard-shelled), sweet potatoes	1 week at room temperature	For longer storage, keep at 50–60°F. but not refrigerated. Keep dry, out of sun, loosely wrapped.
Yeast, active dry	check date on pack	

PREPARED FOODS

Food	Time	Special Handling
Bread, rolls	3 days	
Bread crumbs	6 months	
Cakes	2 days	If butter-cream, whipped-cream or custard fillings, refrigerate.
Cookies, packaged	4 months	
Crackers	3 months	
Pies, pastries	3 days	Refrigerate cream, custard, chiffon fillings.

REFRIGERATOR STORAGE

Keep your refrigerator temperature between 34° and 40°F; above 40°F. food spoilage happens fast. Except as noted, wrap foods in foil, plastic wrap or bags, or place in airtight containers. This keeps food from drying out and odors from transferring from one food to another. Always keep uncooked meat, fish and poultry in the coldest part of the refrigerator. Fresh fruits and vegetables should be kept in the crisper or loosely closed in moisture-resistant bag or wrap. Except for greens, do not wash before storing. All packaged and prepared foods, all leftovers and dairy products should be kept tightly covered or wrapped in moisture-resistant wrap or foil.

FRESH FRUITS AND VEGETABLES

Food	Time	Special Handling
Fruit		
apples	1 month	May also store at 60-70°F.
apricots, avocados, bananas, melons, nectarines, peaches, pears	5 days	If necessary, allow to ripen at room temperature before refrigerating.
berries, cherries	3 days	
citrus fruit	2 weeks	May also store at 60-70°F.
grapes, plums	5 days	Let ripen at room temperature; then refrigerate.
pineapples	2 days	
Vegetables		
asparagus	3 days	
beets, carrots, parsnips, radishes, turnips	2 weeks	Remove any leafy tops before refrigerating.
broccoli, Brussels sprouts, green onions, soft-skinned squash	5 days	
cabbage, cauliflower, celery, cucumber, eggplant, green beans, peppers,	1 week	
tomatoes		If necessary, ripen tomatoes at room temperature, away from light, before refrigerating.
corn	1 day	Leave in husk.
lettuce, spinach, all leafy greens	5 days	Rinse, drain before refrigerating.
limas, peas	5 days	Leave in shell.

DAIRY PRODUCTS

Food	Time	Special Handling
Butter	2 weeks	
Buttermilk, sour cream, yogurt	2 weeks	
Cheese		
cottage, ricotta	5 days	Cut off mold if it forms on surface of cheese.
cream, Neufchâtel	2 weeks	
sliced cheese	2 weeks	
whole pieces	2 months	
Cream	1 week	

Food	Time	Special Handling
Eggs, in shell	1 month	One week for best flavor.
whites, yolks	4 days	Cover yolks with water.
Margarine	1 month	
Milk whole, skimmed	1 week	Do not return unused milk to original container; this spreads bacteria to remaining milk.

MEAT, FISH, POULTRY BEFORE COOKING

Food	Time	Special Handling
Fresh meat beef, lamb, pork, veal		Leave in plastic wrap. Or if not prepackaged in plastic, wrap loosely in waxed paper so surface can dry slightly.
chops, steaks	5 days	
roasts	5 days	
ground, stew meat	2 days	
sausage, fresh	2 days	
variety meats	2 days	
Processed meats bacon, frankfurters	1 week	Times are for opened packages of sliced meat. Check date on unopened vacuum-packed meat.
ham		
canned (unopened)	6 months	
slices	3 days	
whole	1 week	
luncheon meats	5 days	
sausage, dry, semi-dry	3 weeks	
Fish, shellfish (all kinds)	1 day	Keep wrapped.
Poultry (all kinds) fresh, thawed frozen	2 days	If not in plastic wrap, wrap loosely.

PACKAGED AND PREPARED FOODS – LEFTOVERS OR AFTER OPENING

Food	Time	Special Handling
Cooked or canned foods broths, gravy, soup	2 days	
casseroles, stews	3 days	
fruit, vegetables	3 days	
juices, drinks	6 days	
meat, fish, poultry	2 days	
stuffings	2 days	Remove stuffings from poultry and refrigerate separately.
Cakes, pies: cream, custard	2 days	
Coffee, ground	1 week	After opening.
Flour: rye, whole-wheat	1 year	
Nuts (shelled)	6 months	
Pickles, olives	1 month	
Refrigerated biscuits, cookies, rolls		See expiration date on label.
Salad dressings	3 months	
Salads: potato, coleslaw	2 days	
Wine, table	3 days	
Wine, cooking	3 months	

Storage guide

FREEZER STORAGE

Keep freezer at 0°F. otherwise use food within a week or two. To wrap for storage for one month or more, use moisture-proof materials or specially coated or laminated papers. Properly wrapped and frozen, foods will hold full flavor and nutrients for times listed below; after that, flavors may fade but food is still safe to eat. It's safe to refreeze foods if they still contain ice crystals or have been thawed in the refrigerator and held no more than one or two days. Never refreeze, or eat, any food with off-odor or off-color. Do not freeze eggs in the shell, creamed cottage cheese or cream cheese, or custard pies.

COMMERCIALLY-FROZEN FOODS

Food	Time	Special Handling
Breads baked, dough	3 months	Pick up frozen foods immediately before going to check-out counter. Buy only foods frozen solid and with no dribbles on the package, odor or other signs of being thawed. Put all frozen foods together in one bag so they'll stay as cold as possible for trip home. Store in original wrapping. Place in home freezer as soon as possible. Cook or thaw as label directs.
Cakes angel-food layer cake, frosted pound, yellow cake	2 months 4 months 6 months	
Doughnuts, pastries	3 months	
Fish "fatty" fish – mackerel, trout, etc. "lean" fish – cod, flounder, etc.	3 months 6 months	
Fruit	1 year	
Ice cream, sherbet	1 month	
Juices, drinks	1 year	
Main dishes, pies fish, meat poultry	3 months 6 months	
Meat beef roasts, steaks ground beef lamb, veal roasts, steaks pork chops roasts	1 year 4 months 9 months 4 months 8 months	
Pancake, waffle batter	3 months	
Pies	8 months	
Poultry chicken, turkey parts chicken, turkey (whole) duckling goose turkey rolls, roasts	6 months 1 year 6 months 6 months 6 months	
Shellfish Alaska King crab breaded, cooked lobster, scallops shrimp (unbreaded)	10 months 3 months 3 months 1 year	
Vegetables	8 months	

HOME-FROZEN FOODS

Food	Time	Special Handling
Breads baked unbaked doughs	3 months 1 month	Use only special recipes.
Butter, margarine	9 months	
Cakes, baked	3 months	
Cheese dry-curd cottage cheese, ricotta natural, process	2 weeks 3 months	Cut and wrap cheese in small pieces.
Cookies, baked, dough	3 months	
Cream, heavy whipped	2 months 1 month	Thawed cream may not whip.
Egg whites, yolks	1 year	To each cup yolks, add 1 teaspoon sugar for use in sweet, or 1 teaspoon salt for non-sweet, dishes.
Fish, shellfish "fatty" fish – bluefish, trout, etc. "lean" fish – cod, flounder, etc. shellfish	3 months 6 months 3 months	All fish and shellfish. Wrap tightly in heavy-duty foil or freezer wrap.
Fruit pies	8 months	Freeze baked or unbaked.
Ice cream, sherbet	1 month	
Main dishes, cooked meat, fish poultry	3 months 6 months	Freeze in freezer- and ovenproof baking dishes or freezer containers.
Meat bacon frankfurters ground, stew meat ham leftover cooked roasts beef, lamb roasts pork, veal roasts steaks, chops beef lamb, veal pork variety meats	1 month 2 weeks 3 months 2 months 1 year 8 months 1 year 9 months 4 months 4 months	Keep in vacuum packages. If meat is purchased fresh and wrapped in plastic wrap, check for holes. If none, freeze in this wrap up to 2 weeks. For longer storage overwrap tightly with freezer wrap or heavy-duty foil.
Nuts	3 months	
Poultry cooked, with gravy cooked, no gravy uncooked (whole) chicken, turkey duckling, goose uncooked (parts) chicken turkey	6 months 1 month 1 year 6 months 9 months 6 months	Wrap in heavy-duty foil or freezer wrap as airtight as possible. Thaw uncooked poultry in refrigerator or under cool running water. Cook within two days of thawing.
Vegetables	1 year	

Menu planning and entertaining

Whether you are planning a menu for everyday or elaborate entertaining, choose dishes from the Basic Four Food Groups: *Meat and protein-rich foods*, which include meats, fish, poultry, shellfish, eggs or cheese, dry or canned beans, dry peas and lentils, nuts and peanut butter; *Fruits and vegetables*; *Breads, cereals and pasta* and *Milk and milk products*, which include cheese and yogurt. By choosing from these groups, you will be able to supply the foods needed for good health in a variety of food flavors, colors and textures.

When planning a menu there are four important points to bear in mind: You should consider family nutritional needs, especially in everyday meals, the food preferences of family or guests, your budget and the available preparation time.

Another factor to consider in menu planning is the season of the year: for example, Chilled Cucumber Soup is better suited for summer rather than winter menus, while New England "Boiled" Dinner would be far more suitable for a cold winter's evening meal.

BALANCING THE MENU
The Basic Four Food Groups should be used as your guide. In everyday meal planning, work out a day's three menus all at one time so that the right number of servings from all groups are included.

Include two servings a day from the Meat group, four a day from Fruits and vegetables. Try to include one serving of citrus fruit or tomatoes and a serving of dark-green leafy or orange vegetable and fruit every other day.

Provide four servings from Bread, cereal or pasta. A serving equals either 1 slice bread, 1 medium potato, ½ cup starchy vegetable such as corn or ½ cup pasta or rice, or ½ cup cooked cereal.

From the Milk group, plan on two servings for adults, three to four for children. One serving equals either an 8-ounce glass of milk, 1 ounce of cheese, ½ cup cottage cheese or 1 cup plain yogurt.

CHOOSING THE DISHES
Select the main dish first. It should provide a serving from the Meat and protein-rich food group. Next choose the vegetables. Most menus include one starchy vegetable or one from the Breads, cereals and pasta group and at least one non-starchy vegetable chosen from Fruits and vegetables.

Plan vegetables that are varied in color. For example, serve a green or yellow vegetable with white potatoes or rice. You can also vary vegetable shapes to add interest to the plate.

Choose a salad that will add any needed fruits or vegetables for the day. Select a crunchy vegetable to add texture to an otherwise soft menu. A creamy fruit or molded salad can be served when the main dish is broiled or fried and eaten without sauce or gravy.

Select the dessert to balance the main dish. If the main dish is hearty such as beef stew, serve a light dessert such as sherbet or fruit and cookies. If the main dish is light, a salad or soup, top off the meal with a hearty sweet such as apple pie or chocolate cake.

While bread is not an essential part of any menu, it can supply a contrast to other dishes and provides additional interest when other foods are plain. It can provide a serving from the Breads, cereals and pasta group. If the meal is cold, serve a hot bread; if the meal is soft textured, serve a crisp and crunchy bread. Use bread to supply starch in a menu that does not include such food.

Pickles, olives, butter, jam, relishes and garnishes are little touches that add interest to a meal. Use beverages to round out a menu. Include milk if that has been omitted from the day's meal.

The last step to menu planning is to go over the entire menu once again to be sure that flavors are harmonious, colors are varied and attractive and textures and shapes offer agreeable variety.

PLANNING AHEAD
Occasional spur-of-the-moment entertaining can be fun but things will be easier on the hostess if parties are planned ahead. Make a guest list and send out invitations a week or two in advance for an informal function, two or three weeks ahead for a more formal party.

After you decide on the menu, check that you have all the equipment you need to prepare and serve the foods.

Make out a detailed work order so that as much preparation as possible can be done in advance. If you are going to need help, ask the family or close friends or for the day itself, hire outside help – a maid for serving or a bartender. It is important for the host and hostess to be relaxed – so make sure you have enough help.

Make a detailed shopping list, including items needed for a centerpiece and any decorations. Buy staple foods well ahead, perishables a day or two in advance.

ARRANGING AND SERVING FOOD
If the host and hostess jointly serve the main course, the main dish should be brought in from the kitchen after the appetizer dishes are removed. If there's no appetizer, then the main dish should be on the table covered and ready to serve.

The vegetables should be placed in front of the hostess. If the host is carving, he places a serving on a plate and passes it to his left and it is passed on to the hostess. She serves the vegetables and passes the plate left to be passed on up the table to the person to the right of the host.

After serving all guests and the host, the hostess' own plate is last. She should take a bite of food first to signal that it is time to begin eating. If the party is large, however, she may ask guests to begin ahead. Breads, sauces, condiments may be passed around the table.

If a maid is serving the meal, the hostess is served first then the person to her right and so on around the table. If the host is carving, the maid at his left receives the plate, takes it to the hostess; then the person to the hostess' right is served and on up the table to the host, then the person to the hostess' left and up to the host.

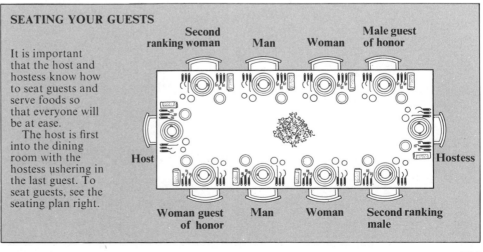

SEATING YOUR GUESTS

It is important that the host and hostess know how to seat guests and serve foods so that everyone will be at ease.

The host is first into the dining room with the hostess ushering in the last guest. To seat guests, see the seating plan right.

Second ranking woman — Man — Woman — Male guest of honor

Host — Hostess

Woman guest of honor — Man — Woman — Second ranking male

Menu planning and entertaining

Brunch

Conveniently timed for late morning, yet early enough to allow for an afternoon of activity, brunch unites the good qualities of lunch and breakfast – it's the ideal way of casually entertaining weekend guests or merely anticipating a quiet day with the Sunday paper. A selection of fresh fruit or a fruit beverage might precede the main dish, while dessert is usually omitted.

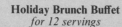

Holiday Brunch Buffet
for 12 servings

Mimosa (orange juice with champagne)
Quiche Lorraine *page 156*
Crab Quiche *page 156*
Colonel's Lady's Salad Bowl *page 318*
Kolacky *page 443*
Coffee served with Crème de Cacao or
Brandy or Whipped Cream

Weekend Brunch
for 4 servings

Chilled Peach Nectar
Eggs Mornay *page 143*
Brown-and-Serve Sausage Links
Pan-fried Apple Wedges *page 300*
Toasted English Muffins
Coffee   Hot Tea

International Brunch
for 8 servings

Company Bloody Mary *page 473*
Orange-Apple Cup with Mint Garnish
Beignets *page 425*
Pan-fried Canadian Bacon
French Hot Chocolate *page 468*

Brunch Before Bridge
for 4 servings

Grapefruit Ambrosia *page 305*
Brunch Eggs Florentine *page 144*
Café au Lait *page 467*

Family Gathering
for 8 servings

Gingered Melon Wedges *page 309*
Chicken à la King *page 268*
Buttered Broccoli Spears
Sour-Cream Coffeecake *page 430*
Tea   Milk   Coffee

Country Brunch
for 8 servings

Pineapple Juice
Buttermilk Waffles *page 427*
(double recipe)
Homemade Sausages *page 243*
Hearty Hot Cocoa *page 468* or Coffee

Quick and Easy
for 6 servings

Cocktail Vegetable Juice
Welsh Rabbit *page 154*
Waldorf Salad *page 322*
Coffee   Hot Tea

Luncheon

A luncheon neither has to be large nor elaborate to be considered a party. A light soup or fruit, optional for first course, could be followed by any of these combinations: a cold salad with hot bread and a rich dessert, or a hot casserole or omelet, plus bread and a light dessert; or a hot main dish with a crisp salad and either a light or a rich dessert.

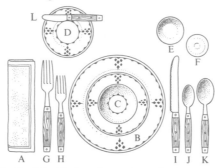

A. *Napkin*; B. *Luncheon plate*; C. *First-course bowl and liner plate*; D. *Bread-and-butter plate*; E. *Water goblet*; F. *Wine glass*; G. *Luncheon fork*; H. *Dessert fork*; I. *Luncheon knife*; J. *Teaspoon*; K. *Soup spoon*; L. *Bread-and-butter knife*

Soup Deluxe
for 10 servings

Bouillabaisse, American Style *page 136*
Sourdough Bread, sliced *page 441*
Tossed Salad with Lemony-Mustard
Dressing *page 318*
Deep-Dish Peach Pie *page 348*
Coffee   Hot Tea

Pre-Game Buffet
for 8 servings

Sacramento Fruit Bowl *page 322*
Chicken Tetrazzini *page 267*
Green Beans Amandine
Crusty Hard Rolls   Butter
Perfection Salad *page 323*
Devil's Food Cake *page 384*
Beer   Coffee

Business Lunch
for 4 servings

Crème Vichyssoise *page 129*
Roast Rack of Lamb *page 227*
Baked Herbed Tomatoes *page 296*
Caesar Salad *page 318*
Strawberries Romanoff *page 303*
Caffè Espresso *page 467*

Summer Pre-Theater
for 4 servings

Crab Louis *page 325*
Bran Muffins *page 424*
Cinnamon Apricots in Cream *page 301*
Sugar Cookies *page 412*
Coffee

Tea

Tea parties range from an afternoon get together with just a few friends to a formal gathering. Four o'clock is the usual hour for serving tea, but any time between two and six is acceptable. Select foods which are suitable for eating in the hand.

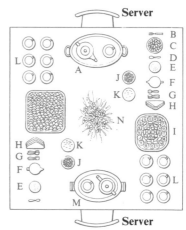

A. *Tea service (teapot and tray)*; B. *Lemon fork*; C. *Plate of lemon slices*; D. *Sugar spoon*; E. *Sugar bowl*; F. *Creamer*; G. *Teaspoons*; H. *Napkins*; I. *Tray of cookies, tea sandwiches*; J. *Bowl of mints*; K. *Bowl of nuts*; L. *Cups and saucers*; M. *Coffee service (coffee pot and tray)*; N. *Centerpiece*

Come-for-Tea Party
for 12 servings

Swans *page 367*
Chinese Fried Walnuts *page 114*
Candied Fruit Tray: Orange Slices,
Figs, Apricots, Dates, Pineapple
Hot Tea   Coffee

Welcoming Tea
for 20 servings

Deviled Ham Pinwheels *page 459*
Pimento-Cheese Finger Sandwiches
Lemon Loaf, sliced *page 428*
Neapolitan Cookies *page 411*
Madeleines *page 409*
Chocolate-dipped Fruit *page 420*
Salted Almonds
Butter Mints
Herbal Tea   Coffee

Spring Reception Tea
for 25 servings

Ribbon Sandwiches *page 459*
Cream Cheese on Raisin-Bread Squares
Citrus Pinwheels *page 411*
Toffee Bars *page 404*
Marzipan Fruits *page 419*
Candied Orange Peel *page 310*
Diced Crystallized Ginger
Hot Tea   Coffee

Dinner

A family dinner is an informal occasion for entertaining visiting relatives or friends, while a party dinner is formal, usually given for very special occasions – for anniversaries, in honor of a community leader, when the boss is invited or for visits of very special friends. For a memorable party dinner, try basing your menu on a theme, and decorating and selecting appropriate dishes.

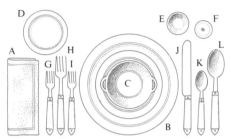

A. *Napkin;* B. *Dinner or service plate;* C. *First-course bowl and liner plate;* D. *Salad plate;* E. *Water goblet;* F. *Wine glass;* G. *Salad fork;* H. *Dinner fork;* I. *Dessert fork;* J. *Dinner knife;* K. *Teaspoon;* L. *Soup spoon*

Candlelit Dinner
for 8 servings

Smithfield Ham on Honeydew Wedges
Chicken Périgord-style *page 256*
Oven-Dinner Rice *page 338*
(double recipe)
Carrots and Celery *page 297*
California Salad *page 318*
Giant Popovers *page 427*
Chocolate Chiffon Pie *page 353*
Dry Sauterne   Coffee

Gala Retirement Party
for 10 servings

Eggs en Gelée *page 141*
Individual Beef Wellingtons *page 192*
Cabernet Sauvignon
Peas with Lettuce
Cauliflower Polonaise *page 282*
(double recipe)
Tomatoes Vinaigrette *page 319*
(double recipe)
Ice-Cream Bombe Les Dames
d'Escoffier *page 379*
Coffee   Hot Tea

Elegant Dinner
for 6 servings

Gravad Lax *page 119*
Veal Forestier *page 237*
Mashed Potatoes *page 291*
Summer Squash Medley *page 294*
Danish Cucumber Salad *page 319*
Vienna Rolls *page 439*
Butter Curls *page 424*
Apricot-Cream Flan *page 360*
Demitasse   Cordials

Mostly Do-Ahead Dinner
for 8 servings

Celery Hearts Vinaigrette *page 321*
Fillets of Sole Thermidor *page 178*
Homemade Spinach Noodles *page 330*
Glazed Carrots *page 282 (double recipe)*
Tomato Aspic *page 323*
Dinner Rolls *page 439*
Very-Berry Compote *page 303*
Coffee   Hot Tea

All-American Christmas
for 12 to 14 servings

Roast Turkey
with Moist Bread Stuffing *page 249*
Spiced Carrots *page 282*
Creamed Onions *page 289*
Brussels Sprouts with Chestnuts
Perfection Salad *page 323*
(double recipe)
Cranberry Relish *page 305*
Corn Sticks *page 428*
Butter Balls *page 424*
Strawberry Shortcake *page 369* or
Apple Pie *page 346*
Coffee   Milk   Hot Tea

Mexican Fiesta
for 6 servings

Guacamole *page 124*
Margarita *page 472 (6 times recipe)*
Sour Cream Chicken Enchiladas
page 269
Mixed Fruit Salad
Caramel Flan
Hot Chocolate with Cinnamon

Festive Fall Meal
for 12 servings

Appetizer Avocados *page 302*
(double recipe)
Prune-stuffed Roast Pork *page 212*
Pan-roasted Potatoes *page 291*
(double recipe)
Confetti Vegetables *page 297*
Colonel's Lady's Salad Bowl *page 318*
Chocolate-Cherry Soufflé *page 361*
Coffee   Hot Tea

Mother's Favorite
for 6 servings

Teriyaki Beef Kabobs *page 198*
Rice Ring *page 341*
Stir-fried Asparagus *page 277*
Avocado and Radish Romaine Salad
Thousand Island Dressing *page 326*
Meringue Shells *page 364*
with Pistachio Ice Cream *page 377*
Hot Green Tea

In Ye Olde English Manner
for 16 servings

Cream of Leek Soup
Standing Rib Roast
with Yorkshire Pudding *page 191*
Potatoes au Gratin *page 292*
(triple recipe)
Sliced Parsnips and Carrots
Cucumber-Watercress Salad
Sherry Trifle *page 372 (double recipe)*
Earl Grey Tea

Far Eastern Dinner
for 6 servings

Mushroom-Snow Pea Soup
Striped Bass with Pungent Sauce
page 175
Hot Fluffy Rice *page 338*
(double recipe)
Stir-fried Broccoli *page 280*
Gingered Kiwi fruit *page 306*
(double recipe)
Oolong or Jasmine Tea

Italian Repast
for 8 servings

Tortellini in Cream Sauce *page 335*
Veal Piccata *page 236*
Risotto alla Milanese *page 339*
(double recipe)
Pepper-and-Tomato Sauté *page 298*
Braised Fennel *page 285 (double recipe)*
Crisp Italian Toast
Strawberry-Orange Ice *page 381*
Caffè Espresso *page 467*
(double recipe)

SETTING UP A BUFFET

A buffet enables you to serve a large crowd in a small dining area and any meal, even dessert and coffee, can be served this way. Arrange plates and food in menu order for smooth service.

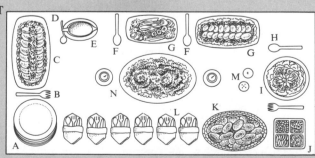

A. *Plates;* B. *Serving fork;* C. *Main dish;* D. *Gravy ladle;* E. *Gravy boat on liner plate;* F. *Serving spoon;* G. *Vegetable dish;* H. *Salad fork and spoon;* I. *Salad bowl;* J. *Relish tray;* K. *Basket of rolls;* L. *Napkins with knives, forks and spoons;* M. *Salt and pepper;* N. *Centerpiece and candles*

Menu planning and entertaining

French Provincial
for 4 servings

Artichokes Béarnaise *page 276*
Coq au Vin *page 266*
Potatoes Anna *page 292*
Sorrel Salad
Crusty French Bread
Camembert with Pears
Burgundy Wine   Coffee

Valencia Olé
for 8 servings

Tapas: stuffed green olives, Curried
Almonds *page 114*, Marinated
Mushrooms, Pickled Shrimp
Sherry
Paella *page 165*
Sliced Orange and Red Onion on
Lettuce
Crème Caramel *page 359*
Sangria *page 471*

Aegean Feast
for 8 servings

Spanakopitas *page 121*
Retsina (wine)
Chicken Avgolemono *page 258*
Greek Salad *page 320*
Baklava *page 371*
Hot Tea with Mint   Espresso

Father's Day
for 6 servings

Shrimp Cocktail with Tangy Dip
page 164
Filets Mignon with
Mustard-Caper Sauce *page 195*
Baked Potatoes *page 291*
Green Beans with Zucchini *page 298*
Poached Pears in Sauterne *page 312*
Irish Coffee *page 467*
(*6 times recipe*)

Anniversary Dinner Buffet
for 16 servings

Tiny Ham-stuffed Tomatoes *page 126*
Pumpernickel-Muenster Triangles
page 117
Cocktails   Appetizer Wines
Châteaubriand *page 195*
Crab Imperial *page 167*
Rice Pilaf with Peas *page 339*
(*double recipe*)
Salad Bar: choice of green pepper
strips, cherry tomatoes, croutons,
spinach, lettuce, salad dressings
Chocolate-Cinnamon Torte *page 373*
Minted Sherbet Ring with Berries
page 380
Champagne   Coffee

Saturday Night Special
for 6 servings

Chilled Cucumber Soup *page 129*
Turkey in Champagne Sauce
with Toast Flowers *page 259*
Zesty Tangelo Salad *page 314*
Walnut Tarts *page 357*
Hot or Iced Tea

Graduation Celebration
for 16 servings

Green Onion Dip *page 124*
Cheese Spreads *page 124* with
assorted crackers
Golden Punch *page 471*
Turkey Roll with Stuffing *page 250*
Spiced Nectarine Slices *page 310*
Ratatouille *page 297 (double recipe)*
Deluxe Coleslaw *page 319*
(*double recipe*)
Walnut-Fudge Cake *page 388*
Iced or Hot Tea

Friday Family Dinner
for 6 servings

Broiled Sesame Trout *page 174*
Brown Rice *page 338*
Whole Green and Wax Beans with
Parsley Sauce *page 278*
Greens with Russian dressing *page 326*
Lemon Meringue Pie *page 351*
Coffee   Hot Tea

Welcome Neighbor
for 8 servings

Marinated Artichoke Hearts and
Mushrooms *page 319*
Hearty Manicotti *page 334*
Baked Creamed Spinach *page 293*
Chianti
Braided Herb Bread *page 437*
Cantaloupe Ice *page 309*
Caffè Espresso with Hot Milk and
Cinnamon Stick

Coffee and dessert

Having family or friends over for coffee
or some other hot beverage and a fancy
dessert is a pleasant way to entertain,
particularly on the weekends, after the
theater or movies, or during the holidays.

Après-Ski
for 12 servings

Six-Layer Eggnog Cake *page 394*
Café Brûlot *page 467 (double recipe)*

Summer Delight
for 8 servings

Raspberry Ribbon Pie *page 354*
Demitasse   Cordials

Spring Dessert Party
for 12 servings

Strawberry Soufflé *page 361*
Chocolate-dipped Butter Cookies
page 410
Coffee   Hot Tea with Mint

A Special Occasion
for 16 servings

Chocolate Fancy *page 374*
Champagne   Coffee

Cocktail party

A cocktail party lets you entertain a few
or a lot of friends with a minimum of space
and money. Have hot and cold food selec-
tions and an assortment of liquors, mixers
and garnishes for popular drinks.

Cocktails at Six
for 6 servings

Blue Cheese Dip (*page 124*)
Tray of Vegetables for Dipping: carrot
sticks, broccoli flowerets, cucumber
wedges
Bacon-broiled Scallops *page 163*
Caviar-Egg Rounds *page 115*
Salted Nuts and Pretzels
Cocktails   Wine

Cocktails for a Crowd
for 20 to 25 servings

Crisp Cheese Twists *page 114*
Chili Dip with Fresh Vegetables
page 125
Pissaladière *page 117*
Chicken Liver Pâté *page 122* with
Melba Toast *page 133*
Homemade Pepper-Herb Cheese
page 123
Rye Crisps or Flat Breads
Tuna-Dill Rounds *page 115*
Steak Bites *page 119*
Cocktails   Appetizer Wines

OPENING A CHAMPAGNE BOTTLE

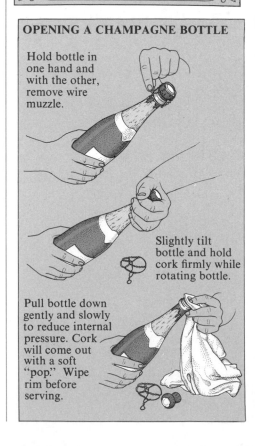

Hold bottle in
one hand and
with the other,
remove wire
muzzle.

Slightly tilt
bottle and hold
cork firmly while
rotating bottle.

Pull bottle down
gently and slowly
to reduce internal
pressure. Cork
will come out
with a soft
"pop." Wipe
rim before
serving.

Bridal or baby shower

Bridal showers may be given at brunch, luncheon, tea, dinner or in the evening, while baby showers are usually afternoon or evening functions.

Spring Luncheon Shower
for 8 servings

Shrimp Bisque *page 130*
Open Sandwiches *page 458*
Hawaiian Fruit Salad *page 322*
Heart-shaped Cake
Party Orange Soda *page 469*

Baby Buffet Tea
for 16 servings

Ribbon Sandwiches *page 459*
Deviled Ham Pinwheels *page 459*
Fresh Coconut Cake *page 386*
Fondant *page 417*
Melt-Away Chocolate Mints *page 420*
Salted Nuts
Hot Tea   Coffee

Wedding reception

The reception after a wedding can be an intimate dinner for the wedding party and immediate family alone, or a large-scale event for all the invited guests. For a simple reception, just serve the Party Cake with nuts, candies and the punch. For the buffet below, set the table as shown on page 480, but place the cake, punch bowl, candies and nuts on another table.

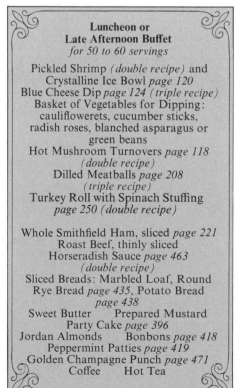

**Luncheon or
Late Afternoon Buffet**
for 50 to 60 servings

Pickled Shrimp *(double recipe)* and
Crystalline Ice Bowl *page 120*
Blue Cheese Dip *page 124 (triple recipe)*
Basket of Vegetables for Dipping:
cauliflowerets, cucumber sticks,
radish roses, blanched asparagus or
green beans
Hot Mushroom Turnovers *page 118*
(double recipe)
Dilled Meatballs *page 208*
(triple recipe)
Turkey Roll with Spinach Stuffing
page 250 (double recipe)

Whole Smithfield Ham, sliced *page 221*
Roast Beef, thinly sliced
Horseradish Sauce *page 463*
(double recipe)
Sliced Breads: Marbled Loaf, Round
Rye Bread *page 435*, Potato Bread
page 438
Sweet Butter   Prepared Mustard
Party Cake *page 396*
Jordan Almonds   Bonbons *page 418*
Peppermint Patties *page 419*
Golden Champagne Punch *page 471*
Coffee   Hot Tea

NAPKIN FOLDING

Add a final decorative touch to your dinner table by folding napkins into any of the shapes below. Napkins may also be placed on the dinner plates.

SILVER BUFFET

Fold the napkin over twice to form a square. Hold the square in a diamond shape.

Take the top 2 flaps and roll them halfway down the napkin.

Fold under the right and left points at the sides. There is now a pocket into which you can place the knife, fork and spoon.

BUTTERFLY

Form a triangle from an open napkin. Fold the right corner to the center.

Take the left corner up to center, making a diamond. Keeping the loose points at the top, turn the napkin over, then fold upward, to form a triangle.

Tuck the left corner into the right. Stand up napkin; turn it round, then turn the petals down; it's now a butterfly.

WATER LILY

Place all 4 points to the center of an opened napkin.

Fold the 4 points to the center of the napkin once more.

Repeat a third time; turn napkin over and fold points to the center once more.

Holding finger firmly at center, unfold 1 petal first from underneath each corner.

Pull out 4 more from between the petals. Then pull out the next 4 under the petals.

The water lily now has 12 points.

Eating outdoors

Cooking outdoors on a grill can be a fun way of entertaining; however, it can be a disaster unless you think of safety first. Since many factors affect the amount of heat from a grill, cooking directions are very general. Follow our tips for successful barbecuing.

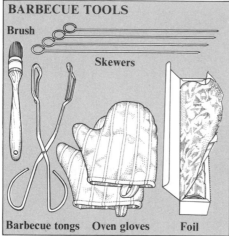

BARBECUE TOOLS

Brush

Skewers

Barbecue tongs   Oven gloves   Foil

LIGHTING THE FIRE
Be sure there is adequate ventilation to remove deadly carbon monoxide formed by the fire. Never grill in a closed camper, porch, garage, trailer or tent.

Place grill away from dry grass, bushes, the house. Never leave it unattended once coals are ignited.

Line the grill with heavy-duty foil. It reflects heat and so speeds cooking, makes cleaning a snap. If bottom of grill has vents, puncture foil so air can circulate.

To get the fire started quickly, push the briquettes into a pyramid.

Use a charcoal lighter to start the fire, choosing from liquid, solid and jelly types; or use a UL-listed electric starter. Follow manufacturer's directions to the letter. NEVER, NEVER use gasoline, alcohol or other highly volatile fluids.

Let briquettes burn until they are covered with a layer of gray ash in daylight or are glowing red at night. This will take 20 to 40 minutes. On a cold day, use more briquettes to offset lower outside temperatures.

If you're grilling fatty meats like hamburger, use fewer briquettes to keep the fire cool, reduce flare-ups. Use more briquettes when grilling lean meats.

Experiment with different brands of briquettes, some are easier to light.

BARBECUING TIPS
Spread hot briquettes in a single layer before placing food on rack.

To judge the temperature of the coals, hold your hand, palm down, at cooking height. If you can hold it there only 2 to 3 seconds, temperature is hot, above 375°F.; for 4 seconds, it's medium, above 300°F.; for 5 to 6 seconds, it's low, above 200°F.

To change the temperature when needed, raise the cooking rack and/or spread out coals to lower the heat. To raise the heat, push coals together.

To minimize flare-ups when grilling fatty meats, try tipping the rack slightly so that hot fat runs down the wires and drips off at the cool edge of the fire.

To put out flare-ups caused by dripping fat, raise the rack and spread out coals or remove the food and douse the flames with water in a plastic pump-spray bottle.

Bon Voyage Party
for 8 servings

Bluefish with Buttery Lemon Sauce
page 174
Potatoes Baked in Coals
Grilled Zucchini Halves
Three-Bean Salad *page 321*
Speedy Biscuits *page 423*
Cold Watermelon
Iced Coffee   Sparkling Wine

Graduation Barbecue
for 8 servings

Yogurt-Cheese Dip *page 125*
Potato Chips Breadsticks Corn Chips
Savory Chicken *page 260*
Corn-on-the-cob with Chive butter
page 283
Sliced Tomato-Green Bean Salad
Chocolate Chiffon Cake *page 389*
Lemonade *page 470*   Iced Tea

Fourth of July
for 8 servings

Lamb Kabobs *page 228*
Spinach Mushroom Salad
Poori *page 431*
Peach Meringue Tarts *page 357*
Beer   Ice Tea, Family Style *page 468*

Mountain Park Barbecue
for 4 servings

Barbecued Spareribs *page 216*
Vegetable Trio *page 298 (foil-wrapped)*
Zesty Lima Beans *page 279*
Whole Wheat Rolls
Pears with Raspberry Sauce
Soft Drinks   Iced Coffee

Steak Grill
for 8 to 10 servings

Stuffed Eggs *page 141*
Deviled Round Steak *page 197*
Stir-fried Cabbage and Zucchini
page 298
Turkish Bean Salad *page 321*
Cherry Cream Tart *page 355*
Hearty Burgundy   Limeade

Picnics
Whether you're planning a light lunch in the park or a feast at the beach, proper food preparation and packing is important. If food is left standing too long at warm temperatures, bacteria such as salmonella can grow to dangerous levels leading to food poisoning. To ensure that food will be fresh when served, follow our suggestions and precautions below.

WHAT AND HOW TO PACK
The best picnic foods are those that keep well. Some favorites: cold fried chicken, marinated vegetable salads, breads.

Keep cooked foods refrigerated in shallow containers so they chill quickly until ready to pack.

Store hot and cold foods in vacuum containers. Line cold food carriers with ice cubes in plastic bags, ice bars made by freezing water in clean milk cartons, or frozen gel-filled containers.

Set out food in portions that will be eaten quickly; replenish only as needed.

For a Day in the Country
for 8 servings

Hot-Pepper Pecans *page 114*
Country Meat Loaf *page 207*
Pickled Onions *page 126*
Macaroni Salad
Olives
Cheese Crackers
Pineapple-Upside-Down Cake *page 384*
Soft Drinks   Dry Red Wine

Concert on the Mall
for 8 servings

Pea Soup *page 130*
Pâté de Campagne *page 122*
Herbed Mushrooms *page 126*
Salade Niçoise *page 324 (double recipe)*
Onion Thins *page 431*
Brie with Seedless Grapes
Iced Tea   Rosé Wine

Lunch in the Park
for 6 servings

Gazpacho *page 129 (double recipe)*
Chicken or Turkey Salad *page 268*
with Alfalfa Sprouts
Pita (pocket bread) *page 447*
Cucumber and Carrot Sticks
Backpacking Bars *page 404*
Apple Juice   Milk

Beach Party
for 10 servings

Tuna Dip *page 125*
Italian Cheese-and-Ham Pie *page 157*
Caponata *page 299*
Bananas or Nectarines
German Gold Poundcake *page 386*
Beer   Soft Drinks

Glossary of food and cooking terms

à la: In the manner of.

à la carte: A meal in which the diner selects individual items, paying for each, rather than taking a table d'hôte (complete) meal at a fixed price.

à la mode: In style. Desserts à la mode are served with ice cream; meats cooked à la mode are braised with vegetables and served with gravy.

Age: 1. To tenderize meat by allowing it to hang for a specified length of time in carefully controlled conditions.
2. To store cheese until it is mature and flavorful.
3. To store wine to improve flavor.

al dente: Italian term used to describe pasta that is cooked until it offers a slight resistance to the bite.

Amandine: Dishes made or garnished with almonds.

Antipasto: Italian term describing an assortment of appetizers.

Aperitif: A drink taken before a meal to stimulate the appetite.

Ascorbic-acid mixture for fruit: A crystalline or powdered mixture used to prevent darkening and loss of flavor of fruits low in ascorbic acid.

Aspic: Jellied meat, fish or poultry stock or vegetable liquid often used for molding meat, fish, poultry or vegetables.

au jus: A French term meaning served with unthickened natural juices that develop during roasting.

au lait: A French term meaning served with milk.

Bake: To cook food uncovered in an oven or oven-type appliance. When applied to meats and poultry, it is called roasting.

Baking powder: A leavening agent which makes foods rise when they are baked. It is a combination of baking soda, a dry acid or acid salt and starch or flour. The acid ingredient reacts with the baking soda to produce gas bubbles in the mixture. Double-acting baking powder (used in the recipes in this book) produces gas bubbles twice: first during mixing and second during baking.

Baking soda: An essential ingredient of baking powder, may be used alone as a leavening agent in mixtures containing an acid ingredient such as buttermilk or in combination with baking powder. Mixtures containing baking soda should be baked as soon as mixed, since the soda starts to react as soon as it comes in contact with the liquid.

Barbecue: To roast or broil food on a rack or spit over coals, or under a heat unit. The food is usually brushed with a highly seasoned sauce during the last of the cooking time.

Baste: To moisten food while it cooks, so that the surface doesn't dry out and flavor is added. Melted fat, drippings, sauce and fruit juice are the liquids generally used.

Basting steak

Batter: A mixture of fairly thin consistency, made of flour, liquid and other ingredients.

Bavarian: A molded cold dessert made with gelatin, eggs, cream and flavorings.

Beat: To make a mixture smooth with rapid, regular motion using a wire whisk, spoon, hand beater or mixer. When using a spoon, the mixture should be lifted up and over with each stroke.

Bisque: A thick, rich cream soup usually made with shellfish or pureed vegetables.

Blanch: To cook a few minutes in boiling water either to help loosen the skin from some foods, or as a step in preparing vegetables for freezing.

Blanquette: A white, creamy stew of veal, chicken or lamb with small onions and mushrooms.

Blend: To mix thoroughly two or more ingredients; or to prepare food in blender until pureed, chopped, etc., as desired.

Blintz: A thin pancake filled and rolled, usually with cottage cheese.

Boil: To cook food over high heat in liquid in which bubbles rise constantly to the surface and break.

Bombe: A dessert of frozen mixtures arranged and frozen in a mold.

Bone: To remove bones from meats, fish or poultry.

Bouillabaisse: A hearty stew made with several kinds of fish and shellfish.

Bouillon: A clear, seasoned broth usually made from beef or chicken; also obtained by dissolving a bouillon cube or envelope in boiling water.

Bouquet garni: A bundle of several herbs, usually including parsley, thyme and bay leaf, tied in cheesecloth. Added to stews, soups and sauces for flavoring, it is easy to remove when desired.

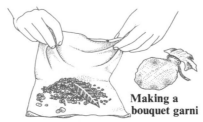

Making a bouquet garni

Braise: To cook food over low heat in a small amount of liquid in a covered pan. (Food may or may not be browned first in a small amount of fat.)

Bread: To coat with bread crumbs, cracker crumbs or cornmeal. Food may first be floured, then dipped in beaten egg or other liquid to help crumbs to adhere.

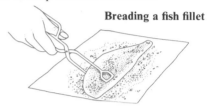

Breading a fish fillet

Brochette: A skewer. Food cooked "en brochette" is cooked on a skewer.

Broil: To cook food by direct heat on a rack or spit.

Broth: Liquid in which meat, poultry or vegetables have simmered. Same as stock.

Brush with: To use a pastry brush to spread food lightly with liquid such as salad oil, melted fat, milk, heavy cream or beaten egg.

Butter: 1. Made from sweet or sour cream, contains not less than 80 percent milk fat. It is available salted or unsalted.
2. To spread butter, margarine or other fat lightly over a dish or pan to prevent food sticking to it.

Canapé: Plain or toasted bread or crackers topped with a savory mixture, served as an appetizer or with cocktails.

Caramelize: To stir sugar in skillet over low heat until it melts and develops characteristic flavor and golden-brown color.

Carve: To cut meat or poultry in slices or pieces for serving.

Chill: To refrigerate food or let it stand in ice or iced water until cold.

Chocolate: Comes in several forms. Each reacts differently and gives a different flavor in recipes (see also page 363).

Chop: To cut food into small pieces with a knife, blender or food processor.

Chutney: A highly seasoned relish of fruits, herbs and spices.

Coat: To sprinkle food with, or dip it into, flour, sauce, etc., until covered.

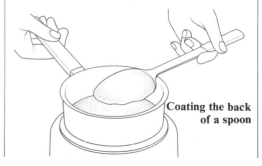

Coating the back of a spoon

509

Glossary of food and cooking terms

Compote: 1. A dessert of fresh or dried fruits cooked in syrup.
2. A deep bowl, often stemmed, from which such desserts and other foods are usually served.

Condiment: 1. Sauces and relishes to add to food at the table, such as catchup or prepared mustard.
2. Seasoning, often pungent, used to bring out the flavor of foods.

Cool: To refrigerate food, or let it stand at room temperature, until no longer warm to the touch.

Corn syrup: Available as light and dark. Both can be used to glaze meats and vegetables and as ingredients in marinades, candies and desserts.

Court bouillon: Seasoned liquid in which fish can be poached (see also page 172).

Cream: 1. The fat portion of milk. Light cream contains at least 18 percent milk fat; light whipping cream, 30 to 36 percent; heavy or whipping cream, at least 36 percent. Half-and-half is a mixture of milk and cream containing not less than 10.5 but less than 18 percent milk fat. Sour cream usually has at least 18 percent and sour half-and-half 10.5 to 18 percent.
2. To cook food in, or serve it with, white or "cream" sauce.
3. To make soft, smooth and creamy by beating with spoon or with mixer (usually applied to blending sugar and a fat).

Crêpe: A thin, delicate pancake.

Croissant: A rich crescent-shaped roll.

Croquette: A mixture of chopped or minced food, usually shaped as a cone or ball, coated with egg and crumbs then deep-fried.

Crouton: A small cube of bread toasted or fried, most often used to garnish soups and salads (see also page 131).

Crustacean: Shellfish such as shrimp, lobster and crab with segmented body covered by crusty outer skeleton.

Cube: 1. To cut food into small cubes (about ½ inch).
2. To cut surface of meat in checkered pattern to increase tenderness by breaking tough meat fibers.

Cubing steak

Cut in: To distribute solid fat in flour or flour mixture by using pastry blender or two knives scissor-fashion until flour-coated fat particles are of desired size.

Deep-fry: To cook food in hot fat deep enough for food to float on it.

Demitasse: A small cup ("half cup") of black coffee, usually served after dinner.

Dice: To cut food into very small pieces (about ¼ inch).

Dijon mustard: A prepared mustard (originally made in Dijon, France) which can be mild or highly seasoned. Our recipes call for highly seasoned Dijon.

Dot: To scatter bits, as of butter or margarine, over surface of food.

Dotting pastry with butter

Draw: To remove entrails from, and clean, poultry or game. Drawn fish are whole fish that have been cleaned (eviscerated) but not boned.

Dredge: To cover or coat food, as with flour, cornmeal, etc.

Dress: To mix salad or other food with dressing or sauce.

Dressed fish: Whole fish with scales and entrails removed. Usually head, tail and fins have also been cut off (see also page 172). Smaller fish are generally called pan-dressed.

Drippings: Fat and juice given off by meat or poultry as it cooks.

Durum: A wheat variety used in making high-quality spaghetti and other pastas.

Enchilada: A tortilla, stuffed, rolled and served with a highly seasoned sauce.

Enriched: Resupplied with vitamins and minerals lost during processing of food.

Entree: The main dish of the meal.

Escargot: An edible snail, usually a land snail imported from France and served in the shell.

Filet (or fillet): A piece of meat, fish or poultry which is boneless or has had all bones removed.

Fines herbes: A mixture of herbs used for seasoning. Traditionally includes parsley, chervil, chives and tarragon, though other herbs may also be used.

Flame: To ignite warmed alcoholic beverage poured over food. Also known as flambé.

Flaming crêpes

Flour: 1. *All-purpose.* Made from a variety of wheats, it produces good results for a wide variety of baked goods (most of our recipes call for it). *Whole-wheat flour* is milled from the entire wheat kernel while *rye flour* is milled from the rye kernel. *Cake flour* is milled especially for cakes and other light baked products. For best results always use the flour called for in the recipe. In recipes calling for all-purpose and whole wheat or rye, a certain proportion of all-purpose to the other flour is needed for best results; so don't substitute flour.
2. To coat lightly with flour.

Flute: To make decorative indentations.

Foie gras: Literally "fat liver", a term usually applied to goose liver.

Fold in: To combine delicate ingredients such as whipped cream or beaten egg whites with other foods by using a gentle, circular motion to cut down into the mixture, slide across the bottom of the bowl to bring some of the mixture up and over the surface (see also page 139).

Fondue: Most often a dish of hot melted cheese and wine, into which bread is dipped and then eaten. For meat fondues, at the table, cubes of meat are dipped in hot fat to cook, then into a choice of sauces. Dessert fondues include chocolate or other sauces for dipping chunks of poundcake or fruit. The term also denotes a baked main dish made with cheese, milk and bread.

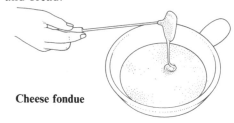

Cheese fondue

Fortified: Supplied with more vitamins and minerals than were present in the natural state.

Freeze-dried: Term applied to food that has been dried by rapid freezing, then had most of its water content removed.

Fricassee: A stew made of chicken or veal cut into pieces and cooked in a gravy.

Fritter: A small quantity of a batter mixture, sometimes containing meat, vegetables or fruit, fried in deep fat until crisp.

Fruit pectin: A natural substance found in many fruits; also available in liquid or powdered forms. When pectin is used in the right proportion with sugar and acid liquid, it forms a jelly.

Fry: To cook food over high heat in a small amount of fat. See also Deep-fry, Pan-fry, Sauté.

Garnish: To add a decorative touch to food, as with parsley, croutons or prepared vegetables.

Gazpacho: A cold Spanish soup made with tomatoes and other fresh vegetables.

Gelatin: Available as unflavored and fruit-flavored. They are not interchangeable.

Glacé: 1. Glazed, as with a frosting. 2. Frozen.

Glaze: 1. To coat with a glossy mixture. 2. Concentrated stock used to add flavor.

Grate: To rub food on a grater (or chop in blender or food processor) to produce fine, medium or coarse particles.

Grating carrot

Gratin: A French term defining a brown crust formed by baking or broiling bread crumbs, cheese, butter or a mixture on top of a casserole or other dish.

Grease: To rub surface of dish or pan with fat, to keep food from sticking.

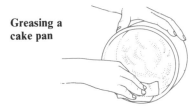

Greasing a cake pan

Grenadine: Pomegranate-flavored syrup used as flavoring and sauce.

Grill: To cook food on a rack by direct heat; also the appliance or utensil used for this type of cooking.

Grind: To reduce to particles in food grinder, blender or food processor.

Gumbo: A thick, Southern-style soup or stew made with meat, poultry, fish, shellfish or vegetables.

Hibachi: Small, portable charcoal grill.

Hoisin sauce: A thick sauce made of soy beans and seasonings used in Chinese cooking.

Homard: French word for lobster.

Homogenized: With fat broken down into such small particles that it stays suspended in liquid, rather than rising to the top.

Honey: Sometimes sold in the comb, but usually as the extracted liquid and in solid and granular forms. Our recipes always use liquid honey.

Hors d'oeuvres: Savory foods used as appetizers.

Jardinière: French term meaning garnished with vegetables.

Kabob: Cubes of meat or poultry and vegetables threaded on a skewer and grilled; also any food that is threaded on a skewer.

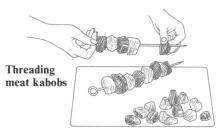

Threading meat kabobs

Knead: To work a food mixture (usually dough) with a press-fold motion (see also page 432).

Kosher: Ritually fit for eating in accordance with Jewish law.

Lard: The white fat of pork, rendered and sold in solid form; used in piecrusts, biscuits, other baked foods and for frying.

Liquor: 1. An alcoholic beverage, such as rum or vodka.
2. Liquid surrounding clams, oysters and other mollusks.
3. In recipe directions, sometimes a broth or juice.

Lukewarm: At a temperature of about 95°F. Lukewarm food feels neither warm nor cold when in contact with inside of the wrist.

Maple sugar: Made from the evaporation of maple sap. It is usually pressed into fancy shapes to serve as a confection.

Maple syrup: The pure variety comes from the evaporation of the sap of maple trees. Maple-flavor syrup is made from a blend of refined, corn and maple-sugar syrups.

Marbled: Term used to describe meat with visible fat running through the lean.

Margarine: Comes in several forms. Regular margarine with 80 percent fat is interchangeable with butter in our recipes.

Marinade: A seasoned liquid, in which food is soaked to enhance flavor.

Marinate: To soak in a marinade.

Marron: Chestnut. Marrons glacés are chestnuts preserved in syrup or candied.

Marzipan: Sweetened almond paste made into confections.

Matzo: Thin, unleavened, cracker-like bread made of flour and water.

Meat tenderizer: Papain from natural tenderizers such as papaya is used to soften meat tissue. It is usually sprinkled on the meat before meat is cooked.

Meringue: Mixture of stiffly beaten egg whites and sugar. Also the cooked soft mixture on desserts or the cooked "hard" mixture as a dessert shell.

Meunière: With sauce of butter, lemon juice and parsley.

Milk: Available fresh, canned and dried. Almost all milk and cream is pasteurized.

Mince: To cut into very small pieces, using knife, food grinder or blender, or food processor.

Mocha: Flavoring of coffee.

Mollusk: Shellfish such as clams and oysters, with soft unsegmented bodies protected by a hard shell.

Monosodium glutamate: White, crystalline salt that enhances natural flavor of foods without adding its own.

Mousse: A cold dessert made with whipped cream or beaten egg whites.

Nuts: May be purchased in the shell or shelled with the exception of cashews which are only available shelled. Shelled nuts are available chopped, ground, halved, blanched, slivered, plain, toasted or salted.

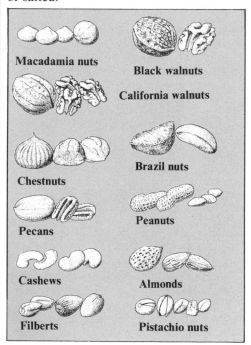

Macadamia nuts

Black walnuts

California walnuts

Chestnuts

Brazil nuts

Pecans

Peanuts

Cashews

Almonds

Filberts

Pistachio nuts

Oeuf: French word for egg.

Olives: Both varieties green and ripe (black) are processed to remove their natural bitterness. Green olives are packed in brine and may be unpitted, pitted or pitted and stuffed with pimento, almonds or anchovies, etc. Ripe olives are packed in light brine and may be pitted or unpitted.

Pan: To cook, covered, in very small amount of liquid.

Pan-broil: To cook food, uncovered, over high heat on ungreased or lightly greased hot surface, pouring off accumulating fat.

Pan-fry: To cook food over high heat in a small amount of fat.

Parboil: To boil until partially cooked, usually before completing cooking by another method.

Glossary of food and cooking terms

Parfait: A dessert made of layers of fruit, syrup, ice cream and whipped cream or beaten egg whites.

Pasta: Spaghetti, macaroni and similar products, usually of Italian origin.

Pasteurize: To destroy, by heating, certain undesirable bacteria in juices, dairy foods.

Pastrami: Highly spiced smoked beef, usually prepared from shoulder cuts.

Pâté: Spread or loaf of ground, seasoned meat, poultry or fish or vegetables.

Patty shell: A shell made from puff paste to hold creamed mixtures or fruit.

Filling patty shells

Peel: To remove outer covering of foods by trimming away with knife or vegetable peeler, or by pulling off.

Petit four: Small, decoratively iced cake.

Pilaf: Seasoned rice, often with meat or poultry added.

Pit: To remove seed from whole fruit.

Poach: To cook food over low heat in simmering liquid.

Polenta: A very thick mush usually made from cornmeal or farina, used in main dishes and as accompaniment.

Pot-roast: To cook large pieces of meat or poultry by braising; also certain meat cuts.

Potage: Soup.

Prawn: Term used primarily on the West Coast for larger shrimp.

Preheat: To heat oven to desired temperature before putting food in to bake.

Pressure-cook: To cook in steam under high pressure, using a special saucepan.

Profiterole: Tiny cream puff, filled with sweet or savory mixtures, served as dessert or hors d'oeuvre.

Prosciutto: Italian-style cured and spiced ham, served sliced paper thin.

Punch down: To deflate a risen yeast dough by pushing it down with the fist.

Purée: 1. A thick mixture made from a puréed vegetable base.
2. To press food through a fine sieve or food mill, or to blend in blender or food processor to a smooth, thick mixture.

Food mill

Quiche: Savory one-crust egg-and-cream main dish pie.

Reduce: To reduce volume of liquid by rapid boiling in an uncovered pan.

Roast: To cook meat or poultry uncovered in oven (see Bake).

Roulade: Rolled meat.

Salad oils: Consist of one or a combination of vegetable oils. They are used for salad dressings, in recipes and for cooking. They cannot be substituted for butter or other solid fats in recipes but can be used in place of melted fats in frying.

Scald: To heat liquid just to below the boiling point.

Scallopine: Small, thin pieces of meat.

Scampi: Shrimp or a dish of shrimp in garlic sauce.

Score: 1. To cut shallow slits in surface of food to increase tenderness or to prevent fat covering from curling.
2. To decorate.

Scoring ham

Shortening: Produced from bleached, refined, hydrogenated vegetable oil or animal fat, this solid fat is good for deep-fat- and pan-frying and as an ingredient in pastry. Can refer generally to fats.

Shred: To cut food into slivers or slender pieces, using a knife or shredder.

Shuck: To remove meat of oysters, clams, etc. from their shells (see also page 162).

Silver dragées: Tiny, ball-shaped silver-colored candies.

Simmer: To cook food over low heat in a liquid just below the boiling point in which bubbles form slowly and collapse just below the surface.

Skim: To remove fat or scum from surface of food.

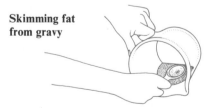

Skimming fat from gravy

Steam: To cook food on a rack or in a colander in a covered pan over steaming hot water.

Stew: To cook food over low heat in a simmering liquid.

Stir-fry: To cook sliced food quickly Chinese-style in a skillet or wok.

Sugar: Available in several forms: Granulated white sugar is the kind used generally in cooking, for the table and in our recipes unless otherwise specified. Confectioners' or powdered sugar, used for frosting, is pulverized granulated sugar; brown sugars contain some molasses.

Table d'hôte: Set-price menu in a restaurant consisting of several courses.

Taco: Fried tortilla with filling rolled or folded inside.

Tamale: Corn mush, spread on corn husk filled with chili-seasoned mixture, rolled, tied and steamed.

Tempura: Japanese dish of batter-dipped, fried seafood or vegetables.

Toast points: Toast slices, cut in half diagonally.

Torte: Cake or meringue-type dessert, usually rich in eggs and nuts.

Tortilla: Very thin, Mexican bread made of cornmeal or flour.

Toss: To mix foods lightly with a lifting motion, using two forks or spoons.

Tostada: Tortilla fried until crisp, served flat topped with refried beans, other savory toppings.

Tournedos: Filet of beef steak.

Truffle: 1. Species of fungus that grows below the ground; used as garnish.
2. A very rich chocolate candy.

Truss: To secure poultry with string or skewers, to hold its shape while cooking (see also page 248).

Vinegar: An acid liquid used for flavoring and preserving. Among the types: Cider vinegar, made from apple juice, has a mellow fruit flavor; distilled white vinegar, usually made from grain alcohol; herb vinegars flavored with herbs; and red or white wine vinegars which also may be flavored with garlic.

Whip: To beat rapidly with mixer, wire whisk or hand beater, to incorporate air and increase volume.

Wok: Chinese cooking utensil with rounded bottom used as a skillet.

Wok and utensils

Yeast: Micro-organisms that produce carbon dioxide and alcohol from carbohydrates to cause baked goods to rise, fruits to ferment, etc. Our recipes call for active dry yeast.

Zabaglione: Delicate dessert made of beaten eggs and wine.

INDEX

Italic numbers indicate recipes with step-by-step illustrations; (m) indicates recipes for microwave cooking

Y

Z